MW01514356

"I've always wanted to hop into a time machine and travel back into the various periods of Rochester. Ray and Pam Bruzan have given readers the arm-chair opportunity to do just that in *Cotton, Violins & Shots in the Night*."
   Carolyn Bowersock Moore (Born - Raised - Stayed in Rochester, Illinois; First President: Rochester Historical Preservation Society)

". . . An enlightening and interesting history of Rochester from the early 1800s pioneer days through the 2010s . . . A fascinating historical documentation with many photos that anyone connected with Rochester will not want to miss."
   Ruth Slottag (President Sangamon County Historical Society)

". . . An amazing assemblage of archival and family lore detailing the rich history of a unique prairie town. Their research is meticulous and compelling."
   J. Michael Lennon (Library of America editions of the work of Norman Mailer [2018] and former Rochester resident)

". . . An extensive account ranging from pre-history into the future. Their combination of bullet points, stories, and photos makes this book feel like a visit to Rochester . . ."
   Mark McDonald (Producer/Host/Illinois Stories, WSEC PBS)

"Many thanks to Ray and Pam for completing this story of Rochester in time for the village's sesquicentennial. I found the book very interesting, and I'm intrigued to think about what it would be like to come back in 50 years to see the changes between now and then."
   David Armstrong (Rochester Village President, 2001-2017)

COTTON, VIOLINS & SHOTS in the NIGHT

A Timeline Visit to ROCHESTER, Illinois

RAYMOND BRUZAN
PAMELA BRUZAN

Copyright © 2017 by Raymond and Pamela J. Bruzan

All rights reserved. No part of this book may be used reproduced, distributed, or transmitted in any form by any means, or stored in any database or retrieval system, without prior written permission from the authors except in the case of brief quotations used in articles or reviews. For information contact Sangamon Valley Writing Associates at www.cottonviolinsandshots.com.

Published by Sangamon Valley Writing Associates, Rochester, Illinois

ISBN: 978-0-9993146-0-9

Library of Congress Control Number: 2017912673

Cover and book design by Polly Danforth | Morning Star Design
Cover and title page illustrations by Daniel G. Moore

Printed in the United States of America by
Faith Printing | Jacksonville, Illinois

DEDICATION

This book is dedicated to our parents: Leander and Reta Hills and Walter and Virginia Bruzan, who gave us life; to our children: Kevin and Michelle Bruzan, and Jennifer and David Bevan, who gave purpose to our lives; and to our grandchildren: Anthony, Ryan, Ash, Tabitha, and Elyssa, who have enriched our lives.

We also dedicate this book to the past, current, and future generations of Rochester citizens, an evolving community that has been our home for nearly a half century.

ROCHESTER TOWNSHIP

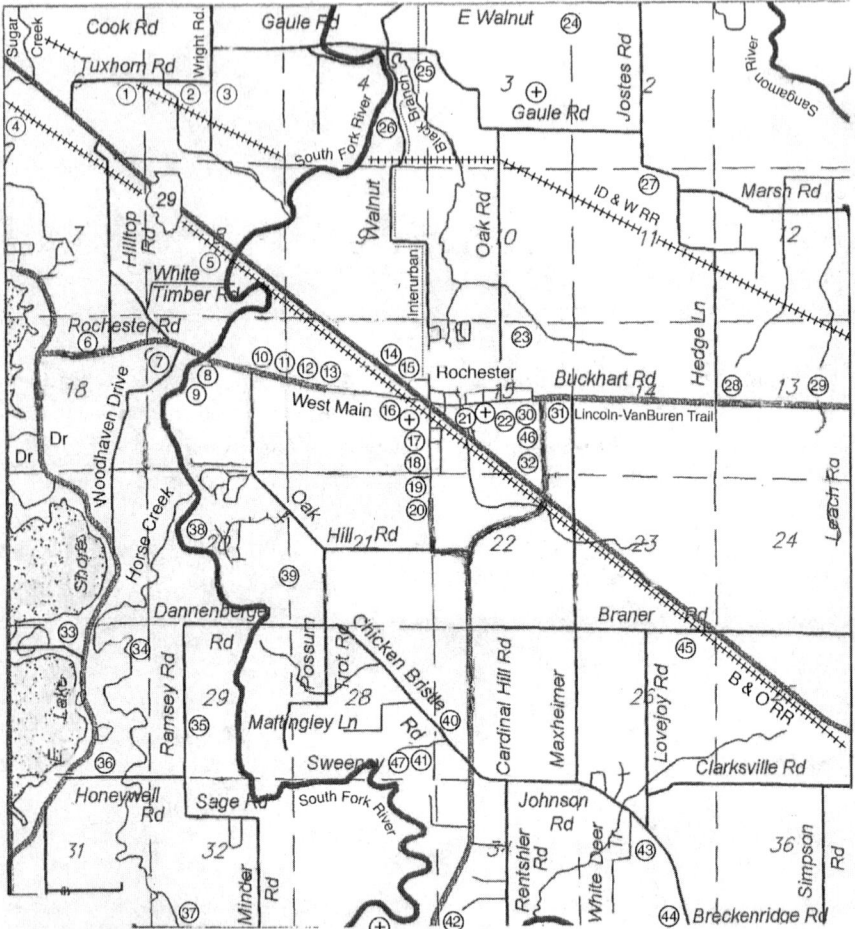

1. Tuxhorn Coal Mine*
2. Keys Station*
3. South Round Prairie School
4. Utt Brothers Brick & Tile Works*
5. Drag City*
6. Flecks Lake View Air Park*
7. Poffenberger School
8. Rochester Road Covered Bridge*
9. Clark's Mill*
10. Stone House / Historical Park
11. Community Park
12. Rochester Cemetery
13. West Main School Campus
14. Good Shepherd Lutheran Church
15. Illinois 29 School Campus
16. Lost Bridge Trailhead
17. Rochester Christian Church
18. Rochester United Methodist Church
19. Catholic Church of St. Jude
20. Twist Brothers Brick & Tile Works*
21. Rochester Train Station*
22. Campbell Park Baseball Field*
23. James McCoy Homestead*
24. Fork Prairie School
25. Glenwood Park Covered Bridge*
26. Glenwood Park*
27. Bluff School
28. Hedge School*
29. Stone House Original Site
30. Fire Department
31. East Main School Campus
32. Village Hall, Police Station, Library
33. Edwards Trace
34. Horse Creek Covered Bridge*
35. Herndon's River Dell Farm
36. Forest Grove School
37. Pensacola Tavern
38. Olcott Indian Mounds*
39. Oil Historical Marker
40. Mottaville School*
41. Mottaville Cemetery
42. Cardinal Hill Road Covered Bridge*
43. Bell School*
44. South Fork Christian Church
45. Rochester Township Office
46. First Baptist Church
47. Stone Quarry

*No longer exists   +Log house

(MAP COURTESY OF DECATUR GENEALOGICAL SOCIETY;
MARK RITTERBUSCH, COMMUNICATION DESIGN; RAY BRUZAN)

Contents

—continued on next page

Appendix, continued

PREFACE

The popular 1990s television show, *Seinfeld*, has often been described as a show about "nothing." This book is a book about "something." In fact, at times, it seemed to become a book about "everything." A timeline history of any community becomes limitless, and it's with that character that this book came to life.

Readers will time travel through Rochester's fascinating stories. It's how a pioneer village came to be a thriving and growing suburb and township a few miles southeast of the Illinois State capital, Springfield. Along the way, the reader will encounter Rochester's stories of gun fights, log houses and home construction, a bank robbery, UFOs, a downtown trolley, a cotton baron, major fires, connections to seven U.S. Presidents, murders, church building, a mountain in Alaska, and a world-renowned violinist.

The genesis of this book began in 1971, when we purchased a large two-story pink house in Rochester. As repair and remodeling began, we discovered a tintype of a man holding two children on his lap. It generated curiosity and a fascination with the previous homeowners and with our new community. After writing a 1977 *Illinois Times* article about our house, we accomplished little research until 2015, when we spearheaded the creation of a walking tour guide of Rochester's historic Orange Judd homes.

As a reader of this book, you will encounter the Orange Judd name multiple times. Judd, whose given name really was Orange, was a writer and well-known publisher of valuable information for farm families. After he died, a Chicago publishing firm acquired Judd's company and, eventually, produced the 1918 Orange Judd Farmer *Pictorial Community Album of Rochester Township and Village*. The pictorial contains 268 photographs of Rochester homes, downtown buildings, schools, and churches.

This original collection of photographs was the basis of Rochester's *Historic Walking Tour Guide* and this book. We thank the hundreds of individuals who were interviewed during the research and writing of both. A special thank you to the website *GenealogyBank* that was extensively used for locating Rochester stories that appeared in local newspapers.

Instead of chapters, this book is arranged by decades from pre-1800 to the present. Each decade begins with a brief timeline, followed by stand-alone, non-sequential storylines and pictures that provide a glimpse into Rochester during that decade. An index and references are provided for readers who wish to carry out extended studies of Rochester history.

—continued on next page

The availability of this book at this time marks a pivotal period in Rochester's history:

- Rochester's first homestead by the McCoy family, 200 years ago;
- Rochester incorporated as a village, 150 years ago;
- Illinois statehood, 200 years ago;
- Production of the Orange Judd *Pictorial* 100 years ago; and
- The authors' golden wedding anniversary.

And so it's time to begin the celebration!! We hope you enjoy your time travel through the fascinating history of our village and also learn to understand the wonderful sense of belonging that comes with living here.

Ray Bruzan
Pam Bruzan
2018

ABOUT THE AUTHORS

(L. RAMSEY PHOTO)

Raymond Bruzan grew up in Southern, Illinois, where he began his formal education in the one-room Hopewell school located northeast of Mt. Vernon. During a 42-year teaching career, he authored articles in the *Journal of Chemical Education*, the *American Biology Teacher*, and *Illinois Times*.

Ray holds degrees from Southern Illinois University, Illinois State University, and the University of Illinois Springfield. After retiring from teaching at Lanphier High School and Ursuline Academy in Springfield, he became a professor of chemistry at Benedictine University Springfield. There he was awarded Student Organization Advisor of the Year in 2010. Earlier, he received the Davidson Award for teaching chemistry in 1992 and was the 1990 Educator of the Year in Springfield schools. His involvement in the nation's first Earth Day led to his contribution of a 1970s Earth Day flag to the permanent collection at the Smithsonian Museum of History in Washington, DC.

Fascination with the history of his Rochester home and community resulted in creating the 2015 *Orange Judd Historic Walking Tour Guide* of Rochester's historic homes and the writing of this book.

Pamela (*Hills*) **Bruzan** is a transplant to the midwest, having grown up in Newark, NY, and graduated from Syracuse University. She originally moved to Springfield and covered city hall for the *Illinois State Register*, but soon put down roots in Rochester.

As a Rochester resident Pam covered local events for both the *Register* and the new *Rochester Times*. After reporting for several years on Rochester-related news, she served on the Rochester School Board and boards of the Rochester Public Library, Friends of the Library, and Rochester Historical Preservation Society. She was named Rochester's 2001 Citizen of the Year.

(R. BRUZAN PHOTO)

Pam established Sangamon Valley Writing Associates in 1995, which enabled her to serve as marketing coordinator for a number of engineering and architectural firms, and also to guide several local public-information campaigns. Her work has included writing dozens of technical articles for professional magazines and co-authoring the book *Greater Springfield: Building on the Legacy*.

This book has provided Pam with an opportunity to learn about Rochester families in much the same way she has learned about her own family through genealogy.

Mistakes

We'd know more if the waters and banks of the South Fork River could reflect on those early Rochester individuals who built a mill and crossed over covered and iron bridges.

But they cannot.

We'd know more if Rochester roads and railroad beds could tell the life stories of those people who traveled along them.

But they cannot.

We'd know more if the walls of Rochester's hundred-year-old buildings could fill in the genealogies of those who lived and worked there.

But they cannot.

We'd know more if the old trees in Rochester Township cemeteries could whisper what they witnessed as families mourned beneath their branches.

But they cannot.

Instead, in order to write this timeline history, we had to rely on newspaper accounts and the memories and artifacts of the fine people of Rochester. We are most grateful for their help. Many sources and hours of research produced what we hope is an accurate description of life in Rochester.

However, we assume full responsibility for any mistakes or misinterpretations in our efforts to produce a valuable book for the current and future generations of the village and township of Rochester, Illinois.

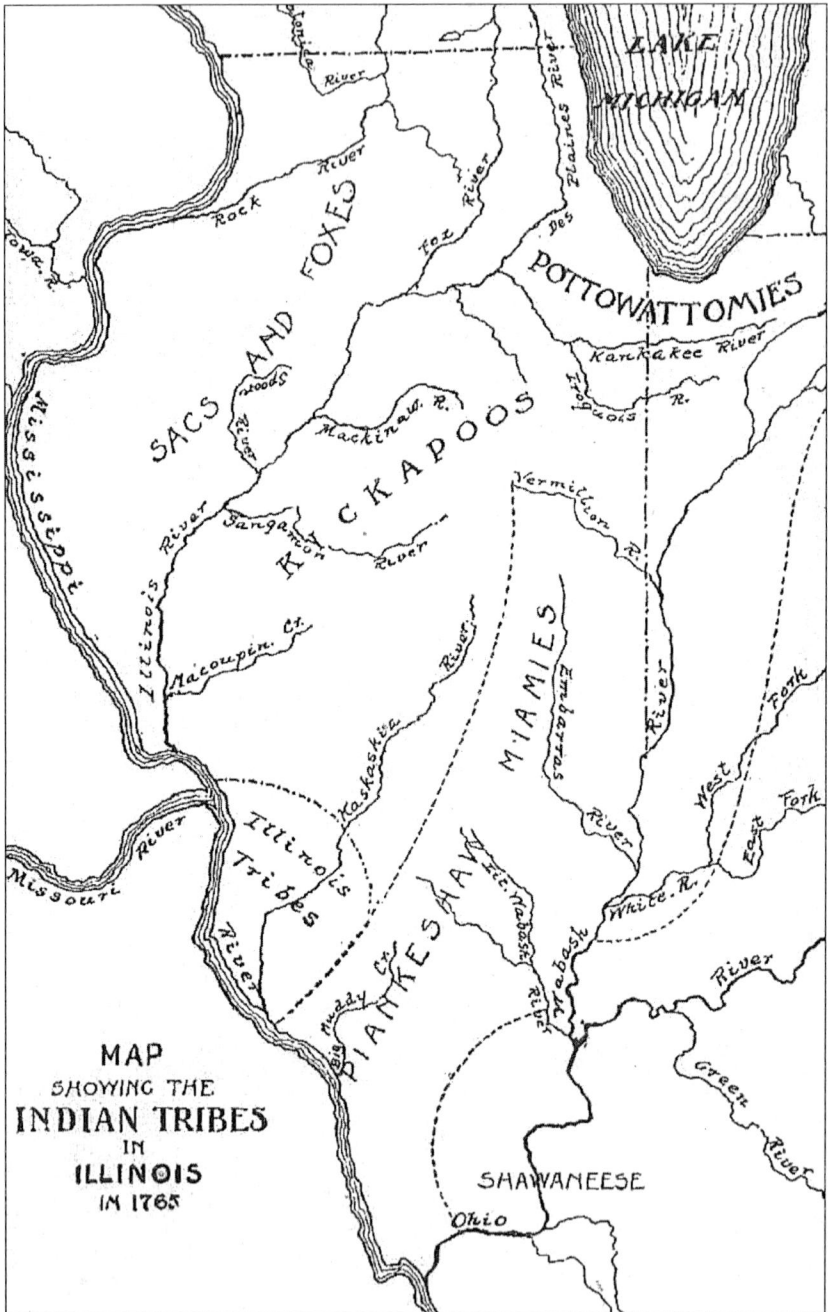

This map depicts the general locations in Illinois of several Native American tribes that existed as Europeans arrived in central Illinois in 1765. (FROM *THE MAKING OF ILLINOIS*, BY IRWIN F. MATHER, A. FLANAGAN CO. PUB., 1900)

PRE-1800S

Pre-1800s Timeline...

1040 BC–1260 AD   Woodland Indian Cultures were present along the Sangamon South Fork River in Rochester Township

300 BC–500 AD   Hopewellian and Mississippian mound builders were present in Rochester Township

1400–1800 AD   Illiniwek and Kickapoo tribes were present in Sangamon County when Europeans arrived in the 1600s

Pre-1800s Storylines...

- When viewed from space, Earth may not appear to have changed a great deal in eons. That distant view is, however, deceiving. Rochester Township has grown during just two centuries from an area thinly populated by Native Americans to what is today a vibrant 34-square-mile township and roughly 5,300 souls. The village of Rochester comprises a 2.5-square-mile area with a population of about 3,700 people. The changes from then to today are what readers will discover on these pages. Welcome to Rochester township and the village of Rochester, Illinois.

- "Time has no beginnings and history has no bounds," sang popular folk singer Gordon Lightfoot in 1967. His reflections could be a major theme of this volume. Scientific evidence estimates that our universe is approximately 13.8 billion years old, and the age of Earth as 4.5 billion years. Life forms first appeared a mere 3.6 billion years ago. Observable evidence indicates that early human beings explored what is now Central Illinois thousands of years ago, having arrived on the North American continent from Asia during an ice age.

- Rochester High School graduate Ron Baumhardt has walked hundreds of miles locally, fueled by his fascination with a search for Native American artifacts. Knowing where to browse in Rochester Township farm fields, he has collected several thousand items, including arrowheads, stone axe heads, spear points, and even rare clovis points that may indicate early inhabitants lived in Rochester 12,000 years ago. Some of Baumhardt's collection were pictured in the landmark book *Legends of Prehistoric Art.*

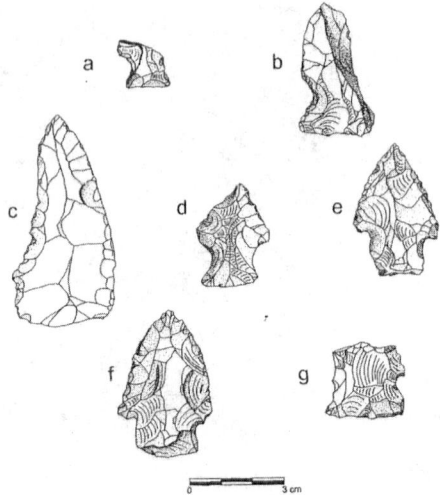

Figure 14: Diagnostic Chipped Stone Artifacts: a) Mound 2 fill; b) Area of Mound 3, Unit N4,W2; c-d) Mound 4 fill; e-f) Mound 5 fill; g) Below Mound 5.

Stone artifacts collected at the Olcott Indian Mounds on the east bluff of the Sangamon South Fork River in Rochester Township. (JOSEPH CRAIG CHART, USED WITH PERMISSION)

The most recent excavation of Olcott Mounds was undertaken in 1994 under the direction of the Illinois Historic Preservation Agency. This is Mound Number 4. (JOSEPH CRAIG PHOTO, USED WITH PERMISSION)

- Burial mounds estimated to have been created by early inhabitants more than 1,000 years ago and stone implements used by those peoples have been found and documented in Rochester Township along the South Fork River and the stream known today as Black Branch Creek.

- James Wickersham described his 19th-century excavations of more than two dozen mounds in an 1885 article that appeared in an annual Smithsonian Institution publication. Five of those mounds, along the east bluff of the South Fork River, were on property owned and farmed by James Olcott. There Wickersham found some human remains as well as stone implements. Olcott Mounds were revisited in 1994 as The Woodlands at South Fork subdivision was being planned. Radiocarbon dating at that time suggested that the mounds were built 1040–1260 AD, and the observed artifacts were determined to be a product of late Woodland cultures.

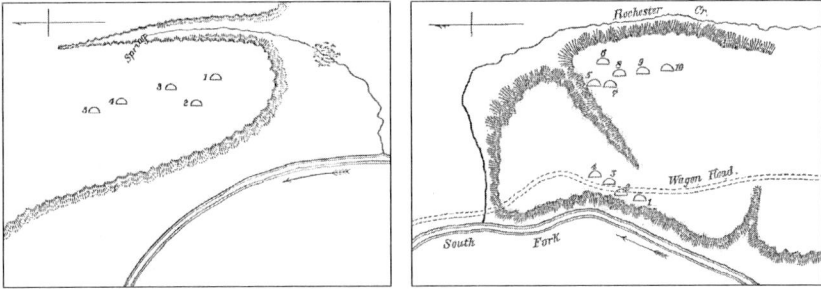

James Wickersham located and examined Olcott Mounds on the east bank of the South Fork River. His research was reported in an 1885 Smithsonian Institution publication. The five identified mounds in Wickersham's drawing (above left) are shown on the east bank of the north-flowing river, shown by the arrow.

Above right: Wickersham also located 10 mounds on the Robert Dawson property north of Rochester. Four of these were found along what is today Walnut Road at what would become Glenwood Park. Six mounds were on the west bank of Rochester Creek (now Black Branch Creek). (ANNUAL REPORT OF THE BOARD OF REGENTS OF THE SMITHSONIAN INSTITUTION, GOVERNMENT PRINTING OFFICE, 1885)

Bob Fairchild, a descendent of early Rochester settler Robert Sattley, found a Native American stone arrowhead point in the 1950s while cultivating a crop on property east of Rochester. Fairchild also retrieved an arrowhead from gravel delivered to his farm from Buckhart. (R. BRUZAN PHOTOS)

- North of Rochester, Wickersham described another ten Native American mounds, identified as Dawson Mounds. Located along what is today Walnut Road between the South Fork River and Black Branch Creek (then called Rochester Creek), the mounds averaged 40 feet long and 20 feet wide. Although Wickersham made no excavation of those mounds, he reported a story that human bones were found during the building of Walnut Road, then called the Wagon Road.

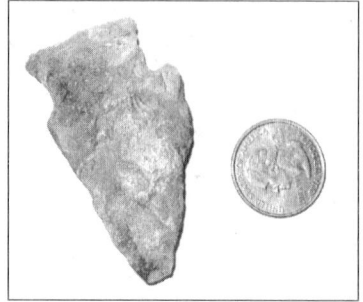

A stone point, discovered by Anna Plessa near the Clark Mill site on the South Fork River in Rochester Township, is an Early Archaic spear/knife that dates from 7500 BC.
(R. BRUZAN PHOTO)

- Disappearance of these mound builders and other early Native American groups, possibly a result of disease and depleted resources, took place prior to the arrival of Europeans in North America. The vacuum left by these earliest inhabitants was filled by Illini and later by Kickapoo tribes. Sharp-eyed visitors walking today east of Lake Springfield can still find remnants of Edwards Trace, originally a tribal corridor for travel through Rochester Township from Kaskaskia to Springfield, and the Illini settlement at Peoria.

Rochester High School graduate Ron Baumhardt displays numerous Native American artifacts thousands of years old that he has collected in Rochester Township.
(R. BRUZAN PHOTO)

Illinois State Treasurer   Judy Baa

A stone celt, found by Rochester resident Carl "Bud" Moore near the Clark Mill site on the South Fork River in Rochester Township was a woodworking tool made by Native Americans between roughly 1000 BC and 1300 AD. (R. BRUZAN PHOTO)

Herbert Roy found this Native American stone axe head in the South Fork River south of the Sandbar Tavern. (CHERYL AND GARRY NIEMEYER PHOTO; USED WITH PERMISSION)

- Treaties in 1818 and 1819 encouraged most Native Americans in the Illinois country, including those near Rochester, to relocate west of the Mississippi River. Through the 1800s, however, stories remained about Rochester Township pioneers seeing and encountering remnants of the peoples who had lived in the area for centuries.

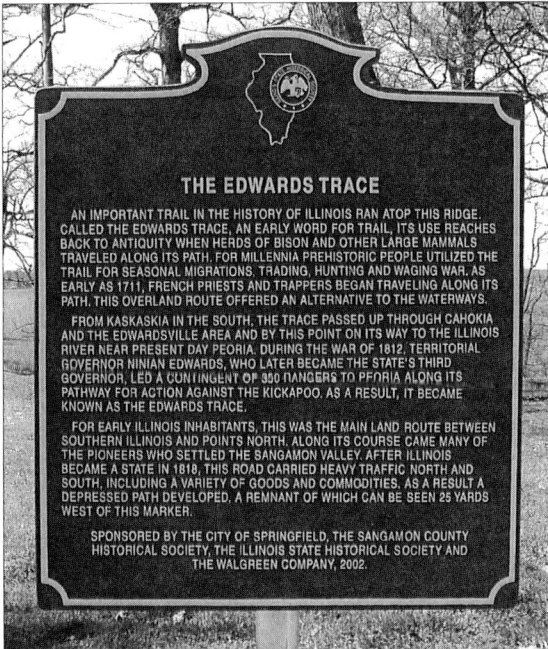

THE EDWARDS TRACE

AN IMPORTANT TRAIL IN THE HISTORY OF ILLINOIS RAN ATOP THIS RIDGE. CALLED THE EDWARDS TRACE, AN EARLY WORD FOR TRAIL, ITS USE REACHES BACK TO ANTIQUITY WHEN HERDS OF BISON AND OTHER LARGE MAMMALS TRAVELED ALONG ITS PATH. FOR MILLENNIA PREHISTORIC PEOPLE UTILIZED THE TRAIL FOR SEASONAL MIGRATIONS, TRADING, HUNTING AND WAGING WAR. AS EARLY AS 1711, FRENCH PRIESTS AND TRAPPERS BEGAN TRAVELING ALONG ITS PATH. THIS OVERLAND ROUTE OFFERED AN ALTERNATIVE TO THE WATERWAYS.

FROM KASKASKIA IN THE SOUTH, THE TRACE PASSED UP THROUGH CAHOKIA AND THE EDWARDSVILLE AREA AND BY THIS POINT ON ITS WAY TO THE ILLINOIS RIVER NEAR PRESENT DAY PEORIA. DURING THE WAR OF 1812, TERRITORIAL GOVERNOR NINIAN EDWARDS, WHO LATER BECAME THE STATE'S THIRD GOVERNOR, LED A CONTINGENT OF 350 RANGERS TO PEORIA ALONG ITS PATHWAY FOR ACTION AGAINST THE KICKAPOO. AS A RESULT, IT BECAME KNOWN AS THE EDWARDS TRACE.

FOR EARLY ILLINOIS INHABITANTS, THIS WAS THE MAIN LAND ROUTE BETWEEN SOUTHERN ILLINOIS AND POINTS NORTH. ALONG ITS COURSE CAME MANY OF THE PIONEERS WHO SETTLED THE SANGAMON VALLEY. AFTER ILLINOIS BECAME A STATE IN 1818, THIS ROAD CARRIED HEAVY TRAFFIC NORTH AND SOUTH, INCLUDING A VARIETY OF GOODS AND COMMODITIES. AS A RESULT A DEPRESSED PATH DEVELOPED, A REMNANT OF WHICH CAN BE SEEN 25 YARDS WEST OF THIS MARKER.

SPONSORED BY THE CITY OF SPRINGFIELD, THE SANGAMON COUNTY HISTORICAL SOCIETY, THE ILLINOIS STATE HISTORICAL SOCIETY AND THE WALGREEN COMPANY, 2002.

Segments of the Edwards Trace are still visible at a site along East Lake Shore Drive at Center Park near the shore of Lake Springfield. (R. BRUZAN PHOTO)

Rochester's first homestead was located in this field on the east side of Oak Street. The McCoy family arrived here in 1818. Artifacts found at the former McCoy homestead site have included blue and green Pearlware Staffordshire, the type often found at New Salem.

The remains of yellow ware crockery, buttons, square iron nails, and fragments of bottles, ceramics, and bricks have also been recovered. (R. BRUZAN PHOTOS)

1800~1819

Rochester's first homestead was settled by James McCoy. Pictured (from left) are Pauline McCoy, Sylvester McCoy, Nina (McCoy) Frame, and unidentified. Nina, in the rocker was married in this log house. (COURTESY OF BARBARA WAGNER)

1800–1819 Timeline ...

1800	United States Congress created the Indiana Territory, which included what is today Illinois
1804	Lewis and Clark Expedition began
1809	Congress organized the Illinois Territory, named Kaskaskia the capital, and appointed Ninian Edwards its governor; Edwards served from 1809-1818
1812	Eleven veterans of the War of 1812 moved to Sangamon County and upon their deaths, were buried in Rochester Cemetery
1817	Robert Pulliam built the first cabin in what became, four years later, Sangamon County
1818–1819	James McCoy explored land along Horse Creek and both the North and South Forks of the Sangamon River; he also built Rochester's first homestead

1818   Illinois was granted statehood, with Shadrach Bond elected the first governor; the state population was listed at 34,620

1819   Joseph E. McCoy and his twin sister were said to be the first white children born in Sangamon County

1800-1819 Storylines…

- A blend of cultures occurred in early Rochester as settlers arrived from both the south and the northeast to settle on Fork Prairie. This area of the future Rochester Township featured abundant water and plentiful trees along the banks of both the North and South Forks of the Sangamon River.
  — Among the homesteaders from the south were McCoys, DeLays, Coes, Coopers, Derrys, and Otts. From the northeast came Staffords, Tafts, Twists, Carters, Locks, Deyos, Fairchilds, Parkers, Hollenbacks, and Sattleys.

- There were several reasons families moved west. Some wanted to homestead bounty lands awarded for their war service. Others decided the East Coast was becoming too crowded. Yet another reason to migrate was the so-called "year without a summer" when crop failures in New England followed climatic changes caused by the 1815 Tambora volcano eruption.

- James and Jane (*Murphy*) McCoy are most often recognized as Rochester's first settlers, arriving in today's Cotton Hill Township from Kentucky in 1818. James and Jane established the first Rochester homestead in 1819. By 1819 Joseph E. McCoy and his twin sister became the first white children born in Sangamon County. Although Joseph's sister died young, the McCoy family eventually included 10 children.

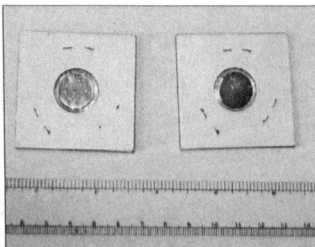

Rochester High School graduate Jacob Dinardo displays coins that he and his sister Kristen found at the McCoy homestead site. Dates on the coins are 1838 and 1853.
(R. BRUZAN PHOTOS)

The McCoy farm mineral spring, as it appeared in 1977, provided water for the family and their livestock. Although the spring is now fenced off and in 2017 overgrown with vegetation, water continues to flow.
(R. BRUZAN PHOTO)

— Identifiable McCoy family members are prominent in a later photograph at the family's homestead site. Although that location is now an actively cultivated field, artifacts from the former McCoy home are still found.

- Family members of former Rochester resident Kathryn Dinardo have often walked the field they now own where James McCoy built the first homestead in what would become the village of Rochester. One such 2006 walk became memorable when 10-year-old Kristen Dinardo found a half dime. Her brother Jacob, years later with the help of a metal detector, found another half dime. Dates on the coins were 1853 and 1838.

— Pottery, glass, stones, horse shoes, buttons, and square nails have also been found at that debris field located on privately owned land. A mineral spring is still visible a short distance north of the McCoy homestead site, where it likely helped provide water for the first Rochester settlers and their livestock.

- Perhaps the oldest and most significant historic artifact of this early decade is Joseph McCoy's Kentucky percussion long rifle passed down through the family since 1810. When early pioneer wives were left alone on the sparsely settled prairie, they also relied on rifles such as this for protection. The McCoy rifle was presented to David Ramsey at his eighth-grade graduation in 1966.

Docent David Ramsey, portrays a McCoy pioneer and displays a rifle handed down from that family. (TOBY McDANIEL PHOTO, USED WITH PERMISSION)

- Brothers Robert and Archibald Sattley from Vermont married, respectively, twin sisters Eliza and Harriet Hawley. Both couples settled in 1819 near what is today Black Branch Creek a stream flowing through and north from the future village of Rochester.

- The Roberts, Keys, Baker, and Bowling families settled in the portion of Fork Prairie that would become Rochester township and village. Philip and Edward Clark, who arrived in 1819, soon built a mill on the South Fork River west of present-day Rochester.

- Elizabeth Bowling, in her 1893 written account of growing up on Fork Prairie, described wildlife that included wolves, snakes, turkeys, deer, and prairie chickens. She also recalled seeing as many as 500 Indians at one time. Her recollections mirrored numerous sightings of Native Americans on Fork Prairie that were recorded well into the 1820s.

- Sattley Street and Oak Street (known earlier as McCoy Lane) remain today as reminders of the those early settlers to Fork Prairie who built the foundations of what would become recognized as the village of Rochester 50 years later.

EARLY ROCHESTER TOWNSHIP ROADS

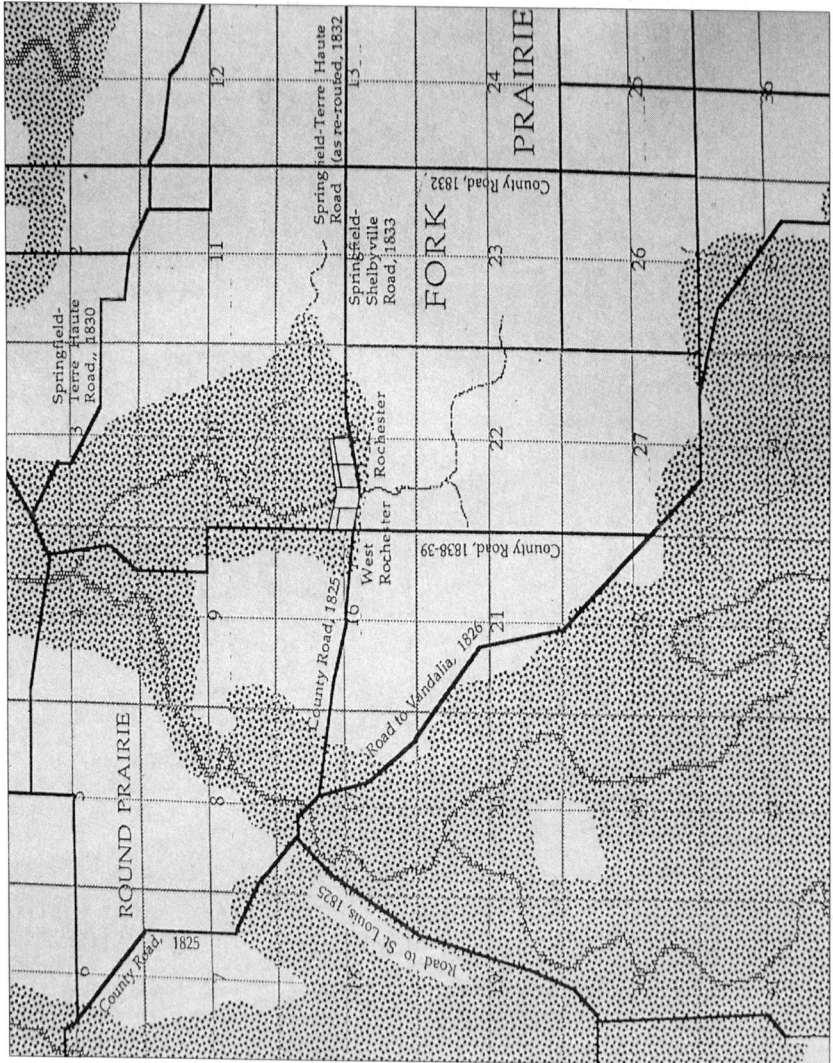

There were few roads in Rochester Township between 1825 and 1858.
(MAP BY THOMAS J. WOOD, 1989, USED WITH PERMISSION)

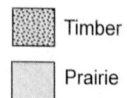

Timber

Prairie

1820s

Four generations of Rochester's original family posed for this photo. M.D. McCoy (right) was the son of Rochester's first settler, James McCoy. M.D.'s son Sylvester (center), and grandson Walter J. McCoy (left), are holding Hester McCoy, the original settler's great-great-granddaughter. (COURTESY OF BARBARA WAGNER)

1820s Timeline...

1820   Vandalia was named the second Illinois state capital
— George Simpson, the first recorded death in Rochester
Township, was the first person buried in what is now Rochester
Cemetery

1821   State legislation was approved that authorized establishing
Sangamon County
— Methodist Bible study was the first religious gathering in
Rochester
— James and Joseph McCoy traded coonskins to Elijah Iles for
four sacks of salt

1822   Clark brothers began work on one of the first saw and flour mills
on the South Fork River west of Rochester
— A May 8, 1822, act of Congress created the Springfield Land
District Office in preparation for land sales in Sangamon County

1823	Birth of Milton D. McCoy, son of James McCoy — Isaac Keys, Sr., Philip Clark, Edward Clark, and William Chilton were Rochester Township's first land owners
1823 – 1824	Richard E. Barker began teaching during the winter at a school in the Sattley settlement near today's village of Rochester
1824	Jabez Capps taught school near Clark's Mill on the South Fork River in Rochester Township
1825	Another school was also built near the Clark Mill — Archibald Sattley bought land in what is today Rochester; he later sold that property to the Hollenbeck brothers
1829	Robert Sattley built a log house on the southeast corner of John and Main Streets
1829 – 1830	L.V. Hollenbeck built a corn-and-carding mill, with distillery, at the north end of Water Street

1820s Storylines...

- The availability of cheap Illinois land became yet another enticing invitation that drew pioneers to the Sangamon frontier, particularly to Fork Prairie and what would become Rochester village. The chart on the following page indicates that the future of Rochester would be in the hands of citizens who arrived from both northern and southern states. Many of these families would go on to play major roles in the village and township.

- During low-water conditions, evidence of logs from Rochester's earliest mill on the South Fork River are still visible on the property of Carl "Bud" Moore. By 1824 Phillip and Edward Clark operated their mill here, providing lumber and trimming logs for various buildings.

Carl "Bud" Moore is shown in 2002 observing a log that washed out of the Clark Mill site on the east bank of the South Fork River west of Rochester. (COURTESY OF DAVID GRUBB)

01/01/2002

1818-1840 Some Families Settling in Rochester Township	Home States / Country of Early Rochester Settlers
Bell, Bowling, Dickinson, Gooden, Jarvis, Keys, Long, McCoy, Taylor, Warrick	Kentucky
Benham, Carter, Lock, Putnam, Sattley, Sherman, Taft, Tracy, Williams	Vermont
Baker, Chilton, Cooper, Giger	Tennessee
Stevens	New Hampshire
Graham, Roberts	Pennsylvania
Hollenbeck, Twist, West	Massachusetts
Fairchild, Gregory, Lock, St. Clair, Williams	New York
Cherry	Georgia
Stafford, Jewett	Rhode Island
Conover, Cox, DeLay, Jones, Turner	Virginia
Clark	England
Stephenson	South Carolina
Cantrill	North Carolina

— Travelers near the Clark Mill used a ferry or toll bridge to cross the river. A covered bridge later existed at this location. Yet another 19th century structure is evidenced by a hand-forged drive pintle on which a door hinge would have been set. The pintle (shown at right) was found by Carl "Bud" Moore near the mill site.

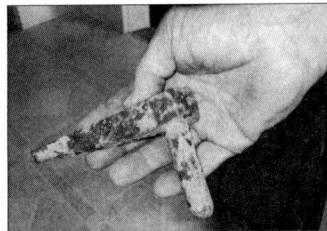

This log, which washed out from the Clark Mill site along the Sangamon South Fork river near Rochester, was retrieved in the fall of 2015 by, from left: David Jostes and Carl "Bud" Moore, along with Ray Bruzan (not pictured). Plans to display the log, currently in storage, are being considered by the Rochester Historical Preservation Society. (R. Bruzan photos)

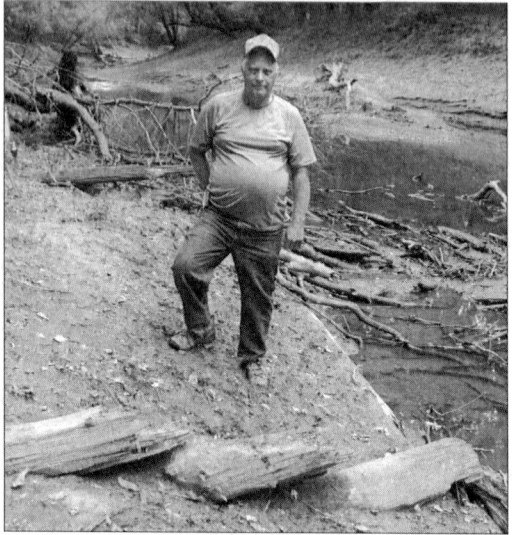

Edmund John Clark (1831-1908) was a son of Edward Clark. Edward, with his brother Phillip, built a mill in 1823 on the South Fork River west of Rochester. (*THE ROCHESTER WEEKLY ITEM*, 25 JAN. 1908)

David Grubb stands near three logs from the 1823 Clark Mill that protruded from the east bank of the South Fork River in 2015. The logs became visible during a period of low water. Grubb is the great-great-grandson of Phillip Clark, one of the two brothers who built the mill. (P. BRUZAN PHOTO)

Above: Local artist and Rochester High graduate Daniel G. Moore posed in 2014 near the South Fork River at the site of the former Clark Mill. (R. BRUZAN PHOTO)

LEFT: The log recovered in 2015 from the Clark Mill site rests in storage. (R. BRUZAN PHOTO)

Above: Rochester artist Daniel G. Moore sketched logs from the 1823 Clark Mill that in 2015 remained embedded in the east bank of the South Fork River and became visible when the river was low. Ray and Pam Bruzan measured distances between these protruding logs as, from left: 9 feet, 15 feet, 19 feet, and 15 feet. The total length of the mill site was an estimated 81 feet.

One of many water-powered mills in Sangamon County was Torrence Mill built along the South Fork River at Cascade by the Hollenbeck brothers, who were major landowners in Rochester. A log from the Torrence Mill dam was recovered in 2007 by Lyle Behl, Kenneth Hobbs, and Gary McKinnon. Although no photograph of Rochester's Clark Mill exists, it may have resembled the Torrence Mill. (PHOTO COURTESY OF SANGAMON VALLEY COLLECTION, LINCOLN LIBRARY, THE HERBERT BARNES COLLECTION)

Phil Southwick, pictured in 2017 with his wife Jerolyn Ann, is a great-great-grandson of Edward Clark, who with his brother Phillip, built a mill west of Rochester on the South Fork River in 1823. (R. BRUZAN PHOTO)

• Born in London, England, Jabez Capps (1796-1896) arrived in Sangamon County in 1819. By 1824 he was teaching school near Clark's Mill on the South Fork River. One local history describes Capps as "a worthy man and an excellent scholar but so easy and indulgent with children in regard to his discipline, that his school was considered by some as very defective."

— Capps may have been "the first teacher in Sangamon County," although different sources have attributed that designation to others. A longtime friend of Abraham Lincoln, Capps sought Abe's advice when he headed northeast a few miles to establish the village of Mount Pulaski. Capps lived most of his life, died, and is buried in that Logan County community.

In 1824 Jabez Capps (1796-1896) taught students in a school located near Clark's Mill on the South Fork River. He later became a good friend of Abraham Lincoln and founded the village of Mt. Pulaski. (*ILLINOIS STATE REGISTER*, 10 SEP. 1895: 8)

This hat and photograph of Jabez Capps are displayed at the *Mt. Pulaski Township Historical Society Museum and Genealogy Center.* Capps, founder of Mount Pulaski and friend of Abraham Lincoln, taught at a school near Clark's Mill in Rochester Township by 1824. Two of his four wives were Rochester women, Prudence Stafford and Elizabeth Baker. (COURTESY OF MARY KNAUER, MT. PULASKI TOWNSHIP HISTORICAL SOCIETY MUSEUM, USED WITH PERMISSION; R. BRUZAN PHOTO)

- Although there had already been as many as 20 burials on the land when William Taft bought it in 1834, he continued to approve burials on the scenic prairie hillside in what today is Rochester Cemetery. The burial grounds were far enough off the road that the earliest mourners had to walk or ride across a cow pasture to reach the grave of their loved one.

- Little is known of the Simpson family except that local histories record George Simpson's 1820 burial as the first in what became Rochester Cemetery. Cemetery historian Steve Leach explains that no official Simpson record, marker, or tombstone exists today. Leach remembers a headstone for early 1819 settler Archibald Sattley, but explains that the Sattley tombstone also can no longer be located, possibly the casualty of a lawn mower.

- Although the Public Land Office opened in Springfield in 1822, five years later only 1,160 acres of the 23,040 acres in Rochester Township had sold. Land sales skyrocketed soon, however, so that most of the remaining Rochester Township land had been purchased by 1835.

- Samuel Williams recalled later in his "Reminiscences" that populations of ". . . wild bees, wild deer, turkeys, raccoons, minks, muskrats, and some others . . ." thrived in the Rochester area. He noted that cotton and flax were grown here.

Milton Darling McCoy and his wife Malcina (*Cooper*) McCoy were both Rochester-born. Milton was a son of James McCoy, Rochester's first homesteader, and Jane (*Murphy*). Malcina's parents were Tennessee natives Jacob and Jane (*Kelley*) Cooper. (RHPS COLLECTION)

Samuel Johnson and his wife Louisa (*Taft*) Johnson were successful Rochester Township farmers. He was the son of millwright Andrew Johnson (1795-1832), who came from Scotland to Sangamon County in 1823 and helped build the Clark Mill. (*PAST AND PRESENT OF THE CITY OF SPRINGFIELD AND SANGAMON COUNTY IL*; JOSEPH WALLACE, VOL. II, S.J. CLARK PUB. CO., CHICAGO, 1904)

Left: Joel Cantrill (1811-1866) was the son of Thomas and Elizabeth (*Murray*) Cantrill, 1828 settlers who built a home along what is today Tuxhorn Road, northwest of Rochester. Joel married Zerelda Branch in 1839. Their son Edward died at the Battle of Vicksburg during the Civil War and was brought back for burial in Rochester Cemetery. (COURTESY OF HAROLD CANTRILL)

The South and North Forks of the Sangamon River provided water, transportation, and mill power for hundreds of early Rochester Township homesteaders. In 1830 the Lincoln family settled west of Decatur on the banks of the Sangamon River, and from there young Abraham Lincoln traveled farther west to New Salem. While riding on the Eighth Judicial Circuit, the lawyer Lincoln crossed the South Fork often as he traveled between Taylorville and Springfield through Rochester Township. (ARTWORK BY MARK RITTERBUSCH, COMMUNICATION DESIGN)

1830S

Seen here in a 1918 photo, the "Old Stone House" was a family home for more than a century after it was built circa 1835 on Buckhart Road east of Rochester. (COURTESY OF COMPASS POINT PRODUCTIONS AND FARM PROGRESS COMPANIES)

1830s Timeline...

1830   Hollenbeck brothers settled in Rochester
          — Early burials in Rochester Cemetery were recorded

1831   James Gregory surveyed and platted the village of Rochester
          — An 18'x20' log structure was the first in the township built specifically as a school

1832   Abraham Lincoln was reported to have delivered one of his earliest political speeches at an East Main Street location in Rochester
          — South Fork Church of Christ was founded

1834   Lewis Sargent and Samuel West built their flouring and saw mill on West Main Street
          — Rochester "became a post office," and C.B. Stafford was named its first postmaster

1835	Estimated year that Samuel Stevens built what is now known as the Old Stone House east of Rochester
1836	Benjamin West built a steam carding and flour mill at the northwest corner of Main and Walnut Streets; it was later the location of the Shreve Coal and Corn Mill
1838	Nathan P. West surveyed Rochester's West Addition
1839	A north-south road was blazed as the forerunner of what is now Walnut Street — Springfield became the Illinois capital

1830s Storylines...

• James Gregory completed a land survey and platted Rochester in 1831, setting the stage for Lawrence V. Hollenbeck (sometimes spelled Hollenback) to create this village on the Illinois prairie. By 1832, Hollenbeck had established his distillery and wool mill at the north end of Water Street and was selling lots along what are today Mill and East Main Streets. Much of this was property he had bought from his wife's uncle, Archibald Sattley. When Hollenbeck died in 1833, just 13 months after his marriage to Jane Stafford, 62 lots he had owned were put up for sale.

• Various stories exist as to how the village was named Rochester:
— Credit is sometimes given to brothers Andrew and Lawrence Hollenbeck for naming Rochester when they laid out the village.
— Lord Rochester of England, visiting from England in the early 19th century, was said to have purchased land in Illinois that now bears his name; no documentation of such a purchase has been found.
— A logical explanation is that some early settlers to this frontier spot were from near Rochester, NY.
— Perhaps the most romantic story relates how Archibald Sattley galloped by horseback to catch up with a family moving west from Vermont to the Sangamo country. The reason for his haste was to marry Harriet Hawley, a member of the group. He overtook them near Rochester, NY, where he and Harriet were married. Archibald later was given the privilege of naming Rochester, IL, to commemorate the happiest event in his life. Research, however, indicates that the couple was actually married February 13, 1819, in the White County, IL town of Carmi.

- A lone walnut tree grows today on the Rochester hillside where our 16th president is said to have given one of his earliest political speeches. Abraham Lincoln campaigned in 1832 for the office of Illinois state representative, an election he lost to the fire-and-brimstone Methodist preacher and politician Peter Cartwright. Although no eyewitness accounts have been documented, stories have repeatedly described how Lincoln gave that 1832 campaign speech under a walnut tree on the East Main Street property of his Rochester friends Robert and Archibald Sattley. Rochester citizens later described the event in no fewer than eight newspaper accounts.

— Souvenirs made from that storied walnut tree have included a walnut box that is now an heirloom of the Terry Campbell family in Missouri.

Above: Close comparisons of a photo taken circa 1880 with Campbell family members and a 1918 picture with homeowner G.A. Wolford strongly indicate both are the Nelson Campbell Homestead. A grove of walnut trees at the Campbell homestead on East Main Street provided the site where young Abraham Lincoln was said to have given his first political speech in 1832. Stories of that Lincoln visit have been handed down ever since. (COURTESY OF JANET AND BRIAN CAMPBELL; COMPASS POINT PRODUCTIONS AND FARM PROGRESS COMPANIES)

Left: Terry Campbell displays a box made of walnut wood harvested decades ago from a Rochester tree that marked the location where, in 1832, Abraham Lincoln was said to have delivered his first political speech. (R. BRUZAN PHOTO)

The Campbell property on East Main Street as seen above is where tradition says Lincoln gave a political speech in 1832. (COURTESY OF JERRY AND NANCY CAMPBELL; R. BRUZAN PHOTO)

— As a child, Theodore Roosevelt witnessed Lincoln's New York City funeral. During his 1900 vice-presidential campaign visit to Springfield, candidate Roosevelt was presented with a cane that featured a head crafted from the Rochester walnut tree. A search for this artifact is ongoing.

— During the 1950s, newspaper carriers Larry Churchill, Wayne Beck, and Jerry Moore recall seeing a plaque that likely commemorated Lincoln's speech on the Sattley property, owned today by Jerry Campbell. The former carriers are uncertain whether the plaque was made of bronze or wood, and the plaque's location and inscription are both unknown today.

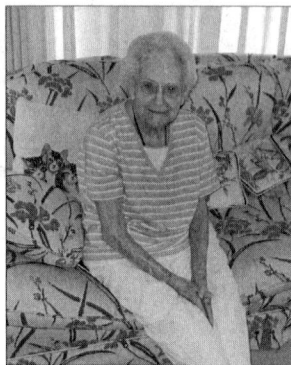

- Benjamin West arrived in Rochester from Boston after graduating from Dartmouth College and, in 1836, from Harvard Law School. Although the location of his Rochester home and law office has not yet been determined, Benjamin did own land in what is now Rochester's downtown. This area was listed as the West Addition after being surveyed and platted in 1838 by Benjamin's brother Nathan.

At the age of 99, Larry Churchill clearly recalled seeing a plaque on the Wolford – Campbell property, where tradition relates that Lincoln gave one of his earliest political speeches in 1832.
(R. BRUZAN PHOTO)

— On the northwest corner of Main and Walnut Streets Benjamin also built a carding and fulling mill, both processes involved in the production of wool cloth. He was known to be successful in business, the law, land speculation, and politics, serving in the 1846-1847 Illinois House of Representatives. In addition, he was an acknowledged artist, including a sketch of the Mormon prophet Joseph Smith that was completed during Smith's 1843 extradition hearing in Springfield.

— Benjamin died of tuberculosis in 1847 at age 35, as described in his obituary found in the *Daily Atlas* of Boston, MA. He is buried in Rochester Cemetery. Two of his three children died at age 18. A daughter, Fanny, died after swallowing her false teeth as she slept, and his son Benjamin, Jr., drowned in the Philippines.

Wood, stone, and metal artifacts were saved from the Old Stone House built circa 1835. (COURTESY OF NORTH AND DORTHY ROSS; R. BRUZAN PHOTO)

- The Old Stone House, originally located east of Rochester on Buckhart Road, was built in the mid-1830s by Samuel H. Stevens. A stone home in Illinois was unusual at that time, but the sturdy structure filled a requirement of Lucetta Putnam's father before he allowed his daughter to marry Stevens and move from New Hampshire to the prairie.

— A pioneer farmhouse, it featured three levels with two fireplaces, one of which included a built-in oven. Because the lowest level included an indoor well, fresh water was readily available. A pegged wall divided the third-level loft into two rooms.

— Lucetta was widowed about three years after her marriage and soon married Benjamin West's brother, Samuel. Lucetta and Samuel are both buried in Rochester Cemetery. The Old Stone House has been relocated to Rochester's Historical Park on West Main Street.

- What became the Ira Twist House on the southeast corner of Main and John Streets may well include portions of Robert Sattley's original log home. This property was owned early in the 1830s by the Sattley family, and visitors to the crawl space under what is now the Wilson Park Funeral Home can see floor joists made of logs with the bark still attached. The cellar stone walls, hand-hewn floor supports, and wood-pegged construction support the strong possibility that part of this home originally belonged to one of the earliest village settlers.

The former Ira Twist residence on East Main Street is among Rochester's oldest homes. It is estimated that part of this building was constructed as early as 1835.

These hand-hewn and bark-covered logs were likely part of the Sattley log house built in 1829-1830. (COURTESY OF PARK FUNERAL HOME; R. BRUZAN PHOTOS)

- Although they were not the first deaths in Rochester, Sarah Sattley and Martha Clark were among the first burials recorded in Rochester Cemetery. Sarah was the three-year-old daughter of

Archibald and Harriet (*Hawley*) Sattley. Martha (*Jessup*) Clark was the 28-year-old second wife of mill owner Philip Clark.

- Christopher B. Stafford arrived in Rochester from Rhode Island in 1824. "Kit" was a justice of the peace and in 1834, established a two-story stagecoach stop, tavern, and post office at the corner of Main and Water Streets. This ordained Baptist minister and his second wife, Sophronia (*Eggleston*), had five children and are buried in Rochester Cemetery. He was married a total of four times.

As of 2017, there are no plans to save the Pensacola Tavern, a building constructed circa 1835 and familiar to early settlers of Rochester and Cotton Hill Townships. (R. BRUZAN PHOTO)

The first floor of the Pensacola Tavern has collapsed into the basement leaving this stairway to the second story without support beneath it. (R. BRUZAN PHOTOS)

- Rochester Township settlers or their families also had connections to adjacent Cotton Hill Township:

  — James McCoy, Rochester's first homesteader, lived briefly in Cotton Hill before settling in Rochester.

  — The Funderburk, Breckenridge, Haines, and Vigal families were also among those with connections in both locations.

  — Built in the 1830s, Pensacola tavern and stagecoach stop was located, and now sits abandoned, a stone's throw from the southwest corner of Rochester Township. It was likely used by residents of both townships.

  —Also located on Horse Creek at Pensacola was Beam's Mill and a bridge. The mill and bridge no longer exist, but in 2017 remains of the tavern still stand tall. They will not, however, be tall enough to break the surface of the proposed Hunter Lake, which would destroy one of Sangamon County's earliest structures.

- A recovered 1839 book of Rochester Methodist Episcopal Church records, misplaced for nearly 90 years, documents the early presence of the Methodist Church in Rochester. It lists well-known revivalist Peter Cartwright as the

Minister Peter Cartwright (1785-1872) rode a Methodist circuit that included Rochester Township. The man who defeated Abraham Lincoln in 1832 for the office of Illinois State Representative also conducted baptisms in Rochester seven years later. (*HISTORICAL ENCYCLOPEDIA OF ILLINOIS AND HISTORY OF SANGAMON CO.*, BATEMAN AND SELBY, VOL 1, MUNSELL PUB. CO., CHICAGO, 1912)

pastor who administered some of the early baptisms in the area. Early Methodist ministers Christopher Houts and Michael Shunk are also listed in the document. Church services were often held at homes of the early settlers or, later, at the parsonage, since a Methodist Church building was not constructed until 1876.

- Mathias Chilton applied to county officials in 1834 for a license to establish a toll on what was called Chilton's Bridge across the South Fork River. The bridge was located on what in 2017 is Gaule Road.

— Ten years later Chilton's Bridge was where the body of 22-year-old Ralph Sattley was recovered after he drowned trying to save the life of a friend.

A Rochester Methodist Episcopal Church record book that had been misplaced for more than 90 years, was found by Mark and Karen Ritterbusch in 2015. The oldest entry in the book lists a number of area residents who were "baptized by P. Cartwright Sept 1st 1839." The book and several other rediscovered church documents were returned to the Rochester United Methodist Church in 2015. (R. BRUZAN PHOTO)

This log-house wall is carefully preserved on a Gaule Road farm in Rochester Township. It is suspected that the original log house was constructed by William Cassity circa 1835. (COURTESY OF MARLENE SPURGEON; R. BRUZAN PHOTO)

• Mathias Chilton was one of several brothers who had moved to Illinois from Tennessee before 1819. It is believed he bought three former slaves, by then called indentured servants, from his father's estate and brought them to Sangamon County.

— Phoebe Bartlett, who had been one of the Chilton family's slaves in Tennessee, was brought to Mathias's property on Round Prairie in Rochester Township, where her daughter Mariah was born in 1819. Mariah married Henry Vance in 1842 and became well known in history as "Aunt Mariah," the woman who, between 1850 and 1860, was largely responsible for cleaning, cooking, and helping to care for the family of Abraham Lincoln.

— Although some of Mathias's considerable property was listed on delinquent-tax rolls, he was apparently highly successful. In 1834 he advertised for sale his 900-acre farm, 250 acres of which were being farmed. That land near Round Prairie also included a brick house, other houses, and barns.

• Rampaging Guatemalan natives spared the life of Dr. Charles F. Hughes in 1827, although they murdered the remaining crew and passengers of the ship on which Hughes had been sailing. This graduate of Maryland Medical College was held captive in Guatemala for seven years. He eventually escaped by hiding among barrels on a ship bound for the United States. After returning to Baltimore, he married Sarah Chambers in 1835 and moved to Sangamon County a year later.

— Hughes was one of the earliest doctors to open a practice in Rochester. After 1843, the family moved to Springfield, where Charles continued to practice medicine, developed a medical drug business, and helped establish the Episcopal Church. Charles died in 1850 and his wife Sarah died in 1871, both in Springfield. The couple had six children.

Melvina and George Reed lived on West Main Street. As a Rochester contractor, George discovered the 1838 day book of general-store owner Samuel West. The book provided a glimpse into the lives of many local residents in 1838-1839. (COURTESY OF JUDITH, JULIA AND MIKE HAMPSON)

• Samuel West died in 1868. His day book was found 53 years later by local builder George W. Reed in the attic of what had been West's general-store building on the north side of Main Street near the Baltimore & Ohio Railroad tracks.

— Reed's 1921 discovery provided a glimpse of Rochester circa 1838. Reed found evidence that whiskey was a particularly popular commodity, exchanged for corn or other items.

— "Corn juice" sold for two-bits a quart, with a gallon selling for as much as 75 cents; brandy was worth $1 a gallon.

— William Graham was credited with $1.12 1/2 cents for three barrels of corn.

— Minos Johnson would have been paid 50 cents for a day's work, but chose a bushel of corn instead.

— Dozens of early Rochester settlers who conducted business at what was believed to be the village's first general store included: Sattley, DeLay, Clark, Fairchild, Hollenbeck, Taft, Turley, Hughes, Neal, Stafford, Bell, Haines, and Samuel's brother, Benjamin.

— Although the building in which the day book was discovered is long gone, hope still exists that at some point the ledger will be found.

Left: The earliest documented burials in Rochester Cemetery took place in 1830.
(R. BRUZAN PHOTO)

Below: This 3-4-foot-high stone foundation remains behind a home on East Main Street, where it was likely built for an outbuilding circa 1835, the same decade as the Old Stone House.
(Courtesy of Nina Duggar; R. BRUZAN PHOTO)

ROCHESTER IN 1840

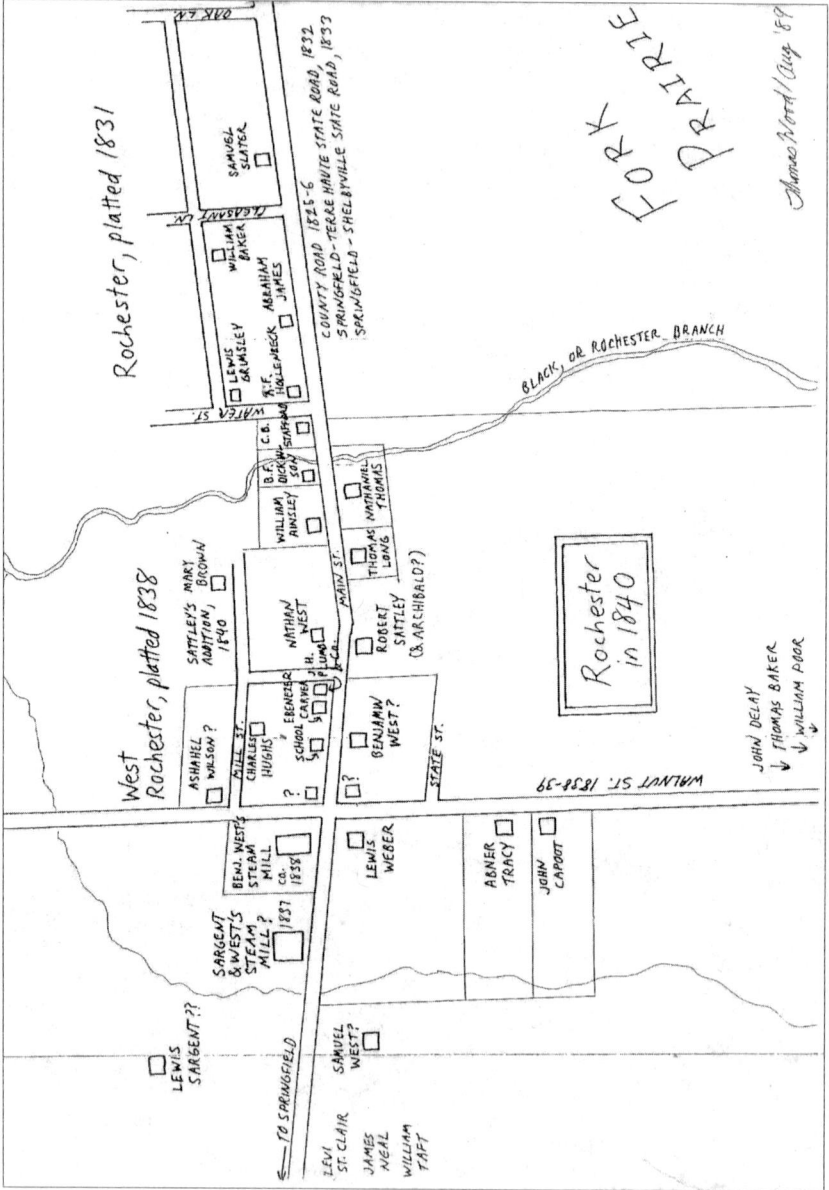

(MAP BY THOMAS J. WOOD, 1989, USED WITH PERMISSION)

1840s

A large mural on the Rochester grain elevator shares history with Route 29 travelers as it depicts Martin Van Buren's 1842 meeting with Abraham Lincoln in Rochester.
(MURAL BY HELEN STANNARD, USED WITH PERMISSION)

1840s Timeline ...

1840	John Capoot, a cooper, moved into a log house along South Walnut Street in Rochester with his wife Elizabeth *(Wilson)*, and son Columbus
1841	The first congregation of the Rochester Christian Church began to meet independently from congregants of the South Fork Christian Church
1842	Abraham Lincoln spent an evening in Rochester with former president Martin Van Buren
1844	Abraham Lincoln was scheduled to be in Rochester for a meeting of the local Whig political party
1846	The log school near South Fork Christian Church hosted a gathering with Abraham Lincoln delivering a temperance address
1848	Revolutionary War veteran and Maryland native Isaac Baker was buried in Rochester Cemetery

1840s Storylines...

* Abraham Lincoln was no stranger to Rochester.
  — Lincoln was scheduled to attend a March 1844 Whig meeting in Rochester—at least *The Sangamo Journal* advertised that Lincoln's attendance was expected.
  — Rochester citizen Richard H. Coe recalled that his dad John C. Coe was a personal friend and legal client of Lincoln. Richard recalled sitting on Abe's knee during a conference between the two adults before Lincoln left for Washington.
  — Mary Ellen *(Herndon)* Thornton of Rochester remembered as a young girl attending President Lincoln's funeral procession in Springfield.

This monument on John Street in downtown Rochester describes Martin Van Buren's Rochester visit with Abraham Lincoln in 1842. (R. BRUZAN PHOTO)

* Such local interactions with the 16th President might lead to the question of whether Lincoln ever spent a night in Rochester. *YES— Lincoln slept here!*
  — The often-repeated story describes Abe's 1842 meeting in Rochester with former President Martin Van Buren, who had arrived after visiting his cousin George Brunk a few miles south in Cotton Hill Township. Rising waters of the South Fork River forced Van Buren's group to spend the night in Rochester. When local Democrats were unsure how to entertain the eighth president in what was viewed as a somewhat primitive

Abraham Lincoln and Martin Van Buren traded stories when they spent the night in Rochester in 1842, as depicted in this sketch of the former and future United States Presidents. (*DAILY REGISTER GAZETTE*, ROCKFORD, IL 11 FEB 1891; GENEALOGYBANK.COM, A DIVISION OF NEWSBANK)

Rochester community, they called on Lincoln, a Whig follower, to cross the river and spend the night.
  — Van Buren recalled for years how he thoroughly enjoyed Lincoln's stories and humor. His fondness for Abe extended to his support for the 16th presi-

dent's efforts against secession that culminated in the Civil War. Van Buren died in 1862.

- With whom and where Lincoln and Van Buren spent the night are uncertain. One report states they were entertained at the home of "Mr. Doty" and spent the night at a country hotel in Rochester. Little is known about Mr. Doty, and the place they stayed is almost as much of a mystery.
  — One possibility is that they stayed at the "Rochester House," sometimes listed in an abstract as the "Tavern House" located on the north side of East Main Street's 200 block. This tavern had been the birthplace of Robert (1837) and Eliza Sattley (1834) and was moved across the street in the 1880s to the Twist property near Black Branch Creek.
  — Facts are scarce about the fate of this "tavern house," although the existing Easley house near that creek contains a log house within it. The possibility that the two structures are in fact the same remains one of Rochester's unanswered questions.

A log house built circa 1840 is concealed within the walls of the East Main Street "Easley House." It has been proposed that the log structure might be the "Tavern House," in which Robert and Eliza Sattley were born and which was later moved by the Twist family from its original location across Main Street. No known study of the the log house has yet taken place. The Easley House was built circa 1900 and is pictured with what is believed to be the W.G. Brown family.
(Photo courtesy of Nina Duggar)

- Clues to life and growth in Rochester are found in Springfield newspaper advertisements.
  — Early in 1840 a man going by the name "John Hancock" advertised his new "Coffee House and Grocery" adjoining Stafford's tavern, which was located on Main Street near Black Branch Creek. Hancock asserted that his new store would "accommodate the inhabitants and travelers with good wine and liquors . . . "
  — By 1845 Benjamin West advertised "great improvements" to his steam carding mill, anticipating "to turn out superior work both in Color and Finish." Within two years he was dead, and his brother Samuel advertised as part of Benjamin's estate the "Steam Engine and Carding Machine" located on a one-acre lot.

Right: The Illinois Weekly State Journal ran this announcement on May 7, 1846, listing Abraham Lincoln as a candidate for the U.S. House of Representatives and Rochester attorney Benjamin West for State Representative. Both Whig candidates won their races.
(ILLINOIS WEEKLY STATE JOURNAL, 7 MAY 1846; PUBLISHED BY GENEALOGYBANK.COM, A DIVISION OF NEWSBANK)

The Sangamo Journal.

SPRINGFIELD:

Thursday, May 7, 1846.

AUGUST ELECTION.

For Congress,

Abraham Lincoln.

of Sangamon County.

For Representatives,
S. T. LOGAN,
BENJAMIN WEST,
JAMES N. BROWN,
R. H. CONSTANT.
For County Commissioner,
ZACHARIAH PETERS.
For Sheriff,
WILLIAM HARVEY.
For Coroner,
JOSEPH A. NEAL.

Grounds of the South Fork Christian Church are near the spot where Abraham Lincoln gave a temperance address at a log school in 1846. A plaque, shown below, commemorates that occasion.

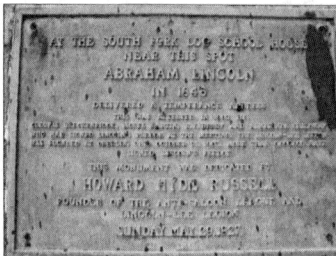

Text shown on the plaque:
"At the South Fork Log School House near this spot Abraham Lincoln in 1846 delivered a temperance address. This was attested in 1903 by Cleopas Breckenridge, Moses Martin, R.E. Berry and Almarinda Galloway who had signed Lincoln's Pledge at the meeting. The Lincoln-Lee Legion was founded at Oberlin, Ohio October 21, 1903. More than 6,000,000 have signed Lincoln's Pledge. This monument was dedicated by Howard Hyde Russell Founder of the Anti-Saloon League and Lincoln-Lee Legion Sunday May 29, 1927" (R. BRUZAN PHOTOS)

— Samuel West also owned a mill, next door to his brother's carding operation. Samuel's mill, which began in the 1830s with partners Samuel Stevens and Lewis Sargent, concentrated on flour, wood, and distilling. Samuel West put that property up for sale in 1848.

— Ads for other estate sales included those for Abner Tracy, administered by Munson Carter; Archibald Sattley, by his son Albert; and Robert Sattley by Aaron Sattley.

• Stafford, whose tavern is mentioned in the earlier bullet, may be the same Christopher B. Stafford who was associated with the Fork Prairie Baptist Church that appeared in Rochester about 1842. Although Stafford himself pastored for about four decades, the church seems to have enjoyed a membership of not more than 10 souls, with no records available after 1866.

- "Washington Societies" and the temperance pledge followed by their members, described in an 1842 article, were active in Rochester. When visiting the South Fork school in 1846, Abraham Lincoln gave a speech endorsing temperance. The event has been commemorated by a bronze plaque on the grounds of the South Fork Christian Church, southeast of Rochester.
  — Three years after this Lincoln speech, Rochester's common counsel heard pros and cons of selling "intoxicating liquors as a beverage." Although they voted ten to seven against granting such liquor licenses, the topic would recur as a social issue for more than 100 years.

- Rochester's political activities during the 1840s included several Whig meetings, such as the planned barbecue involving Benjamin West. His brother, Nathan, was appointed deputy surveyor of Sangamon County, and John Cooper, also of Rochester, ran for county commissioner on the Democratic ticket. Rochester Precinct was one of several in which a Clay Club was organized in the 1840s to honor the five-times presidential candidate Henry Clay.

- Revolutionary War veteran Isaac Baker, who arrived in Rochester Township from Maryland in 1829, had been a fifer during that war. He and his wife Phoebe *(Waddell)* had 12 children, four of whom grew up in Sangamon County. Baker's continued patriotism was legendary, and one of the most often-repeated stories related that during William Henry Harrison's 1840 Presidential campaign, Isaac Baker rode through Springfield "in a log cabin drawn by 32 yoke of oxen." Decorations to the cabin included deer and raccoon skins, plus a barrel filled with cider for the thirsty crowds.
  — Phoebe died in 1845 and her husband died three years later at age 96. The patriot and his wife are both buried in Rochester Cemetery.

- Frequent transportation issues began to appear in the local news:
  — A new bridge across Sugar Creek on the Rochester Road was let to the lowest bidder in 1848. Although the plans wouldn't be available until

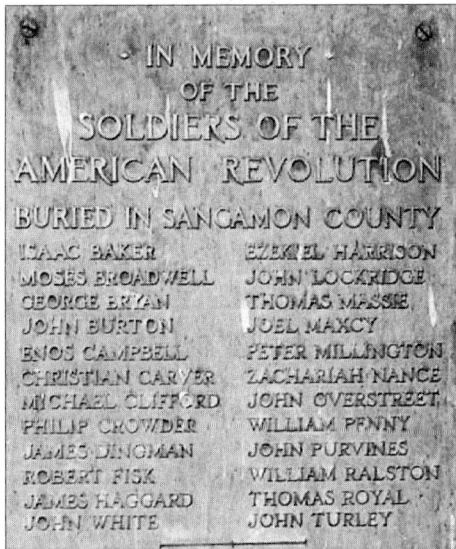

Revolutionary War soldier Isaac Baker died in 1848 and was buried in Rochester Cemetery. This DAR plaque bearing Baker's name is displayed near the Old State Capitol in Springfield. (PHOTO COURTESY OF BEN AND MARY ALICE TUXHORN)

- IN MEMORY -
OF THE
SOLDIERS OF THE
AMERICAN REVOLUTION
BURIED IN SANGAMON COUNTY

ISAAC BAKER	EZEKIEL HARRISON
MOSES BROADWELL	JOHN LOCKRIDGE
GEORGE BRYAN	THOMAS MASSIE
JOHN BURTON	JOEL MAXCY
ENOS CAMPBELL	PETER MILLINGTON
CHRISTIAN CARVER	ZACHARIAH NANCE
MICHAEL CLIFFORD	JOHN OVERSTREET
PHILIP CROWDER	WILLIAM PENNY
JAMES DINGMAN	JOHN PURVINES
ROBERT FISK	WILLIAM RALSTON
JAMES HAGGARD	THOMAS ROYAL
JOHN WHITE	JOHN TURLEY

the letting, bidders were advised the structure was "to be built of good white and burr oak timber."

— A series of "rail road" meetings took place in Springfield, Rochester, and nine surrounding townships to generate farmers' support in 1847 for the proposed Alton and Springfield Rail Road.

— The writer of a letter to the editor of the *Illinois Weekly State Journal* expressed grave concern that a new road from Charleston to Springfield would bypass Rochester to the north. The letter's author suggested that "the People of Rochester" act together so that the "enterprising and thriving village" would be on the planned route.

- A detailed 2003 study was conducted of the "Stafford Site," located in Section 22 south of the Oak Hill Road and Cardinal Hill Road intersection. The study resulted in a unique opportunity to better understand the lives of some of Rochester's earliest settlers. Oliver Stafford purchased and homesteaded the land in 1827. Although Oliver died two years later, his wife Polly *(Sattley)*, children, and other Stafford family members lived on the property

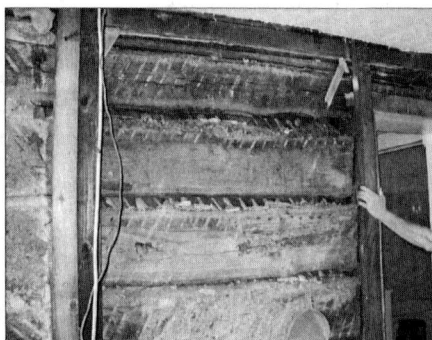

Janelle Melton (left) of Rochester talks with archaeologist Robert Mazrim to glean suggestions for reconstructing the Cotton Hill Township log house she discovered while remodeling in 2014. The 1840-era building was on property owned by early settler Christopher Haines, an ancestor of the Haines family who lived in Rochester decades later. (P. BRUZAN PHOTOS)

Married in 1892, Arthur and Nora *(Lawley)* Haines moved, circa 1906, from a farm near New City to their West Main Street home in Rochester. Arthur was the grandson of Christopher and Myrah Haines, 1829 settlers of Cotton Hill Township where a log house was discovered by Janelle Melton in 2014. (COURTESY OF TOM AND MAGGIE JENSEN)

for a number of years. Their lives at that location led to the recovery of numerous historic artifacts indicative of farm life in the 1830-1850s.

— Excavation, research, and a subsequent report by Robert Hickson and Robert Mazrim described dozens of articles recovered from the Stafford Site that included buttons, coins, tools, bottles, and tableware.

— Mazrim's expertise was again requested in 2014. It was then that Rochester resident Janelle Melton had planned to rehab her Cotton Hill Township home. Instead, she discovered a log house on her property once owned by Christopher Haines, who was an 1830 Sangamon County homesteader. Melton preserved her circa-1840s log house, now part of her renovated home.

Daniel Bailey (1824-1898) and his brother George Washington Bailey (1823-1901) arrived in Sangamon County in 1849. Both lived in Rochester Township, although at different times, and served in the Civil War. It was 1913 when their descendants began gathering as the Bailey Family Reunion, an annual event that continues through 2017 and may hold a county record for reunions by one extended family. (*THE ROCHESTER & LAKE SPRINGFIELD HERALD*, 21 JULY 1993; COURTESY OF FAY JOSTES)

ROCHESTER TOWNSHIP 1858 ROAD MAP

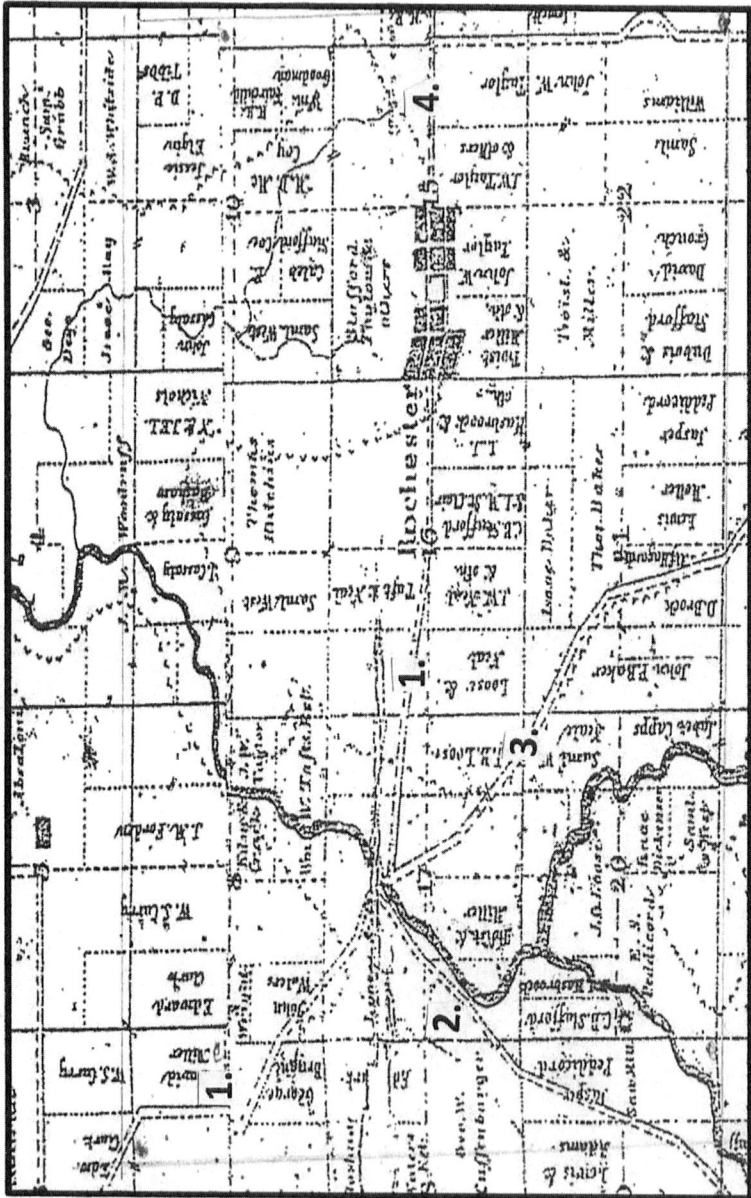

1. Rochester Road; 2. Woodhaven Drive; 3. Springfield-Taylorville Road; 4. Buckhart Road

A portion of Rochester Township, including major roads, is shown on this 1858 map.
(MODIFIED FROM *SANGAMON COUNTY STATE OF ILLINOIS MAP* BY JOSEPH LEDLIE,
WHITLEY AND WHEELOCK, PUB., ST. LOUIS, MO, 1858; COURTESY OF SANGAMON VALLEY
COLLECTION, LINCOLN LIBRARY, SPRINGFIELD, IL)

1850s

The back portion of the S.G. Richardson building, seen as lighter-color brick, was built about 1858 by Munson Carter. The front portion was added by R.H. Coe in 1900. (R. BRUZAN PHOTO)

1850s Timeline ...

1851	Marshall Sattley began manufacturing plows at his Rochester home
1852	Universalist Church trustees obtained property at the northeast corner of Main and Water Streets
1852	South Fork Church of Christ members built their first church
1853	The first Illinois State Fair made its debut in Springfield
1855	Munson Carter was said to be active with fugitive slaves and the Underground Railroad
1858	Munson Carter constructed what later became known as the S.G. Richardson building at the northwest corner of East Main and John Streets

| 1858-59 | Rochester Methodist Episcopal Church purchased their parsonage house and lot on Mill Street |
| 1859 | Rochester Lodge 268 of the Independent Order of Odd Fellows (IOOF) organized |

1850s Storylines ...

- An 1852 property abstract describes acquisition of lot 19 at the corner of East Main and Water Streets by trustees of the Universalist Church in Rochester. While serving Universalist churches in Springfield and Rochester in 1885, Universalist Pastor A.U. Hutchins expressed his hopes of bringing the Rochester and Springfield Universalist congregations together. Until the Rochester Methodist Episcopal and Church of Christ congregations built their own churches in the 1870s, they both used the brick Universalist Church for their worship services.

Property for the former Universalist Church on East Main Street was acquired in 1852. The church structure was converted much later into a private residence. Both the Rochester Methodist and Rochester Christian congregations used this building for their services until their own churches were constructed. (COURTESY OF JERRY "JAKE" MOORE; R. BRUZAN PHOTO)

- An 1858-1859 Methodist ledger entry describes the Rochester Circuit's Second Quarterly Conference that met at the Universalist Church in Rochester on February 12, 1859, with Presiding Elder William Swain Prentice. A vote during this conference approved locating a Methodist parsonage in Rochester rather than in Mt. Auburn, and a committee was authorized to spend up to $500 for the property. Although no longer a parsonage, this home still stands at 117 Mill Street.

- By the time he left his native Vermont for the midwest, Munson Carter had buried two young wives. He arrived in Rochester about 1841, married a former sister-in-law, the widow Ann *(Taft)* Tracy, and began a successful political and business career. To accommodate the eight children of the combined Tracy and Carter families, in 1858 Munson built the Greek Revival house on Main Street now known as the Bell House. Ann's son Carter Tracy (one of Munson's stepsons) grew up in the Bell House and would go on to a colorful political career that will be highlighted in a later decade.

- Munson ran for sheriff, circuit court clerk, and state representative. He served as the village's peace magistrate, post master, and in 1869, Rochester's first

According to church records, the Rochester Methodist Church purchased a Mill Street lot with an existing building in 1858. That home was used as a parsonage and meeting place until their church was completed in 1876. It is uncertain whether this was the existing parsonage when the lot was purchased. (*THE ROCHESTER WEEKLY ITEM*, 23 DEC. 1909)

The former Rochester Methodist Church parsonage was still recognizable as it appeared on Mill Street in 2015. (R. BRUZAN PHOTO)

village president. Munson's first Rochester store was a wooden structure located on Main Street next to where Rochester's first bank now stands. He replaced that store in 1858 with what is today the rear portion of the brick building on the northwest corner of Main and John Streets.

- Rochester folklore includes stories of how Neal's Grove property on West Main Street was a safe haven for fugitive slaves. Although specific Rochester references to the secretive Underground Railroad are rare, an 1855 story, reported in 1903, described how Munson Carter secreted runaway slaves in his downtown store.

- From two-and-a-half miles above Central Illinois, Professor O.K. Harrison observed a panorama of the countryside that included Rochester during an August 1855 "Grand Balloon Ascension." After two hours, the self-described "World-Renowned Fire King and Balloonist" descended near the farm of John Morgan, whose location was not listed in newspaper accounts. Adults were charged 25 cents for admission to the grounds in Springfield where Harrison's balloon, named "Eclipse," was inflated. Admission was 15 cents for "children and servants."

- The Plank Road Company proposed in 1853 to build a plank road from Springfield through Rochester to Taylorville. As it looked for investors, the company predicted that the road would pay a "handsome interest" to those investors and that property values along the route would also increase ten-fold.

- County officials planned repairs and replacements during 1856 for four local bridges, including the one across Sugar Creek on Rochester Road. Their requested sealed bids specified the use of pine for the weather boarding, studs, rafters, and sheeting, with shingles of pine, oak, or walnut. "Two good coats of paint" were to be used on the sides and ends of each bridge.

- Among the items reported this decade that related to animal husbandry were:
  — Rochester Horse Doctor H.R. Clark advertised in the early 1850s that he could "cure all horse diseases that are curable," including big head, weak eyes, ringbone, and other equine afflictions.
  — Samuel West offered a liberal reward in 1853 for the return of his chestnut sorrel horse that had strayed. One identifier he pointed out was that the horse "limps a little."
  — The "copartnership" formed in 1858 by S.A. Jones of Rochester and W.E. Moore of Springfield advertised shipments of "fat cattle, live fat hogs, stock hogs, slaughtered hogs, and fat sheep."

- A new tri-weekly postal route was authorized by the United States Congress in 1856. It would head southeast from Springfield, following closely along what today is Route 29 through Rochester, Blueville (now Edinburg), Taylorville, and Owaneco, to the junction of the Alton / Terre Haute Roads in Pana.

- After John Finney broke into the kitchen of the Rochester House in 1859, Officer David Crouch escorted him to the Springfield jail. Unable to post a $100 bail, Finney was bound over for trial during the next circuit court term.

- Oscar T. St. Clair and Nancy E. Neal, both of Rochester, were married in February 1853 by the Baptist pastor Rev. C.B. Stafford. Oscar lived only eight more months, dying in October at the age of 21. His obituary relates how St. Clair "has left a young wife and a large circle of relatives and friends to mourn his untimely death."

- Rochester businessman Rev. C.B. Stafford ran unsuccessfully on the 1857 Democratic ticket for county school commissioner.

- Shortly after completing his three-year apprenticeship with Rochester blacksmith Abraham Elvy Nichols, Marshall Sattley set to work in 1851 to forge by hand his company's first plow, the "Prairie Breaker." This son of Rochester pioneers would eventually have his name associated with more than 30 patents, all for nationally known farm equipment. Under the company name M. Sattley & Brother, Marshall had moved to Decatur by 1857, a year later to Taylorville, and eventually to Springfield as the Sattley Manufacturing Company. The Springfield factory was housed in a four-story building sprawled over seven acres at the corner of 9th Street and South Grand Avenue.

Racine
SATTLEY

One of Springfield's largest and longest lasting industries was founded by Marshall and Archibald Sattley, Jr., of Rochester. Their father, Archibald Sattley, Sr., was of one of Rochester's earliest land owners. Sattley Manufacturing Co., having already merged with the Racine Wagon & Carriage Co., was eventually bought in 1916 by Montgomery Ward & Co. and continued producing numerous farm implements. The Springfield plant closed in 1958.
(COURTESY OF THE SANGAMON COUNTY HISTORICAL SOCIETY)

SATTLEY MAKES THE BEST SINCE 1851

Your Dad and Grandad bought their implements from Sattley's and bragged about them. And nothing better was made in those pioneer days than Sattley tools.

But look at the contrast between 1868 and 1926! Could you keep your boy on the farm with one of those old-time 1868 Sattley Gang Plows?

Talk over your needs with our "UNCLE BEN" DETRICK and "DICK SMITH."

They Can Save You Money on

PLOWS
TOOTH HARROWS
DISC HARROWS
CORN PLANTERS
CULTIVATORS
MANURE SPREADERS
CREAM SEPARATORS
HARNESS
BINDER TWINE

The first gang plow was built in 1868 by Marshall Sattley.

ITS "SATISFACTORY" IF FROM

SATTLEY FACTORY
OR YOUR "MONEY BACK"
NINTH AND SOUTH GRAND AVENUE
SPRINGFIELD, ILL.

Marshall Sattley, who built his first plow in Rochester in the 1850s, was requested to exhibit his patented three-wheel plow "the Hummer" at the 1892 World's Columbian Exposition in Chicago. Sattley was the son of Archibald Sattley, one of Rochester's earliest settlers.
(ILLINOIS STATE REGISTER, 2 OCT. 1892; USED WITH PERMISSION)

Advertising was as important generations ago as it is today.
(ILLINOIS STATE JOURNAL, 27 MAR. 1926; PUBLISHED BY GENEALOGYBANK.COM, A DIVISION OF NEWSBANK)

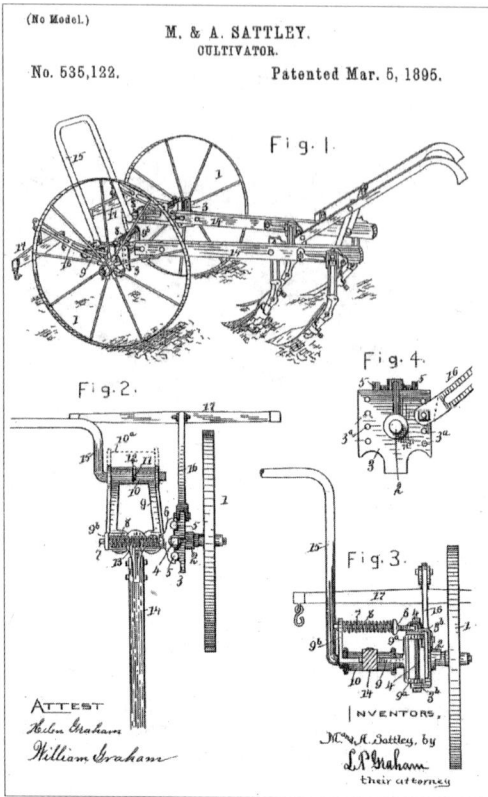

(No Model.)

M. & A. SATTLEY.
CULTIVATOR.

No. 535,122. Patented Mar. 5, 1895.

Fig. 1.

Fig. 2.

Fig. 4.

Fig. 3.

ATTEST
Helen Graham
William Graham

INVENTORS,
M. & A. Sattley, by
L.P. Graham
their attorney

A cultivator invented by Marshall and Archibald Sattley,
shown in this patent drawing, received a patent in 1895.
(WWW.GOOGLE.COM/PATENTS/US535122, 26 MAY, 2016)

Kathryn Dinardo displays the 1857
large one-cent coin, seen below,
that she found in 2014 at the
McCoy homestead site.
(P. BRUZAN PHOTO)

- What appears to be Rochester's first fraternal organization began meeting during this decade. A ledger provided by Clarissa Shockley from the estate of Louise Miller includes a January 24, 1859, hand-written entry that describes Rochester's first meeting of the Independent Order of Odd Fellows (IOOF) Lodge 268. R.F. Price, Munson Carter, Carter Tracy, and J.R. Richards were elected lodge officers. Other early documents list lodge members' names, occupations, rank, lodge office, and reasons for leaving. The most common reason for being dropped was non-payment of dues. In 1869 one member would be "expelled for visiting houses of prostitution."

Dr. Robert F. Price, M.D.,
(1835-1865) one of the first
officers of Rochester IOOF Lodge
No. 268, is buried in Rochester
Cemetery. The handshake and
three interlocking chain links on
his headstone symbolize
Friendship, Love, and Truth.
(R. BRUZAN PHOTO)

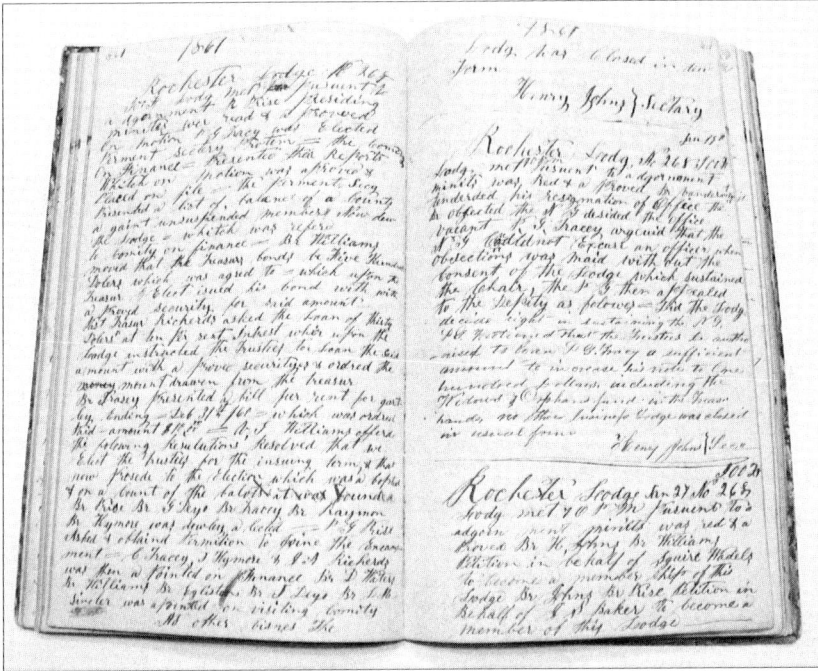

These original records of Rochester's Independent Order of Odd Fellows (IOOF) Lodge No. 268 were acquired by RHPS in 2016. They provide minutes of the lodge's first meeting on January 24, 1859, through the meeting February 21, 1863. (COURTESY OF CLARISSA SHOCKLEY AND LOUISE MILLER, RHPS COLLECTION; R. BRUZAN PHOTO)

The original South Fork Christian Church, was built in 1852 from logs hauled by Isaac Bell to the South Fork Mill owned by Preston Breckenridge. (POSTCARD PICTURE COURTESY OF · DWIGHT AND GRACE POPE)

FORDEN'S BARN

One of Rochester Township's oldest barns is on property homesteaded by
John and Evalina (or Emeline) Forden on what is today Tuxhorn Road.
Support beams are all hand-hewn timbers, and the roof is supported on log rafters.
The estimated construction date of this barn is pre-1860s. (P. BRUZAN PHOTO)

1860s

Rochester's Civil War veterans received honors during a 1912 Memorial Day celebration at the Woman's Christian Temperance Union Temple on East Main Street. They were, from left, Thomas Ridgeway, Thomas J. Shreve*, Uriah King, David Funderburk, James Richardson, Rev. John C. Stevenson, and Willian J. (Jack) Nutt.
(*THE ROCHESTER HERALD*, 18 MAY 1988, JAMES WOODRUFF COLLECTION, SANGAMON VALLEY COLLECTION, LINCOLN LIBRARY)

*This veteran may have been listed incorrectly as Thomas J. Shreve; he may instead be Theodore D. Shreve.

1860s Timeline...

1860	Abraham Lincoln was elected President of the United States
1860–1865	U.S. Civil War
1861	Township 15 of Range 4 West was designated "Rochester Township"
1864	President Lincoln was reelected
	— Section 16 on the west side of South Walnut Street was surveyed and platted
1865	John Wilkes Booth assassinated Abraham Lincoln
	— A two-story frame school was built in downtown Rochester
1868	Carter Tracy built his two-story gothic-style home on Mill Street
1869	Rochester was incorporated as a town with Munson Carter its first president

1860s Storylines...

- With Abraham Lincoln winning the 1860 presidential election and the 1861 firing on Fort Sumter, SC, our nation was plunged into a war that impacted even small communities nationwide. War meetings were held in Rochester to raise volunteers in answer to the President's call. Patriotic resolutions were adopted in Rochester Township pledging to support measures taken by the County Board of Supervisors that encouraged enlistments.

- According to Rochester Cemetery historian Steve Leach, graves of 35 Civil War soldiers are recorded in Rochester Cemetery. Of these, eight cannot be located because some of the early records have apparently been lost. Among the Rochester Township Civil War veterans were the following:

Civil War veteran Uriah King(1842-1913) was wounded and captured during the 1863 Chickamauga Campaign. He then served time in several southern prisons including Andersonville. Uriah and his wife Melvina *(Bailey)* were the parents of 11 children. Uriah died in Rochester in 1913, and Melvina died six years later. Both are buried at Oak Hill Cemetery in Clear Lake Township. (PHOTO COURTESY OF FAY JOSTES)

— Uriah King fought in the Battle of Chickamauga and twice served time in Andersonville prison.

— David Funderburk, Jr. served three years in the 11th Missouri Infantry. He was born in Cotton Hill Township and buried in Pawnee's Zion Cemetery after living on South Walnut Street in Rochester for eight years.

— Virginia-born George W. Everhart initially enlisted in the Confederate army, but fought for the Union forces after he was captured and had served time at Illinois's Rock Island Prison Barracks.

— Theodore D. Shreve was 18 in 1861 when he enlisted in the 106th Regiment, 111th IL Infantry. He was discharged three years later at Bolivar, TN, due to illness.

— Edward T. Cantrill, who lived at Round Prairie in Rochester Township, fought at Vicksburg, where he became ill, dying one week after the Union victory there.

— As postmaster in Co. G 114th Vol's Infantry, D.G. Kalb used a confiscated wheelbarrow for three years to carry regimental mail at such notable battle sites as Gettysburg and Vicksburg.

— John W. Sturdy moved to Rochester after serving in the Confederate army, having enlisted as an armorer at Harper's Ferry, VA.

This gothic-style Rochester house, known in 1918 as the Whiteside Homestead, was built circa 1868 by Carter Tracy. Located on Mill Street, the house features a fireplace in every room and served for years as the home of John W. Sturdy, a Confederate veteran of the Civil War, and his wife Ruth A. *(Saunders)*. (LITHOGRAPH FROM *ILLUSTRATED ATLAS MAP OF SANGAMON COUNTY, ILL*, BRINK & McCORMICK PUB.; DUVAL AND HUNTER, LITHOGRAPHERS, 1874)

- Carter Tracy, a stepson of businessman Munson Carter, spent $7,000-$8,000 in 1868 to build what is now known as the Whiteside Homestead on East Mill Street. Long after leaving Rochester, Carter's son Fred described the house as having four rooms upstairs and five below, each with a fireplace. The full basement included a room for storing produce and another room for the home's coal furnace. A striking lithograph of the house (see above picture) appeared in the 1874 *Illustrated Atlas Map of Sangamon County*. Owner of a grocery store on Main Street, Carter Tracy also became involved in politics. His home was where John W. Sturdy lived after the Civil War.

Multiple wallpaper designs were recovered during 2000s remodeling of the Mill-Street house built by Carter Tracy in 1868. (COURTESY OF BRENDA AND DAVID BERNADIN; R. BRUZAN PHOTO)

John W. Sturdy was a Confederate soldier and Union prisoner of war who was paroled in 1865 at Harper's Ferry, WV. After the war, he farmed in Cooper Township before moving to Rochester, where he joined the Independent Order of Odd Fellows and became an active member of community. He is buried in Buckhart's Oak Hill Cemetery. (P. BRUZAN PHOTO)

This traveling trunk, a Sturdy family heirloom, belonged to John W. Sturdy of Rochester, a Confederate Soldier who in the 1920s lived in the house Carter Tracy had built on Mill Street. (COURTESY OF JOANN STURDY; R. BRUZAN PHOTO)

As seen in 2017, Dr. Mark Sturdy's veterinary clinic is about a half block south of the home formerly owned by his great-grandfather John W. Sturdy. That house is visible in the background. (COURTESY OF MARK STURDY; R. BRUZAN PHOTO)

- Rochester Township officers elected less than two weeks before the Civil War began in 1861 included: Supervisor, Samuel Williams; Town Clerk, Samuel West; Assessor, William Goodrum; Collector, James W. Neal; Overseer of Poor, A.E. Nicols (sic); Commissioners of Highways, William Morttar (sic), Samuel Miller, and Henry Johnson; Justices of the Peace, David Miller and

Christopher B. Stafford; and Constables, George W. Puffenbarger (sic) and David Crouch.

- Winners of the April 1864 Rochester Township elections were: Supervisor, John L. Highmore; Town Clerk, Carter Tracy; Assessor, A.E. Nicholson; Collector, William Goodrun; Overseer of the Poor, John Dickerson; and Commissioner, James H. Bell. Readers will notice the different spellings of some of the candidates' names on both ballots and may recognize different surname spellings between then and today.

Located on what is today Tuxhorn Road, the George Forden Homestead was likely built circa 1860s. George's parents, John and Emeline, or Evalina, *(Sidener)* Forden were 1833 Sangamon County settlers. (COURTESY OF COMPASS POINT PRODUCTIONS; FARM PROGRESS COMPANIES)

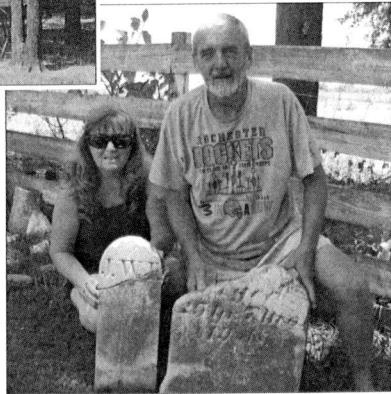

Headstones of Forden family members are carefully displayed by Tim and Teana Scannell in 2016. Today they own the property originally homesteaded in 1833 by John and Evalina (or Emeline) *(Sidener)* Forden. (P. BRUZAN PHOTO)

- There are at least two sides to many stories, and this one is no exception. According to one account, Rochester Constable David Crouch was determined to take possession of a horse that was part of an 1860 Springfield funeral cortege. Crouch asserted that the horse was actually his, and he would use any means to get it back. After Crouch threatened various mourners with his knife, the entire procession descended into chaos, with the driver and the horse in question making a fast escape. Initial reports described the constable as "a reckless desperado" who "could have committed no greater outrage upon humanity, except by stopping in front of the procession and making a levy upon the corpse."

— Crouch saw it differently. He challenged the accuracy of the first news story, alleging instead that some 150 friends of the man with the horse attacked him. As Crouch related his version, the accusers apparently failed to appear in front of a justice, and all charges were dropped.

— One of the county's early settlers, Crouch himself was buried in Rochester Cemetery in 1871.

• Some 56 wagons and 500 people represented Rochester at "The Prairies On Fire For Lincoln" political rally of August 9, 1860, that passed by Lincoln's home in Springfield. Young ladies riding on two of the decorated carriages from Rochester represented each of the states as their part of the "veritable political earthquake" making up the massive "pageant." Lincoln supporters from throughout Illinois, as well as Wisconsin and Missouri, made up the wildly enthusiastic throngs.

A gold-seeking forty-niner and friend of Abraham Lincoln, John C. Coe moved to Rochester with his wife Charity *(Grubb)* in 1863. Square nails were used in the construction of their Mill Street home, where hand-hewn basement-sill timbers are still visible.
(LEFT: COURTESY OF COMPASS POINT PRODUCTIONS; FARM PROGRESS COMPANIES)
(RIGHT: COURTESY OF RANDY LORSCHEIDER; R. BRUZAN PHOTO)

Built in 1860 by Lawson Smith three and a half miles southeast of Rochester, this house remained in the Smith family until it was auctioned in 1996 to provide funds for the care of 96-year-old Dora *(Smith)* Lovejoy. Dora was born and spent most of her life on this farm, where she also raised her daughter, niece and nephew. She died in 1998, not long before a fire destroyed the historic family home. (COURTESY OF DWIGHT AND GRACE POPE)

Abstract records indicate that Robert Dawson bought this property on North Walnut Street Road circa 1865 and soon built this brick two-story home. This picture, taken around 1945, was provided by Lorene *(Baum-hardt)* Schrenk whose family owned the home when she was a child. (COURTESY OF LORENE SCHRENK AND PAT SCHRENK; USED WITH PERMISSION)

The Robert Dawson Homestead as it appeared circa 1985. (DOTTIE TROOP PHOTO; USED WITH PERMISSION)

- Rochester Township accidents:

1863

— **Phillip Austin Richards**, the 10-year-old son of well-known Springfield printer B.A. Richards, was severely injured when his horse fell on him as they plunged through part of a plank bridge. Phillip's thigh was broken, and he lay injured for four hours before help arrived. After the accident, a lot of local finger pointing took place regarding the less-than-ideal way in which Phillip's leg may have been set by Rochester doctors Robert F. Price and Lyman B. Slater. Phillip, however, would go on to a successful career in printing, dying in Waco, TX, at age 59.

— **William King** and his friends only went to the North Fork of the Sangamon River near Rochester to bathe and presumably, enjoy the cool waters during an August day. But when William drowned, his friends were terrified and returned home without telling anyone. The next morning, however, they confessed to a search party what happened to their friend. The 14-year-old teen had been living in Springfield with Spencer Donegan, a co-founder of the St. Paul AME Church.

1864

— **Mrs. John Delahay** may have been thrown, or maybe she jumped, from a rapidly moving mule-drawn wagon owned by John Ryan. She died without ever regaining consciousness.

1866

— Even though he sustained several wounds during the Civil War, **John Morrison** survived. His wartime bravery counted for nothing, however, when a year after the war ended the horses pulling his wagon became uncontrollable. Morrison was thrown to the ground, a wagon wheel fractured his skull, and he died instantly.

- Although he was unnamed in news accounts of the 1863 incident, it was likely Munson Carter's teenage son Charles who may have only been trying to annoy an elephant from Van Amburgh's Circus that was entertaining in Rochester. The pachyderm was not amused. After Charles hit him with a stick, the elephant picked the boy up and threw him, not so gently, about 10 feet. The elephant was uninjured and having made its point, resumed eating. The boy was at first "insensible" but soon recovered.

Although the year the Herndon family built River Dell Farm has not been determined, this lithograph of the property was published in 1874. Records indicate that the Herndon family obtained land in the southwest area of Rochester Township as early as the 1860s. River Dell resident Archer Gray Herndon, Jr., was a brother of attorney William H. Herndon, law partner of Abraham Lincoln.
(LITHOGRAPH FROM *ILLUSTRATED ATLAS MAP OF SANGAMON COUNTY, IL*, BRINK & MCCORMICK PUB.; DUVAL AND HUNTER, LITHOGRAPHERS, 1874)

Archer Gray Herndon, Jr., (1825-1890) owned River Dell Farm that still exists in 2017, located in Section 29 of Rochester Township. (*PORTRAIT AND BIOGRAPHICAL ALBUM, SANGAMON COUNTY, ILLINOIS*, CHAPMAN BROTHERS PUBLISHERS, CHICAGO, IL, 1891)

- Friends of the proposed Pana, Springfield, and Northwestern Railroad met in Rochester on July 12, 1865, shortly after the "Rochester route" was selected from several options. The line was also called the Pana & Springfield Railroad. With a total distance of 41 miles, it was projected to cost $ 8,081.85 per mile, a total cost of $331,355.85.

  — An 1866 strike by about 100 workers, however, halted railroad construction and led to the arrest near Rochester of strike "ringleaders" Samuel Smith and Peter Jacobs. A large crowd, that may have also included strikers, forced the release of both men. Work resumed after the workmen received a pay increase so that teamsters earned $3.50 per day and shovelers were paid $1.75 per day. Service through Rochester on the Pana & Springfield Railroad began in 1870.

Bricks made on his property were used to build the Thomas Thornton Homestead on Ramsey Road around 1860. William Thornton, father of Thomas, was a close friend of Abraham Lincoln. Rochester resident Don Mohler grew up in this house during the 1930s.
(COURTESY OF COMPASS POINT PRODUCTIONS; FARM PROGRESS COMPANIES)

- The Sangamon County Board of Supervisors approved a $1,000 appropriation in 1868 for bridge construction in Rochester. The bridge location in the village was not identified.

- A month after Capt. William T. Day of Co. K 29th Regiment of Illinois volunteers was said to be missing in 1864, the remains

This 2016 photo of the Thornton Homestead depicts the home's current state of collapse.
(COURTESY OF DON AND BETTY MOHLER; R. BRUZAN PHOTO)

of a man were found in Samuel Miller's field near the South Fork River bridge. Miller's hogs had mutilated the body so badly that its identification was impossible. Some soldier's clothing and Camp Butler tickets suggested that the body may have been Capt. Day or possibly another soldier from that camp.

- Lawbreaking:
  — When Erastus G. McDonald talked widely about a robbery from Edward Donahue before the victim had told others, McDonald himself was charged with the theft of $120 from a trunk in Donahue's grocery. The store, "the Donahue Place" near the South Fork River bridge west of Rochester, along with 20 acres of farmland were advertised for rent seven years later.
  — Some sweets, knives, and $45 were stolen from Jacob Flagg's grocery in Rochester during an overnight robbery in 1863.
  — Daniel McAvoy and William O'Hara were both sentenced to a year in the penitentiary at Joliet for their 1863 robbery of Battie's store in Rochester.
  — Thefts in October 1867 included two of David Miller's horses and two harness sets from a neighboring farm.
  — Two horses and a mule were stolen in 1864 from farms along the Rochester Road owned by Joshua Graham and Samuel Miller. Miller's horse escaped and returned home via the Petersburg Road, possibly from the direction the three stolen animals had been taken. Graham offered a "liberal reward" for information about the theft of his "very fat," "considerably knock-kneed" horse and two-year-old "very large size" mule with "two bloody warts" on his right hind leg. Graham then sent men to track down the animals, which were found in Beardstown with two other horses also believed to have been stolen. The thieves were apprehended.
  — John Coe was fined $100 on an assault charge after he was alleged to have attempted killing James Everhart in 1868. Both were Rochester-area residents.

- Ellsley Pugh, who lived near Rochester with his wife Martha and eight children, stole a horse in 1860. After selling the horse in Springfield, Pugh went to the Vinegar Hill area, assumed the last name "Johnson," married a young lady, and left for parts unknown. Martha came searching for her husband, as did the man from whom the horse was stolen. Pugh was nowhere to be found, but police expressed hope at the time they would "captur(e) the rascal."

- Rochester was first incorporated as a town on February 1, 1869, with Munson Carter as its president. The town's first four trustees were John L. Firey (a blacksmith), John A. Richards (wagon maker), Ethan P. May (miller), and Carter Tracy (dry-goods dealer).

Edward T. Cantrill (1842-1863), who died during the Civil War campaign at Vicksburg, is buried in Rochester Cemetery. At the time of his death Edward was carrying the New Testament Bible pictured here. He was the grandson of Thomas and Elizabeth *(Murray)* Cantrill, 1828 settlers on land north of Tuxhorn Road in Rochester Township. (PHOTOS COURTESY OF HAROLD CANTRILL)

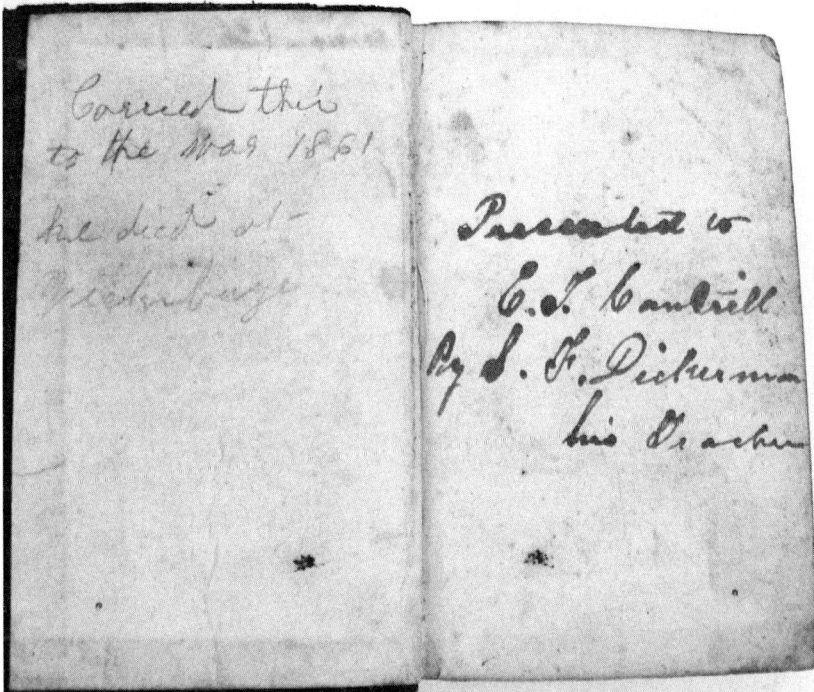

1874 VILLAGE OF ROCHESTER

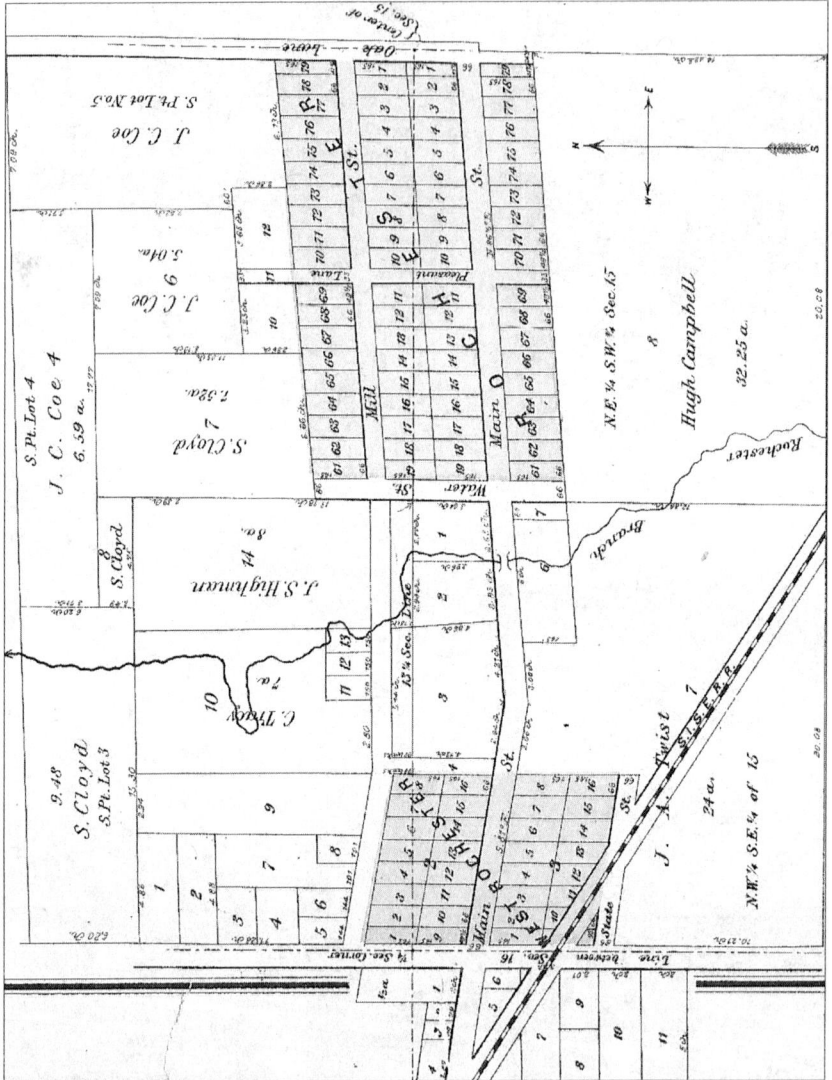

(*ILLUSTRATED ATLAS MAP OF SANGAMON CO., IL*, BRINK AND MCCORMICK PUB. OF IL, 1874)

1870s

This postcard picture of Rochester station is the earliest image the authors found of the rail service that began in 1870. This view looks southeast with South Walnut Street in the foreground and a grain elevator in the distance. (COURTESY OF BILL L. COFFEY)

1870s Timeline ...

1870	Rochester's population: 250
	Rail service was brought to Rochester
1872	Railroad passenger depot was built near South Walnut Street
1875	Rochester Christian Church was built on South Walnut Street
	— W.W. Taft, Jr., house was built on West Main Street
1876	The Independent Order of Odd Fellows constructed their lodge at the northeast corner of East Main and John Streets
	— Rochester Methodist Episcopal Church was built on Mill Street
	— Construction began on James Neal's West Main Street home at Neal's Grove
1877	Carter Tracy began construction of his East Main Street store

1870s Storylines ...

- Rochester flourished during the 1870s. A railroad connection from Rochester north to Springfield and south to Taylorville made the village available as a shipping center and provided new travel options for businessmen and other visitors. The new Odd Fellows lodge, Carter Tracy's store, railroad depot, and two churches reflected the health of Rochester's growing economy.

- The Pana, Springfield and Northwestern (PSNW) Railroad provided Rochester's first rail service in 1870. Undergoing a number of name changes over the years, these railroad tracks were laid at what is now Lost Bridge Trail that bisects the village. The PSNW later became the Baltimore and Ohio Railroad (B&O) and other similar names. To avoid confusion to our readers, this rail service will be referred to only as the B&O.
  — Another set of railroad tracks, owned by the Indianapolis, Decatur, and Western Railroad (ID&W), was laid about two miles north of the village in 1902. These tracks also underwent several ownership changes and later became part of the B&O line. However, the authors will refer to this northern trackage as the ID&W.

- Once the railroad passed through Rochester, it was possible to bring visitors to attend a variety of meetings.
  — The day-long Teachers Institute generated glowing praises from a reporter in 1872.
  — A special train brought a group of Odd Fellows to Rochester from Springfield in 1873 for an evening gathering that included speeches, singing, and refreshments.
  — Special trains brought Grange members to Rochester from the surrounding area in 1875 for that year's annual "pic-nic." Young and old enjoyed the vast quantities of food and heard poetry, speeches, and band selections throughout the day-long event.

This undated picture of the Rochester IOOF building may have been taken soon after the building was completed in 1876. According to the sign, the first floor was also Rochester's Post Office. Note the buggy on the left, wood plank sidewalk, and dirt Main Street. (COURTESY OF ROCHESTER PUBLIC LIBRARY, RHPS COLLECTION)

  — Political meetings were also common, as illustrated by a Republican gathering in 1872. According to one report, some of Rochester's oldest residents termed it "one of the largest and most enthusiastic ever held at this place." The Springfield Glee Club entertained, and at least one of the speakers gave "a straight-forward, sensible and manly address at some length."
  — An estimated 2,500 people attended the 1879 Old Settlers' Society reunion held in Rochester. The annual event, which took place in different communities, was an opportunity for area residents who braved "the deep snow of

1830-31" to meet again, share recollections and enjoy picnicking with old and new friends.

- Township taxes were approaching $11,000 and businesses thrived. The bustling flour mill of Walton and Sharp produced a "splendid grade of flour," although six months after that observation, miller R.C. Walton gave up the business.

- Several correspondents visited Rochester during the decade, and their various observations were quickly published in Springfield newspapers, although their politics, statistics, and opinions did not always agree.
  — One correspondent was less than kind in reporting his 1870 visit. The positives included the village's 250 citizens, one of them a doctor; a boot-and-shoe store; the post office; butcher shop; Universalist Church; two-story school for about 200 students; a steam-operated flour mill; and a blacksmith shop.
  — However, the same writer recalled that in prior years the roads to reach Rochester were "almost fathomless mud" that made stage-coach travel "appall the strongest heart." The writer pointed out that the now-abandoned tavern was "a relic of the past" where "the belles and beaux of the town whiled away the long winter nights in the mazy dance," and large groups from Springfield arrived to enjoy the "Rochester hops."
  — That writer concluded that the village's history demonstrated how "enterprise had failed to reach the slow-moving town" of Rochester. But looking ahead, he anticipated that future growth "will make it a good town."

- Eight months later another visitor listed an amazing build up in village commerce: two stores, two doctors, two wagon-makers, three blacksmiths, and one shoemaker. That writer also admired the "very neat cottages" along quiet streets and pointed to the Springfield & Southeastern Railroad as one reason the community "has become 'quite peart.'"

- Alcohol sales were a major topic of conversation by several visiting writers. As a result of the "anti-license" stance taken by the 1871 Town Board, made up of E.R. Babcock, J. Twist, J.A. Richards, B.P. Abel, and M. Lock, Rochester had no saloons. There was, however, a "confectionery store" where "fancy pop" was sold. "Viator" wrote two years later "Rochester is almost literally deluged with whiskey and beer, and almost all the men seem to think it is their duty to drink to intoxication."

- After worshipping in the Universalist Church on East Main Street for more than two decades, two of Rochester's congregations erected their own churches.
  — Guernsey Smith donated land for the Christian Church across from the depot on South Walnut Street in what was known as Walnut Grove. The new house of worship was dedicated September 16, 1877, and a special train

brought visitors from Springfield for the occasion.

— Some of Carter Tracy's property on Mill Street was donated for the new Methodist Episcopal Church, which was built by contractor Perry Money. This church cost $2,100, much of which was donated by the congregation. Rev. William M. McElfresh invited the public to its dedication on August 13, 1876.

Above: The first Rochester Christian Church, dedicated in 1875, was on South Walnut Street. The Rochester Methodist Episcopal Church on Mill Street (left) was dedicated in 1876. The church bell seen in this photo was relocated to a new church building in 1924 and restored in 2017. (PHOTOS COURTESY OF ROCHESTER PUBLIC LIBRARY, RHPS COLLECTION)

• Perry Money completed several two-story Italianate-style homes near Rochester. Two of these still sit across from each other near the Rochester Cemetery lane on what was at that time the Rochester-to-Springfield Road. Local legends suggest that before these homes were built in the mid-1870s, their sites may have played a role in the Underground Railroad.

Two of Rochester's historic Italianate-style homes were built on West Main Street during the 1870s. The W.W. Taft house (left) was built on the original 1834 Taft homestead. Neal's Grove (right), built on the 1830 homestead of James and Mary Neal, was the home of several generations of the Neal and St. Clair families. (R. BRUZAN PHOTOS)

— On the north side of West Main Street, the William Webb Taft house was built on land previously owned by other members of the Taft family, settlers who came to Rochester from Vermont in 1832. W.W. Taft, Jr., was a fifth cousin of U.S. President William H. Taft.

— Across the street, Neal's Grove was where James and Mary *(Cassity)* Neal settled after their 1830 arrival from Kentucky. The two-story home was built for their son, William. Neal's Grove itself became the site of numerous Rochester social events.

— East of Rochester, along what is today Buckhart Road, Money also built a home in the same Italianate style for Charles Fairchild.

— Farther west on the Rochester-to-Springfield Road near Hilltop, a fourth home was built in the same Italianate style for farm owner Joshua Graham. The name of that home's builder is uncertain.

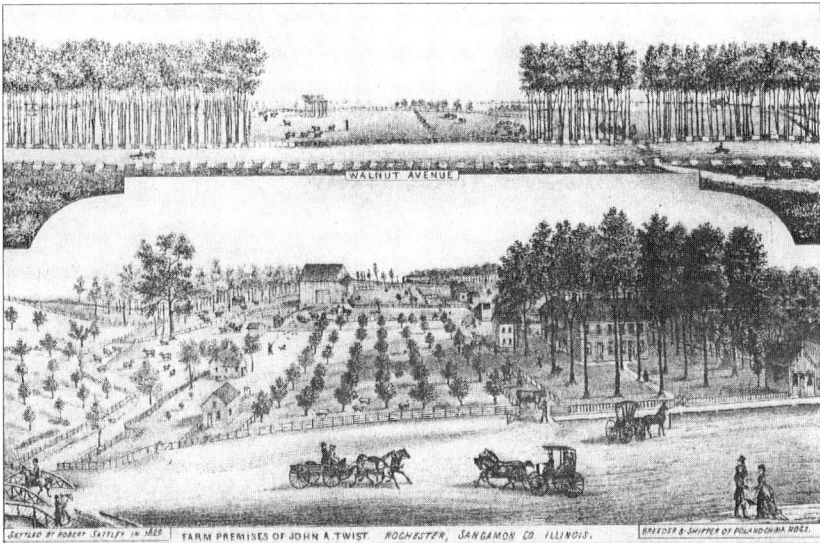

The John A. Twist farm is shown in this 1874 lithograph. The Twist family arrived in Rochester Township from Seneca Falls, NY, in 1822 and brought with them the first apple trees planted in Sangamon County. The horses and carriages are pictured on what would later become Main Street, with the bridge (far left) crossing Black Branch Creek. In 2017 the large house is a family residence and the location of Wilson Park Funeral Home. (LITHOGRAPH FROM *ILLUSTRATED ATLAS MAP OF SANGAMON COUNTY, ILL,* BRINK & MCCORMICK PUB.; DUVAL AND HUNTER, LITHOGRAPHERS, 1874)

• A lithograph of John A. Twist's Rochester farm in the 1874 *Illustrated Atlas Map of Sangamon County, ILL,* indicates the Twist family's depth of success.

— Twist bred and shipped Poland China hogs, a breed that had been developed in Ohio only about 30 years earlier.

— As a conscientious merchant, Twist's 1878 ledger listed the names of customers who bought cows, hogs, hay, corn, watermelons, and potatoes, as well as those who paid rent for Twist's multiple rooms and houses.

— John A. Twist and his wife Eliza *(Sattley)* were major Rochester land owners whose children would impact the community well into the 1900s.

- Interesting turmoil arose occasionally. Charles W. Decker sued William Clark for $10,000 in damages that resulted when Clark shot Decker in the groin. Prior to the shooting Decker and others had been outside Clark's house, serenading Abe Richardson and his new bride as part of a mock wedding custom known as shivaree. Decker claimed that the inflicted injuries had left him "a eunuch." The jury returned a verdict for Decker, awarding damages of $30, one dollar per day for 30 days of home confinement following his injury.

The 1878 ledger from a Rochester business owned by John A. Twist lists his customers, their purchases and costs. The ledger was taken to Arkansas about 1920, but was returned to Rochester in 2014 by Jean Brickey and Christine Cary. (RHPS COLLECTION; R. BRUZAN PHOTO)

- A Rochester branch of the Y.M.C.A was organized in 1875, with Cottage Prayer meetings. R.P. Abel was the first president.

- Robberies in Rochester:
— Thieves robbed the stores of Carter Tracy and Munson Carter at least twice during the decade, removing money and goods with a total value of about $500.

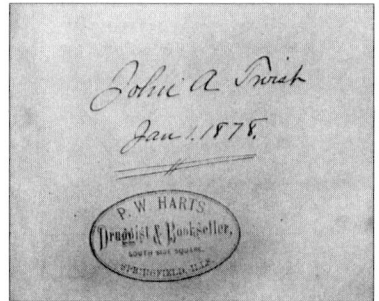

The signature of John A. Twist and date, Jan. 1, 1878, are visible in a ledger from his Rochester business. (COURTESY OF JEAN BRICKEY AND CHRISTINE CARY, RHPS COLLECTION; R. BRUZAN PHOTO)

— John Twist was a victim of horse thieves in 1876, although his stolen horses were recovered after they had apparently been abandoned.
— Eleven "fat cattle" were taken from the J.W. Dalby farm near Williamsville in 1870. Rochester Constable William Vickers arrested William Goroy for stealing the animals.

- While he was watching some sheep with Daniel Ott in 1875, Henry Lock shot a "huge" timber wolf. Both of those Rochester residents were convinced that the wolf was the same one that had been stealing sheep for some time.

- Accidents:
  — In separate accidents, **James Kernsan** was thrown from his horse and Samuel Torrence from his wagon. Both died from their injuries.
  — **George Enlow** survived a compound fracture when his leg became caught in weed-cutting machinery.
  — **Perry Money** had to have his left arm amputated near the shoulder after the home builder fell beneath a moving freight train car. Upon recovering, he continued to build homes and other area structures.
  — When the five-year-old son of **J.G. Crouch** tried to light an oil lamp one morning, he only succeeded in lighting his mother's clothing and a nearby carpet. Although his mother's foot was badly burned, further injuries were averted when J.G. wrapped her in a quilt. The little boy and his dad were uninjured.
  — Such was not the case when 26-year-old **Dona Herndon** spilled burning kerosene on her clothes, igniting herself almost instantly. She died within hours. The daughter of farmer Archer Gray Herndon, Jr., lived at the River Dell Farm in southwest Rochester Township. She was the niece of Abraham Lincoln's law partner, William Herndon.

- An argument between two township men followed an early-morning card game in a Springfield saloon. It ended when Armstrong D. Young stabbed Higginson Peddicord several times. Although both men were fined for fighting, Young was arrested and spent the night in the county jail. It was not long before Amanda Peddicord sued the bar owner, William Beckmeyer, for the loss of Peddicord's money during the evening's card games and the loss of wages as her husband recovered. Although she also asked for "exemplary damages," Amanda received just $40 for the lost wages. Young would be deeply involved in Rochester law-enforcement efforts in the future.

- An 1872 Rochester death began with the boyish prank of setting off firecrackers behind Taylor Dickerson and the young miss he was escorting home on July 4th. Dickerson challenged the scoundrel to a fight, which over several days escalated to what news reports termed a "riot." Friends, neighbors, and family members took sides, and "the little village of Rochester became a fearful pandemonium." One attempt to arrest two individuals by the name of Kendall for fighting and disturbing the peace came to a violent end when one of the hastily deputized peace officers, Dr. J.M. Burch, shot and killed one of the men as he tried to escape.

- Another death occurred when a war of words led to a fight between William Craig of Rochester and a man by the name of McCord from Morrisonville. McCord kicked Craig's head repeatedly and stomped on his body. The assailant pleaded guilty to assault and battery.

- Munson Carter and Edward Clark, two of Rochester's early pioneers, died this decade. Carter, Rochester's first village president, died in 1877 and is buried in Rochester Cemetery with his wife Ann *(Taft)* Carter, who died in 1882. Clark, who built Rochester's earliest mill on the South Fork River, is buried in Rochester Cemetery with both of his wives, Sarah *(Viney)* Clark and Nancy Ann *(Trotter)* Clark.

Edward Samuel and Carrie (Olcott) Clark, gathered here with the entire family, lived in a home that was estimated to have been built in the late 1870s. From left: Edward, Carrie with baby Fred,· Carroll, Floyd, Bertha, Ray, Mable, Ethel, Allie, and Alice. Edward is a direct descendent of the Clark Brothers who built a mill on the South Fork River. (PHOTO COURTESY OF PHIL SOUTHWICK)

The Edward S. Clark home on what is today Sweeney Drive was included in the 1918 Orange Judd *Pictorial*. Pieces of the home's stone foundation were most likely carried from Samuel Williams's stone quarry located a short distance south of the house. Edward was a grandson of early Rochester settlers Edward (1790-1875) and Sarah *(Viney)* (1803-1897) Clark. (COURTESY OF COMPASS POINT PRODUCTIONS; FARM PROGRESS COMPANIES)

An 1874 map indicates that the Samuel Williams's stone quarry was located on the property of Henry Clark west of Mottarville Cemetery. The stone from this quarry was used to build a mid-1800s Rochester school. The author located that quarry site in 2017 and photographed some of the remaining stones. (COURTESY OF DENNIS MCEVOY; R. BRUZAN PHOTO)

- At various points during the decade Rochester area farmers reported wheat production of 47 bushels per acre, which sold for 85 cents a bushel; 300-pound hogs selling for $3.25 per hundred; shipments of cattle weighing more than 1,600 pounds; and several unsuccessful mule sales in New Orleans.

  — Late July storms in 1873 drastically reduced apple, pear, corn, hay, oat, and wheat crops.

  — More than a dozen cows east of Rochester died the same year from a suspected infection of dry murrain, a disease of various names that is usually fatal.

- A successful downtown merchant with a newly constructed brick building, Carter Tracy, stepson of Munson Carter, also became an important political figure. He served as village president, a Sangamon County supervisor, and was elected as a Democrat to the Illinois General Assembly.

  — He married Louisa *Jaquays* in 1857 and built their imposing two-story gothic-style home, which still stands, on Mill Street. Their daughter, Jessie, who died at age two, is buried in Rochester Cemetery.

  — Soon after being elected as a state representative, Carter's social life began to draw considerable attention. His association with the Springfield soiled dove Bertha Eugene became apparent when one of their frequent altercations resulted in Carter receiving serious head wounds from a severe beating with a poker and the butt end of a gun.

  — Newspaper reports also detailed one occasion during which an intoxicated Bertha

Erected by Carter Tracy circa 1878 for his store, this East Main Street building has served variously as a dry goods store, restaurant, Masonic meeting hall, church, and office building. As of 2017, it houses an antique store and apartments. (R. BRUZAN PHOTO)

Eugene demanded that he leave a House session in the state's General Assembly, and another in which she led "her little lamb away" from a dance by his whiskers. Besides being asked to resign his legislative seat, Carter was also expelled from the Rochester lodges of the Odd Fellows and Masons.

  — Carter's marriage was also precarious. His "invalid" wife Louisa caught him with Emma Bailey late one evening in his Rochester second-floor office. Because Carter deflected Louisa's arm, she only shot her husband in the leg and then fainted immediately. Fearing Louisa's wrath, Carter escaped out a side window and down a tree. He grabbed a ladder for Emma to climb down, and the two drove to Springfield by horse and buggy.

— Louisa Tracy died in 1881. Carter Tracy, his son Fred and daughter Carrie moved to Beaver, OK, in 1885. Opening a store and law office, he also served there as a probate judge for six years. Carter died in 1905 and is buried in Beaver.

Carter Tracy moved to Beaver, OK, circa 1885. Some people attributed the poor performance of his Rochester store as the reason behind Tracy's relocation. He became a successful land owner, lawyer, judge, and business man in Beaver. (COURTESY OF THE BEAVER COUNTY HISTORICAL SOCIETY AND THE JONES AND PLUMMER MUSEUM)

- The July 22, 1879, edition of the short-lived *Sangamo Daily Monitor* reported that Henry Johnson of Rochester had just recovered from "a very severe case of sickness." Born in Vermont in 1816, Johnson arrived in Rochester at age 16. He married Joanna Twist in 1838, and they had nine children. Their son, Orson, died during the Civil War at Memphis, TN, and his body was brought back to Rochester for burial. Henry, who had served in the Blackhawk War, was a highly respected horseman, and served for five years on the Sangamon County Board of Supervisors. He died in 1889. Joanna died eight years later, and both are buried in Rochester Cemetery.

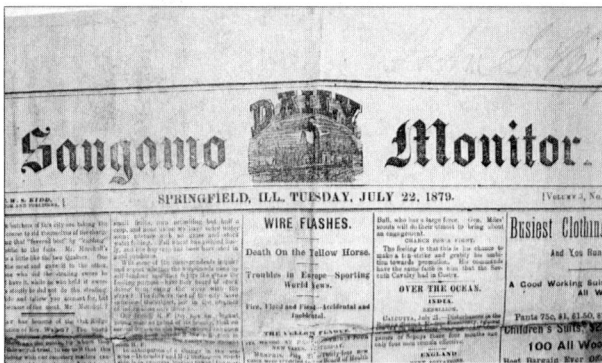

A July 22, 1879, issue of this short-lived Springfield newspaper mentioned Rochester Township land owner Henry Johnson. (COURTESY OF CLARISSA SHOCKLEY AND LOUISE MILLER; RHPS COLLECTION; R. BRUZAN PHOTOS)

—Henry Johnson, Esq., of Rochester, who has just recovered from a very severe case of sickness, was in the city yesterday, the guest of Henry Ramstetter, the good-natured host of the Brilliant House.

- During one Springfield-bound railroad trip soon after service began through Rochester, a train engineer saw some pigs on the tracks west of the village. The swine moved off the track at the sound of the train whistle, and the trip continued. When the train arrived in Springfield, however, a large uninjured hog was found comfortably snuggled in front of the train's warm "smoke box."

The Richard H. Coe house on West Main Street dates back to the mid-1800s. Richard's father, John C. Coe, traveled to Sacramento, CA, as a gold-seeking forty-niner. As a child, Richard sat on Abraham Lincoln's knee while his father and the future president talked. As of 2017, descendants of the Coe family own and reside in this historic Rochester home. (R. Bruzan photo)

Newspapers as early as 1872 mention "Bell's School," located four miles southeast of Rochester on the Springfield-to-Taylorville Road that passed across the land owned by Robert M. Bell. Bell homesteaded this area in 1830. Few students were present at Bell School on this day circa 1918. (Courtesy of Compass Point Productions; Farm Progress Companies)

The school pictured here was demolished in 1971 by Diana and Wayne Graham, who recovered a board with a list of students who had attended the school. The Grahams reused much of the wood from the school to build their home on the former school site. (Courtesy of Fay Jostes and Diana Graham; used with permission)

Rochester Circa 1880

1 Munson Carter Store & G. Phillips
2 His residence
3 Munson, (later his opp) and Tracy store.
4 Tracy store after he and half Bro divided stocks
5 School house
6 Odd Fellows Hall
7 Old Tavern, historical landmark
8 Tvist res. and farms
9 Tracy Res. and pasture
9½ Ma Neill (tent) Res.
10 Old (fur mill) Res.
11 Depot
12 Christian Church
13 Methodist Church
14 Universalist Church Oldest church
14½ Taft res. and farms
15 Neill res.
16 Cemetery, entrance through Taft est.

Frederick Carter drew this map in 1950 based on his childhood memories of Rochester circa 1880. Note that North is toward the bottom of the map, and east is on the left.
(COURTESY OF JAMES R. TAFT)

1880S

The Rochester Weekly Item began publication in 1882 and continued for 40 years. As of 2017, the authors have located only 10 issues of the paper. Editor Ethelbert Kalb became well known for his newspaper, as well as for his creation of Glenwood Park on the South Fork River.
(SANGAMON VALLEY COLLECTION, LINCOLN LIBRARY, SPRINGFIELD, IL)

1880s Timeline...

1880	Rochester population: 307
	— Baltimore & Ohio freight depot built
	— Two-story brick school built on East Main Street
1882	Ethelbert Kalb began publishing *The Rochester Weekly Item* newspaper
	— A central telephone office was installed in the Parker, Firey & Twist Store
1883	The Rochester Village Board accepted the plat of Henry John's Addition
1884	Milton D. McCoy built his home on East Main Street

1880s Storylines...

• Beginning in late 1882, regular news about Rochester was distributed throughout the village with publication of its first newspaper, *The Rochester Item*. Printed by *The Illinois State Journal*, it began as a "semi-monthly" publication. Within a few weeks, however, it grew to be *The Rochester Weekly Item*.

Daniel G. Kalb (1815-1905) came to Sangamon County from Maryland in 1849, served in the Civil War, and settled on a farm in northwest Rochester Township. His son, Ethelbert Kalb, established *The Rochester Weekly Item* in 1882 and developed the Glenwood Park recreation area on the South Fork River.
(*PAST AND PRESENT OF THE CITY OF SPRINGFIELD AND SANGAMON CO., VOL. 1*; JOSEPH WALLACE, S. J. CLARK PUB. CO., CHICAGO, 1904)

The early *Rochester Weekly Item* newspaper office was located on East Main Street, but in 1915 moved two doors west to the first floor of the Independent Order of Odd Fellows building.
(*ILLINOIS STATE JOURNAL*, 7 JUNE 1915; PUBLISHED BY GENEALOGYBANK.COM, A DIVISION OF NEWSBANK)

Its creator, Ethelbert Kalb, drew praise from Springfield newspapers that de-scribed him as having "an enviable reputation as a country journalist" and described his paper as "thoroughly reliable." Although *The Rochester Weekly Item* may have been a model weekly paper, it is believed that only about 10 issues remain as a source of information about life in turn-of-the-twentieth-century Rochester.

- One of Rochester's early large homes was built in 1884 on East Main Street by Milton D. McCoy. Milton had been born in the origi-nal McCoy cabin built by his fa-ther, Rochester's first homesteader James McCoy. The house later became the residence of M.D.'s son, Sylvester, a man who enjoyed racing horses. Milton and his wife Melcina *(Cooper)*, and Sylvester and his wife Pauline *(Able)* are all buried in Rochester Cemetery.

Milton D. McCoy, who built this home in 1884, had been a steward and class leader in the Rochester Methodist Episcopal Church for 40 years before his death in 1908 at age 85. His death came eight years after the death of his wife, Melcina *(Cooper)* McCoy. Their son, Sylvester, and daughter-in-law, Pauline *(Able)*, later lived in this house on East Main Street.
(COURTESY OF COMPASS POINT PRODUCTIONS; FARM PROGRESS COMPANIES)

Sylvester McCoy poses with his race horse, "Festus," and carriage at the intersection of North Walnut and East Main Streets. Shreve's Mill is visible on the left and a paint and hardware store on the right, where an unidentified man is sitting. (COURTESY OF BARBARA WAGNER)

Rochester's two-story brick school was built on East Main Street in 1880 at a cost of $5,000. It was the only school in the village until it was replaced in 1920 by a new building on North Walnut Street. The Rochester Masonic Lodge bought this building the same year. Notice part of the Woman's Christian Temperance Union temple to the right of the school and the dirt Main Street across the front. This photo was taken circa 1905.
(COURTESY OF THE ROCHESTER PUBLIC LIBRARY, RHPS COLLECTION)

- A rapid response to rebuild Rochester's wood school that was destroyed in a September 1880 fire resulted in a commanding two-story downtown brick school that was ready for students by January 1881. The new school was built at a cost of $5,000 on East Main Street west of Carter Tracy's store. The building would serve Rochester students for 40 years.

- Rochester remained a "dry town" when a newly seated village board voted in 1880 against a resolution to permit liquor sales. To the delight of the Temperance Party, the resolution and all liquor license requests were rejected immediately following that vote.

- Troublemaking:
  — John Sommers and Robert Vickers were arrested in 1882 for blowing open a safe owned by Rochester resident John Tobin and taking $100. They later claimed false imprisonment and made loud protests over having been vaccinated while in jail.
  — A year earlier the same pair, along with Charles Carter and Judson Horn had been arrested for breaking open the door of Rochester's "calaboose" jail in order to release the prisoner, Charles Vickers.
  — Charles Carter of Rochester was arraigned on a charge of assaulting Constable George W. Everhart with a double-barreled shotgun.
  — Constable Everhart was himself arrested in 1882 for the brutal beating of a black man with a billet. Details about that Rochester incident or disposition of the case were not found.

Lida Twist
Mamie Ott
John Twist
Chas. Goodrum
Burt Lyons
Samuel May
Chas. Vickers
Fred Everhart
Gussie May
Ada Davis
Carrie Shue
Minnie Workman
Gracie Lyons
Mattie Vickers
Frank Carter
Tracy Carter
Sadie Kerns
Henry Money
Fred May
Willie Lock
John Kerns
Herman Ott

It may have brought joy to some Rochester parents and embarrassment to others when student test scores became public knowledge throughout the community. After a series of exams during four months of school, these students' grade averages were published in the March 13, 1884, edition of *The Rochester Weekly Item*. (COURTESY OF LINCOLN LIBRARY, SANGAMON VALLEY COLLECTION)

- True love in Rochester apparently defied any age boundaries as village resident John T. Benham, age 93, was united in marriage to 24-year-old Catharine O'Donnell. It was his third marriage and her first. Their marriage ended soon, however, as the Black Hawk War veteran died just three years after the ceremony. Soon after John's death, Catharine relocated to Peoria.

Wedding picture of Deborah *(Bell)* and James Wickersham. James Wickersham, who studied Sangamon County Indian burial mounds extensively, lived with the Bell family in southeast Rochester Township. Wickersham married Deborah on October 27, 1880, in Rochester, and they lived briefly in Springfield before leaving for Tacoma, WA. (COURTESY OF HOUSE OF WICKERSHAM, JUNEAU, AK; USED WITH PERMISSION)

- The Preston Breckenridge Post of the Grand Army of the Republic was chartered in 1883 with 16 members. It recognized Breckenridge, who served for three years in the Illinois Infantry and died less than one day after returning home. Officers leading this Post #355 included C.F. Humphrey, C.C. Breckenridge, and D.F. Auxier. G.A.R. members were all Rochester Township veterans of the Civil War who had fought for the Union.

- Unwelcome wildlife in Rochester Township created hunting opportunities for some residents. Alexander Dunnavan claimed a record in 1885 when he and two friends killed 220 rats on a 200-acre farm whose owner was not identified.
  — Fewer snakes were alive on Sam Johnson's farm after he and Harry Taft executed 14 of the reptiles, nine of them rattlesnakes. Johnson, of Rochester, reported there were seven rattles on one of the snakes.

- With the availability of rail transportation, Rochester became a popular meeting location. The Masons and Odd Fellows often drew interested members from Springfield and other area lodges.

This undated early photo of the Independent Order of Odd Fellows building at the northeast corner of East Main and John Street was possibly taken between 1876-1890. (COURTESY OF THE ROCHESTER PUBLIC LIBRARY, RHPS COLLECTION)

— One major gathering was the 1889 Anti-Horse Thief Association picnic attended by 1,200–1,500 people on the grounds of Dan Ott's grove, about three-fourths of a mile west of Rochester. Besides the basket dinner, speeches, and music selections, a waltzing horse entertained the crowd.
— Another 1,500–2,000 participants of all ages from throughout the county and beyond enjoyed the 1887 Prohibition Picnic during which food, music, and speeches were the entertainment.
— When the 1888 Old Settlers of Sangamon County meeting was called to order at Ott's Grove by M.D. McCoy, an estimated 5,000 enjoyed seeing old friends and hearing stories from decades past. Participants also read the

names of Old Settlers who had died since the last annual meeting. Of particular interest was a display of relics that included a working flax wheel, kettle, 125-year-old plate, clock, plug hat, and a trammel brought to this country on the Mayflower. M.D. McCoy displayed a gun used in the War of 1812 and the Black Hawk War.

- Prostitution was common in Springfield, and multiple Rochester citizens were among those arrested in the city for "being inmates" of a "house of ill fame." — In a related matter, fines of $200 were assessed in 1885 to each of the campers who partied for several weeks along Sugar Creek near the wagon bridge on the Rochester Road. According to area farmers, the accused had been nude when they paraded in public and swam together. It was alleged that the party goers were "hard cases" and soiled doves.

- Both Democrat and Republican political party members met in Rochester at different times during 1884. — The Mechanicsburg band and the Rochester Glee Club entertained about 1,000 Democrats who gathered from nearby villages. A special train from Springfield brought 100 Democrats, including the featured speaker, former Texas Governor Richard Bennett Hubbard, Jr., who made a two-hour speech. — Special train service was also available for the Republican rally. The 2,500 attendees listened to speeches, enjoyed music of the Hibernian Band, and paraded with 745 torch lights. Hooligans, however, attacked their departing train, throwing bricks and exchanging gunfire with train riders. Although many train windows were broken, there were no serious injuries.

- The parents of a nine-year-old Rochester boy alerted police to search for the youngster, who, barefoot and wearing jeans and a straw hat, was making his way to Springfield for a chance to meet Buffalo Bill. The western show entertainer was scheduled to appear in two shows at the Sangamon County Fairgrounds. Among the featured acts were American cowboys, Mexican vaqueros, groups from American Indian tribes, and a menagerie of trained and wild animals "faithfully depict(ing) Life in the Wild West." The show was modestly advertised as "the most thrilling, romantic, and novel exhibition ever known."

- Illnesses and accidents:
  — Rochester had its very own "little" epidemic of measles in 1881.
  — **Mattie Coe**, the nine-year-old daughter of Richard and Helen Coe, died from diphtheria and scarlet fever in 1889.
  — As his mother absentmindedly held him on her lap, the 18-month-old son of Ira and **Julia Twist** reached for a bottle of carbonic acid and drank from it causing serious injuries.

— Two days after **August Thielmann** left the Brown farm to hunt, his body was found in a pasture on neighboring Graham property along the Rochester Road. Thielmann had apparently shot himself in the head accidentally while loading his gun.

— **Mitchell Kirkpatrick's** plan was to continue digging a well on John Clark's farm on Rochester Road. However, he sustained a massive head wound when he fell from the bucket that was being used to lower him into the ground. Doctors removed most of the skull from Kirkpatrick's forehead even before the man was moved to St. John's hospital. He died two days later.

— A **Rochester mother** sustained relatively minor injuries when she and her young son were thrown from their runaway horse and buggy. Her husband went head first over the dashboard at the same time, but was uninjured.

— In another runaway, "Humpy" Campbell became a hero when, not thinking of his own danger, he sprang toward **Lizzie Baker's** horse and buggy as it careened out of control through downtown Rochester. Grabbing one of the buggy shafts and lines he succeeded in slowing the horse and bringing the situation under control.

- Horses were still valuable to their owners. George E. Jones and Daniel Ott even raised Clydesdale horses for show.

  — Because horse thieves also prowled Sangamon County, a Rochester branch of the Anti-Horse Thief Association was created in 1884. The vigilance committee elected John S. Highmore president; Daniel A. Ott, William J. Sterling, and William J. Cooper, vice presidents; Samuel J. Smith, secretary; Edmund Miller, treasurer; and A.D. Young, director.

  — In spite of the association's efforts, a horse, buggy, and harness were stolen from Christian E. Miller of Rochester. Although an arrest warrant was issued for the thief, his capture was unreported.

- In 1882, just six years after Alexander Graham Bell received his patent for the telephone, a central telephone was established in Rochester. This connected the village to Springfield and other surrounding towns. Residents could make calls by visiting the telephone office, which was installed in the counting room of the Parker, Firey, and Twist store.

- Disease, weather, and trains took their toll on local livestock:

  — The severe losses of swine to hog cholera were exemplified by William Derry, who lost 66 of his 70 hogs in 1884.

  — Three years later the extreme heat caused the death of several hogs belonging to Henry Clark.

  — William and Henry Taft sued the Ohio and Mississippi Railroad for $140 in 1881 for the death of four steers.

- Deaths of key community members:
1881 & 1882
— It was 1832 when Vermont natives John Lock (1799-1881) and his wife, Maria *(Jaques)* arrived in Rochester. John donated both the timber and labor to build the village's first steam mill, the location of which has not been determined. It was at Lock's tavern where young people of Rochester learned square dances and the polka. Maria died a year after John and is buried with him in Rochester Cemetery.

1883
— Dr. Richard J. McNeil, who had moved to the village in 1869, died of consumption at age 43. Dr. McNeil was known for never allowing the weather to keep him from the sick, traveling by foot when the roads were impassable for his horse. He was a charter member of the Rochester Masonic Lodge in 1869, and 50 members attended his funeral.

— Dr. Edwin R. Babcock was a New York native who served at the Camp Yates post hospital near Springfield during the Civil War. After relocating to Rochester, he

An elaborate memorial card remembers John A. Twist, who was born November 11, 1826, and died March 17, 1880. His Rochester-born son Ira would become one of the largest cotton farmers in the country. (COURTESY OF JOHN RUNIONS; USED WITH PERMISSION)

Dr. Oliver Brewster Babcock posed circa 1918 at his "Hylo Farm" on Poffenberger Lane (now Woodhaven Drive) west of the South Fork River. He and his family had come to Sangamon County in 1863 from New York. Oliver's father, Dr. Edwin Babcock, was a surgeon at Springfield's Camp Yates during the Civil War. After settling in Rochester, the father and son practiced medicine together. (COURTESY OF COMPASS POINT PRODUCTIONS; FARM PROGRESS COMPANIES)

Right: Dr. O.B. Babcock poses with his daughter Madeline. She was born in 1887 and died in 1952, after becoming nationally known for her book *The Lemon Jelly Cake*. Characters in the book were based on individuals she remembered from Rochester. (COURTESY OF THE ROCHESTER PUBLIC LIBRARY, RHPS COLLECTION)

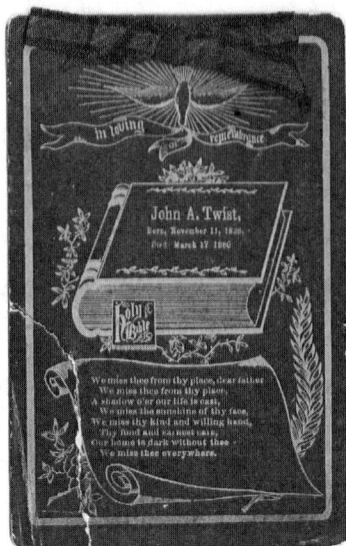

joined the Methodist Church. His son, Oliver Brewster Babcock, also became a doctor, serving the Rochester area with his father.

- When Louis Persinger was born in 1887 to Rochester Christian Church members Susan *(Humphrey)* and Amos Persinger, no one in Rochester could have imagined the international recognition Louis would gain as a violinist and pianist. The year after Louis was born his father was elected village clerk; Amos was listed as Rochester's railroad agent in 1889. The little family moved west shortly thereafter.

- Roads into Springfield were difficult to navigate during January 1882. However, one writer to the *Daily State Journal* described how visitors would despair upon their arrival in Springfield. This writer claimed that, between the city limits and Springfield's downtown business district, visitors could only "contemplate the vast sea of mud, sometimes with a frozen crust on top."
  — The writer concluded that because of Springfield's travel challenges, business in Rochester was booming as local merchants stocked a large supply of goods to meet every need. Besides thriving dry-goods and grocery stores, the writer observed that Mr. Tobin's new hog slaughtering and packing business was showing signs of success. Creation of a Rochester bank was even mentioned.

- By accepting the 1883 survey and plat of Henry John's Addition, the Rochester Village Board indicated its support of continued orderly growth. John's Addition included a number of properties north of Main and east of John Streets that included residential and commercial opportunities. Lots were soon offered for sale at $100–$185.

Rochester merchant and politician Carter Tracy left Rochester in 1885, relocating to Beaver, OK, where he ran a mercantile business and served as probate judge. This 1900 picture was taken during a picnic of Beaver's Modern Woodmen of America. With a full white beard, Tracy is the third man from the left in the back row. His son, Fred Carter Tracy, is fourth from the left in the middle row. Fred sketched the Rochester map used in this decade.
(*BEAVER COUNTY HISTORY BOOK, VOL. 2*; COURTESY OF BEAVER COUNTY HISTORICAL SOCIETY AND THE JONES AND PLUMMER MUSEUM; USED WITH PERMISSION)

ROCHESTER CIRCA 1894

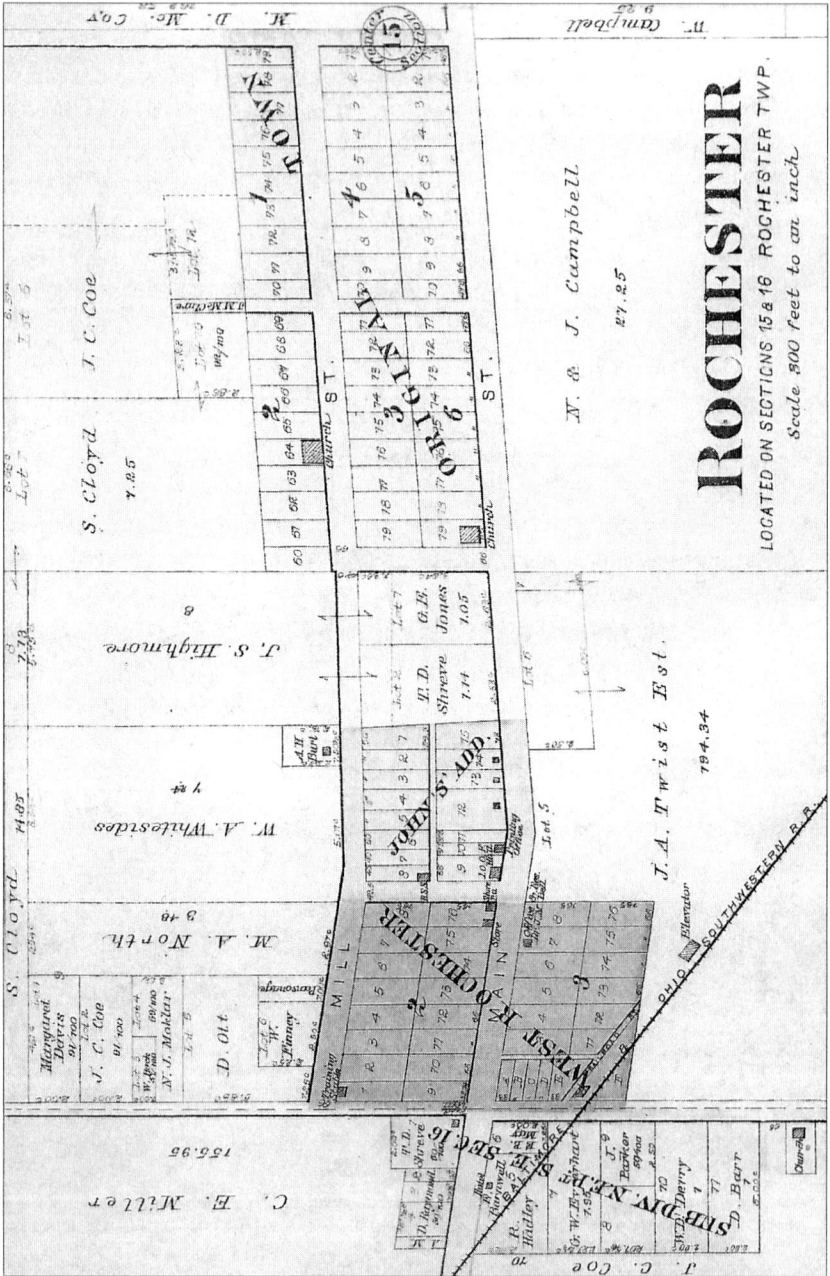

This 1894 Rochester map identifies the original town layout as well as West Rochester, John's Addition, and Section 16 subdivision. (*PLAT BOOK OF SANGAMON COUNTY ILLINOIS*, FIELD PUBLISHING CO., CHICAGO, IL, 1894)

1890s

Ira Twist became the nation's second largest cotton producer, owning 25,000 acres of land in Arkansas and 1,500 acres of land in Sangamon County. Pictured here are, from left: Clarence, Ira, and Frank Twist, all originally of Rochester. (COURTESY OF TERRY AND MIKE TWIST; SECURED BY JEAN BRICKEY AND CHRISTINE CARY)

1890s Timeline...

1890	Rochester population: 330
1891	Woman's Christian Temperance Union (WCTU) temple was completed on East Main Street
1893	Twist Brothers Lumber & Grain elevator business was established
1894	Ethelbert Kalb created Glenwood Park along the South Fork River
1896	A steel Baltimore & Ohio Railroad bridge was erected over the South Fork River west of Rochester
1898	Rev. T.B. Wright home built on East Main Street

The Woman's Christian Temperance Union temple on East Main Street was dedicated in 1891. This postcard is dated 1909. (COURTESY OF THE ROCHESTER PUBLIC LIBRARY, RHPS COLLECTION)

1890s Storylines...

- A $4,000 Woman's Christian Temperance Union (WCTU) temple on East Main Street was dedicated in 1891. Located downtown next to the two-story school, this structure remained a vibrant part of Rochester until its demolition 77 years later. The WCTU auditorium was a meeting place for political, religious, and school gatherings that drew hundreds of people from Springfield and other communities.

  — High school commencements, attracting more than 600 graduates, families, and friends, were held at the WCTU. Early in the school district's history, Rochester students graduated after their junior year because the district provided just three years of high school.

A gathering of young and old took place at the Rochester WCTU temple in downtown Rochester circa 1895. (COURTESY OF THE ROCHESTER PUBLIC LIBRARY, RHPS COLLECTION)

  — Rochester citizen Edmund Miller, who ran for political office on the Prohibition Party ticket, spoke frequently at WCTU meetings.

- Little remains today of the 50-acre park that thousands of recreation seekers enjoyed in Rochester Township around the turn of the 20th century. Multitalented newspaper man Ethelbert Kalb developed Glenwood Park in the early 1890s on the east bank of the South Fork River about two miles north of Rochester.

A short cruise on the little steamboat "Lalla Rookh" and a pleasurable afternoon of rowing on the South Fork River were two of the diversions available at Glenwood Park, north of Rochester. (COURTESY OF *THE STATE JOURNAL-REGISTER*; SANGAMON VALLEY COLLECTION, LINCOLN LIBRARY, SPRINGFIELD, IL; USED WITH PERMISSION)

— A dance pavilion, bowling alley, dining hall, row boats, and livery with feed barns attracted visitors from Central Illinois even beyond Rochester and Springfield. Ice skating was available during the winter. An estimated crowd of 1,500-1,800 people attended an 1897 Odd Fellows picnic at the park.

— When Kalb had a dam built, enough water backed up that his 25-passenger steamboat, the "Lalla Rookh," could travel up river as far as the Baltimore and Ohio Railroad bridge west of Rochester.

— The picnic resort was just 100 yards from the Indianapolis, Decatur and Western (ID&W) Railroad station. The Springfield and Rochester Interurban also served the park briefly during the 1900s.

The covered bridge over Black Branch Creek on Walnut Street Road circa 1900 led to Glenwood Park, located on the east bank of the South Fork River. It appears that the photographer is looking south through the bridge. To the left of the words Glenwood Park, the bridge portal has written on it "no liquor or improper persons allowed." (COURTESY OF *THE STATE JOURNAL-REGISTER*; USED WITH PERMISSION)

The dam at Glenwood Park across the South Fork River provided a pool of water upon which recreational boats could navigate. Also visible in the background of this photograph, taken about 1895, is the covered bridge across Black Branch Creek south of the dam. The authors found no evidence of the covered bridge or dam during a 2015 site visit. (JAMES A. WOODRUFF COLLECTION; SANGAMON VALLEY COLLECTION, LINCOLN LIBRARY, SPRINGFIELD, IL; USED WITH PERMISSION)

By the time this 1918 photo of the Glenwood Park pavilion was taken, the park had been largely abandoned. In earlier decades, however, its dance hall, bowling alley, boat rides, buggy rentals, ice cream parlor, and fried-chicken dinners had been enjoyed by thousands of visitors. (COURTESY OF COMPASS POINT PRODUCTIONS; FARM PROGRESS COMPANIES)

— Alcoholic beverages were prohibited, although it was known that some of society's "rough element" went into the nearby woods to guzzle beer and "have a time." Glenwood Park began to decline after Kalb's death in 1903.

- When Emma Wright died in 1896, 12 years after the death of her two-year-old son David, her husband Thomas had to rebuild his life. Their college-age daughter Mary also survived. Rev. Wright, pastor of Rochester's Methodist Episcopal Church, married Lillian *McCoy* in 1897. The couple welcomed their only child Helen a year later at about the same time they moved into a new house on the corner of Oak and East Main Streets.

Rev. Thomas B. Wright, his wife Emma, and daughter Mary may have already moved to Rochester when this photo was taken. Mary attended Northwestern University to study for the ministry, and in 1896 Emma died of a heart condition. Rev. Wright took a second wife in 1897 when he married Lillian McCoy, granddaughter of Rochester's first homesteader James McCoy. (COURTESY OF CAROLE STRICK AND THE ROCHESTER UNITED METHODIST CHURCH)

The Rev. Thomas B. Wright house on East Main Street was built in 1898. It was the home of Thomas and his wife Lillian until their deaths in the 1920s. (COURTESY OF COMPASS POINT PRODUCTIONS; FARM PROGRESS COMPANIES)

— Lillian was the granddaughter of Rochester's first homesteader, James McCoy, and the new home was built on what was still McCoy-owned land.

— While continuing many of his pastoral duties, T.B. Wright would also go on to edit *The Rochester Weekly Item*, buy and sell land actively, and become involved with other farm-related businesses.

Twist family members who gathered circa 1917 are, from left: Clarence with son Ira, Edith with the baby Giltner, Florence, Claribel, Frank, and Ira. (COURTESY OF TERRY AND MIKE TWIST; SECURED BY JEAN BRICKEY AND CHRISTINE CARY)

• The son of a local pioneering family, Rochester merchant John A. Twist passed his local business to sons Ira and Ralph. In turn, those men and their younger brothers, Noah and John, created the Rochester-based Twist Brothers Lumber & Grain Company in 1893.

— They also experienced phenomenal growth in both Illinois and Arkansas. Seven grain elevators in Sangamon County and 1,500 acres of farmland in Illinois were eventually under their ownership.

Ira Twist's house on the southeast corner of East Main and John Streets is pictured circa 1918. (COURTESY OF COMPASS POINT PRODUCTIONS; FARM PROGRESS COMPANIES)

In 1922 the life of Twist, AR, centered around the nearby Twist cotton plantation. (COURTESY OF JEAN BRICKEY AND CHRISTINE CARY)

TWIST 4
JCT AR 149 10

Twist, Arkansas, was named after Ira Twist. In 2017 this highway sign still directed travelers to the tiny community that was a hub of cotton production around the turn of the 20th century. (COURTESY OF JEAN BRICKEY AND CHRISTINE CARY)

— As Ira acquired about 25,000 acres of delta land in Arkansas, he became the second largest cotton producer in the United States. The small community of Twist, AR, was named for Ira Twist.

Servants for the Twist family may have lived in this two-level brick building located directly east of their house. In this 1946 photograph June *(Gaddey)* Park and Fay *(Gaddey)* Fields stand in the doorway, shortly before the building was removed to make room for an addition to the Park Funeral Home. Visible in the background are the C.E. Miller and A.D. Young homes on East Main Street. (COURTESY OF GREG PARK)

- Armed with a fire extinguisher, an alert John Twist saved Murphy & Everhart's restaurant from certain destruction in 1895 when a leaking gas stove caused a fire. Not so lucky were two other Rochester buildings.
  — C.E. Miller's two-story home was completely destroyed by a fire that started in the kitchen stove. Although Rochester did not yet have a fire department, citizens helped to rescue some of the home's contents.
  — A defective chimney flue sparked the rapidly moving fire that leveled Mrs. Esther Ann *(Coe)* Barnwell's two-story boarding house on West Main Street in 1899. An 1894 Rochester map identifies the boarding house as a hotel.

- Marriages:
  — A newspaper account described the October 14, 1890, double wedding of sisters Ella and Lydia Twist as a "brilliant society event." The daughters of Eliza and the late John A. Twist were described as both "handsome and accom-

plished." Ella married William P. Troxell, while Lydia wed William H. Kernoll. Only four months later, however, Ella died of consumption at age 27 and was buried in Rochester Cemetery.

— Sixty-three-year-old bachelor James M. Coe surprised everyone when he brought home a wife, Virginia native Miss Nettie Sanbouer, who was 36. Rochester residents greeted the occasion with a noisy shivaree. Again, death was not far behind this celebration as the groom died of typhoid in 1894, one year and two days after his marriage.

— Several teens used rail services to escape their stern parents and elope. Seventeen-year-old Ora Torrence was thought to have left by train with 35-year-old widower John Ruthrauff to begin what would become 40 years of marriage. J. Brewster Highmore, 19, and Lulu Poffenbarger, age 17, took the train to St. Louis to say their wedding vows.

This quietly haunting tombstone was erected in Rochester Cemetery to honor 26-year-old Eliza (Twist) Troxell, who died in 1891 just a few months after her marriage to William P. Troxell. (R. BRUZAN PHOTO)

— Marriage longevity was celebrated in Rochester on March 29, 1898, with the golden wedding anniversary of Milton and Malcina (Cooper) McCoy. Their children surprised them with gifts of $50 in gold coins and two bottles of gold dust. One of their sons, Jacob, sent his parents more than $100 in placer gold and gold quartz from Cripple Creek, CO, to commemorate the occasion.

• Diseases recorded in Rochester during a single week in the spring of 1895 included pleurisy, heart trouble, malaria, neck abscess, sore throat, lung trouble, and the grip, a respiratory disease.

• Diphtheria was sufficiently widespread at one point to close Rochester Township schools, and 16-year-old Moselle Miller, daughter of Christian and Martha Miller, was one of several typhoid-fever victims.

• Other deaths included:

1890
— **Archer G. Herndon, Jr.,** (b. 1826) farmed extensively southwest of Rochester and is buried in Springfield's Oak Ridge Cemetery. He was a brother of William H. Herndon, Lincoln's friend and law-office partner.

1891
— **Robert Sattley** (b. 1837]), a descendent of one of the village's earliest settlers, was born in the "old tavern." That building was later moved across East Main Street to Twist property. At the time of his death, Robert lived about three miles east of Rochester.

1894
— **Andrew Hollenback** (b. 1807) moved to Sangamon County in 1830 and worked with his brother Lawrence to lay out early Rochester. Some historians have also given the brothers credit for selecting the village's name.

1894 & 1895
— **Daniel Barr** (b. 1817), a blacksmith by trade, at one time owned a log house on South Walnut Street that was rediscovered in 1988. His wife, **Elvira** *(Bowling)* (b. 1820), who was among the first white children born in what was to become Rochester Township, died one year after her husband.

1895
— **Ebenezer Coe** (b. 1812) farmed land east of Rochester, and at the time of his death was said to be one of Rochester Township's largest landowners.
— **Julia** *(Atkinson)* **Twist,** the wife of businessman Ira Twist, died of an "abscess on the hip" at age 32. In addition to her husband, survivors included three children.

• After enjoying "too much of that which . . . causes the soul to flow," Rochester Constable Samuel W. Hankins was escorted to a Springfield police station by city officers. Reports theorized that since Hankins lived in a "dry town," he was not used to intoxicants. He was released after having "squared matters."

• Mrs. Esther Barnwell's hotel was the focus of an 1896 report that involved local "nice guy," Joe Murphy. One of Mrs. Barnwell's daughters had caught Murphy's fancy and after a few relaxing drinks, the would-be suitor would come to visit the object of his affections. Hotel residents were not amused and "bolted and barricaded" the doors and windows.
— Someone would also run to get the constable, but he would usually arrived after Murphy left the premises. One day, however, Constable Hankins arrested the local character on a peace warrant.
— Although the accused opted for a bench trial, he declined to join "the entire population of the town" who had apparently come to testify or witness the event. Murphy was only fined $50 since the worst that could be proven against the would-be wooer was that he once said "of the women of the hotel that he 'would drive all those jay birds up a tree.'"

• An estimated 3,000 people attended the 1890 Farmers Mutual Benefit Association meeting at Ott's Grove near Rochester. All enjoyed the picnic lunch, speakers, and music of Springfield's Germania Band. The Association had been formed in Illinois during the 1880s by farmers in order to promote fair sales of their produce and add their collective voices to a variety of other agriculture-related issues.

This photo from the collection of Netty *(Bailey)* Coe was taken during an 1896 camping party near Buckhart. Present were Mr. and Mrs. S.B. Coe, Mrs. C.E. Miller, Mrs. G.E. Jones, Mollie Campbell, Anna and Ruth Parker, Jessie Peddicord, Nannie and Florentine St. Clair, Etta and Clara Johnson, Ora Troxell, Lulu Renfrow, Gussie and Bettie King, L.F. Peddicord, Elmer Jones, Johnny Coe, Ed McCoy, Fred Poffenberger, Lyman Wright, Ben Richardson, Fred Glenn, Charles DeLay, Everett Campbell, George Troxell, C.E. Miller, and F.B. Everhart.
(*THE ROCHESTER & LAKE SPRINGFIELD HERALD*, 27 AUG. 1987)

- Local law-breakers:
  — Three chicken thieves were ambushed on Rochester Road in 1896 by five Rochester citizens who had been waiting to rescue the plundered fowl. Although those citizens emptied five revolvers and two shotguns at the backs of the fleeing thieves, their prey escaped, apparently unscathed.

Members of the Anti-Horse Thief Association also worked to reduce farm vandalism including chicken theft, orchard looting, and reckless hunting. Rochester members of the active Cooper Township AHTA included Henry D. Geiger, Daniel Ott, A.D. Young, and J.M. Bell. This association Constitution and By-laws booklet is dated 1894.
(COURTESY OF KENT KURNISKIE)

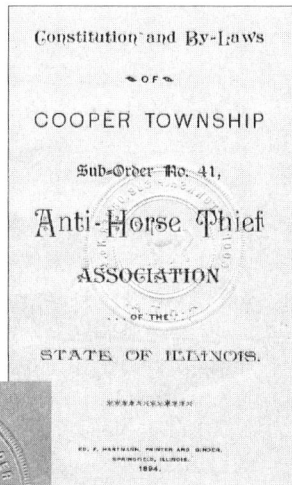

Constitution and By-Laws

OF

COOPER TOWNSHIP

Sub-Order No. 41,

Anti-Horse Thief

ASSOCIATION

OF THE

STATE OF ILLINOIS.

ED. F. HARTMANN, PRINTER AND BINDER,
SPRINGFIELD, ILLINOIS.
1894.

— Two years earlier one of three chicken thieves was captured, but only after Rochester residents sprayed his buggy with buckshot and then brought the abandoned vehicle to the Springfield police station. When the alleged thief reclaimed the buggy he was arrested and brought back to Rochester.

— Everhart and Woodruff's general store was robbed of an estimated $100 worth of items that included canned goods, a telescope, and 1,000 cigars.

Because Rochester did not have a bank until 1900, most Rochester citizens banked in Springfield. This 1899 Ridgely National Bank check was made out to Rochester store owner F.M. DeLay by Rochester livestock dealer and resident C.E. Miller. (COURTESY OF KELLY GRIFFIN)

— Several thieves tried to burgle F.M. DeLay's store and the post office before hitting the store of Parker & Coe. Although that was the only one of the three targets where the thieves could have found money, an upstairs tenant, Admiral Campbell, heard them and commanded them to "halt." The thieves escaped on a B&O Railroad handcar after the 17-year-old Campbell fired three shots at them.

— Marshal A.H. Burt arrested five tramps after R.S. Twist noticed them wearing what turned out to be stolen Stetson hats with price tags still attached. The thieves had apparently robbed a Chatham store and seemed to enjoy wearing their stolen headwear and other finery.

• Equine accidents:
   — D.A. Ott lost a horse that fell into an uncovered well.
   — Horses owned by Samuel Wolford and William Ginther were killed instantly when struck by lightning during two separate storms.
   — Thomas Norris lost four horses when they decided to eat their way through a wheat stack and died after eating too much of the grain.

• Accidents incurred by humans:
   — **Nicholas Haynes** died four days after a cider press crank he had released hit him above his right eye, slicing his head to the bone.
   — **James Gardner**, "a colored boy" who worked for C.E. Martin, was swimming with friends under the Rochester Road wagon bridge when he drowned in the South Fork River.
   —When brakeman **Charles Greenwood** was thrown from a freight car in Rochester, the train rolled over him, cutting off one foot and part of his other.
   — While butchering hogs, **J.C. Dawley** sliced off one finger tip.
   — When **James Derry's** horse team ran away, Derry was tossed from the wagon into a telegraph pole. He received a concussion and bruises.
   — A horse kicked four-year-old **Harry James**, fracturing his skull.

- Wildlife:
  — Two cents a head for dead sparrows was the going rate in February 1895, as John Johnson caught 300 of them with a string-sprung trap.
  — Thanks to the cold that same winter, other wildlife was also easily caught including rabbits, quail, carp, and buffalo fish.
  — Samuel Fairchild and two brothers, Albert and Phillip Leaderbrand, trapped mink and raccoons during the winter of 1894.
  — Weasels were unwelcome farm invaders, known to kill 50 chickens per visit.
  — Farmer-fisherman Theodore Derry was served an arrest warrant for building an illegal dam used to trap fish. Because Derry removed the dam and agreed not to violate fish laws in the future, he was not arrested.

- Sangamo Lodge No. 509 Knights of Pythias began to meet in Rochester during 1895. Founded in 1864 by Justus H. Rathbone, this international fraternity continues to promote understanding among men of good will in order to reach universal peace and harmony. Rochester members were initiated by 75 knights from Springfield who arrived by a special B&O train.

- New buildings and infrastructure improvements went hand in hand during the decade.
  — Wood plank sidewalks began to be replaced by bricks in 1893, and 2,000 feet of brick sidewalks were expected to be laid in 1897.

Bricks were used to replace Rochester's plank sidewalks beginning in the 1890s. Remnants of those brick sidewalks still exist as shown in the above 2016 photograph taken on the east side of Pleasant Lane. (R. Bruzan photo)

Two Utt Bros. bricks were found in the South Fork River bank near the Clark Mill site in 2015. Two brick companies, the Utt Bros. on Rochester Road in Woodside Township and the Twist Bros. on South Walnut Street in Rochester, provided building and paving bricks during the 1890s. The top brick is black shale, and the bottom brick is red. (R. Bruzan photo)

Left: The original wooden railroad trestle across the South Fork River west of Rochester was replaced in 1896 by this steel bridge. Although the tracks have been removed, the bridge deck was rebuilt for use today by bikers and hikers on the Lost Bridge Trail. (R. BRUZAN PHOTO)

Right: The wooden railroad trestle that was built circa 1896 across West Main Street was removed in 1995 as street improvements were made at this location. (DANIEL G. MOORE PHOTO; USED WITH PERMISSION)

— Work on a railroad trestle over West Main Street began and the new steel B&O Railroad bridge over the South Fork River was completed in 1896.

— The Twist Brothers built a new ice house.

— Ira Twist joined A.H. Lakin, J.S. Highmore, and H.P. Clark to incorporate the Rochester Creamery Company.

— Ideas were considered for a new road in southwest Rochester Township, a new town hall, and a telephone line between Rochester and Pawnee.

• Besides the occasional shots in the night, other forms of assault also took place:

— At first report, it was an on-going feud between Rochester residents Charles McCoy and William Dolly that led to a clubbing, a face slapping, and Dolly stabbing McCoy in the right arm, right shoulder, right side, and over the right eye. That report said that Dolly ran, making good his escape and leaving McCoy with life-threatening wounds. After further review, however, it seems that Dolly and McCoy had been partying with some friends and were passing by the home of Edward Bennett, north of Rochester. One thing led to another, and Bennett stabbed McCoy, but not seriously. Dolly was uninjured.

— Another knifing took place between Republicans Cooper Funderburk of Rochester Township and O.B. Grubb of Cotton Hill Township, who got into a

A notation in the lower left corner of this photograph reads, "Star Bridge, Rochester Road, 1895." Several Illinois covered bridges with a star on their portal have been recorded. It has not been confirmed if this bridge carried Rochester Road across the South Fork River or Sugar Creek. (COURTESY OF KAREN ALEXANDER AND HAZEL PARK)

heated political argument that degenerated into a brawl in a Springfield bar. The fight ended when Funderburk slashed Grubb across the face, his eye, and down his chin with a razor-sharp knife. Grubb survived.
— Not everyone supported the prohibition cause. Rochester residents Edward Henry and Edmund Miller were among the targets of egg and whiskey-bottle throwers as they rode home from an 1882 Prohibition rally in Buckhart.

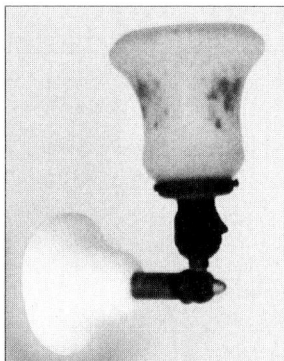

Before electricity came to Rochester homes in 1915, gas lights were common. Few original gas light fixtures still exist in Rochester like this one pictured in an East Main Street home. Note the gas line extending out of the wall to the frosted-glass Victorian light fixture. (PATT PATTERSON PHOTO; USED WITH PERMISSION)

- About 400 baseball fans at Coe's grounds enjoyed watching the Rochester Invincibles decisively beat the visiting Springfield Infants 18 to 8. The 1893 Rochester team roster included: Conley, Campbell, Wolford, T. May, Riddle, S. May, Miller, E. Campbell, and Morgan. The umpires were Clifford from Springfield and Twist from Rochester.

- Early settler Daniel Ott, a farmer until 1872, developed a livery business in Rochester on the southeast corner of Mill and North Walnut Streets. There he provided seven to ten horses and buggies to his customers. Ott sold his property to George Doane in 1894 for $4,700 and moved his family to Oklahoma, where he died in 1916. Ott is buried in the Yukon, OK, Cemetery.

- Train-related incidents became common:
  — A west-bound train full of grain jumped its tracks at the Sugar Creek bridge with 300 feet of track ripped up and train cars thrown willy nilly around the site. Train travel was discontinued until repairs were made.
  — Weather conditions sometimes affected train travel, as when an east-bound early-morning B&O train encountered fog so thick that the engineer passed beyond the Edinburg station before realizing that he had missed stops miles back at the Rochester and Breckenridge stations.
  — Ten of Samuel Smith's horses trotted away from their cornfield in 1896. Several made it to the B&O tracks and started across a trestle. An oncoming train stopped before hitting them, and the farmer successfully removed three of his injured horses from the bridge. Two other horses died, however, when they jumped from the trestle.
  — Another accident was averted when J.W. Richardson and C.H. Schwartz reported a broken rail along what was identified as the Ohio and Mississippi tracks, but may have been the B&O. The men were rewarded with complimentary passes for train travel.

- The following teachers were assigned their teaching positions for the 1890 school year, although the year's length was not specified for each of them:
  — Rochester: Horace N. Foltz, principal, $75/ month (nine months); Laura A. Taylor, intermediate, $40/month (six months); Agusta (sic) May, primary, $35/month (nine months);
  — Bluff School: Charles Foss, $35/month (eight months);
  — Hedge School: Florence Dallman, $37.20/month;
  — Bell School: Alice Daigh, $35/ month;
  — Mottarville School: Charles King, $60/month (six months) and $50 (two months);
  — Round Prairie School: Mary E. Cockrell, $45/month (five months) and $40/month (three months);
  — Poffenbarger School: J.R. Morgan, $45/month;
  — Buckhart School: H.D. Giger, $52.50/month (eight months); and
  — Clear Lake School: J.F. Cooper, $50/month (six months).
  All of these were one-room country schools, except the school in the village of Rochester.

Rochester Public School commencement ceremonies were held at the Rochester Christian Church on South Walnut Street in 1894 and at the WCTU temple on East Main Street the following year. (COURTESY OF RUTH DRILLINGER)

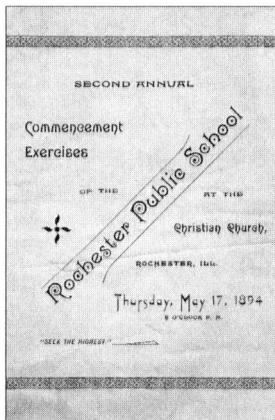

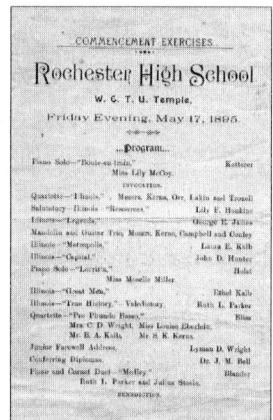

More than a century after someone wrote "May 11, 1890," and their initials on a wall of the Harcourt house on Mill Street, the current homeowners discovered the notation as they removed wallpaper from a bedroom in the 2010s. (HOUSE PICTURE COURTESY OF COMPASS POINT PRODUCTIONS; FARM PROGRESS COMPANIES; WALL NOTATION COURTESY OF ANDY AND JANE LUNT; R. BRUZAN PHOTO)

Jacob McCoy, right, was visited at least once in Cripple Creek, CO, by Rochester residents, from left: Nannie and Jasper Easley, his mother Malcina McCoy, and sister Mary McCoy. Although Jacob was a successful gold miner, ill-health led him to take his own life in 1901 at the McCoy family home. (RHPS COLLECTION)

Seated on a fence in 1916 are, from left: Thomas Bennett, his wife Gertrude *(King)* Bennett, Ester Chandler, and Persis *(King)* Chandler. Standing is Frank Chandler. The Bennetts, who farmed land north of the village, are the couple whose marriage was commemorated with an ornate certificate. Frank Chandler was a well-known builder of several Rochester homes around the turn of the 20th century. (COURTESY OF FAY JOSTES)

According to this marriage certificate of Thomas Bennett and Gertrude King, both of Rochester, they were married by the Rev. Thomas B. Wright of the Rochester Methodist Episcopal Church. Mr. and Mrs. S.B. Coe witnessed the ceremony on February 5, 1896. (COURTESY OF FAY JOSTES)

(Right): Rev. Montreville L. Browning, with his wife Etta and children Hugh and Flossie are pictured in 1893. Rev. Browning was a minister at the Rochester Methodist Episcopal Church from 1892 to 1895. (SANGAMON VALLEY COLLECTION, LINCOLN LIBRARY, SPRINGFIELD, IL)

Rochester Circa 1906

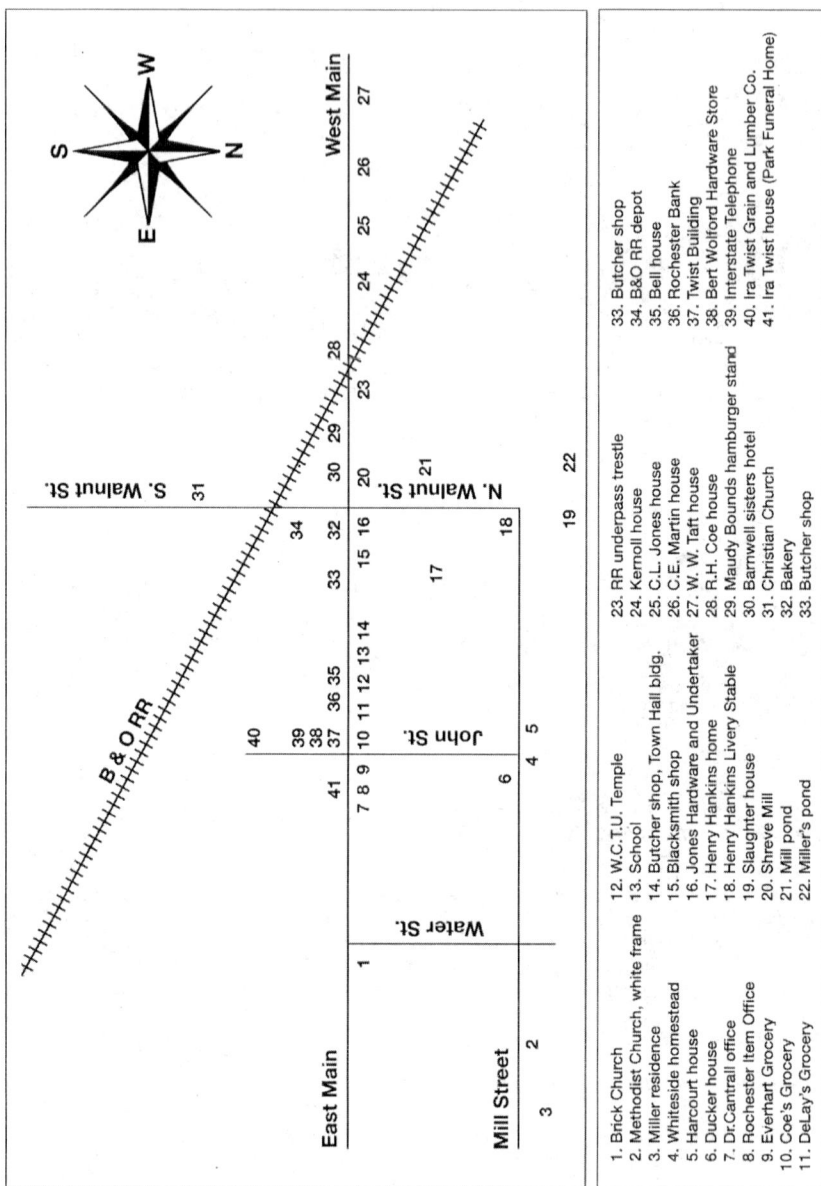

1. Brick Church
2. Methodist Church, white frame
3. Miller residence
4. Whiteside homestead
5. Harcourt house
6. Ducker house
7. Dr.Cantrall office
8. Rochester Item Office
9. Everhart Grocery
10. Coe's Grocery
11. DeLay's Grocery
12. W.C.T.U. Temple
13. School
14. Butcher shop, Town Hall bldg.
15. Blacksmith shop
16. Jones Hardware and Undertaker
17. Henry Hankins home
18. Henry Hankins Livery Stable
19. Slaughter house
20. Shreve Mill
21. Mill pond
22. Miller's pond
23. RR underpass trestle
24. Kernoll house
25. C.L. Jones house
26. C.E. Martin house
27. W. W. Taft house
28. R.H. Coe house
29. Maudy Bounds hamburger stand
30. Barnwell sisters hotel
31. Christian Church
32. Bakery
33. Butcher shop
33. Butcher shop
34. B&O RR depot
35. Bell house
36. Rochester Bank
37. Twist Building
38. Bert Wolford Hardware Store
39. Interstate Telephone
40. Ira Twist Grain and Lumber Co.
41. Ira Twist house (Park Funeral Home)

This was based on a map drawn by Hazel Park. It represents the village of Rochester circa 1906.
(Original courtesy of Karen Alexander; Graphic by Mark Ritterbusch, Communication Design)

1900s

Mt. Deborah, Alaska, was named in 1907 by Judge James Wickersham for his wife Deborah *(Bell)* Wickersham of Rochester. The mountain's name became official in 1917. (MOUNTAIN PHOTO BY JONATHAN GRIFFITH; USED WITH PERMISSION; INSET PHOTO COURTESY OF HOUSE OF WICKERSHAM, JUNEAU, AK; USED WITH PERMISSION)

1900s Timeline...

1900	Rochester population: 365
	— Bank of Rochester was established and building constructed on East Main Street
1901	Tracks for the Indianapolis, Decatur, and Western (ID&W) Railroad were laid north of Rochester
	— Twist Addition east of South Walnut Street was surveyed
1902	Twist Building erected at East Main and John Streets
	— Keys Station built along what is today Tuxhorn Road
	— Estimated year a meat market was built on East Main Street
	— Rebekah Lodge #573 established in Rochester
1903	Twist Brothers installed the telephone office in their new building
	— Concrete sidewalks were placed in much of the village
	— Coal mine at Keys Station became operational
1907	A steel bridge replaced the condemned covered bridge over the South Fork River on the Rochester-to-Springfield Road

— Mt. Deborah in Alaska was named for Deborah Bell of Rochester

1908 Springfield, Clear Lake & Rochester Railroad (Interurban) began service

— Springfield race riot

1900s Storylines...

- The 20th century brought major growth and changes to Rochester village and township. Three major downtown buildings brought additional customers to the downtown area: Rochester Bank, Twist Building, and the butcher shop, which would later become the Town Hall. Coupled with completion of an interurban train connecting Rochester with Springfield and more than 20 new homes, Rochester was established as a bustling community. A major infra-structure problem, however, remained—dirt streets and roads. The Rochester Road was described in 1901 as among the "worst roads out of the city of Springfield."

Transportation technologies met in Rochester circa 1909 as represented on this postcard, with horses and buggies on the left and the electric Interurban trolley on the right. (COURTESY OF BILL L. COFFEY)

The South Fork bridge became so decrepit that it was condemned and closed. With the occasional sighting of automobiles and the promises of more in the near future, roads and bridges were improved to accommodate this emerging technology.

- A Rochester marriage was in some ways responsible for bringing the flat prairies of Central Illinois together with the mountainous terrain of Alaska. After township residents Deborah S. Bell and James Wickersham were mar-ried, his work assignment took them to their new home in Eagle, AK.

James and Deborah (Bell) Wickersham (on the right) stand in front of their log home in Eagle, Alaska, about 1900. The person on left is Lillian (Whitaker) Heilig, wife of James's legal associate Albert. (ALASKA STATE LIBRARY WICKERSHAM STATE HISTORIC SITE PHOTO COLLECTION; USED WITH PERMISSION)

Writing to her Rochester family in 1900, Deborah *(Bell)* Wickersham described this room in her Eagle City, AK, home. (ALASKA STATE LIBRARY WICKERSHAM STATE HISTORIC SITE PHOTO COLLECTION; USED WITH PERMISSION)

Rochester Township farmer Isaac B. Bell (1820-1880) and his wife Susan *(Stokes)* Bell (1822-1877) were the parents of Deborah Bell and are buried in the South Fork Church cemetery. Deborah married James Wickersham, who became a U.S. District Judge in Alaska. (COURTESY OF DWIGHT AND GRACE POPE)

— Judge Wickersham, who was also a territorial delegate to Congress from Alaska, demonstrated his love for his wife Deborah by naming a mountain after her. Mt. Deborah, officially identified by the Board of Geographic Names, has an elevation of 12,339 feet and is among the major peaks of the eastern Alaska Range.

— Deborah died in 1926 in the state of Washington. She is certainly one Rochester woman whose life took her to heights she never dreamed of as a child.

• A covered bridge over the South Fork River on the state road between Rochester and Springfield was condemned in 1903. It was, however, still the target of scorn in a 1905 *Illinois State Journal* editorial describing it as a bridge "that hangs and totters on its abutments and is likely to exist in this condition until it goes down carrying with it life and limb." A $2,640 contract to build an iron replacement was finally let in 1907. Some 50 years earlier area trees had been used to build the original picturesque, but eventually dangerous structure. It was said that Abraham Lincoln had surveyed the road.
— In 1904, after several years of debate, a covered bridge was also replaced with an iron bridge over Sugar Creek on the Rochester-to-Springfield Road.
— A low-water bridge over the South Fork River on an unnamed road near New City was replaced with a $4,000 span in 1905.

• The B&O Railroad delivered Rochester's first street car on June 8, 1908, and a celebration was set for the June 10th inaugural run of the Springfield, Clear Lake & Rochester (SCL&R) Interurban. Complete operations started only a segment at a time over several months. The eight-mile trip for this electric trolley, Number 4 Rochester, typically took about an hour, or two in bad weather, between downtown Rochester and Springfield. The rail line headed north from the village and paralleled Walnut Street and Gabriel Road to Mechanicsburg Road, where it turned west toward Springfield.

A downtown reception was held in Rochester on July 28, 1908, to celebrate completion of the Springfield, Clear Lake, and Rochester interurban railway. Note the rails in the dirt street and the utility poles needed to operate the electric trolley cars. Electricity to Rochester homes was not available until 1915. (JAMES WOODRUFF PHOTO; COURTESY OF ROCHESTER PUBLIC LIBRARY; RHPS COLLECTION)

Jim Bennett (inset) with several pictures of the Rochester Interurban Railroad that ran across his ancestors' property north of Rochester. Bennett Stop was the first place the trolley stopped after leaving the village on its way to Springfield. A uniformed motorman and a conductor, pictured in the photo at left, served riders on their eight-mile 50-minute trip from Springfield. (COURTESY OF JIM BENNETT; *ROCHESTER HERALD*; PHOTO INSET BY R. BRUZAN)

— Creation of this interurban was the dream of Springfield entrepreneur John E. Melick. He first incorporated the company in 1906 and planned the SCL&R track with a two-and-a-half-mile spur to a Clear Lake amusement park. Problems, however, soon developed when projected profits from that park never materialized. A poor balance sheet, coupled with poor materials and shoddy construction, led the Illinois Railroad and Warehouse Commission to shut the operation down in 1912 until track and bridge repairs were completed.

This time card for trips to Springfield and back to Rochester included an ad for an August 1909 Chautauqua at Clear Lake, which was also served by the Interurban. (COURTESY OF DICK WALLIN)

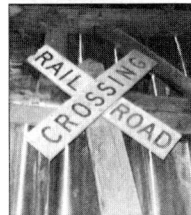

—After foreclosure in 1913 by the First Trust and Savings Bank of Springfield, several Rochester investors attempted in vain to re-open the rail line. Investors included: William Brown, Thomas Smith, Ralph Twist, Daniel Waters, S.J. McCoy, T.B. Wright, and Henry Schwartz. The two Interurban cars that had served Rochester became the property of William Brown, who sold them in Decatur.

— SCL&R creator Melick died in 1918 from injuries sustained when he was attacked by a track worker on a Calhoun County railroad venture. Today, other than an occasional railroad spike found along the Interurban track bed, little remains to remind village citizens of the brief period when Rochester's little street car carried excited riders to downtown Springfield.

- In other railroad news, a major extension of the Indianapolis, Decatur & Western (ID&W) Railroad was constructed about two miles north of the village in 1901. Several cases of smallpox were identified in the fall among the two dozen or so graders working on the new line. A Rochester doctor, John W. Cantrall isolated these men for treatment in hospital tents erected in a field of wheat stubble on one of the Twist Brothers' farms.

Artifacts from the ID&W RR that ran north of Rochester are still found occasionally. The kerosene switch lamp, top, and the target, center, were used to signal that a train should change tracks. The railroad crossing sign (bottom) had been posted where the tracks crossed Tuxhorn Road. (TOP AND CENTER PHOTOS COURTESY OF DAVE JOSTES; BOTTOM PHOTO COURTESY OF TIM AND TEANA SCANNELL; R. BRUZAN PHOTOS)

- Railroad mishaps:
  — In 1904, B&O brakeman Logue Jones fell from an eastbound train as it departed from Rochester. Jones sustained serious head and shoulder injuries when he attempted to move from a coach car to the engine, but slipped and fell to the ground. The accident was witnessed by another train employee, and Jones was taken back to Springfield on the next west-bound train to receive treatment.
  — Three years earlier Albert Lenz's fall from another train-car platform went unnoticed, and the Rochester resident lay on the ground all night until he regained consciousness and made his way to a station in Philadelphia, IL. There he caught another train home. He later lost his suit against the B&O for $5,000 in damages.
  — William Taft was awarded $750 in damages for four horses killed in 1908 by a B&O passenger train.
  — A failed attempt to derail a B&O passenger train west of Rochester occurred at the Sugar Creek bridge on Christmas Eve in 1902. Because the train left Rochester late, the engineer ran at full speed down the grade from Hilltop, smashing into a rail placed across the tracks. It was widely believed that a derailment there would have caused the train to roll down a 10-to-15-foot embankment, almost certainly resulting in deaths. Robbery was suspected to be the motive behind the vandalism.

Thomas and Caroline *(Conant)* Dillon were Rochester residents at the turn of the 20th century. Having no children of their own, they adopted two daughters, Dora and Virginia. Thomas was an ordained Methodist minister and served at the Rochester Methodist Episcopal Church. He was also an editor of the *The Rochester Weekly Item* and was once caned by the Edinburg Mayor for writing a story in which he called the mayor "un-American, ungentlemanly, un-Christian, and insane." (HISTORICAL ENCYCLOPEDIA OF ILLINOIS AND HISTORY OF SANGAMON CO., BATEMAN AND SELBY, VOL. 1, MUNSELL PUB. CO., CHICAGO, 1912)

- As publisher of *The Rochester Weekly Item*, T.M. Dillon verbally took on Edinburg Mayor W.H. Vigal in 1901. Although many Edinburgh residents had wanted a bandstand built, the mayor refused. Dillon wrote in the Rochester paper that Vigal was "ungentlemanly, anti-American, anti-Christian and insane." The next time Dillon showed up in Edinburg, Vigal took his cane to the publisher, break-

The Rev. Dillon House on East Main Street as it appeared in 2017. Five generations of the Fairchild family have made this historic Orange Judd house their home. (R. BRUZAN PHOTO)

ing it in the process. He turned himself in to authorities, pled guilty to assault, and paid a $3 fine.

- A 1905 ad in the *Illinois State Register* listed the following Rochester businesses:
  — Bank of Rochester
  — F.M. DeLay & Sons, General Merchandise
  — Everhart & Woodruff, Groceries . . .
  — H.S. Hankins, Livery, Feed, and Sale Stable
  — Jones & Woodruff, Undertakers and Funeral Directors
  — H.W. Olinger, Restaurant and Café
  — H.D. Parker & Co., Druggists
  — Twist Bros., Grain Shippers and
    Lumber Dealers
  — J.C. Windsor, City Bakery

The Twist Building was constructed in 1902 on the southwest corner of East Main and John Streets adjacent to the bank. As well as being Twist Brothers's home offices, it housed the telephone office upstairs and a hardware and a drug store on the first floor. Fire destroyed the building in 1932. (COURTESY OF BILL L. COFFEY)

This was one of the many Central Illinois grain elevators owned by the Twist Brothers of Rochester. It was located on the north side of the Baltimore & Ohio Railroad tracks east of the Rochester train station. Sparks from a B&O train started a fire that destroyed the elevator in 1910. (COURTESY OF BILL L. COFFEY)

Left: An undated postcard of the meat market at 117 East Main Street is believed to have been taken about 1905. The building would be purchased in 1912 for use as the Rochester Town Hall. (COURTESY OF BRAD BUCHER)

This postcard depicts the Bank of Rochester, on the right, and the H.D. Parker & Co. Drug Store in the Twist building, circa 1900. (COURTESY OF ROCHESTER PUBLIC LIBRARY; RHPS COLLECTION)

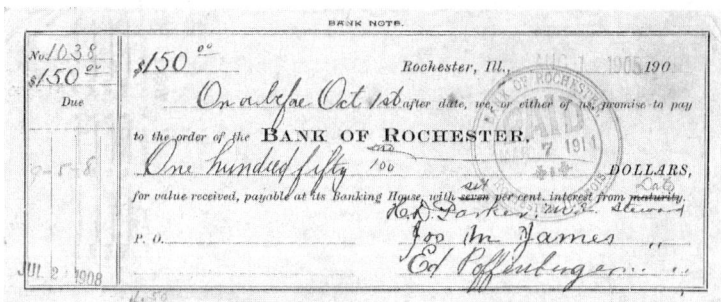

The Bank of Rochester opened in its downtown Main Street building in 1900. It became Rochester State Bank in 1912. This 1905 bank note for $150 has the signatures of three Rochester homeowners; H.D. Parker, Joseph M. James, and Edwin Poffenberger. (COURTESY OF MARK AND KAREN RITTERBUSCH; RHPS COLLECTION)

The Jones and Woodruff Hardware, Paint, and Undertaking store was located on the northeast corner of East Main and North Walnut Streets. The view in this 1907 photograph is to the north, where a Walnut Street stable is also visible. (COURTESY OF GREG PARK)

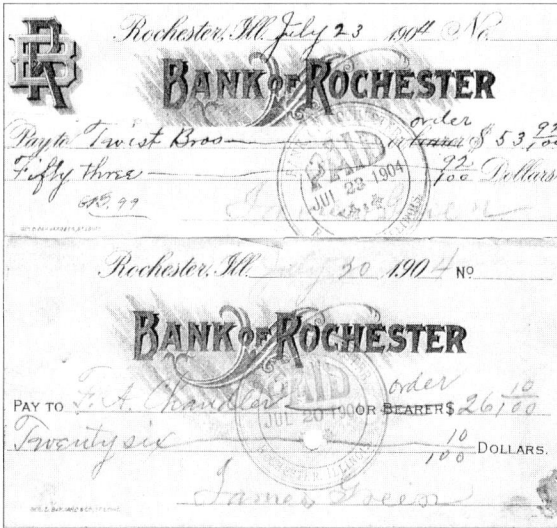

James Green signed both of these 1904 checks on his Bank of Rochester account. The top check was written to the Twist Brothers and the bottom check to Rochester builder Frank Chandler. (COURTESY OF KENT AND BRENDA KURNISKIE)

This eight-inch-diameter plate was sold in Rochester about 1905 and bears the name of the seller, "F.M. DeLay & Son, Rochester." (PLATE IS IN A PRIVATE COLLECTION, R. BRUZAN PHOTO)

The F.M. DeLay store at 129 East Main Street was photographed circa 1900. (COURTESY OF GRETCHEN (WEISSBERG) QUISTGAARD)

Dirt streets dominated downtown Rochester as this circa-1905 postcard illustrates. Looking west, the Twist building and bank are on the left, with the S.G. Richardson store on the right. (COURTESY OF ROCHESTER PUBLIC LIBRARY; RHPS COLLECTION)

- Other business notes included the following:
  — In 1902, C.W. Fairchild bought Fred Poffenberger's butcher shop;
  — After studying the necessary courses, J.B. Highmore, remodeled his livery barn in 1903 to accommodate a new undertaking business.

R. T. SHREVE

DEALER IN

Corn, Oats, Ship-Stuff, Meal, Bran, Coal and All Kinds of Ground Feed

This mill has the reputation of making the best meal in Central Illinois

I carry in stock at all times a supply of the best grades of coal.

Your Patronage Solicited

R. T. SHREVE

Shreve's Mill.   Rochester · · · · Illinois

This ad for the R.T. Shreve Mill was taken from a Christmas edition of *The Rochester Weekly Item*. The Shreve family lived on East Main Street in a house that still exists as of 2017. (*THE ROCHESTER WEEKLY ITEM*, 23 DEC. 1909)

- The July 1908 stabbing of white mining engineer Clergy A. Ballard on the north side of Springfield near Reservoir Park led to the arrest of a Negro, Joe James, for murder. James was convicted and sentenced to die by hanging. Rochester residents J.M. Bell, J.W. Cantrall, S.B. Coe, and Thomas Thornton were among the hundred people formally invited to witness James's October 23, 1908, execution on gallows erected in a jail corridor.

- Rochester's G.W. Everhart served on grand jury investigations of both the Clergy Ballard murder and the August 1908 Springfield race riot. At least 11 people died during the two-day mass civil disturbance with $200,000 in property damage, mostly in the black community. Hundreds of articles and books have detailed the escalating racial tensions in Springfield, some of which was attributed to circumstances surrounding the Clergy Ballard murder one month earlier. The riot led to formation of the National Association for the Advancement of Colored People (NAACP) in 1909.

- Joseph Miller of Rochester was among the village's earliest automobile accident victims when, in 1905, a speeding horseless carriage driven by Taylorville citizen Ernest Hoover grazed him. Miller had been trying to calm the frightened horses pulling his buggy when Hoover roared past. Chief of Police Anderson arrested Hoover, who was by that time partying at Springfield's Leland Hotel. Even as the police confronted him, Hoover laughed and joked about the incident. The driver was later indicted for his deliberate actions.

- Led by Fred Poffenberger, about 20 men took part in the 1902 ice harvest of the South Fork River. The crystal-clear ice blocks measured 10-12-inches thick.

- A sensational story developed when Rochester citizen Charles W. Fairchild shot and killed a colored farm worker, George Hayes, at a Springfield saloon on Christmas Day, 1901. Fairchild was charged with murder. Prominent

Rochester citizens who witnessed the shooting were Sylvester McCoy, Everett Campbell, Bruce Highmore, and Al Grubb.

— Fairchild's Springfield trial, held one year later, was labeled one of the most interesting in the county's history. Because some testimony contended that the two men had a long-time feud, one segment of the public felt Fairchild should be found guilty. Hayes, on the other hand, was described by others as a physically powerful and at times quarrelsome man whom Fairchild shot in self-defense. The jury found Fairchild not guilty.

— Hayes, a farm hand who worked for C.E. (Elva) Miller of Rochester, had been described in an 1898 news account as the only colored resident of Rochester. He is buried in Barrows Cemetery, Lincoln County, KY. Fairchild left Rochester after the trial, and news accounts six years later described him as owning a meat market in Hoople, ND.

• Edward Keys created the new village of Keys Station in 1902. Located northwest of Rochester, on what is today Tuxhorn Road, named after the coal mine that operated between 1903 and 1919. A station there served the ID&W Railroad, and the little community provided housing for the miners. Significantly,

Many who worked at the Tuxhorn Coal Mine lived in the mining community of Keys Station located in Rochester Township on what is now Tuxhorn Road. The ID&W RR transported Tuxhorn coal to Springfield. The Tuxhorn Coal Mine and the community of Keys Station no longer exist. (COURTESY OF COMPASS POINT PRODUCTIONS; FARM PROGRESS COMPANIES)

South Round Prairie Methodist Church was located east of Keys Station in 1918, but no longer exists. (COURTESY OF COMPASS POINT PRODUCTIONS; FARM PROGRESS COMPANIES)

The French-born widow Rosa Ducker (also spelled DeCroix) sold groceries from her Keys Station store in 1918. (COURTESY OF COMPASS POINT PRODUCTIONS; FARM PROGRESS COMPANIES)

electricity was extended to Rochester homes in 1915 from the mine at Keys Station. Although the active coal mine and railroad have been gone for decades, the one-room South Round Prairie school serves today as a family home in what was the village of Keys Station and is a reminder of that early coal mining community.

As of 2017, just three Keys Station houses remained. One is a family home on Tuxhorn Road pictured here. It has had several renovations including the addition of a second story. (COURTESY OF MIKE AND REBECCA MELTON; R. BRUZAN PHOTO)

• Sports teams provided community-wide diversions.

— With his racing outfield catch, Rochester's Bert Wolford amazed 300 fans during an August 1904 home baseball game. The Rochester Merchants posted a 10-to-3 victory over Springfield's Athletic Blues during that matchup.

— A month later, Rochester teams, some of which had not played for 35 years, competed as the Fat Men versus the Lean Men. Witnessed by a large, enthusiastic crowd, the Fats beat the Leans, 24-21.

— As football gained in popularity, Rochester's Frank Twist lettered at the University of Illinois in 1908, an award earned by meeting the school's standards of both playing time and scholarship.

• About 100 Rochester students received a day off in January 1903 when their school had to close because of insufficient coal to heat their building. The situation, labelled a "coal famine," resulted when Rochester coal supplier T.D. Shreve received a single car of coal for the entire village. Although the nearest coal mine was just a few miles away, winter road conditions made access difficult.

- Wildlife seemed at times to congregate around travel byways. Such was the case when so many quail gathered along the Interurban right-of-way in 1908 that they brought at least one trolley car to a stop. The motorman was forced to climb down from the car in order to scatter the birds.
  — In another case, while grading a local farmer's roadbed, a crew led by Theodore Wolford uncovered a nest of rattlesnakes. They killed 22 of the 23 snakes that slithered from the nest.

- Crime reports:
  1901
  — A January 1901 *Illinois State Journal* account from Rochester opined that "there seems to be an organized gang in the village who make it a practice to raid their neighbor's chicken roosts."

  1904
  — During a hold-up and assault by two men at the South Fork River bridge, James Brown of Rochester sustained a fractured skull and a paralyzed left eye when he was knocked unconscious. A similar crime the following night at the same place caused no such injuries when the thieves' target pulled out his own firearm.
  — After a few too many drinks in Springfield, two Roby men went on a crime spree in Rochester. They threw bricks at several women, the Twist Brothers business, and the home of T.F. Ridgeway. They smashed a window at Coe's store, and broke three mailboxes and the Buckhart School pump handle. Pursuing villagers fired shots after them, and the birdshot in Frank Prather's shot gun even hit their fleeing buggy. Both vandals were arrested the following day and paid for their crimes.
  — One news article said his wife's name was Emma, while another said it was Annie. In either case, George Cooper of Rochester was lucky to be alive after his wife tried to poison him with mercury. George alleged that his wife's prior abuse often included threats on his life. Becoming aware that she spiked his coffee with quicksilver, George drank a mixture of fresh milk and lard, which his doctor said probably saved the aggrieved husband's life. Mrs. Cooper readily admitted the attempted murder, although she had no explanation for her action. Their divorce was granted three months later.

  1905
  — A 150-pound hog was taken one night from Edward Poffenberger's farm and replaced by a noticeably lighter porker.

  1908
  — At least one robber broke into the F.M. DeLay & Sons store in February, making off with eight pairs of shoes, 600 cigars, 12 pocket knives, some candy, and 15 cents.

- Just as Ray Brown was about to commit suicide by jumping in front of an ID&W train north of Rochester in 1903, his wife pulled him from the tracks. Brown soon moved to California; his wife moved back to live with her parents.

  — No one came to the rescue of prominent Rochester resident Jacob C. Mc-Coy. At the home of his father in 1901, Jacob killed himself instantly by firing a 38-caliber revolver into his right temple. McCoy had been a successful Colorado gold miner worth $75,000 at the time of his death. He had, however, sustained injuries earlier in a bronco-riding accident at Cripple Creek, CO, and had been told those injuries would likely lead to paralysis. Anticipating this inevitability drove him to suicide. He is buried in Rochester Cemetery.

- Because electricity and electric lights would not arrive in Rochester until the next decade, numerous homes and businesses installed acetylene gas plants that produced the fuel for gas lights.

  — R.H. Coe installed an acetylene gas plant in his store in 1903, and J.H. Logan of Edinburg was called upon to repair and maintain various gas-producing systems in this village.

  — Mishaps did occur, such as the 1906 incident at the four-year-old home of William Everhart. The kitchen was "irrevocably damaged" and his wife was injured when their acetylene stove exploded, blowing off the oven door and throwing her to the floor. The explosion was felt for a mile around Rochester.

- Deaths:

  1901

  — Mayme E. Hall, daughter of John S. Highmore of Rochester, died of fright almost a week after three drunk men accosted her and her husband on the road home to Mechanicsburg from a Springfield carnival. She went into hysterics and never recovered.

  1903

  — The death of Ethelbert Kalb marked an end of what was to many an admired life. A Civil War veteran, Kalb was the founder and first publisher of *The Rochester Weekly Item* and also established Glenwood Park.

  — Less than a month before Kalb's death, his successor as publisher of *The Rochester Weekly Item* also died. Rev. T.M. Dillon died suddenly at Rochester's B&O Railroad station as he waited for a train to Springfield.

  — Mary *(Wright)* Pease, an expectant mother, was memorialized during services at the Rochester Methodist Episcopal Church marking her death at the Singapore Straits Settlement in Malasia. Despite her father's pleas, Rev. Thomas B. Wright was told that government regulations would not permit the return of her remains to Rochester. The young missionary, who had married Kingsley Pease in 1901, was buried in Singapore.

Missionaries Mary *(Wright)* Pease and her husband Kingsley were assigned to Singapore in 1901. After Mary died there in 1903, her father, Rev. T.B. Wright, was unable to have her body returned for burial in Rochester. (COURTESY OF METHODIST ARCHIVES AND HISTORY LIBRARY, SINGAPORE; USED WITH PERMISSION)

"In memory of Mary Wright Pease who died in Singapore March 1903 after 15 months of joyful missionary service. Her life was fragrant with love and good works. This tablet is erected by her fellow missionaries and friends." This memorial plaque in Singapore's Wesley Methodist Church still honors Mary *(Wright)* Pease. (COURTESY OF WESLEY COMMUNICATIONS, SINGAPORE; USED WITH PERMISSION)

1908

— John Richardson died in September 1908, four months after a mule kicked him.

• Other notable Rochester deaths:

1900: Malcina *(Cooper)* McCoy

1901: Archibald Sattley, Jr.; William and Rachel *(James)* Coe

1902: James W. Everhart

1903: Henry P. Clark; Oliver C. Stafford; John S. Highmore

1904: Bettie *(Hoover)* Everhart

1905: Carter Tracy

1906: George E. Graham; Louisiana *(Branch)* Miller

1907: Marshall Sattley

1908: Milton D. McCoy

A Rochester businessman, politician, and builder, Carter Tracy died in 1905 in Beaver, OK, where he had become a successful landowner, lawyer, and judge. Pam Bruzan is shown during a 2015 visit to Tracy's grave. (R. BRUZAN PHOTO)

The wooden covered bridge that previously spanned the South Fork River on the Rochester-Springfield road west of the village was replaced in 1907 by this steel bridge. The photographer was looking west across the river. (PHOTO BY JACK TAFT; COURTESY OF CARL "BUD" MOORE)

- Fifty-year anniversaries:
  — An Ohio native, 91-year-old Mary Ann Ducker of Rochester won a parlor chair in 1909 for being the oldest woman at the 50th anniversary of the **San-gamon County Old Settlers Reunion.**
  — **Rochester's Odd Fellows Lodge #268** celebrated 50 years of community service in 1908 with a celebration at the Rochester temple of the Woman's Christian Temperance Union (WCTU).
  — **Michael** and **Eva** *(Phillips)* **Wahlsmith** of Rochester celebrated their golden anniversary in 1909. Natives of Germany, the Wahlsmiths, were the parents of 10 children and had 19 grandchildren.
  — **John** and **Charity** *(Grubb)* **Coe** celebrated their 50th wedding anniversary in 1903 at the Rochester home of their son Richard. The couple had traveled in covered wagons with their families to Illinois from Virginia in 1851, two years before they were wed.

- Any Rochester anniversary was apparently an occasion to celebrate. On May 1, 1903, "Willie" DeLay had already retired to bed when 90 friends and relatives showed up to celebrate the 23rd wedding anniversary of "Willie" and husband, "Frannie," who at that moment was still working at his F.M. DeLay & Son General Store. Fortunately, guests brought all the celebration foods and decorations, and a fine evening was reported.

- The Rebekah's were established in Rochester on October 25, 1902, as the Moreland Rebekah Lodge # 573, Independent Order of Odd Fellows (IOOF). Their sister lodge from Mechanicsburg helped organize the event, which included installing the first Noble Grand, Nettie Enlow. After a dinner and appropriate ceremonies, oysters were served at 11 p.m.

- Numerous speakers, a "bounteous basket luncheon," and music by the Edinburg Band were features of the ninth annual county Prohibition Picnic at Olcott's Grove south of Rochester in 1901. The all-day festival drew about 1,500 people.

- Insanity has occasionally been suspected to be a result of marriage. A 1909 wedding proposal, however, involved insanity prior to the marriage. According to James Clark, during a brief conversation with him on a short train ride from Rochester, Mrs. Sarah Auxier accepted his marriage proposal. When Clark arrived in Rochester on their wedding day ready to marry his betrothed, he casually mentioned to Sarah that he was sane now, but had been in an "insane asylum" three times. According to Mr. Clark, they decided to postpone the wedding for two weeks. Mrs. Auxier, a mother of four, later denied that she ever intended to marry Mr. Clark.

- Fire dangers:
  — A bucket brigade in 1904 was unable to save the Twist barn from a fire that threatened the entire village. A lightning bolt started the late-afternoon blaze that consumed the barn and its contents. All the horses and mules were saved, but one horse had to be put out of its misery when its eyes were burned out and its ears burned off. A change in the wind direction saved the remaining town.
  — C.E. Hazlett's farm north of Rochester also sustained a lightning-caused fire in 1904. Along with the loss of hay, corn, and farm wagons, seven horses burned to death.
  — The valuable library and enormous home of D.G. Kalb, located on Glenwood Road north of Rochester, burned to the ground the result of a 1903 stove fire. No lives were lost. Glenwood Road is probably what is known today as Gaule Road.

JULY 4

1776   Rochester, Ill.   1906

...PROGRAM...

Morning Program
9:00 Parade; best decorated rig 2.50, most comical outfit 2.50.
9:30 Song, "America."
9:35 Address of Welcome. Rev. T. B. Wright.
10:00 Address by Hon. Wm. Stevens.
10:15 Ball Game, Farmingdale vs. Rochester.
10:30 Recitation, Miss Mary Thornton.
10:30 Free Platform Attractions.

Afternoon Program
1:15 Band Concert.
1:30 Free Platform Attractions.
2:00 Races—Sack race, 50 yds. free for all, prize 50c; Fat Men's Race, 200 lbs. and over, 50 yds., prize 50c; Lean Men's Race, 135 lbs. and under, 100 yds., prize 50c; Boy's Race, 16 years and under, 100 yds., prize $1; Free For All Race, open to the world, 200 yds., prize $2.
3:00 Ball Game, Mt. Pulaski vs. Rochester. Address by Hon. Geo. Morgan, of Springfield.
3:30 Recitations by Misses Edna Nutt and Elsie Denton.
4:00 Baby Show, babies 18 months and under, prize $2 gold ring.
4:45 Fiddlers' Contest, prize $1.

Evening Program
7:00 Band Concert.
8:00 Free Platform Entertainment.
8:30 Fireworks.

Band concerts, speakers, ball games, a baby show, a fiddlers' contest and fireworks were all part of Rochester's 1906 July 4th celebration.
(COURTESY OF RUTH DRILLINGER)

— A restaurant cook stove ignited Mrs. C.D. Turner's hair in 1909. Fortunately, Ben Fairchild was entering the building at that moment and smothered the flames that caused extensive, non-fatal burns.

- A "brilliantly illuminated" meteor the size of a barrel crashed into the C.W. Murphy farm field near Rochester on November 15, 1902. This object from outer space was said to have taken hours to cool before area farmers were able to dig it out. Although plans at that time were to send the meteorite to a science museum for analysis, nothing more was reported about the object.

- Pete Jones of Rochester and Al Grubb of Springfield caused area-wide excitement during their 1909 fishing trip on the South Fork River southwest of Rochester. When the men failed to return as expected, someone started a rumor that they must have drowned. The possible double drowning generated a flurry of conversation throughout Rochester and Springfield. Among those showing up to search for the missing men or just be part of the excitement were local residents, divers, and men with grappling irons. More ominously, undertakers and the coroner were also present. The search ended when the men were found, quite alive, in a box car at a dairy-farm siding, totally unaware that they had been the object of an all-day search. Although one searcher said that the missing men had a jug with them, he declined to speculate what the jug contained.

- Rochester was well represented at an August 1903 party held along the Sangamon River where the Joe Miller bridge crossed that stream north of Buckhart. The adults and young people included Lester Baldwin, Tony Baxter, Calista Breckenridge, Mary Anna Breckenridge, Ralph Breckenridge, Eillie Byers, Otis Byers, Junius Chapman, Mrs. J.A. Clemens, Bertha Clemens, Phillip Coe, Jessie Foster, Elizabeth Furrow, Ethel Gore, Edna Hayes, Lydia Kernoll, Russell Kernoll, Cleavy McCoy, Jake Middlekauff, Mayme Pearson, Pearl Reed, Joe Taft, Lida Taft, Chelsea Tobin, Frank Twist, and Andy Woodruff. Dinner and supper were served, and the group enjoyed a wonderful summer day.

- In what today might be described as a "cat fight," two well-known Rochester matrons began their June 1900 public argument by hurling words at each other. It escalated until one threw a shoe "at the velocity of a Kansas cyclone," striking her adversary and causing a "badly bruised . . . epidermis." The immediate storm soon died, although village residents anticipated the potential of more on the horizon. The participants were not identified.

- As J.B. Highmore and Robert McLaughlin were returning from Springfield on the Rochester Road near the Sugar Creek bridge one noon in April 1902, they noticed a market basket at the side of the road. To their surprise, inside they found a newborn girl with only a blanket and sheet to protect her. The baby was initially given into the care of A.D. Young and then taken to Springfield's Home for the Friendless. John and Sarah Denton of Rochester soon adopted the infant they named Hazel. Hazel married Herman Sperry 18 years later, and that couple raised four sons in Macon County. Hazel died 56 years after her abandonment and was buried in Harristown, IL.

— A similar story of abandonment had unfolded tragically, however, about a year earlier when Alfred H. Hutchinson of Rochester placed the newborn son of his unwed daughter on the steps of a Washington Street family's home near Springfield. Exposure to the cool April night and lack of food doomed this baby before the homeowner found him in the morning. Among those items found with the unfortunate infant was a copy of *The Rochester Item* newspaper with Hutchinson's name and address, leading authorities directly to the baby's birth family.

- Rochester was among the 21 Sangamon County townships that voted "dry" when the question of approving saloons was on the April 1908 ballot. Rochester voters were 221 against saloons to 68 in favor. Capital and New Berlin Townships were the only two townships in which voters approved saloons.

- Serious horse-and-buggy accidents involved **Fred Poffenbarger** and **Dr. S.E. Munson** in 1901, **G.W. McFadden** and members of his family in 1903, and **Dr. J.W. Cantrall** and **Earl Conner** in 1904. Other notable accidents of the decade included the following:

1900
— A thorn punctured the eye of **James Baker** as the man climbed through a hedge fence.

1903
— While stirring up the embers in a stove one January night, **Elizabeth Baker's** clothing caught fire, producing painful, although not serious burns.
— After **William T. McNeil's** drowning in Harvey, ND, his uncle, Henry Taft, brought the body back for burial in Rochester Cemetery.
— **Joseph Cheery** lost the tip of the third finger on his left hand when one of his "fine bred hogs" ate it.

1904
— Twenty stitches were needed to close **George Miller's** two wounds inflicted when the farmer's pig attacked him, tearing the flesh of the farmer's right hip with its tusk.

1905
— While traveling west to Kansas, Rochester's **Rev. Thomas B. Wright** was involved in two train wrecks. The first happened in Missouri without any serious injuries. The second accident occurred when a Missouri Pacific Railroad train hit a broken rail near Fort Scott, KN. Rev. Wright was thrown through a train window resulting in wounds requiring 18 stitches. One eye was almost

cut out, and in a message back to Rochester, his wife said doctors expected the pastor would lose sight in that eye.

1908
— Lightning killed **Archie Ralston** on a farm field one mile north of Rochester.
— Hauling water on the Rochester Road, 18-year-old **Floyd Henderson** fell beneath his wagon, and two wheels ran over the youth's leg breaking it in two places. As in a scene from the Bible, although Henderson was in agony and begging for help, two passing travelers declined to help. A good samaritan finally transported Henderson the short distance to a farm near Sangamon Station where he received medical assistance.

- An early July 1902 storm flooded bridges over both the South Fork River and Sugar Creek. Due to bottomland flooding, a number of Rochester Township farmers lost dozens of acres of wheat, corn, and rye crops.
 — A July storm seven years later tore through several Twist tile-and-brick-factory buildings on South Walnut Street. It also demolished almost a mile of telephone wire, destroyed hundreds of acres of crops, and damaged numerous trees.

- In 1902, prominent Rochester businessman H.D. Parker had established his popular drug store in the new Twist Building at the corner of East Main and John Streets. In addition to a wide stock of drugs and other products of the

The H.D. Parker's drug store was in the Twist Building located on Main Street next to the bank. This postcard picture, taken about 1905, includes from left, Homer D. Parker, "Uncle Jake," Margaret *(Lawrence)* Parker, and Roscoe Lakin. (COURTESY OF RUTH DRILLINGER)

The John Street residence of Homer and Margaret Parker, and their five daughters was located just a block from their Main Street drug store. Their daughters, Edith and Bertha, became professors at the University of Chicago and authored several successful books. The Rochester State Bank now occupies this corner. (COURTESY OF COMPASS POINT PRODUCTIONS; FARM PROGRESS COMPANIES)

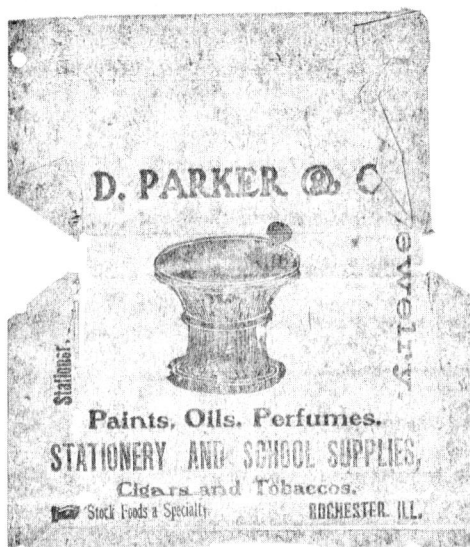

In 2014, Jacob Dinardo found numerous old medicine bottles in a creek bank north of Homer Parker's residence. That site appears to have been a disposal spot for the Parker Drug Store. (COURTESY OF JACOB DINARDO; P. BRUZAN PHOTO)

D. PARKER & C

Stationer.

Jewelry.

Paints, Oils, Perfumes.

STATIONERY AND SCHOOL SUPPLIES,

Cigars and Tobaccos.

Stock Foods a Specialty.   ROCHESTER. ILL.

H.D. Parker & Co. ads included this handbill, which gives an idea of his wide-ranging stock. (COURTESY OF DORTHY ROSS)

day, Parker built a soda fountain in the store. The Parker family home was on the corner of John and Mill Streets, now the site of Rochester State Bank.

- J.C. Brunk of Rochester won three prizes at the 1904 World's Fair horse show in St. Louis. All three of his horses, Sonata, Does Daisy, and Fenelluad, received first- and second-place prizes.

- A more unusual 1901 horse show at the Coliseum at the State Fair grounds featured Prof. O.R. Gleason, who claimed the ability to master horses previously thought to be uncontrollable. He promised to subdue the vicious, man-eating stallion Royal John, shipped to Springfield from Iowa in a special train car. J.B. Highmore of Rochester also provided horses that were fighters, strikers, and kickers for the professor to tame. Thousands watched to see the celebrated horse trainer, although Royal John's temper that Sunday failed to match his reputation. Music was provided by the Watch Factory Band.

• Rochester enjoyed its own band beginning in 1907. Nineteen band members took weekly lessons, met for weekly practices, and played for weekly concerts during the summer as well as at other local events. Albert Knotts led the band, which included Christopher Wahlsmith, William Bennett, Archie Thornton, Philip Coe, Jesse Corey, Morris Moklar, Earl Bell, Allen Cantrill, John Bennett, Charles Frame, Earl Hankins, Charles DeLay, William Evers, Jake Middlekauff, Cleavy McCoy, Sherring Highmore, Park Cantrill, and Fred King.

According to life-long Rochester resident Hazel Park, "there was a band of local boys and a band concert every Wednesday night in Rochester." She recalled many ice cream socials on the lawn of the Twist house and the fun of dancing the tango, polka, two-step, and waltz. This photo is dated 1907. (COURTESY OF KAREN ALEXANDER; ROCHESTER PUBLIC LIBRARY, RHPS COLLECTION)

• While on a trip to the St. Louis World's Fair, Joseph Taft and Vida Almeda Conner, both of Rochester, decided to get married. Their secret marriage took place on July 5, 1904, at the Belleville courthouse.

— Another elopement occurred in 1903 when, without the consent of their parents, 19-year-old Julia Wright of Riverton and 20-year-old James Johnson of Rochester traveled with friends on the Chicago & Alton (C&A) train to St. Louis. They were wed in the St. John's Catholic Church rectory and announced their wedding to their parents by sending the following telegram: "In St. Louis, married, and glad of it."

Shown in 2014, David "Cotton" Taft displays the tool box used by his grandfather, Frank Chandler, a well-known carpenter who built several Rochester homes during the early 1900s. Chandler was known to rely on hand tools for the buildings he constructed and never used power tools. (COURTESY OF DAVID "COTTON" TAFT; R. BRUZAN PHOTO)

This was the West Main Street home of the William and Lydia *(Twist)* Kernoll family, built in 1903. (COURTESY OF COMPASS POINT PRODUCTIONS; FARM PROGRESS COMPANIES)

This young lad is William Kernoll, who was born in 1865, married Lydia Twist in 1890, and built their family home on West Main Street in 1903. Funeral services were held at the home in 1923 for William's mother Elmira *(Moore)* Kernoll, seen on the right. The home became the Rochester Methodist Episcopal Church Parsonage in 1925 and is now a private residence. (PHOTOS COURTESY OF GEORGE AND DONNA ALEWELT)

This wallpaper artifact saved from the Kernoll House on West Main Street is believed to be original to its 1903 construction. William and Lydia *(Twist)* Kernoll lived in the house with their children Russell and Jeanette. (COURTESY OF GEORGE AND DONNA ALEWELT)

Uriah and Melvina *(Bailey)* King are surrounded by their 11 children, many of whom lived in Rochester when this 1907 photo was taken. Uriah (1843-1913) and Melvina (1850-1919) are buried in Clear Lake Township's Oak Hill Cemetery. (COURTESY OF FAY JOSTES)

* * Program * *

The Class 1905

Extends You an Invitation to

The Sixth Annual Commencement

Sangamon County

Rural and Village Schools

Chatterton Opera House, Tuesday, Aug. 22, 1905
2 o'clock, P. M.

DOORS OPEN AT 1 O'CLOCK

GRADUATES—Concluded.

Name	School	Address
Lizzie Burtle	Oak Ridge	Glenarm
Flossie Leona Davidson	" "	"
James Hyden	Patton (Auburn Twp.)	Auburn
Edythe Annie Sterriker	Prosperity	Loami
Claude Malsbury	Prospect	Lowder
Kenneth Parkinson	"	Maxwell
Allen Cantrill	Round Prairie	Springfield R. R. 7
George Hemp	Ray	Illiopolis
Frank Trotter	Riverton	Riverton
Lillian Kline	"	"
Hilda Rentschler	"	"
Bertha V. Melahn	"	"
Martha Morris	"	"
William Smith	"	"
John Miller	"	"
Pearl Stone	Rochester	Rochester
Edna Nutt	"	"
Harlan Hayes	"	"
Beryl King	"	"
Jason Taft	"	"
James Walker	"	"
Myron Williams	"	"
Golda Mae Gordon	Salisbury	Farmingdale
Willard Stevens	"	Salisbury
Leona Mounce	"	"
Russell Hurley	South Fork	Loami
Grace Brooks	Sand Hill	Springfield R. R. 5
Marie Kohl	"	"
Martha Brooks	"	"
Emma Telfer	Smith	Buffalo Hart
Bessie Pool	Tucker	Divernon
Opal Woodyard	Union	Glenarm
Mayme Parkes	Winchell	Farmingdale
Fred Schuppel	Wright	Riverton
Ethel B. Wright	"	"
William Pursell, Jr.	Washburne	Farmingdale
Walter Mowry	Yankeetown	Pleasant Plains

This program marks the annual commencement hosted in 1905 at Springfield's Chatterton Opera House. Students from Rochester and other county schools were honored. (COURTESY OF KAREN ALEXANDER)

Buffalo Bill brought his Wild West show to Sangamon County several times, attracting Rochester's young and old to his wide-ranging productions. (*DAILY ILLINOIS STATE REGISTER*, 21 SEP. 1901; PUBLISHED BY GENEALOGYBANK.COM, A DIVISION OF NEWSBANK)

Where, when, or why these young ladies are wading in what might be the South Fork River are unknown. However, the authors hope their readers will enjoy this unusual picture. Identified members of the McCoy family are Elda, third from left; Nina, fourth; Eva, fifth; and Mary, seventh. (COURTESY OF RHPS COLLECTION)

ROCHESTER CIRCA 1914

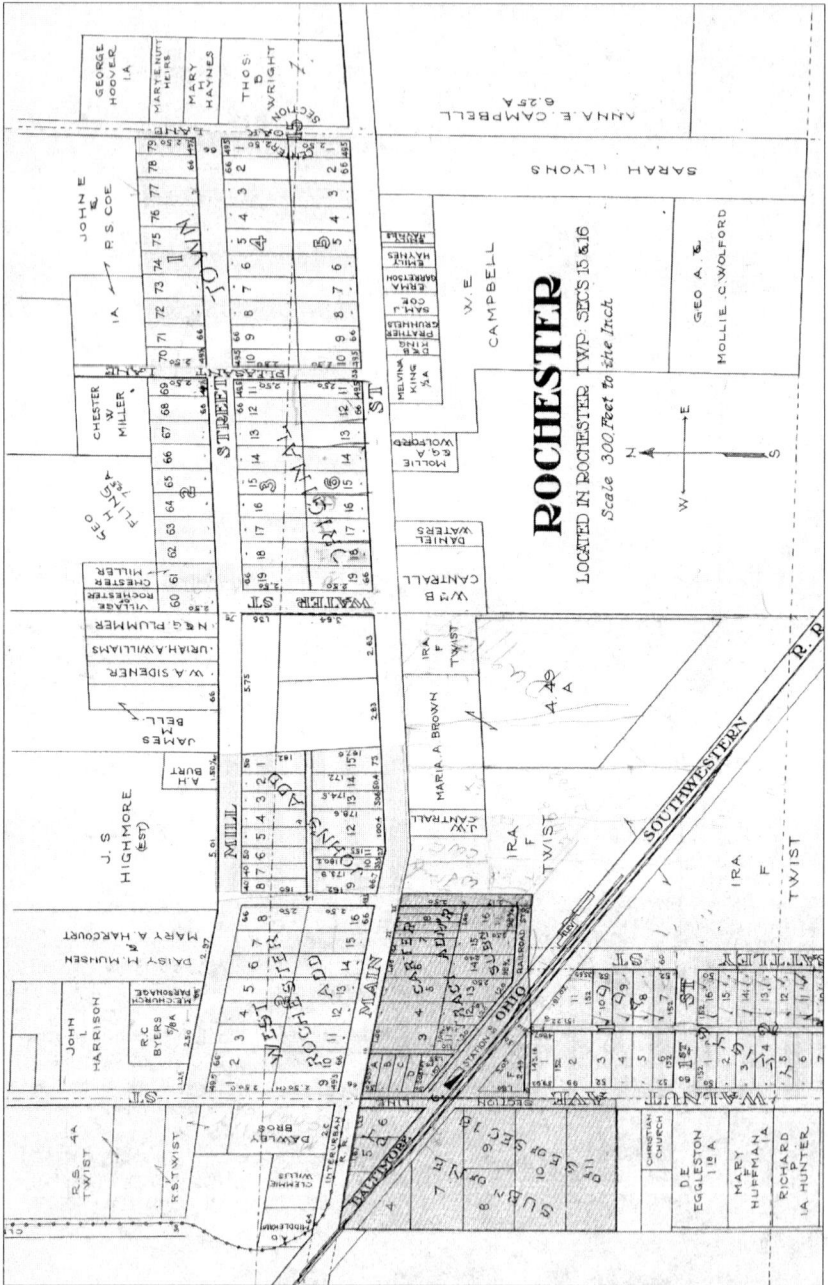

(*PLAT BOOK OF SANGAMON COUNTY ILLINOIS*, SANGAMON COUNTY ABSTRACT CO., SPRINGFIELD, IL, 1914)

1910s

Pilot Meryl Fairchild of Rochester posed with this de Havilland airplane while serving in France during World War I. (COURTESY OF ROBERT FAIRCHILD)

1910s Timeline...

1910	Rochester population: 444
	— Twist Brothers Grain Company built a new elevator
1912	Rochester State Bank opened
	— Henry Taft built Maplehurst on West Main Street
	— Interurban went bankrupt and discontinued service
	— Village bought the building at 117 East Main Street for use as a Town Hall
1914	W.S. Woodruff house built on East Main Street
	— B&O train snowbound in 12-foot snowdrifts at Rochester
1915	Electricity installed in Rochester homes
	— Dr. J.M. Bell bought the Twist Building
	— Three-year high school opened
1916	Christian Church destroyed by lighting-caused fire
1917	U.S. declared war on Germany, and Rochester enlistees joined World War I fighting
	— New Christian Church was dedicated

— B&O Railroad takes ownership of the ID&W Railroad
— Officials confirmed the name Mt. Deborah for the mountain in
Alaska that honors Deborah S. *(Bell)* Wickersham of Rochester
1918   Orange Judd Company published *Pictorial Community Album of
Rochester Township and Village*
— Word War I ended with the signing of an Armistice on
November 11

1910s Storylines...

- One of the most impactful changes in this decade was the availability, in 1915, of electricity to Rochester homeowners. World War I changed the lives of soldiers, their families, and friends. Colliding technologies of the horse and buggy with the auto industry changed not just the most common mode of transportation, but also the concept of travel time. A photographer from the Orange Judd Company of Chicago recorded 268 pictures of village and township homes and businesses in a 1918 pictorial. Existing businesses included a grain-and-lumber yard, hardware store, drugstore, tile-and-brick yard, florist, coal-and-ice company, blacksmith, grist mill, bank, three general stores, barber shop, jeweler, livery stable, two contractors and builders, two doctors, and an undertaker.

- After passage of the 1917 Selective Service Act, 2.8 million men were drafted into military service. Of the 13,412 men registered from Sangamon County, 142 were from the Rochester precinct. Fifty-four of those are listed, many with pictures, in the *Sangamon County Honor Book and Record of WW I.*
  — At the conclusion of what some termed "the war to end all wars," a great homecoming celebration was held in Rochester for returning soldiers. More than a thousand area citizens attended the tribute that consisted of music by the Capitol (sic) City Band, a range of speakers, athletic events, and a lunch counter that served attendees and from which "no service man is being permitted to leave the grounds hungry."
  — Sergeant Harry L. Fogle, however, did not attend, for this son of John E. and Rosa A. Fogle had died in France, a victim of cerebro-spinal meningitis. Fogle was a Rochester High School graduate who had worked at *The Rochester Item* office. He was 22 years old at the time of his death in 1919 and is buried at St. Mihiel American Cemetery in Thiaucourt, France. Rochester's American Legion Post 274 was named in his honor in 1928.

  Army Sergeant Harry L. Fogle from Rochester, who died overseas during WW I, is buried in France. (*THE HONOR BOOK* BY NELLIE BROWNE DUFF, A.P. BICKENBACH, PUB. 1920)

The Rochester Item.

Good Furniture
Sullivan-Reisch
Springfield, Illinois.
Published Weekly

ROCHESTER, ILLINOIS, THURSDAY, SEPTEMBER 12, 1918

Rochester Item
One Year $1.50
Six Months $0.75
W. F. Lacey, Pub.

Thirty-Seventh Year, No. 21

WOLFORD & OLCOTT
ROCHESTER, ILLINOIS.

S. G. RICHARDSON
ROCHESTER ILLINOIS

A. EGGLESTON
Rochester, - - Illinois.

As of 2017 only 10 issues of the *The Rochester Item* newspaper have been located. This 1918 edition includes Rochester merchant ads encouraging patriotism during World War I. (*THE ROCHESTER ITEM*, 12 SEP. 1918; COURTESY OF KENT AND BRENDA KURNISKIE)

- A red-letter event that attracted thousands of residents and visitors took place July 9, 1915, to celebrate the arrival of electricity throughout Rochester. The celebrants, many of whom arrived by automobile, enjoyed the music, ice cream, cake, and dignitaries' speeches.
  — The Utilities Company of Springfield signed a 20-year agreement with the village board to provide commercial lighting and a 10-year contract to light village streets.

The date July 1915, written on the inside of a Rochester home's fuse box, marks the year electricity became available to Rochester homeowners. (R. BRUZAN PHOTO)

Power provided by the plant at Tenth Street and Capitol Avenue was delivered via a new power line from the Tuxhorn Mine northwest of Rochester.
  — Newspaper ads soon appeared to wire "already-built houses" for as little as $10.00. Rochester had entered the age of electricity.

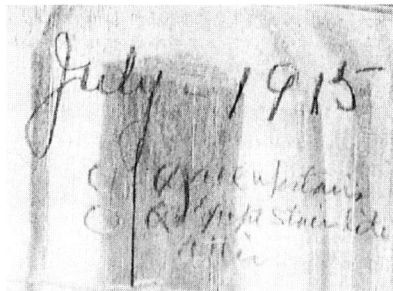

- Several remaining carriage house "barns" in Rochester testify to the horse-and-buggy era that continued into this decade. Still visible in 2017, a few horse hitching posts and curb-side stoops are also reminders of a transportation mode that was quickly being replaced by "the automobile."

Only a few artifacts remain in 2017 that are reminders of 100 years ago when horse-related transportation was being replaced by the automobile. One of the few remaining carriage houses in Rochester is on West Main Street. (COURTESY OF GEORGEANNE DAILY; R. BRUZAN PHOTO)

Above: This carriage stoop harkens back to when the J.M. James family lived on West Main Street. (COURTESY OF RICK AND JEANNE EILERING; R. BRUZAN PHOTO)

These horse hitching posts are at homes on Rochester's Main Street. (LEFT PHOTO COURTESY OF RICHARD AND LYNN BUECKER; CENTER PHOTO COURTESY OF TIM AND BENÉ NUDING; R. BRUZAN PHOTOS)

Maplehurst, located on what is today the southeast corner of West Main Street and Oak Hill Road, was built by Henry and Mary Jane (Eckels) Taft in 1912. Note the horse hitching posts and the vintage automobile. (COURTESY OF COMPASS POINT PRODUCTIONS; FARM PROGRESS COMPANIES)

The horse-drawn sleigh, originally used by Henry and Mary Jane Taft, is now an annual front-porch Christmas decoration at Maplehurst. (COURTESY OF STEVE AND ROBIN TAFT; R. BRUZAN PHOTO)

This 1918 Orange Judd *Pictorial* photo illustrates the importance of both the automobile and the horse to the Olcott homestead farm on the Springfield-Taylorville Road in Rochester Township. (COURTESY OF COMPASS POINT PRODUCTIONS; FARM PROGRESS COMPANIES)

— No fewer than three Rochester auto dealerships offered their customers choices of Hupmobile, Haynes, and Willys Knight automobiles at a price range of $1,000 to $1,950.

Willis Cleveland Copeland advertised the Hupmobiles he sold in Rochester for $1,000 as "fully equipped" with 32 horse power. Copeland's farm was located on East Townline Road (now Leach Road). (*ILLINOIS STATE REGISTER*, 12 JUNE 1913; USED WITH PERMISSION)

• Newspaper stories in the 1910s took on a different tone, with fewer reports of injuries from horses and more stories related to automobiles.
— Rochester citizen John Hutchinson broke his leg while cranking to start his car, and J.E. Shine, also of Rochester, was the victim of a speeding car that struck his horse-drawn buggy. By 1919 Springfield was rigidly enforcing traffic laws by using "motorcycle cops."
— Speeding—within the law—encouraged growth of the popular sport of auto racing. Rochester race-car driver E.H. Donovan was featured in 1913 during one five-mile race hosted by the New Berlin Driving Club. Donovan lost before a crowd of 1,600 eager fans that included Illinois Governor Edward F. Dunne. The winning time was 7 minutes, 46 seconds.
— The popularity of automobiles necessitated improved roads and bridges throughout Sangamon County and Illinois.

• A 1916 *Illinois State Register* ad promoted the auction of "twenty beautiful lots" in Rochester. The ad extolled this as a suburb where residents enjoyed the convenience of four daily trains between the village and Springfield or, for automobile owners, a drive on oiled roads between the communities.
— Determined to have a "dustless town," Rochester residents donated $400 toward a public drive for 14,000 gallons of oil to be spread over their streets. Other township infrastructure improvements during the decade included the

1914 completion of Herndon Road, today's Dannenberger Road, and the steel bridge that carried it over the South Fork River, as well as 9,000 square feet of new concrete sidewalks in the village.

— Sangamon County road commissioners considered a brick road from Springfield through Rochester east to Buckhart and south to New City as early as 1913. Instead, they supported a 1916 petition for action from 50 Rochester citizens and in 1917 oiled the Springfield-to-Buckhart Road.

This 1914 Oak Street photo taken about a mile north of East Main Street displays the muddy conditions that travelers often faced during that decade. (*THE ROCHESTER & LAKE SPRINGFIELD HERALD*, 20 JUNE 1984)

- No one today knows why the Orange Judd Farmer Company of Chicago sent a photographer to Rochester Township in 1918 to take 268 photographs of village homes and businesses and township farms.

— Rochester Township families are pictured at their homes or businesses with their prized possessions: horses, dogs, and automobiles. Published as the Orange Judd Farmer *Pictorial Community Album of Rochester Township and Village*, the book is a 1918 time capsule that captures the community in that era. Where applicable, names of homes from that era that are used in this book are names that appeared in the *Pictorial*.

The Orange Judd Farmer Company from Chicago produced the *Pictorial Community Album of Rochester Township and Village* in 1918. Its 268 black-and-white photographs of downtown Rochester, village homes, churches, schools, and township farms document life in Rochester as it was 100 years ago. (COURTESY OF FARM PROGRESS COMPANIES; R. BRUZAN PHOTO)

— The Rochester Public Library maintains an original copy of the *Pictorial*, and remaining originals of the large-format paperback book are today prized possessions of many current and former residents. Excellent copies of the original, also valued by their owners, were sold as the 21st century dawned.

In 2016 Dwight and Grace Pope, right, provided the Orange Judd photograph, seen at the left, taken about 1918 as part of the Orange Judd *Pictorial* project. Grace's mother, Mary Smith, is seen with her mother Ada and Grace's uncle, Joseph Smith, is posed with his father Ira. Ada and Ira Smith lived in Rochester Township. Grace is also a descendant of Revolutionary War soldier Isaac Baker, who is buried in Rochester Cemetery. (LEFT PHOTO COURTESY OF GRACE POPE; COMPASS POINT PRODUCTIONS; FARM PROGRESS COMPANIES; RIGHT PHOTO BY R. BRUZAN)

- Rochester Christian Church members quickly rebuilt their South Walnut Street church that had been destroyed by a disastrous fire after being struck by lightning in July 1916. More than 1,000 members and guests attended dedication of the new church just nine months after the fire. Congregants came forward during that day's morning and afternoon services with sufficient contributions to retire the church's remaining $1,000 building debt.

This Rochester Christian Church on South Walnut Street, was built in 1917 to replace the 1875 church, which had been destroyed by fire a year earlier when struck by lightning. (COMPASS POINT PRODUCTIONS; FARM PROGRESS COMPANIES)

  — Attendees were treated to lunch, special choir selections, Springfield's Temple Boy Choir, and solos by Beulah Martin and Hazel Jones. Under the leadership of Rev. Thomas Shaw, the all-day event concluded with an evening sermon. The dedication so involved the entire community that the Rochester Methodist Church and their pastor, Rev. C.A. Ward, cancelled their own service, and assisted with dedication of the new church.

- Elementary teacher Margaret Parker prevented a disaster in 1913 when she successfully put out a fire at the school that started when a candle ignited a nearby drapery and Christmas tree. No one was seriously injured and the school sustained minimal damage.

  — The Twist Brothers Company was not so lucky when their Rochester grain elevator caught fire in 1910, probably caused by sparks from the engine of a passing Baltimore & Ohio (B&O) train. Thanks to the efforts of a 250-person bucket brigade, nearby residences were saved. However, the elevator, its grain, and two railroad cars were totally destroyed at an estimated loss of $20,000.

• Rochester never seemed short of political candidates.
— Dr. James M. Bell was a successful 1910 Democratic candidate for representative from the 45th District; J.S. Derry was unsuccessful in his 1912 primary bid to be the Sangamon County Republican Coroner candidate; and Rochester native Noah Twist was soundly defeated by his Republican challenger in the 1918 election for county sheriff.
— Women's suffrage played a significant role in Illinois politics. In 1913, women in Illinois were the first living east of the Mississippi River to secure limited voting rights. Women not only voted, but they would follow in the footsteps of Rochester Prohibition candidates Emma Baldwin, Mary Poffenberger, Harriet Waters, and Armiza Miller, who ran for village clerk and trustees on the Prohibition ticket in 1914. They lost their bids for office. As many enthusiastic women voters as men were reported during the decade. The 19th Amendment to the U.S Constitution, guaranteeing the right of all women to vote, was ratified on August 18, 1920.

• The popularity of train travel produced several Rochester-related stories.
— Quick action by a railroad employee in 1916 saved the life of Rochester's Rev. T.B. Wright. Rev. Wright had slipped from the Union Station platform under the rail cars, but was saved by an unnamed brakeman who saw his tumble in time to perform a rescue. This was Rev. Wright's third train-related accident in 11 years. It would not be his last.

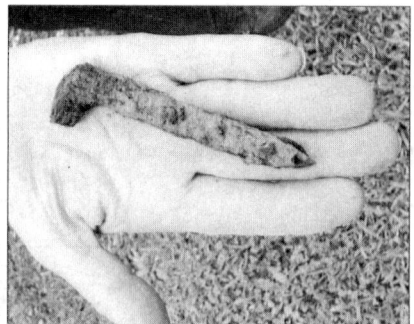

Although Rochester's Interurban disappeared almost 100 years ago, artifacts of the short-lived trolley line to Springfield are still found. Using a metal detector, Pam Bruzan located a rail spike in 2016 on the property of David and Debbie Taft. The two-foot-diameter RR sign, which has been in the Bennett family for several generations, was most likely posted at the Interurban's Bennett Stop north of Rochester. (RR SIGN COURTESY OF JIM BENNETT; RAIL SPIKE COURTESY OF DAVID AND DEBBIE TAFT; R. BRUZAN PHOTOS)

Waiting passengers in 1918 look southeast toward an oncoming train that will take them to Springfield. The first rail tracks through Rochester were laid in the 1870s as a line was built from Springfield to Rochester, Taylorville, and Pana. Passenger travel and transportation of livestock and grain served the township. (COMPASS POINT PRODUCTIONS; FARM PROGRESS COMPANIES)

— Two young boys came face to face with an oncoming train traveling toward them at full speed over the Rochester trestle. Ray Gaffney jumped to the ground, but Henry Willett dangled from the trestle until the train had passed. Both were scared but uninjured.

— As B&O passenger train No. 121 was heading west toward Springfield on a spring evening in 1911, a single set of wheels on the coal car derailed east of Rochester. The rest of the train remained on the track, and all the passengers escaped injury.

— Another 1911 B&O derailment occurred one-and-a-half miles east of Rochester when one car of an east-bound train dragged another 10 off the tracks at full speed. Six hundred feet of tracks were destroyed in the melee. No injuries were reported, although State Fair train traffic was seriously delayed.

Twelve-foot snow drifts in Rochester during February 1914 almost hid this B&O train and prevented it from proceeding farther. J.E. Coe of Rochester took the picture near where the tracks crossed Black Branch Creek. (COURTESY OF CARL "BUD" MOORE, BARBARA WAGNER; *ILLINOIS STATE JOURNAL*, 24 FEB. 1914; USED WITH PERMISSION)

• A February 1914 snowstorm all but shut down rail traffic in Central Illinois. It took two additional engines and two days of shoveling to free the original two B&O engines that were stuck in 12-foot snowdrifts at Rochester. Local farmers gave refuge to the train's passengers. An estimated four miles of snowdrifts up to four feet deep covered the B&O tracks between Taylorville and Springfield.

- Self-proclaimed "champion skunk slayer" S.B. Smith of Rochester Township killed 16 skunks in 1912 after locating a nest of them in his farm field. Skunks had been killing chickens in the area, and only one from the nest successfully escaped Smith's skilled attack. He then issued a general dare to anyone else interested in a skunk-killing contest.

- The 1911 launch from Springfield of the hot air balloon "Million Population" entertained more than 5,000 spectators. Captain John Berry and his passenger Roy Donaldson came prepared with warm clothes, plenty of food, and souvenirs to drop from aloft. As they slowly rose, the wind floated them toward the southeast along the Rochester-to-Springfield Road. Captain Berry reported an altitude of 1,600 feet and speed of 12 miles per hour. After arriving at the Rochester viaduct, the balloon traveled south, where local audiences last saw them over New City. Although they were prepared for days of travel, air currents conspired against the pair who landed the next morning in LaPlace, IL, southeast of Decatur.
  — Forced to land their hot-air balloon because of atmospheric conditions, seven U.S. soldiers surprised Rochester citizens at 5:30 a.m. one August day in 1917 when they descended onto the farm field owned by C.M. McArthur. The McArthur family provided breakfast to their unexpected guests who soon thereafter resumed their flight.

- While walking along a street in 1911, Rochester citizen James Richardson was attacked and bitten by a dog that was later shot by blacksmith John Dunn. The dog's head was sent to Chicago for testing, where the canine was determined to have been rabid. Richardson traveled to the Pasteur Institute in Chicago for successful treatment and survived.
  — Less fortunate was eight-year-old Olive Eggleston who died from tetanus after a cut she sustained when lifting a pail became infected. Her death at St. John's Hospital in Springfield was the result of lockjaw. She is buried in Rochester Cemetery next to her parents, grocery-store owner Alonzo Eggleston and his wife, Flora.

- Minor crimes in this decade may be viewed with amusement today:
  — At different times, thieves broke into stores owned by F. DeLay, A. Eggleston, and H.D. Parker, as well as Twist Brothers' offices and J. Lynch's blacksmith shop. The thieves were sometimes caught, but sometimes escaped even when bloodhounds chased them.

The DeLay family in 1919 included, from left, Francis M., Wilhelmina "Willie," and their son Charles. (COURTESY OF SHARON DUDLEY)

Built originally by Carter Tracy, the East Main Street store owned by F.M. DeLay sold general merchandise. (*THE ROCHESTER ITEM*, 23 DEC. 1909)

— When thieves stole 150 chickens from George Admiral's farm in 1915, the theft was labeled "one of the biggest hauls of this kind."

— William Hinds was fined $1 in 1917 for swearing as he tried to open a Rochester Methodist Church window prior to an evening service in June.

— Rochester's two Snyder brothers were tracked by bloodhounds and arrested in 1912 for throwing "hen fruit" at Deacon M.P. Buckles and his family as they were returning home from church.

The DeLay home on East Main Street is seen as it appeared in a 1932 ad. (*ILLINOIS STATE JOURNAL*, 27 APR. 1932; USED WITH PERMISSION)

- Serious crimes:
  — Six sticks of dynamite were found on the Rochester B&O trestle in 1914. An evening train from Taylorville with 200 passengers was delayed until an inspection of the track determined no other dynamite had been placed.
  — A dispute at Glenwood Park north of Rochester over a 13-year-old girl led to the 1910 shooting death of Bill Knight by Edward Johnson. Johnson was charged with murder.

— Barbershop gossip about a woman emerged as the cause that took George Everhart and Joseph Murphy to the streets of Rochester in 1914 for a pistol duel. Although they exchanged seven shots, no one was injured. An owner of one nearby Rochester home, however, awoke to find that two bullets had passed over her head as she slept. Both men were charged with disorderly conduct and paid a $3 fine.

- Horseless carriage accidents:
  — A team of horses owned by Rochester Township resident William Hinsey was frightened in 1910 by an automobile as the horses drove through downtown Springfield. The wagon crashed and its occupants were flung to the brick pavement. The horses sped away, as did the automobile driver.
  — As he bicycled his way to deliver a Sunday-afternoon sermon at Round Prairie, Rochester Methodist Episcopal Church Pastor E.L. Carson was hit by an auto at the B&O hilltop bridge. In another early example of a hit and run, the car sped up and left the scene with none of its occupants offering help to Rev. Carson.
  — Another accident occurred in 1916 near Rochester when a racing horse and rig collided with an oncoming motorcycle. All the people involved survived, but the horse was killed and the motorcycle was destroyed.

Although this location had been the Jones and Woodruff Hardware, Paint, and Undertaking store about 10 years earlier, by this decade Joseph Murphy's barber shop occupied the northeast corner of East Main and Walnut Streets. (*THE ROCHESTER WEEKLY ITEM*, 23 DEC. 1909)

A Civil War veteran who served as both a Confederate and Union soldier, 70-year-old Rochester shoe maker George W. Everhart had a shootout with barber and jeweler Joseph Murphy at East Main and Walnut Streets in 1914. Both men were charged with disorderly conduct and fined $3. (*PAST AND PRESENT OF THE CITY OF SPRINGFIELD AND SANGAMON CO.*, VOL. II; JOSEPH WALLACE, S.J. CLARK PUB. CO., CHICAGO, 1904)

- Unusual accidents:
  — C.F. Fairchild and J.P. Dawley rescued Nettie Woodruff in 1910 after she had fallen into a backyard well at her home on East Main Street.
  — Harold Brown lost two fingers and a thumb in 1910 when he lit a dynamite cap with a match while playing at home after school.
  — A.G. Haines of Rochester was seriously injured in 1911 when two bleacher sections at the State Fairgrounds collapsed during an "Old Soldiers Day" celebration.
  — Lightning-rod salesman William Whitcomb was hit by lightning in his yard during a 1915 storm. His clothes were charred, but although Whitcomb was knocked unconscious, he survived.
  — Russell Kernoll saved brothers William and Henry Steinhauer from drowning in 1916 after the boys fell through the ice while skating. After pulling them from the water, Kernoll took the boys home to their mom, Ella, and dad, Frederick, who was the town barber.

- Rochester hosted numerous community-wide events:
  — The 1916 annual homecoming drew 3,000 people from Sangamon County who enjoyed the picnic, multiple speeches, music of Springfield's Watch Factory Band, and contests for a wide variety of athletes. These included the 100- and the 50-yard dashes, fat man's race, three-legged race, bicycle race, horse-shoe pitching contests, judging of various food items, and a baseball game.

Rochester's 1913 baseball team are, from left front row: Fred King, Manager Joe Hamel, Clarence Twist, and Sam Wolford; middle row: Art Haney, George Richardson, Arch Thornton, Meryl Fairchild, and Bert Wolford; and back row: Mick McCoy, Russell Kernoll, Jap Easley, Hosea Ross, and Justin Taft, Sr. (COURTESY OF ROCHESTER PUBLIC LIBRARY; RHPS COLLECTION)

  — Baseball was often played at the Rochester Merchants' home field on East Main Street, known as Campbell Park. Ed Campbell owned the property where team manager Joe Hamel was given credit for building a covered grandstand to shelter enthusiastic fans.
  — A week-long 1916 Chautauqua in Rochester entertained hundreds of people with music, literary programs, and lectures.
  — G.L. Rousseau remodeled and reopened the 20-acres of Glenwood Park in 1911. He had limited success, however, and by 1918 the park had failed for its second and final time.
  — U.G. Huffman, assistant state superintendent of public instruction, and S.G. Pruitt, county superintendent of schools, presented an evening of talks at

The Rochester Merchants baseball team played their home games at Campbell Park, located on the south side of the 600 block of East Main Street. This picture was taken in April 1912. (COURTESY OF CARL "BUD" MOORE AND BARBARA WAGNER)

Rochester's Woman's Christian Temperance Union (WCTU) temple. In addition to five movies, the duo used a forerunner of future technology, lantern slides.

- After the heavy-set star played center on the Springfield High School football team, Frank Twist made news in 1910 as "keystone of the (University of) Illinois defense and strong on the offensive." His brother Clarence, a former Springfield High baseball team captain, was selected, also in 1910, as a U of I outfielder who traveled with the team through the south. Frank and Clarence grew up in Rochester and were sons of prominent Rochester businessman Ira Twist and his first wife, Julia.

- Rochester's business community continued to grow.
  — Rochester State Bank was incorporated in 1911 and chartered one year later, taking over the Bank of Rochester. The new bank occupied the Main Street building that had been constructed downtown for the former institution.
  — After 25 years in a small frame building, *The Rochester Item*, by now under the ownership of Ira R. George and T.B. Wright, moved in 1915 two doors west to the first floor of the Odd Fellows Hall.

Edward Bennett's one-year subscription to *The Rochester Weekly Item* began 23 June 1915. He paid $1.00 for a year's worth of local news. (COURTESY OF ROCHESTER PUBLIC LIBRARY; RHPS COLLECTION; *THE ROCHESTER TIMES*, 29 OCT. 1976)

— In addition to new painting and decorating inside and out, the remodeling of Rochester's B&O train station in 1916 included a waiting room for ladies, a larger freight room, and bay window.
— G.A. Wolford in 1919 bought out J.H. Olcott's interest in the downtown hardware store they had previously owned jointly.

— Plans in 1910 foresaw out-of-town interests constructing a new grain elevator in Rochester.

— The Mississippi Pearl Button Company of Iowa briefly set up a camp in 1916 on the South Fork River as part of their operation to harvest clams for button manufacturing.

— Efforts of former Rochester farmer and businessman Marshall Sattley were recognized in 1914. More than 8,000 visitors watched 500 workmen manufacturing agricultural implements during the Racine-Sattley Manufacturing open house in Springfield. The Sattley plow, a handmade creation of then 20-year-old Rochester farmer Marshall Sattley, was the basis of his factories in Decatur, Taylorville, and Springfield. Sattley Manufacturing Company of Springfield joined with the Racine Wagon and Carriage Works in 1903. Sattley was recognized as one of Rochester's most successful businessmen.

G.A. Wolford Hardware Store, located in the Twist Building, billed the Rochester M.E. Church $15.31 in 1914 for chimney and furnace repairs at the church and parsonage.
(COURTESY OF ROCHESTER PUBLIC LIBRARY; RHPS COLLECTION)

Over a four-month period, the Rochester M.E. Church bought $16.41 worth of coal from the Shreve Mill. Owner Roy T. Shreve acknowledged payment on 1 Feb. 1912. (COURTESY OF ROCHESTER PUBLIC LIBRARY; RHPS COLLECTION)

Invoices and bills reflect the businesses that existed in Rochester a century ago. This 1914 bill for $10.32 was sent to the Methodist Episcopal Church from Twist Brothers Lumber Company of Rochester. (COURTESY OF ROCHESTER PUBLIC LIBRARY; RHPS COLLECTION)

The person or business receiving 2,200 pounds of coal from the Tuxhorn Coal Co. was not listed on this February 1911 receipt. The coal company was located at Keys Station in Rochester Township. (COURTESY OF ROCHESTER PUBLIC LIBRARY; RHPS COLLECTION)

THE TUXHORN COAL CO.

N° 1149

Springfield, Ill.,_____190___

Load of_____Coal to_____

Gross_____lbs.

Tare_____lbs.

Net_____lbs.

Net_____Bus.

Teamster_____

This 3,700-pound chunk of coal displayed in Springfield was taken from the Tuxhorn Mine in Rochester Township. (COURTESY OF THE STATE JOURNAL-REGISTER, 25 FEB. 1976; COURTESY OF MARY ALICE TUXHORN)

Four generations of the Tobin family are together in this photo taken about 1910. Far right is James Tobin, who brought his family to Sangamon County in 1856. John F. Tobin (center) lived with his wife Mary (Ehrler) on West Main Street in Rochester. Active in the Rochester community, John served as village president in 1919. His son (far left), James Ralph Tobin became well known for his Springfield jewelery store. James holds his eight-month-old son J. Willard Tobin, who would join his father in business. (COURTESY OF ANN (TOBIN) HART)

- Some Rochester deaths:

1912
— Christian E. Miller, international stock dealer;
— John C. Coe, pioneer farmer, '49er, and friend of Abraham Lincoln;
— William H. Neal, public servant;
— George W. Poffenbarger, farmer;

1915
— Mary Ann Ducker, a widow who earned her livelihood by selling chickens;

1916
— Daniel Waters, farmer and landowner;
— Richard P. Hunter, Civil War veteran;

1917
— John W. Byers, rural mail carrier;
— Daniel Ott, livery-business owner;

1918
— George W. Everhart, shoe-and-harness shop owner.

An 1874 Sangamon County map located a school at the site of the one-room Hedge School on Buckhart Road about 1.5 miles east of Rochester. The John Hunter farm, later owned by the Fairchild family, is visible on the far right of this 1913 Hedge School photo. The school was no longer used when the building was demolished around 1950. (SANGAMON COUNTY SCHOOLS ANNUAL REPORT, JOURNAL CO. PRINTERS, SPRINGFIELD, IL, PAGE 11, 1913-1914; COURTESY OF LYLE BEHL)

- One-room schools dotted Rochester Township, many of them built based on standards that included the building's size, the number of windows, and placement of desks. The goal for each small school was to achieve the designation of a "Standard School." Among the 27 goals were measurable and subjective details:
  — "Ample play ground."
  — "Heated with jacketed stove in corner, or a room heater and ventilator in corner, or basement furnace which brings clear air in through the furnace and removes foul air from room."

— "Good book case."

— "Set of good maps, a globe, dictionaries, sanitary water supply."

— "School well organized."

— "At least seven months school."

— (Teacher) "Education: The equivalent of a high school course."

— (Teacher) "Must receive at least $360 per annum."

Located at the northwest corner of Walnut Road and Etherton Lane, Fork Prairie School appears on maps as early as 1874. Although located near the boundary between Clear Lake and Rochester Townships, many Fork Prairie students continued their education in Rochester. As of 2017, the building is a family residence. (SANGAMON COUNTY SCHOOLS ANNUAL REPORT; EDWARD F. HARTMANN CO. PRINTERS 1916; COURTESY OF LYLE BEHL)

This "fine Punctuality Pin" was presented to county students who "are neither absent nor tardy for forty school months." County school officials gave assurances that awards such as this would "encourage regular attendance at school." (SANGAMON COUNTY SCHOOLS ANNUAL REPORT; JOURNAL CO. PRINTERS, SPRINGFIELD, IL, PAGE 11, 1913-1914; COURTESY OF LYLE BEHL)

- Education appears to have always been a top priority in the Rochester community, the first school having been established as early as 1823.

— Voters in 1917 authorized a $10,000 bond issue to build a new school on a three-acre North Walnut Street site.

— It was observed in 1915 that numerous Rochester graduates had become educators, with teaching assignments that extended from rural districts in Central Illinois to Chicago. The assignments of several former Rochester students included:

Elizabeth Furrow, primary department, Rochester;

Eva James, Hedge School;

Hazel Jones, South Cotton Hill School;

Grace Martin, Bluff School;
Elsie Martin, intermediate department, Rochester;
Rose Middlekauf, grammar department, Rochester.

— Other teachers from Rochester that year included Calista Breckenridge, Dora Dillon, Francis Funderburk, Minerva Furrow, Etta Harwood, Maude James, Bertha Nickols, Bertha Parker, Edith Parker, Pearl Stone, and Maude Tobin. Previous teachers who had recently married included Beryl *(King)* Jones, Nettie *(Enlow)* Martin, Emma *(Baldwin)* Taft, Anna *(Parker)* Twist, and Della *(King)* Woodruff.

The family of Charles and Julia *(King)* Martin posed in front of their West Main Street home about 1910. Frank Chandler had built their house in 1905. (COURTESY OF ROCHESTER PUBLIC LIBRARY; RHPS COLLECTION; GEORGEANNE DALY)

Outhouses were sometimes hidden out of sight in a barn, as is this two holer at J.B. Highmore's Orange Judd house on John Street. (COURTESY OF ADAM BLOODWORTH; R. BRUZAN PHOTO)

The Forsythe House is one of only four brick homes of the 60 village houses featured in the 1918 Orange Judd *Pictorial* album. The date this house was built has not yet been determined. As of 2017, the Forsythe house has been converted into apartments. (COURTESY OF BILL RODGERS, SUNNIE FLATT; COMPASS POINT PRODUCTIONS; FARM PROGRESS COMPANIES)

The Forsythe House is among the few Rochester homes with drawn plaster crown molding, much of which still remains in the house on Mill Street. (COURTESY OF BILL RODGERS, SUNNIE FLATT; R. BRUZAN PHOTO)

The 1917 congregation of the South Fork Christian Church was identified decades ago by Myrtle Nave and Josephine Weaver. The congregants included, from left: back row George Weaver, Billie Weaver, Albert Cary, Fred Gregory, Milton Green, Maggie Gregory and her daughter Grace, Mary Westbook, Alice Dickerson, Mrs. Ferrel, Lillie Self, Mary Smelly, Verna Weaver, Mrs. Breckenridge, J.B. Westbrook, John Smelly, John Simpson, Oscar Dickerson, Bill Runyon, Elmer Simpson, and Jess Martin. Middle row: Florence Green, Mary Derry, Elsie Campbell, Anna Derry, Geraldine Smelly, Ada Cary, and Ruby Bell. Front row: Leslie Simpson, John Westbrook, Noel Westbook, Russell Simpson, Arlo Dickerson, Harold Dickerson, Luke Bell, Velma Green, Mary Ellen Gregory, Edna Green, Ruth Westbrook, Fanny Runyon, Mabel Sharp, Edith Sharp, and Margaret Green. (COURTESY OF HAROLD WEAVER AND THE ROCHESTER HELLO, 15 APR. 1982)

Horses were hitched up to two wagons on the Henry A. Cantrill farm about 1915. The farm was located on the north side of Tuxhorn Road. (COURTESY OF HAROLD CANTRILL)

Enjoying a child-size buggy ride circa 1915 are, from left: a goat, Nelson, Isabell, Hugh, and Lyman Campbell. This view looking north across East Main Street includes two homes that have since been torn down. (COURTESY OF CATHY LEAHY, BRIAN CAMPBELL, AND JANET CAMPBELL)

Charles and Carrie (Ross) Fairchild posed with their children, Ross, Charles, and Meryl, in 1912 at their farm on Buckhart Road east of Rochester. Their Fairchild ancestors were early Rochester settlers who traveled here from New York in 1833. (COURTESY OF ROBERT FAIRCHILD)

Rochester Village Board President Charles W. Frame, who served 1911-1912, was the grandfather of former local resident Barbara (Watkins) Wagner. (COURTESY OF BARBARA WATKINS)

A (MUDDY) ROAD LESS TRAVELED

This 1920 picture of the Rochester Road to Springfield highlights the drastic need for highway improvements. (*THE ROCHESTER & LAKE SPRINGFIELD HERALD*, 26 NOV. 1986; RHPS COLLECTION)

1920S

The Shreve Mill was located at the northwest corner of Main and Walnut Streets. It was demolished in 1923, and a new Methodist Episcopal Church was built on the site. (COURTESY OF ROCHESTER PUBLIC LIBRARY; RHPS COLLECTION)

1920s Timeline...

1920	Rochester population: 399
	— Brick school built on North Walnut Street for grades 1-11
1922	*The Rochester Weekly Item* ceased publication
	— Masons purchased the downtown school
	— Village purchased fire-fighting equipment
1923	Shreve Mill was demolished
	— W.H. Kernoll had a radio "installed" in his West Main Street home
1924	Rochester Woman's Club established
	— New Methodist Episcopal Church was dedicated
	— Chapel built at the Rochester Cemetery
1925	Robert Fairchild and H.T. Campbell each had a radio "installed" in their home
1926	Methodist Episcopal Church purchased a parsonage on West Main Street
1927	Homes in Rochester Township were being wired for electricity

— A hard road parallel to the Baltimore & Ohio Railroad (B&O) tracks was paved from Springfield to Rochester
— Downtown Main Street home of R.S. Twist was destroyed by fire

1928   Harry L. Fogel American Legion Post 274 was chartered in Rochester

1920s Storylines...

- During the "Roaring Twenties," major upgrades to roads and bridges were necessary to accommodate the continued influx of automobile travelers. Creation of a hard road from Springfield to Pana had a major impact on merchants and community events. Pioneer-era bridges were being replaced and a new school, church, and cemetery chapel pointed to an energetic village.

- The increasing number of automobiles were a driving force to improve the horrible roads and bridges of Sangamon County, notably the Springfield-Rochester connection. Bridges crossing the South Fork River and Sugar Creek were subject to flooding, and oiled road surfaces were inadequate.
  — Echoing discussions from 10 years earlier, plans were made to build a concrete road from Springfield to the Christian County line that would link with a hard road to Taylorville and Pana.
  — A legal dispute ensued in 1925 when a Rochester contingent fought for the road to link into Springfield at South Grand Avenue instead of at Cook Street, as preferred by state officials. Rochester landowners in the lawsuit included William Taft, George Bigelow, Milton Green, Isham Taft, J. Earl Bell, John F. Vigal, Charles E. Fairchild, H.D. Parker, George G. Oliver, John A. Dickerson, and Conrad Heissinger. The year-long court case was settled in favor of the Cook Street approach to Springfield, and work soon began on the nine-mile section of Route 24 from Springfield to the Christian County line.
  — A portion of the new alignment, from Hilltop to Rochester, established this hard road along the north side of the B&O tracks. That two-lane highway, now known as Route 29, was completed in 1928.

- The community lost a valued media source when *The Rochester Item* newspaper ceased publication in 1922. A creation of Ethelbert Kalb, the weekly publication served Rochester for 40 years under a series of editors and publishers. An editorial in the *Illinois State Journal* had high praise for the *Item*, stating it "represented conscientious, painstaking work of the highest order." Only 10 copies of the *Item* have been found by the authors to exist today.

- A June issue of *The Rochester Item* during its last year included an ad by Alonzo Eggleston listing "Prices on a Few of the Many Items We Carry in Stock." No doubt anticipating bounteous gardens, Eggleston listed canning-related items, including half-gallon mason jars ($1.20), quart jars ($.85), pint jars ($.75), two packages of jar rings ($.15), and jar caps ($.25 per dozen).

Maurice W. Scott, shown in the 1928 photo on the right, described in his 1982 oral history how Rochester school was dismissed before lunch so that students could watch the 1923 dynamiting of the Shreve Mill chimney, as recorded in the larger photo. (LEFT: COURTESY OF ROCHESTER PUBLIC LIBRARY; RHPS COLLECTION; RIGHT: *ILLINOIS STATE JOURNAL*, 17 JUNE 1928; PUBLISHED BY GENEALOGYBANK.COM, A DIVISION OF NEWSBANK)

- Demolition of the Shreve Coal and Corn Mill in 1923 made way for the new Rochester Methodist Church built a year later on the northwest corner of Main and Walnut Streets. Present at the dedication of the new church were 11 members who had attended the 1876 dedication of the first church building on Mill Street. The new church belfry housed the original bell from the Mill Street church.

Millstones saved from the Shreve Mill on Main Street are maintained by a private collector. (COURTESY OF BLAINE AND JUANITA SMITH; R. BRUZAN PHOTOS)

The original Rochester Methodist Episcopal Church on Mill Street was replaced in 1924 by this new church on East Main. (R. BRUZAN PHOTO)

— A day-long church dedication drew guests from around Central Illinois and celebrated the new brick church built with a 300-seat sanctuary, a choir loft, pulpit, a parlor with a fireplace, Sunday School rooms, kitchen, dining room, and a basement gymnasium. Fourteen memorial stained-glass windows filtered natural light into the sanctuary. The church cost $20,000.

• Mr. and Mrs. Edmund Miller contributed $5,000 in 1926 toward the purchase price of $6,000 for the new Methodist Church parsonage on West Main Street. The first Rochester Methodist parsonage, purchased by the church in 1858 and located on East Mill Street, was later sold.

— Donations by members of the Methodist congregation toward the purchase of their new church property were also made public earlier in the decade. A front-page article in *The Rochester Item* listed all donors by name and detailed each donation, which ranged from $5 to $100.

The 1924 Rochester Methodist Episcopal Church included 14 memorial windows surrounding the loft and sanctuary. Several of these historic windows are now displayed at the church's new South Walnut Street location. (COURTESY OF LYNN CHARD, RICHARD METCALF; P. BRUZAN PHOTO)

Left: Rev. Henry Curtis Munch was minister of the Rochester Methodist Episcopal Church when the new Main Street church was dedicated in 1924. He is shown here in 1923 holding his daughter Mary and posing with his wife, Mary *(Curry)*, son Joseph, and older daughter Florence. (COURTESY OF ROCHESTER PUBLIC LIBRARY; RHPS COLLECTION)

Right: The Rochester Methodist Episcopal Church is seen as it appeared on Mill Street for almost half a century. (COURTESY OF ROCHESTER UNITED METHODIST CHURCH)

Eleven members of the Rochester Methodist Episcopal Church were present at the dedication of both their Mill Street church, built in 1876, and the Main Street Church, dedicated in 1924. They are, from left: Richard Coe, Mary Poffenberger, Mrs. Mary *(Derry)* Woodruff, S.B. Coe, Mrs. E. Nichols, Mrs. H. Waters, I.F. Twist, John Kerrney, Edwin Miller, and Mrs. Edwin Miller. (COURTESY OF ROCHESTER UNITED METHODIST CHURCH)

The original 1876 Rochester Methodist Church bell spent more than a decade in Lynn Chard's storage barn. The bell had been removed from the original Mill Street church and installed in the East Main Street church in 1924. Placed in storage in 2001 when the church moved to South Walnut Street, the bell refinishing became an Eagle Scout project for RHS student Alex Baylor. The church is finalizing plans in 2017 to display the refurbished historic bell. (COURTESY OF LYNN CHARD; R. BRUZAN PHOTO)

- A picturesque little brick building comes into view as drivers navigate the narrow lane toward Rochester's historic cemetery. Prominent Rochester Township farmer William Cantrill provided $3,000 in his will for this one-room chapel built at the cemetery by George and Jesse Reed in 1924. Cemetery trustees at that time were John F. Tobin, Benjamin F. Waters, and R.F. Fairchild. The chapel still provides a peaceful location in which to conduct services.

Paid for by the William Cantrill Memorial Fund, the Rochester Cemetery Chapel was completed by George W. Reed and Son in 1924. William and his wife, Elizabeth *(Derry)* Cantrill both died in 1917 and are buried in Rochester Cemetery. (R. BRUZAN PHOTO)

- The high cost of materials prevented construction of a new school with the $10,000 that voters had approved in 1917. A second bond issue, approved three years later for an additional $9,900, provided the necessary funding to begin construction of the new school on North Walnut Street. The school, which housed grades 1-11, opened in 1921, and was described as "one of the most modern and up-to-date in the county." Students wishing to attend a

The new Rochester School on North Walnut was built for grades 1-11 in 1920 by the construction company of G.W. Reed and Son. It is seen between two wings added decades later. (COURTESY OF STEVE LEACH)

The cornerstone of the 1920 Rochester School building that was demolished in 2006 is displayed at the RHPS Historical Park on West Main Street. Directors listed on the stone are Everet Campbell, Charles Martin, and Annie Twist. (P. BRUZAN PHOTO)

The 1923-24 third-grade class at Rochester Grade School is pictured on the front steps of their recently completed building. (COURTESY OF ROCHESTER PUBLIC LIBRARY; RHPS COLLECTION)

The Rochester High School boys basketball team in 1926 included, from left: George Beck, Orville Gathard, George Duffey, Ross Fairchild, Glenn Irvin, and Clarence Denton. Coach O.D. Gabel is on the right. (STATE JOURNAL-REGISTER, 29 DEC. 1977; PUBLISHED BY GENEALOGYBANK.COM, A DIVISION OF NEWSBANK)

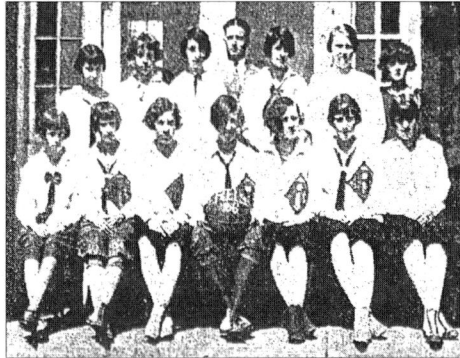

The 1926 Rochester High School girls basketball team included, front row from left: Francis Taft, Eva Neich, Norma Taylor, Irene Huffman, Clara Dickerson, Margaret Green, and Edna Green. Back row: Beatrice Fogle, Fannie Wolford, Pauline Frame, Coach O.D. Gabel, Virginia Coontz, Mary Shrives, and Alice Bigelow. (*STATE JOURNAL-REGISTER*, 29 DEC. 1977; PUBLISHED BY GENEALOGYBANK.COM, A DIVISION OF NEWSBANK)

fourth year of high school went to Springfield High. After 41 years as a school, the old building on Main Street was sold in 1922 for $1,500 to the Rochester Masons and was remodeled to became their temple the following year.

- Rochester created a fire department of sorts as early as 1922 when the village purchased a chemical tank that could be pulled to the site of local fires. Stored in the former jail, the tank failed, however, to prevent total destruction of a 12-room two-story brick home owned by R.S. Twist. This stately Main Street residence was apparently set ablaze in 1927 by a spark on the roof. Sustaining a $20,000 loss, the Twist home was never rebuilt.

— The house had been owned about 40 years earlier by Dr. E.R. Babcock and was the birthplace of internationally acclaimed violinist Louis Persinger.

— On the east side of the burning Twist home, the James Drillinger residence owned by Rose Middlekauff, incurred $400 in fire damages. As of 2017 that house is still part of the Main

The Drillinger home (lower left), still located on East Main Street near downtown, was saved from a 1927 fire that destroyed the Ralph Sattley Twist home (above) next door. The Twist house, the former home of Dr. E.R. Babcock, was the birthplace of internationally known violinist Louis Persinger.

(ABOVE PHOTO COURTESY OF COMPASS POINT PRODUCTIONS; FARM PROGRESS COMPANIES; LEFT: R. BRUZAN PHOTO)

Street scene. L.A. Rule's gas station, located immediately west of the blazing home, was not damaged, but no longer exists.

- Mollie *(Campbell)* Wolford was elected in 1924 as the first president of a newly organized 15-member Rochester Woman's Club. For its first six years the club affiliated with the Sangamon County Farmer's Institute. From the beginning, their colors were yellow and turquoise and their flower was the chrysanthemum. Over the years, this community-service organization has been responsible for a wide variety of activities:
— Decorated veterans' graves in Rochester Cemetery with fresh flower wreaths;
— Established the Rochester Public Library;
— Began Rochester's first Girl Scout troop;
— Sponsored style and flower shows;
— Led efforts that, with help from the Rochester Lions Club, completed tennis courts at the high school;
— Granted scholarships to school students for summer arts programs;
— Established the village's first recycling drive to collect newspapers, magazines, and bottles;
— Planted trees and shrubs on the high school campus; and
— Planted an evergreen tree in the village triangle at the corner of Route 29 and Walnut Street, decorating it annually for Christmas.
— As it approaches the centennial of its organization, the club continues in spite of decreased membership.

C.L. Jones of Rochester and embalmer Jim Ellinger owned the hearse and horses, providing and promoting their services at the Illinois State Fair about 1920. (COURTESY OF GREG PARK)

- After arresting a 16-year-old self-proclaimed "tough guy," who had drawn a revolver during a 1924 fight, Village President Henry Schwartz believed that the young man's behavior would change after a few hours in the Rochester calaboose. Instead, within 15 minutes the teen managed to destroy a large portion of the jail roof, requiring his transfer to the county jail in Springfield. There he was charged with carrying a concealed weapon and disorderly conduct.
  — Rochester authorities were left to repair the jail roof. The calaboose was located behind the building at 125 East Main Street. Although they searched diligently, the authors were unable to locate a picture of the much-talked-about jail.

- After falling into a 30-foot-deep water well on the Poffenberger farm east of Rochester in 1927, three-year-old Jane Thornton was rescued when her ten-year-old brother, Gene, slid into the well and Fred Poffenberger, Jr., ran for help. Gene kept his sister's head above water until their mother and friends used a lawn rake to help pull the siblings to safety. Jane was reported to be "none the worse for her experience," and Gene certainly earned his status as a hero.

- Members of the Rochester Rebekahs cooked a noon-time dinner for 29 Odd Fellows, neighbors, and friends who came to the aid of Leo M. Boehme. Illness had confined the Rochester farmer to his home during much of the 1925 harvest season. By the end of the day they had husked 1,300 bushels of corn.

- The retired Rev. T.B. Wright experienced a challenging auto trip in 1923 when driving to conduct a church revival. As he drove across the Allen Street railroad crossing in Springfield, a northbound Alton Limited train hit his car's spare tire, launching it more than a hundred feet into the air.
  — Once the tire landed and he retrieved it, Rev. Wright continued, but soon realized his car was on fire. Wright put out the flames before finding another car and driver who deposited him safely at the church only a few minutes behind his original schedule.

- Early in the decade "good orchestra music" was the incentive to attend dances advertised at "the Rochester Hall" or the "Old Legion Hall." An evening's entertainment cost just $1.10 per couple. For those who preferred to dance at home instead, Springfield Dry Goods Co., in the 100 block of South Sixth Street, advertised Orophone Talking Machines on sale for $6.95 and Regal 10-inch records for 49 cents. A dime bought 100 Brilliantone phonograph needles, advertised to produce a "perfect clear tone."

- Rochester deaths included:

1921
— **Winn Fairchild**, killed by a speeding train in Yakima, WA;

1922
— **Ella Barnwell**, whose hotel boarding house was identified on an 1894 Rochester map;

1923
— **John W. Sturdy**, a Confederate soldier and member of the Rochester Odd Fellows Lodge who is buried in Buckhart Cemetery;

1924
— **Mary Jane Neer**, a pioneer whose family settled in the stone house east of Rochester after arriving from Virginia in a one-horse wagon;
— **Clara** *(Vigal)* **Jones**, wife of Rochester undertaker Charles L. Jones;
— **Thomas B. Wright**, Methodist minister, newspaper editor, and real-estate agent died in September. His wife, **Lillian** *(McCoy)* **Wright**, followed him in death almost exactly three months later; she was a granddaughter of Rochester's first settler James McCoy;

1929
— **Florence Twist**, daughter of cotton mogul Ira F. Twist, died in Taylorville at an uncle's home.

A.D. Young (1837-1927) lived in Rochester most of his life. He was a Sangamon County deputy sheriff, jailer, and Rochester Township constable "where he was known as a fearless official." His home was on East Main Street. (*ILLINOIS STATE JOURNAL*, 28 FEB. 1925; PUBLISHED BY GENEALOGYBANK.COM, A DIVISION OF NEWSBANK)

- Dangerous storms:
— A June 1922 storm, possibly a twister, caused thousands of dollars of damage. Many farm buildings owned in Rochester Township by the Richardson, Knotts, Green, Howell, Martin, Copeland, Mottar, and Fairchild families were damaged or destroyed. Part of the Methodist Church roof was damaged, as was a chimney on the Mill Street home of J.W. Sturdy. Clarence Gabrael (sic) suffered a fractured skull and was knocked unconscious when he was hit by a large tree limb that came through his bedroom window. Two Auburn men were seriously injured as they camped near the South Fork River covered bridge south of Rochester.
— Two years later a lightning bolt hit the John Morris barn causing a fire that consumed the barn and killed three horses. More lightning from the same storm struck and killed one of Martin Pillischafske's horses.

- Nineteen-year-old Claude F. Bell avoided becoming mired in almost impassable February roads when he walked from Rochester to Springfield to participate in the *Illinois State Journal*'s 1928 Amateur Vaudeville contest. The harmonica-playing Bell "regaled the crowd with his musical offering." Audience applause placed him second in the preliminary round and third in the final senior division of the contest, which was part of the newspaper's Food Show and Household Appliance Exposition.
  — Claude was presented his $10 award on stage at the Illinois State Arsenal. Claude's son, Paul, recalled in 2015 the stories he had heard of his dad playing harmonica at Glenwood Park northwest of Rochester on the South Fork River.

- Members of the Twist family had already relocated from Rochester to their cotton plantation in Arkansas by the 1920s. Milton Green of Rochester bought a controlling interest in Twist-owned grain elevators at Berry and Breckenridge. Most Twist family members returned, however, for burial in Rochester Cemetery. Clarence Twist, who died in 1938, was originally buried in Rochester, but his wife, Edith, had him moved in 1954 for reburial in Earl, AR.

Thanksgiving Day 1923 brought families together at "Locustholm," the S.B. Coe farm east of Rochester on the Lincoln Highway (today Buckhart Road). (ABOVE: COURTESY OF COMPASS POINT PRODUCTIONS; FARM PROGRESS COMPANIES; LEFT: JAMES A. WOODRUFF COLLECTION)

- Birthdays, achievements, anniversaries, and weddings:

1922

— Bringing together two families whose ancestors were among the early settlers of Rochester, Iva Lucile Campbell married Meryl Robert Fairchild.

1923

— Sylvester J. and Pauline *(Abel)* McCoy celebrated their 50th anniversary. Sylvester was a grandson of Rochester's first settler, James McCoy.

— Charles and Martha *(Billings)* Dickerson celebrated their golden wedding anniversary.

1925

— Former Sangamon County jailer and Rochester Township constable Armstrong Dawson Young celebrated his 88th birthday at home.

1927

— After delivering an estimated 1,500,000 pieces of mail as a Rochester Township mail carrier, Uriah Alexander Williams retired to enjoy his well-earned pension. He delivered mail by horse-drawn cart for 17 years of his 25-year career.

1927

— Jeanette Coe, the daughter of R.H. Coe, married Rochester School Superintendent Otto Gabel.

Charlie Dickerson (1849-1929) and his wife Martha *(Billings)* (1849-1943) lived five miles southeast of Rochester, where they celebrated their golden wedding anniversary in 1922. They are buried in Mottarville Cemetery. (*ILLINOIS STATE JOURNAL*, 2 JULY 1922; PUBLISHED BY GENEALOGYBANK.COM, A DIVISION OF NEWSBANK)

1928

— Fourteen-year-old Maurice Scott was recognized as the best history student in Sangamon County when he was awarded a Daughters of the American Revolution medal for earning the highest score on a competitive test.

Maurice W. Scott recalled in his oral history how, much to the distress of Rochester-area beaus, "the beautiful Jeanette Coe" married one of his favorite teachers, Otto D. Gable, on Christmas Eve 1927. "Everyone was invited and everyone was there," said Scott. The Gables celebrated their 50th wedding anniversary in 1977. (*ILLINOIS STATE JOURNAL*, 27 NOV. 1927; PUBLISHED BY GENEALOGYBANK.COM, A DIVISION OF NEWSBANK)

- Crimes of the decade included:
  — One Rochester citizen bound over to the grand jury in 1922 accused of stealing 31 chickens belonging to Henry Schwartz;
  — An unsuccessful attempt to blow open a Post Office safe in the S.G. Richardson store;
  — Theft and later recovery of a Ford sedan from the home of C.E. Fairchild;
  — Charges of assault with a deadly weapon against Harry Baker for firing a shotgun at John A. Densmore; and
  — Charges that resident George Hass had made threats against Joe Murphy, also of Rochester.

- Rochester Mayor, Henry Schwartz, was arrested in July 1926 on charges of assault with a deadly weapon and then released on $500 bond to appear before a justice of the peace. The charge occurred after Schwartz, wearing only his night shirt, shot at an automobile driven by Loren B. Taft. The mayor claimed he was enforcing an ordinance that limited the use of fireworks in the village to July 4th. He became angry when Taft set off fireworks in the Schwartz front yard the night before the celebration, actually scheduled that year on the "legal holiday" Monday July 5th. The case was settled out of court but the often-elected mayor was long remembered as "Shotgun Schwartz."

- A jail-break attempt made front-page news on January 12, 1922. Rochester citizen James Laubourge's attempt to deliver a gun and ammunition to Sangamon County jail prisoner Grover Hill was derailed by Deputy Sheriff Willard Mester. Laubourge's grocery delivery to Hill included the contraband in five pounds of flour. A young boy later delivered cornmeal containing two steel saw blades and a bottle of muriatic acid.
  — Officials suggested that prisoners would have thrown the acid into the jailer's eyes when he delivered breakfast, thus providing an escape opportunity. Laubourge was captured as he waited to board a Rochester-bound B&O train.

- Rochester authorities were criticized in 1920 when several local cases of smallpox were reported to the state department of public health. Changes were soon made to administer vaccinations when needed for Rochester citizens, diagnose the disease more accurately, and strictly quarantine homes where smallpox had surfaced.

- As Rochester Methodist Church Pastor H.C. Munch conducted a revival service for 600 people on December 9, 1923, he was interrupted by four hooded Klansmen. One of them spoke highly of Munch's efforts against immorality and handed the pastor an envelope with money and a letter. Although Munch requested the crowd to attend the next meeting and hear him read the KKK note, subsequent events went unreported. Rochester Christian Church Pastor C.C.

Hull and members of his congregation were also attending the revival. Reports suggested that some Rochester citizens were members of the Ku Klux Klan and that they met in a large tract of timber west of the village.

— Apparently Rochester was not the only Illinois community to experience a December 1923 Klan visit. Eleven white-robed individuals visited a Sunday-night Colchester Methodist congregation. The Klansmen received cheers from church members when they left an envelope containing $24 and instructions to distribute that money to the poor of Colchester. Other reports of the Klan visiting churches with donations and Klan information were noted a year earlier in Winchester and Jacksonville.

Apparently Rochester's December 1923 visit by Ku Klux Klan members was one of several similar appearances. Eleven white-robed Klansmen also visited a 1923 Sunday-night Colchester Methodist Church service. Church members there cheered when the KKK provided an envelope with $24 and instructions to distribute their donation to the poor. (Photo taken by R. Bruzan during a 2016 visit to The Henry Ford. The Henry Ford does not sponsor, endorse, or affiliate with R. Bruzan or any others associated with this book.)

• Checkers was a serious sport in Rochester, where it was bragged "more expert checker players (lived) than any town of its size in the world." The East Main Street veterinary office of Harold Campbell was the site of many afternoon and evening matches. Campbell, Milton Green, J.W. Cantrall, Robert Fairchild, Admiral Campbell, Frank Horning, and Leslie Williams were among the players who were eager to justify this self-proclaimed honor.

VOTE FOR
J. BRUCE HIGHMORE
FOR SHERIFF

• Former Rochester mayor J. Bruce Highmore ran for sheriff in the 1922 Democratic primary. His political ad stated, "I have never double crossed a man or woman in my life" and he had "never made an obligation that I did not meet." Regardless of his statements, Highmore lost the primary, placing fourth out of four candidates.

Former Rochester Mayor J. B. Highmore lost this 1922 election for sheriff. (Illinois State Journal, 14 Apr. 1922; Published by GenealogyBank. com, A Division of NewsBank)

- Farm-related news during 1927 was of great interest in this farming community.
  — In July, Howard McCoy, James Duffy, Samuel B. Coe, Ralph S. Twist, Charles Frame, Elmer McCoy, and G.A. Wolford were all cutting wheat.
  — Isham Taft's corn was looking good by July, whereas Clarence Rude had just finished planting corn.
  — Ruth Sturdy's head lettuce was also doing well in July.
  — In August, four carloads of C.E. Fairchild's well-fed cattle were shipped to Chicago, John Davis's four-year-old cow give birth to twins, and Charles Frame bought 70 head of feeding cattle in Kansas City, MO.
  — G.A. Wolford and Charles E. Frame both lost mules due to the September heat. Charles E. Frame bought carloads of stock cattle in Southern Illinois, and Fred Poffenbarger made four carloads of cattle ready for shipment to Chicago.

- New homes and home improvements dominated village news in November 1922.
  — Electricity came to the farm homes of S.B. Coe and Charles E. Fairchild.
  — While occupying the Old Stone House three miles east of Rochester, Charles Darneiden had a new eight-room home built on that farm property.
  — Contractor George Reed built a five-room bungalow on West Main Street.
  — C.E. Fairchild built a new seven-room house near Breckenridge for his son Meryl and new daughter-in-law Lucile.

The home of Preston Parish and Mary Anna *(Twist)* Breckenridge on South Walnut Street is shown about 1920. A farmer and building contractor, Preston was a cousin of John C. Breckenridge, vice president of the United States from 1857 to 1861 and an unsuccessful 1860 presidential candidate.
(COURTESY OF JOHN RUNIONS)

Telephones appeared in Rochester in the early 1880s. This $2.54 Illinois Bell Telephone Company bill was sent to Julia Crockett of Rochester for the month of November 1920.
(COURTESY OF FAY JOSTES)

• Rochester's share of train stories continued:

— The state utilities commission okayed the B&O request for a new 300-foot-long industrial track across Walnut Street to service a grain elevator under construction in 1920.

— After the B&O and Indianapolis, Decatur, and Western (ID&W) railroads combined in 1917, plans developed to merge the two existing tracks. Construction of a new short section between Keys Station west of Rochester and the B&O would eliminate four miles of ID&W track and an extremely long trestle over Sugar Creek.

— This track-merger plan was not completed until 1963, when a railroad bridge was built over Route 29 just east of Sugar Creek. Although those tracks and bridge were removed in 1999, the spot where the two tracks joined may be seen from Lost Bridge Trail.

— Flames from an ID&W trestle burning two miles east of Rochester could be seen in the village during a spectacular June 1923 fire. Firefighters put out the flames in an hour, but damages closed that rail line until repairs were made. Cause of the fire was undetermined.

— A B&O engineer was not seriously injured even though he had lost his balance and fallen from his locomotive in 1927. The accident occurred after he had stopped at the Rochester water tank. He sustained injuries to his left side when he fell on the rail.

— Rochester tin-shop proprietor Antone Smith died in 1923 as a result of injuries he received when the car he was riding in crashed into the Rochester B&O railroad trestle over West Main Street. His brother Frank was driving and lost control as they approached the curve under the trestle. Missing the curve, the car drove directly into the structure.

• A pleasant 1923 outing of the DMC Embroidery Club to Mrs. J.H. Olcott's farm about two miles south of Rochester turned exciting as the mule team under rein of Mrs. F.E. Poffenbarger decided to stage a runaway. Unable to slow them down, Mrs. Poffenbarger sought assistance from Mrs. John B. (Louela)

Highmore, who also had no luck at slowing the running mules. It was up to Mrs. Roy T. (Estella) Shreve to control the cantankerous animals.
— Estella knew from her previous "Kentucky experience" that mules will run until they become tired. So she kept the mules on the road until they simply came to a halt, right at the Olcott farm. Shaken but not stirred, all seven passengers survived without injury.

- Nettie Woodruff was not as lucky when she leaped from a runaway buggy in 1924. In falling, she hit her head on the street, sustaining a concussion and severe bruising. Although the early prognosis was bleak, Nettie actually lived another 38 years.

- Rochester hosted what was billed in 1924 as the largest farm exhibit in the county. The four-day Sangamon County Farmer's Institute and Domestic Science Association took over the downtown area with displays of poultry, pet stock, cattle, swine, horses, mules, and numerous farm products and implements. Hundreds of visitors enjoyed the farm displays, speakers, music entertainment, school-work display, needlework, livestock judging, and fine food. Rochester also hosted the Farmer's Institute a year later.

- When G.A. Wolford sold two of his walnut trees in 1926, he realized a nice profit of $200. The sale brought back memories of the many visitors who had been drawn to his East Main Street home looking for pieces of the walnut tree under which Abraham Lincoln was said to have campaigned in 1832.

- Two Rochester citizens recalled their experiences in the Civil War:
— James W. Richardson, who celebrated his 80th birthday in 1921, served three years in the war. His first engagement was at Jackson, MS, and his second at Vicksburg. He served at New Orleans and had returned to Vicksburg just before President Lincoln was assassinated. One of Rochester's best known residents, Richardson died at his North Walnut Street home in 1922 and is buried in Oak Hill Cemetery, Riverton.

Rochester-born farmer George Brunk Boyd (1839-1930) recalled on his 90th birthday many of the major events of his life that included seeing Abraham Lincoln in Springfield and serving in the Union army during the Civil War. He opined that radios were the greatest invention and that Charles Lindbergh's trans-Atlantic flight was only rivaled by the discoveries of Christopher Columbus. (*ILLINOIS STATE JOURNAL*, 22 DEC. 1929; PUBLISHED BY GENEALOGYBANK.COM, A DIVISION OF NEWSBANK)

— George Brunk Boyd turned 90 in 1929. Born in Rochester Township, Boyd earned the rank of sergeant after enlisting in 1862. He engaged in combat in Tennessee, Mississippi, Missouri, and Arkansas, fighting under Union generals Grant, Sherman, and Smith. Boyd remembered well the occasions when he saw Abraham Lincoln and Stephen Douglas. He died in 1930 and is buried in Oak Ridge Cemetery.

• Rochester's American Legion Harry Fogle Post 274 was established in 1925 and chartered in 1928. The post was named after the Rochester sergeant, who died in World War I and is buried in France. H.L. Campbell was the Post's first commander.

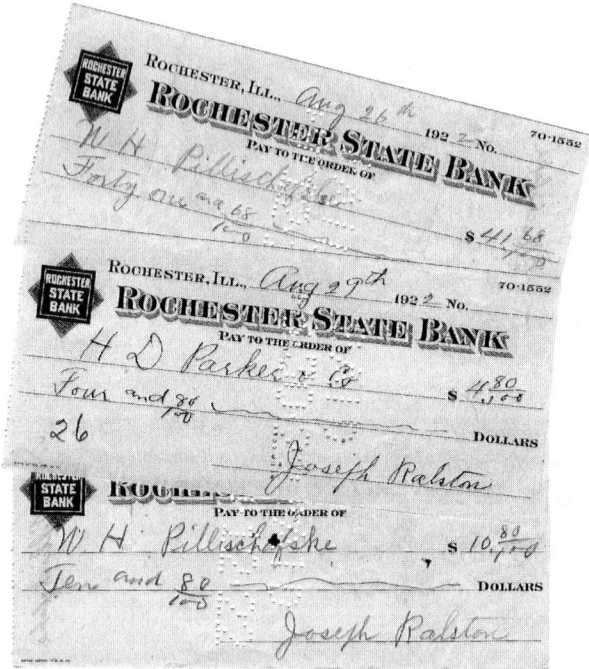

Joseph Ralston (1864-1950) and his family lived on the east side of what today is East Lake Shore Drive. (COURTESY OF KENT AND BRENDA KURNISKIE)

Artifacts such as these checks and check register page can sometimes provide a glimpse into the lives of people who died decades ago. The middle check and check register page from Rochester State Bank show that on August 29, 1922, Joseph Ralston spent $4.80 at H.D. Parker & Co. drug store for ice cream. The treat may have been a delayed celebration of the August 27 birthday of his daughter Goldie. The other two checks are written out to his neighbor, W.H. Pillischafske, for threshing wheat. (COURTESY OF KENT AND BRENDA KURNISKIE)

Joseph and Emma *(Green)* Ralston lived for about 50 years in their historic Orange Judd home on what is today East Lake Shore Drive. They both died in 1950. Their daughter, Goldie, is also seen in this photo. (COURTESY OF COMPASS POINT PRODUCTIONS; FARM PROGRESS COMPANIES)

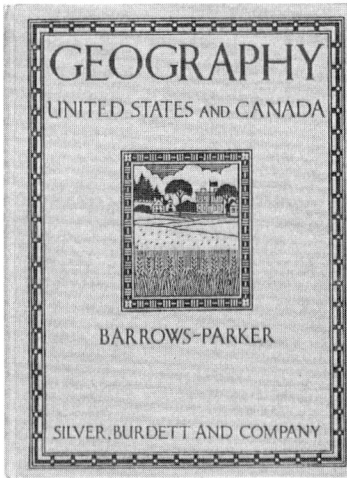

It was 1925 when Rochester native Edith Putnam Parker co-authored the textbook *Geography / United States and Canada.* This was one of many books she wrote or co-authored. (COURTESY OF SILVER BURDETT AND COMPANY, NY, 1925)

Rochester born and educated, Justin Taft (1924-2010) holds a 1920s-era homemade basketball hoop that was once attached to a utility pole on a cindered lot behind the North Walnut Street school. Home games on the outside court began at 4 p.m., after school ended. Taft recalled that some games were also played inside the Rochester Methodist Church or WCTU building, both on East Main Street. This historic hoop artifact is part of the RHPS Collection. (TOBY MCDANIEL PHOTO; USED WITH PERMISSION)

DOWNTOWN ROCHESTER 1930

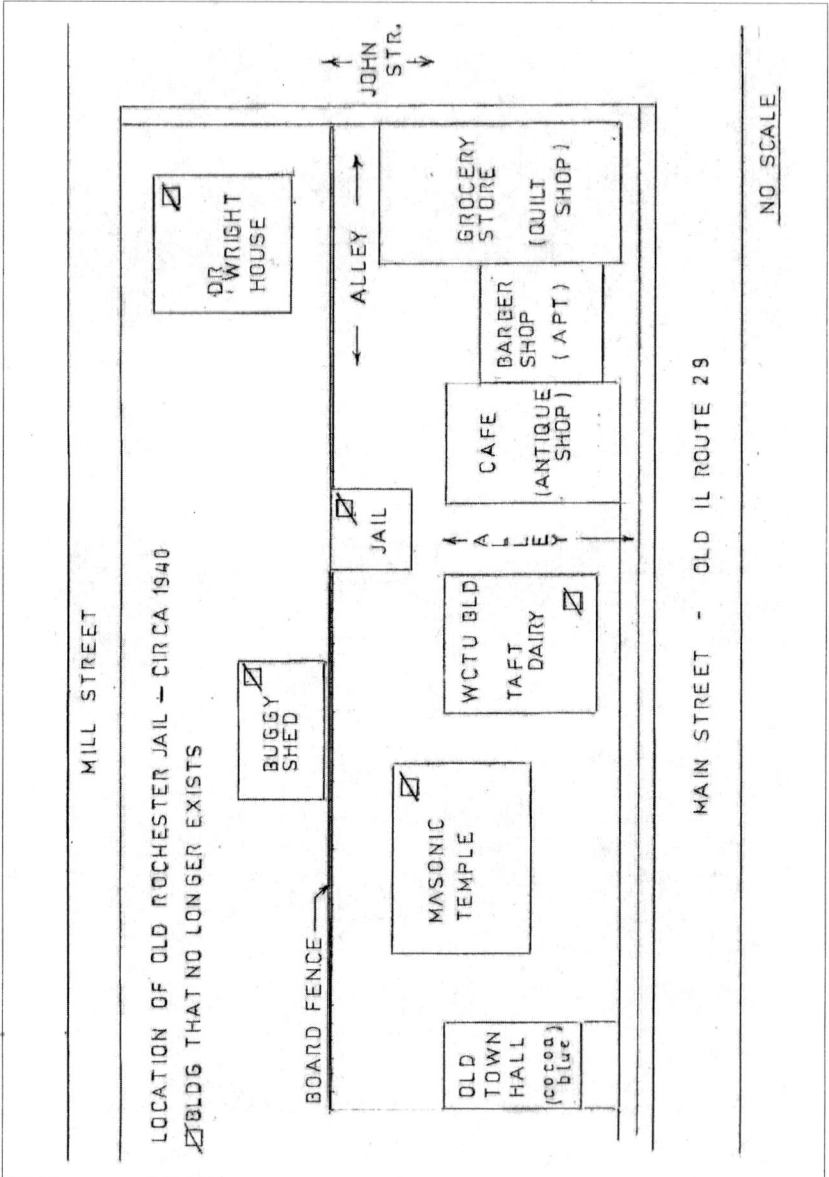

Although several downtown Rochester buildings of the 1930s remain in 2017, those that have been demolished are the "calaboose" jail, the Masonic Temple in the former school, the WCTU / Taft Dairy building, and the buggy shed. Rochester State Bank is now located where the Dr. Wright /H.D. Parker house once stood. (MAP COURTESY OF "BUD" MOORE)

1930s

Illinois State Journal
FOR THE HOME—THE NEWS—THE RIGHT

MAKE RAIDS HERE FOR ROBBERY CLUES

Bank That Was Held Up, 4 Bandits Captured And Their Bullet Riddled Auto

Two of these suspects were later convicted of the November 26, 1930, Rochester State Bank robbery. (*ILLINOIS STATE JOURNAL*, 27 Nov. 1930; PUBLISHED BY GENEALOGYBANK.COM, A DIVISION OF NEWSBANK)

1930s Timeline ...

1930	Population: 427
	— Rochester State Bank robbery
	— Rochester Grain Company elevator fire
	— A concrete-and-steel bridge replaced the wooden covered bridge south of Rochester over the South Fork River
1932	Fire destroyed the Twist Building
	— Concrete road completed between Rochester and Buckhart
1935	Village water system installed as a Public Works Administration (PWA) project
1936	Dial telephone system was established
1937	Two-story brick high school was built facing Illinois Route 29
1938	Works Progress Administration (WPA) awarded a grant for village sewers

1930s Storylines...

- An exciting bank robbery and two village-threatening fires highlighted the early half of the 1930s. In spite of those destructive fires and a nation-wide depression, Rochester continued to grow and perform as an agricultural center for crops and livestock. By the end of the decade, a dozen new homes had been planned or completed. With a new high school and a new, reliable source of water from Springfield, Rochester citizens demonstrated their commitment to the future.

- Twenty-two-year-old Fred Drillinger was living in the third house west of the Rochester State Bank, when he witnessed the bank being held up and saw the robbers as they drove away with a hostage, bank cashier J. Earl Bell.
— Entering the bank at 11 a.m. on November 26, 1930, the three armed thieves climbed over the cage and broke glass in the counting-room door. Two bankers and a customer were pushed into a back room before the men forced Bell to collect about $2,800 in cash and silver from the vault and cash drawers.
— The robbers released Bell as they reached the west side of Rochester and sped out of

Fred Drillinger, who lived three houses west of the Rochester State Bank, witnessed the robbers making their escape after their 1930 bank holdup. (COURTESY OF RUTH DRILLINGER)

town. All three men were apprehended after Springfield's Chief of Detectives C.W. Jesberg fired his sub-machine gun into their car, hitting two of the suspects. A fourth man was also charged once he admitted to being ready with a second getaway car.
— Multiple trials followed the arrest of these robbers: the first guilty verdict was set aside because women had been on the panel from which jurors were selected; the second guilty verdict was invalidated because of an underage juror. All of the men served some prison time.

- A 1930 inferno, with a fiery glow that was visible 20 miles away, destroyed the Rochester Grain Company elevator and threatened nearby homes and a gas station. Lack of water limited the ability of Rochester volunteer firemen to control the blaze,

The Rochester Grain Elevator, owned by Edmund Chard, burned to the ground in 1930, at a loss of $65,000 to $85,000. (*ILLINOIS STATE JOURNAL*, 16 FEB. 1930; PUBLISHED BY GENEALOGYBANK.COM, A DIVISION OF NEWSBANK)

even with help from the Springfield Fire Department. Destruction of the grain elevator, two railroad cars full of wheat, plus 6,000 bushels of wheat, and 600 bushels of corn in the elevator brought the estimated lost to $65,000. Because his insurance failed to cover those losses, elevator owner Edmund Chard said he had no plans to rebuild the structure, which was only about 10 years old. Cause of the fire was unknown.

- Art Warnke, former owner of the original Rochester State Bank building, has seen charred wood in the attic of the century-old structure. That charring reflects how the structure was saved from a tremendous 1932 fire that destroyed the adjacent two-story Twist Building.

Illinois State Journal

FOR THE HOME—THE NEWS—THE RIGHT

SPRINGFIELD, ILL., MONDAY, FEBRUARY 29, 1932.

ROCHESTER SWEPT BY DISASTROUS FIRE

The Twist Building, Rochester's largest downtown structure, was destroyed by fire in 1932. Located directly west of the Twist Building, the Rochester State Bank building was saved and still exists as of 2017. (*ILLINOIS STATE JOURNAL*, 29 FEB. 1932; PUBLISHED BY GENEALOGYBANK.COM, A DIVISION OF NEWSBANK)

— Lyman L. Easley discovered and reported the fire caused by a defective electric light wire. Damages of more than $50,000 were the result of flames destroying a drug store, hardware store, telephone office, grain office, garage, and home. Night telephone operator Leo Beck stayed in the blazing building, calling for help until the telephone wires burned. Firefighters from Springfield and Edinburg helped Rochester volunteers save the slightly damaged bank building.

- After Rochester was awarded a Public Works Administration (PWA) loan and grant of $33,000, the village of Rochester was connected to the water system of Springfield. This relationship between the communities continues today. Firefighting was made more certain and 115 homeowners of Rochester no longer had to rely on well water after work was completed on the 1935 water line constructed from Rochester to Lake Springfield. Seventeen fire hydrants were hooked up to the new village water mains.

- The Works Progress Administration (WPA) granted Rochester $43,432 in 1938 to construct a sewer system and treatment plant. The project required a $19,403 bond sale by the village. Rochester would not construct a sewer system, however, until 1959.

- The Illinois state highway department approved and funded construction of a 60-foot-wide concrete road between Rochester and Buckhart. A bridge across Buckhart Creek, which cost $17,015, was completed in 1931. The $96,494 worth of concrete pavement was completed and open to traffic in 1932.
  — The state also provided $1,700 in 1939 for bituminous surfacing to portions of Oak Lane and Walnut, Mill, Twist, and West Main Streets.
  — Rochester received $8,351 from the WPA in 1939 to repair curbs, gutters, sidewalks, and install manholes.
  — A new steel-and-concrete bridge built in 1930 replaced the wooden covered bridge south of Rochester across the South Fork River on New City Road. Five years later voters turned down bonds for a new $15,000 Walnut Road bridge over Black Branch Creek north of town near the former Glenwood Park.

— As construction proceeded in 1937 on a new Clear Lake Road bridge across the South Fork River, the Rochester Woman's Club joined other area citizens in unsuccessful efforts to preserve the site's 53-year old covered bridge.

The 1877 covered bridge over the South Fork River south of Rochester on Cardinal Hill Road, was replaced by an iron-and-concrete structure in 1930. (PHOTOS FROM THE WILEY GORDON FUNDERBURK ESTATE; COURTESY OF BILL WALDMIRE)

Left: Rochester High School students arrived in October 1937 to their new school, the first separate high school in the township. Enrollment tallied 45 boys and 45 girls. Guided by Principal Paul Comer, their teachers were Clarence Coe, John Churchill, Nelrose Corkill, Pauline Frame, and Mary Cordis. (*ILLINOIS STATE JOURNAL*, 3 DEC. 1937; PUBLISHED BY GENEALOGYBANK.COM, A DIVISION OF NEWSBANK)

Below: Rochester's first high school opened in 1937, facing south toward what is today Route 29. Until it was demolished in 2006, it had also been used as the junior high, middle school, and district offices. (PHOTO BY STEVE LEACH; USED WITH PERMISSION)

- Rochester voters in 1936 chose to buy land and build a new four-year high school. The new building allowed students to attend all four years of high school in Rochester, rather than requiring them to attend Springfield High for their senior year.

— The school district purchased 10 acres of land along Route 24 (later to become Route 29) two blocks west of the village limits. Work was underway in January 1937 and the $85,000 building opened 10 months later. The two-story fireproof brick structure included a gymnasium.

— The 90 high school students present for opening day were divided exactly between boys and girls. An all-senior cast of the play *Fingerprints,* viewed by an audience of 300, dedicated the new school's stage in 1938.

Rochester High School's 1931-32 boys basketball team members were, from left: John Morris, Maurice Green, Raymond Woodruff, Delmar Denton, Elmer Boehme, Fredrick Poffenberger, Robert Scott, and James Conner, who was not present for the photo. (COURTESY OF *THE ROCHESTER HELLO*, 25 MAR. 1982)

- Criminal activities:

— A whopping $8 was the haul for thieves who in 1939 exploded the door off a safe in the new Rochester High School.

— Thieves made off with 13 cartons of cigarettes, a battery, a tire, and $1 from Kenneth Jones's gas station in 1936 when they burglarized gas stations owned by Jones and Milton Green. The take at Milton Green's station two years later was 600 packages of cigarettes, plus $10.50 and their own self-service gas fill-up.

— Coming upon a gory crime scene, George Graham found only the remains of a

Many questions remain about Rochester's jail, known for decades as the calaboose. When was it built? When was it demolished? Exactly what did it look like? Although a photograph of the little building was not found, Daniel G. Moore created this original artwork based on recollections of his father, Carl "Bud" Moore, and others. Town Marshal D.R. Beck is depicted outside the calaboose about 1930. References to the calaboose date as early as the 1880s, and it was probably torn down in the late 1960s before construction of Rochester's downtown fire station on East Main Street. (ARTWORK BY DANIEL G. MOORE; USED WITH PERMISSION)

calf and a hog that had been killed before their meat was taken from his farm in 1933. A second calf was also stolen.

— Sensational crimes also involved the July 1930 discovery of two murdered men near Rochester within four days. Both appeared to have been tortured and were possibly members of a Chicago gang. Velma Ebinger found the first body along a country road. Carrie Kimball and Nettie Durham discovered the second corpse as they picked berries.

— Rochester's reputation as a speed trap traced as far back as 1930 when Village Marshal David R. Beck arrested 13 speeders in two days. Springfield AAA representatives traveled to Rochester, investigating the great number of tickets. Two justices of the peace denied existence of a speed trap, assuring the visitors "that no driver as yet had been hanged for driving through Rochester at a speed greater than that made by an aged turtle." They stressed that fines were handed out only to the worst speeders.

— Speaking of speeders, one sweet "flapper incarnate," was brought before Justice Albert H. Burt in May 1930. Although her appearance was caused by roaring into Rochester, the memory of her was indelibly etched when she snatched her papers from the judge's desk and sprinted out the door. She easily outran the judge, who noted dryly that she "was pretty and fast on her feet." An octogenarian, Burt said he had never seen her before but hoped to meet her again someday.

- Business reports included a wide variety of opportunities. During this decade, residents could buy "natural milk and cream" when the Coontz Brothers Dairy opened in 1939; purchase their gasoline from Richardson's Sinclair station at the southwest corner of East Main and John Streets; receive medical or surgical attention from Dr. Frederick Bornstein, who moved to town in 1937; and listen to an orchestra while enjoying two beers and fish for 15 cents at the Hill-Top Inn west of town.

Richardson's Service Station, located next to Rochester State Bank on East Main Street in 1939, later became Kessler's Sinclair gas station. (*ILLINOIS STATE JOURNAL*, 30 MAY 1939; PUBLISHED BY GENEALOGYBANK.COM, A DIVISION OF NEWSBANK)

- Non- fatal accidents:
  — Candidate for sheriff Robert J. Harrison and nearby farmers rescued four men who became stranded with their car by the April 1938 flooding of the South Fork River near the Rochester-New City bridge. Swiftly flowing waters made it necessary to rescue each man separately by boat. The candidate's heroism didn't help his standing at the ballot box, however. Harrison came in fourth out of nine Democrats in that primary contest.
  — One of Alexander M. Dunnavan's chickens wounded her owner in 1933 with a shotgun he had previously rigged to surprise chicken thieves. The hen committed the assault when she flew into a string that triggered the firearm. Dunnavan's leg and hand wounds reportedly recovered, and there was no inference that Dunnavan's sale of personal property a month later, which included two feather beds, was related to the accident.
  — Seven-year-old Justin Taft, Jr., lost his left eye as the result of a 1931 accident, when the car driven by his father was sideswiped and forced down an embankment. His injury, which came as the result of a shattered window, was the only one from this accident.
  — A team of runaway horses severely injured Oscar Meyer, Jr., in 1938 when they pulled a wagon wheel over the man's right foot. He was treated at St. John's hospital. Five years earlier, Justin Taft, Sr., had been awarded $400 from Meyer in a suit brought for the 1931 injuries to Justin Taft, Jr., and car damages when Meyer sideswiped Taft's car.
  — Three men were injured in 1937 when a steam-powered threshing machine exploded on the Jason Taft farm. William Ginder was seriously burned while John Grubb and Earl Jones received less serious injuries. Ginder had also been

injured on a Fox Road bridge-construction project five years earlier when the firebox on a piece of construction equipment exploded.

- Fatal accidents:
  — Betty Jane Easley died in 1935 after being struck by an automobile as she crossed West Main Street. Services for the 10-year-old fifth grader were held at the Rochester Christian Church, and she was buried in Rochester Cemetery. Her parents were Robert and Ermyn Easley.
  — Another car accident took the life of 74-year-old Michael Moklar who was struck by an automobile in 1938 as he walked on Route 29. His services were also held at the Rochester Christian Church, and he was buried in Rochester Cemetery.
  — Both Edith Matthew and her seven-year-old daughter Marjorie died in 1935 from burns when Edith mistakenly poured gasoline instead of kerosene when trying to stoke a small fire in their stove. The resulting explosion ignited their clothing, and they died a few hours later at St. John's Hospital. Funeral services were held at the Rochester Methodist Church before burial in Rochester Cemetery.

- Beyond serving as a more rapid form of transportation, airplanes also provided exciting entertainment. The Kluzek brothers, Hill-Top Inn proprietors in 1933, chartered a two-day air show on the Kluzek landing field west of Rochester. The free event featured a Texas parachute jumper and five licensed pilots. One of the pilots was Inn co-owner Stanley Kluzek, who claimed more than 400 hours of flight time. He later served in the Royal Canadian Air Force during World War II, flying bombers across the Atlantic to England. A colorful man, Kluzek died in 1987 and is buried in Calvary Cemetery.

- Occupations and events in the lives of Rochester citizens led to some interesting stories.
  — School bus driver **Bessie Raney** became known in 1939 as one of the few such women in the country. At the time her unusual profession was highlighted, Bessie already had seven years of experience. She drove a 35-passenger bus between the Rochester consolidated grade school and

Although Bessie Raney was active in Rochester's Woman's Club and Eastern Star, she is still remembered for being one of the few women in the nation to drive a school bus during the 1930s. (*ILLINOIS STATE JOURNAL*, 27 JAN. 1939; PUBLISHED BY GENEALOGYBANK.COM, A DIVISION OF NEWSBANK)

students' homes in nearby hamlets such as Berry, Breckenridge, and Buckhart. Carolyn Wanless, who grew up in Rochester, fondly remembers Bessie driving her bus when Carolyn was a first grade student some years later.

— Bert Wolford, known as a baseball player when he was young, delivered a 14-foot, eight-inch stalk of corn to Governor Henry Horner's office in 1937 as part of a corn-growing contest among neighboring Midwest states. He said that ears of corn on his stalks were growing seven feet above the ground.

— It was 1938 when well-known Rochester gardener John W. Campbell grew some of the first local "Boyesen berries," now known as boysenberries. Campbell explained this new variety was a cross between loganberries and dewberries, producing fruit as large as black walnuts. He supported claims of the California originators that Boyesen berries made excellent pies.

John W. Campbell's home and fruit garden on East Main Street are seen, left, as they appeared in the 1950s. The picture on the right is thought to be the same house in 1918 when it was owned by William Campbell. (LEFT: PROVIDED BY JANET AND BRIAN CAMPBELL; RIGHT: COURTESY OF COMPASS POINT PRODUCTIONS; FARM PROGRESS COMPANIES)

Rochester truck gardener John W. Campbell grew "Boyesen berries." (ILLINOIS STATE JOURNAL, 26 JUNE 1938; PUBLISHED BY GENEALOGYBANK.COM, A DIVISION OF NEWSBANK)

— Rochester's only living Civil War widow, Eliza Ann Gobin, donated two rare flags for a 1935 Rochester Grade School exhibit. Previously owned by her husband David, who died in 1903, one flag had 37 stars and the other 42 stars. David Gobin enlisted as an 18-year-old drummer boy in the 114th Illinois Regiment and received a military pension after the war. The 37-star flag was created after Nebraska became a state on March 1, 1867. The 42-star symbol was unofficial, representing the addition of Washington State to the union; it had been superseded by the official 43-star flag designed after Idaho became a state.

— Rosa A. Fogle, Rochester's only Gold Star Mother, traveled to France in 1931 to view the grave of her son, Harry, who died during World War I.

• John Bennett's marriage on March 26, 1930, was memorable on several accounts. Other couples may have also been married that day. Few, however, arrived at the ceremony using horses to pull their car across snow-covered fields to the nearest plowed road. Bennett's horses helped get him to his wedding on time, but drifts created by a 54-inch-deep blizzard didn't allow a complete return trip. Seventy-five feet from home, Bennett abandoned his vehicle, returning the next day to dig a path home.

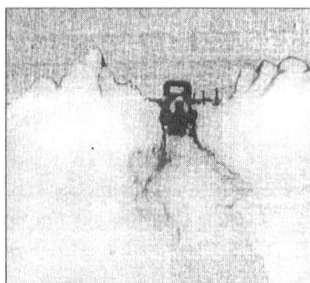

Fifty-four inches of snow on March 27, 1930, forced John Bennett to leave his snow-bound car in a drift just 75 feet from his home north of Rochester. He returned the next day to shovel it out. (*ILLINOIS STATE JOURNAL*, 28 MAR. 1939; PUBLISHED BY GENEALOGYBANK.COM, A DIVISION OF NEWSBANK)

- Two hundred members of the Twist family were expected to show up for the 1937 family reunion in Lovington, IL. All were descended from John and Phoebe Twist, who settled near Rochester in 1822 and brought with them from Seneca Falls, NY, the first apple trees in Sangamon County. John and Phoebe are buried in Rochester Cemetery.

- Scarlet fever, a streptococcal infection spread by inhalation and skin contact, was a dangerous disease until antibiotics became available. When two members of the D. Gilson Taft family came down with scarlet fever in 1935, the state health department quarantined their home, and the dairy's milk deliveries were suspended.
— One year later public gatherings such as Sunday church activities and club meetings in Rochester were cancelled after several scarlet fever cases were again reported in the area.

- It was 1937 when George Donagan, a black resident of Springfield, recalled memories of the Underground Railroad, "copperhead" attacks on him, and the work of well-known abolitionist Erastus Wright. Using the terminology of the time George related how his father, Wiley, had let "colored folks" stay on his farm, located three miles south of Rochester, because at that time black farm workers were not allowed to sleep at the same farms where they worked.
— During the early hours of the 1908 race riot, George's uncle, William Donagan, was hanged from a Springfield schoolyard tree, largely for having married a white woman. Based on the experiences he had seen and been part of, it was George's opinion that "equality of the colored race will never be recognized."

- Significant anniversaries and birthdays continued to be publicly noted and celebrated.
— Golden wedding anniversaries were celebrated by **George** and **Melvina (*Workman*) Reed** in 1930, **Turner** and **Etta (*Johnson*) Abel** in 1933, and **James** and **Mary (*Middlekauff*) Drillinger** in 1937.

— **Margaret** *(Gibson)* **Campbell** celebrated her 89th birthday in 1931 at the Rochester home of her daughter, Eugenia Bremer.

— **Sylvester J. McCoy**, who turned 85 in 1934, was born in one of the first houses in Sangamon County, built in 1818.

George Christian Turner Abel (1857-1948) and his wife Etta *(Johnson)* Abel (1863-1950) of Rochester celebrated their golden wedding anniversary in 1933. George was born in Harpers Ferry, WV, and recalled stories of John Brown's anti-slavery demonstration of 1859. He was a Republican, as was his father who voted for Abraham Lincoln. (*Illinois State Journal*, 28 Feb. 1933; Published by GenealogyBank.com, a Division of NewsBank)

This 140-acre farm of George and Etta Abel on the west edge of Rochester Township was purchased by the city of Springfield and was one of the properties partially or completely inundated under the new Lake Springfield during the 1930s. (Courtesy of Compass Point Productions; Farm Progress Companies)

Sylvester and Pauline *(Abel)* McCoy celebrated their 50th wedding anniversary in 1923. Sylvester was born in one of Rochester's first log houses, but celebrated his 85th birthday in 1934 at his East Main Street home, shown on the right as it appeared in 2015. He was a grandson of Rochester's first settler James McCoy. (Left: Courtesy of Barbara Wagner; Right: R. Bruzan photo)

- Four prominent members of the Twist family died in this decade: Ira, 80, in 1937; John A., 65, in 1935; Ralph, 70, in 1931; and Clarence, 49, in 1938.

Other notable deaths included:

1930

— **Henry Taft**, 80, was buried in Rochester Cemetery, which is on some of the same land his father, William Taft, had first homesteaded 100 years earlier.

— Former resident **Susie Persinger**, was the mother of Louis Persinger, esteemed around the world for his violin talents.

1931

— Well-known farmer **Thomas Thornton**, 81, was a son of English emigrants.

— **Theodore Shreve**, 87, had been a Civil War veteran and Rochester mill owner and operator.

1932

— British-born **Margaret Bennett**, 90

— **George W. McFadden**, 90, was a Civil War veteran who had been with Ulysses S. Grant at Vicksburg. Four of his brothers, all from Ohio, had perished in that war.

— **William J. Nutt**, known to his friends as Jack, was the oldest Civil War veteran in Rochester Township when he celebrated his 90th birthday in July 1931. He died just six months later.

1934

— **William Dawley**, who farmed north of Rochester, sustained severe burns in 1934 after burning brush ignited his clothes. The burns to his legs and feet proved fatal a few days after the accident.

— Retired Rochester druggist **Homer D. Parker**, 81, died in Chicago. His parents traveled from Vermont, settling in Rochester in 1855.

— Former deputy sheriff **Samuel B. Coe**, 71, was a son of early settlers Ebenezer and Julia Coe who came to Rochester from Loudoun County, Virginia.

1936

— Rochester's oldest native, Justice of the Peace **Albert H. Burt**, 88, was a victim of the heat.

— Descendent of an early pioneer family, farmer and contractor **Preston P. Breckenridge** died at age 77.

— **Noah L. Baxter** died at age 87. He had travelled to Illinois from North Carolina by covered wagon in 1867. A former Rochester School Board member, he had promoted planting trees around several schools.

1938

— **John Kierstein**, Springfield's first baby in 1938, died a few days after his birth at St. John's Hospital,.

William J. Nutt (1841-1932) from Newburg, NY, arrived in Rochester in 1857 and served with the Illinois infantry at the battles of Nashville and Vicksburg. At the age of 90, he was the oldest Civil War veteran living in Rochester Township. Nutt is buried in Buckhart Cemetery. (*ILLINOIS STATE JOURNAL*, 9 JULY 1931; PUBLISHED BY GENEALOGYBANK.COM, A DIVISION OF NEWSBANK)

James Wickersham died in 1939. He was born in Patoka, IL, studied area burial mounds, married Deborah (*Bell*) of Rochester, and served as a U.S. District Judge in Eagle, AK. Mount Wickersham and the Wickersham Wall of Mt. McKinley are named in his honor. (ALASKA STATE LIBRARY PHOTO COLLECTION; USED WITH PERMISSION)

— Fourteen-year-old **Shirley Fairchild** died at her parent's home. She was president of the freshman class at Rochester High School.

- Although numerous banks closed during the Great Depression, Rochester State Bank remained open, working with depositors during one period to waive some of their deposits or defer withdrawing a portion of their deposits. — It was one of the first banks in the county to pay back those waived deposits. As of April 2, 1938, the bank had paid $9,002.50, which was the balance of deferred deposits. The bank became a member of the recently created Federal Deposit Insurance Corporation (FDIC) that insured deposits up to $5,000.

Elyssa, Tabitha, and Ash Bevan are seen crossing the Black Branch Creek bridge north of Mill Street. Built circa 1932, the pedestrian bridge with an iron-and-wood deck remains widely used as of 2017. (R. Bruzan photo)

The dial telephone became available in Rochester in 1936, although this "Princess Phone" did not debut until the 1960s. The authors still use this phone in 2017. (R. Bruzan photo)

Rose Middlekauf, seen in the back, taught these Rochester Junior High students in 1935. As identified almost 50 years later, the students were, front from left: Robert Ritterbusch, Kenneth Licklider, Russell Hill, Lucien Young, ____ Painter, Maxine Curry, Frances Campbell, Mary Ellen Bennett; middle row: Mary Trader, Carol Rule, Virginia Glover, Margaret Hatfield, James Waters, Lyman Ginder, John Beck, Justin Taft; back row: Carl Young, Robert Easley, Estill VanFossen, Dale Curry, Dorothy Carpenter, Eileen Richardson, Hazel Trader, Evelyn Gaddey, Iva Wright. (COURTESY OF THE ROCHESTER HELLO, 18 MAR. 1982)

The Poffenbarger one-room school is shown (upper left) as it appeared in 1918 with teacher Gertrude Griffin. Above, Nova Blankenship taught in the same Poffenbarger one-room school circa 1939. As of 2017 the building is actively used as a family residence. (UPPER LEFT: COURTESY OF COMPASS POINT PRODUCTIONS; FARM PROGRESS COMPANIES; ABOVE: COURTESY OF CARL "BUD" MOORE)

Goldie Ralston received this Certificate of Award in 1904 for perfect attendance at Poffenbarger School. (COURTESY OF KENT KURNISKIE)

Brothers Joseph and William Dawley are pictured on the front step of their home on North Walnut Street, property owned in 2017 by David and Debbie Taft. The cellar and its access door, visible to the left of the house, are still functional. The Dawley brothers' father, Harrison Dawley (1817-1883) drove the stage coach between Rochester and Beardstown. (COURTESY OF COMPASS POINT PRODUCTIONS; FARM PROGRESS COMPANIES)

Several of the stones from abutments previously supporting the Horse Creek covered bridge were still visible at the bridge site in 2016. (R. BRUZAN PHOTO)

This covered bridge over Horse Creek was reported in 1936 as located on an abandoned road on the John Tobin farm west of what is today Ramsey Road in Rochester Township. Township resident Don Mohler has childhood memories of a covered bridge at this site. Richard Ramsey, owner of the property in 2017, reports that some of the bridge's stone abutments still exist. This image was previously published in Thelma Eaton's 1968 book *The Covered Bridges of Illinois*. (PHOTO IS COURTESY OF THE ILLINOIS DEPARTMENT OF TRANSPORTATION (IDOT), SPRINGFIELD, IL. THIS BOOK REFLECTS THE VIEWS OF THE AUTHORS WHO ARE RESPONSIBLE FOR THE FACTS AND ACCURACY OF THE DATE HEREIN AND DO NOT NECESSARILY REFLECT THE VIEWS OR THE POLICIES OF IDOT.)

PROPOSED RESERVOIRS
FOR SANGAMON COUNTY

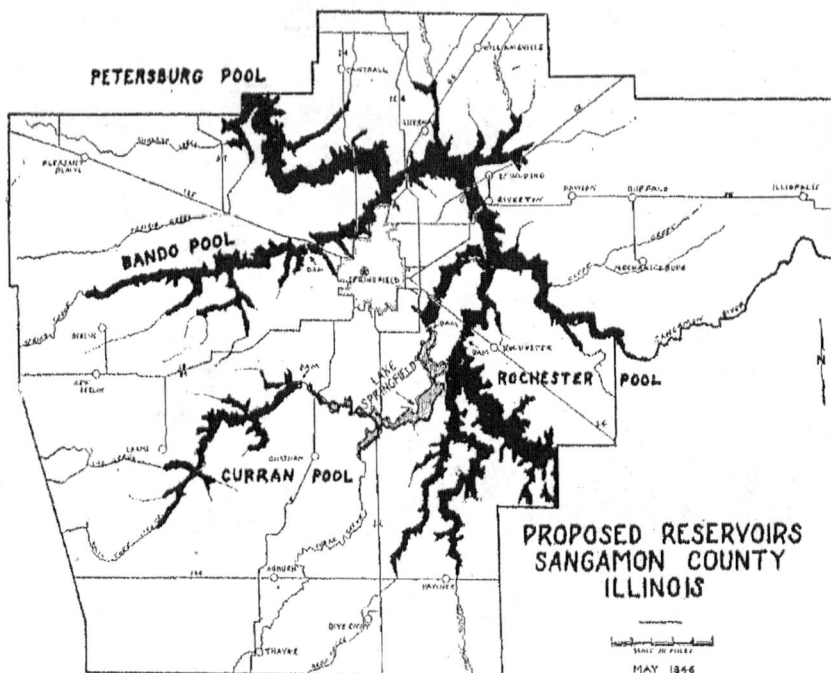

A controversial plan of U.S. district engineers to dam the South Fork River near Rochester as part of a flood-control project was defeated in 1946. (*ILLINOIS STATE JOURNAL*, 29 MAY 1946: 21; PUBLISHED BY GENEALOGYBANK.COM, A DIVISION OF NEWSBANK)

1940s

Brothers and Rochester High School graduates, from left: Robert and Joseph Ritterbusch, were among those from Rochester who served their country during World War II. (*SERVICE RECORD BOOK OF MEN AND WOMEN OF ROCHESTER, ILLINOIS AND COMMUNITY*, CIRCA 1949)

1940s Timeline ...

1940	Rochester population: 464
1939–1945	World War II
1941	Taft & Sons' Dairy opened on Main Street in the former WCTU building
	— Rochester Boy Scout troop organized
	— Rochester chapter, Future Farmers of America was organized
1943	Rochester jail became headquarters for the newly organized Girl Scout troop
1945	Fleck's Lakeview Air Park was dedicated
1946	Rochester schools consolidated, and one-room schools closed in Rochester Township
1947	Rochester Christian Church was destroyed by fire
	— Rochester Athletic Club purchased a Willys Jeep fire truck for the village
	— Rochester voters approved a bond issue of $125,000 to build a grade-school addition

1940s Storylines...

- The 1940s brought to Rochester Township the horrors of World War II, another notable fire, rebuilding of the Rochester Christian Church, a new downtown dairy, and major changes in Rochester schools.

- Members of the armed services during World War II came from some families who had lived in Rochester Township for generations. Taft, Fairchild, Coffey, Grubb, and Sturdy are only some of the Rochester families represented among the village's 52 WW II veterans. Some of these are now buried in Rochester Cemetery.

  — **S/Sgt. Emery Eugene Richardson** died April 25, 1945, in Germany and was buried in Saint-Avold, Lorraine, France. The son of George and Arvia Richardson, Emery's survivors included his wife, Leota, and four children.

  — **Pvt. Russell Twist Kernoll, Jr.**, son of former Rochester residents Russell and Florence Kernoll, died on D-Day, June 6, 1944, and is buried at St. Laurent-sur-Mer, Normandy, France. His brother Sherrick was in active service for three years during WW II.

  — **Pvt. Donald E. Ray**, son of Mrs. Harold Miller of Rochester, was killed June 24, 1944, and is buried at Colleville-sur-Mer, Normandy, France; he also left a wife and son.

- Rochester had its share of war heroes who received recognition, among them:

  — **Robert F. Scott** – Bronze Star for counter-intelligence work;

  — **Delbert Taft** – two Battle Stars for war efforts in Germany;

Killed in action June 6, 1944, Russell Twist Kernoll, Jr., was buried at Normandy, France. A Rochester Cemetery plaque honors the sacrifice of this former village resident. (R. BRUZAN PHOTO)

Lt. Ernest Taft of Rochester (top row, second from left) served combat duty in Europe as a B-24 bomber pilot. (*ILLINOIS STATE JOURNAL*, 13 NOV. 1944; PUBLISHED BY GENEALOGYBANK.COM, A DIVISION OF NEWSBANK)

— Jack Campbell—three Purple Hearts and three Bronze Stars, all for battles in the Pacific theater;

— Orville E. Fortner—medal of bravery for his actions in Holland;

— Ernest Taft piloted B-24 bombers while stationed in Italy;

— Earl Taft served in several Pacific-theater campaigns;

— Joseph Spengler completed at least 23 combat strikes against Japanese forces;

— Brothers William, Robert, and Arthur Kessler all served in the navy during WW II. Following the war, Bill also worked with electronics associated with atomic bomb tests.

Katherine Smith of Rochester served as a Navy WAVE commander during World War II. (*STATE JOURNAL-REGISTER*, 8 Nov. 2004: 2A; PUBLISHED BY GENEALOGYBANK.COM, A DIVISION OF NEWSBANK)

- "Milk so rich it tastes like cream" was only one of the many slogans used by Delbert Gilson Taft, who in 1941 opened his Taft & Sons' Dairy in the former Woman's Christian Temperance Union (WCTU) building on East Main Street. The Dairy was an expansion of the home delivery service that began from the family farm the previous decade.

— Taft credited his herd of Guernsey cows, a breed that originated on the English Channel Island of Guernsey, with producing "perfect milk." Prior to the dairy's March grand opening, the building was completely remodeled for new milk-pasteurizing equipment, a sales room, and soda-fountain counter.

Don Taft displays artifacts from the Taft & Sons' Dairy that was located during the 1940s and 1950s in the former Woman's Christian Temperance Union building on East Main Street. (P. BRUZAN PHOTO)

Two unidentified friends were visiting the Taft Dairy in downtown Rochester when this photo was taken. (COURTESY OF DON TAFT)

During the 1930s and 1940s, Taft's Guernsey Dairy truck delivered a variety of products, including "milk so rich it tastes like cream," throughout the Rochester area. Pictured are (from left) Wayne and Don Taft. (COURTESY OF DON TAFT)

A model Taft Dairy Truck in a Taft milk bottle was created by Carl "Bud" Moore and presented to his friend Don Taft. (COURTESY OF DON TAFT; P. BRUZAN PHOTO)

This dairy token, "Good for 1 Quart Milk," was distributed by Rochester's Willhite Dairy. Although little is known about this particular business, several dairies operated in the Rochester area, including Taft's, Tinch's, Coontz's and Todd's Dairies. (TOKEN ARTIFACT OF RHPS COLLECTION; COURTESY OF JEAN AND HERB WILKINSON)

Wayne Andrews (left), owner of the Rochester Food Store is pictured with meat department manager Harold Eggleston as they celebrated the store's grand opening on October 4, 1940. Fay Wolford was in charge of the grocery department at the store on the northwest corner of East Main and Water Streets. (ILLINOIS STATE JOURNAL, 4 OCT. 1940; PUBLISHED BY GENEALOGYBANK.COM, A DIVISION OF NEWSBANK)

- The Rochester Food Store, which opened in 1940, also served the community. Wayne Andrews operated the business on the northwest corner of East Main and Water Streets until it closed several months later.

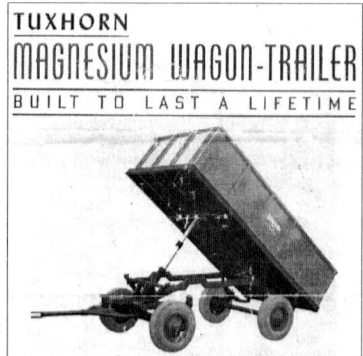

In the 1940s, Ben Tuxhorn of Rochester manufactured light-weight farm trailers made with the metal magnesium at Tuxhorn Manufacturing Co. near Rochester. (COURTESY OF DWIGHT AND GRACE POPE)

- In 1949, Tuxhorn Manufacturing Co. of Rochester may have been the world's only manufacturer to produce farm wagons made of magnesium metal. The light-weight wagons made it possible to carry heavier loads across wet fields. The Heliarc welding equipment the Tuxhorns had used earlier to weld aluminum on farm trailers turned out to be useful when welding magnesium. The new-style trailers weighed only 1,600 pounds, but could carry five tons of grain, equivalent to 150 bushels. They were produced by Ben Tuxhorn and his sons Elmer and Harold at their shop on Route 29.

• After only 30 years, the strength of the Rochester Christian Church congregation was once again sorely tested when their church burned to the ground in a February 1947 conflagration. Rev. John Honey alerted fire departments in both Rochester and Springfield as church pews, the pulpit and other items were being rescued. Homes north of the church were saved, but the church loss was estimated at $30,000.

Above: For the second time in 31 years, fire destroyed the Rochester Christian Church on South Walnut Street. A defective flue was one of the suspected causes of this 1947 blaze. Plans were soon in place to rebuild the church. (ILLINOIS STATE JOURNAL, 10 DEC. 1947; COURTESY OF ROCHESTER CHRISTIAN CHURCH; USED WITH PERMISSION)

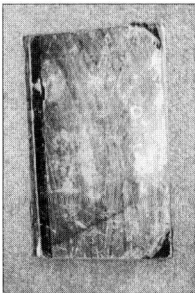

The bell from the 1875 Rochester Christian Church, a collection plate, and the church's record ledger with dates back to 1878 were saved from the 1947 church fire. (COURTESY OF LAURA WELCH AND THE ROCHESTER CHRISTIAN CHURCH; R. BRUZAN PHOTOS)

— Decades later, Rochester resident Carl "Bud" Moore recalled seeing the fire from the back yard of his grandfather's home a half mile away. He remembered being amazed as the flames raged above a distant line of trees.

— It was determined that this fire was caused by either a defective chimney flue or faulty wiring. As plans were set forth to build a new church structure, worship services were held in the Rochester High School gym. An October 1947 ground breaking for the new building signaled the start of work on the church basement, which provided a meeting place for the congregation beginning later that year until the new church sanctuary was ready for use seven years later.

- The 1946 efforts of Ernest J. Rentschler, Maurice Scott, Jr., and Gilson Taft led to the state granting a non-profit charter for the Rochester Athletic Club, the forerunner of today's Rochester Fire Protection District.

— After the 1947 Christian Church fire, that Club solicited money to buy a fire truck. Community support and need for fire protection throughout Rochester Township was demonstrated when it took only one week to collect enough donations to purchase a Willys Jeep fire truck.

Rochester's first fire truck was a Willys Jeep purchased by the Rochester Athletic Club in 1947. (COURTESY OF CARL "BUD" MOORE)

— Efforts of the Athletic Club, the Independent Order of Odd Fellows (IOOF), and the American

The Rochester Fire Protection District had the Jeep restored to its former glory in the 2010 decade. (COURTESY OF MIKE WEAVER AND THE ROCHESTER FIRE PROTECTION DISTRICT)

Legion Post 274 combined to build a firehouse on John Street in 1948. The Athletic Club and fire truck were housed on the first floor, while the American Legion occupied the second floor. Cost of the new cement-block building and most of the labor were donated by Rochester citizens.

— By the following summer, the Athletic Club fire department had also bought a resuscitator for use by residents needing emergency breathing assistance.

- Soon after the Rochester Athletic Club bought a Willys Jeep fire engine in 1947, the equipment was called on to challenge a house fire at the home of

F. Ray Smith. The structure and contents sustained significant damage from smoke and water, as well as the flames that were, early in the two-hour fight, concentrated in the upper parts of the home.

— It took only 30 minutes, however, for the Athletic Club fire department to control a 1949 fire at the Taft & Sons' Dairy on Main Street. The dairy building café and second-floor apartment of Mr. and Mrs. Howard Berry sustained several hundred dollars in damage from that fire, caused by an overheated boiler and defective flue.

- Rochester voters went to the polls to determine four major school issues during the 1940s.

— Sixteen school districts in Rochester, Cooper, Cotton Hill and Clear Lake townships voted in 1946 to consolidate with the Rochester Grade School. Declining enrollment in the one-room country schools led to a majority of 258 to 104 in favor of establishing a Community Consolidated School district. Surplus items from the closed schools were sold at auction and included pianos, teacher and student desks, bells, maps, slate blackboards, chairs, clocks and many other items. The one-room schools were also put up for auction. Several were demolished to salvage the wood, while others were converted into homes, five of which remain today.

— One such converted home was the Poffenbarger School on Woodhaven Drive that became home to the Russell Fetter family. Russell, principal of the Rochester Grade School, along with his wife Hilda, daughter Brenda, and their dog Dickie, enthusiastically enjoyed their school home, especially when they compared it to their former trailer. The former Poffenbarger School is, in 2017, still a single-family home.

— One year after the grade-school consolidation, Rochester voters approved by 238 to 88 a $126,000 bond issue to enlarge the 1920 grade school.

— Also in 1947, voters approved creating a community unit school district for grades one through 12. Polling places were set up within the village limits and in Rochester and Cooper Townships. The vote favored the proposal 317 to 18. By October 1947, one month after the vote, Rochester had become District 3.

Russell and Hilda Fetter turned the abandoned Poffenbarger one-room school into their new home when they moved to Rochester in 1946. They are shown with their daughter, Brenda, and Dickie, the canine family member. They moved in after Russell was named Rochester Grade School principal. Their home, located on Woodhaven Drive, continues in 2017 to be used as a family residence. (*ILLINOIS STATE JOURNAL*, 20 SEP. 1946: 19; PUBLISHED BY GENEALOGYBANK. COM, A DIVISION OF NEWSBANK)

Dave Jostes (front row, second from the right) recalled that Bluff School had no electricity when he was a student there in the 1940s. Mrs. Martha Newman taught this 1944-45 class in the school barely visible behind the car. (COURTESY OF DAVE JOSTES)

Left: John Baker provided this 1907-08 picture of Bluff School. Carrie F. Abel was his teacher in the one-room brick school. Located on Jostes Road, this building replaced a nearby wood frame school that burned in 1881. The school closed in 1946 and exists as a family home in 2017. (COURTESY OF DORTHY ROSS)

When one-room schools in Rochester Township closed in 1946, students had to be driven by bus to the Rochester School on North Walnut Street. Lloyd Hart was driving along Jostes Road about 1949 when this photo was taken. The boy on the left by the fence is Fred Jostes. (COURTESY OF DAVE JOSTES)

— However, a 1948 proposal to merge Rochester schools with the Springfield school system and other area schools met with overwhelmingly defeat. A local campaign against the proposal was led by a coalition that included the Rochester Methodist Church, Rochester Christian Church, American Legion Post 274, and the Rochester Athletic Club. The Rochester vote was 9 for and 287 against.

- Although consolidation of one-room schools was hailed by many, not everyone was excited by the enormous changes it brought. Two decades later Mrs. Margaret *(McKee)* Ayers wrote in a Sangamon County newspaper about Cascade School in Cotton Hill Township, "The Cascade School house faded from the picture with the advent of consolidation and the appearance of that modern orange-yellow monster shuttling down the highway to transport our

In addition to coaching, "Mr. Scott" taught Rochester's eighth grade in 1941. (COURTESY OF KAREN ALEXANDER)

younger generation off to realms of higher learning." Former Cascade student Lyle Behl reflected in 2017, "I love that statement. I think she sensed that was the beginning of the end of our close-knit rural communities."

- Student news in 1947 involved immunizing youngsters for diphtheria, small-pox, and whooping cough. In 1948, the Rochester Parent Teacher Association (PTA) held a rummage sale and a card party-bake sale as fundraisers to buy student Christmas treats and to start a community library.

- The Fortnightly Book Club decided to raise members' annual dues to 25 cents in 1948. Although the minutes of that September 20 meeting only recorded the increase, there was no reason listed or the previous dues given. It would perhaps be more noteworthy to point out that 69 years later, although the membership would be limited to 20 women, the dues had not increased.

- A 1948 petition from Rochester Township citizens asked that the state high-way department provide patrols along Route 29 after a horrendous accident demolished Raymond Estes's car and seriously injured six members of his family. A truck careened out of control, smashing the vehicle, which was parked at Kenneth Jones's service station on the west edge of the village. All survived but the injured were expected to endure long-term pain and scars. The truck driver was arrested on charges of reckless driving and carrying a concealed weapon.

- Wilbern Dugger spent decades leading a Rochester Boy Scout troop that organized in 1941. He oversaw numerous local trips such as canoeing the Sangamon

W.W. Dugger became scoutmaster for Rochester's Boy Scout Troop 40 in the 1940s. He was Rochester's 1979 Citizen of the Year, and the National Eagle Scout Association named him Scoutmaster of the Year in 1984. (ILLINOIS STATE JOURNAL-REGISTER, 1 DEC. 1985, P.23.)

River, as well as scout activities that included trips to Wisconsin, Michigan, Minnesota, and New Mexico. Dugger served Rochester Troop 40 for about half a century. Wayne Beck was the Troop's Scoutmaster from 1992 to 2008, when Jim Hefley became leader.

Looking south in 1945, when this aerial photo of Fleck's Lakeview Air Park was taken, several planes, three hangars, and the Theodore Wolford home are clearly visible. Heavily populated subdivisions today occupy the air strip property, as well as what was then an empty field south of the Rochester-Springfield Road. (COURTESY OF GARY FLECK)

- A thriving subdivision with dozens of homes now occupies the former landing strip along the Rochester Road near East Lake Shore Drive, where Fleck's Lakeview Air Park was dedicated in 1945.

   — The air park was located just east of Theodore Wolford's historic home that is pictured in the 1918 Orange Judd *Pictorial* and is still a home in 2017. Thousands of spectators in 1945 and 1946, including Rochester citizens, enjoyed the air shows there that featured formation flying, aerial aerobatics, gliders, mock bombing, parachutes, rides in army ducks capable of traveling on land and water, and orchestral music. The free show in 1945 helped promote war bond sales.

   — Created by Frank "Bud" Fleck of Springfield, the airport offered aviation classes, plane rentals, and private instructions. Rochester High School

Fleck's Lakeview Air Park, located on the north side of the Rochester-Springfield Road near Lake Springfield, provided the landing strip for this unnamed pilot during World War II. (COURTESY OF GARY FLECK)

The historic Theodore Wolford home, seen in this 1918 Orange Judd *Pictorial* photo, was built on the north side of what is today the Rochester-Springfield Road near its intersection with East Lake Shore Drive. Fleck's Air Park landing strip was built immediately east of this property several decades later. (COURTESY OF COMPASS POINT PRODUCTIONS; FARM PROGRESS COMPANIES)

aeronautics students also visited Fleck's Air Park to inspect various planes and watch mechanics work on aircraft and engines. One of the budding pilots was Jerome "Jerry" Daley, Sr., who lived and worked just east of the airport at Maplehurst Farm, owned by Isham Taft. Jerry soloed when he was 17 and served in the U.S. Air Force during the Korean War.

— Tragedy occurred in 1948 when two pilots took off from Fleck's Air Park one minute apart and crashed in mid-air 10 minutes later over Clearlake Township. Both pilots were killed. A decline in the Air Park's fortunes seems to have become public knowledge soon after the crash. Most of the air park was sold off by 1949 and the remaining hangars became home to a variety of businesses.

— Founder Bud Fleck died in a 1970 automobile accident at age 61. At his death, Fleck owned a Springfield liquor store, although he had also owned an auto-sales business after the air park closed.

• Although the Works Progress Administration (WPA) approved more than $43,000 in the late 1930s for Rochester sewers, the issue was still pending in 1946 when the WPA's administrative successor, the Federal Works Agency, approved preliminary plans for a $63,281 sewage treatment plant and sanitary sewers in Rochester. The announcement noted that a voter-approved bond issue would be necessary to finance the plant that Village President Lyman E. Campbell said would likely be located on the village's north side. It would be another 13 years before village sewers were constructed.

• Springfield policeman Selea L. Myers found a strange copper ball-like object covered with spikes in 1943 on his South Fork River property south of Rochester. Deciding to turn the unidentified object over to the FBI, Myers mused about a story of $20,000 in gold paid by the government to area Native Americans who then buried it near his land. As of 2017, no one has either identified the strange object or acknowledged finding the treasure.

• How often is there an open house at a jail? The newly formed Rochester Girl Scouts hosted just such an event in 1943 after Mayor Earl Bell gave permission

Girl Scout Gloria King welcomes Village Marshal D.R. Beck to the calaboose that had been converted into the headquarters for Rochester's new Girl Scout troop. Note the heavy iron door. (*ILLINOIS STATE REGISTER*, 18 Nov. 1943; COURTESY OF WAYNE BECK)

Organized in 1943, the Rochester Girl Scouts obtained village board permission to use the former Rochester calaboose for their meetings. After renovation, the Scouts moved into the building in November 1943. Pictured on the left is Girl Scout leader June Park. The Scouts are, front from left: Gloria King, Doris Tulpin, and Charlotte Fairchild; back from left: Rose Miller, Carol Moore, Betty Pennington, Rigmor Christiansen, and Patricia Turley. Located behind the Taft Dairy in the 100 block of East Main Street, the jail included the wavy steel window bars seen here. (*ILLINOIS STATE REGISTER*, 18 Nov. 1943)

Rochester Village Marshal D.R. Beck and Girl Scouts Carol Moore (left) and Charlotte Fairchild examine a window newly added to the former Rochester jail. Known for decades as "the calaboose," the building had been transformed into headquarters by members of the new Girl Scout troop. (*ILLINOIS STATE REGISTER*, 18 Nov. 1943; COURTESY OF WAYNE BECK)

to transform the empty Rochester calaboose jail into their headquarters. There, under the leadership of June Park, they enjoyed serving tea in the same spaces formerly used by local prisoners.

— Under the direction of Dorothy Dugger, the local troop earned national recognition in 1949 for shipping 250 pounds of clothes overseas through the national Girls Scouts organization and through friends of village residents.

• Voters in the village and township of Rochester took part in separate 1941 spring elections, both choosing to remain "dry." The township precinct voted 210 to 173 on April 1 to prohibit alcohol sales. Village voters went to the polls two weeks later, with 156 deciding to keep the town dry versus 53 who favored selling alcohol.

- As for birthdays and anniversaries:

1940
— **Admiral Dot** and **Anna M.** *(Campbell)* **Campbell** celebrated their 40th wedding anniversary in 1940. These parents of four children had lived in Rochester for 10 years. While working in the Rochester store of Parker and Coe in 1894, Admiral fired shots at four would-be-robbers who escaped on a stolen B&O Railroad handcar. He worked 39 years as a linotype operator for the *Illinois State Journal*.

East Main Street residents Admiral Dot and Anna M. *(Campbell)* Campbell celebrated their 40th wedding anniversary in 1940. Their son George was a graduate of the U.S. Naval Academy. (*ILLINOIS STATE JOURNAL*, 5 JULY 1940; PUBLISHED BY GENEALOGYBANK.COM, A DIVISION OF NEWSBANK)

1945
— **John W. Simpson** celebrated his 75th birthday by walking seven miles to Springfield. He left Rochester at 7:20 a.m. and arrived in Springfield at 9:45 a.m. Born in 1870, Simpson had been a Sangamon County resident for 55 years. After arriving at the *Illinois State Journal* office, the septuagenarian challenged any man at least his age to do better.

- Twenty years after their first day-long homecoming at South Fork Christian Church in 1920, members continued their annual tradition in 1940. The congregation is one of the oldest in Sangamon County, first organized in April 1832. The original church was built in 1852, about five years after Abraham Lincoln delivered his famous temperance speech nearby at the South Fork School. Bell and Breckenridge families were among those who actively helped in the church construction, and their descendants also contributed to the Rochester community.

- As the war ordnance plant east of Springfield was expected to increased local traffic on Route 36, state government considered in 1942 constructing a new highway south of the Sangamon River from Springfield to Decatur. The new pavement would connect Route 29 at Rochester to Route 48 south of Decatur. — In addition to relieving Route 36 traffic, that alignment would give travelers a more convenient opportunity to visit historic sites such as the Lincoln Homestead west of Decatur and the grave of General Samuel A. Whiteside in Mt. Auburn's Hunter Cemetery. Although the proposal had been floated a few years earlier, it was not carried forward because of the uncertain need for this new highway and potential war-related construction issues.

Rochester's old Post Office at 124 North John Street appears well used in this 1948 photo. Located directly north of the IOOF building, this structure later served other functions before being torn down in 1985. The dental office of Dr. Jerry Gies, which replaced this building, became the office of Waters Agency, Inc., Insurance in 2004. (COURTESY OF NINA DUGGER)

- As perpetrators or as victims, Rochester residents were still involved in unique lawbreaking schemes.

    — Chicken thieves were old news by 1945, but the individuals who stole 68 chickens from William Crim also hauled off 20 feet of fence.

    — It was December 1946 when someone walked away with a door from Estol Lechrone's car while Estol worked the second shift at Springfield's Pillsbury Plant. Since he faced a cold drive home to Rochester that frigid night, Lechrone told police that he wished the thief "had taken the car and left the door."

    —It was more serious when two Rochester boys broke in and robbed Carroll Raney's service station of rifles and ammunition in 1949. The juveniles, ages 11 and 15, were caught as they conducted target practice north of town, which was after they had shot out several high-school windows.

    — Hugh A. Campbell thought in 1941 that he was stopping his car in Springfield to help two individuals in trouble, only to find himself kidnapped at gunpoint and robbed of $7. The Rochester man was forced to drive to a spot near Rochester where the two abductors jumped from his car and into another vehicle waiting nearby. Campbell reported the incident to Springfield police but explained he was not able to read the license number of the fleeing car.

- When Ralph Norman of Rochester went to the top of an elevator shaft to repair the lift at the Rochester Grain and Lumber Co. in August 1949, he wasn't prepared for what lay ahead. Thinking he had repaired the lift that some boys had tampered with a day or two earlier, Norman stepped on it to go back to ground level. Instead, he and the lift fell, uncontrolled, 40 feet to the bottom. Miraculously, Norman suffered only a sprained ankle and burned palms, which were attended to at Memorial Hospital in Springfield.

- Within two days in early October 1946, six patients diagnosed with polio were admitted to St. John's Hospital. All were under the age of 15, and they included one teen from a Rochester family. Across the U.S., polio peaked six years later, with about 58,000 cases having been reported. Of those patients, 3,145 died and 21,269 were paralyzed to some degree.

- The Red Cross was a key organization to help alleviate suffering around the world during World War II. For instance, volunteers in 1944 were trained to prepare surgical dressings for wounded soldiers overseas. Rochester was one of many Sangamon County villages where surgical-dressing-preparation rooms were set up. A year earlier, 705 women across the county volunteered 20,700 hours to prepare the dressings.
  — Carl Moore was named chairman of the Rochester Township Red Cross war relief fund campaign in 1942. The Rochester State Bank served as drive headquarters, and contributions were also collected at Rentschler & Sons Clover Farm Store. Wilson Park directed Rochester's 1945 Red Cross drive.

- At its height, the Twist family's Arkansas property, which made up a single township, was estimated to be the world's largest plantation in a single land parcel. After the 1937 death of Ira Twist, a Twist-estate receivership under the direction of his son John F. Twist sorted though the family's affairs in order to

The photographer for this picture was looking north on John Street from the Rochester Grain and Lumber Company elevator in 1946. The elevator office in the building on the left later became a hardware store and as of 2017 was a restaurant, barber shop, and florist. The IOOF building on East Main Street is visible in the distance. (COURTESY OF NINA DUGGER)

Another view of the Rochester Grain and Lumber Company office on John Street is seen circa 1940. This building has since also served as a hardware store, newspaper office, and barber shop. Later additions provided space for other businesses, including an insurance office, florist, Rochester Public Library, and a tanning salon (COURTESY OF NINA DUGGER)

resolve debts. All Illinois properties, except the Twist's Rochester house and lot on East Main Street, had been sold by 1940.

— Of the original 18,000-acre Arkansas plantation, 16,616 acres were leased to the U.S. government under the Farm Security Administration. A portion of that acreage was divided into 285 forty-acre farms leased to landless families who were encouraged to grow both their own food and cash crops.

- Beginning in 1942, community scrap drives were organized throughout the country to support World War II efforts. Salvaged kitchen grease and fats were collected in Rochester and delivered to the Sallenger's grocery store in New City. Mrs. Josephine Clark of Rochester and Mrs. Lottie Sallenger of New City co-chaired that effort.

  — A Rochester High School tin can drive, under the direction of John H. Churchill, collected metal that was then delivered to Springfield for processing. It was part of a county-wide drive coordinated by high school principals, as county schools vied for prizes of $5, $2, and $1.

- Sportsmen of Sangamon County led March of Dimes fundraisers in 1947 that collected donations for the foundation established to fight polio. Under the slogan "those who run must help them to walk," 10% of one Rochester High School basketball game gate receipts were donated to the cause in January. At the same time, the Rochester Athletic Club sponsored a fox hunt with the proceeds directed to the March of Dimes. Sangamon County's goal was $30,000.

- Army Corps of Engineers plans for flood-control dams were met with a public outcry in 1946 that ultimately prevented building just such a structure on the South Fork River. That dam would have created a lake south of the B&O Railroad bridge. Other dam locations were planned in and beyond the county. The Sangamon County Farm Bureau, Springfield Chamber of Commerce, and numerous individuals led opposition to the project. Opponents estimated that the $103 million project would remove 34,000 acres of Sangamon County farmland from crop production and evict hundreds of Sangamon County farmers.

- Rochester citizens often made news:

  — **Justin Taft, Jr.**, and his Shorthorn calf Otis earned a second place award at the 1944 International Livestock Show in Chicago.

  — In addition to being known for gardening, **John W. Campbell** was known for making white-oak-sapling baskets by hand. He completed about 100 baskets of different styles during the winter of 1945-1946.

  — **Elmer Richardson** delivered a note in 1944 that he had found in his cornfield south of Rochester. It was addressed to a mother in Springfield and had been dropped by her son from an airplane on a training flight from Nebraska.

— While she attended a 4-H camp in 1941, **Norma Fairchild** won first place in the annual Sangamon County style show.

— **Robert Ritterbusch** shot and killed a 13-pound red fox during a 1940 hunting trip on the William Coontz farm west of Rochester.

— After completing numerous farm-related activities during their years at Rochester High School, both **Delbert** and **Justin Taft** received scholarships in 1941 to the College of Agriculture at the University of Illinois.

— **Carl Moore** received a frantic call from his wife during the winter of 1941 to please hurry home from work because one of their prize hogs was busy gobbling down the neighbor's chickens. Five chickens were eaten before Moore arrived home to take charge of the situation.

— Fourteen-year-old Rochester eighth-grader **Don Park** won the county portion of the 1941 marble-playing championships in Springfield. He advanced to the western finals, but ultimately lost during that tournament held at Wisconsin Dells.

— It was a competition between friends in 1943 when Rochester's **J. E. Campbell** and Pawnee's A.M. Archer tried to see who would produce that season's first ripe sweet corn. Although they were apparently neck and neck around June 26, a week later Campbell brought his only ripe ear to the office of the *Illinois State Journal*—and won the contest.

— **Charles F. Bailey** had earned a doctorate in chemistry from the University of Wisconsin and went on to conduct research in chemistry at Harvard University. In the 1940s he developed ink to be used in the newly invented "ball point pen." Bailey, who had attended a one-room rural Rochester school, and three years at Rochester High School, graduated from Springfield High. Upon retiring, he settled in Michigan, where he died in 1997.

• Deaths during the 1940s included the following:

1940

— **Josephine** *(Jagla)* **Derry**, who was 77 when she died, sailed from Germany on a ten-week-long trip when she was three years old. She and her husband, Columbus Derry, were Rochester farmers until his death in 1924.

1941

— **Mollie** *(Campbell)* **Wolford**, 64, died in the

Born in 1906, Charles "Fred" Bailey attended a one-room grade school in Rochester Township and went on to earn a doctorate in chemistry from the University of Wisconsin. Fred's later research led him in the 1940s to develop several inks, including one for use in the newly created instrument known as the "ball point pen." (*ILLINOIS STATE JOURNAL*, 30 JAN. 1997; PUBLISHED BY GENEALOGYBANK. COM, A DIVISION OF NEWSBANK)

same East Main Street home where she was born, married G. A. Wolford, and lived most of her life. Mollie was the first president of the Rochester Woman's Club.

1948

— **John E. Fogle**, 83 when he died, had been a Rochester justice of the peace, long-time treasurer of the Rochester IOOF, and worked on maintenance for the Twist Brothers Grain and Lumber Co. John was the father of Harry Fogle, the only Rochester soldier to die during WW I.

— James Bell, 94, was born on Christmas Day in 1853. He and his wife, Balzora, moved from Kentucky in 1909 to Rochester, where they farmed. They were the parents of noted musician Claude Bell and the grandparents of Paul Bell, who in 2017, lives in Dawson.

1949

— Retired Rochester farmer and funeral director **Charles L. Jones**, 89, was born in Cotton Hill township in 1859 and married Clara Vigal in 1880. The family moved to Rochester in 1905, where he opened the C. L. Jones Funeral Home on the corner of East Main and North Walnut Streets. His great-grandson, Greg Park, continues in 2017 to operate that business as Wilson Park Funeral Home, Rochester's longest continuous family business.

Mollie *(Campbell)* Wolford (1876-1941) was born, married, and died in the Nelson Campbell homestead on East Main Street. Mollie was a direct descendant of Hugh Campbell, who homesteaded in Sangamon County in 1823. The childhood memories of Carl "Bud" Moore include recalling the trouble he earned by locking Mollie, a next-door neighbor, in her own shed. (COURTESY OF JERRY CAMPBELL AND JANET CAMPBELL)

- When she died, the remains of Maria Bolden were brought from Bates City, MO, by ambulance to Rochester, where she had faithfully and lovingly served some of the village and township's best-known families: Parker, Twist, Bell, Coe, Fairchild, and others. Only a few months earlier the same ambulance had made a much longer trip to Chicago, where Maria had suffered a debilitating stroke. During that trip, she was moved to the Missouri home of Elizabeth *(Highmore)* Fishback, who had been in Maria's care as a child decades earlier.

Maria Jane Bolden, a beloved black servant who worked for several prominent Rochester families, was buried with honor in Rochester Cemetery. (R. BRUZAN PHOTO)

— All who attended her funeral affectionately remembered Maria's cooking, her smile, her laugh, and above all, her selflessness. She was described as someone who was "a friend of all and all were her friends." The daughter of a Negro slave born near Harper's Ferry, WV, Maria was young when she arrived in Sangamon County and lived as a servant first for the John S. Highmore family. A later census listed her living at the Edward Poffenberger home. Her activities and travels with Rochester families were recorded for years in local news notes.

— Perhaps Maria Bolden, one of only a few black workers in Rochester, would have been surprised when she was carried to her grave by Hugh Campbell, Frederick Poffenberger, Ross Fairchild, R. Coe, and Sherring Highmore, all prominent men of the township. Maria was buried in the Highmore family plot in Rochester Cemetery.

— Rochester Methodist Church minister William H. Day, who conducted the burial service, used terminology of that time when in his tender eulogy he said Maria was "black of skin but white of heart, pure of soul and thoroughly Christian."

This girls' night out in 1943 included, from left: Helen *(Durham)* Poffenberger, Doris *(Park)* Clark, Elizabeth *(Cordis)* Fairchild, Deloris *(Coontz)* Eggleston, Pauline *(Frame)* Watkins, and in front, June *(Gaddey)* Park. (COURTESY OF BARBARA WAGNER)

Carl "Bud" Moore rides the pony and Butch Fairchild watches in this 1940s photo. This property had once been the W.W. Taft farm on West Main Street. (COURTESY OF CARL "BUD" MOORE)

BUSINESSES OF ROCHESTER
CIRCA 1950

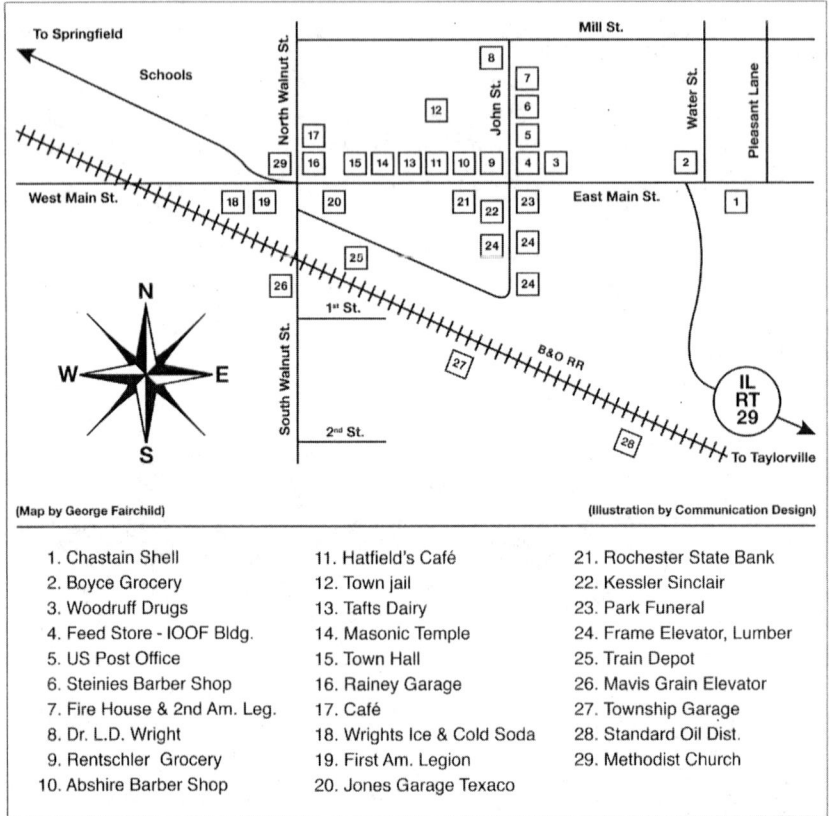

(Map by George Fairchild)   (Illustration by Communication Design)

1. Chastain Shell	11. Hatfield's Café	21. Rochester State Bank
2. Boyce Grocery	12. Town jail	22. Kessler Sinclair
3. Woodruff Drugs	13. Tafts Dairy	23. Park Funeral
4. Feed Store - IOOF Bldg.	14. Masonic Temple	24. Frame Elevator, Lumber
5. US Post Office	15. Town Hall	25. Train Depot
6. Steinies Barber Shop	16. Rainey Garage	26. Mavis Grain Elevator
7. Fire House & 2nd Am. Leg.	17. Café	27. Township Garage
8. Dr. L.D. Wright	18. Wrights Ice & Cold Soda	28. Standard Oil Dist.
9. Rentschler Grocery	19. First Am. Legion	29. Methodist Church
10. Abshire Barber Shop	20. Jones Garage Texaco	

(ORIGINAL MAP BY GEORGE FAIRCHILD; ILLUSTRATION BY COMMUNICATION DESIGN)

1950s

The plate on Rochester's water tank built in 1956 records that the capacity is 60,000 gallons and the bottom of the tank is 100 feet from the ground. This view is looking north with Sattley Street in the foreground.
(COURTESY OF WAYNE BECK)

1950s Timeline...

1950	Population: 506
	— Rochester Fire Protection District organized
	— Dismissal of a high school coach led to a four-day student strike
1952	Former Rochester resident Madeline Babcock Smith authored *The Lemon Jelly Cake*
1954	Springfield City Council approved building a system to pump water from the South Fork into Lake Springfield during droughts
	— Route 29 through Rochester was relocated parallel to the Baltimore & Ohio Railroad tracks
1955	The Rochester Grain & Lumber Co. grain silo was built at the northeast corner of John Street and Route 29
	— A rebuilt Rochester Christian Church was dedicated
	— A monument to armed services veterans was donated by the C.C. Twist family

1956   Rochester's first water tower was built on Sattley Street
            — Central Illinois Light Company (CILCO) installed a natural-gas
            connection to Rochester
1957   Development began for Oak Hills Estates subdivision
1958   Steel bridge on Rochester Road over the South Fork River was
            replaced
1959   White Fence Acres subdivision was developed
            — Coffey Texaco Service station was built at the corner of
            Route 29 and Walnut Street
            — Fire destroyed the Rochester Grain Co. elevator
            — Major oil strike was made in Rochester Township
            — A new high school was built on the Route 29 campus

1950s Storylines ...

- A popular book about a lemon jelly cake, and a major oil strike in Rochester Township brought wide attention to the community. Highway improvements, a new high school, and a new Christian Church were part of the dynamic Rochester scene of the 1950s. Changes to Route 29 and building Rochester's first water tower contributed to the village's infrastructure.

- Her creative imagination and her childhood in Rochester led Madeline Babcock Smith to write her popular 1952 semi-autobiographical novel *The Lemon Jelly Cake*. An immediate success, the book received praise from *The New York Times Book Review*, *The New York Herald Tribune*, and the *Saturday Review* and was named "Book of the Week" by the Associated Press. Paramount Pictures even considered buying the film rights.

  — Based on the nine years she spent in Rochester, Smith described the 1900 community of Tory (Rochester) through the lives of its fictional citizens, who some said were based on actual village residents. The book has been described as "preserving an important moment in the cultural life of Illinois."

  — Smith was born in Rochester in 1887 to Dr. Oliver Brewster and Emma *(Merriam)* Babcock. She died within months after her book was released and is buried in Springfield at Oak Ridge Cemetery.

The Lemon Jelly Cake, a 1952 novel by Madeline Babcock Smith, was based on her 1900s childhood memories of Rochester residents. It was so popular that Paramount Pictures expressed interest in buying film rights to the book. (UNIVERSITY OF ILLINOIS PRESS, URBANA AND CHICAGO, IL, 1998; USED WITH PERMISSION)

- Rochester's 1959 oil strike, Sangamon County's first major oil well, was described as a unique Central Illinois discovery. Late in the afternoon of December 14, gases rising from the well foretold the oil that was close behind. One of the gathered throng soon shouted, "here she comes!" as oil began to flow heavily from the well and into the nearby creek. Storage tanks were soon installed to collect the black gold.

On Today's
Editorial Page:
Ike's Tour A Propaganda
Defeat For Reds

Illinois State Journal

FINAL
EDITION

Journal Washington Bureau—Associated Press—United Press International—U.P.I. Facsimile—N.E.A. Service—Copley News Service

FOUNDED NOV. 10, 1831   VOLUME 129, NO. 30   SPRINGFIELD, ILLINOIS, TUESDAY, DECEMBER 15, 1959   TWENTY-SIX PAGES   TWO SECTIONS   PRICE 7 CENTS

STRIKE OIL NEAR ROCHESTER

Rochester made front-page news in 1959 when oil was discovered on the Scott farm southwest of the village. At left, Rochester farmer Tom E. Scott and geologist W.A. Warren examine oil well core samples. The well soon produced 2,000 to 3,000 barrels per day. (*ILLINOIS STATE JOURNAL*, 15 DEC. 1959: 1-2; COURTESY OF JIM WATERS)

Right: Gushing oil was lit when gas released from the Scott-farm well was set afire by oilmen. The 1959 Rochester Township well was described as a major oil producer unequaled in Central Illinois. (*ILLINOIS STATE JOURNAL*, 15 DEC. 1959: 1; COURTESY OF JIM WATERS)

— Drilled on the farm of Tom E. Scott, a mile southwest of Rochester, the well initially produced an estimated 2,000 to 3,000 barrels a day. Scott commented that his farming on the same property prior to the valuable discovery had resulted in only marginal profits.

— His well preceded several other oil wells drilled in Rochester Township during the 1960s that proved to be profitable for land owners and well shareholders.

HISTORICAL MARKER

Bi-Petro, Inc. Owner   Scott Trust Lease

This well was drilled in 1958. It produced over 400,000 bbls. of crude oil which made 16 million gal. of gasoline and diesel.

As of 2005, this well is producing 1,100 gal. of gasoline and diesel per day.

This operation and ethanol creates jobs, tax dollars and money that stay in Illinois. That's money OPEC and foreign oil production does not receive.

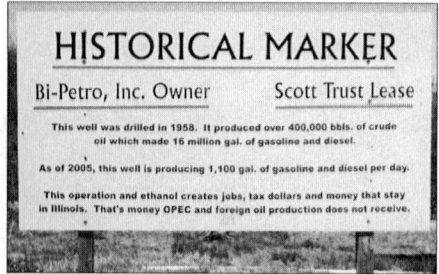

Above: Oil storage tanks and a historical marker are located on Possum Trot Road southwest of the village. The marker reads: "This well was drilled in 1958. It produced over 400,000 bbls of crude oil which made 16 million gal. of gasoline and diesel. As of 2005, this well is producing 1,100 gal. of gasoline and diesel per day. This operation and ethanol creates jobs, tax dollars and money that stay in Illinois. That's money OPEC and foreign oil production does not receive."

Right: Oil wells drilled in the 1950s continued pumping in Rochester Township 65 years later as shown by this 2015 picture. (R. BRUZAN PHOTOS)

- Having endured a horrendous fire that destroyed the Rochester Christian Church on February 9, 1947, the determined congregation began rebuilding the same year. The congregation initially worshipped at the high school and then in a newly completed basement on the church site. Work renewed in 1953 on their above-ground structure, which was dedicated June 19, 1955. As described at its dedication, the new building was "made possible by the labor and generosity of a devout congregation and friends."

The rebuilt Rochester Christian Church on South Walnut Street was dedicated in 1955. It replaced the former church that had been destroyed by fire eight years earlier. (COURTESY OF LAURA WELCH AND THE ROCHESTER CHRISTIAN CHURCH)

- The South Fork Church of Christ held a rededication in 1959 to celebrate a refurnished building and new baptistery. The church, which was originally organized in 1832, continues in 2017 to hold services in the modernized and expanded structure originally built in 1852.

- Two major changes to Rochester's infrastructure were explored during a 1955 public meeting held at the high school. Although Lake Springfield had provided water to Rochester for 20 years, the community lacked a water tower that would store additional water and improve water pressure to the expanding village. Another growing concern was Rochester's lack of a sewage treatment system, as residents still depended on individual septic tanks.

  — With approval of the state public health department, a 60,000-gallon elevated water tank was built in 1956 near the B&O Railroad tracks and Sattley Street at a cost of $27,400.

  — The state sanitary water board granted a sewer system permit the same year. A federal grant for $152,000, approved in June 1959 to construct a sanitary system, was followed a month later by yet another federal grant of $14,793 toward the same project. Rochester Mayor Lyman E. Campbell proclaimed the work would be, "the last utility it takes to make us a modern town."

- Major changes were in store for the campus of Rochester's school system. Voters approved a $125,000 bond issue in 1950 to enlarge the grade school by adding six classrooms, a cafeteria, library, office, and teachers' room.

  — A bus garage, large enough to house six vehicles, was built in 1952 at a cost of $7,539. Facing a district enrollment that almost doubled between 1951 and 1957, a 1958 building proposal earned voter approval for a $300,000 bond issue to construct a new high school and vocation education shop. The old high school building became the junior high school for grades 6 through 8, while the existing elementary school was used for first through fifth grades.

  — The new high school opened in 1959 for 150 students. That year also marked the first in which the Rochester district offered kindergarten, with 20 students in the morning class and 15 in the afternoon.

- Within three years after Senator Joseph McCarthy (R-WI) first claimed that Communists had infiltrated the U.S. government, fears of Communist subversion had spread throughout the country. It was these fears that prompted the 1953 Rochester School Board to request that all school personnel and board members sign an affidavit saying they were not a Communist nor had they been involved in Communist activities.

  One ranking official in the office of state superintendent of public instruction said he believed such a request was legal as a condition of employment. In spite of the fact that requiring employees to sign such an affidavit violated their Fifth Amendment right against self incrimination, an *Illinois State Journal* editorial supported the Rochester School Board position.

- When the school board voted in March 1950 not to renew the contract of basketball coach Henry Starks on the grounds that he had failed to cooperate with other teachers and parents, their action ignited a four-day student strike.

Rochester students were angry when the Rochester School Board asked one of the team coaches to resign. In protest, they boycotted classes and gathered at the courthouse in downtown Springfield to meet with the county superintendent of schools. (*ILLINOIS STATE JOURNAL*, 28 MAR. 1950: 1; PUBLISHED BY GENEALOGYBANK.COM, A DIVISION OF NEWSBANK)

An estimated 60 of the 76 enrolled high school students stayed out of classes at least one day during the protest. The coach, however, encouraged students to return to class.

— The students claimed they had collected 200 names on petitions to reinstate the coach, and a student delegation met during the furor with Sangamon County Superintendent of Schools Wesley O. Withrow. Although it was supported by a number of parents, the student campaign failed to replace three anti-Stark board members who were up for re-election just weeks after the strike.

- Rochester voters in 1950 approved organizing a legal fire-protection district. In addition to the village itself, the new district extended three miles north, five miles east, five miles south, and three miles west. By virtue of being in the district, farms realized a 6-10% decrease in fire-insurance premiums.

  — Ernest J. Rentschler was the first fire chief of what was then a 21-member volunteer fire department, none of whom received compensation for either training or fire calls.

  — By 1951 the fire department was ready for public display of its newly acquired Diamond T truck chassis and 700-gallon water tank. A larger 1,000-gallon auxiliary tank was acquired by the department in 1953 for use on rural fires.

- Rochester's recently organized fire department was tested in June 1959 when a blaze broke out in the Rochester Grain Company elevator.

  — Along with the elevator, owned by Marshall Watkins, 23,500 bushels of government corn and two railroad box cars were also destroyed. The B&O Railroad tracks warped where they ran adjacent to the elevator, confirming the fire's intense heat. Probably caused by an electrical short circuit, the fire was fought by a total of eight area fire departments. The loss was estimated at $75,000.

Left: Dick Rentschler, a 1969 RHS graduate, proudly displays in 2016 a photo of his father, Ernie, who was Rochester's first fire chief. Dick also served as Rochester fire chief beginning in 2003. (R. BRUZAN PHOTO). Right: Rochester's new firefighting equipment was put on display in 1951 at the John Street firehouse. Pictured, from left: Chief Ernie Rentschler, Gerald Abshire, and Marshall Watkins. (COURTESY OF DICK RENTSCHLER)

— In November of the same year, Marshall Watkins suffered a $160,000 loss when another spectacular blaze burned his Berry grain elevator to the ground. Rochester was one of 10 area departments that fought that fire.

• Illinois Bell upgraded Rochester's dial telephone system to modernize direct dialing among four towns. One immediate change in Rochester was to add the number "7" to the previous four-digit phone numbers, which had already started with "7." For instance, the earlier number of "7859" became "7-7859."

— The company spent about $32,000 for a new building on East Main Street and the new equipment needed to improve telephone service. The change went into operation on November 18, 1953, making both local and long-distance calling more convenient.

The Rochester Grain Co. fire in 1959 leveled the company's elevator and destroyed two railroad freight cars, a truck, and 23,500 bushels of corn. The loss totalled $75,000. (COURTESY OF KATHY SMITH AND THE ROCHESTER FIRE PROTECTION DISTRICT)

Illinois Bell built this East Main Street structure in 1953 to house equipment the company would soon use to upgrade Rochester's dial telephone service. (R. BRUZAN PHOTO)

- Road conditions continued to be frequent issues in the village and township.
  — The South Fork bridges at Cascade and Rochester were declared to be unsafe for school buses in 1950, thus requiring alternative routes for student travel.
  — A $13,000 project to improve the road between Rochester and New City was completed in 1956.

Left: Photo looks southeast from the intersection with West Main Street. It includes Bill J. Coffey's Texaco Station.

Below: The Texaco Station was at the corner of Walnut Street and Route 29. (COURTESY OF BILL L. COFFEY)

Above: The Texaco sign was photographed again in 2016, this time between Bill J. Coffey's great-grandson Bill D. Coffey (left) and his grandson Bill L. Coffey. (PHOTOGRAPH BY JOHN GROVES, COURTESY OF BILL L. COFFEY)

— Rochester American Legion Post members installed 14 new signs in 1959 to identify the village streets.

— To straighten and do away with dangerous curves, a new section of Route 29 was built parallel to the B&O Railroad tracks in 1954, replacing its alignment through downtown Rochester.

— A contentious highway project in 1956 involved Rochester and two competing proposals to locate the new Route 66 Springfield bypass. State engineers recommended locating the bypass to the west of Lake Springfield. The Greater Springfield plan commission urged that it be located east of East Lake Shore Drive and extend along the west side of Rochester. Although the new highway was built along the state-recommended alignment, it is entertaining to speculate how such a road with its heavy traffic between Chicago and St. Louis would have impacted future development of the village.

- When Al Mavis developed the 65-acre Oak Hills Estates in 1957, it opened a flood of new home construction. Newspaper ads described Oak Hills as combining country living with city facilities and emphasized the full-grown trees on lots overlooking the South Fork River, a short drive from Springfield.
  — An Oak Hills Estates advertising article listed village amenities awaiting subdivision residents, including the K-12 school system, churches, fire protection district, gas stations, three lumber yards, active Civil Defense Unit, and a variety of useful businesses.
  — Because of its location within one and a half miles of the city limits, the Springfield City Council determined that Oak Hills had to meet street requirements as specified in Springfield's brand new land subdivision ordinance. After review, however, the Springfield Plan Commission recommended waiving ordinance requirements for sidewalks, street signs, and a six-inch water main. The Springfield City Council concurred.

Looking east on East Main in 1955, the downtown Rochester street scene included the Town Hall, Masonic Temple in the former school, Taft Dairy in the former Woman's Christian Temperance Union building, and various stores. (COURTESY OF THE ROCHESTER HERALD, 1 FEB. 1984; SANGAMON VALLEY COLLECTION, LINCOLN LIBRARY, SPRINGFIELD, IL)

- The Illinois Commerce Commission granted authority to Central Illinois Light Company (CILCO) in 1956 for construction of a $120,000 extension of the company's gas distribution system to serve Rochester. A four-inch gas main connection was made at a metering station west of the village.

- Theft and vandalism:
  1956
  — Burglars stole cash and checks worth more than $4,300 from the Rochester Grain and Lumber Co.

  1957
  — A man and young girl entered the Main Street home of deaf-and-blind octogenarian Bert Wolford, stealing his billfold and $210. They were last seen leaving in a dark-colored Cadillac.

— A prowler knocked out a window in Charles Jones's service station and stole 200 pennies, several wrenches, two new tires, and 50 packs of cigarettes.

1958
— An antique organ and historic Bible were destroyed by two 15-year-old vandals who broke into the Rochester Cemetery chapel. The boys, who also admitted to burglarizing a downtown Rochester store and stealing tools from a construction site, were arrested and made wards of the Family Court.

- The first polio vaccine, developed by Jonas Salk in the early 1950s, was at least partially funded by money collected by the March of Dimes. When Springfield and Sangamon County grade schools administered the first series of Salk shots in April 1955, they were on the forefront of those inoculations, which had been officially pronounced safe just two weeks earlier. Rochester first and second graders were among those receiving the anti-polio vaccine.

- Rochester native Hugh A. Campbell was elected Sangamon County sheriff in 1958 and again in 1970. A Navy veteran of World War II, he was a livestock dealer for 20 years and served as Rochester Township Road Commissioner for 12 years.

Long-time Rochester resident Hugh Campbell was elected Sangamon County Sheriff in 1958 and again in 1970. He and his wife Doris *(Hardbarger)* Campbell, both members of the Rochester Christian Church, were married in 1934. (COURTESY OF JANET AND BRIAN CAMPBELL)

- Rochester celebrations:
1950
— **Jasper Easley**, who moved to Rochester from Kentucky with his wife Nannie in 1904, observed his 72nd birthday. Easley was a conductor for the Springfield, Clear Lake, & Rochester Interurban and later worked 23 years for the Interstate Telephone and Bell Telephone companies.
— **Lucille McCormick** of Rushville became the bride of **Carl J. Rule** of Rochester. Carl was employed at Rentschler & Son's grocery in Rochester and Lucille at the Illinois Department of Public Health.

1953
— **Mary Martha** *(Eubanks)* **Miller** celebrated her 96th birthday. It was Mary who hosted a 1915 lawn party celebrating the arrival of electricity to Rochester homes. A Kentucky native, Mary and her husband, C.E. Miller, moved to Rochester in 1880. C.E. was a highly respected farmer and stock breeder.

1954

— **Alonzo** and **Lema** *(Haney)* **Wilson** celebrated their golden wedding anniversary. Their families were early settlers in Central Illinois.

1955

— **Alonzo** and **Flora** *(Windsor)* **Eggleston** celebrated 50 years of marriage. The Egglestons had owned and operated their Rochester grocery business for 40 years.

Married in the Rochester Christian Church, Alonzo and Flora *(Windsor)* Eggleston celebrated their 50th wedding anniversary in 1955, left. The couple was in the grocery business for 40 years. Their store, seen right, was located at the southeast corner of Main and Walnut Streets. (*ILLINOIS STATE JOURNAL*, 21 AUG. 1955; PUBLISHED BY GENEALOGYBANK.COM, A DIVISION OF NEWSBANK; RIGHT: *THE ROCHESTER WEEKLY ITEM*, 23 DEC. 1909)

- The Red Barn Restaurant celebrated its grand opening in 1953. Located on North Walnut Street, the new business served breakfast, lunch, and supper, and promoted its chicken and steak dinners. The restaurant closed four years later, and its inventory was sold at a public auction. As of 2017, the building houses apartments.

GRAND OPENING
Red Barn Restaurant
ROCHESTER, ILLINOIS .... AIR-CONDITIONED
Operated by FRANK and MINNIE ADCOCK

You are invited to visit our restaurant, of which we are very proud.

Serving breakfast, lunch and dinner in a quaint, hospitable atmosphere.

We Specialize In
SAVORY STEAKS
and
CHICKEN DINNERS

Rochester's new restaurant on North Walnut Street had a grand opening in July 1953. The business closed in 1957, and the building was converted into apartments. (*ILLINOIS STATE JOURNAL*, 24 JULY 1953: 2; PUBLISHED BY GENEALOGYBANK.COM, A DIVISION OF NEWSBANK)

- In addition to the Red Barn Restaurant's equipment auction, other such bidding for Rochester land and personal property took place during the 1950s. These included a community sale to raise money for 45 high school band uniforms. Auctions were also held for Joe Elben's Shell service station and launderette at the corner of

A July 4th celebration in Rochester around 1950 included, from left: Joann Taft, Janet Trees, and Carolyn Norman. The background includes Kessler's Service Station and Rochester State Bank.
(COURTESY OF CAROLYN *(NORMAN)* WANLESS)

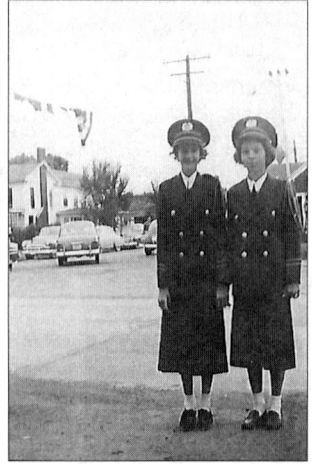

Above: Rochester High School band members, from left: Joann Taft and Carolyn Norman, were part of the downtown July 4th celebration around 1950. Wilson Park Funeral Home is visible on the left. (COURTESY OF CAROLYN *(NORMAN)* WANLESS)

The Rochester High School band provided music for the July 4th celebration in the early 1950s. Buildings seen along John Street in that year were, from left, the American Legion hall and fire station, U.S. Post Office, and the Independent Order of Odd Fellows.
(COURTESY OF CAROLYN *(NORMAN)* WANLESS)

State and East Main Streets, Carroll Raney's Garage and Automotive Store, the house and personal items of both W.S. Woodruff and Jasper Easley, and the estate of Mabelle *(Raney)* Mayes.

- Sweet & Canterbury Seed Co. invited Rochester citizens to view a technicolor film, *The Rumen Story*, detailing the digestive system of cows and steers. Viewers saw food entering the stomach, water mixing with the food, salivary liquids added, and "the birth of a burp." The free film was shown at Rochester High School in 1954.

- A first-hand experience with an animal's internal organs took place in 1954 on the Al Mavis farm when Griff, the family dog, swallowed a marble. A rare operation included cutting the boxer's windpipe to remove the marble that had moved into one of his lungs. Although Griff lost 15 pounds during the ordeal, he did recover, much to the joy of the Mavis family.

- Rochester citizens helped individuals and causes.
  — Rochester neighbors demonstrated their care for each other as they came to the aid of Justin Taft, Jr., when he was unable to combine 30 acres of wheat

in 1952. Similar acts of kindness were provided for George Ratz to combine 35 acres of beans in 1954, and when Virgil Pope received help in 1955 to combine 40 acres of oats.

— When $8,527 was collected in Rochester toward a 1955 Memorial Hospital building-fund program, it completely surpassed the original community goal of $5,400.

— Rochester civic groups and individuals organized summer children's activities and discussed playground improvement plans in 1955.

— A porchlight parade solicited donations for the March of Dimes in January 1956, not quite one year after the first polio vaccinations were given to Rochester first and second graders.

• Worldwide tensions over the Cold War and fears of nuclear attack led to community training programs. Civil Defense programs for Rochester citizens in 1957 began with a five-week home-protection course at the American Legion hall. Among the topics discussed during each two-hour session were fire prevention, radiological detection, panic, evacuation, shelters, and family survival.

• By the early 1940s, Florentine (St. Clair) Sherman, a descendent of early Rochester settlers James McCoy and Leonard St. Clair, was living at the family's West Main Street home, Neal's Grove. Her daughter, professional artist Frances Florentine Morrison, joined her mother during the summer of 1951 and created 19 paintings, many of which depicted Rochester scenes. During Rochester's Labor Day celebration, she presented an exhibit of her art at the American Legion Hall that included the watercolor "Rochester Corners," which she described as "a typical American village scene."

Rochester artist Florentine Morrison, a descendent of the St. Clair and McCoy families of early Rochester, displays her 1950 painting "Rochester Corners" that she described as depicting a "typical American village." (*ILLINOIS STATE JOURNAL*, 28 AUG. 1950: 2; PUBLISHED BY GENEALOGYBANK.COM, A DIVISION OF NEWSBANK)

• Rochester deaths included the following:

1950

— Rochester Township Clerk **Roy T. Shreve** died at age 66. Born near Rochester in 1883, the lifelong area resident first operated a coal-and-corn mill with his father at the northwest corner of Walnut and Main Streets and continued in the ice and coal business after the mill was demolished to make way for the new Methodist Church.

1951

— **William Everett Campbell**, who grew up in Rochester, was killed in an Arizona vehicle accident. He was driving a transport truck at the time.

1952

— **William Sherman Woodruff**, a prominent farmer, who was also known across the country for breeding stock, died as he recovered from injuries caused by a fall. The summer after his death, 240 acres of his farmland were auctioned.

1955

— Seventy-year-old **Albert E. Mavis**, founder of Rochester's Mavis Grain Co., died.

1959

— **G.A. "Bert" Wolford**, who at one time owned a hardware and tin shop in the Twist Building, died at the age of 88. Well known for his baseball skills, Bert had managed the Mattoon baseball club in the Three-Eye League and the local Sangamon County Farm Bureau team.

• Justin Taft described in his book *As I Saw It* how the Rochester Cemetery tombstone of Clarence Twist was donated to the Rochester American Legion after Twist's wife, Edith, moved her husband's body to Arkansas for reburial. The

A monument at the entrance of the Rochester Cemetery, provided in 1955 by the Twist family, was dedicated to those who served in the nation's armed forces. (R. BRUZAN PHOTO)

monument was inscribed with the American Legion symbol and relocated in 1955 to what is locally known as "the triangle" at the corner of Walnut and Main Streets. Wilson Park Funeral Home moved the monument in the early 1990s to a location near the entrance of Rochester Cemetery and added a flagpole and benches on behalf of Rochester American Legion and Veterans of Foreign Wars posts. The marker memorializes service members who served in all branches of the military.

The Rochester Grain & Lumber Co. grain elevator at the northeast corner of Route 29 and John Street was built about 1955. (R. BRUZAN PHOTO)

More than a thousand members of the Land of Lincoln Girl Scout Council met in 1958 at the Illinois State Fairgrounds to display exhibits. Rochester's Troop 14 was represented by, from left: Malinda Mavis, Rita Heissinger, Janet Weaver, and their leader Mrs. John Weaver. (ILLINOIS STATE JOURNAL, 5 MAY 1958: 4; PUBLISHED BY GENEALOGYBANK.COM, A DIVISION OF NEWSBANK)

Rentschler's Clover Farm Store, at the northwest corner of East Main and John Streets, was an important grocery for the community. Looking much different in 2017, the building now houses Peace & Appliqué Quilt Shop. (COURTESY OF DICK RENTSCHLER)

Frederick "Steiny" Steinhaur was a Rochester character. In addition to running the "Ding Bat Café," he was a barber, justice of the peace, and clock repairman. Typical of a "Steiny story" was the time he told a customer whose haircut was half done that he had to leave to catch a train so please come back the next day. This 1952 picture was taken on John Street looking north. (COURTESY OF BONNIE (ABSHIRE) RYDER)

The Abshire family lived at 131 East Main Street, where Helen and Gerald operated their barber and beautician shop in the 1950s. Their daughter, Bonnie, was a 1958 RHS graduate.(COURTESY OF BONNIE *(ABSHIRE)* RYDER)

U.S. Postmaster Earl Thomas is seen in 1952 with his daughter Marilyn standing in the doorway of the Post Office, then on John Street. (COURTESY OF BONNIE *(ABSHIRE)* RYDER)

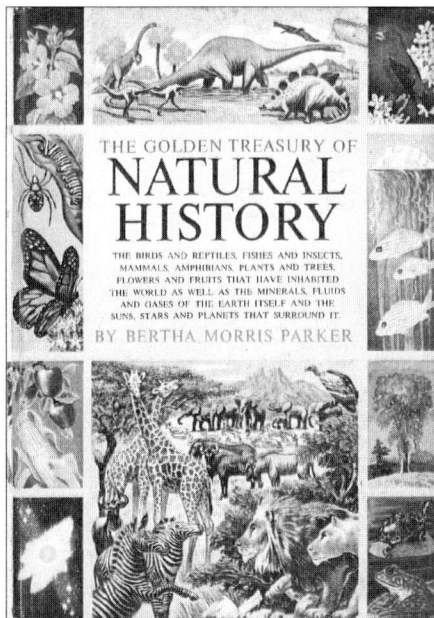

Rochester native Bertha Morris Parker wrote the book *The Golden Treasury of Natural History* published in 1952. (COURTESY OF GOLDEN PRESS, NEW YORK, 1952)

DOWNTOWN ROCHESTER
CIRCA 1960

Downtown Rochester buildings as they appeared in the late 1960s were, clockwise from upper left: Rochester State Bank; DeLay, Abshire-Norman, and Richardson buildings; Town Hall and Masonic Temple; and the Independent Order of Odd Fellows building. (*ROCHESTER & LAKE SPRINGFIELD HERALD*, 18 NOV. 1966; LOWER RIGHT PHOTO COURTESY OF BRAD BUCHER.)

1960s

Rochester-born Louis Persinger (1887-1966) became a world-renowned violinist and taught such young musicians as Isaac Stern, Ruggiero Ricci, and Yehudi Menuhin. He sent this photo and note to his mother in 1902. *"Leipsig - 1902: Dear Mother: I happened to see these cards in a little shop in the Minnig-gasse so thought you might like one. With best wishes for a jolly good Xmas from your loving son Louis."* (PHOTO COURTESY OF BRANDON LOUIS PERSINGER; USED WITH PERMISSION)

1960s Timeline ...

1960	Population: 742
	— Thirty-year water agreement was approved with Springfield's City Water, Light & Power
	— A bowling alley, Rochester Lanes, was built at Route 29 and State Street
	— Drag City opened on Route 29
1961	Rentschler's supermarket opened on State Street
	— New post office on John Street was dedicated
	— Lexington Heights subdivision was developed

1965	Eastgate Meadows subdivision was proposed
	— Rochester Lions Club was chartered
1966	Route 29 became a four-lane highway between Rochester and Springfield
	— Village homeowners were required to connect to village sewers
	— Acclaimed violinist, Louis Persinger, died
	— Good Shepherd Lutheran Church on Route 29 was dedicated
	— Rochester Village Board approved First Illinois Cable TV, Inc. franchise
1967	A gym, cafeteria, 15 classrooms, agriculture shop, and industrial arts facility were added to the Rochester school campus on Route 29
1968	Final plat was approved for Grove Park Estates subdivision
	— Taft Dairy building, formerly the WCTU temple, was demolished to make way for a new Fire Department building
	— Water and sewer services approved for Camelot subdivision
1969	West sewage treatment ponds were constructed
	— Chicken Bristle chapter of Questers was organized
	— Rochester celebrated its Centennial

1960s Storylines...

- "Explosive" defined Rochester growth during the 1960s. New subdivisions required improved water and sewer services, as new stores, churches, and streets also appeared.

- The Rochester Village Board passed a 1967 ordinance to regulate lands that were proposed for annexation, including specifications for subdivision streets and water connections. The creation of several new Rochester subdivisions and anticipation of a new comprehensive plan were driving forces that led to these requirements. Joining Oak Hills Estates and White Fence Acres, which were developed during the 1950s, housing developments in the 1960s included Lexington Heights, Eastgate Meadows, Camelot, and Grove Park Estates.

Karen *(Park)* Alexander enjoyed riding her horse Duke in beautiful Neal's Grove before it was developed into the Grove Park Subdivision in 1968. (COURTESY OF KAREN ALEXANDER)

- Not everyone was in favor of new subdivisions for Rochester. As a 14-year-old horse-riding enthusiast and nature lover, Karen Park was so disappointed to see Grove Park subdivision being planned in one of her favorite riding areas that she repeatedly removed the lot corner stakes in the planned subdivision until she was caught by her mother, Jo *(Park)* Bunn. Pleading guilty, she promised never to do it again. She and her husband, Rick Alexander, would eventually become neighbors of that subdivision.

- The Rochester Village Board voted on several issues that reflected how the once small farming community was rapidly becoming a suburb.

  — Beginning in 1965, the village vowed to enforce a 1908 ordinance requiring owners of horses and other livestock to find housing outside the village for their animals.

  — A village marshal was appointed the same year, and a list of deputy marshals was also prepared.

  — As of January 1, 1966, all homes in the village had to be connected to a sewer line.

  — A series of new sewer ponds was planned for 27.6 acres of land bought from Isham Taft in 1969.

  — The village's first Planning Commission was named in 1966. Two years later an urban planning grant of $4,492 from the U.S. Department of Housing and Urban Development (HUD) would be used to evaluate existing village resources and plan for future development.

- A new 30-year water agreement with Springfield's City Water, Light & Power was approved in 1960. This agreement was necessary in order for Rochester to qualify for a $154,000 Federal Housing and Home Finance Agency loan that would pay for construction of a village-wide sanitary sewer system.

  — Increasing water-pumping capacity to Rochester, new sewers, wastewater treatment facilities, and three water-main projects were also addressed to provide for a village population that almost doubled to 1,300 persons during the first half of the decade.

Construction of a village sewer system in 1960 was a major infrastructure improvement. The picture, looking east, shows laying a sewer line on East Main Street in front of the IOOF building. The C.E. Miller house is visible on the left. (*Illinois State Journal*, 10 Nov. 1960; Published by GenealogyBank.com, a Division of NewsBank)

  — A $290,000 public-facility loan from HUD in 1969 was awarded to improve village water and sewage systems.

— The influx of new residents stressed not only the existing infrastructure, but at times also the spirit of cooperation between the established families and new citizens. Along with the ongoing improvements to Rochester's water and sewer services rose complaints by some residents at the high rates charged in conjunction with the new services. Justin Taft chaired a community council that was set up to increase cooperation and calm ruffled nerves.

- A violin master revered around the world is today largely unknown in the town of his birth. It was 1887 when Louis Persinger was born in Rochester to railroad agent Amos Wilson and his wife, Susan *(Humphrey)* Persinger. The enormous house in which he was born was owned at that time by a doctor and later by R.S. Twist.

— After his parents moved west, Louis's talents attracted the attention of a Colorado gold-mine owner who became his patron. Persinger's aptitude for the violin was so advanced, even at age 11, that it was decided that he should go to Leipzig, Germany, to study under famous cellist Hans Becker. The renowned conductor, Arthur Nikisch later declared Louis Persinger "one of the most talented violinist that the Leipzig Conservatory had ever had."

— He performed with great success throughout Europe, including appearances in London, Liege, Blankenberghe, Munich, Vienna, Hamburg, and Dresden. Persinger also led the Berlin Philharmonic Orchestra and Brussels Royal Opera Orchestra, and he played for the Philadelphia Orchestra. As a teacher at New York's Juilliard School beginning in 1930, Louis taught upcoming violinists including Yehudi Menuhin, Isaac Stern, and Ruggiero Ricci.

— Louis Persinger, who was also a classical pianist and chess aficionado, was 79 years old when he died in New York City on New Year's Eve, 1966. His survivors included his son Rolf and grandson Brandon Louis Persinger. Brandon has helped keep his grandfather's talents alive by posting several of Persinger's recordings on the internet.

— Although they had lived quite a distance apart, Brandon related in 2015 stories of his grandfather's wonderful sense of humor. Brandon also treasures a number of artifacts passed down by the famous violinist who was born in the small village of Rochester, Illinois.

- The surge of new students to Rochester schools that began in the 1950s grew unabated as students living in new subdivisions stressed the existing school facilities. One result was the need to use United Methodist Church classrooms for some elementary students.

— When the number of high school students increased by 15.1% in 1963, it signaled the need for what became a $525,000 bond issue one year later. The bond issue and an operational tax-rate increase were approved soundly. By January 1967, 10 new classrooms and a combined gymnasium and cafeteria were completed. This enabled kindergarten and sixth-grade classes to return to the elementary school, the youngest students from the Methodist Church and older classes from the junior high. By 1969, however, crowded classrooms were at capacity in all three district buildings, the result of continued annual enrollment increases of 7-10%.

— Tennis courts, financed by a joint effort of the Rochester Woman's Club and the Sears-Roebuck Foundation, were added to the school campus in 1967.

— A popular student activity, the Rochester High School Madrigal Singers, was organized in 1966, led by the district's vocal director, Mrs. Melva Jo Sexton.

— The school board voted in 1969 to submit an initial application to join the Springfield Area Vocational School.

• New and expanding churches also reflected Rochester's growing population. With a membership of 500, the Rochester United Methodist Church held a successful 1960 fund drive for an educational wing to be added to their church at the corner of Main and Walnut Streets. The First Baptist Church of Rochester bought four acres of land on State Street in 1969 for a future church building, and Good Shepherd Lutheran Church along Route 29 was dedicated in 1966.

A new Lutheran Church, at the corner of Camelot Drive and Route 29, is seen under construction in 1965. (*ILLINOIS STATE JOURNAL*, 30 SEP. 1965; PUBLISHED BY GENEALOGYBANK.COM, A DIVISION OF NEWSBANK)

Below: Good Shepherd Lutheran Church was dedicated in 1966. (R. BRUZAN PHOTO)

• Increased traffic also brought, yet again, the need for new township roads and bridges. Route 29 from Rochester to Springfield was upgraded in 1966 to a four-lane highway. Maintenance of a portion of Route 29 that had woven its way through the middle of town for decades was turned over to the village in the spring of 1968, and it officially became part of East Main Street.

— Oak Hill Road from Oak Hills subdivision to the Old Rochester Road was blacktopped in 1965.

— A new 265-foot concrete bridge on Gaule Road across the South Fork River two miles north of Rochester was completed in 1967 at a cost of $258,603.

A new concrete bridge carrying Gaule Road across the South Fork River north of Rochester opened to traffic in 1967, replacing an iron bridge pictured on the right. The old bridge had brought visitors to a spot near Glenwood Park decades ago. (LEFT: R. BRUZAN PHOTO; RIGHT: JAMES A. WOODRUFF COLLECTION, SANGAMON VALLEY COLLECTION, LINCOLN LIBRARY)

- A new Rochester Post Office building on John Street was dedicated May 27, 1962. A speaker's stage and folding chairs were set up in the street for the event, and the high school band provided entertainment. Guests included Carlinville resident U.S. Representative Peter F. Mack, Jr., (D-IL) and Palmer G. Boyle, postal field service officer. Boyle and Rochester Postmaster Earl M. Thomas praised the new structure and modern equipment, predicting that employees would be working "under the best of conditions" and "provide the finest postal service in its history."

The community came together in 1962 to dedicate a new Post Office on John Street. (*ILLINOIS STATE JOURNAL*, 28 MAY 1962; PUBLISHED BY GENEALOGYBANK.COM, A DIVISION OF NEWSBANK)

- The object they saw "was about 25 feet in diameter, with green and white lights blinking very fast, and the object seemed to be moving in a circular motion and making no noise." Mrs. Angelo Gresta attempted to describe the UFO that she and her three children observed in 1966 one mile southwest of Rochester. They estimated that it flew just 100 feet above them and saw it last moving rapidly toward the southwest.

— In a 2015 interview, Diane *(Gresta)* Jarosz, who was 13 years old when she saw the UFO from her house, said she, her siblings, and their mother watched the mysterious object in a field east of Oak Hill Road. She remembers being awestruck, but not at all scared. Instead, today Diane remembers the event as a treasured memory during which they all shared a moment of excitement and fun.

- The Campbell Grain & Lumber Company held a huge sale two weeks after a 1968 fire damaged a large quantity of their warehoused merchandise. A malfunctioning oil burner was blamed for the blaze that the Rochester Fire Department brought under control in just a half hour.

- Fears generated by the Cold War resulted in public awareness of the possible dangers from a nuclear war with Russia. The "dangers of communism" were explained in a "Project Alert" program presented in 1961 at the Rochester High School. Rochester Civil Defense Director Robert Ritterbusch explained later in the decade how supplies for more than 250 people had been stocked in the local elementary school for use in case the building was needed as a fallout shelter. The Sangamon County Civil Defense Agency established a radiological monitoring station at the same building in 1969, one of 57 such locations in Sangamon County.

- Several new businesses became community mainstays for years.
  — The Hayshakers, a 1960s Rochester investment group, developed several parcels along State Street where it meets Route 29. In 1960 one of their buildings became the home of Rochester Lanes, an eight-lane bowling alley and snack bar.
  — Village View shopping center, another Hayshakers structure, had its grand opening in 1961. The stores included Village Variety and Rentschler's Super Market, the latter which had moved from downtown. The Lunt family bought the grocery in 1971.
  — Rochester was not without a newspaper. The weekly *Rochester Herald* that originated in the mid-1940s later became the *Rochester & Lake Springfield Herald*. Earl Wilcoxson purchased that weekly in 1967.

Bowling became an entertainment option in Rochester with the 1960 opening of Rochester Lanes. Located at the corner of Route 29 and State Street, the new eight-lane bowling alley included a snack bar and table service for 36 customers. (ILLINOIS STATE JOURNAL 15 JUNE 1960; PUBLISHED BY GENEALOGYBANK.COM, A DIVISION OF NEWSBANK)

- Howard Behl built a new facility for horse riders in 1961. Located east of what is today Pleasant Lane in Lexington Heights, the new 40x104-foot barn was constructed so that Behl could expand his "equitation classes," better known as classes for the art of horseback riding. Some of his students won ribbons at state- and county-fair horse competitions, including former Rochester resident Barbara (*Watkins*) Wagner, a student of Behl's who still recalls winning horse-show ribbons.

- Rochester citizen Ernie Rentschler reported at least six fish kills on the South Fork River during the first half of 1963. Sulfur from Peabody Coal Company mine-slag refuse combined with rainwater to form sulfuric acid that flowed into the South Fork, polluting the river and killing fish and other river organisms. To combat future pollution, the company set about to cover about 200 acres of refuse with two feet of clay in order to encapsulate the sulfur and prevent its escape into the environment.

- The restricted sight lines for trains approaching Rochester's B&O Railroad crossing at South Walnut Street were identified in 1960 as a hazard to school buses. Based on that finding, the Illinois Commerce Commission ordered that trains stop before entering the crossing. However, because they were more difficult to get moving again, long grain trains were, instead, only required to reduce their speed to 15 miles per hour and not come to a halt.
  — The B&O Railroad replacement bridge over the South Fork River north of Rochester was almost complete when it was extensively damaged by a 1968 fire. Rochester firemen Bob Ramsey and Jerry Moore were part of the crew that fought that blaze with assistance from the Springfield Fire Department. Both men recalled in 2015 that the fire had been caused by a spark from a cutting torch that was being used by construction workers on the bridge. Some news reports mistakenly reported this major story as occurring at Sugar Creek.

A new B&O Railroad bridge under construction across the South Fork River north of Rochester in 1968 sustained an estimated $1 million in damage from a blaze that took the Rochester Fire Department, with help from other firefighters, three hours to bring under control. (*ILLINOIS STATE JOURNAL*, 1 MAY 1968: 1; PUBLISHED BY GENEALOGYBANK.COM, A DIVISION OF NEWSBANK)

Eastbound Baltimore & Ohio trains cross the Sugar Creek trestle in 1963.
These tracks, located northwest of Rochester, were abandoned in 1984.
(WALT PETERS PHOTOS; R.R. WALLIN COLLECTION; USED WITH PERMISSION)

- Two oil fields discovered this decade were named for Black Branch Creek, which flows relatively near both. The Black Branch pool, with an initial production of 14 barrels of oil per day, was discovered about a half mile east of Rochester in 1967. The Black Branch East oil pool, located about 2.5 miles east of Rochester, was discovered in 1969 and produced 101 barrels per day. One state geologist described the East pool as a "pretty good well."

- In an attempt to eliminate Rochester Township property-assessment inequities, a complete reassessment of about 1,700 pieces of property was approved in 1960 and conducted by volunteer deputy assessors. The reassessment led to increased valuation of 311 township properties for an assessed value increase of $65,005.

- Rochester citizens were in the news:
  1962
  — **Wilson Park** was sworn in as Sangamon County supervisor of assessments;

  1965
  — The **Robert Hendrickson family** hosted a Paraguay teen for two weeks as part of the 1965 International Farm Youth Exchange program;

  1966
  — After a 1957 trip to Ireland led to his purchase and breeding of Connemara ponies, **Al Mavis** now had 50 ponies and was president of the American Connemara Pony Society;

  1967
  — Nine-year-old **Michael Fred Sexton** exhibited his toothpick Fort Comanche at the Sangamon County Fair;
  — The spinning wheel talents of **Dorothy Dugger** were described as she demonstrated the great wool spinning wheel at Clayville;

1968
— Rochester High School junior **Richard Alexander** attended the National Youth Conference on the Atom as one of seven outstanding Central Illinois high school students;

1969
— Five-year-old **Angie Cook** continued her battle against the muscular disease arthrogryposis.

- Two new Rochester civic groups were organized in the 1960s, and another celebrated its centennial year.
  — Forty-one charter members of the newly established Rochester Lions Club elected Kester Pollock president in 1965.
  — Named for an area south of Rochester that was a former stage-coach route, the Chicken Bristle Chapter of Questers began meeting in 1969 with 12 members.
  — Rochester Masonic Lodge 635, AF&AM celebrated its 100th anniversary in 1969.

- As the decade neared its end, the community learned that 1964 Rochester High School graduate **Richard Gwinn Thunman** had died during the Vietnam War. Killed in action on January 6, 1969, Lance Corporal Thunman was buried in Oak Ridge Cemetery, where the U.S. Marine Corps conducted graveside military services. He has been remembered publicly by comrades as a fun-loving man and a proud Marine.

Calligrapher and Rochester Masonic Lodge member Bud McCafferty created an artistic list of all past masters of Rochester Masonic Lodge 635 from 1869 to the present. Displayed at the lodge on East Main Street and in the appendix of this book, the list contains 150 names that took McCafferty an estimated 50 hours to record. (R. BRUZAN PHOTO)

- Other notable Rochester deaths included one of the village's oldest residents. Born in Cornwall, England, and a Rochester resident since he was 11, **Thomas Bennett** was 91 when he died in 1962.
  — Dr. Lyman Wright, formerly a student of Rochester schools, died in 1962. He had practiced medicine in Rochester, Divernon, and Springfield.
  — Richard O. Coe, who was born in the R.H. Coe house on West Main Street, died in 1966. He had been a Rochester State Bank cashier and supervisor of the Sangamon County Office of Plats and Surveys.

Above: Joe Bonefeste of Springfield won several races at Drag City in this 1966 Chevelle Supersport. (COURTESY OF JOE BONEFESTE; USED WITH PERMISSION)

Left: Drag City, originally named Pleasant Grove Drag Strip, was located in Rochester Township just west of the South Fork River along Route 29. Chuck Weyant and Carroll Heissinger, Sr., created the one-eighth-mile strip. (POSTER COURTESY OF JERRY CAMPBELL; R. BRUZAN PHOTO)

Center: Long-time Rochester resident Jerry Campbell proudly displays two trophies he won at Drag City during the 1960s. (R. BRUZAN PHOTO)

- Joe Bonefeste of Springfield remembers well the noise, dust, excitement, and thrill of winning several first-place trophies with his 1966 Chevelle Supersport at Drag City, the racing strip south of Route 29 and west of the South Fork River. This one-eighth mile racing track, initially known as Pleasant Grove Drag Strip, was built in 1960 by Carroll Heissinger, Sr. Affiliated with the American Hot Rod Association, the drag strip featured well-attended races as it drew big-name dragsters and top drivers for years. After the strip closed in 1971, Drag City pavement was removed and recycled as landfill for Jostes Garage in Rochester. The land soon reverted to a productive farm field.

- New seven-digit telephone numbers made their debut in Rochester in 1960, and direct distance dialing made its Rochester appearance two years later. At last, long-distance calls from Rochester were made by dialing 1 followed by an area code and the seven-digit phone number. Before completing their call, however, callers had to provide their number to the operator.

- Rochester citizens vied for public office beyond the village.
  — In a 1962 political version of dominos, Ernest Rentschler was named Rochester Township clerk, replacing Gerald Abshire, who succeeded Justin Taft as Rochester Township supervisor when Taft was elected probate clerk of the Circuit Court.
  — Taft went on to win the 1968 state-wide election for clerk of the Illinois Supreme Court. Meeting President Richard Nixon and Taft's tour of Washington, DC are described in his 2004 book As I Saw It.
  — Rochester born and educated, Maurice Scott graduated with a law degree from the Lincoln College of Law and was elected in 1969 as a Constitutional Convention delegate.

• A hundred years after Rochester was incorporated in 1869 with Munson Carter as the first village president, the village celebrated its centennial with a three-day gala. Leo Coplea led the centennial celebration committee that put in motion a multi-faceted Fourth of July weekend event.

— The opening parade down East Main Street led to the school grounds, where activities for all ages took place. They included an antique show, art show, dinners, little league all-star game, craft show, soap-box derby, model airplane exhibit, variety talent show, teen dance, community worship service, beard-judging contest, fashion show, ice cream social, garden-tractor pull, and fireworks.

— Centennial pennants, lapel buttons, bumper stickers, and carnival rides were available during the celebration. One of the celebration's highlights was Congressman Paul Findley's dedication of a military memorial at the Main Street-Walnut Street triangle.

Rochester's 1969 centennial celebration included a parade, art show, dinner, antique show, craft show, soap-box derby, teen dance, and fireworks. Centennial plates depicting early Rochester buildings and a brief Rochester history were available for purchase. (COURTESY OF LAURA WELCH AND ROCHESTER CHRISTIAN CHURCH; R. BRUZAN PHOTO)

One highlight of Rochester's centennial celebration was the music-based reunion of Rochester's elementary school class of 1917. They were: John Taft, Lyman Campbell, Ted Coe, Gilson Taft, Eva (Steinhouer) Jones, Vernon Woodruff, Elma (Eggleston) Sargent, Loren Taft, Anna May (Nunes) Turley, and Hazel (Jones) Park. Their rehearsal took place in their former school, which was at this time the Rochester Masonic Temple. (COURTESY OF KAREN ALEXANDER)

The largely abandoned Rochester depot on South Walnut Street was photographed in January 1967. (WALT PETERS PHOTO; R.R. WALLIN COLLECTION; USED WITH PERMISSION)

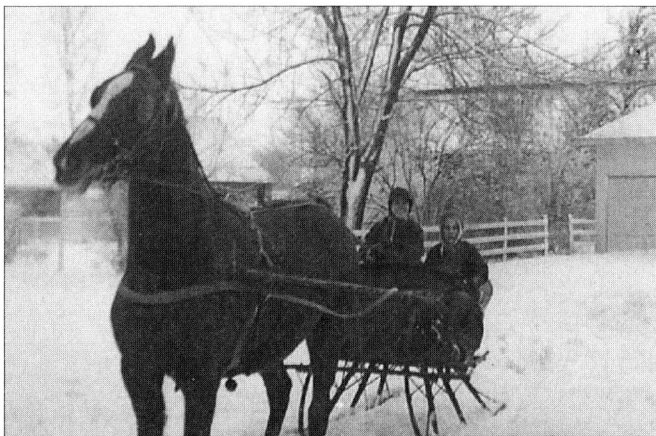

The Park family enjoyed a January 1962 sleigh ride in snowy downtown Rochester. As of 2017, the sleigh is in storage and awaits another snowy winter for its next outing. (COURTESY OF GREG PARK)

Above: Mottarville School served the small community of Mottarville in 1918. Mottarville was located on Chicken Bristle Road south of Rochester. (COURTESY OF COMPASS POINT PRODUCTIONS; FARM PROGRESS COMPANIES)

Left: The same one-room Mottarville School stood almost alone on the Illinois prairie in 1962. (BILL WALDMIRE PHOTO; USED WITH PERMISSION)

INAUGURATION PARADE
WASHINGTON, DC

Several village residents represented Rochester at the 1977 inauguration of President Jimmy Carter in Washington, DC. Al Mavis, riding in front of the flag, was one of several Rochester members of the 7th Illinois Cavalry Mounted Patrol (Reactivated) who rode in the inaugural parade down Pennsylvania Ave. (PHOTO BY CURT MAVIS; USED WITH PERMISSION)

1970s

Work began in 1974 on what became the scenic multi-use Community Park on West Main Street.
(R. BRUZAN PHOTO)

1970s Timeline ...

1970	Population: 1,657
1971	New Rochester firehouse was built at 125 East Main Street
	— MCI tower, Rochester's tallest structure, was erected near Route 29 and State Street
1972	Village offices relocated to 128 North John Street
1973	Rochester train station closed
	— First Baptist Church was built on State Street
	— Village population 1,879 according to a special census
1974	Rochester's first stoplight was installed at Route 29 and West Main Street
	— Rochester Rescue Squad organized
1975	*Rochester Times* began publication February 7
	— Ramblewood subdivision began offering lots for sale southeast of the village
1976	Rochester State Bank moved from Main Street to 133 North John Street

— New library was added to the existing high school
— Helen *(Magill)* Duffey and the Chicken Bristle Chapter of Questers prepared the slide program *Rochester – Yesterday and Today* as part of the nation's bicentennial
— New Masonic Temple was built at 121 East Main Street
— Park Forest Hundred annexed to the village
— Camelot subdivision was platted

1977   History of an Orange Judd home was published in *Illinois Times*
1978   Cottonwood Estates subdivision was platted
1979   Rochester Community Park on West Main Street was first dedicated during the July 4th celebration
— Bike path was built along West Main Street to Community Park
— Church of St. Jude was dedicated on South Walnut Street
— Rochester Station complex was built at South Walnut and Route 29

1970s Storylines...

- The creation of new subdivisions in the 1960s and 1970s continued to stress Rochester's existing services. As a result, the community incurred significant expenses for water and sewer, as well as for police, fire, and rescue squads. A rising population clamored for parks, more sidewalks, and improved streets. New municipal buildings, churches, and schools were built to accommodate the community's needs.

- Adopted in 1967, Rochester's first Comprehensive Plan was relied on throughout this decade as new subdivisions were platted and annexed to the village. The plan document, along with subsequent revisions adopted in the 1970s, were seen by the village board more as development guidelines than rigid rules.
  — Zoning classifications in the plan described permitted land uses.
  — Ordinances related to planned subdivisions including Park Forest Hundred (1976), Camelot (1971), and Cottonwood Estates (1978) were of increasing concern because of the associated expenses to provide sewers, water, lighting, and sidewalks.
  — A related ordinance requiring formal "inspection during construction of commercial buildings" was adopted in 1978. The village board also voiced its intent to enforce the existing requirements that building permits be obtained prior to the start of residential or commercial construction.
  — New laws even impacted pets. Rochester citizens who allowed their dogs to roam freely in violation of a 1973 leash law were subject to fines as high as $100 in addition to impoundment and kennel boarding fees.

- Water shortages, low water pressure, boil orders, fines for watering lawns and gardens, along with an 80% jump in water bills plagued residents.
  — In August 1972, Rochester's increasing water needs combined with a water-main leak under Lake Springfield to drain Rochester's water tank, resulting in low water pressure throughout the village. It happened again a month later. And yet again that November. Besides repairs to Springfield's City Water Light and Power (CWLP) distribution system, part of the solution was to refill the tower using a newer 10-inch emergency water main.
  — After unsuccessful attempts to renegotiate the 30-year CWLP water contract signed with the village in 1960, in 1976 the Springfield utility prohibited use of the 10-inch water main until a new contract was approved, forcing water-usage restrictions in Rochester. A new contract, signed in 1977, resulted in monthly increases of 80% to village water customers. An additional increase was added in order to balance the village's water department budget. Because of the dramatic increase, one Rochester trustee voted against the contract and recommended that Rochester develop its own water supply. This possibility was given serious consideration 21 years later.

- After the Illinois Environmental Protection Agency detected pollution in Black Branch Creek in 1971, Rochester was forced to sell $315,000 in water and sewage revenue bonds to improve sewage treatment and water systems. A new water-supply main and a new sewage treatment system of three ponds west of Rochester were built. The ponds were designed to avoid overloading existing sewage ponds located on the north edge of the village and to accommodate residents of the new subdivisions. In a preview of the future, a 1972 survey of Oak Hills residents revealed their desire to abandon their septic tanks in favor of attaching to Rochester's sanitary sewers.

- As the nation became increasingly familiar with the term "ecology" and the practices of recycling during the decade, Rochester Woman's Club members collected newspapers, magazines, glass, and other items at a Salvation Army truck that parked monthly in front of Lunt's grocery store.

- The Woman's Club also sponsored an Energy Fair in 1979 as a way of inform-ing the community about environmental interests of the decade. The fair in-cluded student and adult displays, talks, and additional activities both inside and outside of the Rochester Middle School. Student displays were side by side information from 21 other groups such as the Internal Revenue Service and Prairie Kaverns. Energy commercials by the Enerjets, a car running on 100% alcohol, and talks about "Energy in the Future," and "How I Made My Home More Energy Efficient" were among the topics designed to appeal to all ages.

• As Rochester grew, road improvements to the east and west became necessary. At just 16-feet wide, Buckhart Road east from Rochester was so narrow that when school buses and gravel trucks met along the road, both were forced to drive partially off the pavement. The five-mile stretch between the two communities was widened by 6 feet in 1974, and the bridge over Buckhart Creek was expanded to 32 feet.

— The Rochester Village Board awarded contracts in 1975 to improve West Main Street. That was only one portion of a complete project that stretched from East Lake Shore Drive to Route 29 in Rochester. The pavement was widened to 24 feet, and new storm sewers, curbs, and gutters were installed. The improvement also widened the West Main curve to improve safety and avoid squeezing beneath the existing Baltimore & Ohio Railroad trestle at Route 29. It was designed in such a way as to preserve most of the existing front-yard vegetation in front of the historic R.H. Coe house.

• As more police calls went unanswered during the early 1970s, Rochester's police coverage grew from one man working four hours a day to 24-hour protection a few years later. The village board hired a full-time and a part-time officer in 1972 and in 1974 organized a volunteer force of four reserve officers who responded to emergencies and other calls for extra police protection. A second full-time policeman was added in 1976 and three more were hired in 1978 to complete around-the-clock protection. The board noted this was not because of increased crime, but rather in response to

Rochester's police force members in 1975 were, from left: Mervin Spurgeon, Sam Gresham, Carl Jiannoni, Police Chief Henry " Hank" Bregenhorn, Bob Rentschler, and Mitch Murdock. (*ROCHESTER TIMES*, MAR. 7, 1975: 1; USED WITH PERMISSION)

the growing population. A part-time officer was hired in 1979 who also served as dog catcher to enforce Rochester's leash laws.

• A 1976 liquor license request by G and K Lanes led the village board to research whether they had the legal right to issue liquor licenses without the topic being brought to a vote of village residents. Their complicated findings first determined that a 1908 village ordinance set fees for liquor licenses. They then found that citizens voted the township, though not necessarily the village, dry in 1931. However, the village was definitively voted dry by a three-to-one margin in a 1941 referendum. Although several businesses attempted in 1979 to bring the issue to Rochester voters again, it failed because their petition lacked the required 25% of the village's registered voters, and it was not filed in time to meet state statutes. As a result, Rochester remained a dry town and no liquor licenses were issued.

The Rochester Fire Protection District station moved from its John Street location to 125 East Main in 1971. (COURTESY OF ROCHESTER FIRE PROTECTION DISTRICT AND MIKE WEAVER; USED WITH PERMISSION)

- The building at 128 North John Street had functioned since 1948 as a fire station with American Legion Post 274 upstairs. However, once the fire department moved to a new home on East Main Street, its former building became Rochester's village offices in late 1972. Those offices had previously been in the Town Hall on Main Street. The village board leased the former fire station, which they also remodeled, assisted by members of the American Legion and Rochester Rescue Squad.

- The agricultural industry that supported Rochester Township since its settlement, continued to grow food for the nation and provide jobs throughout the township.

— The local Soil and Water Conservation District awarded the Robert Hendrickson family their designation as 1972 Conservation Family of the Year for Sangamon County. The award criteria included land use, conservation efforts, community service, and farm beautification.

— The Future Farmers of America later recognized the Hendrickson's son David as one of the best young farmers in the nation, naming him an American Farmer in 1978. Active in Rochester High School's Future Farmers of America chapter, David had raised hogs since grade school and was also farming 350 acres by the time the award was presented.

— The public was invited to witness Rochester Township's vibrant farming community when two farms were opened for a tour in 1974.

Rochester farmer David Hendrickson was recognized by the Future Farmers of America in 1978 as one of the best young farmers in the United States. The award was announced at the national FFA convention in Kansas City. (STATE JOURNAL-REGISTER 17 NOV. 1978: 88; PUBLISHED BY GENEALOGYBANK.COM, A DIVISION OF NEWSBANK)

Visitors were welcome at Fred and Helen Poffenberger's hog operation, which annually produced both hogs and crops, and Robert and Jane Fairchild's grain farm to witness a variety of modern farm equipment.

- Students in a Springfield high school biology lab really enjoyed Spike, a six-foot-long boa constrictor who was the class pet. At one point, however, attempts to feed Spike a live baby chick from the local hatchery repeatedly failed. The problem was not with the snake, which would resume eating once his regular shedding period was over. The problem was with the cute little chick that continued to grow during that month to become a hen much too large for Spike to eat.

Rochester High School's chapter of Future Farmers of America was popular for decades in this largely rural community. FFA members gathered annually to cook up a pancake-and-sausage breakfast for the school's faculty. Taken in 1976, this photo shows the enthusiastic chefs busy in the Methodist Church kitchen. (*ROCHESTER TIMES*, 27 FEB. 1976; USED WITH PERMISSION)

— The biology teacher, who in 1971 had just moved into his Rochester home, decided it was time to relocate the chicken. His first stop was at the farm home of Marlene Spurgeon. She struggled to understand why a stranger wanted to present her with a chicken that was in his car. She suggested that perhaps the Jostes family, who raised chickens, would accept the hen. Dave Jostes gladly accepted the feathered gift.

— Years later, the teacher went to pick up his car that had been repaired at the Jostes Garage and heard the rest of the story. Dave proceeded to tell him about someone who had years ago donated a chicken to his family. Not only had the hen scratched his wife, Fay, who still had a scar, but the chicken had been the toughest one he had ever eaten. Not sure what to say, the teacher got into his repaired auto and slowly drove away. (Note: Names have not been change to protect the innocent. The teacher was one of the authors of this book.)

- Rochester schools were on the forefront of experiencing the area's growing pains.

— Overcrowded classrooms and buses led in 1970 to the creation of elementary classrooms in the basement and a 1972 decision limiting bus riders to students living more than 1.5 miles from the school campus.

— School board members investigated the possibility of year-around school as a way to address school crowding, but dismissed the option because the high school population was not large enough to support that approach.

— It was 1970 when the Rochester School District bought 25 acres of land north of the high school. Envisioned at that time as the site of future buildings and an athletic track, it would indeed become soccer and football fields, after those sports were introduced.

— A successful 1973 bond referendum resulted in construction of a new high school, addition of four classrooms to what was then the junior high, and a broad range of remodeling and safety-related improvements throughout the existing buildings.

- Superintendent Jack K. Taylor, hired in 1975, joined a district that had mushroomed 300% in just 20 years. He soon faced a school budget deficit of $150,000. The school board sought passage of an operational tax rate increase in 1976 to address the deficit. Voters rejected it by a two-to-one margin, leading to budget cuts and teacher layoffs.

— In a 2017 interview, Taylor recalled that when he began his Rochester tenure, the school district lacked an active athletic booster organization and parent-teacher organization. He suggested that this was, in part, because there were so many new families without deep roots in the community. Beginning to build on the district's history and increasing community involvement increased voter awareness of the district's needs.

— Recognizing the drastic nature of the district's finances, voters approved a subsequent November 1977 tax rate referendum by 1,012 to 721, and the board began to restore their previous budget cuts.

- After the school district discontinued busing students within 1.5 miles of the campus, concerns grew over the safety of youngsters crossing Route 29 in front of the school campus. After 50 residents attended a 1972 village board meeting to support increased safety, flashing yellow caution lights were installed. Two years later, despite the $33,200 cost, the village's first traffic signals were installed at the corner of Walnut Street and Route 29. Some village officials opposed the expense, reasoning that students would cross the road wherever they pleased and predicting that a crossing guard would also be needed.

Rochester's first stop lights were installed in 1974 at the intersection of Route 29 and West Main Street. The original Rochester stop light, pictured here, is in a private collection.
(R. BRUZAN PHOTO)

- The ground was scraped and molded by huge machinery in 1978, as Rochester Recreation Advisory Board President Walt Ebel predicted enthusiastically that the land underfoot was "going to be a lovely park." Park designer Richard Williams explained that the village board wanted more than just a "pure baseball park or pure something else." The goal of a "family-oriented city park" was realized when 16 acres of land west of the cemetery, offered by Gail Wanless Realtors in 1972, was transformed into Community Park.

Among the many activities of Rochester's Summer Recreation Program was a trip to Henson Robinson Zoo, where visitors met animals from around the world. (*ROCHESTER TIMES*, 24 JUNE 1977; USED WITH PERMISSION)

— The park was largely completed by volunteers. What became a scenic and well-used area included a fishing pond, shelter, children's playground, ball diamonds, restrooms, bike path, and soccer fields.

— The Rochester Village Board had established the Recreation Advisory Board in 1974 to make recommendations regarding parks, libraries, community centers, and recreation centers.

— News articles listed the park's dedication first during the 1979 July 4th celebration. More extensive dedication activities took place the following June.

• A bike path proposal made to the village board in 1977 by the Rochester Woman's Club became a reality two years later. The bike path was recommended along the north side of West Main Street from what was then the west edge of the village to the new park entrance. It was, however, land that had

The Rochester Woman's Club sponsored a 1977 bike-a-thon to raise funds toward construction of a bike path along West Main Street. Pictured from left: Ed Dellert, Kay Stahr, and Ralph Metcalf. (*ROCHESTER TIMES*, 4 Nov. 1977; USED WITH PERMISSION)

to be annexed before the village would agree to assume liability associated with the path. A $29,000 matching grant through the federal Land and Water Conservation Fund Program, supplemented by more than $3,000 generated during the Woman's Club-sponsored bike-a-thon, helped fund the project. The completed bike path was dedicated in October 1979.

- Dubbed "The Wheel Thing" the October bike-a-thon attracted dozens of riders ages 6 to 16 who solicited pledges of at least 25 cents per mile to ride as far as 20 miles for the event. Jeff Higgins, age 12, topped all money earners with almost $260 in pledges, while 9-year-old Jeff Meyer topped the younger riders with $105 in pledges. Each boy won a new bicycle for his efforts.

- Although the new bike path helped solve some pedestrian-safety concerns, 144 families petitioned the village board in 1978 requesting a crossing guard at the Route 29 stoplights. One month later the board approved hiring a crossing guard on a trial basis for before- and after-school duty. Board members also responded to another 1978 petition requesting a sidewalk between Camelot subdivision and the school campus. Camelot residents pledged $1,800 toward that concrete connection located north of the Good Shepherd Lutheran Church.

- In part, crime control in Rochester included the use of radar equipment acquired in 1971 as a way of discouraging would-be speeders. As the radar was tried out along Route 29 near the school, 40 violations were recorded in just 58 minutes.
  — A 1979 prank by two Rochester High School seniors caused an hour-long student evacuation after the boys ignited a smoke bomb in a restroom. The boys were expelled for the rest of the school year, and each was fined $230 plus restitution.
  — Three teens were arrested by Sangamon County sheriff's deputies in 1976 for burglary and criminal damage to property at the Rochester High School library. Damages totaled $8,000-$10,000 when the boys overturned book shelves and furniture, then emptied a fire extinguisher over the debris.

- Local accidents made the news.
  — A low-hanging branch, snagged by a rear tractor tire in 1971, was pulled across a local farmer, crushing him against the tractor's steering wheel.
  — A 10-year-old Rochester boy drowned in 1979 after falling from a train trestle into a swollen creek while he was fishing with friends. His companions tried in vain to rescue him.
  — One snowmobile driver fell from his vehicle in 1979 and was run over by a companion on a following vehicle. He was treated for cuts and a broken leg, but survived.

Above: Rochester Rescue Squad members pictured in 1979 are, back from left: Steve Tice, Harold Lundberg, Junior Grieme, Mark Adams, and Terry Day; front from left: Dick Rentschler, Phil Spindel, Mike Weaver, Mark Kother, and Mark Poffenberger. (COURTESY OF ROCHESTER FIRE PROTECTION DISTRICT AND MIKE WEAVER; USED WITH PERMISSION)
Right: Training sessions were held to prepare Rescue Squad members to deal with emergencies. Pictured, front from left: Mark Poffenberger, Michael Weaver, Terry Day, and Martin Fairchild; standing from left: Harold Lundberg, Mark Ritterbusch, Bob Rentschler, Dick Rentschler, Ted Clark, and Harry Grieme, Jr. (ROCHESTER TIMES, 2 MAY 1975; USED WITH PERMISSION)

- The Rochester Emergency-Rescue Squad, with village board approval to organize in 1974, had grown from six volunteers to sixteen by 1978. By then the squad had acquired three government-surplus vehicles and additional equipment worth more than $25,000. All volunteers were trained in cardiopulmonary resuscitation and injury management, while most earned advanced certifications. Supported by modest village and township funding, the squad responded to a variety of calls, including the 1978 ice-storm emergency, a 1977 tornado touchdown near Chatham, and searches for drowning victims. It participated in joint disaster drills with the Rochester fire and police departments. The unit was one of three in Sangamon County certified by the state Emergency Services and Disaster Agency (ESDA) and served throughout the fire-protection district.

- When Rochester Police officer Wayne Baker answered a 1979 call for help, he was unaware that he and the Rochester Rescue Squad would be delivering a baby. Judy Adams had gone into labor at home as she and her husband, John, prepared to go to the hospital. After the delivery, the couple and their new-born daughter were whisked to St. Johns Hospital for recovery.

- A variety of businesses appeared in the 1970s:

  — The first of two buildings for Rochester Station opened in late 1978 and included offices for doctor, dental, engineering, and law services, the Illinois Registered Land Surveyors Association headquarters, a restaurant, and shops specializing in gifts, quilting, and art framing.

Rochester Station, a retail and office complex at the southwest corner of Illinois Route 29 and South Walnut Street, has been remodeled since it was completed in 1979. (R. BRUZAN PHOTO)

  — The remodeled Country True Value hardware store celebrated its grand opening in 1976 at 129 South John Street.

  — After more than 70 years on East Main Street, Rochester State Bank built a new facility at the corner of North John and Mill Streets in 1975.

Rochester State Bank relocated in 1976 from its original site on East Main Street to its new location on the southwest corner of John and Mill Streets. (R. BRUZAN PHOTO)

  — Joe's Italian Village opened in 1976 in the former Richardson store on East Main Street and allowed customers to bring their own adult beverages to enjoy during dinner in "dry" Rochester.

  — First Federal Savings and Loan Association broke ground in 1975 for its new building at 441 State Street.

  — Jostes Garage was established in 1977 at 305 East Main Street north of an existing car wash.

TUESDAY NIGHT SPECIAL!
BAKED LASAGNA 2^{50}
REG. PRICE $3.35

WEDNESDAY NIGHT SPECIAL!
HOMEMADE RAVIOLI
REG. PRICE $3.15 2^{50}
EACH SPECIAL INCLUDES
SALAD, GARLIC BREAD & LARGE DRINK

Joe's **ITALIAN VILLAGE**
ROCHESTER, ILL.
2 BLOCKS NORTH OF STOPLIGHT
OPEN 4:30 — CLOSED MONDAY
YOUR HOSTS: JOE & CONNIE SAPUTO   637-7377

Joe's Italian Village, a popular Rochester eatery, was located in the Richardson building on the northwest corner of East Main and John Streets. Because Rochester was a dry town, wine was not sold in the restaurant, but customers were permitted to "bring their own bottle." The restaurant, opened in 1976 by Joe and Connie Saputo, was sold and closed in the 1980s. (STATE JOURNAL-REGISTER, 14 SEP. 1977: 53; PUBLISHED BY GENEALOGYBANK.COM, A DIVISION OF NEWSBANK)

Although they are well speckled with paint, artists Wendy Jostes and Cindy McCoy look as happy as the mural they painted at Jostes Car Wash in 1978. (LEFT: R. BRUZAN PHOTO; RIGHT: COURTESY·OF DAVE AND FAY JOSTES)

- With the nation's bicentennial in 1976, Rochester Grade School students celebrated with a series of monthly activities.

  — Learning to vote was the goal of one such event during which the grade schoolers decided which of three locations would be the site for planting a white oak "Liberty Tree." The exercise included learning about procedures at the polls and the reasons why voting is important.

  — Fifth-grade art students embroidered patriotic designs and U.S. Presidents' names on individual squares that were bordered with plain fabric and stitched into an 84x96-inch quilt and two pillows. These items were then delivered to President Gerald Ford by local Congressman Paul Findley. The President sent a thank you to their teacher, David Behymer, in which he said, ". . . I deeply appreciate the time and effort your students devoted to this symbolically designed remembrance." Ford took the

As part of their involvement in celebrating the nation's 200th birthday, the Rochester Woman's Club presented a bicentennial flag to village officials. (ROCHESTER TIMES, 19 SEP. 1976; USED WITH PERMISSION)

U.S. Rep. Paul Findley (left) is pictured delivering a bicentennial quilt to President Gerald Ford in the Oval Office. Rochester fifth graders made this gift under the direction of Rochester Elementary School art instructor David Behymer. (ROCHESTER TIMES, 1 OCT. 1976; USED WITH PERMISSION)

quilt when he left office, and it was later seen at his presidential museum in Battle Creek, MI.

- Dorothy J. Ogilvie, wife of Governor Richard B. Ogilvie, gave a dedication address during the July 3, 1971, celebration of the flag and flagpole at Rochester's new fire station. The flag had flown over the United States Capitol. The flagpole was recovered by Rochester Mayor Cecil Hyatt from the grounds of the governor's mansion, which was undergoing renovations. Others at the celebration included Illinois Rep. Paul Findley, Supreme Court Clerk Justin Taft, Circuit Judge Harvey Beam, and Sangamon County Sheriff Hugh Campbell. The Springfield Falcon Drum and Bugle Corps provided music.

Standing with Rochester's newest fire truck at the new fire station in 1978 are, from left: Wayne Beck, Jerry Moore, and Bob Ramsey. The bright yellow vehicle stood out at any emergency call or parade. (COURTESY OF ROCHESTER FIRE PROTECTION DISTRICT AND MIKE WEAVER; USED WITH PERMISSION)

- The fears of some village residents that an oil well was being drilled within the village limits were calmed when they learned in 1971 that Rochester's newest structure was being built for microwave transmission. The 180-foot-high computer-relay station was erected west of Black Branch Creek and north of Route 29. Planned as one of a several such towers between Chicago and St. Louis, its successor continues in 2017 to be Rochester's tallest structure.

- Wind and ice caused significant damages.
  — A 1975 tornado touched down east of Rochester. Clarence Coe's farm lost three storage bins, and Clarence's neighbor Charles Fairchild lost his porch roof. Although damages totaled about $8,000, no one was injured.
  — It was known as the "Easter ice storm" because it arrived on Good Friday, 1978. The widespread ice devastated 24 Central Illinois counties, which

Rochester's tallest structure, the microwave transmission tower near State Street and Route 29, stood 180 feet tall when it was built in 1971. That was increased to 342 feet high in 1984. The tower is owned by the American Tower Corporation. (COURTESY OF NINA DUGGER; P. BRUZAN PHOTO)

were declared disaster areas with damages totaling $15–$20 million. Rochester residents endured five to seven days without electricity as they repeatedly heard the unsettling sounds resembling rifle reports when huge limbs crashed to the ground throughout that period. Some rural areas lost power for up to four weeks.

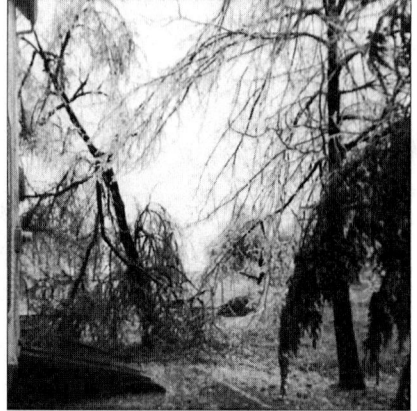

Twenty-four Central Illinois counties were declared disaster areas as a result of the Good Friday ice storm in 1978. These Rochester photos were taken on East Main Street. (P. BRUZAN PHOTO)

- Concerns for student safety during physical education classes were the focus of one 1978 Rochester School Board meeting. The unique use of a trampoline in PE classes concerned some board members, who recognized the potential for serious student injury. Former PE teacher Robin Taft recalled in 2016, "most students loved using the trampoline." She explained that students were not required to use it, spotters were placed on all four sides for safety, and no serious injuries ever occurred during those classes. Taft added, "students were disappointed when the administration finally removed it in about 1980 because of liability."

- Rochester's rising population led to major increases in local church memberships. Many of the new or enlarged churches were completed with significant labor from their respective congregants:
  — The existing Christian Church added a two-story education building in 1970 and broke ground just nine years later for a sanctuary auditorium with seating for more than 400.
  — After organizing as a Rochester mission in 1972, the Rochester First Baptist congregation built a church on Vernon Drive the following year. Even as the new 4,500-square-foot sanctuary and education building were under construction, plans were also being made for a future auditorium and two-story education building.

A Baptist mission church in Rochester began worship in 1965, and four acres of land on Vernon Drive were purchased in 1967 for a future church site. With 48 charter members and the mission church organized as the Rochester Baptist Church, construction plans moved forward. The education wing and sanctuary were dedicated in 1975. (R. BRUZAN PHOTO)

— The Springfield Diocese granted permission in 1973 for Rochester Catholics to form a mission church. After Maurice, Thomas, and Robert Scott donated three acres of land on South Walnut Street, ground was broken for a church in 1976. The Church of St. Jude, designed to serve as a multi-purpose building, and a rectory were completed and dedicated in 1979.

Plans for a Catholic parish began with a mission church in 1973, with selection of a South Walnut Street site two years later. Thomas, Robert, and Maurice Scott donated three acres and sold another five acres of land for the new church. Many of the 75 registered Catholic families physically helped to build the Church of St. Jude, which was dedicated in 1979. (R. BRUZAN PHOTOS)

Standing in a farm field on South Walnut Street at the Church of St. Jude site are, from left: Maurice Scott, Rev. Henry F. Kozak, Tom Scott, and Robert Scott. In memory of their parents, the Scotts donated three acres of land upon which the new church was to be built. (COURTESY OF BARBARA SCOGGINS, CHURCH OF ST. JUDE; STATE JOURNAL-REGISTER, 31 MAY 1976)

The Masonic Temple on East Main Street, previously the Rochester School, is shown just prior to its July 1975 demolition. (*ROCHESTER TIMES*, JULY 4, 1975: 1; USED WITH PERMISSION)

Rochester's Masonic Lodge moved into their new Temple on East Main Street in 1976. (R. BRUZAN PHOTO)

Roy Brunk, the oldest living past master of Rochester Lodge No. 635 AF&AM drove the last nail of the new Temple's exterior framing in 1976. Brunk used a four-inch nail cut from the old temple and drove it behind where the cornerstone would be set. Building committee members present for the event were, from left: Herb Carter, Cecil Hyatt, Gil Easley, Delbert Taft, Stan Shutt, John Rassmussen, Roy Brunk, Floyd Starr, Leonard Siddens, Mike Sexton, Harry Smith, and Carroll Bowersock. (*ROCHESTER TIMES*, 14 MAY 1976: 1; USED WITH PERMISSION)

- The Rochester Lions Club, which often took charge of planning the village's annual July 4th celebration, chose an old-fashioned theme for 1978. In addition to the parade, activities included a softball tournament, horseshoes, garden-tractor pull, children's games, model-airplane show, and a fire-department water fight. A pig roast, old-time movie show, and fireworks rounded out the day's entertainment with refreshments advertised at old-fashioned prices.

- Insects were an unusual topic during a September 1973 school board meeting. Board members gave Superintendent A.B. Miller approval to get bids for termite control in the junior and senior high schools. The biology lab had reportedly sustained insect damage, and the hungry pests had also chewed through a notebook in a student's locker.

- A 1973 leak in one of Rochester's three new sewage treatment ponds was stopped by spreading a chemical developed to sink and coat the pond bottom. At about the same time, a second treatment pond was assaulted by muskrats. An extermination company was called to get rid of the rodents.

- Seeking adequate maintenance funding in 1973, the Rochester Cemetery Society asked Rochester Township to take over cemetery operations. The five-member Society Board requested the change so that tax money levied by the township could be directed toward cemetery care and operations. Society secretary Justin Taft commented that the goal was that "a nice cemetery be provided for our community." The township was also approached with an opportunity to buy seven additional acres of ground to expand the cemetery that had seen its first burial in 1820.

The *Rochester Times* began serving the community on February 7, 1975. Editor and publisher Joe Michelich of Auburn established the new publication. In 1975, South County Publications also provided newspapers for Chatham, Divernon, Auburn, and Pawnee. (*ROCHESTER TIMES*, 7 FEB. 1975: 1; USED WITH PERMISSION)

- Rochester citizens made the news:
  1970
  — **Maurice Scott** was elected to serve as a delegate to the Illinois Constitution Convention.
  — **Alvin Mavis** was named to the U.S. Department of Agriculture's Farmers Home Administration State Advisory Committee.

  1971
  — **James Earl Bell**, who had been president of Rochester State Bank since 1944 and a former mayor of Rochester for eight years, died. He was a charter member of the Springfield Ansar Shriners in 1915 and was a Master Mason for 50 years.

— **L. Forrest Mattingley** was elected president of Navajo Freight Lines of Denver.

1972

— The Central Illinois Chapter of the American Society of Certified Engineering Technicians named **Orville "Bud" McCafferty** its Engineering Technician of the Year.

— Rochester High School graduate **James R. Taft** earned his silver wings from the Air Force.

1973

— The metallurgical research work of engineer **Richard V. Turley** was detailed in a news article. A Rochester High graduate, Turley worked on aircraft development for McDonnell-Douglas Corporation in Long Beach, CA.

1975

— Rochester High graduate **Dana Ross** was elected president of the Illinois Society Children of the American Revolution. She was elected in later years to serve as treasurer and second vice president of the national society.

1977

— **Fred** and **Ada** *(Denkert)* **Braner** celebrated their 60th wedding anniversary in April. Moving to Rochester in 1917, the couple's parents were German immigrants.

— **L. Kent** and **La-Vergne** *(Hutchinson)* **Kyes** observed their 53rd anniversary in December, about 40 years after moving to Rochester.

1978

— **Edith** *(Miller)* **Fairchild** died at age 102, having been recognized earlier as Rochester's oldest resident. One of her grandfathers, Christian Miller, had travelled by covered wagon from Virginia to settle in this area in the 1830s.

1979

— **W.W. Dugger** received Rochester Lions Club's first community service award.

— **Kathleen** (Kitty) **Kelly** was honored for four years of work with the village-sponsored summer recreation program.

• The Bailey family reunion of 1972 marked the 60th annual gathering. Members of

At 101, Edith Fairchild was Rochester's oldest citizen in 1976. She was a descendant of Christian Miller, who settled in Rochester Township in 1835. (*ROCHESTER TIMES*, 12 Nov. 1976; USED WITH PERMISSION)

the extended Bailey family attending the reunions from Rochester included the Bennett, Woodruff, Chandler, Taft, Crockett, Burton, and Jostes families. It was reported that only about 30 attended the first Bailey reunion in 1912, but more than 70 enjoyed the opportunity to share family stories by 1952. The Bailey reunions continue, with the most recent family celebration held in July 2017.

- Ray, Pam, and Kevin Bruzan moved into their faded-pink Rochester house at the corner of East Main and Oak Streets in 1971. Their discovery of a tintype picturing Rev. Thomas B. Wright with his children led to years of researching their home's history. Wright and his second wife, Lily McCoy, built the

The 1970s discovery of a tintype behind a baseboard in their home led the authors of this book to research their 1898 house. They learned about its first owner, Rev. T.B. Wright, and wrote an in-depth article about this historic home. Their article became a forerunner to the *Orange Judd Historic Walking Tour Guide* of Rochester homes in 2015 and to this book. (R. BRUZAN PHOTO)

This tintype of Rev. Thomas B. Wright, taken about 1884, includes from left: his son, David, who died at age two, Wright, and his daughter, Mary. A Methodist Episcopal minister, Wright moved his family to Rochester about 1890. The tintype was found in 1975 behind a baseboard in his home on East Main Street. (COURTESY OF RAY AND PAM BRUZAN)

house in 1898. A 1977 *Illinois Times* story about the house was a forerunner to production of the 2015 *Orange Judd Historic Walking Tour Guide* to the historic homes of Rochester and this history of the village.

- Dan Walker, hopeful Democratic candidate for governor, visited Rochester on his "walking tour of Illinois" in 1971, when he stopped for a reception at the South Walnut Street home of Oscar and Martha Weil.

Young Kevin Bruzan sat in the governor's jeep, speaking with Gov. Dan Walker (left) and office seeker Peter Mack during the governor's October 1976 visit to Rochester. (P. BRUZAN PHOTO)

Illinois Democratic candidate for governor Dan Walker was an August 1971 guest of Oscar and Martha Weil, who lived in the Nunes house on South Walnut Street. Walker was accompanied by two of his seven children on this leg of the candidate's walking tour of Illinois. (*ROCHESTER & LAKE SPRINGFIELD HERALD*, 19 AUG. 1971)

— Governor Walker, who had already lost his 1976 gubernatorial reelection primary, stopped that fall to visit the Rochester Grade School, address first-through-eighth-grade students, and promote the ultimately unsuccessful candidacy of Democrat Peter Mack. Mack was vying for a comeback election to the U.S. Congress. Before the two left Rochester, they stopped at Lunts Grocery store where five-year-old Kevin Bruzan was permitted to sit in the governor's jeep and shake hands with the two politicians.

Rochester Township built this iron bridge to carry Honeywell Road across Horse Creek about 1900 and replaced it in 1972. The early bridge's wood deck is clearly visible in this photo. (BETTY MOHLER PHOTO; USED WITH PERMISSION)

More than 100 Rochester hunters gathered on a cold January day in 1970 and tried to reduce by 500 the fox population of Rochester Township. Organized by Jerry Campbell, Bennie Tuxhorn, and Jim Gaule, the hunt resulted in only two foxes being killed. In spite of the poor results, everyone seemed to have had an enjoyable outing, except for the two foxes.
(ROCHESTER HERALD, 20 JAN. 1970)

Left: The Grieme Implement Company near Rochester provided hot air balloon rides to guests during its 1976 open house.
(ROCHESTER TIMES, 3 SEP. 1976; USED WITH PERMISSION)

Right: The "Old Stone House" on Buckhart Road is seen as it appeared in 1973. (BILL WALDMIRE PHOTO; USED WITH PERMISSION)

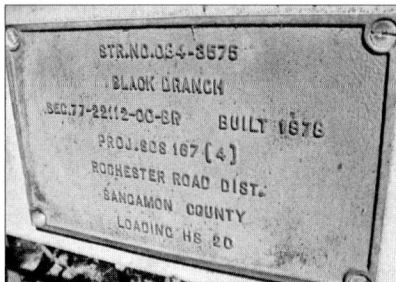

The bridge on North Walnut Road over Black Branch Creek just before that creek enters the South Fork River was built in 1976. This had been the site of a covered bridge leading into Glenwood Park as shown in the 1890s. This picture was taken looking west along the creek. (R. BRUZAN PHOTOS)

ROADS AND RAILS
OF ROCHESTER TOWNSHIP

A Baltimore & Ohio (B&O) train from Decatur crosses over Route 29 west of Rochester. This 1981 picture was taken near Hilltop looking northwest toward Springfield. The overpass bridge was removed in 1999. (WALT PETERS PHOTOS; R.R. WALLIN COLLECTION; USED WITH PERMISSION)

1980S

The discovery of a log house on South Walnut Street in 1987 provided the community an opportunity to witness research of the village's most significant historic artifact. Mel Creviston made the discovery as he began demolishing a house that had been built around the log structure. (DORTHY ROSS PHOTO; USED WITH PERMISSION)

1980s Timeline...

1980   Rochester population: 2,488
      — Dedication activities took place at Community Park on West Main Street
      — Taft farm, "Maplehurst," was listed in the National Register of Historic Places
      — Cable television became available in Rochester

1981   Village offices underwent extensive renovation
      — Rochester voted to remain a "dry" town
      — *The Rochester Hello* newspaper began publication

1982   Sangamon Frontier Canoe Rental was established on John Street

1983   Baltimore & Ohio Railroad was sold to the Prairie Trunk Railroad line

1984   Prairie Trunk Railroad and Springfield-to-Decatur tracks were abandoned

1985   Rochester Public Library held its grand opening at Rochester Station

1987   Log house was discovered on South Walnut Street
        — New Post Office opened in March 1987 on South Walnut Street

1988   Rochester Historical Preservation Society was founded
        — Severe drought restricted water usage
        — A portion of The Meadows subdivision was platted

1989   Prairie Trunk Railroad sold all assets for scrap and disposition

1980s Storylines...

- A 1988 *State Journal-Register* article described how Rochester's 1968 population of 1,300 had more than doubled by 1988 to nearly 3,000. Village President Henry Bregenhorn related that about 15 new homes were being built annually, and the cost of existing or new homes ranged from $40,000 to $120,000.

  — About 60 businesses existed in Rochester at the time, although most middle-class Rochester residents worked in Springfield. In a village where the average family size was 3.23 persons, minorities made up less than 2% of the population. Pointing to the school district's reputation for excellence, Planning Commission Chair Wally Biermann said, "Most Rochester citizens have high educational aspirations for their children."

  — This decade included creation of a public library district, discovery of a historic log house on South Walnut Street, and dedication of a large park.

- After using the Rochester High School library one night a week since 1969, residents listed library service as vital on a 1983 village-wide survey. A Rochester Woman's Club committee, led by Vickie Lattimer, met in 1984 to explore establishing a local public library.

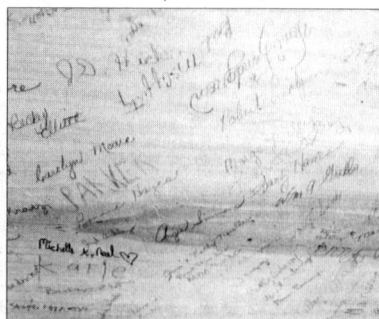

Rochester Public Library's "signature table" is a permanent reminder of those local residents who attended the 1985 grand opening of this library in the Rochester Station building on South Walnut Street. (R. BRUZAN PHOTOS)

— Rolling Prairie Library System in Decatur helped Rochester residents secure a two-year federal grant to "test drive" a new library. The second grant year, however, depended on local voters passing a referendum to generate future local tax support for library services.

— U.S. Representative Richard Durbin and Mayor Nyla Hardwick participated in the May 25, 1985, ribbon-cutting celebration for the Rochester Public Library at its Rochester Station location. On March 18, 1986, Rochester voters approved the referendum by 979 to 438, thereby creating a library taxing district. One month after the vote, seven people were appointed to Rochester's first library board: John E. Daly, Joanne Fairchild, Vickie Lattimer, Ralph Moore, Robert Ritterbusch, Jennifer A. Sciera, and Sharon Zara.

• Perhaps Rochester's most significant historic artifact was discovered unexpectedly in 1987 when Mel Creviston began demolishing a house at 317 South Walnut Street. The property was owned by the Rochester Christian Church, which planned a church expansion or parking lot at that location.

— As Creviston removed siding, he realized that a log house was part of the structure. Unknown to him at the time, this was only the second log house known to exist in Sangamon County. Creviston, a 1966 RHS graduate, was excited about his discovery and wanted area school children to have an opportunity to view the historic artifact. He was, however, uncertain how to make that happen.

— Extensive on-site archeological excavating and detailed library research by volunteers, including Sangamon State University graduate student Carol S. Jenkins,

The log house, taken down in 1987, remains in storage as of 2017.
(Dorthy Ross photo; used with permission)

generated information about the house that helped identify the most likely pioneer builder. Guiding Rochester volunteers during the excavation were representatives of Fever River Research, Illinois State Museum, the Illinois Historic Preservation Agency and Kampsville Archeological Center.

— An abstract of a lot near the log house describes how Maryland native John Capoot purchased one acre of land for $30 in 1840 and sold it the following year for $300, the increased value possibly the result of a new log house and well. This theory was supported when Capoot's name was found on a window-framing lintel.

— With plans to rebuild it, the log house was dismantled in December 1988. As of 2017, the house remains in storage awaiting the day that the pioneer structure will provide a living history lesson.

- Discovering the Capoot log house generated community-wide enthusiasm and was the impetus to organize the Rochester Historical Preservation Society (RHPS) in 1988. Since then, the Society focused on researching the log house, documenting Rochester's history, providing history-related programs, restoring historic structures, and preserving local history for future generations.

— Under the guidance of some early officers, the Society obtained land for a historical village that could feature historic structures such as the log house. Those dreams of the founding Society officers would become realities as the park and a reconstructed 1830s stone house now provide a place where Rochester citizens and visitors can begin to understand the village's unique history.

One year after the historic log house was discovered, the Rochester Historical Preservation Society organized and elected Carolyn Moore as president. (COURTESY OF CAROLYN MOORE; USED WITH PERMISSION)

- *The Rochester Hello* newspaper, a creation of Jim and Ann Rominger, began publishing in 1981. Although the Rochester community was enthusiastic about the new weekly, publication was discontinued in 1982, just 18 months after its debut.

Through the efforts of Jim and Ann Rominger, Rochester once again had a newspaper. The first edition of *The Rochester Hello* is dated April 2, 1981. Many area residents were disappointed when it ceased publication September 30, 1982. (COURTESY OF JIM AND ANN ROMINGER; USED WITH PERMISSION)

- The 1980s was another decade of major changes within the Rochester School District.

— Use of educational television and discussion of a high school computer system in 1980 ushered Rochester schools into the age of electronics. Although the school board had earlier denied a request to add a computer programming course to the high school math curriculum, by the 1985-86 school year the district was advertising for a "Mathematics/Computer Science Teacher." It was not long after that the district remodeled two high school classrooms for computer lab spaces.

— With a seven-to-zero vote in 1982 the school board rejected a "Kick-Off Committee" request to begin a football program at Rochester. Although School Superintendent Jack K. Taylor had recommended against adding that program, board members each explained why they were also against the re-quested sport. At its next meeting, the board approved introducing a girls' basketball program in the 1982-83 school year.

— The Rochester School Board expressed no interest in consolidating with nearby districts in 1986. Consolidation legislation, part of the state's 1985 education-reform package, allowed local districts to remain intact without consolidation.

— Negotiation efforts to settle teacher contracts and avoid a teachers' strike in 1986 and 1989 required the help of federal mediators to reach an agreement between the Rochester School Board and the teachers' union.

— The 1988 Vision 2000 School Committee recommended that the Rochester School District build a new school and make numerous renovations to exist-ing buildings. Predicted increases in student enrollment caused by growing populations had led, once again, to packed classrooms and a need for new fa-cilities to meet the district's evolving educational programs. District voters in 1989 passed a $5.75 million bond issue by 1,235 to 1,124 votes. The money was used for a new grade school at a new campus on West Main Street and for building renovations.

— Due to the popularity of the school's first computer, the high school's Math Club successfully raised money in 1981 to buy a second "Apple microcom-puter." The first system included "a communication device that enables the Apple to 'talk' to other computers over the phone lines."

- As a way of encouraging Rochester Elementary students to meet the school's 1989 reading goals, Principal John Rigg agreed to kiss a pig for each class success over the five-month program. Seven classes met the goal and in front of the student body, the principal went "hog wild," kissing the cross-bred pig seven times. As the pig grunted, Rigg was "not sure if it was complaining or experiencing ecstasy." In honor of their guest, Rigg made sure that pork was not part of that day's school's lunch menu.

- A comment by the school district's Vision 2000 Chair John Day in 1988 resonated throughout the district and generated head shaking along with some smiles. In referring to the widely respected school district having been a key motivation for the area's growth, Day said, "People come here to raise families. They don't come because of the bowling alley." It wasn't long before bumper stickers affirmed, "I live in Rochester for the bowling alley." References were to Chapin's Country Lanes.

- After being one of the Rochester High School's extracurricular activities since 1941, the Future Farmers of America (FFA) chapter was discontinued after the 1986 school year.

- Several road proposals made news during the decade.

  — The impetus to expand Route 29 to four lanes from Rochester to Taylorville was enhanced in 1988 as the Grand Trunk Prairie Railroad appeared ready to abandon its railroad bed running parallel to the highway. That step would make the land available for use as right-of-way. The Route 29-widening proposal was estimated to cost $75 million in 1988, but the actual cost was $88.4 million by the time the four-lane expansion was dedicated in 2017.

Rochester's FFA Chapter promoted leadership, cooperation, and citizenship among high school students interested in careers related to agriculture. Members in 1982 posed for a photographer. (*THE ROCHESTER HELLO*, 18 FEB. 1982; CECIL WITHROW PHOTO; USED WITH PERMISSION)

  — Another potential project was creation of a Rochester-to-Riverton road. Rochester and Clear Lake townships along with Sangamon County earmarked $30,000 in 1989 for a location-and-feasibility study of the road.

  — The 89-year-old Dannenberger Road bridge across the South Fork River about 1.5 miles southwest of Rochester was deemed substandard in 1989. It topped the county's bridge-replacement list, with costs estimated to be $750,000.

- After nine years of wrestling with sewage-treatment problems, the village board recommended that voters approve joining the Springfield Metro Sanitary District (SMSD). Their recommendation came after Illinois Environmental Protection Agency (IEPA) warnings that Rochester must upgrade operation of its sewage treatment lagoon system to meet effluent requirements. The agency said that failure to do so would open the possibilities of a ban on additional sewer connections or fines as high as $1,000 a day. Projected population increases were going to make it more difficult to reach the required goals.

  — Rochester voters, however, rejected the proposal to join SMSD, prompting the IEPA to require operating modifications to the lagoon system. Further solutions to Rochester's sewage treatment problems would confront future village boards.

— The village board paid an engineering firm $132,000 in 1989 for several key studies: existing water and sewer systems, along with the projected needs and cost estimates for each; existing street conditions and future maintenance costs; and updates to Rochester's Comprehensive Plan and Subdivision Ordinance.

• For the second time in seven years the village hall on John Street was remodeled, with this work completed in June 1981 for more than $70,000. The building itself dated back to 1947 when American Legion Post 274 leased the ground from Rochester's Independent Order of Odd Fellows. The Legion promised to build a two-story structure worth at least $2,500 in which fire-department equipment was kept on the first floor, which was also where the Rochester Athletic Club met.

— Legion members met on the second floor. When the fire department moved in 1971 and village offices needed to expand, the Legion offered use of the building's first-floor space, which the village board accepted.

— By 1980, however, the police department had expanded, a larger office for village utility records was necessary, and the village board sought to present a more professional image to visitors. It was about that time that the IOOF offered to sell to the village land on which the building sat, an offer that was also accepted.

Rochester's old Post Office on John Street was torn down in the mid-1980s. It was replaced by a dental office that became, in 2004, home of Waters Insurance Agency, Inc. (COURTESY OF SANGAMON VALLEY COLLECTION, LINCOLN LIBRARY, SPRINGFIELD, IL)

Rochester's current Post Office opened on South Walnut Street in 1987. There have been at least five other U.S. Post Office locations during Rochester's history. (R. BRUZAN PHOTO)

- Written to address problems generated by animal-control issues, a controversial 1988 village pet ordinance was based on complaints of children bitten or scared by loose pets, dog and cat feces left in neighboring yards, and damage to yards and landscaping. The ordinance specified that domesticated animals could leave their owners' property only if they were on a leash shorter than six feet. Some pet owners, however, interpreted that the ordinance could ban them from walking their pets on streets, sidewalks, or alleys without permission. Violators faced fines of $100 to $500, plus impound charges of $50 to $100 before getting their animals back. Mayor Henry Bregenhorn said that the ordinance could be reworked if necessary.

- The first two plats of The Meadows subdivision on the west edge of Rochester were approved by the Rochester Planning Commission in 1988 and 1989. The two plats comprised a total of 44 lots on the former Justin Taft farm that lay along the north side of Route 29 adjacent to Camelot subdivision. The lot prices were advertised for $10,000 to $24,000, with homes in the range of $80,000 to $110,000.

Rather than move from the property at Mill and Oak Streets, where they had lived since 1952, Arthur Lewis and Erma *(Hames)* Kessler built a new home in 1981. They then watched their house of almost 30 years move without them. In this series of photos, from left: the house has been secured on wheels; it is being driven south on Oak Street; and is being settle on a new foundation at the East Main Street location where it remains as of 2017. (*THE ROCHESTER HELLO*, 9 APR. 1981)

- Villagers overwhelmingly voted in 1981 against the sale of alcohol in Rochester. By more than a two-to-one margin, 569 to 226, voters again chose to keep a "dry" village.

- A wide range of Rochester age groups found in 1988 that they all had something in common: they did not want Rochester to become the site for low-level nuclear-waste disposal, which many people referred to as a "dump." Not only did adults circulate a petition opposing the site, but school children did as well. In the face of opposition from Rochester and the other potential county location in New Berlin, the Sangamon County Board voted to reject locating the waste site in Sangamon County.

- Rochester dedicated Community Park on West Main Street during a Flag Day celebration June 14, 1980. Guest speaker for the occasion was U.S. Rep. Paul

Finley. The event also included a parade to the park, a one-mile fun run, and a performance by the Statesmen Drum and Bugle Corps. A more brief dedication had also taken place during July 4th celebrations a year earlier.

- Several members of Rochester Boy Scout Troop 40 contributed to the development of Community Park with candidate projects for their Eagle Scout badges. On a May 1981 weekend their attention focused on building a footbridge over a park stream.

- Several long-time Rochester citizens celebrated milestones:
  — Marshall and Pauline *(Frame)* Watkins, William and Ruth *(Painter)* Coe, Thomas and Antoinette *(Scarnier)* Scott, Ralph and Thedelma *(Gray)* Cox, and John and Margaret *(Green)* Foster celebrated golden anniversaries.
  — Russell and Chelsea *(Jett)* Simpson observed their 60th anniversary.
  — Rochester's oldest resident, Charles Story, observed his 100th birthday in 1988, four years after he and his wife Emma *(Harter)* celebrated their 70th anniversary.

- The hot summer of 1983 that caused the pavement of Route 29 to buckle west of the South Fork River was not close to the heat and drought of 1988, when Central Illinois went 31 consecutive days without rain.
  — Lake Springfield plunged to alarming levels, farmers feared for their crops, and water levels in area wells dropped. Mandatory water restrictions were enacted in Rochester, and water was pumped from the South Fork River into Lake Springfield, at a rate of as much as 70 million gallons a day. Above-normal rainfall brought relief in the fall, and Lake Springfield returned to its full pool.
  — Some area residents thought that the drought would convince previous doubters of the need to build Lake Springfield II, sometimes called Hunter Lake. As of 2017, debate continues to swirl around a second lake, which could impact the South Fork River in Rochester Township.

- World-renowned violinist Isaac Stern performed in 1984 at Sangamon Auditorium on the campus of what was then called Sangamon State University. Few people, perhaps no one, in the auditorium was aware that Ukraine native Stern had been a student of Rochester-born Louis Persinger, who taught him in New York City. A portion of the concert's ticket price benefited the Hope School for the Blind. Stern, born in 1920, died in 2001.

- The Franzen Brothers Circus brought its show to the grounds of the Church of St. Jude in 1987. Included in the featured lineup were "the world's only place-kicking elephant," and Tonto, a mathematically gifted horse. Proceeds helped support the church.

- Business reports:

  — Hook-ups for cable tv became available January 1, 1980, with cable services for most village residents available by March. First Illinois Cable TV offered a 30-day free installation period, charging $7.50 for basic monthly programs and an additional $8.25 per month for Home Box Office (HBO).

  — Country Custard Ice Cream shop on John Street, which was opened in the mid-1970s, was bought by the Ray Bruzan family in 1980 and operated until 1984, when they sold it to the Terry Day family. Between 1982 and 1984, the Bruzans also established the Sangamon Frontier Canoe Rental on John Street. The canoe rental offered put-in and pick-up services on the Sangamon River and Sangchris Lake.

Country Custard, an ice cream store on John Street, also sold sandwiches and penny candy. The business was owned and operated by the Bruzan family from 1980 to 1984, when it was sold to Terry and Donna Day. (P. BRUZAN PHOTO; FLYER ARTWORK BY MARK RITTERBUSCH, COMMUNICATION DESIGN)

Below: From 1983-1984 Sangamon Frontier Canoe Rental, located on John Street, provided livery services on the Sangamon River and Sangchris Lake. (R. BRUZAN PHOTO; FLYER ARTWORK BY MARK RITTERBUSCH, COMMUNICATION DESIGN)

IT MUST BE SPRING

Country Custard

IS OPEN

SPRING HOURS:
Sunday - Friday 1 p.m. - 9 p.m.
Saturday - 11 a.m. - 9 p.m.

Sangamon Frontier CANOE RENTAL

We Also Provide
PUT IN/PICK UP SERVICE
On
• The Sangamon River • Lake Springfield
• Sangchris Lake

For Reservations or Brochure
(217) 498-8140 or 498-7325
ROCHESTER, ILLINOIS 62563

Left: Jennifer Bruzan canoes with her father through rocks and rapids on the Sangamon River near Niantic in June 1984. (BOB RITTERBUSCH PHOTO)

— RHS graduate Mark Sturdy opened his Rochester Veterinary Clinic in 1988 on John Street within view of the house where his great grandfather, John W. Sturdy, lived for several years until his death in 1923. John was a Civil War veteran who served in the Confederate army.

— A hog processing plant proposed in 1980 for an 80-acre location north of Eastgate Meadows subdivision was never built.

— Sangamon Valley Writing Associates was founded by Pam Bruzan on East Main Street in 1985 to provide technical writing and editing services to civil engineers, architects, educators, authors, and healthcare professionals.

- The Illinois Department of Conservation was pursuing state funding in 1989 to help purchase five miles of the abandoned Baltimore & Ohio Railroad bed for construction of a bike path. The land was owned at that time by the Prairie Trunk Railroad. The former B&O Railroad line ran parallel to Route 29 from Springfield, through Rochester and Edinburg, to Taylorville, and the proposed bike path would follow the former railroad bed between Springfield and Rochester.

Left: Dave Jostes stands on a railroad tie that he recovered in 2016 from along the old B&O Railroad bed. Train travel through Rochester ceased in the late 1980s. Below: A tie plate and two spikes were found by the author in 2016 along the B&O Railroad bed, which by then had become Lost Bridge Trail. (R. Bruzan photos)

- Local accidents:

— A bank president from Rantoul lost his life in 1983 when his plane crashed in a field southeast of Rochester.

— While repairing a flat tire, a Rochester gas-station owner died when pieces of the station's tire-mounting machine flew into the air, striking the man.

— A Sangamon County deputy escaped injury in 1987, but the unmarked county-owned car he was driving was destroyed when the deputy hit the railroad trestle on West Main Street as he swerved to avoid an oncoming motorist.

— Two Rochester teens survived serious injuries in 1988 when their car hit a fence post along North Walnut Road outside of Rochester.

— An unusual traffic accident caused by a hydraulically powered tree transplanter occurred in 1981. Attached to the back of a pickup truck, the transplanter was being moved along West Main Street when the top failed to clear the railroad trestle underpass. Although no injuries and no serious damage occurred, the transplanter initially swiveled, lifting the back of the truck to about a 45-degree angle off the ground.

— As MCI Communications workers erected a taller, 340-foot tower in 1984, one of them was hit by a pole that had snapped. The Rochester Emergency Squad spent close to an hour lowering the man about 150 feet from the tower located between Route 29 and State Street. The worker, who was from Iowa, was taken to Memorial Medical Center with a broken right hip and left leg.

- The Rochester Lions Club and the village of Rochester worked together in 1989 to sponsor Rochester's annual July 4th celebration. The parade, "Rochester, God, and Country," included some 75 parade units competing for cash prizes and ribbons. Activities for all ages included a giant auction, banjo band concert, ribeye steak dinner, and fireworks.

Jennifer Bruzan shares a moment of celebration with her cat Smudge. In her hand is the $1,000 check she received as winner of the 1983 Rochester Lions Club 4th-of-July drawing. (P. BRUZAN PHOTO)

- The Rochester Fire Department was kept busy in October 1983 controlling three brush fires, two of them simultaneously. Two building fires were far more destructive.

— An electrical short was blamed for a 1980 fire that totally destroyed a two-and-a-half story wood-frame house and its contents at 417 East Main Street. The loss was estimated at $90,000.

— Arson was suspected in a 1989 fire that destroyed the Rochester Cemetery chapel. Plans began immediately to repair the $14,500 in damages and restore the 65-year-old building.

- After lightning damaged an oil tank northeast of Rochester in 1981, about 5,000 gallons of crude oil leaked into Black Branch Creek that flows into the South Fork River. Damage included some dead carp, as well as oil-covered river banks and vegetation. The U.S. Attorney's office filed suit three years later against Aladdin Oil Development Company to recover the $23,618 in clean-up costs incurred along both streams.

- The first apartment complex built specifically for senior citizens and people with handicaps was completed early in 1980. Walnut Hill Village, located directly across Walnut Street from the Rochester Grade School, offered 24 units. MFC Development, Inc. of Taylorville spearheaded the project.

- Rochester police chased a car on Route 29 at speeds up to 90 miles an hour toward Springfield in 1987. With assistance from state and county officers, the driver was apprehended on the northbound entrance ramp to Interstate 55. The lawbreaker was found to have been driving under the influence and in possession of a 22-caliber handgun. Charges included speeding, driving under the influence, and unlawful use of a weapon.
  — A less-serious, but perhaps more widely noticed crime took place in 1980 when three high school seniors climbed to the top of Rochester's water tower and spray painted messages over the 60,000-gallon tank. After their arrest, the boys agreed to pay the $500 repainting cost.

Left: Full-time members of the Rochester Police Department in 1982 were, from left: Larry Dobson, Steve Rutledge, Bill Marass, Terry Day, Chief Mike Upchurch, and Police Trustee Herb Benson. (*THE ROCHESTER HELLO*, 30 SEP. 1982)

Right: Part-time Rochester Police Department patrolmen in 1982 were, from left: Mervin Spurgeon, Mike Grim, and Sam Gresham. (*THE ROCHESTER HELLO*, 30 SEP. 1982)

- The Rochester Police Department and Rochester Mothers' Club sponsored two "Safety Days" at the village office in 1983. Children's fingerprint records were given to their parents in case they were needed in the future. Rochester Fire Department, Emergency Squad, and Police Department vehicles and equipment were also on display.
  — Within two years almost three dozen businesses and homes were named "McGruff Safe Houses," where children could seek safety if strangers or other emergencies caused them to sense danger. Large yellow signs with black letters identified those locations. The effective program was a joint effort by school,

police, and community members. Crime-prevention classes for students in second, fourth, and sixth grades explained the safe-house program.

- Rochester newsmakers:

— **Don Chard** had the gift of dowsing also known as "water witching." Using a forked willow branch, Chard was widely sought after to help determine where to drill a new water well. He had realized his dowsing talents when he was just 10 years old.

— Former YWCA Woman of the Year **Dorthy Ross** of Compass Point Farm east of Rochester was named the assistant state conservation chairman for the Illinois organization of the Daughters of the American Revolution in 1989.

— **Margaret Honey** celebrated her 97th birthday in 1981. She arrived in Rochester with her husband the **Rev. John Honey** in 1939 and was a charter member of the Sangamon County Home Extension.

— Well-known cook **Malinda Church** earned the honor "Best Pie" in the 1983 *State Journal-Register*'s "Best of Springfield" listings. Of the pastries she served at Petticoat Junction Restaurant in Rochester Station, her banana cream pies, which weighed a hefty seven pounds, were particularly popular.

— When **Wiley Funderburk** celebrated his 80th birthday in 1988, a special guest at his party was 93-year-old **Hazel Park**. Hazel had been Wiley's first-grade teacher in 1914 at the one-room South Cotton Hill Grade School near New City.

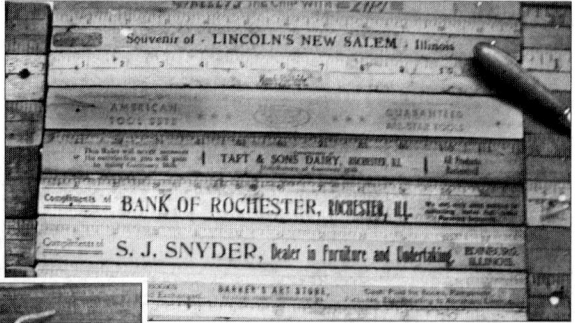

Kim Klickna of Rochester has an unusual collection of more than 1,000 yardsticks that includes one from the Bank of Rochester, circa 1910, and Taft & Sons Dairy, circa 1945. Kim's collection was featured in a 1987 *State Journal-Register* article.
(R. BRUZAN PHOTOS)

— **Kim Klickna** of Rochester now has a unique collection of more than 1,000 rulers and yardsticks. When he had only about 300, a 1987 Best of Springfield survey awarded him the honor of "Best Yardstick Collection." As of 2017, the collection covered his basement walls and included several from early Rochester businesses such as Taft Dairy and Bank of Rochester.

— **Bob Church** was named "executive director" for Springfield Mayor Ossie Langfelder in 1987. At that time, Church was executive director of the Illinois Land Surveyors Association and owned the Rochester Station business complex.

— A Rochester resident, attorney **Robin Cona**, chaired the April 1981 statewide drive to collect money for cancer research. With a $6.5 million goal, she worked with more than 100,000 volunteers on behalf of the American Cancer Society.

— After holding multiple local offices and receiving several recognitions, **Charles Newhouse** was

Bob Church (right) of Rochester served for eight years as executive director for Springfield Mayor Ossie Langfelder (left). This 1989 picture was taken in Norfork, VA, during commissioning events for the USS Abraham Lincoln (cvn-72) air craft carrier. Church was Rochester's 1987 Citizen of the Year. (COURTESY OF BOB CHURCH; USED WITH PERMISSION)

elected governor of Lions Club District 1-L comprising about 50 Lions Clubs in Central Illinois.

— High school Rubik's Cube Team members **David Jostes**, **Ralph Metcalf**, and **Jenny Nuding** beat Riverton's team, coming in more than three minutes faster than their rivals. Ralph's time of 1 minute, 12 seconds was the fastest of the meet.

— High school sophomore **Stephanie Brogdon** brought home the title Best Junior Homemaker from the 1981 Illinois State Fair. Thanks to a love of baking, she earned multiple best-in-class rosettes, as well as blue and red ribbons.

• Some Rochester deaths during this decade included the following:

1980
— **Ron Coffman**, school board member and former Rochester High School guidance counselor who had contracted Rocky Mountain Spotted fever

1981
— **Carl E. Moore**, a real estate broker, Rochester Township clerk, 50-year member of Rochester Lodge 635 AF&AM, and Rochester Lions Club charter member
— **Helen Prather**, an East Main Street resident, an enthusiast of dining at all new restaurants in the area, and a loving neighbor whose kindness is still remembered fondly by the authors

1982
— **Ernest J. Rentschler**, a World War II veteran, owner of Rentschler & Son's Grocery, and Rochester's first fire chief

1983

— **Hugh Campbell**, a long-time Rochester resident and former Sangamon County sheriff

1984

— **Anthony "Tony" Mazzara**, who played in the U.S. Navy Band and later directed Rochester school district bands for 20 years

1987

— **D. Gilson Taft**, who started the Taft & Sons' Dairy in 1933 and opened Rochester's Taft Dairy on East Main in 1941

1988

— **Marshall Fay Beck**, who was class salutatorian in 1938, the first year Rochester had a four-year high school; had been a medic during the D-Day invasion at Omaha Beach; and was Rochester's 1982 First Citizen

1989

— **Meryl Fairchild**, a World War I veteran who served in France and was a charter member of Harry Fogle Post 274 American Legion in Rochester

— **R. Earl Sidener**, a 20-year member of the Rochester School Board who played a significant roll in the consolidation of rural schools and the subsequent student-transportation program

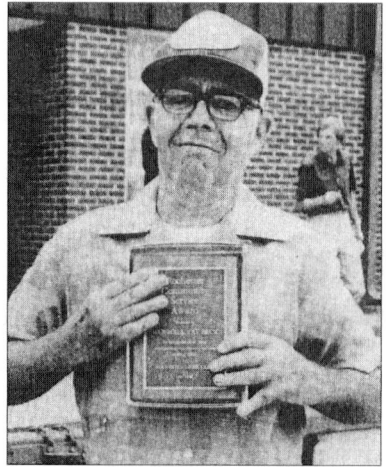

World War II veteran Marshall Fay Beck was named Rochester's First Citizen at the village's 1982 Independence Day celebration. (*THE ROCHESTER HELLO*, 8 JULY 1982)

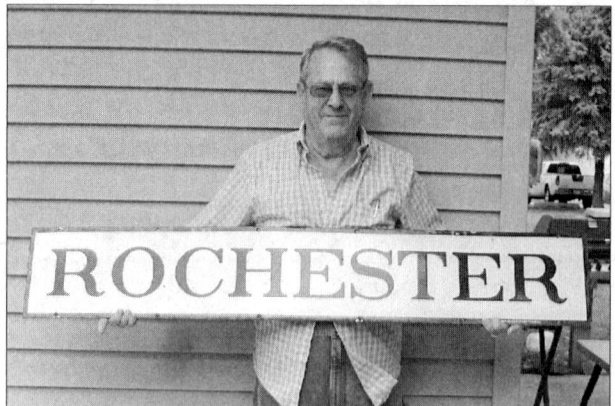

When the Rochester railroad station was demolished in the late 1980s, Bud Beck saved the station sign. (COURTESY OF BUD BECK; R. BRUZAN PHOTO)

- Maplehurst, a farm house on West Main Street, was listed in the National Register of Historic Places in 1980. Henry and Mary Jane *(Eckels)* Taft built their home for $12,000 in 1912. Reminiscent of a southern plantation, this home in the classical revival style features two-story-high ionic columns, transported to Rochester from the south by wagon, and a second-floor balcony. As of 2017, Maplehurst has been occupied continuously by members of the Taft family. The original owner, Henry, was a fifth cousin of U.S. President William H. Taft.

Above: Maplehurst, a unique home on West Main Street, was listed in the National Register of Historic Places in 1980. (R. BRUZAN PHOTO)

Left: Aloft Horizon, with an office and launch site on John Street, made hot air balloon trips available from downtown Rochester during the early 1980s. This photo was taken looking northeast from Oak Hill Road. (*THE ROCHESTER HELLO*, 9 SEP. 1982)

LOST BRIDGE TRAIL

Many Lost Bridge Trail users enjoy the Hilltop Road Tunnel. (R. BRUZAN PHOTO)

1990s

The Rochester Library and Village Hall, located at the corner of Route 29 and Community Drive, also includes the Rochester Police Department and a multipurpose room. It was dedicated in 1995. (R. BRUZAN PHOTO)

1990s Timeline...

1990	Population: 2,676
	— Rochester annexed to the Springfield Metro Sanitary District
1991	Elementary school was built on West Main Street
	— Village board approved 20-year Comprehensive Plan
1992	Rochester teachers go on strike
1993	New 300,000-gallon water tower was built at the North Park
	— Multipurpose facility was built at Rochester High School
	— Village-wide curbside recycling began
1994	Development began at The Woodlands subdivision
	— Rochester School Board approved a high school football program
	— Grace Bible Chapel was built on Woodhaven Drive
1995	Rochester Library and Village Hall on Community Drive were dedicated
	— Rochester Police Department relocated from John Street to the newly dedicated Rochester Village Hall
	— Maplehurst subdivision was developed
	— A contract was let to remove the train trestle at West Main and Route 29
	— Traffic signals were installed at Walnut Street and Route 29

	— Phone-line modem internet connections became available in the village
1996	Sangamon County Board approved a proposed Riverton-to-Rochester Road alignment
	— Rochester Lodge 268 of the Independent Order of Odd Fellows (IOOF) closed after 138 years
1997	Lost Bridge Trail opened
1998	South Fork River bridge on Rochester Road was replaced
1999	Friendship Fort children's playground was constructed in Community Park
	— Water contract between Rochester and Springfield was renegotiated
	— Traffic lights were installed at Route 29 and State Street
	— Baltimore & Ohio Railroad bridge over Route 29 at Hilltop was removed

1990s Storylines...

- A new village hall, elementary school, and water tower were major additions to Rochester during the 1990s. The population continued to grow as new subdivisions added to the ongoing challenges of securing an adequate water supply and sewage treatment. When Lost Bridge Trail opened, citizens of all ages could enjoy Rochester Township's prairie and waterway scenes. Issues confronting the community included the proposal to build a Rochester-to-Riverton Road and the school district's first teachers' strike.

A new Rochester Elementary School on West Main Street opened in 1991. Its completion marked the first time in 71 years that a school was built apart from the campus bordered by North Walnut Street and Route 29. (R. BRUZAN PHOTO)

- The Rochester School District enjoyed new opportunities and endured new challenges during the 1990s.

  — Four Rochester High School band fund drives in 1990 paid for a trip to play at Disney World in Orlando, FL.

  — A record enrollment of 1,575 students in 1991 was 45 students more than the previous year. Classroom crowding eased with the October 1991 opening and dedication of a new kindergarten-through-fourth-grade school on West Main Street. This building marked the first construction on a new campus in 71 years.

— When the 1992 contract negotiations between the school board and teachers broke down over salary increases and class size, Rochester's first teachers' strike took place. An agreement reached with the help of a federal mediator brought an end to the 11-day work stoppage.

— At a bid price of $1.6 million, a 10,000-square-foot multipurpose facility was added to the west side of the high school in 1993. It was designed to accommodate band and choral performances, as well as physical education classes and practicing sports teams.

— A 1996 head-lice outbreak among Rochester elementary students pushed district officials to take a series of extermination measures. In addition to hiring a company to wash the buildings and desks thoroughly, they banned Beanie Babies because lice could be transmitted when students shared and traded the wildly popular pellet-filled toys.

— A tie vote doomed a $7.5 million school bond issue in March 1998. A modified $6.5 million school bond issue passed by a 2-to-1 margin six months later. The new bonds enabled building a new school for grades four through six on the West Main campus, as well as new and remodeled high school science labs. The new labs were dedicated in a 1999 ceremony.

• The Rochester Village Board and Library Board approved major changes in 1994 when they planned a joint complex on five acres of land made available by the Church of St. Jude. As the result of what was then a unique intergovernmental agreement, the new 16,000-square-foot structure was built to house the Rochester Public Library, the combined Rochester Village Offices and Police Department,

A plaque at the entrance of the new community center honors those people and companies that were largely responsible for the new Rochester Library and Village Hall. (R. BRUZAN PHOTO)

The Rochester Police Department is on the east side of the village hall on Community Drive. (R. BRUZAN PHOTO)

and a large public commons area. The new structure was dedicated in 1995, and the former John Street village office building was sold.

— The street leading to that multi-purpose building was named Community Drive, and the section of Route 29 within Rochester was designated Illinois Avenue.

— In other 1994 action, the village board faced a lawsuit from the Rochester Developers Association, which asserted that a village "fair share assessment," or impact fee, of about $2,300 per lot for new sewer and water hook ups was unconstitutional. The village prevailed when the state appeals court upheld the impact fee.

After moving into their new building in 1995, the village sold their former village hall and police department located on John Street. (COURTESY OF THE ROCHESTER POLICE DEPT.)

— To increase the size of Community Park, the 1995 village board bought 26.6 acres of school district land located adjacent to and north of the existing park.

- Instead of a traditional announcement of dedication ceremonies at the new library and village hall complex, it was a "birth announcement." Two storks were pictured delivering the new building with a weight of 2,100,000 pounds and height of 23'8." The "Proud Parents" were listed as the Rochester Public Library District and the Village of Rochester.

- The sometimes uneasy relations between Rochester and Springfield's City Water, Light & Power (CWLP) deteriorated to new lows over water. After continuing to buy water from CWLP under a contract that had officially expired in 1989, Rochester filed a 1994 lawsuit over the price charged to the village for water. Rochester lost the case that claimed water charges to Rochester generated more revenue than CWLP needed for "reasonable" profits.

— By January 1998 Rochester and Chatham village representatives had agreed to study the feasibility of forming a joint water district to address long-term water supplies for each community. Robert Church, James Finley, and Scott Miller were Rochester's representa-

Water Advisory Team: Evaluate *and* **Recommend**

In 1998, Rochester and Chatham began to explore the option of creating their own water-supply system in order to discontinue purchasing water from Springfield's City Water, Light & Power. A joint task force evaluated the options and costs. (ARTWORK BY MARK RITTERBUSCH, COMMUNICATION DESIGN)

tives on the "Water Advisory Team: Evaluate and Recommend" (WATER). Chatham also had three WATER representatives. CWLP was blindsided by the announcement made jointly by Village Presidents Grant Blasdell of Rochester and Chatham's Linda Koester.

— A state bill was approved and signed later that year to allow formation of the joint water district, and officials of both villages closely studied using the Sangamon River Valley aquifer east of Rochester as the water source. Even after Rochester signed a renegotiated water contract with CWLP in 1999, consideration of that new water district continued.

- Despite the certainty of sewer rates tripling if the answer was affirmative, the village board asked voters in 1990 "Is It Time to SOS?" The "Ship Our Sewage" question was approved by a 624 to 442 vote, thus annexing the village to the Springfield Metro Sanitary District (SMSD). By joining the district, Rochester avoided Illinois Environmental Protection Agency (IEPA) actions to limit the number of new homes and impose fines for repeated discharges that did not meet EPA standards. The other alternative, building a wastewater treatment facility in Rochester, was likely to have required even larger rate increases. Oak Hills Estates, Park Forest Hundred, and The Woodlands were annexed to SMSD in mid-decade. What had been the village's wastewater treatment ponds became used as excess flow lagoons, relied on primarily to capture heavy storm-water flows.

- Described by some Rochester citizens as "the best thing to happen here in a long time," Lost Bridge Trail opened in 1997. The original five-mile asphalt trail was built on the abandoned Baltimore & Ohio (B&O) Railroad bed and stretched from the Illinois Department of Transportation building on the east edge of Springfield to Walnut Street in Rochester. Plans for two trail extensions, one a connector trail to Community Park and one from Walnut Street east to Community Drive were unveiled in 1999.

— In preparation for the trail, studies discovered that a 165-foot-long trestle over Sugar Creek had been removed. IDOT suggested it was done "surreptitiously" during railroad salvage operations. However the bridge was removed, the action generated the name

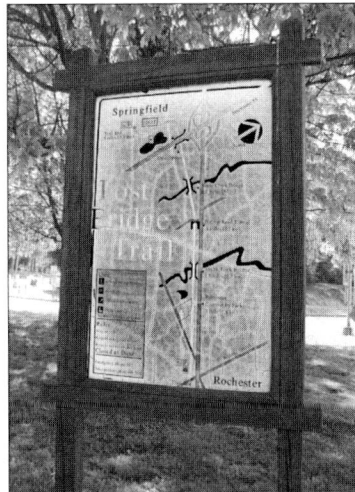

The Lost Bridge trailhead, at the corner of Route 29 and West Main Street, was opened in 1997. The five-mile trail to Springfield quickly became a Rochester attraction enjoyed by villagers and visitors of all ages for biking, hiking, and skating. (R. BRUZAN PHOTO)

Left photo: Built in 1896, this iron bridge carried B&O Railroad trains across the South Fork River west of Rochester. Although the tracks were removed decades ago, the bridge is still used in 2017 as part of Lost Bridge Trail.

Inset photo: Sugar Creek is seen here from the "lost" replacement bridge.

Top photo: Early in the process to convert a portion of the abandoned B&O Railroad track bed to a hike-bike trail, planners were surprised to discover that the Sugar Creek bridge had been removed. It thus seemed that "Lost Bridge Trail" would be an appropriate trail name. This replacement bridge now crosses Sugar Creek. (R. BRUZAN PHOTOS)

"Lost Bridge Trail." Featuring a parklike atmosphere where visitors often see wildlife, the trail was designed for walkers, runners, cyclists, rollerbladers and riders in strollers and even wheelchairs.

— At 102 years old, Rochester's oldest citizen, Hazel Park, enjoyed a two-mile outing on the new trail in 1997 when her granddaughter, Karen Alexander, pushed Hazel in a wheelchair from the trail's east end to the South Fork bridge. Hazel recounted fond memories of when she and her teenage friends spent many Sunday afternoons sitting on the edge of that bridge and talking for hours.

- A $334,000 study in 1995 paved the way for a major controversy regarding a potential Riverton-to-Rochester Road. Proponents of the estimated $12-to-$14-million 6.5-mile project said the road would decrease emergency response times, reduce road hazards and driving time, and promote commercial growth. Road opponents countered that saving a few minutes driving time and destroying several existing homes, farmland, and established neighborhoods were simply not worth the project cost.
  — Several options were set forth at public meetings in Rochester, Riverton, and Springfield. At one point, a petition with more than 30 signatures from Oak Street residents opposed the proposed alignment through their neighborhood. Village trustees said that petition was one reason why another proposed route was chosen, overruling the Rochester Township Road Commissioner's recommendation to use the Oak Street option.
  — The Sangamon County Board approved an alignment for the proposed two-lane road in 1996. With no funding in sight, however, as of 2017 the Riverton-to-Rochester Road remained only a proposal.

- In addition to the Riverton-to-Rochester Road, various other road and bridge improvements were planned or completed throughout the township.
  1990
  — Five-and-a-half miles of Cardinal Hill Road were resurfaced, and the abandoned B&O Railroad crossing on South Walnut Street was removed.

  1991
  — A timber bridge over the abandoned B&O Railroad tracks at Hilltop was removed and replaced with a new road and 16-foot-diameter pipe culvert in preparation for the construction of Lost Bridge Trail.
  — The Route 29 bridge across Black Branch Creek was replaced.

  1992
  — East Main Street was resurfaced between Route 29 and the east edge of Rochester.

  1994
  — The June heat raised the surface temperature of Route 29 to 130 degrees, although the soil beneath it remained about 80 degrees. The result was a "pavement blow up" that shattered a segment of the two-lane road about a mile southeast of Rochester. No accidents occurred as a result.
  — During this election year, Governor Jim Edgar promised to direct as much as $2 million of the fiscal 1995 road budget toward an engineering study to widen Route 29 to four lanes between Rochester and Taylorville. The 1996

fiscal year budget included more than $800,000 for an archeological study also in anticipation of that road widening.

1995

— A total of $751,000 in state highway construction money for fiscal year 1996 enabled plans to move forward to improve the Route 29 intersection at West Main, in part by eliminating the wooden railroad trestle underpass. Replacement traffic signals at Walnut and Route 29 were also funded.

Above: This view of the Route 29 and West Main Street intersection, looking east circa 1990, is from the Baltimore & Ohio (B&O) Railroad track viaduct, visible on the right. The former United Methodist Church is seen to the left.
(DANIEL G. MOORE PHOTO; USED WITH PERMISSION)

Above: The B&O Railroad trestle at Route 29 and West Main Street was removed in July 1995. This photo was taken looking south across Route 29.

Left: As seen across Route 29 from the former United Methodist Church parking lot, a new alignment was cut through the abandoned B&O Railroad bed to connect West Main Street with Route 29. The railroad trestle, which would soon be removed, was located just to the left of this photo.
(PHOTOS COURTESY OF CLAUDIA CROSS)

1998

— The 25-foot-wide South Fork River bridge on Rochester Road, built in 1958, was replaced by one 40 feet wide and designed to better accommodate daily traffic of about 5,700 vehicles.

1999

— Traffic signals were installed at Route 29 and State Street as part of an extensive project that also removed the abandoned B&O Railroad bridge over Route 29 near Hilltop. Route 29 bridges over the South Fork River and Sugar Creek were also rehabilitated.

Bud McCafferty used a special ink and fabric marker to pen in calligraphy the names of more than 700 Rochester citizens on a quilt that was pieced and quilted by Debbie Taft and Nanci Kieffer in 1996. On display at the Rochester Public Library, the quilt project helped raise funds to relocate the Old Stone House. A similar quilt is displayed at the Old Stone House at Rochester's Historical Park. (COURTESY OF ROCHESTER PUBLIC LIBRARY, RHPS COLLECTION; R. BRUZAN PHOTOS)

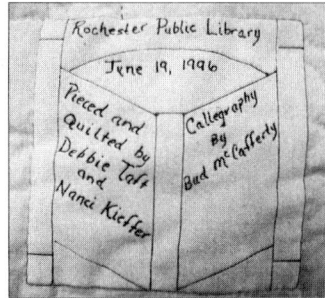

- Rochester's new library quickly became popular with the community. By 1997, library card holders were given access to the internet by using a library computer dedicated to this usage. Parents had to accompany children age 12 or younger, and those using the internet inappropriately could see their privileges suspended.

  — A library-sponsored baking contest, based on the 1952 book *The Lemon Jelly Cake* by former Rochester resident Madeline Babcock Smith, drew 23 entries in 1998. Leslie Fotre-Leach of Rochester baked the winning cake using modern techniques and her grandmother's recipes.

- A July 1990 car-truck accident north of Rochester trapped 17-year-old Don Deason for almost three hours before Rochester Emergency Squad and Rochester Fire Department volunteers, aided by the Sangamon County Rescue Squad and America Ambulance, extracted the teen from his flattened car. Rochester's Gary McBride and Gary Moore were among those who were later

Don Deason was trapped in his car, seen here under the truck, for three hours in 1990 before members of the Rochester Rescue Squad and Rochester Fire Department were able to extract him safely. The accident happened at the intersection of Gaule and North Walnut Roads. (COURTESY OF THE ROCHESTER FIRE PROTECTION DISTRICT AND MIKE WEAVER; USED WITH PERMISSION)

honored by the Illinois Department of Public Health for their parts in saving Deason's life. A report of the rescue was scheduled to appear on the CBS-TV program *"Rescue 911."*

— The Rochester Rescue Squad hosted an open house in 1999 to celebrate 25 years of service to the village and township.

- The Rochester Police Department's visible image was reworked in 1991. Blue became the "in" color for the RPD as new police uniforms were switched from brown and tan to navy and light blue. Squad cars also took on a new identity that distinguished the Rochester Police vehicles from those of the Sangamon County Sheriff's Department. A year later two police squad cars were equipped with mobile data terminals that enabled police to conduct from their squad cars any background checks on individuals stopped for traffic infractions.

The Rochester Police Department "Coat of Arms" patch, designed by members of the department in 1991, is used on all police uniforms. The design is registered nationally by the American College of Heraldry. (COURTESY OF ROCHESTER POLICE DEPT.)

— Rochester's reputation as a speed trap widened when an Internet web site in 1999 warned drivers to slow down or get ticketed when driving through the village. Rochester officers wrote an average of 3.25 traffic tickets per day in 1999.

- His Ford pickup was located near the Sangamon River at Buckhart, but the body of William Emmitt Chastain, Jr., of Rochester was never found. The Rochester Rescue Squad was joined by the Sangamon County Emergency Services and Disaster Agency rescue squad and the Springfield Underwater Search and Rescue Team. They searched the river and its banks for several weeks after Chastain was reported missing on June 11, 1999. As of 2017, the whereabouts of Chastain remains one of Rochester's unsolved mysteries.

- In 1997 Compass Point Productions, owned by F. North and Dorthy Ross, reproduced the 1918 Orange Judd *Pictorial* of Rochester homes and made it available for purchase. They added an index, maps, and page numbers for more convenient referencing.

— Also in 1997, the Mendenhall family, owners of the "Old Stone House" on Buckhart Road, offered to donated the crumbling structure to the Rochester Historical Preservation Society (RHPS) if members would move it off the farm property.

— Additionally, in order to help RHPS document local history, members asked area residents to donate or make available for copy historic artifacts and pictures they owned that were connected to Rochester's history.

- Eighty-one-year-old resident Esther Taft recalled in 1991 how two issues were frequent topics of conversation in the village decades earlier. One was the horrible mud roads of the early 1900s that slowed horses to a walk. She explained it was so muddy that visitors to Springfield had to take the train (the Interurban) instead of their horse and buggy. The other issue was that Rochester was a dry town in which the sale of alcohol was prohibited, and that was just fine with most people.
  — Rochester was still a dry town in 1994. The village's July 4th alcohol-free celebration drew 2,000 to 3,000 people, indicating that the family-friendly event was successful even without the sale of alcohol.

- A 1994 design competition sponsored by the Rochester Lions Club led to creation of "Welcome to Rochester" signs for travelers entering Rochester on Route 29. That competition attracted entries from Rochester Police Officer Lonnie Stivers and Polish exchange student Benita Walasczyk. The village, Rochester Lions Club, and Rochester Woman's Club were among the groups paying for the signs.

Travelers to Rochester on Route 29 are greeted and welcomed.
(R. Bruzan photo)

- A brush fire combined with high winds to generate smoke and dramatically reduce visibility for drivers along Route 29 south of Rochester in March 1994. Rochester Assistant Fire Chief Wayne Beck, who noted there had been several brush fires on the same day, warned against burning on gusty days.
  — Rochester firefighters also responded in 1996 to a house fire at 112 North Oak Street. Believed to have started in the fireplace chimney, the fire destroyed the garage and badly damaged the home.

- Steve Taft had long been among the enthusiastic supporters in favor of establishing a Rochester High School football program. A 1973 RHS graduate, Taft felt that by 1994 the growing school district was in a better position to launch a football team than in 1982, when a parent-based request was unsuccessful. The seven-member support group moved their proposal through months of planning, meetings, and discussions until April 1994, when on a 5-2 vote, the school board approved a football program to begin its first season in 1995. Dave Jacobs was hired to be Rochester High School's first football coach, as a freshman and junior-varsity program was fielded the first year, and varsity games began the following season.

- *The Rochester Times* resumed publication in 1993. It continues in 2017 to provide weekly coverage of village and township news.

- Rochester history has included frequent church-related construction. Dedication ceremonies were held in April 1990 for a new parish center at the Church of St. Jude and for a new 7,300-square-foot sanctuary and education facility at the Rochester First Baptist Church.

About 50 congregants of Grace Bible Church built a new chapel on Woodhaven Drive in 1994. They were first established in Springfield in 1953. Floyd Pierce is the church president in 2017. (R. BRUZAN PHOTO)

- Rochester IGA supermarket owner Andy Lunt was not present in September 1995 to meet the country music star. However, he heard reports that 1994 Country Music Hall of Fame legend Merle Haggard had been shopping with his band members at Lunt's State Street store, restocking their tour bus before playing that night at Nashville North USA in Taylorville.

- Fifteen lots were added in 1990 as the final plat of The Meadows subdivision, which was first opened in 1988. Additional new and expanded subdivisions emerged in Rochester after village board approval of a 20-year comprehensive plan, a subdivision ordinance, and a zoning ordinance in 1991. In 1993, 64 lots became available in Maplehurst Estates on some of the land farmed decades earlier by Taft brothers Isham, Elwin, and Gilson. Ninety-four single-family lots were planned one year later in The Woodlands at South Fork, located south of Oak Hills Estates.

- Facing a situation unique in Rochester's history, plans for The Woodlands subdivision came to a halt in 1994 after interest was renewed in Olcott Mounds, a Native American

Rochester's North Park water tower went into service in 1993. (R. BRUZAN PHOTO)

burial site located on planned subdivision property. The land at the heart of the controversy is on the east bluff of the South Fork River and was owned at one time by local farmer Rufus W. Olcott.

— The mounds, studied by James Wickersham in the 1880s, were once again examined for artifacts and human remains. Native Americans, led by Daniel Wolfshadow of Springfield, conducted public awareness vigils and powwows in Rochester and Springfield, urging that the mounds not be disturbed if they were found to contain human remains.

— The subsequent detailed mounds study reported that fragmentary remains of one human burial were located, as well as Late Woodland, circa AD 700, pottery and Late Archaic, circa BC 1500, projectile points. Due to the lack of what would have been considered significant tribal artifacts at the mounds, the subdivision was allowed to proceed.

- With well and groundwater levels low due to several years of below-normal precipitation, numerous Rochester township farmers found it necessary to truck water for themselves and their livestock. One farmer in 1990 was hauling 1,300 gallons of water every other day for his 1,100 hogs. Thousands of Central Illinois property owners bought white plastic tanks in order to carry water, and bulk water sellers saw their business double from 1988 to 1990. Another issue emerged when it became known in the middle of the dry spell that the Illinois Commerce Commission had for years required commercial water haulers to buy a $600 permit. That mandate had been largely ignored previously.

- A Rochester business group resembling a local chamber of commerce organized in 1990. Goals of the Rochester Business Association were to promote economic, educational, and cultural life in the immediate area. Owners of Rochester's 80 businesses and others interested in the town's economic future were invited to join.

The Rochester Business Association honored veterans in 1991 with a monument erected among a grove of trees at Community Park.
(R. BRUZAN PHOTOS)

- Although residents could recycle as early as the 1970s by taking items to village locations according to a posted schedule, by the 1990s these programs had ceased. That left residents to find their own options for recycling newspapers, metal cans, plastics, and glass. In 1993, however, the village board authorized garbage haulers to begin curbside recycling using bins that were distributed free to every home. Through the Sangamon County Solid Waste Management Grant Program, Rochester received funding to buy bins and establish the program that included a community forum, educational materials for adults and students, and even refrigerator magnets distributed prior to the first curbside pickups in March. The campaign was dubbed "Rochester Recycles Responsibly" or R^3.

The village board approved Rochester's first curbside recycling program in 1993. A public information campaign, named Rochester Recycles Responsibly, R^3, provided the initial guidance for people interested in taking part in the program. (ARTWORK BY MARK RITTERBUSCH, COMMUNICATION DESIGN)

- In the wake of Iraq's 1990 invasion of Kuwait, gasoline prices increased across the country, including at both of Rochester's gas stations. In less than one week, regular unleaded and premium gas at Strode's full-service station went up 26 cents a gallon to $1.29 and $1.39 per gallon respectively. Several weeks later, Glen Bruce, owner of the Standard gas station, was looking at the potential of another increase, this time 3 cents a gallon for each of the three grades of gas he sold. Some area station owners explained that the invasion had led to motorists' jitters about gasoline availability and a perceived need to fill their tanks more frequently, thus increasing both demand and prices.

- Rochester crimes included an extensive 1999 tire-slashing spree on 18 cars in the State Street neighborhood and a gang symbol that two local teens spray painted on a roadside "Welcome to Rochester" sign in 1994.
  — Efforts of Rochester teens culminated in passage of a 1997 village ordinance making it illegal for anyone under age 18 to possess cigarettes or tobacco products. Violators faced an initial $25 fine and $50 fines for repeat offenses. The students' efforts came as a result of their participation in the drug-and-alcohol prevention program called Operation Snowball.
  — Two men arrested in 1991 were connected to an attempted burglary and subsequent murder that took place 1.5 miles north of Rochester at an Oak Street home. One resident of the house claimed he shot the burglar in self-defense. Local residents' fears were calmed when both surviving suspects had been rounded up within two weeks of the incident. Each man was given a multiple-year prison sentence.

— Like a scene right out of the popular late-1960s TV show *"Mayberry R.F.D,"* a Rochester police officer saw his squad car stolen by a double-jointed woman who had been pulled over on potential sobriety issues. She slipped out of her handcuffs, gained access to the squad car's front seat by sliding around a heavy floor-to-ceiling dividing screen, and left the officer standing by the side of Route 29 as she drove to Springfield in his police vehicle with its lights flashing. She left the lights flashing as she abandoned the car at 11th Street and South Grand Avenue, then walked about 1.5 miles home. Although the woman had been scheduled to be admitted to McFarland Mental Health Center for care, she was welcomed there a few days early.

- Among township citizens who were recognized were the following:

1990
— Beloved music teacher **Melva Jo Sexton** retired after teaching 32 years in the Rochester School District;
— **James Chandler**, former Illinois State Police chief psychologist, published the book *Modern Police Psychology* that included chapters on hostage negotiations and creating personality profiles of wanted criminals;

1993
— **Delores Palmer**, Rochester Library's first director, began working full time at her writing and publishing company Wee Write Keepsakes, Inc., which focused on stories written by children for children;

1994
— After 19 years as superintendent of Rochester School District 3A, **Jack K. Taylor** retired. Sort of. For the next 15 years he continued one of his favorite avocations, driving Rochester school buses.

1995
— **Bob Waldmire** a 1963 RHS graduate, became the caretaker of the International Bioregional Old Route 66 Visitor Center and Preservation Foundation in Hackberry, AZ;
— **Erin Duesterhaus** was crowned Sangamon County Fair queen just weeks after graduating from RHS in 1994; six months later Erin was named Miss Illinois County Fair, and went on to serve as the official hostess of that year's State Fair;

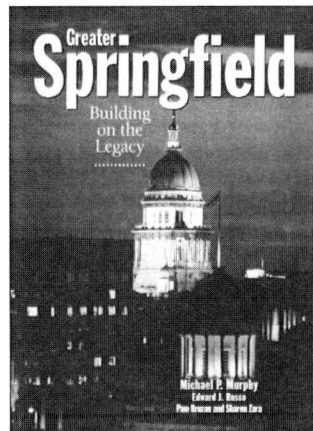

Co-authors of the 1993 book *Greater Springfield: Building on the Legacy* included Rochester writers Sharon Zara and Pam Bruzan. The publication was sponsored by The Greater Springfield Chamber of Commerce. (PHOTO BY TERRY FARMER PHOTOGRAPHY, SPRINGFIELD, IL; USED WITH PERMISSION)

1999

— On behalf of the Veterans of Foreign Wars State Headquarters, **Bill Waldmire** was presented a certificate honoring his 15 years of dedication to place American flags each Memorial Day on the graves of veterans buried in Mottarville Cemetery.

- Emergencies and accidents included the following:
  — An employee at the composting site along Route 29 west of the South Fork River was seriously injured in 1991 when his arm became caught in a conveyer belt.
  — An uninjured parachutist from Rochester was rescued by the Taylorville Rescue Squad in 1990 when she was blown into a tree rather than landing in an open field.
  — Although a local farmer lost a portion of one leg in 1990 after it became entangled in a grain auger, he was back to farming the following spring.
  — Rochester eighth and ninth grade students, along with a 1988 RHS graduate, were killed when hit by a car as they walked along the Mechanicsburg Blacktop in 1991.
  — A few weeks later another high school student died from burns received when a campfire ignited his clothes that may have had gasoline spilled on them.
  — A natural gas explosion at Springfield Clinic killed a Rochester boiler serviceman in 1992.

- Any deaths may give readers a chance to reflect, but after living in Rochester for 20 years, the authors lost five immediate neighbors during the 1990s.
  — **Robert L. Ritterbusch**, a Marine Corps veteran of World War II and a leader in supporting veterans' organizations and promoting village-wide emergency services, died in 1996.
  — Rochester native, 40-year employee of Illinois Bell Telephone Co., and livestock dealer **Nelson V. Campbell** died in 1990.
  — **William B. Pfeiffer** died in 1996. A 49-year member of Laborers Local 477, and a noted gardener, he was always ready to plow neighbors' snow-covered driveways with his tractor.
  — **William** and **Delores** *(Hubbard)* **Mayer** died in 1996 and 1997 respectively.

- Other Rochester deaths included :
  1991
  — Rochester Village President **Henry Bregenhorn**, a former state trooper and Rochester police chief, died during his second term.

1992
— **Ruby** *(Thornton)* **Bell**, 99, had been the wife of James Earl Bell and a granddaughter of Long-Nine member Archer G. Herndon.
— **Harrison Earl Wilcoxson** was a former *State Journal-Register* reporter and publisher of weekly newspapers that included *The Rochester Herald*.

1993
— **Charles M. Newhouse**, co-owner of Helen's Flower Shop in Rochester, was a World War II Naval instructor, and a Lions Club district governor.
— **Edwin S. Waldmire**, was known as a farmer, inventor, food processor, and 1949 founder of Springfield's Cozy Dog Restaurant.
— **Ross E. Fairchild**, a retired farmer and lifelong Rochester resident, was a past master of Rochester Lodge 635 AF&AM, and past president of the Rochester Fire Protection District.
— Korean War veteran, and farmer **H. Wayne Taft** was a founder of the Heritage House Restaurant in Springfield.

1994
— **Doris** *(Hardbarger)* **Campbell**, was a Rochester Christian Church member for 60 years and a 50-year member of Sangamon Order of the Eastern Star 746 chapter.
— **James Marshall Bell**, Rochester State Bank President, was a grandson of the bank's founder and a World War II veteran.

1996
— A charter member of the Church of St. Jude and Rochester Lions Club, **Thomas E. Scott** had also served as Rochester Township Supervisor and township director of the American Red Cross.
— **Raymond W. Woodruff** moved to the historic Spring Valley Farm north of Rochester in 1920 and earned a distinguished flying cross for World War II missions in North Africa, China, Burma, and India.

1998
— **Hazel** *(Jones)* **Park**, who taught in two one-room schools, was a past Rochester Woman's Club president, and member of the Royal Neighbors of America, died at age 102.
— **Dora** *(Smith)* **Lovejoy**, born in the home her grandfather built in 1860 southeast of Rochester and in which she raised her daughter, a nephew and niece, died at age 98.

Hazel *(Jones)* Park, lifelong Sangamon County resident, was born in 1895 on a farm near New City, and lived much of her life in Rochester. (COURTESY OF KAREN PARK ALEXANDER)

—Rochester native **Delbert D. Taft** was a World War II veteran and originator of the Illinois State Fair's rib-eye sandwich.

1999
— **Wilbern W.** and **Dorothy** *(Flynn)* **Dugger** both died in 1999. His scouting activities included serving as scout master of two troops, skipper of a sea scout ship, and director of Camp Illinek. She was an early Girl Scout leader in Rochester and was widely known for her skills at early-American fiber arts, especially spinning.

• Reunions, birthdays, and anniversaries were often shared with family and village friends. As readers may recognize, notable celebrations of the decade occasionally included some families who would later come together to honor family and friends who died in this decade:
— The 78th annual Bailey reunion, one of the oldest family gatherings in Sangamon County, was held at Community Park in 1990. It was notable that three attendees of that year's reunion had also attended the very first Bailey Reunion in 1913.

Golden wedding anniversaries:
— **Alvin** and **Joan** *(Williams)* **Mavis,**
— **Ross** and **Elizabeth** *(Cordis)* **Fairchild,**
— **Ralph** and **Alice Mae** *(Strode)* **Leach,**
— **Fred** and **Ruth** *(Minser)* **Drillinger,**
— **Justin** and **Mardell** *(Kieffer)* **Taft,** and
— **Dean** and **Sarah** *(Truxal)* **Wisleder.**

Other notable events included:
— **Robert** and **Jane** *(Brubaker)* **Fairchild's** 45th anniversary,
— **F.M.** and **Helen** *(Durham)* **Poffenberger's** 45th anniversary,
— 60th anniversary of **Charles** and **Ruby** *(Mangold)* **Beam,**
— **Dora** *(Smith)* **Lovejoy's** 98th birthday, and
— **Hazel** *(Jones)* **Park's** 100th birthday.

F.M. (Sid) and Helen *(Durham)* Poffenberger celebrated their 45th wedding anniversary in 1993. Sid is a descendent of Christian and Mary Poffenberger, who came from Maryland in 1839 to settle in the Rochester area. (COURTESY OF THE *ROCHESTER & LAKE SPRINGFIELD HERALD*; 24 MAR. 1993)

• "What they did is what Rochester is all about: togetherness and people helping people," observed Rochester Village President Henry Bregenhorn in 1991. His words were illustrated through several 1990s community activities.
— When three teens won prize money in a contest sponsored by Dimension Cable Services, they immediately donated it toward the needs of a seriously burned Rochester student.

— Furniture and household goods were provided by village residents to a family displaced by their 1999 house fire.

— Fundraisers were held to help a seventh-grader fighting a brain tumor, a fifth-grade Rochester teacher preparing for a bone marrow transplant, and a Rochester resident with cystic fibrosis awaiting a lung transplant.

— In 1991 Rochester residents recognized soldiers in the Persian Gulf War by covering the pine tree in the village triangle with yellow bows. "It's a way to show we're remembering them," said Village President Henry Bregenhorn.

The Rochester community again demonstrated the spirit of giving when dozens of volunteers completed a new playground, named Friendship Fort, at Community Park in 1999. The playground was dedicated to Rochester student Rachel Anne Sperry, who had died from cancer at age 12. (COURTESY OF THE ROCHESTER TIMES, 29 APR. 1999)

Local woodworking artist F. North Ross created a collection of detailed wood miniatures of Rochester buildings. They are displayed at the Rochester Public Library in 2017. (COURTESY OF DORTHY ROSS; R. BRUZAN PHOTO)

A Central Illinois train authority, Rochester author Dick Wallin has written four books and two dozen magazine articles, and has produced hundreds of photographs on train-related topics. He is co-founder of the GM&O (Gulf Mobile & Ohio) Historical Society. (LEFT: R.R. WALLIN COLLECTION; USED WITH PERMISSION; RIGHT: COURTESY OF FOUR WAYS WEST PUBLICATIONS, LA MIRADA, CA, 1996)

ENCOUNTERS WITH THE PAST;
CONNECTIONS TO THE FUTURE

In addition to the rebuilt Old Stone House, Historical Park on West Main Street may become the future location of other historic Rochester Township buildings and artifacts. (R. BRUZAN PHOTO)

2000s

The "Old Stone House" connects current and future Rochester generations with those of the past.
(TOBY MCDANIEL PHOTO; USED WITH PERMISSION)

2000s Timeline...

2000 Population: 2,893
   — Village board approved Wyndmoor subdivision zoning
   — New middle school for grades 4-6 was built on the West Main Street campus

2001 Rochester resident Toby McDaniel wrote the book *Honk If You're A Hoosier*
   — Rochester Fire Department and Rochester Rescue Squad merged
   — Rochester United Methodist Church dedicated their new church on South Walnut Street

2003 Rochester Fire Department relocated to a new building at 700 East Main Street
   — Rolling Prairie Baptist Church began worship in Rochester
   — Lost Bridge Trail was extended from Walnut Street to Community Drive

2004 Route 29 opened as a four-lane road between Rochester and Berry
   — Population: 2,943

— Rochester resident Justin Taft wrote the book *As I Saw It*
— Rochester resident Nadene Lynch Miller wrote the book
A Haunt of Memories
— Oak Mills Estates subdivision began development

2005   Bank & Trust expanded at its original location on South Walnut
Street
— The Old Stone House was dedicated at Historical Park

2006   The two oldest buildings still used as Rochester schools were
demolished
— Traffic signals were installed on Route 29 at Hilltop
— Population: 3,442
— Wireless internet service became available in Rochester

2007   Rochester voters ended the ban on alcohol sales
— Cardinal Hill Road was extended north to Buckhart Road
— Lincoln – Van Buren Trail was dedicated
— Traffic signals were installed at the intersection of Route 29 and
Cardinal Hill Road
— Rochester resident Justin Taft wrote *The Tafts of Rochester*
— Rochester Township Building was completed on Braner Road

2008   An auditorium, 14 new classrooms, junior high, and cafeteria were
added to the Route 29 campus
— The East Main Street concrete bridge over Black Branch Creek
was replaced

2000s Storylines...

- New roads, bridges, schools, fire station, subdivisions, businesses, and new
residents helped lead Rochester into the new century. Problems associated
with providing proper sewage treatment and a water supply continued, push-
ing the village board to reconsider those issues. Alcohol sales appeared on the
ballot again, while video gaming provided a new topic for consideration. The
Rochester Historical Preservation Society cultivated interest in village history,
as some community groups
kept one foot in the distant
past, while also focusing their
eyes toward Rochester's future.

- Improvement to Rochester
roads and bridges resulted in
safer and more rapid travel in
the village and township.
— When a 5.2-mile stretch of
Route 29 from Rochester to
Berry was completed in 2004,

The East Main Street bridge over Black Branch Creek
is seen before its demolition and replacement in 2008.
(DAVE JOSTES PHOTO; USED WITH PERMISSION)

Left: Visible behind Fay Jostes is the iron-and-wood pedestrian bridge that she and her husband, David Jostes, saved from demolition during the 2008 Black Branch Creek bridge replacement.

Below: David Jostes displays horse shoes, bottles, tires, shoes, and numerous other artifacts he collected from Black Branch Creek during the 2008 East Main Street bridge replacement. (R. BRUZAN PHOTOS)

it marked the initial step to convert 18 miles of a two-lane state road between Rochester and Taylorville to a four-lane divided highway. The final section of this massive project was completed 13 years later.

— From a realigned intersection of Oak Hill and Cardinal Hill Roads at the southeast corner of the village, Cardinal Hill Road was extended on a new alignment north to Route 29. It then extended farther north to Buckhart Road. Traffic signals were installed the same year at the new Cardinal Hill Road intersection with Route 29.

— Another new set of traffic signals on Route 29 was installed in 2006 where it intersected with Hilltop Road.

— Part of East Main Street was closed much of the summer in 2008 during replacement of the bridge over Black Branch Creek, which had been listed as "structurally deficient."

- The village board continued to monitor Rochester's rapid growth.

— More than 600 residents signed petitions in 2000 opposing 23 duplexes originally planned for the new Wyndmoor subdivision on the southwest edge of Rochester. Sixteen duplexes were eventually approved.

— Oak Mill Estates, a 50-acre, 114-lot subdivision on the northeast side of Rochester, began development in 2004. Initial plans called for 100 homes and 14 duplexes with an anticipated value between $175,000 and $225,000.

— Almost half of all village households responded to a survey that questioned, among other issues, residents' use of current village amenities such as parks and what new businesses and services they wanted to see in Rochester. The survey was conducted by the Rochester Planning Commission with help from the University of Illinois Extension. The results were used to help prepare a new Comprehensive Plan.

— In 2009, the village board approved new and replacement sidewalks on Walnut Street and prohibited video gaming terminals in Rochester.

- By a vote of 419 to 189, Rochester taxpayers rejected in 2006 a proposed one-year property tax increase that would have enabled the Illinois Municipal Retirement Fund to begin covering village employees.

- Reporting that Rochester School District 3A underwent major changes during this decade would be an understatement. Bond issues passed, old schools were demolished, land for another new campus was purchased, and new schools were built.

  — Middle school grades four through six moved in 2000 to their new 63,000-square-foot brick middle school on the West Main Street campus. Tele-

Right: A second school on the West Main Street campus opened in 2000 as a grades 4-6 middle school. In 2017 it had been redesignated as Rochester Elementary 2-3.

Below: Located on the Route 29 campus, a new junior high school was dedicated in 2008. (R. BRUZAN PHOTOS)

Rochester High School's Fine Arts Auditorium opened in 2008. It was the first such facility in the history of the Rochester School District. (R. BRUZAN PHOTO)

phone, voice mail, intercom, internet, and TV hookups were installed in the new "dustless" classrooms where dry-erase marker boards replaced traditional chalkboards.

— Approval was two to one in 2002 when Rochester voters passed an $8-million bond issue to demolish what was then the junior high, a vocational building, and bus garage. When combined with a promised $10 million state grant, the referendum was also targeted to fund construction of junior-and-senior-high classrooms, an addition to the elementary school, and the district's first dedicated auditorium.

— Because the state's grant funding promised in 2002 had not yet materialized three years later, Rochester voters approved another bond issue that enabled the district to move forward with construction projects planned earlier but not yet started. The bond issue totaled $11.2 million.

What had started as Rochester's school for grades 1-11 (left) and Rochester High School (right) are seen as they appeared in 2006 prior to their demolition. (P. BRUZAN PHOTOS)

— A year later, a new eight-lane, all-weather track was completed around the football field.

— Valerie Presney was part of a community group that raised more than $125,000 in 2004 to pay for enlarging the planned high school stage, as well as other changes to allow adding stage-related enhancements.

— After an unexpected flood of the district office building, the school board decided to demolish that structure and replace it with one to house both district offices and a weight facility. Pressure problems had caused a water main break with more than eight feet of water filling the basement, flowing across the first floor, and destroying numerous stored records. The building had opened in 1937 as the high school.

— The auditorium and new junior high school were dedicated in 2008. Both are on the Route 29 campus.

— As enrollment continued to grow, up 8.6% between 2004 and 2006, the 2006 school board bought 65 acres of land on Rochester's east side. No definite plans existed for another building at that time.

— Yet another building referendum faced voters this decade, and in 2008 voters approved a $26-million bond issue. With total student enrollment at an all-time high of 2,252, this massive project included an 88,000-square-foot intermediate school for grades four through six on the newly acquired East Main property and a 48,000-square-foot fieldhouse on the Route 29 campus. Geothermal heating and cooling systems were installed for both. The middle school at that time was also remodeled for second and third grades, and the elementary school retrofitted for early childhood, pre-kindergarten, kindergarten and first-grade classes.

— Construction of the new East Main Street intermediate school and fieldhouse on the Route 29 campus began in 2009.

• The decades-long ban on alcohol sales in Rochester ended in 2007 when, by a vote of 659 to 443, the village become a "wet" town that allowed alcohol sales. Opponents of the change feared more crime and a reduced quality of life. Proponents predicted sales-tax-revenue increases and opportunities to attract new business.

—The village board passed a liquor ordinance, and liquor licenses soon became available for banquet halls, restaurants, retail stores, and caterers. The liquor ordinance was soon amended when a planned winery and outdoor wine garden applied for a license in 2009. The annual license fee was established at $600, and an annual outdoor-permit fee was set at $100.

- Mandatory water restrictions after a January 2003 water-main break included avoiding showers and baths, and closing car washes, bulk water businesses and coin-operated laundries. Using disposable plates and eating utensils allowed schools to avoid using dishwashers. The broken pipe was located along Rochester Road, 100 yards west of Oak Hill Road. Freezing temperatures and a parallel gas main slowed repairs that required a hole 18-feet deep, 6-feet long, and 6-feet wide. Restrictions were lifted the day after repairs were completed, but a boil order was issued for residents in that area. Although broken water mains are not uncommon, that Rochester-Road break may have been among the most challenging to locate and repair.

- An adequate water supply and sufficient wastewater treatment for residents continued to be among top village board priorities. An upgrade was proposed in 2009 to improve sewer capacity and meet the demands of the new school on East Main Street. The first phase was to install a larger main between Main Street and the northeast pump station on Black Branch Creek.

— The Chatham-Rochester Water Commission in 2003 considered drilling into a local aquifer for well water in order to discontinue buying water from Springfield. By 2005, however, Rochester decided to discontinue its participation in the Commission's efforts due to the finances involved. The village signed a new 20-year water agreement with City Water, Light & Power (CWLP) four years later. Chatham went forward and constructed an $18-million water plant east of the village on Buckhart Road, as well as transmission lines from there to Chatham.

- The Rochester Fire Department underwent major changes and controversial events.

— During five months early in 2000, a six-member citizens committee met to consider the possible merger of the Rochester Fire Department and Rochester Rescue Squad. After talking with more than three dozen individuals and visiting the headquarters of both agencies, the committee wrote a 22-page report recommending merger of the Rescue Squad into the Fire Protection District.

— Rescue Squad governance was transferred from the Rochester Village Board to the Rochester Fire Protection District Board the following year. The merger

Left: The Rochester Fire Department and Rescue Squad merged in 2001. (COURTESY OF MIKE WEAVER, ROCHESTER FIRE PROTECTION DISTRICT)

Below: Rochester Fire Department's new station at 700 East Main Street was dedicated in 2003. (R. BRUZAN PHOTO)

Above: Assisted by Gary McBride in 2001, four-year-old Ryan Bruzan learns how to drive one of Rochester's firefighting vehicles. (P. BRUZAN PHOTO)

was seen as an avenue to improve coordination between the two groups and ensure financial stability for the Rescue Squad.

— Within months of the merger, Fire Protection District voters approved doubling their fire tax to build a new fire station, improve training, and fund the Rescue Squad.

— With the fire station at 125 East Main Street ready to be sold at auction in 2003, Rochester Fire-Rescue moved into their newly completed $1.6 million station at 700 East Main Street. The new 20,000-square-foot station featured offices, kitchen, meeting rooms, fitness rooms, lockers, training area, and eight drive-through vehicle bays. Fire and Rescue Chief Dick Rentschler said plans were to build a showcase that would display memorabilia from as far back as when his father, Ernie Rentschler, was Rochester's first fire chief in 1952.

— The department purchased a new multi-purpose rescue truck in 2004, but two referenda to buy more equipment failed two years later.

— Controversy swirled throughout the district in 2008 when two former members of the department filed allegations of sexual harassment by a Rochester firefighter with the Illinois Department of Human Rights. At the time, the Rochester Fire Board did not have established policies regarding any form of harassment. The complaint was settled, and later that year the Board adopted a series of job descriptions and policies against harassment.

— A concern about adequate background checks for fire and rescue personnel and volunteers surfaced after the 2009 arrest of a Rochester firefighter for child pornography.

— During the same year, district residents voted to elect future members of the Rochester Fire Protection District Board, rather than rely on appointments by the Sangamon County Board.

- The village board voted in 2003 to extend Lost Bridge Trail from Walnut Street east to Cardinal Hill Road. Federal and state grants funded the new pavement and a bridge over Black Branch Creek.

Looking south near the intersection of State Street and Route 29, viewers can see two bridges crossing Black Branch Creek. In the background is the wooden Lost Bridge Trail bridge, built in 2003, and in the foreground is the concrete Route 29 bridge.
(R. BRUZAN PHOTO)

- In 2007, Police Cpl. Jon Schwartz was named the first police investigator in the history of the Rochester Police Department (RPD). Police Chief Bill Marass explained that Schwartz would be following up with information and individuals who could assist in closing investigations.

— In the early 1970s, just one police officer was needed four hours a day. By 2008, one part-time and eight full-time officers made up the Department.

— As auto accidents in the village decreased from 54 in 2007 to 33 two years later, police credited additional stoplights and better roads.

— RPD held its first citizens police academy in 2009. The four-week program included information about officer training and responsibility, use of force, search and seizure, police equipment, and traffic stops.

— It took two hours in 2006 for police to determine that a reported shooting-and-hostage situation at a West Main Street house was a hoax. Rochester schools had been put on lockdown and Illinois State Police and Sangamon County officers joined RPD in responding to the alleged incident location, which turned out to be an empty house.

- February 2003 brought with it an invasion of the meteorological oddi-ties known as snow rollers, formations that appeared on fields around the

A rarely seen phenomenon, snow rollers, appeared across Rochester Township fields in February 2003. (P. BRUZAN PHOTOS)

township. Snow rollers develop when snowflakes hit the snow cover, are pushed forward by wind, and collect other flakes until hollow log-shaped rolls form. Snow rollers can be as small as tennis balls but have also been seen larger than a car.

— Other unusual weather occurred in January 2005, when severe rains flooded Dannenberger and Ramsey Roads. Six months later, the winds of a June storm caused power outages and felled trees on about 10 Rochester homes.

Homes damaged in a 2005 storm included the J.B. Highmore house at the southeast corner of John and Mill Streets. (STATE JOURNAL-REGISTER, 15 JUNE 2005)

- A voter-approved property tax increase in 2004 allowed the Rochester Public Library to offset taxes from properties that had recently de-annexed from the local district and annexed to other taxing districts. It also enabled increased staffing hours and the purchase of books and materials.

  — An unusual library-sponsored activity in 2003 was a Library Book Brigade, community members who marched in unison during the 4th of July parade to share their joy of reading.

  — Celebrating the Apollo 11 anniversary in 2004, Rochester Librarian Nancy Atkinson gave a multimedia presentation and displayed a moon rock borrowed from NASA.

  — Rochester-born Justin Taft held a 2004 book signing at the library for his autobiography *As I Saw It*. This collection of stories from Taft's life also entwined with the history of the village.

- "We don't have a sense of community like we used to have in the old days," remarked Rochester Police Chief Bill Marass during an RPD-sponsored community meeting in 2009. He felt this contributed to neighbors being less likely to call police if they saw a possible crime. He also pointed out that Rochester burglaries, thefts, and instances of criminal damage were usually committed by local teens and had almost doubled from 26 in 2008 to 47 through September 2009. He described many of the residential burglaries as "garage hopping" by thieves stealing from open garages. Community meetings were held to educate the public about these crimes and to encourage information sharing among officers, residents, and business owners.

- A rather unusual election occurred in 2002 when Rochester biology teacher Don Wohlers and a former student, Sarah Moore, competed for the same Sangamon County Board seat. After a respectful and upbeat campaign, voters chose the student over the teacher. Wohlers graciously said later that the election loss was not a bitter defeat but that he took "a fatherly pride" when he saw any student achieve success.

- Church news:
— Rolling Prairie Baptist Church was established in 2003, holding worship services at the Rochester Elementary School. Offering the advice not to "drive faster than your guardian angel can fly," its pastor and motorcycle enthusiast Mark Estrop blessed about two dozen motorcycles and their riders in Springfield at Hall's Harley-Davidson as the 2008 motorcycle-riding season began.
— The South Fork Church of Christ, founded in 1832, celebrated its 175th anniversary, a terquasquicentennial, in 2007. The church is still recognized as a spot near where Abraham Lincoln delivered a temperance address in 1846.
— Dedication of a new building addition in 2001 was part of the Rochester Christian Church's 125th anniversary celebration. Two years later the church received a charter from the Boy Scouts of America to sponsor Troop 58, the second troop in the village.

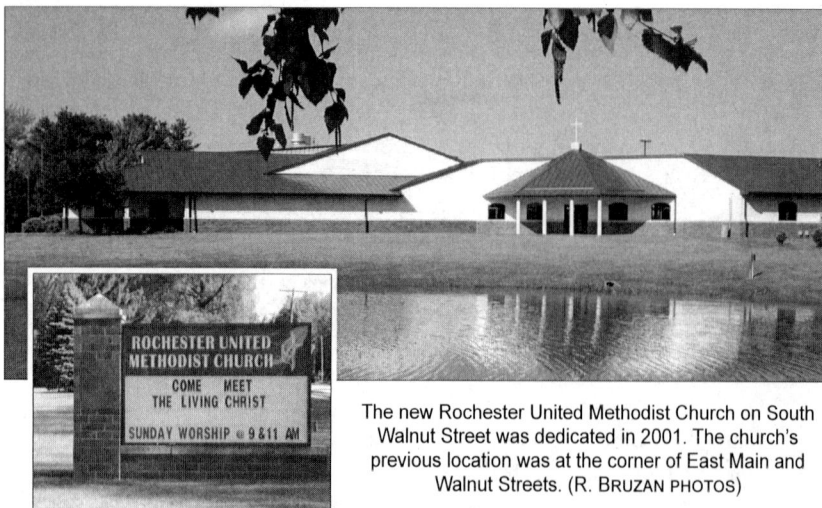

The new Rochester United Methodist Church on South Walnut Street was dedicated in 2001. The church's previous location was at the corner of East Main and Walnut Streets. (R. BRUZAN PHOTOS)

- During the 2006 construction of a 342-foot replacement cellular phone tower between State Street and Route 29, a member of the ground crew became caught in equipment and was pulled up the tower. The worker then fell 60 to 70 feet to the ground. He spent more than a week in critical condition, but survived the accident.

- Hunter Lake, first proposed in the wake of a 1954 drought, was still being considered in 2009 as a backup water source to Lake Springfield. Creating the lake as proposed would dam Horse Creek, which flows into the South Fork River, and flood some Rochester Township land. Although some property had already been purchased for the lake, the necessity and feasibility of the water source remained in question.

- Having sold its land along Route 29 back to the Rochester Lutheran Church in 2000, the Rochester Historical Preservation Society (RHPS) made ready for the monumental task of relocating and rebuilding the Old Stone House on newly acquired property adjacent to Community Park. Stones from the house, originally built on Buckhart Road, were donated to RHPS by Allen and

When a strong 1997 wind blew in part of an Old Stone House wall, the Rochester Historical Preservation Society moved quickly to salvage the historic structure. The house was relocated to the Rochester Historical Park on West Main Street. (COURTESY OF ROCHESTER PUBLIC LIBRARY, RHPS COLLECTION)

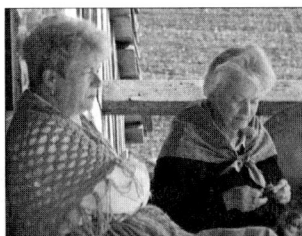

Above: Ann Rowley and Fay Jostes are two of the docents who share the fascinating history of the Old Stone House with visitors.

Left: Every year, students receive lessons in Rochester history during field trips to the Old Stone House. Attentive children here enjoy stories of the Old Stone House told by docent Carolyn Moore. (TOBY MCDANIEL PHOTOS; USED WITH PERMISSION)

Barbara Mendenhall. The house's cornerstone was laid during a 2003 public celebration, followed the next day by a cemetery walk, "A Whisper in Time." The walk featured stories of former Rochester residents buried in cemeteries at Rochester, Mottarville, and Buckhart, with costumed RHPS members portraying those residents at the cemeteries in which they are at rest.

— One year later, visitors to the RHPS-sponsored Potato Festival at Historical Park also saw how far the Stone House reconstruction had progressed. Period home furnishings were actively solicited, and a formal dedication ceremony with music and refreshments was held in October 2005. Since then, the Old Stone House has been open regularly for public and school-group tours.

— David Grubb was recognized as Rochester's 2006 Citizen of the Year, in part to honor his work on the Old Stone House reconstruction.

— Because Abraham Lincoln represented Stone House owner Lucetta Stevens in an inheritance lawsuit after the death of her husband, a Lincoln Text Rail was installed and dedicated in 2009 at Rochester's Historical Park.

- The 2007 dedication of a mural, stone monument, and "Lincoln–Van Buren Trail" signs celebrated the night a former U.S. President spent the night in Rochester with a future President. The 1842 visit to the village by Martin Van Buren and Abraham Lincoln has been documented.

Right: A portion of Buckhart Road is designated as the Lincoln–Van Buren Trail. This image looks east from the village. (R. BRUZAN PHOTO)

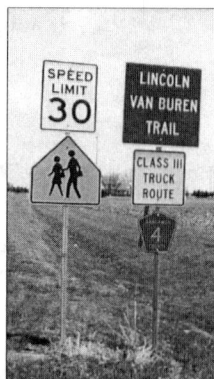

Below left: R.L. Moore displays a historic marker and road sign at the 2007 dedication of the Lincoln–Van Buren Trail. (COURTESY OF ROCHESTER PUBLIC LIBRARY, RHPS COLLECTION)

Above: The "Looking for Lincoln" rail, located on John Street, describes Lincoln's evening in Rochester with former President Martin Van Buren. (R. BRUZAN PHOTO)

— The story relates how Lincoln was asked to join a group of politicians in Rochester to visit with Van Buren, who had become mired by flooded roads on his way to Springfield.

— Commemoration of the 165th anniversary of their visit included patriotic songs, prayer, Lincoln and Van Buren impersonators, a reception, and a dinner that included the two presidents' favorite foods. Posted "Lincoln–Van Buren Trail" signs now officially designated the road Van Buren traveled.

— A former park ranger at the Martin Van Buren National Historic Site traveled from Van Buren's hometown of Kinderhook, NY to take part in the celebration.

- F. North Ross had a unique way of educating the public about Rochester history. The descendant of 1829 Sangamon County pioneers, North painted watercolor pictures from photographs of Rochester buildings and then laminated them onto wood blocks shaped for each painting. After North's death in 2008, his wife, Dorthy, donated nearly 50 of these Rochester depictions to the Rochester Public Library where they are on public display.

- Phone-line modems connecting to the internet, which had arrived in the village in 1997, underwent major changes nine years later. Verizon Wireless launched internet service that brought users of laptops and wireless phones connection speeds comparable to high-speed cable and landline wireless networks. The new wireless system also enabled access to short video clips, music downloads, 3D games, news, weather, and sports.

- Fearing environmental risks and reduced property values, the Rochester-Buckhart Action Group filed a lawsuit in 2007 to stop construction of a large hog-confinement farm east of Rochester. When a 2008 Illinois Supreme Court ruling upheld a lower court decision, construction proceeded on the planned 3,600-hog operation. A 4th District Appellate Court decision the following year determined that the farmer was entitled to collect financial damages sustained in connection with the lawsuit.

- As he walked across the Rochester High School stage to receive his diploma in 2007, senior class president Matt Felts received heartfelt applause from the crowd. Most in attendance were aware of the 18 year old's lifelong heart condition and the 10-hour surgery just six months earlier during which Matt received a heart from an 18-year-old Georgia teen. The Rochester community helped raise money to offset expenses related to Matt's medical care. Felts said he was determined to honor the donor by taking the best care of himself possible. He worked toward his goal of becoming a pediatric cardiologist, became engaged, and was scheduled to graduate from Southern Illinois University at Edwardsville when, in December 2012, he became sick and passed away.

- A variety of business reports:
— The Peace & Appliqué Quilt Shop celebrated its fifth anniversary in downtown Rochester in 2003 by sponsoring a charity quilt show and collecting

donations for the Rochester Fire Department and Rescue Squad.

— Rochester State Bank relocated in 1976, but its original building on East Main Street found new life in 2004 as the Dollars & Cents coin shop. The business changed hands in 2008, but kept the same name.

— A gas station had been at the corner of East Main and State Streets for more than 50 years when the Strode family sold in 2003 what was by then a Marathon outlet. The new owner continued what had been the "full service" tradition followed by Charles and Mary Strode - pumping gas for customers, washing car windows, and checking the oil. The sale of gasoline ended in 2008 when the building became the home of Creekside Service Lawn Care.

— Walnut Street Winery, the first such business in Rochester, opened in 2009 on South Walnut Street after voters had approved the sale of alcohol two years earlier and the village's liquor ordinance was modified to approve such an operation. At one time the building had been the Rochester Christian Church parsonage, and earlier businesses in the building had included a feed-and-bait store.

Walnut St. Winery opened in 2009 at 309 South Walnut in what had been the Rochester Christian Church parsonage. (R. BRUZAN PHOTO)

The Rochester Christian Church used the home on South Walnut Street as a parsonage in 1909 (left). A hundred years later, Walnut St. Winery moved into the building. (LEFT: *THE ROCHESTER WEEKLY ITEM*, 23 DEC. 1909; RIGHT: R. BRUZAN PHOTO)

— When Bank & Trust Co. finished remodeling its full-service Rochester branch in 2005, it occupied the entire building. During the previous eight years the bank had operated from a sliver of the Get-It-N-Go gas station and convenience store at the corner of Route 29 and South Walnut Street.

— Wyndcrest, a 37-unit assisted-living facility, opened in 2005 on Oak Hill Road. Plans called for eventual expansion to as many as 64 units.

— Rochester Station, built in 1979 as a commercial and office building on South Walnut Street, underwent major changes in 2007 when, under new ownership, interior and exterior renovations were carried out.

— Petals & Co. owner and 1981 RHS graduate Michelle O'Neal-Babicky was one of an area florist trio who prepared backdrop decorations when President Barack Obama spoke in Springfield in 2009. The occasion was the 16th president's 200th birthday banquet, hosted by the Abraham Lincoln Association. Although the three were thrilled to be selected, they soon realized that the event was scheduled for the day before Valentine's Day, one of any florist's busiest days of the year. They still enjoyed their opportunity.

— The Illinois Stewardship Alliance, a not-for-profit network organized to help area farmers market their products locally, was founded in Rochester. It later relocated to Springfield.

— Communications Made Easy, a Rochester business founded by Michelle Tjelmeland and Mark Roberts, was a 2009 finalist in the nationwide What Works for Business Contest. Their company was established to help people such as those with disabilities communicate rapidly at critical times.

When the photo above was taken in 2008, the Town Hall building looked significantly different than when it was built as a butcher's shop 90 years earlier. (COURTESY OF BRAD BUCHER)

Rochester Township completed a new building at 7950 Braner Road in 2007. (R. BRUZAN PHOTO)

• Derek Leonard was named varsity football coach in 2005 to succeed Dave Jacobs, who had built the program during its first 10 years. The fall football season that year would be Leonard's first as a head football coach.

• Deaths of some Rochester residents:
2000
— A lifelong Rochester resident, **John R. Foster** was, at one point, simultaneously the village police chief, fire chief, and a member of the public works staff. He also drove a school bus and was president of the fire board.

2002
— Cardinal Hill Candle and Craft store founder **Virginia *(Pierce)* Waldmire** also co-founded the Cozy Dog Drive In. She was a 1992 inductee into the Route 66 Hall of Fame, and a life member of the North American Bluebird Society.

2003

— 102-year-old **Lucile *(Campbell)* Fairchild**, a past president of the Sangamon County and the Rochester Woman's Clubs, was a county native. An 80-year member of the Rochester United Methodist Church, she was also a 75-year member of the Sangamo Chapter Order of the Eastern Star, and a founder of the Rochester PTA.

— Full-time Rochester Library Director and part-time Village Manager **Linda K. *(Pride)* Shaw** was an almost endless source of clever ideas. These included new library programs "Topics to Chew On" and "Cabin Fever," as well as reimagining Rochester's 4th of July as "Sparks in the Park," and introducing baking contests associated with those summer celebrations.

— **Raymond L. Ramsey**, a Korean War veteran, was key to the operations of Ray Ramsey Trucking, Ramsey Grain Inc., and Berry Fertilizer Inc. A 40-year member of the Midwest Truckers Association, he had been a Rochester Fire Board member and Township Road Commissioner.

— **Marshall H. Watkins**, age 94, had owned Rochester Grain and Lumber Co. and farmed in Rochester and Warrensburg. He had been chief and assistant chief of the Rochester Volunteer Fire Department for 20 years, and his memberships included Rochester Masonic Lodge 635 AF&AM, Ansar Shrine, and Sangamon County Farm Bureau.

2004

— The 1986 Citizen of the Year, 95-year-old **Esther M. *(Chandler)* Taft**, was a lifetime member of the Rochester United Methodist Church, and 58-year member of Moreland Rebekah Lodge. She was well known as a church organist and for more than 30 years, was the organist at Wilson Park Funeral Home.

— WW II Army Air Corp veteran **Alvin M. Mavis** had been widely known as Mr. Gasohol for his work on ethanol fuels. The former owner of Mavis Grain Co. and Mavco Fertilizer, he was a colonel in the Illinois Seventh Cavalry reactivated Civil War unit, and a member of Rochester VFW Post 11463 and American Legion Post 274.

— **Helen K. *(Lynch)* Newhouse** had been the owner and operator of Helen's Flower and Gift Shop for 25 years. The shop filled the ground floor of both the Odd Fellows Temple and the adjoining small building that had served at various times as a newspaper office and market.

2005

— **Army Cpl. Jacob Palmatier** was killed while serving in Iraq. The husband of Bridget *(Hendrickson)* Palmatier of Rochester, he was laid to rest with full military honors in Camp Butler National Cemetery.

2007

— **Fred E. Drillinger**, age 99, had been a lifelong resident of Rochester and witnessed the 1930 holdup of Rochester State Bank just three doors east of his home. He had worked at Sangamo Electric Company in Springfield for 29 years.

2008

— **Franklin North Ross**, a descendant of 1829 Sangamon County pioneers and a charter member of the Rochester Historical Preservation Society, maintained a keen interest in local history and historical structures. A long-time local farmer, he was a member of the Rochester United Methodist Church, Rochester Masonic Lodge, and Ansar Shrine. He had been awarded the Illinois Patriots Medal from the Illinois Society of Children of the American Revolution.

— **Althea** *(Vanderburg)* **Pfeiffer**, a member of the Rochester Christian Church for more than half a century, was always interested in neighborhood activities. Her gentle spirit and handcrafted gifts brought joy to the authors of this book and their family.

— **Harry Hopkins**, a multiple-sport athlete who graduated from Rochester High School in 1965, was an urban planner and executive director of the Springfield-Sangamon County Regional Planning Commission for more than 30 years. Planning projects he shepherded during his tenure included White Oaks Mall and the Abraham Lincoln Presidential Library and Museum.

2009

— **Bowen "Skip" Watts**, founder of Watts Copy Systems, had been a former president of the Rochester Education Foundation, and member of the boards of Springfield College in Illinois-Benedictine College and Springfield SPARC. He was also a member of the citizens committee that evaluated the Rochester Fire Department and Rescue Squad merger.

— After **Bill Roy** died in 2009, a new bench was dedicated to honor the spot in Community Park where he enjoyed feeding "his" ducks. Bill served the Navy in WWII, and because Bill had loved animals and the small-town feel of Rochester, his son Tom termed the bench "a fitting tribute."

— RHS graduate and professional pen-and-ink artist **Robert "Bob" Waldmire** was known around the world for efforts to document and preserve Old Route 66. He received the national Historic Route 66 Federation's John Steinbeck Award for his work. This "ethical vegetarian" firmly declined a Pixar/Disney offer to name the VW minibus in their animated movie *Cars* for him when he learned that the character would also become a giveaway toy in McDonald's Happy Meals. The bus, recognizable to many as Bob's own beloved VW, was eventually named Fillmore.

Rochester High School graduate and nationally known artist Bob Waldmire, who championed historic U.S. Route 66, died in 2009. (COURTESY OF THE WALDMIRE FAMILY)

CARDINAL HILL CANDLES & CRAFTS, ROCHESTER, ILLINOIS—
FOR A JOURNEY BACK IN TIME, VISIT CARDINAL HILL, THE STORE IN A TURN-OF-THE-CENTURY CORN CRIB NAMED FOR THE ABUNDANCE OF CARDINALS THERE. ED & GIN WALDMIRE CONVERTED THE CORN CRIB & OPENED FOR BUSINESS IN 1972. IT RETAINS THE ORIGINAL CHARACTER OF ITS TIME.
HERE YOU WILL FIND A RICH REPOSITORY OF ARTIFACTS & HISTORY & A WIDE VARIETY OF HAND CRAFTED CANDLES, CRAFT SUPPLIES & MANY OTHER GIFT ITEMS & IDEAS.
A WARM WOOD STOVE & SEASONAL TREATS LIKE CIDER, PEANUT BRITTLE & COFFEE INVITE VISITORS TO RELAX & WATCH CANDLES BEING MADE.
ARLENE & BILL WALDMIRE & FAMILY CONTINUE THE CARDINAL HILL TRADITION TODAY, "PRESERVING THE PAST."
Just off OLD ROUTE 66 Scenes 47
OPEN 10 to 6 EVERY DAY
RR2, ROCHESTER, ILLINOIS 62563 phone (217)498-9375

Cardinal Hill Candles and Crafts in Rochester Township was the home base of artist Bob Waldmire. This drawing is representative of Waldmire's unique art form. (COURTESY OF THE WALDMIRE FAMILY; USED WITH PERMISSION)

Everyone seems to know Rochester's Toby McDaniel. His popular columns were among 37 years worth of articles he wrote in *The State Journal-Register* until his retirement in 2004. As he wrote, he often related stories of the village where he and his family lived. (PHOTO USED WITH PERMISSION)

- Notable activities of Rochester residents:

— After a career of 40 years in journalism, well-known resident, columnist, and author **Toby McDaniel** retired in 2004 at age 69. He first became active in the Rochester Lions Club in 1979, was named "Citizen of the Year" in 1998, and has published two books.

— **Bob Church** spearheaded efforts to create the sculpture *"Lincoln the Surveyor"* that was unveiled and dedicated at New Salem in 2003. One year earlier he had annotated and republished the Adin Baber book *A. Lincoln With Compass and Chain*, which described the 16th president's surveying career. Led by Church, the Illinois Professional Land Surveyors Association was active in both projects.

— RHS graduate **Jim Waters** received a Lions Club Special Lifetime Achievement Award in 2004. Among the activities of this WWII veteran were member of the Rochester Zoning Board, 50-year American Legion membership, and a charter member of St. Jude's Catholic Church.

— When **Louise Dill** celebrated her 102nd birthday in 2006, the Rochester Historical Preservation Society recognized her as their oldest citizen.

— **Les Eastep**, who had already won state chilli-cook-off championships in Ohio, Louisiana, and Missouri, brought home his first Illinois State title from Taylorville in 2004.

— Among the people **Bill Waldmire** photographed before he retired in 2004 were five Illinois governors, folk singer Burl Ives, and former President Jimmy Carter. He had spent more than three decades with the Illinois Office of Communication and Information,

— The Illinois Society of Professional Engineers presented hydraulic and hydrology engineer **Nathan "Nate" Wilcoxon** with its Illinois Award in 2005. The annual honor recognized Nate's work as a professional engineer and his contributions to the public.

— By 2006 **Richard Metcalf** had used his woodworking skills in a home wood shop to craft multiple useful items for the Rochester United Methodist Church. In addition to desks, cabinets, and tables, he also fashioned lighted display cases for several stained glass windows that had been moved from the church's 1924 building.

— **Greg Park**, director of Rochester's Wilson Park Funeral Home, volunteered in St. Gabriel, LA, to help identify and process the remains of many people who died as a result of Hurricane Katrina in 2005.

— **Richard Ramsey**, recognized in Central Illinois as a beekeeping expert, described beekeeping in the 1800s when he spoke at a 2008 Rochester Historical Preservation Society meeting.

— **Dave Jostes Sr.**, a 1954 RHS graduate, was featured in a newspaper article about his wide-ranging support of Rochester sports. Dave, who himself earned 11 varsity letters on school basketball, track, and baseball teams, was pointed out as a favorite among athletes, hundreds of whom he drove to games or meets during his 20 years as a bus driver. Building confidence in athletes is a priority with Jostes, who owned Jostes Garage and Car Wash until he retired in 2000.

Rochester writers contributed in multiple ways to local and area histories.
Left to right: *As I Saw It* by Justin Taft, Jr., 2004; *The Tafts of Rochester, Illinois* by Justin Taft, Jr., 2007; *A Haunt of Memories* by Nadine Lynch Miller, 2004; *Honk If You're A Hoosier* by Toby McDaniel, 2001; and *The Sangamon River: A Sense of Place*, Director: Charles Schweighauser; Contributor: Ray Bruzan, 2006. (IMAGES USED WITH PERMISSION)

VILLAGE OF ROCHESTER 2012

Rochester subdivisions are shown on this map, beginning with what is labelled "Original Town." (COURTESY OF CRAWFORD, MURPHY AND TILLEY, INC., AND THE VILLAGE OF ROCHESTER; USED WITH PERMISSION)

2010s

^ 1818

1918 >

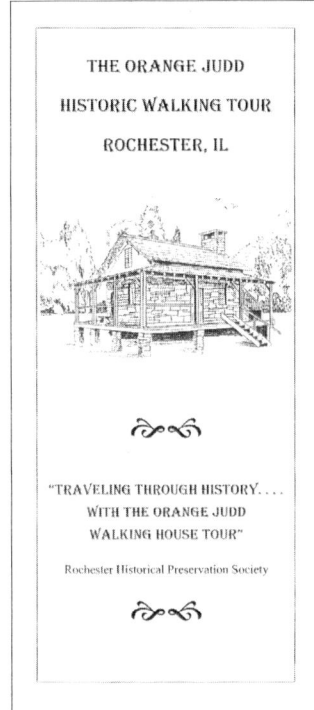

THE ORANGE JUDD

HISTORIC WALKING TOUR

ROCHESTER, IL

"TRAVELING THROUGH HISTORY....
WITH THE ORANGE JUDD
WALKING HOUSE TOUR"

Rochester Historical Preservation Society

^ 2018   (R. BRUZAN PHOTOS)

2010s Timeline...

2010	Population: 3,689
	— RHS Athletic Complex opened on the Route 29 campus
	— Lost Bridge Trail comfort station was dedicated on West Main
	— St. John's Health Center opened on Sattley Street
2011	Rochester Intermediate School opened on Jack Taylor Drive
2013	Former Rochester resident Professor Michael Lennon completed Norman Mailer's biography, *A Double Life*
2014	RHS football team won its fifth straight state championship
	— Rochester Police Department continued its investigations of two local homicides
2015	North Park playground equipment was installed west of Oak Mill Estates subdivision
	— Record-setting flood closed almost all access roads to Rochester
	— *The Orange Judd Historic Walking Tour Guide* was published

2016	Village board approved video gambling terminals
	— An outdoor classroom at the Rochester Arboretum was dedicated in Community Park
	— Rochester High School football team won its sixth state championship
	— Rochester Historic Preservation Society received state recognition for *The Orange Judd Historic Walking Tour Guide*
	— Route 29 widening to four lanes between Rochester and Taylorville was completed
2018	100th anniversary of Rochester's *Orange Judd Pictorial Community Album*
	— 200th anniversary of Rochester's first settlement, the 1818 McCoy homestead
	— 200th anniversary of Illinois statehood
2019	Rochester Sesquicentennial will celebrate 150 years as a village

2010s Storylines...

• It's unlikely that James McCoy, the first homesteader to arrive in Rochester township in 1818, could relate to what exists 200 years later in what has become the village of Rochester. The few cabins from that initial settlement have been replaced by subdivisions and dozens of homes in a village with more than 3,000 people.

— In fact, James would see duplexes, single-family homes, paved streets, an electric substation, and a 300,000-gallon water tower from the front door of his log homestead. Visiting from the past to glimpse events 200 years later, James McCoy would witness a record-setting flood, dedication of a new school not far from his homestead, the discovery of two murders, legalized village gambling, and a record-setting high school sports team.

— And if James McCoy were to be amazed at the village that had grown near his humble Illinois homestead, he might be equally surprised to find his name 200 years later in a book about the history of his adopted home.

Evidence of Rochester's continued growth was seen in 2015. This basement for a new house being built in Oak Mill Estates was within sight of the 1818 homestead of Rochester's first settler, James McCoy.
(P. BRUZAN PHOTO)

- New sidewalks and a major street resurfacing were combined in 2010 when the village board joined with the Illinois Department of Transportation to install new sidewalks from Camelot Drive east along Route 29 to Rocket Road and resurfaced East Main Street from North Walnut to John Street.

- Based on input from a citizen survey three years earlier, a proposed Comprehensive Plan was reviewed during a 2011 public hearing and approved soon after, replacing the previous plan approved in 1992. Among the issues it addressed to help meet anticipated growth were the possible location of future subdivisions, additional sidewalks, more recreation facilities, and expanded village infrastructure. Village President Dave Armstrong explained that the new Comprehensive Plan could also aid in securing grants to help pay for future village projects.

This picture was taken from Route 29 entering Rochester from the southeast. The field on the right is, in 2017, the focus of potential future developments. The Library and Village Hall is seen in the distance. (R. BRUZAN PHOTO)

- Predictions in 2015 were for Rochester to grow along Maxheimer Road east of the village hall. The Catholic Diocese of Springfield announced that year its plans to sell 40 acres of farmland owned along Cardinal Hill Road once a pre-annexation agreement was approved.

— Another school could be built when needed on 60 acres of school-district-owned land adjacent to the intermediate school, which opened in 2011.

— Village officials saw the need for a pharmacy and grocery store, neither of which existed in Rochester at the time.

— Seeing a potential new source of revenue, village trustees approved video gambling to begin in 2016. Gaming licenses were soon approved for several businesses that hoped to attract more customers. During the first 11 months of video gambling, $1.091 million was wagered in Rochester, with $13,050 coming to the village based on a percentage set by the state.

- By a tally of 672 to 205, Rochester voters rejected a 2014 proposal that the village become a home-rule municipality. Approval would have given more flexibility to take actions such as setting tax rates, passing local ordinances, and attracting lower interest rates on future borrowing.

- Muddy, impassible roads and rickety, unsafe bridges made 1800s travel between Rochester and Springfield impossible at times. Rochester was isolated in a similar fashion after Christmas 2015 as Black Branch Creek flooded, the South Fork River rose to record heights, and Rochester Road, Route 29, North

A record-setting December 2015 flood isolated Rochester from Springfield by closing almost every road to and from the village. Route 29 (left) looks from Hilltop southeast toward Rochester; the picture on the right was taken from the Oak Hill Road intersection with West Main Street looking west toward the South Fork River bridge. (R. BRUZAN PHOTOS)

The 2015 photo at left was taken looking north as water flowed over the North Walnut Road bridge where Black Branch Creek enters the South Fork River. Photo at right was taken from the Dannenberger Road bridge that crosses the South Fork River.
(LEFT: R. BRUZAN PHOTO; RIGHT: P. BRUZAN PHOTO)

Walnut Road, Dannenberger Road, and Cardinal Hill Road were completely closed. Carl "Bud" Moore, who took pictures of the previous record flood in 1943, concluded those 2015 water heights were higher. The five-to-eight inches of rain that fell over four days also led to four drowning deaths and 38 flooded homes in Christian County southeast of Rochester.

- It wasn't mud or floods, but incredible dust that made headlines in the spring of 2017. Roads across Central Illinois were closed and traffic accidents abounded during what was described as a "total blackout" at some locations. That description was demonstrated on Cardinal Hill Road, where it was almost impossible to see a car with its headlights on that was stopped across the intersection with Route 29.

- It was 2010 when the state of Illinois finally paid the Rochester School District a $10.18 million construction grant promised in 2002. Such delays were common throughout the state during that decade, and Rochester's work had been completed several years before the state funds arrived.

— The new Intermediate School for grades four through six was dedicated and opened in 2011. The road leading to the school was named "Jack Taylor Drive" in honor of the former Rochester Schools superintendent, who retired from that post in 1994.

— A $5.5 million athletic complex had opened on the Route 29 campus in 2010. Two years later the Rochester School Board filed a $500,000 lawsuit against the company it held responsible for repeated failures of the gymnasium's automated telescoping bleacher system. A $400,000 settlement was reached, and a completely new system was installed in 2014.

Left: The Rochester School District dedicated the new Intermediate School in 2011. Located on Jack Taylor Drive, it houses grades 4-6.

Below: The Rochester Athletic Complex on the Route 29 campus opened in 2010.

Left: The main entrance to Rochester High School is seen in 2016. The school is located on the Route 29 campus. (R. BRUZAN PHOTOS)

— The 2012-2013 school year introduced a three-year plan to provide all students in grades 4 through 12 with laptop computers. Teachers took a week-long summer program that prepared them to blend computer learning with traditional class plans. Beginning in 2013, Rochester families with students in 4th through 12th grades were charged a $75.00 technology fee for three years to pay for their student's Chromebook laptop. Students then owned their computer at the end of three years.

• The goal of a four-lane expressway from Rochester to Taylorville had emerged after repeated fatalities along that stretch of Route 29. Completed in late 2016, that milestone was celebrated in January 2017. It took more than two decades to prepare plans, target funds for the $88 million project, and complete construction in three major stages, including the final segment from Berry to the south edge of Edinburg. Shortly after that completion, speed on the four-lane roadway was raised to 65 mph.

- The electronic notification system Nixle became available through the Rochester Police Department (RPD) in 2011. Using text messages or email, the system allowed the department to send alerts about such time-sensitive information as missing children, road closures, water main breaks, and other public safety concerns, or events.
  — Another RPD community-involvement opportunity was a Youth Police Academy for those age 14 through 20. The program consisted of four evening sessions held at the Department offices.

- Former Rochester antique-store owners Tom and Davyd Dalys became Sangamon County's first same-sex couple to obtain a marriage license on the day the law became effective, June 1, 2014. In all, 12 same-sex couples showed up on that day to get marriage licenses. Tom and Davyd had celebrated their civil union three years earlier.

- Serious crimes created headlines during the decade.
  — A former Rochester volunteer firefighter who pleaded guilty to child molestation and production of child pornography in 2011 was sentenced to 30 years in prison.
  — The Sangamon County coroner determined that the 2013 death of 78-year-old Norma Lipskis was a homicide. The former owner of Petticoat Junction Restaurant in Rochester Station had been found in her Oak Hills Estates home. Police Chief Bill Marass said this was the first murder within the village during his 32 years with the department. The case remained unsolved as of 2017.
  — The skeletal remains of Decatur resident Tracy Trimby were discovered in 2014, wrapped in a blanket or rug and hidden in a storage shed behind a Park Street home. Her body was found as the shed was being cleaned out. A former resident pleaded guilty in 2015 to concealment of a homicidal death and was sentenced to five years in prison.

- Rochester community-service groups continued to provide entertainment and beautify the village.
  — Rochester Women's Club fundraisers helped the village purchase lighted carolers and "Sno" people for the 2013 winter holiday season. The new decorations were seasonally located along Route 29 at the intersections of West Main and North Walnut Streets.
  — After 15 years of Halloween hauntings at increasingly larger locations, the 2014 Rochester Lions Club's enthusiastic "Boo Crew" moved its corpses, roaches, and other gory props into a permanent 7,200-square-foot warehouse. The new digs were on a six-acre lot five miles east of Rochester on Buckhart Road. About 90 volunteers who made up the "Boo Crew" have contributed hundreds of hours annually since about 2000 when the fundraiser first be-

Artist David Shaw created Rochester's sesquicentennial logo in preparation for the village's 150th birthday in 2019. Shaw, a favorite teacher in the Rochester schools, retired in 2016 having shared his artistic talents with students and the community for 32 years.
(R. BRUZAN PHOTO)

gan. The Haunted House has generated money for Lions Club scholarships and to purchase Christmas gifts for children at Springfield's Hope Institute.

- Plans began in 2016 for Rochester's sesquicentennial celebration in 2019. It will mark 150 years since Rochester incorporated and Munson Carter became Rochester's first village president. Committee co-chairs are Ruth Ann Theis and Carolyn Moore, along with initial committee members Ann Rowley, Raetta Laningham, David Jostes, Toby McDaniel, Robert Church, and Wynne Coplea.

— With David Shaw's creation of an official Rochester sesquicentennial logo, the committee is planning celebration elements such as a series of calendars, a cookbook, musical programs, quilt shows, tree plantings, and historic home tours. Moore explained that the goal is to "celebrate our heritage and background to build on a legacy for the future."

— Coplea recalled when her father, Leo, chaired Rochester's centennial in 1969. Although she now lives in Springfield, Wynne says she is ". . . originally a Rochester girl, and still a Rochesterite at heart."

- The April 2011 election marked the first time the Rochester Fire Board was elected rather than appointed by the Sangamon County Board. Those elected were Joseph Suerdieck, Tim Cravens, Teresa Sturdy, Andrew Beck, and William Riggs.

- Rochester firefighters responded in 2012 to a major fire east of the village near Buckhart Road and Parks Lane. A historic drought teamed up with summer heat and winds to set the stage for a hard-to-control fire that destroyed a historic barn, small shed, and 200 field acres. Firefighters succeeded in their concentrated efforts to save a large two-story brick home that ended up almost surrounded by charred fields.

- Interest in a backup water source for Springfield and its water customers has existed for more than 50 years. Another study of such a project, including alternative water sources, was suggested in 2014. One possible avenue, constructing a second lake, has led City Water, Light & Power (CWLP) to buy land along Horse Creek in Rochester Township as part of the more than 3,000 acres of land that would flood in creation of what has long been dubbed "Hunter Lake." Another land parcel on Brunk Cemetery Road was bought in September 2016, leaving an estimated 20 properties remaining in private ownership. As of 2017, the original project is being scaled back and additional information is being gathered for federal and state reviews.

The 29-foot-deep $400,000 southeast regional sewage lift station was completed north of the village hall in 2016. The lift station was necessary for future development on Rochester's east side. (R. BRUZAN PHOTO)

A gravity-flow sewage receiving pit on Cardinal Hill Road northeast of the village hall directs wastewater under that roadway to the new southeast regional sewage lift station. The pit was completed in 2016. (R. BRUZAN PHOTO)

- Water and sewer rates increased during the decade, as a result of repairs needed by the village's aging infrastructure and rate increases passed on from CWLP or the Sangamon County Water Reclamation District, previously known as Springfield Metro Sanitary District. The most recent of these were water and sewer rate increases that each took effect May 1, 2017.

— Some village water lines are more than 75 years old. During 2012, Rochester experienced six water mains breaks along Walnut Street and another three on Rochester Road. One of these forced closure of Rochester Road for several days.

— The village board received an estimated cost of $110,000 to paint Rochester's water tower in 2011. That estimate did not include the rocket logo added to the tower stem.

— Water began flowing in 2012 from the aquifer tapped by the South Sangamon Water Commission east of Rochester to provide water for Chatham, New Berlin, and some residents along the transmission line. Rochester had chosen to withdraw from the Commission in 2005.

- An annual average of 97 home sales in Rochester were tallied from 2010 through 2015. The median price of Rochester homes was $158,000 in 2010 and $180,000 in 2016. This increase was due, at least in part, to new home construction, explained a member of the Capital Area Association of Realtors.

Ameren Illinois began to replace aging steel natural-gas pipes with polyethylene lines in 2016. Replacement of the original gas lines, some of which had been in service since 1958, included new six-inch mains as well as individual service lines to homes and other buildings.
(R. BRUZAN PHOTOS)

- New businesses in other areas of Rochester included:

— A historic downtown building that in the previous century had been a meat market and offices for the township and village opened in 2013 as Cocoa Blue Chocolates.

— Beginning in 2016, the former Lunt's grocery store on State Street underwent major remodeling in anticipation of attracting several new businesses.

— A decades-old gas station site at the corner of East Main and State Street reopened as the Alibi bar and restaurant.

— Hank's Gym, designed for personal fitness training, occupied another former gas station on State Street.

The Rochester office of Bank & Trust Co., which had been completely remodeled in 2005, promoted village history in 2014 with an ongoing display of the historic Orange Judd homes of Rochester.
(ABOVE: R. BRUZAN PHOTO; BELOW: P. BRUZAN PHOTO)

Left: Established in 1904, the Wilson Park Funeral Home and its family-owned predecessors represent in 2017 Rochester's oldest, continuously operated family business.
(R. BRUZAN PHOTO)

- Although Rochester's only grocery store went out of business in 2015, Rochester's slow-moving business climate seemed to gain momentum with the introduction of several new businesses during the decade. Sattley Street became an active, new business hub with construction of several new buildings.

St. John's Hospital established a healthcare facility in 2010 at the southeast corner of Route 29 and Sattley Street. (R. BRUZAN PHOTO)

— In 2010 St. John's Hospital brought medical options to the village with a new $1.4 million Priority Care Clinic. Located near the corner of Route 29 and Sattley Street, the clinic offered walk-in, non-emergency medical care in addition to scheduled visits and physical therapy. By mid-decade the clinic was known as HSHS Medical Group Family Medicine, Rochester.

— As a way to encourage additional commercial development, the village board agreed in 2013 to more than $20,000 in financial incentives to build the Village Center. Directly behind the Clinic, the two-building Village Center opened the following year. Developed by Bill and Trent Rodgers, this $1.7 million complex included Public House 29 family restaurant, a dental office, and the 24-hour Rocket Fitness Center. The fitness center features a 4,000-square-foot gym and an adjacent 5,000-square-foot area with a wide selection of fitness equipment.

- The village board approved Rochester's first tax increment financing (TIF) district in March 2017. Their unanimous vote culminated years of planning in order to define areas designated as the TIF district and to minimize negative impacts on other units of local government. Projects eligible under this complex and highly regulated program could include improvements to roads, water, and sewers that would in turn create incentives for new business development.

- A ribbon-cutting ceremony in 2010 marked the opening of a comfort station at West Main Street and Route 29, along Lost Bridge Trail. Costing about $90,000, the building features an open pavilion, a unisex, handicap-accessible bathroom, a water fountain, and picnic table. Rochester Women's Club fundraisers and village funds supplemented a state grant to pay for the new structure.

A comfort station on West Main Street, built for people using Lost Bridge Trail, was dedicated in 2010. (R. BRUZAN PHOTO)

— In the spring of 2017, a bicycle repair station supported by the Capital Area Realtors of Springfield was added at the comfort station.

• The Orange Judd *Pictorial* of Rochester, described in the 1910 decade, became in 2015 the basis for a *Walking Tour Guide* of Rochester's historic homes. The 68-page *Guide* describes histories of the 57 remaining buildings that had been photographed 97 years earlier in the village.

— Endorsed by the Rochester Historical Preservation Soci-

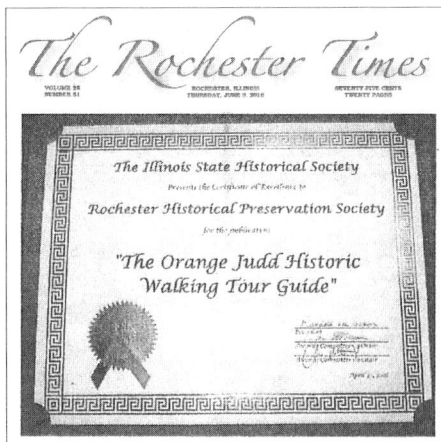

The Orange Judd Historic Walking Tour Guide of Rochester's historic homes received state-wide recognition with a 2016 Award of Excellence from the Illinois State Historical Society. (*THE ROCHESTER TIMES*, 9 JUNE 2016)

RHPS Orange Judd committee members Tris and Debbie Schnepper (at right) presented Orange Judd Recognition Awards in 2015 to, from left: Diane Arthur and Todd Howe, of Bank & Trust Company, and local historian Dorthy Ross for their support of the *Walking Tour Guide* of Rochester's historic buildings. (P. BRUZAN PHOTO)

In 2015, Karen Ritterbusch, a member of the Orange Judd Committee, recovered Methodist Church documents that had been misplaced for 90 years. Karen, seen on the right, presented those materials to Rev. Kathy Sweet, pastor of the Rochester United Methodist Church, and church historian Bud McCafferty during an RHPS meeting. The documents dated as far back as 1839 and included records such as a baptism administered by the famous preacher and politician Peter Cartwright. (P. BRUZAN PHOTO)

ety (RHPS) in 2012, the *Guide* received state-wide recognition in 2016 when the Illinois State Historical Society presented the project with a Certificate of Excellence. A major result of the Orange Judd home studies was location and acquisition of numerous Rochester historic artifacts, property abstracts, and pictures represented in this timeline history. Several Orange Judd homes were found to have been built around log houses that dated back to some of the village's earliest years.

One of the authors rests on a stack of more than 50 Rochester property abstracts used to research the history of village homes for the *The Orange Judd Historic Walking Tour Guide* and this book. The authors are grateful to the many homeowners who have granted permission to study their historic documents. Additional information about Rochester's history will continue to be welcomed. (R. BRUZAN PHOTO)

- The April 2016 dedication of the Rochester Arboretum in Community Park capped nine years of work on this living "museum of plants." The Operating Engineers Local 965 Training Program started the area when they moved 5,000 cubic yards of soil dredged from a nearby pond to the one-acre site in 2007. The Local later carved out a bowl into which tiered benches were installed to provide seating for classes and other groups learning about the arboretum.

Walking trails wind around about 160 native Illinois trees and shrubs that were planted, including white oaks, burr oaks, cypress, and flowering dogwood. Rochester Lions Club and individuals who made donations to the effort look forward to a time when the area will have matured into a native forest.

The Rochester Arboretum in Community Park was dedicated in 2016. Diverse Illinois trees and shrubs are featured as well as an outdoor classroom. (R. BRUZAN PHOTOS)

- The Rochester High School Envirothon Team used the Community Park pond as an outdoor study area in 2011 when they evaluated the chemical, physical, biological, and geographical characteristics of that aquatic ecosystem.

- Long ago, so the story goes, two neighboring women who lived near the area south of Rochester known as Mottarville got into a dustup over who owned some chickens. When the dust settled, their neighbors commented as to how the quarrelers "had their bristle up." Ever since then, the road they lived on has been known, somewhat infamously, as Chicken Bristle Road.

  — This storyline, however, is not about chickens, but about a mule that escaped from his farm pen along that road. As Jean Carnes traveled toward Springfield on Chicken Bristle Road in 2013, she saw ahead a man chasing a mule. Jean stopped her car, but Willie, the mule, went into a slide and smashed into Jean's windshield causing more than $1,000 in damages.

  — Willie's owner, Donald Siddons, said the mule "tried to stop but his hooves slid on the asphalt." Willie wasn't badly hurt, and as they waited for the vet, Carnes reflected that it was nice to meet all the neighbors who stopped to see what happened. She was a bit peeved, however, that the friends who called her after the accident asked first about Willie, who had only needed some stitches to his head. A mule story on Chicken Bristle Road—only in Rochester.

- Rochester Boy Scouts experienced a temperature range of more that 100° F during two camping trips. Seven scouts from Troop 58 traveled to northern Minnesota in March 2010, where they participated in dog sledding, cross-country skiing, and winter camping in temperatures that fell to -4° F. Record-setting temperatures of 104° F greeted 10 scouts from Troop 40 two years later when they traveled to Camp Ingersoll west of Peoria. There they participated in climbing, shooting, and swimming in weather so hot that most of the scouts left their cabins at night to sleep under the stars.

Involved with scouting for 61 years, Wayne Beck helped provide canoeing experiences for hundreds of Rochester Boy Scouts. A 1965 RHS graduate, Beck was chosen Rochester's 1993 Citizen of the Year. (R. BRUZAN PHOTO)

- Early in the 20th century, men's baseball teams thrilled spectators at the East Main Street baseball field. As the century moved forward, high-school teams brought sports thrills to new generations. Rochester's strong showing in both boys and girls competitions were documented by teams' trips to Illinois High School Association-sponsored championship tournaments.

The Rochester Times

VOLUME 24
NUMBER 24

ROCHESTER, ILLINOIS
THURSDAY, DECEMBER 4, 2014

SEVENTY-FIVE CENTS
SIXTY PAGES

RELOAD AND REPEAT

Rockets thump Chicago Phillips 49-28 for fifth straight Class 4A football state championship

The Rochester High School football program received state-wide recognition in 2014 when they became state champions for the fifth year in a row. Coached by Derek Leonard, the Rockets again won the state title in 2016. (*THE ROCHESTER TIMES*, 4 DEC. 2014; IHSA VISUAL IMAGE PHOTO: WWW.VIPIS.COM; USED WITH PERMISSION)

The Association's tallies of championship and second-place awards are the following:

— State championships:

Girls golf (2015-16)

Girls track and field (1993-94)

Girls soccer (2008, 2015, and 2016); the most recent championships marked the first time an Illinois high school soccer team had won championships consecutively in two different classes

Boys golf (1999-2000)

Boys football (2010, 2011, 2012, 2013, 2014, and 2016)

— Second-place state trophies:

Girls basketball (2007, 2008, 2015, 2017)

Girls cross country (2013-14)

Girls golf (2012-13, 2013-14)

Girls soccer (2013-14)

Girls track and field (1994-95)

Boys golf (1980-81)

Boys track and field (1981-82)

• When Coach Derek Leonard was hired as the Rochester football team's varsity coach in 2005, it was his first year as a head coach. Five years later, he and his teams initiated a football dynasty, winning the first of six IHSA state championships over the next seven years.

— Rochester High School football teams were the first Illinois public school to bring home five consecutive state championships. The end of their streak came with a 2015 playoff loss. Coach Leonard reflected on his pride for that team, predicting that the special season, rather than their final loss, would be what players would remember.

The Rochester High School girls' soccer team won back-to-back state championships in 2015 and 2016 under the leadership of coach Chad Kutscher. (*THE ROCHESTER TIMES*, 9 JUNE 2016; IHSA VISUAL IMAGE PHOTO: WWW.VIPIS.COM; USED WITH PERMISSION)

— Among the many notables of those winning football seasons were the sons of Andy and Jane Lunt, Wil and Wes, who were both record-setting quarterbacks. Wil and Wes were selected as *Chicago Tribune* All State players, combining for 162 passing touchdowns and more than 16,000 passing yards. Wil was the nation's number-two passer and became the team captain at Western Illinois University. Wes set an IHSA record for passing yards and became

Two products of the Rochester High School football program were brothers, from left, Wil and Wes Lunt. Both were record setters in high school, and the unusual happened in 2012 when both earned starting quarterback roles at major universities, Wil at Western Illinois University and Wes at Oklahoma State University. (JANE LUNT PHOTOS; USED WITH PERMISSION)

starting quarterback at Oklahoma State University. In another unusual twist, both were starting quarterbacks at their respective schools in 2012.

- On May 1, 2017, the Minnesota Vikings, a member of the National Football League, announced that Wes Lunt had been signed as a rookie free agent. He was due to take part in various team camps during May.

- Okay, this may be significant to only a segment of Rochester residents, but the authors just had to toss in that the Chicago Cubs won the World Series in 2016. First time in 108 years.

- As this book is being written, the faces of Rochester's leadership are changing, perhaps more completely and more rapidly than at any comparable length of time in the village's history. Within less than a year,
  — **David Armstrong**, village president for 16 years, was unseated by Joe Suerdieck in the April 2017 election;
  — **William Marass**, who had served as Rochester Police Chief for 19 years, retired in August 2016, and 20-year RPD veteran Kent Bragg took his place;
  — When Fire Chief **Mark Poffenberger** retired in late 2016, after eight years in that post, veteran Springfield and Rochester firefighter Greg Surbeck was named as his replacement;
  — School Superintendent **Dr. Thomas Bertrand** announced early in 2017 his plans to retire at the end of the 2017-2018 school year, setting in motion a search for his replacement.

Dave Armstrong will go down as one of Rochester's longest serving village presidents, 16 years. Prior to his election as village president, he was a village trustee. (COURTESY OF DAVID ARMSTRONG; USED WITH PERMISSION)

Former Rochester Police Chief Bill Marass retired in 2016 after serving 35 years with the Rochester Police Department, 19 of those as chief. He joined the force in 1981. (R. BRUZAN PHOTO)

After 42 years as a Rochester paramedic and firefighter, including eight years as Rochester Fire Department chief, Mark Poffenberger retired late in 2016. (COURTESY OF ROCHESTER FIRE PROTECTION DISTRICT)

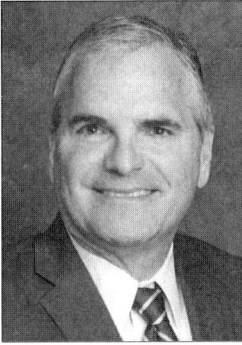

Dr. Thomas Bertrand will retire as superintendent of Rochester School District 3A at the end of the 2017-2018 school year after serving 26 years in a number of district administrative positions. (COURTESY OF DR. THOMAS BERTRAND; USED WITH PERMISSION)

Mike Weaver has been an active member of Rochester Fire-Rescue since 1968. His 48 years of service to the current organization and its predecessors make him the longest-serving active member of the department. (R. BRUZAN PHOTO)

The one-room Forest Grove School, seen above, was built before 1874. A few decades later, young Rachel Kussmaul was a student at the school, followed some decades later by her son Don Mohler. The school on Honeywell Road became the home of Don and Betty *(Morman)* Mohler in 1950, and the couple continues to live in the former school 66 years later. Pictured at left is how the school looks in 2017. (ABOVE: COMPASS POINT PRODUCTIONS; LEFT: R. BRUZAN PHOTO)

Above left: Don and Betty Mohler of Rochester celebrated their 66th wedding anniversary in 2016. The former one-room Forest Grove school they now call home was pictured in the 1918 Orange Judd *Pictorial*. (OLAN MILLS PHOTO; COURTESY OF DON AND BETTY MOHLER)

- Some Rochester Township deaths included:

2011
— Radio personality **Theodore "Ted" McCoy**, 1999 Rochester Citizen of the Year, past president of the Rochester Public Library District Board and Rochester Lions Club, and chair of Rochester United Methodist Church trustees

2012
— Former RHS teacher, 101-year-old **Sarah "Sally" Grace** *(Truxal)* **Wisleder**, who taught fifth grade for 16 years and senior high English for two years

2013
— **Sharon Kay** *(Mosebaugh)* **McDaniel**, Realtor Hall of Fame member and recipient of the Realtor Emeritus Award
— **Norma Ellen** *(Fairchild)* **Ritterbusch**, who was a great-granddaughter of pioneers to Central Illinois, another of the authors' gentle neighbors, an artist talented in many media, and indispensable in the Bob Ritterbusch Insurance Agency office
— **Dr. Gregory Foltz**, a 1981 RHS graduate who had intended to study piano, but instead became known for neurosurgery and research, especially through his founding of the Ben & Catherine Ivy Center for Advanced Brain Tumor Treatment in Seattle, WA

2015
— **James F. Waters**, age 93, was a WWII veteran and recipient of the 2004 Special Lifetime Achievement Award honoring his service on multiple local boards including the Fire Protection District and School District
— RHS graduate and world traveler **Emylee Darneille** died in Spain at age 24, and her brother, classical tubist **Ben Darneille**, died two months later in Wyoming at age 21

2016
— **Larry Louise** *(Swiney)* **Churchill**, age 99, was named by her dad, who had wanted to continue through a fourth generation of a Larry in the family; when Larry died, she was still living on East Main Street and was one of Rochester's most enthusiastic and well-known citizens
— **Margaret** *(Story)* **Beck**, 92, had been Springfield's first Western Union bicycle messenger and was for many years the nursery director at Rochester United Methodist Church

James "Jim" Waters was one of Rochester's most well-known and respected citizens for decades. Waters shared his deep knowledge of local history with the authors of this book before his 2015 death at age 93. (ARTISTIC IMAGES, DIRECTORY OF THE CHURCH OF ST. JUDE, 2012; USED WITH PERMISSION)

— **Melvin L. Creviston**, who received two Purple Hearts for his Army service during WW II, discovered the log house as he started to tear down the structure, a discovery that led to organization of the RHPS; a champion horseshoe pitcher, he had retired in 2008 from his concrete construction business

2017
— **DrexEllen** *(Beggs)* **Armstrong** was the first executive director of the Illinois State Labor Relations Board and for 16 years, the "first lady of Rochester"
— **R.L. Moore**, 2008 Citizen of the Year and an early president of the Rochester Historical Preservation Society, was passionate about the history of Rochester and his Mayflower ancestors
— **Betty** *(Long)* **Etherton** developed West View Park subdivision with her husband, Jack, and took an active role in their farm
— **Stephen B. Schnorf**, was active in state political circles, including director of Central Management Services and state budget director for two Illinois governors

• Some recognized Rochester citizens:
— **Cinda Klickna** was elected president of the 133,000-member Illinois Education Association in 2011. She had been secretary-treasurer of IEA for several years and president of the Springfield Education Association, as well as a high-school English teacher in Springfield.
— **Lynn Chard** was honored as a 2012 State Fair Illinoisan of the Day to recognize her volunteerism.
— **Evan Stevens** was recognized by the United Service Organization as 2012 National Guardsman of the Year for helping to save a fellow airman who had stepped on an improvised explosive device during deployment in Afghanistan.
— **Phillip Clemens**, a 1984 RHS graduate and a member of the 183rd Communications Flight, 183rd Fighter Wing, was named the Illinois Air National Guard Outstanding Senior Noncommissioned Officer of the Year in 2013.
— National Guardsman Staff Sargent **Mathew Arnett** was presented the 2013 Outstanding Guardsmen Award for having helped pull a semi-truck driver from his vehicle after it was involved in a fiery collision on Interstate 57. Arnett turned parts of his uniform into a pressure bandage to stop the driver's bleeding until emergency help arrived.
— **Donna Day** retired in December 2016 after driving a Rochester School District bus 35 years; part of that time she was also the assistant transportation director.
— **Dr. Careyana Brenham** was named Family Medicine Teacher of the Year in 2013 by the Illinois Academy of Family Physicians. A graduate of RHS and the Southern Illinois University School of Medicine, she was also a practicing family physician, and supervisor of family-medicine residents.

— **Dr. Tom Bertrand** was named 2015 Illinois Superintendent of the Year by the Illinois Association of School Administrators. He became superintendent of the Rochester district in 2002-2003 after serving as district assistant superintendent and principal for the elementary and high schools.

— **Lisa Nieves**, a Rochester mom to five and grandmother of three, was named the Illinois 2016 Mother of the Year by the organization "American Mothers." A registered nurse, Lisa had also helped organize the Rochester Rocket Pageant as part of the July 4th Sparks-in-the-Park celebration and the Rochester Olde Towne Fall Festival.

— **Philip Shelato** was honored in 2014 on his 60th birthday with a timeline of his life spray painted on the family garage, with appropriate dates highlighted in colored markers. Family and friends came up with and embellished the idea, but his wife, Ginger, made sure it was waiting when her husband arrived home from work. The timeline was dismantled when new garage siding was installed.

Right: Richard Ramsey is shown in 2016 at his Ramsey Road farm with two of his 50 beehives. He was the 2007 Beekeeper of the Year and in 2015 received the Pioneer Award from the Illinois State Beekeepers Association. (R. BRUZAN PHOTO)

Left: Evelyn Ramsey, who has been an active IOOF Rebekah since 1957, displays the organization's 1902 charter. As of 2017, she is the only remaining member of the Rochester Rebekahs. (R. BRUZAN PHOTO)

Above: Friendship, love, and truth are symbolized by the three joined links of the Odd Fellows and Rebekahs fraternal organization. (COURTESY OF EVELYN RAMSEY)

Former Rochester resident J. Michael Lennon wrote the 2013 book *Norman Mailer, A Double Life*. Mailer spent a night in Rochester in 1983, a guest of Mike and his wife Donna who lived in the C.L. Jones house on West Main Street. (LEFT: MOLLY MALONE COOK PHOTO; SIMON & SCHUSTER, NEW YORK, 2013; USED WITH PERMISSION. RIGHT: R. BRUZAN PHOTO)

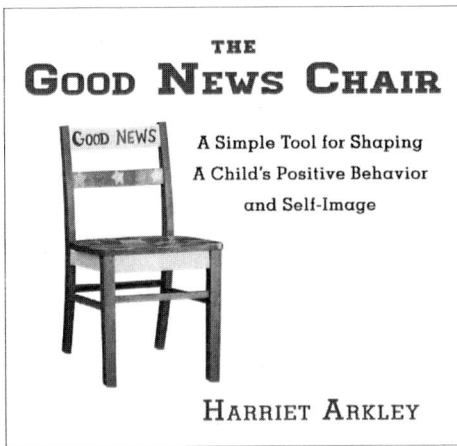

THE
GOOD NEWS CHAIR

GOOD NEWS · A Simple Tool for Shaping A Child's Positive Behavior and Self-Image

HARRIET ARKLEY

Left: Former Rochester resident Harriet Arkley published *The Good News Chair* in 2014. Her book describes an effective alternative to improve communication between adults and children. (COURTESY OF HARRIET ARKLEY)

Oh! Those Maple Creams!!

A Sweet Sampling of Memories, Recollections & Reflections of Hazel Jones Park

- Local and international stories with Rochester connections:

— Artist **Bob Waldmire**, who died in 2009, was remembered a few months later as his ashes were spread at several key locations along the Historic Route 66 he had so enjoyed. A portion of his remains were also put to rest in Mottarville Cemetery next to his parents. Dave Jostes's 1970 Chevelle was at the cemetery observance, where on lookers admired Waldmire's artwork under the car's trunk lid and hood. The car with Bob's artwork was displayed in Milwaukee during the summer of 2014 as part of the Harley-Davidson Museum's "American Road" display.

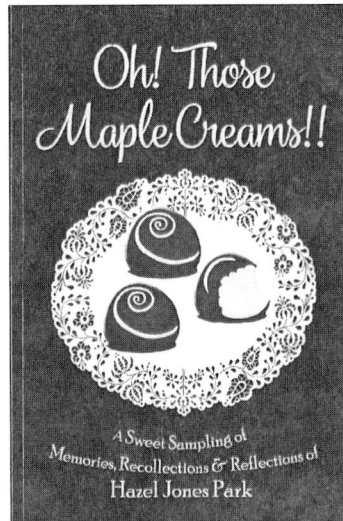

The 2016 publication of Hazel *(Jones)* Park's memories in the book *Oh! Those Maple Creams!!* offers a first-hand look at Rochester's past. Hazel's grand-daughter, Karen Alexander, edited this "sweet sampling of memories." (COVER BY MORNING STAR DESIGN; COURTESY OF KAREN *(PARK)* ALEXANDER)

— Even after a massive 2010 earthquake in Haiti destroyed an orphanage that had been home to five-year-old twins who were bound for the U.S., **Mike** and **Sandy Hurtubise** were able to bring the two safely to Rochester and adopt the youngsters, who have since become American citizens.

— Rochester pastry chef **Kathryn Elder** was a member of the pastry team that prepared thousands of individual desserts for fans at Super Bowl XLV between the Green Bay Packers and Pittsburgh Steelers at Cowboy Stadium in Dallas, TX.

— **Kevin Ramsey**, an assistant English teacher in Ashikaga City, Japan, was reported safe following the massive 2011 earthquake and tsunami that devastated a large swathe of Japan. His parents are Rochester residents Richard and Ann Ramsey.

— **Lucas Denney** was a 2017 RHS senior when he came in second during the 2017 National History Bowl. He was a one-person team in the small schools division, competing against teams with up to four students.

— **Brad Sturdy**, a 1987 RHS graduate, was inducted into the Illinois Amateur Softball Association Hall of Fame in 2017. His long history with the sport included coaching softball at Buffalo Tri-City High School, and earning a number of his own softball titles between 1992 and 2011.

— Rather than use chemical pesticides, **Marvin Hubbell**, owner of Hubbell's Grove Christmas tree farm, explained in 2012 his success in relying on praying mantises to control potentially harmful insect pests. In addition to avoiding chemical pesticides, Hubbell explained that he also avoided chemical herbicides or fertilizers on his 29-acre tree farm.

— As one of those highlighted in the "Springfield Area's Most Interesting People" series, **Harry Hendrickson**'s wide-ranging career was described in 2013. He began as a biology teacher in Laos during the Vietnam War, and was also the state's groundwater education coordinator and the Illinois Science Teachers Association's executive director. A village trustee, he also played a major role in developing Rochester's Arboretum in Community Park.

— A large community turnout met at the Rochester Christian Church to celebrate RHS 1954 graduate **David L. Jostes**'s 80th birthday. Jostes, owner and operator of Jostes Garage for more than 20 years, drove a school bus for 29 years, and served on the Rochester School Board.

• Long-time Rochester residents **Richard** and **Lorine Wallin** have one of the more unusual "how we met" stories. It started, however, decades before the couple first saw each other, when Lorine's mother was born in 1922 on a Chicago, Peoria & St. Louis Railroad trip between Petersburg and Springfield. That line went broke, and the Chicago & Illinois Midland (C&IM) Railroad took over the tracks.

— Move ahead to 1953, when the last C&IM passenger train made the same Petersburg-to-Springfield trip. Train enthusiast Dick Wallin was taking pic-

tures of the occasion, and saw the guest of honor, Anna Mae Batterton and her family, including her nine-year-old daughter Lorine. (See where this is going?)
— It was eight years later when Dick, working in Springfield, was asked to check job references and background of a young lady, Lorine Batterton, for a possible job. She was hired, they fell in love, and it was only after the couple married, that Lorine mentioned in passing that her mother had been born on a train. Dick then realized that his wife had been the nine-year-old daughter of "the lady born on a train" he saw in 1953.
— Dick and Lorine moved to Rochester in 1978, where their children, Jeff and KymmAnn, grew up and graduated from RHS. The Wallins celebrated their 53rd wedding anniversary in 2016.

- The "liar's bench" of the early 1900s has been reincarnated. Today's members are some of the most knowledgable, mature men of the township who meet regularly at Rochester's Subway sandwich shop.
— One faithful member, D.J., announced to his learned brethren early in May 2017 that he was seeking donations for the displaced Beaver family, victims of the recent flood. While not one of the gathering reached into his pockets, the group was surprised when a lady, who was visiting from Colorado, came over to their table. Having heard D.J. call for donations, this kind soul contributed a $20 bill as her donation and walked away.

— Dumbfounded, D.J. rapidly explained to the woman that he was just kidding and that the Beaver family was actually a den of beavers that had set up housekeeping in nearby Black Branch Creek. The lady, unfazed at her misinterpretation, urged D.J. to, "just keep the donation and give it to someone in the community who needs it." D.J. did just that.

Above: Some of Rochester's newest residents set up housekeeping in this beaver dam, which they built across Black Branch Creek south of the East Main Street bridge in 2016.

Sharing their favorite Rochester stories over lunch at the Buckhart Tavern are, from left: Carl "Bud" Moore, George "Butch" Fairchild, David Ramsey, and Don Taft.
(R. BRUZAN PHOTOS)

When former owner Helen Taft sold the Cockrell house in 2012, she left behind a unique sample of her art talents painted on a door. The artwork is highly prized by the home's new owner. (COURTESY OF COMPASS POINT PRODUCTIONS; FARM PROGRESS COMPANIES)

A sample of Helen Taft's artwork decorates a door at her home in the Cockrell house on East Main Street in Rochester. (COURTESY OF CAITLIN WALDEN; R. BRUZAN PHOTO)

- Some of Rochester's heroes:

— **Jeanne Sims** was 82 in 2010 when she was in the spotlight for the dozens of sweaters she had hand knit and donated to the needy through Midwest Mission Distribution Center and Kumler Outreach Ministries. One admirer noted that Jeanne "puts her whole heart and soul into knitting those."

—Retired Rochester teachers **Jane Byram**, **Marsha Menzel**, and **Melody Thomas** began in 2010 to collect and distribute new books to needy children through *The State Journal-Register* annual holiday charity Friend-in-Deed. Even after that charity suspended book distributions, the trio continued collecting new books that local agencies then distributed during the holidays to children from birth to age 12. In the first six years, the book drives collected more than 15,000 books.

— Six-year-old **Anicka Brenham** followed the earlier example of her nine-year-old sister **Cadence** when she donated her birthday presents in 2011 to Toys for Tots. Not one to over-explain her actions, she simply said she wanted children who may not otherwise have gifts to receive the donations.

— **Micah Anderson** and **Daniel Buckley**, RHS band members, came to the aid of a Pana man who experienced a heart attack in 2012 during Pana's annual Labor Day parade. Because the 17-year-olds applied CPR, well-known local photographer Gene Reed lived six more weeks. Although the story ended sadly, Gene's family and friends spoke highly in praise of the boys' efforts to save Reed's life.

— When tests confirmed that Rochester eighth-grader **Rene Runions** had the form of muscular dystrophy known as Charcot-Marie Tooth, she actively found ways to help herself and those with any of the related group of inherited conditions. Rene was named the Muscular Dystrophy Association's State Goodwill Ambassador for Illinois in 2012 and set to work raising donations through numerous fundraisers. Two years later, as a high school sophomore, she was named a Top Teen finalist by *The State Journal-Register's* teen section "The Voice." Nominees for the annual award were recognized because of their contributions to make a difference in their communities. Rene has traveled around Illinois to raise awareness of muscular dystrophy, and she hopes both to help those battling the disease and to prevent it from affecting others.

The Rochester Cemetery Chapel was rebuilt in 2014, long after a 1980s fire. Cemetery Board member and Rochester Cemetery historian Steve Leach is pictured visiting the chapel in 2015. (R. BRUZAN PHOTOS)

Development of North Park was moved forward in 2015 to help meet recreational needs for Rochester's growing population. Located in the shadow of the village's water tower west of Oak Mill Estates subdivision, park additions included new trees and playground equipment. (R. BRUZAN PHOTOS)

ABOUT THE FUTURE...

It's a gamble to predict the future, but in 2018 Rochester appears to be poised for another major growth period. The authors hope that Rochester's future will be well documented so that, 50 years from now, a followup book may celebrate the village's bicentennial.

The authors offer the following suggestions to help keep Rochester's history alive.
- Dedicate a building in which to display Rochester's historic artifacts.
- Bring together village and RHPS leadership in order to rebuild the log house discovered in 1987.
- Provide a speakers' forum on local history for students at all grade levels.
- Increase communications among elected officials, Rochester Public Library, and RHPS to broaden awareness of Rochester's history.
- Incorporate youthful leadership within RHPS to blend with the organization's experienced officials and directors.
- Designate Rochester's first homestead with an appropriate marker.
- Provide visible connections to village history by placing an Interurban trolley or a B&O train engine in downtown Rochester.
- Name or rename village streets to honor people who played important roles in Rochester history: Bell, Bolden, Campbell, Carter, Coe, Fairchild, Hollenbeck, McCoy, Persinger, Taft, and Twist.
- Actively encourage Orange Judd homeowners to preserve their historic buildings.
- Support research of the remaining Orange Judd homes in Rochester Township.
- Use the *Historic Walking Tour Guide* of Rochester's Orange Judd buildings as a stepping stone for potential tourism.

Even after 200 years, Rochester's historic artifacts continue to be found. A stone point, a brick, porcelain dinnerware, a railroad spike and tie, a horse hitching post, old coins, bottles, a log from a mill, or a log house are among the items that have already been identified. What artifacts will be found 200 years from now that will represent today's Rochester community? We can only imagine.

APPENDIX

ROCHESTER VILLAGE PRESIDENTS

1869 — Munson Carter
1871 — R.P. Abel
1873 — Ethan P. May
1874 — Carter Tracy
1876 — E.R. Babcock
1877 — Carter Tracy
1879 — O.C. St. Clair
1880 — Carter Tracy
1882 — Daniel Ott
1883 — H.D. Parker
1886 — Daniel Ott
1887 — Samuel A. Tobin
1889 — Daniel Ott
1890 — O.B. Babcock
1891 — G.W. Everhart
1892 — Ira F. Twist
1895 — J.M. Bell
1897 — F.B. Harcourt
1901 — John T. Dunn
1903 — J.M. Bell
1905 — W.G. Brown
1908 — J.B. Highmore
1909 — Fred B. Everhart
1911 — Charles W. Frame
1913 — J.B. Highmore
1917 — George Feldhausen
1919 — J.F. Tobin
1921 — J.M. Easley
1923 — Henry Schwartz
1937 — J. Earl Bell
1945 — L.E. Campbell
1961 — Frank Foster
1965 — H.E. Montgomery
1969 — Cecil Hyatt
1973 — Robert L. Martin
1975 — Everett J. Turner
1979 — Ernest Bartels
1985 — Nyla Hardwick
1987 — Henry P. Bregenhorn
1991 — James A. Finley
1997 — Grant A. Blasdel
2001 — David L. Armstrong
2017 — Joseph C. Suerdieck

Rochester Law Enforcement

Constables
1878 — A.H. Burt
1895 — S.W. Hawkins

Marshals
1915 — A.B. Crawford
1923 — H.C. Gilbert
1928 — D.R. Beck
1931 — W. Dickerson
? — Lyman Campbell
1965 — Donald Dike
1966 — John Foster

Chiefs of Police
1976 — Michael Upchurch
1987 — Stephen Rutledge
1997 — William Marass
2017 — Kent Bragg

Officers with 30 years of service
Mervin Spurgeon
Sam Gresham
Steve Rutledge
Michael Grim
William Marass
Jon Schwartz

ROCHESTER FIRE PROTECTION

Department Chiefs

1949 — Ernest Rentschler
1964 — Marshall Watkins
1968 — John Foster
1977 — Jerry Moore
2003 — Dick Rentschler
2008 — Mark Poffenberger
2017 — Greg Surbeck

Original Department Members

Ernest Rentschler • Marshal Watkins • Ben Barnes • Nelson Campbell
Floyd Crow • Wilson Park • Frank Price • Lyman Campbell • GeorgeWohlers
Carl Rule • Ralph Norman • Damion Coker • Lloyd Upchurch • George Chastain
Robert Krimmel • George Fisher • Dave Halm • Don Park • Sam Miller
Jack Abshire • Dale Curry • Robert Ritterbusch • William Crim • Robert Dickerson
Blaine Livingston • Harold Shipman • Phillip Grieme • Jim Taylor • Robert Gum
Roland Geiger • Howard Chiles • Lewis Bennett • Ernest Taft
Ernest Dannenburger • Joe Weaver • Charles Strode, Jr.

Members with 20 or More Years of Service

Ernest Rentschler • Marshall Watkins • Ralph Norman • Dave Halm
Jack Abshire • Robert Ritterbusch • Lewis Bennett • Joe Weaver
Harry Grieme, Jr. • Doug Logsdon • Jack Moore • Jerry Moore • Jeff Ramsey
Bob Ramsey • Ray Ramsey • Bob Rentschler • Mark Rentschler • Joe Ross
John Sharp • Bob E. Young • Dan Young • Charles Strode • Barney Flatt
Wayne Beck • John Foster • Randy Prasun • Hank Bregenhorn • Bud Beck
Frank Purnell • Dwight Pope • Bob Ealey • Dale Barthel • Louis Ealey
Loren Beard • Don Kyes • David C. Jostes • Jerry Davis • Marty Fairchild
John Fox, Sr. • John Groves • Larry Kaiser • Gary McBride • Neil Passfield
Mark Poffenberger • Randy Romadka • Michael Weaver • John Archer

ROCHESTER POST OFFICE

Postmasters and Officers in Charge

1834	Christopher B. Stafford
1842	Nathan P. West
1844	William Ainslie
1847	Daniel C. Eggleston
1849	Munson Carter
1856	James H. Neal
1868	Munson Carter
1877	Charles Carter
1881	Homer D. Parker
1885	James M. Firey
1889	Homer D. Parker
1893	Armstrong D. Young
1897	Homer D. Parker
1915	Samuel D. Richardson
1923	Chester W. Miller
1924	Myla M. Oliver
1928	Alonzo Eggleston
1940	Earl M. Thomas
1964	Josephine Campbell
1966	Fred D. Naffziger
1972	Emil F. Naschinski
1981	Georgia L. Leonard
1982	Lori J. Kimble
1983	Jack W. Morrison
1984	Gerald W. Weinheimer
1984	Alice O. Griffin
1990	Beverly S. Held
1991	Mark E. Kleiss
2010	Sarah Drone
2011	Randy Campbell
2011	Jerry L. Thixton

ROCHESTER CITIZENS OF THE YEAR

1979	W.W. Dugger
1980	Walt Ebel
1981	Delbert Taft
1982	Marshall Fay.Beck
1983	Wilson J. Park
1984	Robert L. Ritterbusch
1985	Vickie Lattimer
1986	Esther Taft
1987	Robert E. Church
1988	Roy W. Upham
1989	Rev. George Schmink
1990	Teri Neff
1991	Henry Bregenhorn
1992	Elizabeth Fairchild
1993	Wayne Beck
1994	Gary McBride
1995	Rev. Robert Foulk
1996	Marilee Waters
1997	Hugo Zahn
1998	Toby McDaniel
1999	Ted McCoy
2000	Andy Lunt
2001	Pamela J. Bruzan
2002	John Shoudel
2003	Randy Hawkins
2004	Mike Greer
2005	Lisa Sandidge
2006	Dave Grubb
2007	Nancy Kruse
2008	R.L. and Carolyn Moore
2009	Greg Park
2010	Dave Hicks; Steve Leach
2011	Jerry Robertson
2012	Harry Hendrickson
2013	Larry Shoudel
2014	Dale Laningham
2015	Maribeth Eandi
2016	Gael Kent
2017	Jeff Ramsey

ROCHESTER WOMEN'S CLUB

Presidents

1924	—	Mollie Wolford	1975	—	Barb Carney
1925	—	Nettie B. Coe	1976	—	Judy Hampson
1926	—	May M. Vigal	1977	—	Sandy Williams
1927	—	Fannie Olcott	1978	—	Sue Lascari
1928	—	Grace Montgomery	1979	—	Karen Surina
1929	—	Sabina Coe	1980	—	Judy Eveloff
1930	—	Alma Cantrall	1981	—	Maude Higgins
1931	—	Edna Baker	1984	—	Jenny Sciera
1932	—	Flora Eggleston	1985	—	Shirley Stoldt
1933	—	Grace Chard	1986	—	Judy Hampson
1934	—	Lucile Fairchild	1987	—	Kay McKee
1935	—	Hazel Park	1987	—	Sally Schaefer
1936	—	Edna Gaddey	1988	—	Janet Stover
1937	—	Virginia Taft	1990	—	Carol Craig
1938	—	Margaret Scott	1991	—	Maude Higgins
1939	—	Adele Carswell	1992	—	Lori Tucker
1940	—	Ida Chapin	1993	—	Carolyn Riggs
1942	—	Minerva Durham	1995	—	Joan L. Mason
1944	—	Esker Davey	1997	—	Diana Nevitt
1946	—	Helen J. Goby	1998	—	Lucy Breitung
1948	—	Ruth Carswell	2000	—	Janie File
1950	—	Ethel Lundberg	2001	—	Raetta Laningham
1952	—	Josephine Campbell	2003	—	Amee Lee
1954	—	June Park	2004	—	Maude Higgins
1956	—	Helen Duffey	2005	—	Diana Nevitt
1958	—	Pauline Watkins	2006	—	Janie File
1960	—	Joan Mavis	2007	—	Carol Cross
1962	—	Dolores Church	2008	—	Janie File
1964	—	Lorraine Andruskevitch	2009	—	Carol Cross
1966	—	Jane Auby	2010	—	Nancy Stites
1968	—	Dottie Anderson	2011	—	Jane Hendrickson
1970	—	Melinda Ratliff	2012	—	Carol Knoblock
1971	—	Rosalind LaMarche	2013	—	Jane Hendrickson
1972	—	Betty McKirahan	2014	—	Carol Cross
1973	—	Helen Poffenberger	2015	—	Janie File
1974	—	Nancy Mavis	2016	—	Mary Beth Ramsey

INDEPENDENT ORDER
OF ODD FELLOWS

IOOF Lodge 268 Noble Grands

1859	—	R.F. Price	1882	—	John F. Tobin
1860	—	R.F. Price	1899	—	William F. Clark
1861	—	Carter Tracy	1940	—	Don Lederbrand
1862	—	John L. Jones	1941	—	Harold Chandler
1863	—	James W. Everhart	1942	—	John Miller
1864	—	John A. Richards	1943	—	George Carpenter
1865	—	Levi J. Hasbrouck	1944	—	William Bennett
1866	—	Levi J. Hasbrouck	1946	—	George Miller
1867	—	Thomas Deyo	1947	—	Chester Miller
1868	—	Carter Tracy	1948	—	John Miller
1869	—	Calvin C. Johnson	1949	—	K.M. Elkins
1870	—	A.H. Laken	1950	—	John Miller
1871	—	Henry Williams	1952	—	O.R. Evans
1872	—	A.H. Burt	1953	—	Nelson Vaughn
1873	—	Carter Tracy	1954	—	O.R. Evans
1874	—	William David	1955	—	Homer Cearlock
1875	—	W.B. Prather	1956	—	Nelson Vaughn
1876	—	Lewis Money	1957	—	K.M. Elkins
1877	—	Samuel J. Smith	1958	—	O.R. Evans
1878	—	William Bashaw	1959	—	K.M. Elkins
1879	—	John S. Highmore	1960	—	O.R. Evans
1880	—	A.H. Burt	1961	—	Loren Taft
1881	—	O.C. St. Clair	1996	—	John Miller

(Some years unavailable)

Odd Fellows Lodge 268 of Rochester closed in 1996

MORELAND REBEKAH LODGE 573

1902 Instituting Officers

W.H. Hocke
Augusta Withrow
Ora Burcham

First Noble Grand, 1902

Nettie Enlow

Although records are incomplete,
other Noble Grands have included:

Ethel Bennett
Margaret Dannenberger
Mary Dike
Minerva Durham
Florence Flat
Nevera Fleming
Rosie Fogle
Vera Hankins
Vanita Hiessinger
Grace King
Mrs. Charles Libby
Louise Miller
Margaret Morris
Elizabeth Nelch
Marguerite Price
Ricki Pruitt
Theodosia Pyle
Carrie Ralston
Marjorie Rath
Esther Taft
Irene Taft

2016 Noble Grand

Evelyn Ramsey
As of 2017, Evelyn Ramsey is the only remaining member of
Moreland Rebekah Lodge 573.

Rochester Lodge No. 635, A.F. & A.M.
Chartered October 5, 1869
Past Masters

Name	Year	Name	Year	Name	Year
John F. Burrell	1869	Elma Price	1913	Albert Hopkins	1957
Richard J. McNeil	1870	James H. Walker	1914	Jordon M. Hood	1958
Richard J. McNeil	1871	Charles W. Frame	1915	Damian R. Coker	1959
Ethan P. May	1872	Charles W. Frame	1916	Delbert D. Taft	1960
Carter Cracely	1873	Charles W. Frame	1917	Anthony Mangalavite Sr.	1961
Richard J. McNeil	1874	Robert F. Fairchild	1918	F. North Ross	1962
William Finney	1875	Robert F. Fairchild	1919	Charles W. Libby	1963
Richard J. McNeil	1876	John R. Baker	1920	George G. Easley	1964
Dennis T. Farrell	1877	John R. Baker	1921	George E. Campbell	1965
Richard J. McNeil	1878	Herman Newcomer	1922	Alvin W. Hardy	1966
William Finney	1879	Herman Newcomer	1923	Everett J. Turner	1967
Dennis T. Farrell	1880	Roy Brunk	1924	James L. Campbell	1968
William J. Cooper	1881	Roy Brunk	1925	John L. Pyle	1969
Dennis T. Farrell	1882	Carroll L. Raney	1926	David A. Easley	1970
Dennis T. Farrell	1883	Carroll L. Raney	1927	H. Vere Dawson	1971
Dennis T. Farrell	1884	Charles H. James	1928	Herbert Carter	1972
William Finney	1885	Charles W. Frame	1929	J. E. Johnson	1973
James M. Firey	1886	Arthur G. Haines	1931	Stanley G. Shutt	1974
Richard P. Hunter	1887	Arthur G. Haines	1932	Leonard P. Siddens	1975
Richard P. Hunter	1888	Ernest Darnell	1933	Forrest Sexton	1976
Richard P. Hunter	1889	Edwin Chard Sr.	1930	Cecil W. Hyatt	1977
Richard P. Hunter	1890	Isham H. Taft	1934	John H. Rasmussen	1978
Homer D. Parker	1891	Isham H. Taft	1935	Loren E. Douglas	1979
Homer D. Parker	1892	Charles L. Turley	1936	Floyd A. Starr	1980
James M. Bell	1893	Edwin A. Chard Jr.	1937	William E. Ward	1981
James M. Bell	1894	Lyman E. Campbell	1938	Phillip H. Ulrich	1982
Henry Taft	1895	Harry A. Smith	1939	F. Dwight Pope	1983
James M. Bell	1896	Charles H. Fairchild	1940	Robert W. Smith	1984
Charles B. McClelland	1897	Hugh A. Campbell	1941	Dean A. Bricker	1985
Richard P. Hunter	1898	George G. Easley	1942	Howard Earl Carr	1986
James M. Bell	1899	Clarence S. Coe	1943	Mark J. Schmidt	1987
John H. Pressley	1900	Robert A. Rentschler	1944	David W. Hilton	1988
Richard P. Hunter	1901	George W. Duffey	1945	Timothy L. Spengler	1989
Thomas D. Farrell	1902	Wilson J. Park	1946	Harry H. Hopkins	1990
Thomas D. Farrell	1903	Ernest J. Rentschler	1947	Richard A. Rentschler	1991
James M. Bell	1904	Frederick M. Poffenberger	1948	Grant A. Blasdell	1992
James M. Bell	1905	Marshall H. Watkins	1949	Robert B. Dellert	1993
James M. Bell	1906	Ross E. Fairchild	1950	Adolf E. Fullgrabe	1994
James M. Bell	1907	William R. Crim	1951	Justin Taft Jr.	1995
John D. Hunter	1908	Carroll Bowersock	1952	John W. Ash & Dwight Pope	1996
John D. Hunter	1909	David L. Halm	1953	Andrew T. Carrier	1997
John E. Coe	1910	Lowell B. Miller	1954	David E. Purdy	1998
John D. Hunter	1911	Charles H. Strode Jr.	1955	Brian D. Siddens	1999
John D. Hunter	1912	Ralph L. Leach	1956	Oren D. Dutton	2000

Ronald S. Womack	2001
Martin R. Fairchild	2002
Mark A. Van Dyke	2003
Gary C. Matthews	2004
Harold Lee Shaw, Jr.	2005
Harold Lee Shaw, Jr.	2006
Loren C. Heiple	2007
Ronald S. Womack	2008
David A. Eiter	2009
John F. Preuss	2010
David E. Purdy	2011
Paul D. MacDonna	2012
Mark C. White	2013

Calligraphy by Bud McCafferty

Order of the Eastern Star

Worthy Matrons Rochester Chapter

1905 — Mayme Taft
1907 — Mollie Wolford
1909 — Osie Hunter

Worthy Matrons Sangamo Chapter 746

1914	— Mollie Wolford		1955	— Ruth Sprouse
1915	— Mary B. Fairchild		1956	— Helen Hood
1916	— Nettie Coe		1957	— Mae Leach
1919	— Edith Fairchild		1958	— Mardell Taft
1921	— Edna Baker		1959	— Harriet Beckey
1923	— Ida J. Bell		1960	— Audree Libby
1924	— Carrie Ralston		1961	— Dorthy Ross
1925	— Edna Nichols		1962	— Rachel Shutt
1926	— Bessie Raney		1963	— Betty Hardy
1927	— Lucy Young		1964	— Mary Campbell
1928	— Chelsea Houk		1965	— Dorthy Ross
1929	— Lucy Young		1966	— Mary Brown
1930	— Grace Montgomery		1967	— Ann Huddleston
1931	— Eva Poffenberger		1968	— Ruby Beam
1932	— Lucile Fairchild		1969	— Marian Thomas
1933	— Adele Carswell		1970	— Priscilla Taft
1934	— Emma Brunk		1971	— Thelma Dickey
1935	— Fannie Olcott		1972	— Mary Campbell
1936	— Virginia Taft		1973	— Mabel Bowersock
1937	— Louise Dill		1974	— Rose Armstrong
1938	— Jennie Taft		1975	— Birdiebel Johnson
1939	— Josephine Campbell		1976	— Betty Shackelford
1940	— Grace Chard		1977	— Carolyn Moore
1941	— Edith Greenwalt		1978	— Vivian Coffey
1942	— Renolla Coe		1979	— Peg Cordell
1943	— Virginia Harford		1980	— Grace Pope
1944	— Elizabeth Fairchild		1981	— Vivian Coffey
1945	— Edna Graham		1982	— Audree Libby
1946	— Hazel Park		1983	— Denise Johnson
1947	— June Park		1984	— Peg Cordell
1948	— Mary Frances Ross		1985	— Mary Strode
1949	— Helen Poffenberger		1986	— Molly Schmidt
1950	— Anne King		1987	— Birdiebel Johnson
1951	— Pauline Watkins		1988	— Mabel Bowersock
1952	— Mary Strode		1989	— Denise Johnson
1953	— Mabel Bowersock		2001	— Molly Elmore
1954	— Helen Duffey		2002	— Cathy Hauger

ROCHESTER LIONS CLUB

Presidents

1965	—	Kester Pollock	1992 —	Art Warnke
1966	—	Phil Williams	1993 —	Harry Hendrickson
1967	—	Richard Housel	1994 —	Joe Hill
1968	—	Trevor Samuel	1995 —	Dan Brogdon
1969	—	Parker Kious	1996 —	David Taft
1970	—	James Major	1997 —	Ted McCoy
1971	—	Lawrence Auby	1998 —	Dave Hicks
1972	—	Joe Cordell	1999 —	Larry Shoudel
1973	—	Wilson Park	2000 —	Dave Armstrong
1974	—	Jerry Walter	2001 —	Tim Cravens
1975	—	Robert Fairchild	2002 —	Ken Roy
1976	—	Charles Newhouse	2003 —	Dan Brogdon
1977	—	Sam Gresham	2004 —	Bill Marass
1978	—	Ron Bortmess	2005 —	John Shoudel
1979	—	Wally Biermann	2006 —	Dean Clough
1980	—	Robert Neal	2007 —	Wally Biermann
1981	—	Glen Brachear	2008 —	Dennis Ferguson
1982	—	Nate Wilcoxon	2009 —	Dick Sprinkel
1983	—	Dan Ghere	2010 —	Louie Daugherty
1985	—	Tom Walker	2011 —	Joe Hill
1986	—	Forrest Holsapple	2012 —	John Shoudel
1987	—	Larry Shoudel	2013 —	Gael Kent
1988	—	Herb Benson	2014 —	Bob Church
1989	—	Bill Bowlby	2015 —	Ron Wright
1991	—	Jim Rominger	2016 —	Chris Wright

American Legion
Harry Fogle Post 274

Commanders

1925	—	H.L. Campbell
1927	—	Floyd Clark
1930	—	C.F. Clark
1942	—	Otho Van Fossen
1944	—	Clarence O. Derry
1945	—	Carroll Young
1946	—	William T. Fairchild
1947	—	Arthur H. Beam
1948	—	Robert Ritterbusch
1950	—	Hugh A. Campbell
1951	—	Walter Baumhardt
1952	—	Jack Goby
1953	—	Meryl Sturdy
1954	—	James Waters
1955	—	Earnest Rentschler
1956	—	Carl Rule
1957	—	Ernest Taft
1958	—	John Fredrick
1959	—	Elmer L. Schoeneberg
1961	—	Harrison E. Thurman
1962	—	Eugene Holmes
1963	—	Bryce Griffin
1964	—	Lyman Beck
1965	—	Julian Rothenberger
1966	—	Gayle Beck
1967	—	Raymond K. Gustin
1968	—	Willard J. Hasselbring
1969	—	Dale Barthel
1971	—	William Wiggins
1973	—	David Prior
1974	—	George Shackelford
1975	—	Milo Olson
1976	—	Hugh Campbell
1981	—	Kenneth Maxheimer
1982	—	Dale Barthel
1993	—	Jack Goby
1996	—	Leslie Shipman
1997	—	Paul Bell
2017	—	Gael Kent

QUESTERS 390
CHICKEN BRISTLE CHAPTER

Presidents

1969 — Marge Estrop	1993 — Marietta Bowlby
1970 — Sally Wisleder	1994 — Peg Cordell
1971 — Francis Leek	1995 — Suzi Pettyjohn
1972 — Dottie Troop	1996 — Marge Estrop
1973 — Helen Duffey	1997 — Dottie Troop
1974 — Wilma Bayer	1998 — Suzi Pettyjohn
1975 — Ginny Myers	1999 — Carolyn Moore
1976 — Dorothy Dugger	2000 — Linda Grimm
1977 — Ann Scott	2001 — Marcia VanPelt
1978 — Jane Cross	2002 — Wilma Bayer
1979 — Carolyn Moore	2003 — Wilma Bayer
1980 — Renee Housel	2004 — Jane Fairchild
1981 — Ginny Ludwig	2005 — Sharon Evans
1982 — Linda Grimm	2006 — Priscilla Kluge
1983 — Peg Cordell	2007 — Ruth E. Liken
1984 — Mary Lou Holsapple	2008 — Debbie Schnepper
1985 — Trudy Hubbell	2009 — Trudy Ballinger
1986 — Jane Fairchild	2010 — Trudy Ballinger
1987 — Lois Weissberg	2011 — Cari Carlson
1988 — Phyllis Clemens	2012 — Peg Cordell
1989 — Polly Jamison	2013 — Sandie Nuding
1990 — Marcia Van Pelt	2014 — Ann Rowley
1991 — Trudy Hubbell	2015 — Ann Rowley
1992 — Sharon Evans	2016 — Suzi Pettyjohn

ROCHESTER HISTORICAL PRESERVATION SOCIETY

Presidents

1988	Carolyn Moore
1990	Joe Hill
1993	R.L. Moore
1994	David Ramsey
1996	Bob Fairchild
1998	Bob Church
2001	Dorthy Ross
2002	Justin Taft, Jr.
2006	Kathleen Winhold
2008	Jerry Robertson
2010	Larry Watkins
2013	David Taft
2015	Lyle Behl
2017	John E. Runions

ARTIFACTS & ACQUISITIONS

During the research for this book, dozens of artifacts have been photographed, copied, or donated to the Rochester Historical Preservation Society's collection. This list provides an overview of those items, several of which are held in private collections. Readers who wish to donate additional artifacts to the collection or make them available to be photographed or copied should contact the authors or the current RHPS president.

From the McCoy homestead debris field: nails, glass, brick, pieces of porcelain cups and dishes, crockery

Three coins from the McCoy-homestead debris field, dated 1838, 1853, 1857

Hundreds of family and community photographs

B&O Railroad tie, plate, and spikes

Four original editions of *The Rochester Weekly Item*: 1886, 1916, 1918, 1909, 1922

One log from the 1824 Clark Mill

Ledger books of John Twist, 1878

Ledger books of the Rochester IOOF, 1859

One 1879 edition of the *Sangamo Daily Monitor* newspaper

Mill stones from Shreve Mill

Bottles from H.D. Parker drug store

Rochester School's 1920 corner stone

Methodist Church ledger records, beginning 1839

Rochester Christian Church ledger records, beginning 1878

Cancelled checks from the Bank of Rochester (1904) and Rochester State Bank (1922)

Stone axes, spear points, and arrowheads

Copies of more than 50 abstracts recording Rochester property activity

Bills from H.D. Parker, S.G. Richardson, G.A. Wolford, R.T Shreve, and Twist Brothers

Utt Brothers bricks c1895: one black shale and one red clay

One brick from Pensacola Tavern

Crossing sign and two rail spikes from Rochester's Interurban trolley line

Tool chest owned by Rochester carpenter Frank Chandler

Original copies of the 1918 *Orange Judd Pictorial*

Commemorative plate from Rochester's centennial celebration

Original Rochester Methodist Church bell, 1876

Original Rochester Christian Church bell, 1875

McCoy rifle, held in a private collection

Original 2016 Daniel G. Moore artwork of the Clark Mill site

Door frame pintle found near the Clark Mill site

Hand-hewn logs in several existing buildings

Walnut box from a Rochester tree where Abraham Lincoln spoke

Several log homes within houses that are occupied today

Artifacts & Acquisitions, continued

Partial stone-wall building and stone-wall foundations

Trunk owned by a Confederate soldier who moved to Rochester

Pre-1900 wallpaper from two Orange Judd homes

Tintype of Rev. T.B. Wright, pre-1900

Coin sent to Rev. T.B. Wright from Malaysia

John A. Twist memorial card

1899 check drawn by C.E. Miller on his account at Ridgely National Bank of Springfield

Marriage certificate copies

Constitution and by-laws of the Anti-Horse Thief Association

ID&W Railroad crossing sign, switch lamp, and target

1918 Rochester State Bank calendar

Horse hitching posts and carriage stoops

Two horse-drawn sleighs, c1900

Rochester United Methodist Church memorial windows

C.L. Jones undertaker thermometer gift, c1920

Iron pedestrian bridge and wood deck

Taft & Son's Dairy milk bottles

Texaco sign from Coffey's service and gas station

Poster and trophies from Drag City, c1960

The Rochester Hello newspapers, 1981-82

Sangamon Frontier Canoe Rental sign, 1983

Rochester train station sign

Yard sticks: Bank of Rochester c1900; Taft's Dairy c1940

Rochester Public Library quilt, 1996

Literary and visual art works created by Rochester citizens

Rochester Woman's Club 1935-1945 meeting ledger

Two Rochester Unit Homemakers Extension ledgers, 1956-1974

First Route 29 traffic light in Rochester

Abutment stones from Horse Creek covered bridge

Two bricks from the Thomas Thornton Homestead

Tombstones commemorating members of the Forden family

South Fork Church Ledger, 1877-1902

Token from Rochester's Willhite Dairy

Recordings of Louis Persinger

Video of Mt. Deborah, Alaska

Illinois Stories video of Orange Judd homes

Illinois Stories video of Haines log house

Original Route 29 road sign

THANK YOU . . .

Residents throughout Rochester Township and Sangamon County have been continual sources of help and support as this book moved forward. What surprised us, however, was how far we needed to search for information about Rochester people and events. People as far away as Vermont, Alaska, North Carolina, California, Singapore, London, and South Africa were uniformly gracious and helpful. We could not have done it without any of the contacts we made. Thank you all.

A grand thank you to *GenealogyBank* and the *Illinois State Journal-Register*, incredibly important research sources.

The fear of omitting deserving individuals is always a concern, and we sincerely apologize if we have inadvertently left off the name of someone who should appear on this list.

Akins, Nan; Alewelt, Donna; Alewelt, George; Alexander, Karen; Alexander, Rick; Antonacci, Greg; Antonacci, Melanie; Armstrong, David; Armstrong, DrexEllen; Arthur, Diane; Artistic Images; Bain, Angela; Bakke, Dave; Bank and Trust Rochester; Barber, Evan; Bartels, Bill; Baumhardt, Ron; Beck, Helen; Beck, Lyman "Bud"; Beck, Wayne; Becker, Cecile; Becker, Josh; Beckham, Raymond; Behl, Lyle; Bell, Paul; Bennett, Jim; Bernardin, Brenda; Bernardin, David; Bertrand, Dr. Thomas; Bevan, Ash; Bevan, David; Bevan, Elyssa; Bevan, Jennifer; Bevan, Tabitha; Bloodworth, Adam; Bonefeste, Joe; Bozarth, Sue; Bradley, Martha; Brickey, Jean; Browning, Tamara; Bruzan, Albert; Bruzan, Florian; Bruzan, Kevin; Bruzan, Michelle; Bruzan, Ryan; Bucher, Brad; Buecker, Lynn; Buecker, Richard; Burrell, Lester; Button, Steve; Campbell, Janet; Campbell, Brian; Campbell, Jeff; Campbell, Malou; Campbell, Jerry; Campbell, Linda; Campbell, Terry; Cantrill, David; Cantrill, Harold; Capital Blueprint; Caruso, Jim; Cary, Christine; Chard, Lynn; Chestnut, Tim; Church, Bob; Church, Malinda; Churchill, Larry; Clark, Charles; Clark, Martha; Coffey, Bill; Coffey, Rita; Collings, Leanne; Compass Point Productions; Creviston, Melvin; Creviston, Pat; Cross, Claudia; Culp, Joan; Daley, Dorothy "Dot"; Daly, Georgeanne; Danforth, Polly; Davis, Brian; Davis, Jerry; Davis, Karen; Davis, Lu Ann; Day, Jennifer; Day, Terry; Dinardo, Jacob; Dinardo, Kathryn; Doherty, Cherie; Doherty, Tom; Drillinger, Ruth; Dudley, Sharon; Dugger, Nina; Eberhardt, Michael W.; Eilering, Jeanne; Eilering, Rick; Fairchild, Bob; Fairchild, Brian; Fairchild, Diana; Fairchild, George; Fairchild, Jane; Fairchild, Marty; Farm Progress Co.; Farrar, Fletcher; Flatt, Sunnie; Flores, Kristina; Flores, Lupe; Folder, Todd; Fountain, Cindy; Furry, William; *GenealogyBank*; Gentry, Jennifer; Gorbett, Sharon; Greer, Mike; Griffin, Kelly; Grubb, David; Guy, Teresa; Hamilton, Mike; Hampson, Dawn; Hampson, Doug; Hampson, Judith; Hampson, Julia; Hampson, Mike; Harris, Kathryn; Heissinger, Carrol; Hendrickson, David; Hendrickson, Harry; Hendrickson, Jane; Hendrickson, Jo; Hodges, V. Pauline; Hoover, Tom; House of Wickersham; Howe, Todd; Hughs, Jackie; Humphrey, Gregg; Humphries, Bryan; Hundley, Elaine; Isbell, Chris; Jakaitis, Anne; Jakaitis, Mike; Jeffers, Dorinda; Jeffers, Mark; Jeffers, Mike; Jeffers, Rindie; Jeffers, Shirley; Johnson, Mike; Johnson, Pat; Jones, Kassie; Jones, Lance; Jostes, Dave; Jostes, Fay; Jostes, Mary;

Thank You… , continued

Kaufmann, Phillip C.; Kent, Gael; Kerwin, Joe; Kerwin, Lori; Kessler, Erma; Kienzler, Mike; Klickna, Cinda; Klickna, Kim; Klienschmidt, Kim; Klobnak, Jim; Klobnak, Renee; Knauer, Mary; Kumerow, Sara; Kurniskie, Brenda; Kurniskie, Kent; Laningham, Dale; Leach, Steve; Leahy, Cathy; Lennon, Donna; Lennon, Mike; Leone, Christopher; Leone, Tamara; Lewis, Ann; Long, Glenda; Long, Mike; Lorscheider, Randy; Lunt, Andy; Lunt, Jane; Lunt, Wilda; McPherson, Ann; Mann, Curtis; Marass, Bill; Martin, Stephanie; Mavis, Curt; Maxheimer, Steve; Mazrim, Robert; McAllister, Janet; McCafferty, Bud; McCord, Barb; McDaniel, Toby; McDevitt, Larry; McDevitt, Stephanie; McDonald, Mark; McEvoy, Dennis; McMillan, Sandy; McMillan, Stuart; Melton, Beth; Melton, Janelle; Melton, Mike; Melton, Rebecca; Menderski, Maggie; Messmore, Diane; Metcalf, Francis; Metcalf, Richard; Methodist Archives and History Library, Singapore; Michelich, Joe; Miller, John E.; Miller, Ken; Miller, Nadene Lynch; Miller, Nancy; Mitchell, Ken; Mohler, Betty; Mohler, Don; Moore, Carl "Bud"; Moore, Carolyn; Moore, Daniel G.; Moore, Jack; Moore, Jerry; Moore, Jody; Moore, Ralph; Mt. Pulaski Township Historical Society Museum; Nation, David; Nation, Marge; Nuding, Bené; Nuding, Sandy; Nuding, Terry; Nuding, Tim; O'Connor, Erich; Pahde, Jacob; Park, Greg; Park, Kathy; Parr, Bonnie; Pasley, Cindy; Patterson, Patt; Persinger, Brandon Louis; Pierce, Dennis; Poffenberger, Mark; Pope, Dwight; Pope, Grace; Purdy, Lorachelle; Quistgaard, Gretchen; Ramsey, David; Ramsey, Evelyn; Ramsey, Rich; Ransom, James; Raps, Bob; Reed, Joe; Reid, Barbara; Rentschler, Dick; Rentschler, Jody; Rentschler, Mark; Rentschler, Virginia; Richards, Barbara; Riedel, Bridget; Riedel, Paul; Ritterbusch, Karen; Ritterbusch, Mark; Robertson, Jerry; Robertson, Reba; Rochester Public Library; *Rochester Times*; Rodgers, Bill; Rominger, Ann; Rominger, Jim; Ross, Dorthy; Rowley, Ann; Rubano, Anthony; Ruddy, Walt; Rule, Lucille; Runions, John; Runions, Teri; Ryder, Bonnie; Saal, Rich; Scannell, Teana; Scannell, Tim; Schleder, Rod; Schleder, Missy; Schnepper, Debbie; Schnepper, Tris; Schrenk, Lorene; Schrenk, Pat; Schweighauser, Charlie; Scoggins, Barbara; Sexton, Melva; Sexton, Mike; Shaver, Nancy; Schudel, Mark; Shockley, Clarissa; Shockley, Scott; Shockley, Wayne; Sloan, Bob; Slottag, Ruth; Smith, Blaine; Smith, Carolann; Smith, Juanita; Soerensen, Cheryl; South County Publications, Ltd.; Southwick, Jerolyn; Southwick, Phil; Sperry, Robert "Buzz"; Spurgeon, Marlene; Stannard, Helen; *State Journal-Register*; Strick, Carole; Struble, Leslie; Struble, Robert; Sturdy, JoAnn; Sturdy, Mark; Sturdy, Teresa; Sumner, Tim; Swann, Tina; Sweet, Kathy; Taft, David "Cotton"; Taft, Debbie; Taft, Don; Taft, James; Taft, Robin; Taft, Steve; Taylor, Jack K.; Theis, Ruth Ann; Thurman, Dorothy; Thurman, Susan; Troop, Dottie; Turner, Glennette; Tuxhorn, Ben; Tuxhorn, Mary Alice; Twist, Mike; Twist, Terry; Vineyard, Crystal; Wagner, Barbara; Walden, Caitlin; Waldmire, Bill; Wallin, Richard; Wanless, Carolyn; Ward, Carolyn; Warnke, Art; Warnke, Karen; Washburn, Megan; Waters, Jim; Waters, Perry; Watkins, Larry; Weaver, Harold; Weaver, Mike; Weissberg, John; Weissberg, Lois; Weistart, Jim; Weistart, Rosemary; Welch, Laura; Wiant, Dr. Michael; Wilkinson, Herb; Wilkinson, Jean; Williams, Roger; Winhold, Kathleen; Wire, Bob; Wood, Thomas J.; Woodruff, Lyle; Yates, Debbie; Yeck, Mary Jane; Young, Susan; Zimmers, Mike; Zimmers, Nancy

REFERENCES

Pre-1800s References

Kilav. "Globe North and South America Illustration." *Thinkstock, by Getty Images* 2 July 2017.
<http://www.thinkstockphotos.com/search/##618752406/s=DynamicRank/f=CPIHVX>

Lightfoot, Gordon. *Canadian Railroad Trilogy*. United Artists, 1967.

Schweighauser, Charles A. *Astronomy From A to Z*. Springfield, IL: Illinois Issues, Sangamon State University, 1991.

United States Census Bureau. "American Fact Finder: Population, Housing Units, Area, and Density: 2010 - County Subdivision and Place: 2010 Census Summary File." 21 Oct. 2016.
<http://factfinder.census.gov/faces/tableservices/jsf/pages/productview.xhtml?src=bkmk>.

Bankston, Karen. "Welcome To Springfield, Illinois." *State Journal-Register* [Springfield, IL] 27 May1984: 20-21. Published by GenealogyBank.com, a division of NewsBank.

Wiant, Michael. "Re: Artifacts." E-mail to Raymond Bruzan. 25 May 2015.

Fairchild, Robert. Interview with Ray Bruzan. Mar. 2015.

Fairchild, Robert. Interview with Ray Bruzan. 10 Jun 2015.

Moore, Carl, Jr. Interview with Ray Bruzan. 7 May 2015.

Moore, Carl, Jr. Interview with Ray Bruzan. 11 May 2015.

Howard, Robert P., *A New Eden: The Pioneer Era in Sangamon County*. Ed. Cullom Davis. Sangamon County Historical Society. Springfield, IL. 1974.

Baumhart, Ronald. Interview with Ray Bruzan. 27 Apr. 2016.

Niemeyer, Cheryl. "Re: Nutting stone." E-mail to Pamela J. Bruzan. 2 Nov. 2015.

Carstens, Caryl. "Prehistory on the Prairie," *State Journal-Register* [Springfield, IL] 16 Mar. 1984: 44. Published by GenealogyBank.com, a division of NewsBank.

Enos, Zimri A. "The Old Indian Trail: Sangamon County, Illinois." *Journal of the Illinois State Historical Society* 4, No. 2, July 1911: 218-222. 28 Mar. 2015. <http://www.jtor.org/stable/40193854?seq=4>.

Lindstrom, Andy. "Salt Creek: Waterway Channels Illinois History." *State Journal-Register* [Springfield, IL] 22 Apr. 1976: 64. Published by GenealogyBank.com, a division of NewsBank.

"Find an Indian Cemetery: Discovery Is Made by Children in Edgar County." *State Journal-Register* [Springfield, IL] 7 Oct. 1901: 1. Published by GenealogyBank.com, a division of NewsBank.

"Three Skeletons Are Dug up Near Lincoln; Ground Believed Indian Graveyard." *State Journal-Register* [Springfield, IL] 19 July 1921: 1. Published by GenealogyBank.com, a division of NewsBank.

Muraro, Joan. "Focus on Elkhart Hill: Tour of Historic Homes July 22-24." *State Journal-Register* [Springfield, IL] 17 July 1966: 44. Published by GenealogyBank.com, a division of NewsBank.

Craig, J. "The Olcott Mounds Site: Mortuary Site Investigations in the Sangamon River Drainage — Report of Investigations No. 2." Rochester, IL, 1997.

Wickersham, James. "Mounds of Sangamon County, Illinois." Annual Report of the Board of Regents of the Smithsonian Institution. Washington: Government Printing Office, 1885.

Deuel, T.D. *American Indian Ways of Life: An Interpretation of the Archaeology of Illinois and Adjoining Areas*. Story of Illinois Series, No. 9. Springfield: Illinois State Museum, 1968.

Temple, Wayne C. *Indian Villages of the Illinois Country: Historic Tribes*. Scientific Papers, Vol. II, Part 2. Springfield: Illinois State Museum, 1987.

Kaku, Michio. *Parallel Worlds*. New York: Anchor Books, 2005.

Mazrim, Robert. *The Sangamo Frontier: History and Archaeology in the Shadow of Lincoln*. Chicago: University of Chicago Press, 2007.

Onken, Bobby J. *Legends of Prehistoric Art: Museum Quality Authentic Native American Relics, Volume II*. Richland Center, WI: Hynek Printing, 2001.

1800-1819 References

Blankmeyer, Helen Van Cleave. *The Sangamon Country.* 1935. Preface: George Edward Feldhausen, John R. Chapin. Springfield, IL: Phillips Bros. Inc., Printers and Publishers, 1965.

Bruzan, Ray, and Bruzan, Pam. "Houses Have Roots, Too." *Illinois Times* [Springfield] 2-8 Dec. 1977, 22-23.

History of Sangamon County, Illinois. Chicago: Inter-State Publishing Company, 1881. Evansville: Unigraph, Inc. 1977.

Power, John Carroll. *History of the Early Settlers of Sangamon County: Centennial Record.* Springfield, IL, 1876. 9 Apr. 2015 <http://sangamon.illinoisgenweb.org/1876/mccoy.htm>.

Wood, Thomas J. *Fifty Years on Fork Prairie: The Rochester Community 1819 - 1869.* University of Illinois at Springfield, Feb. 1997.

Klingaman, William K., and Nicholas P Klingaman. *The Year Without Summer: 1816 and the Volcano That Darkened the World and Changed History.* New York: St. Martin's Griffin, 2013.

Ramsey, David. Interview with Ray Bruzan. 26 Aug. 2012.

Kathryn Dinardo. Interview with Ray Bruzan. 24 June 2016.

Jacob Dinardo. Interview with Ray Bruzan.13 Mar. 2016.

1820s References

Church, Robert. "The History of Rochester" Rochester Historical Preservation Society Meeting. Rochester Fire Department, Rochester, IL. Oct. 2000.

History of Sangamon County, Illinois. Chicago: Inter-State Publishing Company, 1881. Evansville: Unigraph, Inc. 1977.

Illinois State Archives. "U.S. General Land Office (Springfield)." Springfield, IL: 2010. <http://archon.ilsos.net/?p=collections/controlcard&id=2110> 25 Oct. 2016.

Leach, Steve. Telephone interviews with Ray Bruzan. n.d. 2015.

Mazrim, Robert F. "Re: Artifacts." E-mail to Raymond Bruzan. 11 May 2015.

Moore, Carl, Jr. Interviews with Ray Bruzan. n.d. 2014-1015.

Power, John Carroll. *History of the Early Settlers of Sangamon County: Centennial Record.* [Springfield, IL], 1876. 9 June 2011 <http://sangamon.illinoisgenweb.org/1876/mccoy.htm>.

Taft, Justin Jr. *The Tafts of Rochester, Illinois.* Bloomington, IN: AuthorHouse 2007

Wiant, Michael D. "Re: Artifacts." E-mail to Raymond Bruzan. 25 May 2015.

Wood, Thomas J. *Fifty Years on Fork Prairie: The Rochester Community 1819 - 1869.* University of Illinois at Springfield, Feb. 1997.

1830s References

History of Sangamon County, Illinois. 1881. Chicago: Inter-State Publishing Company. Evansville, IN: Unigraphic, Inc., 1977.

"The History of Rochester." Rochester High School Second Year English Class. 1936.

"U.S. Appointments of U.S. Postmaster, 1832-1971." Volume: 12B; Volume Year Range: 1832-1844. 14 Nov. 2016. <http://interactive.ancestry.com/1932/30439_065416-00031>

New Wool Carding Establishment. Advertisement. *Sangamo Journal* [Springfield, IL] 28 June 1832: 4. Published by GenealogyBank.com, a division of NewsBank.

Wool Carding. Advertisement. *Sangamo Journal* [Springfield, IL] 16 Aug. 1834: 1. Published by GenealogyBank.com, a division of NewsBank.

Sale of Real Estate. Advertisement. *Illinois Weekly State Journal* [Springfield] 25 July 1835: 3. Published by GenealogyBank.com, a division of NewsBank.

"Naming of Places." *Daily Illinois State Journal* [Springfield] 12 April 1896: 6. Published by GenealogyBank.com, a division of NewsBank.

"Veteran Jewels." *Illinois State Register* [Springfield] 28 Jan.1894: 5. Published by GenealogyBank.com, a division of NewsBank.

Reep, Thomas P. *Lincoln at New Salem*. Petersburg, IL: The Old Salem Lincoln League, 1927.

Wood, Thomas J. *Fifty Years on Fork Prairie: The Rochester Community 1819-1869*. University of Illinois at Springfield, Feb. 1997.

Blankmeyer, Helen Van Cleave. *The Sangamon Country*. 1935. Preface: George Edward Feldhausen, John R. Chapin. Springfield, IL: Phillips Bros. Inc., Printers and Publishers, 1965.

"The Election." *Illinois Weekly State Journal* [Springfield] 11 Aug. 1832: 3. Published by GenealogyBank.com, a division of NewsBank.

Beck, Wayne. Personal interview. 2 Jan. 2015.

Moore, Jerry. Personal interview. 19 Dec. 2014.

Campbell, Terry. Personal interview. 10 Apr. 2015.

"Abe Lincoln's First Speech." *Rockford-Daily Register Gazette*, 27 Dec. 1907: 9. Published by GenealogyBank.com, a division of NewsBank.

Historical Encyclopedia of Illinois and History of Sangamon County, Ed. Newton Bateman, LL. D. and Paul Selby A.M., Vol. 2. Chicago: Munsell Publishing Company, 1912.

Vaughn, John E. "A Handful O' Sorts." *Illinois State Journal* [Springfield] 12 Jan. 1926: 6. Published by GenealogyBank.com, a division of NewsBank.

"Relics of Lincoln." *Illinois State Journal* [Springfield] 16 Nov. 1896: 6. Published by GenealogyBank.com, a division of NewsBank.

McCullough, David. *Mornings on Horseback*. New York: Simon & Schuster, Inc., 1981.

"The Epworth League." *Illinois State Register* [Springfield] 13 July 1897: 6. Published by GenealogyBank.com, a division of NewsBank.

"Mollie C. Wolford Dies at Rochester." *Illinois State Journal* [Springfield] 11 Jan. 1941: 2. Published by GenealogyBank.com, a division of NewsBank.

"Making Ready for the Crowd." *Springfield Sunday Journal* 7 Oct. 1900: 1. Published by GenealogyBank.com, a division of NewsBank.

Power, John Carroll. *History of the Early Settlers of Sangamon County: Centennial Record*. Springfield, IL, 1876. 9 Apr. 2015 <http://sangamon.illinoisgenweb.org/1876/mccoy.htm>.

Dept. of State. *Enumeration of the Inhabitants and Statistics of the United States: Sangamon County*, Washington: Thomas Allen, 1841.

Benjamin West: Attorney & Counsellor at Law. Advertisement. *Sangamo Journal* [Springfield, IL] 18 Mar. 1842: 1. Published by GenealogyBank.com, a division of NewsBank.

"Candidates for Nomination." *Sangamo Journal* [Springfield, IL] 7 Mar. 1844: 4. Published by GenealogyBank.com, a division of NewsBank.

Rice, Nathan. Letter to Harold G. Roy. 26 Mar. 1953. Baker Memorial Library, Dartmouth College, Hanover, N.H.

"Deaths." *Boston Daily Atlas* 26 July 1847: 2. Published by GenealogyBank.com, a division of NewsBank.

Steam Mills and Distillery for Sale. Advertisement. *Sangamo Journal*, [Springfield, IL] 1 June 1843: 3. Published by GenealogyBank.com, a division of NewsBank.

For Sale or Rent. Advertisement. *Illinois Journal* [Springfield] 30 Dec. 1847: 4. Published by GenealogyBank.com, a division of NewsBank.

Jenkins, Carol S. " Report to the Rochester Historical Preservation Society" ms. 13 Apr. 1990. Rochester Public Library: 27-34.

Wood, Thomas J. *Fifty Years on Fork Prairie: The Rochester Community 1819 - 1869*. University of Illinois at Springfield, Feb. 1997.

Munks, Jamie. "Building Hunter Lake Would Affect Houses, Businesses, Cemeteries." *State Journal-Register* [Springfield, IL] 23 Aug. 2015: 5.

McCafferty, Orville "Bud. "*History of the Rochester United Methodist Church*," Rochester, IL, 2014.

Rochester Methodist Church. *Register of Baptism* and *Proceedings: Quarterly Conferences in the Rochester Circuit Springfield District*. [Rochester, IL] n.p., [c 1839 - 1876].

Elder Christopher B. "Kit" Stafford. Find A Grave Memorial #39041850. Added 3 July 2009. 4 Nov. 2016.

"U.S. Appointments of U.S. Postmasters, 1832-1971." Vol. 12B 1832-1844. ancestry.com, 2010. 3 Nov. 2016.

"The History of Rochester." *Rochester Herald* [Rochester, IL] nd 1969: np.

Notice—I shall apply . . . Advertisement. *Sangamo Journal* [Springfield, IL] 1 Mar. 1834: 1. Published by GenealogyBank.com, a division of NewsBank.

Paull, Bonnie E. and Richard E. Hart. *Lincoln's Springfield Neighborhood*. Charleston, SC: The History Press, 2015.

Farm For Sale. Advertisement. *Sangamo Journal* [Springfield, IL] 18 Oct. 1834: 4. Published by GenealogyBank.com, a division of NewsBank.

"Drowned." *Sangamo Journal* [Springfield, IL] 4 July 1844: 2. Published by GenealogyBank.com, a division of NewsBank.

Dr. C. F. Hughes. Advertisement. *Sangamo Journal* [Springfield, IL] 19 Jan. 1839: 1. Published by GenealogyBank.com, a division of NewsBank.

"Estate of Charles F. Hughes." *Illinois Daily Journal* [Springfield] 23 Sep. 1850: 3. Published by GenealogyBank.com, a division of NewsBank.

Vaughn, John E. "A Handful O' Sorts." *Springfield Sunday Journal* [Springfield, IL] 4 Dec. 1921: 22. Published by GenealogyBank.com, a division of NewsBank.

Sarah J. Sattley. Find A Grave Memorial #53228156; Added 04 June 2010. 3 Nov. 16.

Martha (Jessup) Clark. Find A Grave Memorial # 50363201; Added 28 Mar. 2010. 3 Nov. 16.

1840s References

United States Census. *The Seventh Census of the United States: 1850*. Sangamon, IL.

"Van Buren Was Guest in City 3 Days During 1842." *Illinois State Journal* [Springfield] 8 Nov. 1931: 117. Published by GenealogyBank.com, a division of NewsBank.

"Six Fateful Groups." *Daily Register Gazette* [Rockford, IL] 11 Nov. 1891: 3. Published by GenealogyBank.com, a division of NewsBank.

"Richard H. Coe, Rochester, Who Knew Lincoln, Is Dead." *Illinois State Journal* [Springfield] 13 Dec. 1940: 6. Published by GenealogyBank.com, a division of NewsBank.

"Recalls Stories of Abe Lincoln." *Illinois State Journal* [Springfield] 19 Feb. 1912: 2. Published by GenealogyBank.com, a division of NewsBank.

Russell, H.H. "At the South Fork Log School House. . ." Plaque: South Fork Church [Sangamon County, IL] 29 May 1927.

White, Charles T. *Lincoln and Prohibition*. New York: The Abingdon Press, 1921.

"Whig Meetings." *Sangamo Journal* [Springfield, IL] 7 Mar. 1844: 3. Published by GenealogyBank.com, a division of NewsBank.

Isaac Baker. Find A Grave Memorial #9421491; Added 04 Sep. 2004. 20 Feb. 2014.

"The Mortuary Record: Robert H. Sattley." *Illinois State Journal* [Springfield] 20 Nov. 1891: 5. Published by GenealogyBank.com, a division of NewsBank.

"Rochester." *Illinois State Journal* [Springfield] 4 Oct. 1923: 12. Published by GenealogyBank.com, a division of NewsBank.

Rochester Coffee House. Advertisement. *Sangamo Journal* [Springfield, IL] 20 May 1840: 3. Published by GenealogyBank.com, a division of NewsBank.

Steam Carding and Cloth Dressing Works. Advertisement. *Sangamo Journal* [Springfield, IL] 4 Sep. 1845: 2. Published by GenealogyBank.com, a division of NewsBank.

Steam Engine and Carding Machine. Advertisement. *Illinois Journal* [Springfield] 5 Sep. 1849: 2. Published by GenealogyBank.com, a division of NewsBank.

Sale of Real Estate: Abner Tracy. Advertisement. *Sangamo Journal* [Springfield, IL] 2 Jan. 1845: 3. Published by GenealogyBank.com, a division of NewsBank.

Notice: Estate of Robert Sattley. Advertisement. *Sangamo Journal* [Springfield, IL] 13 May 1842: 1. Published by GenealogyBank.com, a division of NewsBank.

A Great Bargain. Farm and Mill Property for Sale. Advertisement. *Illinois Journal* [Springfield] 6 July 1848: 1. Published by GenealogyBank.com, a division of NewsBank.

"Church and Family History Research Assistance for Primitive Baptist Churches in Sangamon County, Illinois." Primitive Baptist Library of Carthage, Illinois. 4 Nov. 2016 <http://pblib.org/FamHist-Sang.html>.

Power, John Carroll. *History of the Early Settlers of Sangamon County: Centennial Record*. Springfield, IL, 1876. 28 June 2015 <http://sangamon.illinoisgenweb.org/1876/stafford.htm>.

Bridge to Let. Advertisement. *Illinois Journal* [Springfield] 27 Sep. 1848: 2. Published by GenealogyBank.com, a division of NewsBank.

"Rail Road Meeting." *Sangamo Journal* [Springfield, IL] 27 May 1847: 2. Published by GenealogyBank.com, a division of NewsBank.

Justice. "To the Editor of the Journal." *Sangamo Journal* [Springfield, IL] 12 Nov.1841: 2. Published by GenealogyBank.com, a division of NewsBank.

Sangamon Democratic Ticket. Advertisement. *Illinois State Register* [Springfield] 19 Apr. 1844: 3. Published by GenealogyBank.com, a division of NewsBank.

N.P. West, Esq. Advertisement. *Sangamo Journal* [Springfield, IL] 20 May 1842: 2. Published by GenealogyBank.com, a division of NewsBank.

"Whig Meeting." *Sangamo Journal* [Springfield, IL] 25 Mar. 1842: 2. Published by GenealogyBank.com, a division of NewsBank.

"The Barbecue." *Sangamo Journal* [Springfield, IL] 7 Sep. 1843: 2. Published by GenealogyBank.com, a division of NewsBank

"No License in Rochester." *Daily Register* [Springfield, IL] 19 May 1849: 2. Published by GenealogyBank.com, a division of NewsBank.

"Thousands Present at Old Settlers' Reunion despite the Weather." *Illinois State Register* [Springfield] 26 Aug. 1910: 9. Published by GenealogyBank.com, a division of NewsBank.

Rochester Christian Church. *A Brief History of Rochester Christian Church*. Rochester, IL. 18 June 1955.

Mazrim, Robert. *More from the Illinois Frontier: Archaeological Studies of Nine Early-Nineteenth-Century Sites in Rural Illinois*. Illinois Transportation Archaeological Research Program / Transportation Archaeological Bulletin No. 2, 2008.

1850s References

Taft, Justin, Jr. *The Tafts of Rochester, Illinois*. Bloomington, IN: AuthorHouse, 20 June 2007.

"Sangamon Democratic Ticket." *Illinois State Register* [Springfield] 15 Oct. 1852: 2. Published by GenealogyBank.com, a division of NewsBank.

Recorder's Office, Sangamon County, IL. "Property Abstract of Rochester Universalist Church." Lot 19 on Main St., Transfer No. 24, Vol 61, page 54. 3 May 1852.

"Sunday Services (Universalist Church)." *Illinois State Journal* [Springfield] 25 Apr. 1885. Published by GenealogyBank.com, a division of NewsBank.

Universalist Church Register and Almanac, Containing the Statistics of the Denomination for 1871. Boston: Universalist Publishing House, 1871, pp. 26-27.

"Rochester and Springfield." *The Universalist* [Boston] 6 June 1885: np. Published by GenealogyBank.com, a division of NewsBank.

The Rochester Circuit. "Record of Proceedings of Rochester Quarterly Conference." 20 Nov. 1858 - 3 June 1876.

"U.S. Appointments of U.S. Postmaster, 1832-1971." Volume: 18; Volume Year Range: 1845-1855. 14 Nov. 2016. <http://interactive.ancestry.com/1932/30439_065416-00034>.

"U.S. Appointments of U.S. Postmaster, 1832-1971." Volume: 32; Volume Year Range: 1865-1878. 14 Nov. 2016. <http://interactive.ancestry.com/1932/30439_065416-00039>.

Taft, Justin Jr. *The Tafts of Rochester, Illinois*. Bloomington, IN: AuthorHouse 2007

Kidd, T.W.S. "An Old Time Dance And Meeting." *Illinois State Register* [Springfield] 28 Dec. 1903: 8. Published by GenealogyBank.com, a division of NewsBank.

"The Balloon Ascension." *Daily Illinois State Journal* [Springfield] 20 Aug. 1855: 3. Published by GenealogyBank.com, a division of NewsBank.

Grand Balloon Ascension. Advertisement. *Illinois State Register* [Springfield] 17 Aug. 1855: 3. Published by GenealogyBank.com, a division of NewsBank.

"Plank Road Company." *Illinois Daily Journal* [Springfield] 14 Mar. 1853: 3. Published by GenealogyBank.com, a division of NewsBank.

To Bridge Builders. Advertisement. *Daily Illinois State Journal* [Springfield] 26 Jan. 1856: 3. Published by GenealogyBank.com, a division of NewsBank.

Horses Cured of Every Disease. Advertisement. *Illinois Daily Journal* [Springfield] 22 July 1850: 3. Published by GenealogyBank.com, a division of NewsBank.

Strayed. Advertisement. *Illinois Daily Journal* [Springfield] 11 June1853: 3. Published by GenealogyBank.com, a division of NewsBank.

Copartnership Notice. Advertisement. *Daily Illinois State Journal* [Springfield] 30 July1858: 1. Published by GenealogyBank.com, a division of NewsBank.

"New Mail Routes." *Daily Illinois State Register* [Springfield] 14 Oct. 1856: 2. Published by GenealogyBank.com, a division of NewsBank.

"Burglary at Rochester." *Daily Illinois State Register* [Springfield] 12 Jul 1859: 3. Published by GenealogyBank.com, a division of NewsBank.

" Married: St. Clair." *Illinois Daily Journal* [Springfield] 11 Feb. 1853: 3. Published by GenealogyBank.com, a division of NewsBank.

"Died: Oscar St. Clair." *Illinois Daily Journal* [Springfield] 19 Oct. 1853: 3. Published by GenealogyBank.com, a division of NewsBank.

"Democratic County Ticket." *Daily Illinois State Register* [Springfield] 28 Oct. 1857: 3. Published by GenealogyBank. com, a division of NewsBank.

"Sangamon County Election." *Daily Illinois State Journal* [Springfield] 6 Nov. 1857: 3. Published by GenealogyBank.com, a division of NewsBank.

"Pioneer Plow Maker Dead." *Illinois State Register* [Springfield] 2 Jan. 1907: 2. Published by GenealogyBank.com, a division of NewsBank.

"One of Springfield's Greatest Industrial Expansion Periods Came in the Years following the Civil War." *Illinois State Journal / Illinois State Register* [Springfield] 7 Oct. 1956: 17. Published by GenealogyBank.com, a division of NewsBank.

Sattley Makes the Best since 1851. Advertisement. *Illinois State Journal* [Springfield] Mar. 27 1926: 10. Published by GenealogyBank.com, a division of NewsBank.

Odd Fellows Lodge Rochester Lodge 268, Meeting Minutes 24 Jan. 1859 - 21 Feb. 1863.

Odd Fellows Lodge Rochester Lodge 268, "Register of Members." Beginning 1859.

1860s References

Wallace, Joseph, M.A. *Past and Present of the City of Springfield and Sangamon County Illinois*. Chicago: The S. J. Clarke Publishing Co.: 1904.

History of Sangamon County, Illinois. Chicago: Inter-State Publishing Company, 1881. Evansville: Unigraph, Inc. 1977.

Leach, Steve. Service Members Buried in Rochester Township Cemetery. Received by Ray Bruzan 4 Nov. 2015.

"U.S., Civil War Soldier Records and Profiles, 1861-1865." ancestry.com. 16 Nov. 2016.

Cantrell, Carmi G. *The Cantrell Family: A Biographical Album and History . . .* Springfield: Illinois State Register Printing House, 1898. 16 Nov. 2016 <https://archive.org/stream/cantrellfamilybi00byucant/cantrellfamilybi00byucant_djvu.txt>.

Allen, L. P. *The Genealogy and History of the Shreve Family From 1641*. Greenfield, IL, 1901. 16 Nov. 2016 <https://archive.org/stream/genealogyhistory00alle/genealogyhistory00alle_djvu.txt>.

Libby Prison War Museum Association. "Catalogue And Program – Chicago's Tribute: Libby Prison War Museum." Chicago. 1889. 16 Nov. 2016 <http://msa.maryland.gov/megafile/msa/speccol/sc5400/sc5458/000051/001000/001473/restricted/msa_sc_5458_51_1473-4.pdf>.

"Uriah King." *Past and Present of the City of Springfield and Sangamon County Illinois*. Joseph Wallace, M.A. 1904. The S.J. Clarke Publishing Co. Chicago: 1904 16 Nov. 2016. <http://sangamon.illinoisgenweb.org/1904/kingu.htm>.

Recollections of No Man's Land from the Memoirs of Fred Carter Tracy. Ed.V. Pauline Hodges, Ph.D. Goodwell, OK: No Man's Land Historical Society, 1998.

Combined Atlases of Sangamon County, Illinois: 1874, 1894, 1914. Evansville, IN: Whipporwill Publications, nd. Rpt. of *Illustrated Atlas Map of Sangamon County, ILL*. Brink, McCormick and Co. of Illinois, 1874.

"Veteran Dies At Rochester." *Illinois State Journal* [Springfield] 30 May 1919: 11. Published by GenealogyBank.com, a division of NewsBank.

"The City: Rochester Township." *Illinois Journal* [Springfield] 5 Apr. 1861: 3. Published by GenealogyBank.com, a division of NewsBank.

"Rochester Township." *Illinois Journal* [Springfield] 8 Apr. 1864: 2. Published by GenealogyBank.com, a division of NewsBank.

"The City: Funeral Procession Stopped." *Illinois Journal* [Springfield] 15 Feb. 1860: 3. Published by GenealogyBank.com, a division of NewsBank.

"The City: Constable Crouch's Statement." *Illinois Journal* [Springfield] 16 Feb. 1860: 3. Published by GenealogyBank.com, a division of NewsBank.

"A Political Earthquake! The Prairies on Fire for Lincoln." *Illinois Journal* [Springfield] 9 Aug. 1860: 2. Published by GenealogyBank.com, a division of NewsBank.

"The City: Dead." *Illinois Journal* [Springfield] 12 Aug. 1864: 3. Published by GenealogyBank.com, a division of NewsBank.

"The City: Serious Accident." *Illinois Journal* [Springfield] 10 Oct. 1863: 3. Published by GenealogyBank.com, a division of NewsBank.

"Defense of Dr. Price." *Illinois Journal* [Springfield] 18 Nov. 1863: 3. Published by GenealogyBank.com, a division of NewsBank.

Texas Department of State Health Services: 1903-1982. "Texas, Death Certificates, 1903-1982 for Phillip Austin Richards." 19 Nov. 2016. <http://interactive.ancestry.com/2272/33154_B061795-01702/40085337?backurl=&ssrc=&backlabel=Return>.

"The City: Fatal Accident." *Illinois Journal* [Springfield] 2 Nov. 1866: 4. Published by GenealogyBank.com, a division of NewsBank.

"The City: Drowned." Illinois *Journal* [Springfield] 19 Aug. 1863: 3. Published by GenealogyBank.com, a division of NewsBank.

Mann, Curtis, Melinda Garvert, and Ed Russo. "Springfield Community Service: A Pictorial History." St. Louis: G. Bradley Publishing, 1999.

"The Pana, Springfield and Northwestern Railroad." *Illinois Journa*l [Springfield] 5 June 1865: 2. Published by GenealogyBank.com, a division of NewsBank.

"Springfield and Pana Railroad - Engineer's Estimates." *Illinois Journal* [Springfield] 4 July1865: 2. Published by GenealogyBank.com, a division of NewsBank.

"The City: Railroad Meeting." *Illinois Journal* [Springfield] 8 July 1865: 3. Published by GenealogyBank.com, a division of NewsBank.

"Railroad Strike." *Illinois Journal* [Springfield] 8 May 1866: 4. Published by GenealogyBank.com, a division of NewsBank.

"The Railroad Strike." *Illinois Journal* [Springfield] 9 May 1866: 4. Published by GenealogyBank.com, a division of NewsBank.

"The City: Work Resumed." *Illinois Journal* [Springfield] 17 May 1866: 4. Published by GenealogyBank.com, a division of NewsBank.

"The City: Board of Supervisors." *Daily Illinois State Register* [Springfield] 25 June 1868: 4. Published by GenealogyBank.com, a division of NewsBank.

"The City: Mysterious Disappearance, Rumors, &c." *Daily Illinois Journal* [Springfield] 21 July 1864: 3. Published by GenealogyBank.com, a division of NewsBank.

"The City: Mysterious Affair—Probable Murder." *Daily Illinois Journal* [Springfield] 27 Aug. 1864: 3. Published by GenealogyBank.com, a division of NewsBank.

"The City: Not Identified." *Daily Illinois Journal* [Springfield] 29 Aug. 1864: 3. Published by GenealogyBank.com, a division of NewsBank.

"Larceny." *Daily Illinois State Register* [Springfield] 1 Aug. 1863: 3. Published by GenealogyBank.com, a division of NewsBank.

"The City: Police Court." *Illinois Journal* [Springfield] 4 Aug. 1863: 3. Published by GenealogyBank.com, a division of NewsBank.

For Rent. Advertisement. *Daily Illinois State Register* [Springfield] 9 Feb. 1870: 4. Published by GenealogyBank.com, a division of NewsBank.

"The City: Robbery." *Illinois Journal* [Springfield] 11 May 1863: 3. Published by GenealogyBank.com, a division of NewsBank.

"The City: Sangamon Circuit Court." *Illinois Journal* [Springfield] 5 Nov. 1863: 3. Published by GenealogyBank.com, a division of NewsBank.

"Taken to Joliet." *Daily Illinois State Journal* [Springfield] 18 Nov. 1863: 3. Published by GenealogyBank.com, a division of NewsBank.

"Horse Thieves." *Daily Illinois State Register* [Springfield] 30 Oct. 1867: 4. Published by GenealogyBank.com, a division of NewsBank.

"Horse Stealing." *Daily Illinois State Register* [Springfield] 23 Apr. 1864: 3. Published by GenealogyBank.com, a division of NewsBank.

Stolen. Advertisement. *Daily Illinois State Register* [Springfield] 26 Apr. 1864: 2. Published by GenealogyBank.com, a division of NewsBank.

"A Den of Thieves." *Daily Illinois State Register* [Springfield] 26 Apr. 1864: 3. Published by GenealogyBank.com, a division of NewsBank.

"A Heartless Wretch." *Illinois Journal* [Springfield] 27 Oct. 1860: 3. Published by GenealogyBank.com, a division of NewsBank.

S.H. Clark and C. Tracy. "Ordinances of the Village of Rochester, Illinois." [Springfield] Daily State Register Steam Print. 1874.

1870s References

Viator. Letter. "A Trip to Rochester." *Daily Illinois State Journal* [Springfield] 18 July 1873: 1. Published by GenealogyBank.com, a division of NewsBank.

Nostaw. "From Rochester." *Illinois State Journal* [Springfield] 21 Oct. 1870: 4. Published by GenealogyBank.com, a division of NewsBank.

Benjamin. Letter. *Illinois State Journal* [Springfield] 10 June 1871: 4. Published by GenealogyBank.com, a division of NewsBank.

"From Rochester." *Daily Illinois State Journal* [Springfield] 24 Feb. 1876: 4. Published by GenealogyBank.com, a division of NewsBank.

"Special Train." *Daily Illinois State Journal* [Springfield] 15 Sep. 1877: 4. Published by GenealogyBank.com, a division of NewsBank.

"Church Dedication." *Illinois State Register* [Springfield] 8 Aug. 1876: 4. Published by GenealogyBank.com, a division of NewsBank.

"From Rochester." *Illinois State Journal* [Springfield] 14 Sep. 1876: 1. Published by GenealogyBank.com, a division of NewsBank.

Combined Atlases Of Sangamon County, Illinois: 1874, 1894, 1914. Evansville, IN: Whipporwill Publications, nd. Rpt. of *Illustrated Atlas Map of Sangamon County, ILL.* Brink, McCormick and Co. of Illinois, 1874.

"Poland China: Breed of Pig." *Encyclopedia Brittanica*. 2017. 10 Jan. 2017 <https://www.britannica.com/animal/Poland-China>.

Scrip. I. Letter. "Republican Meeting at Rochester." *Daily Illinois State Journal* [Springfield] 21 Oct. 1872: 4. Published by GenealogyBank.com, a division of NewsBank.

"The Teachers in Council: Sayings and Doings at Rochester, at the Teachers' Institute." *Illinois Journal* [Springfield] 3 Mar. 1874: 4. Published by GenealogyBank.com, a division of NewsBank.

"The Grange Pic-nic." (sic) *Daily Illinois State Register* [Springfield] 9 Sep. 1875: 4. Published by GenealogyBank.com, a division of NewsBank.

"Visit of Delegation of Odd Fellows to Rochester." *Daily Illinois State Journal* [Springfield] 19 May 1873: 4. Published by GenealogyBank.com, a division of NewsBank.

"Auld Lang Syne: Annual Reunion of the Old Settlers' Society." *Daily Illinois State Journal* [Springfield] 21 Aug. 1879: 4. Published by GenealogyBank.com, a division of NewsBank.

"Rochester Items: Charivari and Shooting." *Daily Illinois State Register* [Springfield] 11 Oct. 1877: 4. Published by GenealogyBank.com, a division of NewsBank.

"The Court Record: Sangamon Circuit Court." *Daily Illinois State Journal* [Springfield] 18 Mar. 1879: 4. Published by GenealogyBank.com, a division of NewsBank.

"Circuit Court." *Daily Illinois State Register* [Springfield] 20 Mar. 1879: 4. Published by GenealogyBank.com, a division of NewsBank.

"Arrested for Stealing Cattle." *Daily Illinois State Journal* [Springfield] 9 Mar. 1870: 3. Published by GenealogyBank.com, a division of NewsBank.

Americas. "Correspondence: From Rochester." *Daily Illinois State Journal* [Springfield] 8 Oct. 1875: 4. Published by GenealogyBank.com, a division of NewsBank.

"Burglary, Etc." *Daily Illinois State Journal* [Springfield] 19 July 1876: 4. Published by GenealogyBank.com, a division of NewsBank.

"Stores Robbed." *Daily Illinois State Journal* [Springfield] 19 Feb. 1870: 3. Published by GenealogyBank.com, a division of NewsBank.

"Horse Thief Arrested." *Daily Illinois State Register* [Springfield] 22 May 1871: 4. Published by GenealogyBank.com, a division of NewsBank.

"Shot a Wolf." *Daily Illinois State Journal* [Springfield] 22 May 1875: 4. Published by GenealogyBank.com, a division of NewsBank.

"Accident at Rochester." *Daily Illinois State Journal* [Springfield] 28 Mar. 1873: 4. Published by GenealogyBank.com, a division of NewsBank.

"A Broken Leg." *Daily Illinois State Register* [Springfield] 1 May 1876: 4. Published by GenealogyBank.com, a division of NewsBank.

"Citizen of Rochester, Ill., Thrown from a Wagon and Killed." *Daily Illinois State Journal* [Springfield] 22 Sep. 1875: 1. Published by GenealogyBank.com, a division of NewsBank.

"County Items—Fire—Fatal Accident, Etc." *Daily Illinois State Journal* [Springfield] 17 Oct. 1873: 4. Published by GenealogyBank.com, a division of NewsBank.

"Lamp Accident." *Daily Illinois State Register* [Springfield] 28 Jan. 1876: 4. Published by GenealogyBank.com, a division of NewsBank.

"Another Kerosene Horror." *Illinois State Journal* [Springfield] 19 Jan. 1876: 4. Published by GenealogyBank.com, a division of NewsBank.

"Police Matters—Cutting With a Knife." *Daily Illinois State Journal* [Springfield] 23 Aug. 1875: 4. Published by GenealogyBank.com, a division of NewsBank.

"The Liquor Law." *Illinois State Journal* [Springfield] 25 Nov. 1875: 4. Published by GenealogyBank.com, a division of NewsBank.

"Brutal Murder." *Daily Illinois State Journal* [Springfield] 8 Sep. 1873: 4. Published by GenealogyBank.com, a division of NewsBank.

"Riot at Rochester—Fatal Shooting Affray." *Illinois State Journal* [Springfield] 17 July 1872: 4. Published by GenealogyBank.com, a division of NewsBank.

"A Dead Head." *Daily Illinois State Register* [Springfield] 1 Dec. 1870: 4. Published by GenealogyBank.com, a division of NewsBank.

"Death of the Venerable Edward Clark." *Daily Illinois State Journal* [Springfield] 12 Jan. 1875: 4. Published by GenealogyBank.com, a division of NewsBank.

"Dead: Munson Carter." *Daily Illinois State Journal* [Springfield] 2 Jan. 1877: 4. Published by GenealogyBank.com, a division of NewsBank.

"New Wheat." *Daily Illinois State Register* [Springfield] 3 July 1879: 4. Published by GenealogyBank.com, a division of NewsBank.

"Crops." *Daily Illinois State Journal* [Springfield] 14 July 1873: 4. Published by GenealogyBank.com, a division of NewsBank.

"Returned." *Daily Illinois State Register* [Springfield] 3 Mar. 1874: 4. Published by GenealogyBank.com, a division of NewsBank.

"Hog Shipment." *Daily Illinois State Journal* [Springfield] 5 Nov. 1873: 4. Published by GenealogyBank.com, a division of NewsBank.

"From Rochester: Good Prospects Ahead—Improvements of that Place—Shipments of Grain and Stock—Public Sale, Etc." *Daily Illinois State Journal* [Springfield] 17 Oct. 1876: 1. Published by GenealogyBank.com, a division of NewsBank.

"Is It Dry Murrain?" *Daily Illinois State Journal* [Springfield] 26 Aug. 1873: 4. Published by GenealogyBank.com, a division of NewsBank.

Haygood, Tamara Miner. "Texas Fever." *Handbook of Texas Online*. 2010. 14 Jan. 2017 < http://www.tshaonline.org/handbook/online/articles/awt01>.

Vaughn, John E. "Recalled to Life." *Illinois State Journal* [Springfield] 21 Oct. 1937: 6. Published by GenealogyBank.com, a division of NewsBank.

"Married: Tracy—Jaquayese." *Daily Illinois State Journal* [Springfield] 23 June 1857: 2. Published by GenealogyBank.com, a division of NewsBank.

"New Business Block." *Daily Illinois State Register* [Springfield] 11 Aug. 1877: 4. Published by GenealogyBank.com, a division of NewsBank.

The City in Brief: Carter Tracy." *Illinois State Journal* [Springfield] 23 Nov. 1878: 4. Published by GenealogyBank.com, a division of NewsBank.

Announcements - For the Legislature: Carter Tracy. Advertisement. *Daily Illinois State Register* [Springfield] 23 July 1878: 1. Published by GenealogyBank.com, a division of NewsBank.

"Love among the Roses." *Illinois State Journal* [Springfield] 27 Jan. 1879: 4. Published by GenealogyBank.com, a division of NewsBank.

"Carter and Bertha." *Illinois State Journal* [Springfield] 28 Mar. 1879: 4. Published by GenealogyBank.com, a division of NewsBank.

Baker, Michael. Letter: Carter Tracy. *Daily Illinois State Register* [Springfield] 11 Feb. 1879: 4. Published by GenealogyBank.com, a division of NewsBank.

"Carter Tracy's Latest." *Illinois State Journal* [Springfield] 23 Sep. 1879: 4. Published by GenealogyBank.com, a division of NewsBank.

"Rochester Racket: An Abused Wife Attempts to Kill Her Husband—Minor Matters." *Daily Illinois State Register* [Springfield] 23 Sept. 1879: 4. Published by GenealogyBank.com, a division of NewsBank.

"Tracy's Record." *Illinois State Journal* [Springfield] 1 Mar. 1880: 4. Published by GenealogyBank.com, a division of NewsBank.

"Mortuary: Tracy." *Illinois State Register* [Springfield] 27 Apr. 1905: 9. Published by GenealogyBank.com, a division of NewsBank.

"Personal - And Other Reflections of the Monitor Man: Henry Johnson." *Sangamo Daily Monitor* [Springfield] 22 Aug. 1879: 4.

"The Mortuary Record: Johnson." *Illinois State Journal* [Springfield] 5 Aug. 1889: 5. Published by GenealogyBank.com, a division of NewsBank.

Power, John Carroll. *History of the Early Settlers of Sangamon County: Centennial Record*. [Springfield, IL] 1876. 6 Mar 2016 <http://sangamon.illinoisgenweb.org/1876/johnsonlu.htm>.

"The History of Rochester." Rochester High School Second Year English Class. 1936.

1880s References

"Interesting Figures from the Census." *Daily Illinois State Journal* [Springfield] 20 Mar. 1883: 4. Published by GenealogyBank.com, a division of NewsBank.

The Sangamon County Abstract Company. "Abstract of Title for Lot 6 John's Addition to Rochester." Beginning 30 Dec. 1828.

"Local Brevities: Rochester *Item*." *Illinois State Journal* [Springfield] 10 Feb. 1883: 6. Published by GenealogyBank.com, a division of NewsBank.

"Local Notes and Personals: E. Kalb." *Illinois State Journal* [Springfield] 8 Dec. 1882: 6. Published by GenealogyBank.com, a division of NewsBank.

"Old Resident of County Is Dead." *Daily Illinois State Journal* [Springfield] 20 Oct. 1908: 6. Published by GenealogyBank.com, a division of NewsBank.

"Rochester's Record—Farmers Happy—Temperance Men Jubilant—Other Notes." *Illinois State Journal* [Springfield] 26 May 1880: 5. Published by GenealogyBank.com, a division of NewsBank.

"Police Courts: Justice Fosselman's Court —George Everhart." *Illinois State Journal* [Springfield] 6 Apr. 1882: 8. Published by GenealogyBank.com, a division of NewsBank.

"Justice Courts: Rochester Rowdyism." *Daily Illinois State Register* [Springfield] 26 July 1881. Published by GenealogyBank.com, a division of NewsBank.

"The Justices—Before Schroyer: Charles Carter." *Daily Illinois State Register* [Springfield] 16 Dec. 1881: 3. Published by GenealogyBank.com, a division of NewsBank.

"Local Notes and Personals: John Sommers." *Illinois State Journal* [Springfield] 4 Feb. 1882: 6. Published by GenealogyBank.com, a division of NewsBank.

History of Sangamon County, Illinois. Chicago: Inter-State Publishing Company, 1881. Evansville, IN: Unigraphic, Inc., 1977.

Building Notice. Advertisement. *Illinois State Journal* [Springfield] 16 June 1881: 3. Published by GenealogyBank.com, a division of NewsBank.

"May and December." *Daily Illinois State Register* [Springfield] 11 Dec. 1881: 5. Published by GenealogyBank.com, a division of NewsBank.

Power, John Carroll. *History of the Early Settlers of Sangamon County: Centennial Record.* [Springfield, IL] 1876. 27 Jan. 2017 <http://sangamon.illinoisgenweb.org/1876>.

"Local Brevities: Mr. A.M. Dunnavan." *Illinois State Journal* [Springfield] 27 Apr. 1885: 8. Published by GenealogyBank.com, a division of NewsBank.

"General and Personal: Sam Johnson." *Illinois State Journal* [Springfield] 10 Aug. 1889: 5. Published by GenealogyBank.com, a division of NewsBank.

"Masonic: Dedication of a New Hall at Rochester—A Good Time." *Illinois State Journal* [Springfield] 28 May 1880: 4. Published by GenealogyBank.com, a division of NewsBank.

"Jovial Odd-Fellows." *Illinois State Journal* [Springfield] 18 Aug. 1883: 8. Published by GenealogyBank.com, a division of NewsBank.

"Prohibition Picnic." *Daily Illinois State Register* [Springfield] 20 Aug. 1887: 3. Published by GenealogyBank.com, a division of NewsBank.

"Anti-Horse Thief Society." *Illinois State Journal* [Springfield] 16 Aug. 1889: 4. Published by GenealogyBank.com, a division of NewsBank.

"Sangamon Old Folks." *Daily Illinois State Journal* [Springfield] 17 Aug. 1888: 2. Published by GenealogyBank.com, a division of NewsBank.

"To Dispense Justice: Justices' Courts." *Daily Illinois State Register* [Springfield] 6 Oct. 1888: 3. Published by GenealogyBank.com, a division of NewsBank.

"The Law: Justices' Courts." Daily Illinois State Register [Springfield] 6 Feb. 1889: 3. Published by GenealogyBank.com, a division of NewsBank.

"A Just Fine." *Illinois State Journal* [Springfield] 26 June 1885: 8. Published by GenealogyBank.com, a division of NewsBank.

"Rally at Rochester." *Illinois State Journal* [Springfield] 18 Oct. 1884: 5. Published by GenealogyBank.com, a division of NewsBank.

"The Political Pot: Hubbard at Rochester." *Illinois State Journal* [Springfield] 2 Oct. 1884: 7. Published by GenealogyBank.com, a division of NewsBank.

"Local Brevities: Little Barefoot Boy." *Illinois State Journal* [Springfield] 14 May1884: 8. Published by GenealogyBank.com, a division of NewsBank.

"Amusements: The Wild West." *Daily Illinois State Register* [Springfield] 9 May 1884: 3. Published by GenealogyBank.com, a division of NewsBank.

Buffalo Bill's Wild West! Advertisement. *Illinois State Journal* [Springfield] 10 May 1884: 5. Published by GenealogyBank.com, a division of NewsBank.

"Frightful Fall." *Daily Illinois State Register* [Springfield] 16 Aug. 1880: 4. Published by GenealogyBank.com, a division of NewsBank.

"Kirkpatrick's Death." Daily Illinois State Register [Springfield] 28 Aug. 1880:4. Published by GenealogyBank.com, a division of NewsBank.

"Frightful Accident." *Daily Illinois State Register* [Springfield] 18 Sep. 1880: 4. Published by GenealogyBank.com, a division of NewsBank.

"Minor Mention: Measles." *Daily Illinois State Register* [Springfield] 19 Feb. 1881: 5. Published by GenealogyBank.com, a division of NewsBank.

"Deaths: Coe." *Daily Illinois State Register* [Springfield] 3 Nov. 1889: 5. Published by GenealogyBank.com, a division of NewsBank.

"Accident at Rochester." *Daily Illinois State Journal* [Springfield] 5 Dec. 1889: 4. Published by GenealogyBank.com, a division of NewsBank.

"Minor Mention: A Little Child . . ." *Daily Illinois State Register* [Springfield] 6 Dec. 1889: 8. Published by GenealogyBank.com, a division of NewsBank.

"Runaway Accident." *Illinois State Journal* [Springfield] 19 Aug. 1885: 8. Published by GenealogyBank.com, a division of NewsBank.

"Neighborhood News: Rochester." *Daily Illinois State Register* [Springfield] 18 Oct. 1887: 2. Published by GenealogyBank.com, a division of NewsBank.

"Local Brevities: The People of Rochester." *Illinois State Journal* [Springfield] 26 Jan. 1884: 8. Published by GenealogyBank.com, a division of NewsBank.

"Justices' Courts: Fosselman." *Daily Illinois State Register* [Springfield] 2 July 1887: 3. Published by GenealogyBank.com, a division of NewsBank.

"County Fair Notes." *Illinois State Journal* [Springfield] 23 Aug. 1881: 6. Published by GenealogyBank.com, a division of NewsBank.

Squire. "Rochester Notes and News." *Illinois State Journal* [Springfield] 21 Aug. 1882: 8. Published by GenealogyBank.com, a division of NewsBank.

"Minor Mention: United States Circuit Court. . ." *Daily Illinois State Register* [Springfield] 11 Sep. 1881: 3. Published by GenealogyBank.com, a division of NewsBank.

"Hog Cholera Prevalent." *Illinois State Journal* [Springfield] 19 Aug. 1884. Published by GenealogyBank.com, a division of NewsBank.

"Minor Mention: Henry Clark." *Daily Illinois State Register* [Springfield] 30 July 1887: 3. Published by GenealogyBank.com, a division of NewsBank.

Smith, Madeline Babcock. *The Lemon Jelly Cake.* 1952. Introd. Dan Guillory. Urbana, IL: University of Illinois Press. 1998.

"Obituary: Dr. E.R. Babcock." *Illinois State Journal* [Springfield] 19 Feb. 1883: 6. Published by GenealogyBank.com, a division of NewsBank.

"Dr. R.J. McNeil - His Death and Burial - Masonic Funeral." *Daily Illinois State Register* [Springfield] 16 Dec. 1883: 2. Published by GenealogyBank.com, a division of NewsBank.

" Local Notes and Personals: Mr. John Lock." *Illinois State Journal* [Springfield] 10 Jan. 1881: 6. Published by GenealogyBank.com, a division of NewsBank.

Blankmeyer, Helen Van Cleave. *The Sangamon Country.* 1935. Preface: George Edward Feldhausen, John R. Chapin. Springfield, IL: Phillips Bros. Inc., Printers and Publishers, 1965.

"Gold On Exhibition." *Illinois State Register* [Springfield] 21 Apr. 1898. Published by GenealogyBank.com, a division of NewsBank.

" Wedded Fifty Years." *Illinois State Journal* [Springfield] Illinois 30 Mar. 1898: 3. Published by GenealogyBank.com, a division of NewsBank.

"The Matrimonial Record: Kalb-Cockrell." *Illinois State Journal* [Springfield] 15 June 1891: 4. Published by GenealogyBank.com, a division of NewsBank.

"Church Record." *Rochester Christian Church* (Rochester, Illinois, [n.d.]).

"Rochester." *Hendrix & Co.'s Directory and Gazetteer of Sangamon County, Illinois.* Springfield: Illinois State Register Book and Job Print, 1889.

"Remembering Louis Persinger: Born on This Day 129 Years Ago." 2016. *The Violin Channel* 19 Jan. 2017. <https://theviolinchannel.com/remembering-louis-persinger-born-on-this-day/>.

"Purely Personal." *Daily Illinois State Register* [Springfield] 21 Oct. 1890: 6. Published by GenealogyBank.com, a division of NewsBank.

"Village Elections: At Rochester." *Daily Illinois State Register* [Springfield] 18 Apr. 1888: 4. Published by GenealogyBank.com, a division of NewsBank.

"Rochester Matters." *Illinois State Journal* [Springfield] 24 Jan. 1882: 8. Published by GenealogyBank.com, a division of NewsBank.

"Real Estate: Henry Johns." Illinois State Journal [Springfield] 7 Nov. 1883: 7. Published by GenealogyBank.com, a division of NewsBank.

Atwood, Evangeline. *Frontier Politics: Alaska's James Wickersham.* Portland, OR: Binford & Mort Publisher, 1979.

1890s References

"Rochester W.C.T.U. Temple." *Illinois State Register* [Springfield] 29 Nov. 1892: 5. Published by GenealogyBank.com, a division of NewsBank.

"Neighborhood News: Rochester—The Union Bridge . . ." *Daily Illinois State Register* 21 Feb. 1896: 7. Published by GenealogyBank.com, a division of NewsBank.

"Let Us All Give Thanks: The Day at Rochester." *Illinois State Journal* [Springfield] 26 Nov. 1891: 1. Published by GenealogyBank.com, a division of NewsBank.

"Rochester Commencement." *Springfield Sunday Journal* [Springfield] 19 May 1895: 1. Published by GenealogyBank.com, a division of NewsBank.

"Rochester High School." *Illinois State Register* [Springfield] 12 May 1895: 5. Published by GenealogyBank.com, a division of NewsBank.

Official Ballot—Sangamon County, Illinois - Election, Tuesday, November 8, 1898. Advertisement. *Illinois State Register* [Springfield] 5 Nov. 1898: 7. Published by GenealogyBank.com, a division of NewsBank.

"Rochester." *Illinois State Register* [Springfield] 22 May 1895:16. Published by GenealogyBank.com, a division of NewsBank.

Smith, J. Emil "Making Conversation: That reminds me . . . Lala Rook." *Illinois State Journal* [Springfield] 23 June 1936: 6. Published by GenealogyBank.com, a division of NewsBank.

"No Rowdyism Tolerated." *Illinois State Journal* [Springfield] 6 July 1893: 4. Published by GenealogyBank.com, a division of NewsBank.

"In Glenwood Park." *Illinois State Journal* [Springfield] 3 Sep. 1897: 8. Published by GenealogyBank.com, a division of NewsBank.

For Sale—By Melton & Snape: Glenwood Park. Advertisement. *Illinois State Journal* [Springfield] 18 July 1904: 7. Published by GenealogyBank.com, a division of NewsBank.

"The Matrimonial Record: Wright-McCoy." *Illinois State Journal* [Springfield] 9 July 1897: 6. Published by GenealogyBank.com, a division of NewsBank.

"Death of Mrs. Wright." *Illinois State Journal* [Springfield] 22 June 1896: 3. Published by GenealogyBank.com, a division of NewsBank.

Wallace, Joseph. *Past and Present of Springfield and Sangamon County.* Chicago: S. J. Clark Publishing Co.: 1904. Transcriber Mary Ann Kaylor. Sangamon Co. GenWeb, 16 July 2013. <http://sangamon.illinoisgenweb.org/1904kingu.htm>.

"Missionaries Wed: Kingley Pease and Miss Mary Wright Married at Rochester." *Illinois State Register* [Springfield] 28 June 1901: 5. Published by GenealogyBank.com, a division of NewsBank.

"Dies In Far Off Land." *Weekly Illinois State Register* [Springfield] 27 Mar. 1903: 1. Published by GenealogyBank.com, a division of NewsBank.

"Rochester and Vicinity: Rev. T. B. Wright's . . . " *The Rochester Weekly Item"* [Rochester, IL] 25 Aug. 1898: n.p.

Power, John Carroll. *History of the Early Settlers of Sangamon County: Centennial Record.* [Springfield, IL], 1876. 26 July 2015 <http://sangamon.illinoisgenweb.org/1876/twist.htm>.

Power, John Carroll. *History of the Early Settlers of Sangamon County: Centennial Record.* [Springfield, IL], 1876. 27 July 2015 <http://sangamon.illinoisgenweb.org/1876/coe.htm>.

"Ira F. Twist, 80, Native Of County, Dies In Arkansas." *Illinois State Journal* [Springfield] 5 Oct. 1937: 1. Published by GenealogyBank.com, a division of NewsBank.

"Fire at Rochester: Boarding House of Mrs. E.A. Barnwell . . . " *Illinois State Journal* [Springfield] 16 Feb. 1899: 2. Published by GenealogyBank.com, a division of NewsBank.

"Rochester: Burglars attempted . . . " *Illinois State Register* [Springfield] 18 Dec. 1895: 8. Published by GenealogyBank.com, a division of NewsBank.

"Fire at Rochester: The Dwelling of C. E. Miller . . ." *Illinois State Journal* [Springfield] 27 Feb. 1891: 8. Published by GenealogyBank.com, a division of NewsBank.

"A Double Wedding." *Daily Illinois State Register* [Springfield] 4 Oct. 1890: 2. Published by GenealogyBank.com, a division of NewsBank.

"Funerals: Troxell." *Daily Illinois State Register* [Springfield] 21 Feb. 1891: 5. Published by GenealogyBank.com, a division of NewsBank.

"Finally Caught." *Illinois State Register* [Springfield] 14 Oct. 1893: 6. Published by GenealogyBank.com, a division of NewsBank.

"Mortuary: Coe." *Daily Illinois State Register* [Springfield] 14 Oct. 1894: 8. Published by GenealogyBank.com, a division of NewsBank.

"Off With a Widower." *Daily Illinois State Register* [Springfield] 6 Mar. 1890: 1. Published by GenealogyBank.com, a division of NewsBank.

"Love Seeks a Way." *Illinois State Journal* [Springfield] 15 Sep. 1894: 1. Published by GenealogyBank.com, a division of NewsBank.

"Wedded Fifty Years." *Illinois State Journal* [Springfield] 30 Mar. 1898: 3. Published by GenealogyBank.com, a division of NewsBank.

"Gold on Exhibition." *Daily Illinois State Register* [Springfield] 21 Apr. 1898: 6. Published by GenealogyBank.com, a division of NewsBank.

"Sick Country People." *Illinois State Journal.* [Springfield] 16 Mar. 1895: 5. Published by GenealogyBank.com, a division of NewsBank.

Jenkins, Carol S., "History Note of the Barr Family" Report to the Rochester Historical Preservation Society, ms. 13 Apr. 1990.

"Funerals: Barr." *Illinois State Register* [Springfield] 12 Dec. 1894: 4. Published by GenealogyBank.com, a division of NewsBank.

"Mortuary: Barr." *Illinois State Register* [Springfield] 31 May 1895: 6. Published by GenealogyBank.com, a division of NewsBank.

"Mortuary Record: Hollenback." *Illinois State Journal* [Springfield] 21 Feb. 1894: 8. Published by GenealogyBank.com, a division of NewsBank.

"Mortuary Record: Sattley." *Illinois State Journal* [Springfield] 20 Nov. 1891: 5. Published by GenealogyBank.com, a division of NewsBank.

"Mortuary: Herndon." *Daily Illinois State Register* [Springfield] 15 Oct. 1890: 1. Published by GenealogyBank.com, a division of NewsBank.

"Rochester Schools Close." *Illinois State Register* [Springfield] 4 Mar. 1898: 8. Published by GenealogyBank.com, a division of NewsBank.

"Mortuary Record: Miller." *Illinois State Journal* [Springfield] 31 Oct. 1898: 6. Published by GenealogyBank.com, a division of NewsBank.

"The Mortuary Record: Coe." *Illinois State Journal* [Springfield] 1 Aug. 1895: 5. Published by GenealogyBank.com, a division of NewsBank.

"Charged With Forgery: Rochester is a Dry Town . . ." *Illinois State Register* [Springfield] 26 Feb. 1899: 5. Published by GenealogyBank.com, a division of NewsBank.

"Excited the Town." *Illinois State Journal.* [Springfield] 23 July 1896: 3. Published by GenealogyBank.com, a division of NewsBank.

"Rochester's Picnic." *Daily Illinois State Register* [Springfield] 10 Aug. 1890: 1. Published by GenealogyBank.com, a division of NewsBank.

"Fought Chicken Thieves." *Illinois State Register* [Springfield] 22 Jan. 1896: 8. Published by GenealogyBank.com, a division of NewsBank.

"Despoilers of Hen Roosts." *Illinois State Journal* [Springfield] 20 Aug. 1894: 1. Published by GenealogyBank.com, a division of NewsBank.

"Burglary at Rochester." *Springfield Sunday Journal* [Springfield] 6 Nov. 1898: 4. Published by GenealogyBank.com, a division of NewsBank.

"Burglars at Rochester." *Illinois State Journal* [Springfield] 5 Feb. 1894: 3. Published by GenealogyBank.com, a division of NewsBank.

"Evidently Got the Burglars." *Illinois State Register* [Springfield] 30 Dec. 1891: 5. Published by GenealogyBank.com, a division of NewsBank.

"Personal And General: A horse. . ." *Illinois State Journal* [Springfield] 30 Sep. 1893: 5. Published by GenealogyBank.com, a division of NewsBank.

"Personal and General: William Ginther . . ." *Illinois State Journal* [Springfield] 8 Apr. 1893: 5. Published by GenealogyBank.com, a division of NewsBank.

"Pranks of Lightning: The Universalist Church Steeple is Damaged—Horses Killed." *Illinois State Journal*. [Springfield] 15 Aug. 1894: 4. Published by GenealogyBank.com, a division of NewsBank.

"General and Personal: Six horses. . . " *Illinois State Journal* [Springfield] 25 Aug. 1894: 5. Published by GenealogyBank.com, a division of NewsBank.

"The Mortuary Record: Haynes." *Illinois State Journal* [Springfield] 16 Oct. 1897: 6. Published by GenealogyBank.com, a division of NewsBank.

"Was a Fatal Blow." *Daily Illinois State Journal* [Springfield] 15 Oct. 1897: 2. Published by GenealogyBank.com, a division of NewsBank.

"Drowned near Rochester." *Illinois State Journal* [Springfield] 13 June1892. Published by GenealogyBank.com, a division of NewsBank.

"A Quiet Return Day: Charles Greenwood." *Illinois State Journal* [Springfield] 25 Aug. 1894: 4. Published by GenealogyBank.com, a division of NewsBank.

"Minor Mention: Charles Greenwood." *Daily Illinois State Register* [Springfield] 16 Aug 1893: 5. Published by GenealogyBank.com, a division of NewsBank.

"Personal and General: J.C. Dawley." *Illinois State Journal* [Springfield] 9 Dec. 1893: 5. Published by GenealogyBank.com, a division of NewsBank.

"Injured in a Runaway." *Illinois State Register* [Springfield] 25 Feb. 1894: 5. Published by GenealogyBank.com, a division of NewsBank.

"Kicked by a Horse." *Illinois State Journal* [Springfield] 7 Nov. 1891: 4. Published by GenealogyBank.com, a division of NewsBank.

"Personal and General: Rochester is replacing . . ." *Illinois State Journal* [Springfield] 25 Nov. 1893: 5. Published by GenealogyBank.com, a division of NewsBank.

"Neighborhood News: Rochester – Our village dads. . . " *Illinois State* Register [Springfield] 31 Aug. 1897: 7. Published by GenealogyBank.com, a division of NewsBank.

"General and Personal: Rochester wants. . ." *Illinois State Journal*. [Springfield] 30 Mar. 1895: 5. Published by GenealogyBank.com, a division of NewsBank.

"Want a New Road to Rochester." *Illinois State Register* [Springfield] 30 July 1895: 5. Published by GenealogyBank.com, a division of NewsBank.

"Supervisors Meet: Mr. Bell presented . . ." *Illinois State Journal*. [Springfield] 15 Sep. 1897: 8. Published by GenealogyBank.com, a division of NewsBank.

"Neighborhood News: Rochester—The big pile driver. . ." *Illinois State Journal* [Springfield] 11 July 1896: 3. Published by GenealogyBank.com, a division of NewsBank.

"Neighborhood News: From Rochester Item – The new steel bridge. . . " *Illinois State Journal* [Springfield] 25 Feb. 1896: 3. Published by GenealogyBank.com, a division of NewsBank.

"Neighborhood News: Rochester – Twist Brothers." *Illinois State Journal* [Springfield] 18 Jan. 1897: 6. Published by GenealogyBank.com, a division of NewsBank.

" A Creamery at Rochester." *Illinois State Journal* [Springfield] 22 Apr. 1892: 4. Published by GenealogyBank.com, a division of NewsBank.

"A Rochester Lodge." *Illinois State Journal* [Springfield] 23 Feb. 1895: 2. Published by GenealogyBank.com, a division of NewsBank.

"About the Order." *Supreme Lodge Knights of Pythias*. 27 July 2015 <http://pythias.org/index.php?option=com_content&view=section&layout=blog&id=13&Itemid=27>.

"Out of the Ordinary." *Illinois State Journal* [Springfield] 18 Feb. 1895: 3. Published by GenealogyBank.com, a division of NewsBank.

"General and Personal: Rochester Item." *Illinois State Journal* [Springfield] 11 July 1891: 4. Published by GenealogyBank.com, a division of NewsBank.

"Personal and General: Rochester Item." *Illinois State Journal*. [Springfield] 3 Feb. 1894: 5. Published by GenealogyBank.com, a division of NewsBank.

"Protecting the Fish." *Illinois State Journal*. [Springfield] 30 May 1890: 1. Published by GenealogyBank.com, a division of NewsBank.

"Destroyed a Fish Trap." *Daily Illinois State Register* [Springfield] 30 May 1890: 6. Published by GenealogyBank.com, a division of NewsBank.

" A Murderous Assault." *Daily Illinois State Register* [Springfield] 29 Sep. 1891: 6. Published by GenealogyBank.com, a division of NewsBank.

"The Row near Rochester." *Daily Illinois State Register* [Springfield] 30 Sep. 1891: 8. Published by GenealogyBank.com, a division of NewsBank.

"Republicans Fight." *Daily Illinois State Register* [Springfield] 1 Nov. 1896. Published by GenealogyBank.com, a division of NewsBank.

"A Cowardly Performance." *Daily Illinois State Journal* [Springfield] 21 Oct. 1892: 4. Published by GenealogyBank.com, a division of NewsBank.

"Rochester the Winners." *Illinois State Journal* [Springfield] 22 Aug. 1893: 4. Published by GenealogyBank.com, a division of NewsBank.

"General and Personal: Mr. D. A. Ott." *Illinois State Journal.* [Springfield] 3 Nov. 1894: 5. Published by GenealogyBank.com, a division of NewsBank.

History of Sangamon County, Illinois. Chicago: Inter-State Publishing Company, 1881. Evansville, IN: Unigraphic, Inc., 1977.

"Freight Cars Demolished." *Springfield Sunday Journal* [Springfield, IL] 30 Mar. 1890: 5. Published by GenealogyBank.com, a division of NewsBank.

"Personal and General: Rochester Item." *Illinois State Journal.* [Springfield] 20 Jan. 1894: 5. Published by GenealogyBank.com, a division of NewsBank.

"Horses Stampeded." *Springfield Sunday Journal* [Springfield, IL] 12 Jan. 1896: 4. Published by GenealogyBank.com, a division of NewsBank.

"Personal and General: Rochester Item." *Illinois State Journal* [Springfield] 15 Apr. 1893: 5. Published by GenealogyBank.com, a division of NewsBank.

"Schools and Their Teachers." *Illinois State Journal* [Springfield] 30 Aug. 1890: 4. Published by GenealogyBank.com, a division of NewsBank.

1900s References

"Rochester's Bank." *Weekly Illinois State Register* [Springfield] 1 May 1900: 2. Published by GenealogyBank.com, a division of NewsBank.

"Neighborhood News: Rochester—The excavating was begun . . ." *Weekly Illinois State Register* [Springfield] 27 July 1900: 3. Published by GenealogyBank.com, a division of NewsBank.

"Rochester Township: Schwartz." *Illinois State Register* [Springfield] 16 July 1900: 11. Published by GenealogyBank.com, a division of NewsBank.

"Neighborhood News: Rochester—P. P. Breckenridge . . ." *Illinois State Journal* [Springfield] 27 Sep. 1902: 2. Published by GenealogyBank.com, a division of NewsBank.

"Neighborhood News: Rochester—Twist Brothers . . ." *Illinois State Journal* [Springfield] 5 July 1902: 2. Published by GenealogyBank.com, a division of NewsBank.

"Neighborhood News: Rochester—Edmund Miller. . ." *Weekly Illinois State Register* [Springfield] 11 Aug. 1903: 2. Published by GenealogyBank.com, a division of NewsBank.

"Rochester: W. H. Kernall (sic) . . ." *Illinois State Register* [Springfield] 14 Oct. 1903: 5. Published by GenealogyBank.com, a division of NewsBank.

"Neighborhood News: Rochester—Twist Brothers . . ." *Weekly Illinois State Register* [Springfield] 7 Apr. 1903: 4. Published by GenealogyBank.com, a division of NewsBank.

"Neighborhood News: Rochester—New brick walks . . ." *Illinois State Journal* [Springfield] 24 Oct. 1903: 3. Published by GenealogyBank.com, a division of NewsBank.

"Suburban: Rochester—Charles E. Martin . . ." *Weekly Illinois State Register* [Springfield] 8 Nov. 1904: 7. Published by GenealogyBank.com, a division of NewsBank.

"Suburban: Rochester—Charles A. DeLay . . ." *Illinois State Register* [Springfield] 13 Jan. 1905: 10. Published by GenealogyBank.com, a division of NewsBank.

"Suburban: Rochester—C. L. Jones . . ." *Illinois State Register* [Springfield] 21 Apr. 1905: 3. Published by GenealogyBank.com, a division of NewsBank.

"Will Build Fine Residence." *Illinois State Register* [Springfield] 16 June 1905: 10. Published by GenealogyBank.com, a division of NewsBank.

Wickersham, Deborah. Letter to her sister Emily. 8 Aug. 1900. Courtesy of Mary Alice Tuxhorn.

"News of Central Illinois Counties: Rochester—The village board . . ." *Illinois State Journal* [Springfield] 6 June 1907: 3. Published by GenealogyBank.com, a division of NewsBank.

"News of Central Illinois Counties, Sangamon County: Rochester—The village board . . ." Illinois State Journal [Springfield] 22 June 1907: 2. Published by GenealogyBank.com, a division of NewsBank.

"Suburban: Rochester—Mr. and Mrs. Thomas Thornton . . ." *Illinois State Register* [Springfield] 8 Feb. 1907: 3. Published by GenealogyBank.com, a division of NewsBank.

"Neighborhood News: Rochester." *Illinois State Register* [Springfield] 14 Aug. 1900: 4. Published by GenealogyBank.com, a division of NewsBank.

"Neighborhood: Rochester—W. C. Campbell . . ." *Illinois State Journal* [Springfield] 5 June 1901: 2. Published by GenealogyBank.com, a division of NewsBank.

"Neighborhood News: Rochester—William Cantrall . . ." *Illinois State Journal* [Springfield] 28 Mar. 1900: 2. Published by GenealogyBank.com, a division of NewsBank.

"Neighborhood News: Rochester—A. Parker moved. . ." *Illinois State Journal* [Springfield] 1 Sep. 1903: 3. Published by GenealogyBank.com, a division of NewsBank.

"Suburban: Rochester—C. L. Jones . . ." *Illinois State Register* [Springfield] 27 Aug. 1904: 7. Published by GenealogyBank.com, a division of NewsBank.

"Bad Roads." *Illinois State Register* [Springfield] 29 Aug. 1901: 5. Published by GenealogyBank.com, a division of NewsBank.

"Rochester: The new bridge . . ." *Illinois State Register* [Springfield] 13 Jan. 1905: 8.m Published by GenealogyBank.com, a division of NewsBank.

"Bridge Open for Traffic." *Weekly Illinois State Register* [Springfield] 31 May 1904: 6. Published by GenealogyBank.com, a division of NewsBank.

Eaton, Thelma. *The Covered Bridges of Illinois.* Ann Arbor, MI: Edwards Brothers, Inc. (Distributors), 1968.

"Bridge Contract Let." *Illinois State Journal* [Springfield] 10 Sep. 1907: 1. Published by GenealogyBank.com, a division of NewsBank.

Atwood, Robert B." Winter Proves Hard on County and City Roads; Spring Work is Begun" *Illinois State Register* [Springfield] 16 Mar. 1930: 8. Published by GenealogyBank.com, a division of NewsBank.

"Bridge Accidents." *Illinois State Register* [Springfield] 22 Aug. 1905: 4. Published by GenealogyBank.com, a division of NewsBank.

"Old Bridge Condemned." *Illinois State Journal* [Springfield] 27 Aug. 1907: 1. Published by GenealogyBank.com, a division of NewsBank.

"To Erect New Bridge." *Illinois State Register* [Springfield] 30 Aug. 1907: 13. Published by GenealogyBank.com, a division of NewsBank.

"Interurban to Rochester." *Illinois State Register* [Springfield] 9 Apr. 1906: 2. Published by GenealogyBank.com, a division of NewsBank.

"Ready To Begin Track Laying." *Springfield Sunday Journal* [Springfield, IL] 17 June 1906: 5. Published by GenealogyBank.com, a division of NewsBank.

"Bridge is Built; Now Closing Gap." *Illinois State Journal* [Springfield] 14 July 1908: 7. Published by GenealogyBank.com, a division of NewsBank.

"New Line is Completed." *Illinois State Register* [Springfield] 26 July 1908: 9. Published by GenealogyBank.com, a division of NewsBank.

"First Street Car in Rochester." *Illinois State Register* [Springfield] 10 June 1908: 11. Published by GenealogyBank.com, a division of NewsBank.

"Ask Receiver for Railroad." *Illinois State Register* [Springfield] 10 Sep. 1911: 8. Published by GenealogyBank.com, a division of NewsBank.

"Rochester Line to be Re-opened." *Illinois State Register* [Springfield] 20 Aug. 1913: 9. Published by GenealogyBank.com, a division of NewsBank.

Jenkins, Dale. "SCL&R: Springfield, Clear Lake & Rochester." Illinois Traction Society: *The Flyer,* Fall 2002.

"I., D. & W. Survey." *Illinois State Register* [Springfield] 2 Sep. 1900: 5. Published by GenealogyBank.com, a division of NewsBank.

"Work on the New Road." *Illinois State Journal* [Springfield] 14 Oct. 1901: 5. Published by GenealogyBank.com, a division of NewsBank.

Wanted—At Once—100 Good Teams. Advertisement. *Illinois State Journal* [Springfield] 28 Aug. 1901: 7. Published by GenealogyBank.com, a division of NewsBank.

"Neighborhood News: Buckhart—Track has been laid . . . " *Illinois State Journal* [Springfield] 26 Nov.1901: 2. Published by GenealogyBank.com, a division of NewsBank.

"New Road is Started: The Bridges." *Weekly Illinois State Register* [Springfield] 18 June1901: 1. Published by GenealogyBank.com, a division of NewsBank.

"Grading on the New Road." *Illinois State Journal* [Springfield] 16 Aug. 1901: 3. Published by GenealogyBank.com, a division of NewsBank.

"Smallpox at Rochester." *Illinois State Journal* [Springfield] 24 Nov. 1901: 2. Published by GenealogyBank.com, a division of NewsBank.

"Smallpox at Rochester: Three Fully Developed Cases Have Been Discovered." *Illinois State Register* [Springfield] 13 Oct. 1901: 2. Published by GenealogyBank.com, a division of NewsBank.

"Fell from Special Train." *Illinois State Journal* [Springfield] 24 June 1904: 2. Published by GenealogyBank.com, a division of NewsBank.

"Files a Damage Suit." *Springfield Sunday Journal* [Springfield, IL] 16 Mar. 1902: 5. Published by GenealogyBank.com, a division of NewsBank.

"Taft Awarded $770 Damages." *Illinois State Register* [Springfield] 12 July 1908: 23. Published by GenealogyBank.com, a division of NewsBank.

"Dastards Try to Wreck Train." *Illinois State Journal* [Springfield] 24 Dec. 1902: 1. Published by GenealogyBank.com, a division of NewsBank.

"Bullets for Christmas." *Illinois State Register* [Springfield] 27 Dec. 1901: 2. Published by GenealogyBank.com, a division of NewsBank.

"Fairchild is Acquitted." *Weekly Illinois State Register* [Springfield] 5 Dec. 1902: 3. Published by GenealogyBank.com, a division of NewsBank.

"Killed: George Hays. . . " *Semi-weekly Interior Journal* [Stanford, KY] 31 Dec. 1901: 3. George Hays. Find a Grave memorial # 115052702 . 7 Aug. 2013. 24 Aug. 2015.

Untitled. "The white man, Fairchild. . ." *Semi-weekly Interior Journal* [Stanford, KY] 3 Jan. 1902: 3. George Hays. Find a Grave memorial # 115052702 . 7 Aug. 2013. 24 Aug. 2015.

George Hays. Find a Grave memorial # 115052702 . 7 Aug. 2013. 24 Aug. 2015.

"Neighborhood News: Rochester—George Hayes . . ." *Illinois State Journal* [Springfield] 8 Jan. 1898: 7. Published by GenealogyBank.com, a division of NewsBank.

"Rochester: Mrs. C.W. Fairchild . . ." *Illinois State Register* [Springfield] 11 Aug. 1908: 11. Published by GenealogyBank.com, a division of NewsBank.

"Meteor Falls near Rochester." *Illinois State Journal* [Springfield] 18 Nov. 1902: 6. Published by GenealogyBank.com, a division of NewsBank.

Farquhar, Francis P. "Naming Alaska's Mountains." *American Alpine Journal.* 19 Jan. 2017. <http://publications.americanalpineclub.org/articles/12195921100/Naming-Alaskas-Mountains>.

"Mayor Canes an Editor." *Illinois State Register* [Springfield] 12 July 1901: 3. Published by GenealogyBank.com, a division of NewsBank.

Business Houses of Sangamon County: Rochester. Advertisement. *Illinois State Register* [Springfield] 15 Sep. 1905: 2. Published by GenealogyBank.com, a division of NewsBank.

"Officers Arrest Reckless Driver." *Illinois State Journal* [Springfield] 28 Aug. 1905: 5. Published by GenealogyBank.com, a division of NewsBank.

"Ernest Hoover Indicted." *Illinois State Register* [Springfield] 21 Oct. 1905: 6. Published by GenealogyBank.com, a division of NewsBank.

Coroner's Jury Says Ballard was Murdered by Joe James; Ask for a Special Grand Jury." *Illinois State Register* [Springfield] July 7 1908: 1. Published by GenealogyBank.com, a division of NewsBank.

"One Hundred May Witness Hanging." *Illinois State Journal* [Springfield] 10 Oct. 1908: 5. Published by GenealogyBank.com, a division of NewsBank.

News of Central Illinois Counties: Sangamon County—Rochester: J. M. Bell . . ." *Illinois State Journal* [Springfield] 24 Oct. 1908: 5. Published by GenealogyBank.com, a division of NewsBank.

Kienzer, Mike (Ed.) "Race riot of 1908." Sangamon County Historical Society: *SangamonLink*. 12 Oct. 2013. 25 Aug. 2015 <http://sangamoncountyhistory.org/wp/?p=1486>.

"Grand Jury Which Indicted Joe James to Hear Riot Cases." *Illinois State Register* [Springfield] 18 Aug. 1908: 1. Published by GenealogyBank.com, a division of NewsBank.

"Rochester: Fred Poffenberger . . . " *Illinois State Journal* [Springfield] 12 Aug. 1902: 2. Published by GenealogyBank.com, a division of NewsBank.

"Neighborhood News: Rochester—The ice harvest. . . " *Illinois State Journal* [Springfield] 7 Feb.1902: 2. Published by GenealogyBank.com, a division of NewsBank.

"Minor Games: Athletic Blues Meet Defeat." *Illinois State Journal* [Springfield] 18 Aug. 1904: 3. Published by GenealogyBank.com, a division of NewsBank.

"Extremes at Base Ball." *Illinois State Register* [Springfield] 17 Sep. 1904: 2. Published by GenealogyBank.com, a division of NewsBank.

"Twist Honored By The U. of I." *Illinois State Register* [Springfield] 30 Nov. 1908: 2. Published by GenealogyBank.com, a division of NewsBank.

"Famine in Coal Closes School." *Illinois State Journal* [Springfield] 8 Jan. 1903: 1. Published by GenealogyBank.com, a division of NewsBank.

"New Point for the Map." *Illinois State Journal* [Springfield] 10 Feb. 1902: 6. Published by GenealogyBank.com, a division of NewsBank.

Illinois State Geological Survey. *Directory of Coal Mines in Illinois: Sangamon County.* Champaign, IL: Prairie Research Institute, Jan. 2015: 12. Published by GenealogyBank.com, a division of NewsBank.

"Official Proceedings." *Illinois State Register* [Springfield] 16 June 1915: 9. Published by GenealogyBank.com, a division of NewsBank.

"Central Rolling Stock Increased: Quail Halt Interurban Car." *Illinois State Journal* [Springfield] 15 Oct. 1908: 12. Published by GenealogyBank.com, a division of NewsBank.

"Farmers Kill Snakes." *Illinois State Journal* [Springfield] 20 July 1906: 1. Published by GenealogyBank.com, a division of NewsBank.

"Neighborhood News: Rochester—There seems to be . . ." *Illinois State Journal* [Springfield] 22 Jan. 1901: 2. Published by GenealogyBank.com, a division of NewsBank.

"Suburban: Rochester—One of Edward Poffenberger's . . . " *Illinois State Register* [Springfield] 16 Mar. 1905: 7. Published by GenealogyBank.com, a division of NewsBank.

"General Store was Robbed." *Illinois State Register* [Springfield] 27 Feb. 1908: 6. Published by GenealogyBank.com, a division of NewsBank.

"Are Attacked by Footpads." *Illinois State Journal* [Springfield] 15 Nov. 1904: 2. Published by GenealogyBank.com, a division of NewsBank.

"Two Young Men Bombard Town." *Illinois State Journal* [Springfield] 9 Sep. 1904: 5. Published by GenealogyBank.com, a division of NewsBank.

"Wife Tries to Poison Husband." *Illinois State Journal* [Springfield] 11 May 1904: 3. Published by GenealogyBank.com, a division of NewsBank.

"Tried to Poison Him." *Weekly Illinois State Register* [Springfield] 13 May 1904: 6. Published by GenealogyBank.com, a division of NewsBank.

"Husband Saved by Fickle Wife." *Illinois State Journal* [Springfield] 12 June 1903: 2. Published by GenealogyBank.com, a division of NewsBank.

"Illness Caused Suicide." *Illinois State Journal* [Springfield] 17 Oct. 1901: 6. Published by GenealogyBank.com, a division of NewsBank.

"Jacob McCoy." Find A Grave Memorial #53161017; 2 June 2010. 23 May 2016.

"Neighborhood News: Rochester—R. H. Coe. . . " *Illinois State Register* [Springfield] 20 Nov. 1903: 4. Published by GenealogyBank.com, a division of NewsBank.

"Neighborhood News: Edinburg—J. H. Logan . . ." *Illinois State Register* [Springfield] 14 Dec. 1902: 7. Published by GenealogyBank.com, a division of NewsBank.

"Neighborhood News: Rochester—William Everhart . . ." Illinois State Journal [Springfield] 16 Sep. 1902: 2. Published by GenealogyBank.com, a division of NewsBank.

"Explosion of Acetylene Stove." Illinois State Register" [Springfield] 6 May 1906: 10. Published by GenealogyBank.com, a division of NewsBank.

"Death Claims Bright Brain." Illinois State Journal [Springfield] 6 Nov. 1903: 6. Published by GenealogyBank.com, a division of NewsBank.

"Mortuary: Dillon." Illinois State Journal [Springfield] 26 Oct. 1903: 6. Published by GenealogyBank.com, a division of NewsBank.

"Died from Injuries Caused by Kick of a Mule." Illinois State Register [Springfield] 19 Sep. 1908: 2. Published by GenealogyBank.com, a division of NewsBank.

"Mortuary: Hall." Illinois State Register [Springfield] 11 Oct. 1901: 5. Published by GenealogyBank.com, a division of NewsBank.

"Licensed to Marry." Illinois State Register [Springfield] 13 Dec. 1893: 1. Published by GenealogyBank.com, a division of NewsBank.

"Mrs. Pease to Be Buried in Orient." Illinois State Journal [Springfield] 31 Mar. 1903: 1. Published by GenealogyBank.com, a division of NewsBank.

Lee, Jack and Vanessa Lee. "Pioneers' Plaques: Mary Wright Pease: A Nightingale in Our Midst" Wesley Tidings November-December 2012: 30-31.

"Mortuary Record: McCoy." Illinois State Journal [Springfield] 17 Dec. 1900: 6. Published by GenealogyBank.com, a division of NewsBank.

"Archibald Sattley Dead." Illinois State Journal [Springfield] 24 July 1901: 2. Published by GenealogyBank.com, a division of NewsBank.

"Died within Few Hours." Illinois State Register [Springfield] 8 Jan. 1901: 3. Published by GenealogyBank.com, a division of NewsBank.

"James W. Everhart Dead." Illinois State Journal [Springfield] 28 June 1902: 6. Published by GenealogyBank.com, a division of NewsBank.

"Mortuary: Clark." Illinois State Register [Springfield] 16 Jan. 1903: 5. Published by GenealogyBank.com, a division of NewsBank.

"Sangamon County Pioneer Has Passed Away." Weekly Illinois State Register [Springfield] 13 Nov. 1903: 2. Published by GenealogyBank.com, a division of NewsBank.

"Mortuary Record: Highmore." Illinois State Journal [Springfield] 23 Apr. 1903: 6. Published by GenealogyBank.com, a division of NewsBank.

"Mortuary: Everhart." Illinois State Journal [Springfield] 13 May 1904: 6. Published by GenealogyBank.com, a division of NewsBank.

"Mortuary: Tracy." Illinois State Register [Springfield] 27 Apr. 1905: 9. Published by GenealogyBank.com, a division of NewsBank.

"Mortuary: Graham." Illinois State Register [Springfield] 17 Jan. 1906: 5. Published by GenealogyBank.com, a division of NewsBank.

"Mortuary: Miller." Illinois State Journal [Springfield] 6 Oct. 1906: 6. Published by GenealogyBank.com, a division of NewsBank.

"Pioneer Plow Maker Dead." Illinois State Register [Springfield] 2 Jan. 1907: 2. Published by GenealogyBank.com, a division of NewsBank.

"Mortuary: McCoy." Illinois State Register [Springfield] 23 Oct. 1908: 11. Published by GenealogyBank.com, a division of NewsBank.

"Sangamon County Old Settlers Hold Fiftieth Reunion Yesterday." Illinois State Register [Springfield] 26 Aug. 1909: 1. Published by GenealogyBank.com, a division of NewsBank.

"Rochester Odd Fellows." Illinois State Register [Springfield] 18 Dec. 1908: 1. Published by GenealogyBank.com, a division of NewsBank.

"Couple Observe Golden Wedding Anniversary." Illinois State Journal [Springfield] 27 Sep. 1909: 5. Published by GenealogyBank.com, a division of NewsBank.

"Wedded Half Century." Illinois State Register [Springfield] 14 Aug. 1903: 8. Published by GenealogyBank.com, a division of NewsBank.

"Neighborhood News: Rochester—Many friends surprised . . ." *Illinois State Journal* [Springfield] 2 May 1903: 2. Published by GenealogyBank.com, a division of NewsBank.

"Rochester Odd Fellowship." *Weekly Illinois State Register* [Springfield] 28 Oct. 1902: 6. Published by GenealogyBank.com, a division of NewsBank.

"Rebekah Lodge Here Since 1902." *Centennial Edition: The Herald* [Rochester] 2 July 1969: np.

"Prohibition Picnic." Weekly *Illinois State Register* [Springfield] 9 Aug. 1901: 2. Published by GenealogyBank.com, a division of NewsBank.

"Wedding Was Postponed." *Illinois State Register* [Springfield] 7 Sep. 1909: 4. Published by GenealogyBank.com, a division of NewsBank.

"Will Not Marry James L. Clark." *Illinois State Register* [Springfield] 8 Sep. 1909: 4. Published by GenealogyBank.com, a division of NewsBank.

"Fire Threatens at Rochester." *Illinois State Journal* [Springfield] 19 Aug. 1904: 5. Published by GenealogyBank.com, a division of NewsBank.

"Seven Horses Burn to Death," *Illinois State Journal* [Springfield] 1 July 1904: 5. Published by GenealogyBank.com, a division of NewsBank.

"Flee from Fire on Bitter Night." *Illinois State Journal* [Springfield] 14 Dec. 1903: 2. Published by GenealogyBank.com, a division of NewsBank.

"Rochester Woman Badly Burned." *Illinois State Register* [Springfield] Feb. 8 1909: 2. Published by GenealogyBank.com, a division of NewsBank.

"Fear Drowning; Men are Found." *Springfield Sunday Journal* [Springfield, IL] 27 June 1909: 1. Published by GenealogyBank.com, a division of NewsBank.

"Neighborhood News: Rochester—A party of young people . . ." *Illinois State Journal* [Springfield] 14 Aug. 1903: 3. Published by GenealogyBank.com, a division of NewsBank.

"Neighborhood News: Rochester—A lovely time. . ." *Weekly Illinois State Register* [Springfield] 15 June 1900: 3. Published by GenealogyBank.com, a division of NewsBank.

"Two Men Find a Girl Baby." *Illinois State Journal* [Springfield] 23 Apr. 1902: 6. Published by GenealogyBank.com, a division of NewsBank.

"Foundling Finds a Home." *Weekly Illinois State Register* [Springfield] 25 Apr. 1902: 2. Published by GenealogyBank.com, a division of NewsBank.

"Increased Their Shame." *Illinois State Journal* [Springfield] 6 June 1901: 2. Published by GenealogyBank.com, a division of NewsBank.

"County Went Dry by Two Majority." *Twice-a-Week Illinois State Register* [Springfield] 10 Apr. 1908: 2. Published by GenealogyBank.com, a division of NewsBank.

"Eye Penetrated with a Thorn." *Illinois State Journal* [Springfield] 19 Jan. 1900: 3. Published by GenealogyBank.com, a division of NewsBank.

"Stirs up Fire; Badly Burned." *Illinois State Journal* [Springfield] 16 Jan. 1903: 1. Published by GenealogyBank.com, a division of NewsBank.

"McNeil Funeral Held." *Illinois State Journal* [Springfield] 17 July 1903: 1. Published by GenealogyBank.com, a division of NewsBank.

"Lightning Kills Man." *Illinois State Journal* [Springfield] 26 May 1908: 1. Published by GenealogyBank.com, a division of NewsBank.

"Hog Attacks Farmer." *Weekly Illinois State Register* [Springfield] 17 Apr. 1903: 1. Published by GenealogyBank.com, a division of NewsBank.

"Farmer Attacked by Vicious Boar." *Illinois State Journal* [Springfield] 20 Sep. 1904: 5. Published by GenealogyBank.com, a division of NewsBank.

"Doctor's Buggy is Wrecked." *Springfield Sunday Journal* [Springfield, IL] 1 Sep. 1901: 5. Published by GenealogyBank.com, a division of NewsBank.

"Serious Runaway Accident." *Illinois State Register* [Springfield] 24 July 1903: 1. Published by GenealogyBank.com, a division of NewsBank.

"Dr. Cantrall in a Runaway." *Illinois State Register* [Springfield] 28 May 1904: 1. Published by GenealogyBank.com, a division of NewsBank.

"Refuse Help to Man Lying Hurt." *Illinois State Journal* [Springfield] 30 Nov. 1908: 1. Published by GenealogyBank.com, a division of NewsBank.

"Rev. T.B. Wright Injured in Wreck." *Springfield Sunday Journal* [Springfield, IL] 22 Oct. 1905: 5. Published by GenealogyBank.com, a division of NewsBank.

"Rev. Wright is Injured." *Illinois State Register* [Springfield] 24 Oct. 1905: 3. Published by GenealogyBank.com, a division of NewsBank.

"Rev. T.B. Wright in Critical Condition." *Daily Illinois State Journal* [Springfield] 26 Oct. 1905: 6. Published by GenealogyBank.com, a division of NewsBank.

"Neighborhood News: Rochester—The rain storm . . ." *Illinois State Journal* [Springfield] 4 July1902: 2. Published by GenealogyBank.com, a division of NewsBank.

"Storm Maims Three at Riverton Mine: Three injured at Riverton—The wind unrooted . . ." *Illinois State Journal* [Springfield] 13 July 1909: 3. Published by GenealogyBank.com, a division of NewsBank.

"One of Rochester's Pioneer Business Men." *Rochester Weekly Item* [Rochester, IL] 23 Dec. 1909. Reprinted: Rochester: The Herald Publications, Christmas, 1984: np.

"Neighborhood News: Rochester—The firm of H. D. Parker & Co. . ." *Illinois State Journal* [Springfield] 2 May 1903: 2. Published by GenealogyBank.com, a division of NewsBank.

"Rochester Man Secures Prizes." *Semi-Weekly Illinois State Journal* [Springfield] 30 Aug. 1904: 7. Published by GenealogyBank.com, a division of NewsBank.

"Prof. Gleason at the Fair Grounds." *Illinois State Register* [Springfield] 20 Oct.1901: 6. Published by GenealogyBank.com, a division of NewsBank.

"Royal John Would Not Fight." *Illinois State Journal* [Springfield] 21 Oct. 1901: 5. Published by GenealogyBank.com, a division of NewsBank.

"The Rochester Band in 1909." *Rochester & Lake Springfield Herald.* [Rochester, IL] 18 June, 1986: 2. From *The Rochester Item* [Rochester, IL] Dec. 1909.

"Rochester Couple Secretly Wedded." *Illinois State Journal* [Springfield] 12 July 1904: 2. Published by GenealogyBank.com, a division of NewsBank.

"They Eloped to St. Louis." *Illinois State Register* [Springfield] 2 Feb. 1903: 6. Published by GenealogyBank.com, a division of NewsBank.

1910s References

"Rochester Bidding Fair to be Model Town of Sangamon." *Illinois State Journal* [Springfield] 7 June 1915: 9. Published by GenealogyBank.com, a division of NewsBank.

"Rochester Jumps into Ring of Model Towns in Sangamon." *Illinois State Register* [Springfield] 12 July 1915: 5. Published by GenealogyBank.com, a division of NewsBank.

Sangamon County Abstract Company. "An Abstract of Title." (A portion of Lot 13, Block 2, West Addition) Springfield, IL. Beginning 27 Nov. 1863.

"Sangamon, Garden Spot of World, Has Romantic and Interesting History: Rochester Township." *Daily Illinois State Register: Centennial Edition* [Springfield] 23 June 1918: 97.

"United States in World War I." *Wikipedia The Free Encyclopedia*, 12 Oct. 2015. <https://en.wikipedia.org/wiki/United_States_in_World_War_I>.

"Men Registered Number 13,412." *Illinois State Register* [Springfield] 14 Sep. 1918: 2. Published by GenealogyBank.com, a division of NewsBank.

Duff, Nellie Browne. *The Honor Book: Sangamon County Illinois 1917-1919.* Illiopolis, IL: A.P. Bickenbach, 1920.

"Troops Feted at Rochester." *Illinois State Register* [Springfield] 10 Sep. 1919: 5. Published by GenealogyBank.com, a division of NewsBank.

"Tribute Paid Service Men." *Illinois State Journal* [Springfield] 11 Sep. 1919: 5. Published by GenealogyBank.com, a division of NewsBank.

"Rochester Boy Dies in France from Meningitis Says Message to Parents." *Illinois State Journal* [Springfield] 25 Jan. 1919: 11. Published by GenealogyBank.com, a division of NewsBank.

"Harry L. Fogle." *HonorStates.org*, 3 June 2016. <http://www.honorstates.org/index.php?id=134838>.

"Celebration at Rochester." *Illinois State Register* [Springfield] 7 July 1915: 5. Published by GenealogyBank.com, a division of NewsBank.

"Rochester in Gala Event." *Illinois State Register* [Springfield] 10 July 1915: 6. Published by GenealogyBank.com, a division of NewsBank.

"Will Light Rochester." *Illinois State Journal* [Springfield] 26 May 1915: 9. Published by GenealogyBank.com, a division of NewsBank.

"Utility Company to Light Rochester." *Illinois State Register* [Springfield] 10 Mar. 1915: 16. Published by GenealogyBank.com, a division of NewsBank.

Already Built Houses. Advertisement. *Illinois State Journal* [Springfield] 29 Mar. 1916: np. Published by GenealogyBank.com, a division of NewsBank.

"Neighborhood News From Our Special Correspondents: Rochester—Several farmers . . . " *Illinois State Register* [Springfield] 20 July 1911: 11. Published by GenealogyBank.com, a division of NewsBank.

Hupmobile. Advertisement. *Illinois State Register* [Springfield] 12 June 1913: 3. Published by GenealogyBank.com, a division of NewsBank.

The Haynes. Advertisement. *Illinois State Journal* [Springfield] 19 Sep. 1915: 56. Published by GenealogyBank.com, a division of NewsBank.

Willys Knight. Advertisement. *Illinois State Register* [Springfield] 10 Sep. 1917: 29. Published by GenealogyBank.com, a division of NewsBank.

"Rochester Man Breaks Leg." *Illinois State Register* [Springfield] 24 Sep. 1914: 14. Published by GenealogyBank.com, a division of NewsBank.

"Reckless Auto Driver Escapes." *Illinois State Register* [Springfield] 12 May 1915: 5. Published by GenealogyBank.com, a division of NewsBank.

"Local Coppers to 'Pinch' All Speed Fiends." *Illinois State Register* [Springfield] 26 Apr. 1919: 3. Published by GenealogyBank.com, a division of NewsBank.

"Hunter to Race Rochester Man." *Illinois State Register* [Springfield] 23 July 1913: 6. Published by GenealogyBank.com, a division of NewsBank.

"Governor Visits Racing Matinee." *Illinois State Register* [Springfield] 24 July 1913: 2. Published by GenealogyBank.com, a division of NewsBank.

Orange Judd Farmer. *Pictorial Community Album of Rochester Township and Village.* Chicago: Orange Judd Company, 1918.

Walton & Son. Advertisement. *Illinois State Register* [Springfield] 30 July 1916: 23. Published by GenealogyBank.com, a division of NewsBank.

"Rochester Will Have 'Dustless Streets.'" *Illinois State Journal* [Springfield] 20 May 1915: 5. Published by GenealogyBank.com, a division of NewsBank.

"To Complete New Bridge Today." *Illinois State Journal* [Springfield] 20 June 1914: 9. Published by GenealogyBank.com, a division of NewsBank.

"Rochester to Have New Sidewalks." *Illinois State Journal* [Springfield] 4 Aug. 1914: 7. Published by GenealogyBank.com, a division of NewsBank.

"City Center of Highway Scheme." *Illinois State Journal* [Springfield] 26 Nov. 1913: 14. Published by GenealogyBank.com, a division of NewsBank.

"Rochester Residents Want Road Conditions Improved." *Illinois State Register* [Springfield] 27 Apr. 1916: 2. Published by GenealogyBank.com, a division of NewsBank.

"Will Oil Rochester Road into This City." *Illinois State Register* [Springfield] 27 Jan. 1916: 9. Published by GenealogyBank.com, a division of NewsBank.

"Starts Oiling Roads about Rochester." *Illinois State Register* [Springfield] 4 July 1917: 12. Published by GenealogyBank.com, a division of NewsBank.

"To Build New Church." *Illinois State Register* [Springfield] 5 Aug. 1916: 9. Published by GenealogyBank.com, a division of NewsBank.

"Raise Fund Rapidly." *Illinois State Register* [Springfield] 18 Sep. 1916: 9. Published by GenealogyBank.com, a division of NewsBank.

"1,000 Present at Dedication." *Illinois State Register* [Springfield] 23 Apr. 1917: 5. Published by GenealogyBank.com, a division of NewsBank.

"Tree Afire Alarms School Children." *Illinois State Journal* [Springfield] 25 Dec. 1913: 1. Published by GenealogyBank.com, a division of NewsBank.

"Twist Elevator at Rochester Burns." *Illinois State Register* [Springfield] 12 Aug. 1910: 5. Published by GenealogyBank.com, a division of NewsBank.

For Representative—Dr. J. M. Bell . . . Political Advertisement. *Illinois State Register* [Springfield] 12 Sep. 1910: 8. Published by GenealogyBank.com, a division of NewsBank.

"Morris High Man with 2111 Lead." *Illinois State Register* [Springfield] 10 Nov. 1910: 1. Published by GenealogyBank.com, a division of NewsBank.

J. S. Derry. Political Advertisement. *Illinois State Journal* [Springfield] 8 Apr. 1912: 11. Published by GenealogyBank.com, a division of NewsBank.

"Total Vote Cast in Sangamon County." *Illinois State Register* [Springfield] 11 Apr. 1912: 11. Published by GenealogyBank.com, a division of NewsBank.

"Noah Twist May Enter Race for Sheriff's Office." *Illinois State Register* [Springfield] 13 Dec. 1917: 3. Published by GenealogyBank.com, a division of NewsBank.

"Republicans Sweep County Electing Their Candidates by Overwhelming Majorities." *State Journal Register* [Springfield] 6 Nov. 1918: 1. Published by GenealogyBank.com, a division of NewsBank.

"All Women on Prohibition Ballot." *Illinois State Journal* [Springfield] 11 Mar. 1914: 1. Published by GenealogyBank.com, a division of NewsBank.

"Women's Suffrage in Illinois." 4 Nov. 2013 Sangamon County Historical Society *SangamonLink* [Springfield]. 11 Oct. 2015 <http://sangamoncountyhistory.org/wp/?p=2666>.

"Railroads are Recovering." *Illinois State Journal* [Springfield] 25 Feb. 1914: 12. Published by GenealogyBank.com, a division of NewsBank.

"How the Snow Stopped Railroad Traffic." *Illinois State Register* [Springfield] 27 Feb. 1914: 1. Published by GenealogyBank.com, a division of NewsBank.

"Champion Skunk Killer Issues Defi." (sic) *Illinois State Journal* [Springfield] 26 July 1912: 5. Published by GenealogyBank.com, a division of NewsBank.

"Balloon Starts On Its Journey." *Illinois State Register* [Springfield] 18 July 1911: 2. Published by GenealogyBank.com, a division of NewsBank.

"Donaldson and Captain Berry Begin Flight in Effort to Set Record." *Illinois State Journal* [Springfield] 18 July 1911: 2. Published by GenealogyBank.com, a division of NewsBank.

"Balloon Lands after Safe Trip." *Illinois State Journal* [Springfield] 19 July 1911: 5. Published by GenealogyBank.com, a division of NewsBank.

"Government Balloon Lights at Rochester." *Illinois State Register* [Springfield] 4 Aug. 1917: 6. Published by GenealogyBank.com, a division of NewsBank.

"Mad Dog at Rochester." *Illinois State Journal* [Springfield] 21 Apr 1911: 1. Published by GenealogyBank.com, a division of NewsBank.

"Bitten by Mad Dog in Rochester." *Illinois State Register* [Springfield] 23 Apr. 1911: 20. Published by GenealogyBank.com, a division of NewsBank.

"Test Shows Dog Had Rabies; Victim Rushed to Pasteur Institute." *Illinois State Journal* [Springfield] 23 Apr. 1911: 8. Published by GenealogyBank.com, a division of NewsBank.

"Rochester Girl Dies of Lockjaw." *Illinois State Journal* [Springfield] 14 May 1919: 16. Published by GenealogyBank.com, a division of NewsBank.

"Death Summons Rochester Man." *Illinois State Journal* [Springfield] 13 Nov. 1912: 9. Published by GenealogyBank.com, a division of NewsBank.

"Pioneer Resident of County Dead." *Illinois State Journal* [Springfield] 17 June 1912: 7. Published by GenealogyBank.com, a division of NewsBank.

"W.H. Neal Dies Aged 76 Years." *Illinois State Register* [Springfield] 28 Jan. 1912: 7. Published by GenealogyBank.com, a division of NewsBank.

"Dies Aboard Electric Car." *Illinois State Register* [Springfield] 8 Apr. 1912: 3. Published by GenealogyBank.com, a division of NewsBank.

"Aged Rochester Resident Dead." *Illinois State Journal* [Springfield] 2 Apr. 1915: 13. Published by GenealogyBank.com, a division of NewsBank.

"Aged Rochester Resident Dead." *Illinois State Register* [Springfield] 3 Mar. 1916: 10. Published by GenealogyBank.com, a division of NewsBank.

"D.A. Ott Dead." *Illinois State Register* [Springfield] 21 Feb. 1917: 5. Published by GenealogyBank.com, a division of NewsBank.

"Aged Resident of Rochester Is Dead." *Illinois State Journal* [Springfield] 13 Jan. 1916: 7. Published by GenealogyBank.com, a division of NewsBank.

"Rochester Mail Man Kills Self." *Illinois State Register* [Springfield] 4 Apr. 1917: 5. Published by GenealogyBank.com, a division of NewsBank.

"Former Local Crier Dies." *Illinois State Journal* [Springfield] 19 Jan. 1918: 5. Published by GenealogyBank.com, a division of NewsBank.

"Three Rochester Stores Entered." *Illinois State Journal* [Springfield] 23 Jan. 1916: 12. Published by GenealogyBank.com, a division of NewsBank.

"Rob Rochester Store." *Illinois State Journal* [Springfield] 31 Dec. 1911: 8. Published by GenealogyBank.com, a division of NewsBank.

"Bloodhounds Are Put on Tracks." *Illinois State Register* [Springfield] 16 July 1913: 2. Published by GenealogyBank.com, a division of NewsBank.

"Many Rochester Chickens Taken." *Illinois State Journal* [Springfield] 23 June 1915: 7. Published by GenealogyBank.com, a division of NewsBank.

"Janitor Arrested for Swearing in Church." *Illinois State Register* [Springfield] 12 June 1917: 6. Published by GenealogyBank.com, a division of NewsBank.

"Ambush Deacon with Raw Eggs." *Illinois State Register* [Springfield] 21 June 1912: 13. Published by GenealogyBank.com, a division of NewsBank.

"See Attempt to Dynamite Train." *Illinois State Journal* [Springfield] 24 Sep. 1914: 9. Published by GenealogyBank.com, a division of NewsBank.

"Rochester Men in duel with Pistols." *Illinois State Journal* [Springfield] 7 July 1914: 1. Published by GenealogyBank.com, a division of NewsBank.

"Rochester Men Engage in Duel." *Illinois State Register* [Springfield] 8 July 1914: 5. Published by GenealogyBank.com, a division of NewsBank.

"Murders Rival in Wild Night Orgy?" *Illinois State Journal* [Springfield] 25 Oct. 1910: 11. Published by GenealogyBank.com, a division of NewsBank.

"Are Injured in Runaway." *Illinois State Register* [Springfield] 18 Apr. 1910: 2. Published by GenealogyBank.com, a division of NewsBank.

"Motorcycle and Rigs Crash at Rochester." *Illinois State Register* [Springfield] 12 Sep. 1916: 7. Published by GenealogyBank.com, a division of NewsBank.

"Minister is Hit by Automobile." *Illinois State Register* [Springfield] 8 May 1916: 14. Published by GenealogyBank.com, a division of NewsBank.

"Lightning Strikes Lightning Rod Agent." *Illinois State Register* [Springfield] 18 May 1915: 7. Published by GenealogyBank.com, a division of NewsBank.

"Boys are Rescued from Death by Rochester Man." *Illinois State Register* [Springfield] 18 Jan. 1916: 5. Published by GenealogyBank.com, a division of NewsBank.

"Explosion Hurts Boy." *Illinois State Journal* [Springfield] 12 Feb. 1910: 5. Published by GenealogyBank.com, a division of NewsBank.

"Bleachers at Illinois State Fair Grounds Collapse; Two Hundred Fall; Fifteen Persons Suffer Injuries." *Illinois State Journal* [Springfield] 5 Oct. 1911: 1. Published by GenealogyBank.com, a division of NewsBank.

"Rochester Woman Falls into Well." *Illinois State Register* [Springfield] 16 Sep. 1910: 9. Published by GenealogyBank.com, a division of NewsBank.

"Minister Dragged from under Train." *Illinois State Journal* [Springfield] 3 Feb. 1916: 7. Published by GenealogyBank.com, a division of NewsBank.

"Hangs From Trestle as Train Passes." *Illinois State Register* [Springfield] 3 Mar. 1910: 2. Published by GenealogyBank.com, a division of NewsBank.

"Engine and Cars On; Tender is Off." *Illinois State Journal* [Springfield] 20 Apr. 1911: 4. Published by GenealogyBank.com, a division of NewsBank.

"Wreck Ties up Fair Traffic." *Illinois State Journal* [Springfield] 5 Oct. 1911: 7. Published by GenealogyBank.com, a division of NewsBank.

"Rochester Has Big Homecoming." *Illinois State Register* [Springfield] 25 Aug. 1916: 3. Published by GenealogyBank.com, a division of NewsBank.

"Rochester Program Drawing Big Crowd." *Illinois State Register* [Springfield] 6 July 1916: 3. Published by GenealogyBank.com, a division of NewsBank.

(Untitled) *The Rochester and Lake Springfield Herald.* [Rochester, IL] 28 May 1986: 6.

Park, Hazel Jones. *Oh! Those Maple Creams!!* Compiled by Karen Park Alexander: Rochester, IL. 2016

"Glenwood Park to be Opened." *Illinois State Register* [Springfield] 23 Apr. 1911: 5. Published by GenealogyBank.com, a division of NewsBank.

"Give Illustrated Talk at Rochester." *Illinois State Register* [Springfield] 5 Apr. 1918: 12. Published by GenealogyBank.com, a division of NewsBank.

"Frank Twist Making Good." *Illinois State Register* [Springfield] 9 Nov. 1910: 2. Published by GenealogyBank.com, a division of NewsBank.

"Twist with Illini Team." *Illinois State Journal* [Springfield] 25 Mar. 1910: 3. Published by GenealogyBank.com, a division of NewsBank.

"Rochester State Bank is Incorporated." *Illinois State Register* [Springfield] 5 May 1911: 10. Published by GenealogyBank.com, a division of NewsBank.

"New Bank Chartered." *Illinois State Journal* [Springfield] 5 Oct. 1912: 2. Published by GenealogyBank.com, a division of NewsBank.

"Will Operate by Telephone: Repairing 'Neer's Depot.'" *Illinois State Register* [Springfield] 4 Feb. 1916: 2. Published by GenealogyBank.com, a division of NewsBank.

"Rochester: G. A. Wolford has. . . " *Illinois State Journal* [Springfield] 14 Feb. 1919: 3. Published by GenealogyBank.com, a division of NewsBank.

"Elevator Company Increases Capital." *Illinois State Register* [Springfield] 18 June 1910: 1. Published by GenealogyBank.com, a division of NewsBank.

"Camp Manager Gives Bond on a Check Charge." *Illinois State Register* [Springfield] 21 Aug. 1916: 5. Published by GenealogyBank.com, a division of NewsBank.

"Open House at Racine-Sattley." *Illinois State Register* [Springfield] 2 Jan. 1914: 7. Published by GenealogyBank.com, a division of NewsBank.

"Big Implement Plant." *Illinois State Register* [Springfield] 8 Aug. 1903: 5. Published by GenealogyBank.com, a division of NewsBank.

"Rochester to Vote on School Today." *Illinois State Register* [Springfield] 20 Jan. 1917: 11. Published by GenealogyBank.com, a division of NewsBank.

"School Voted for Rochester." *Illinois State Register* [Springfield] 21 Jan. 1917: 2. Published by GenealogyBank.com, a division of NewsBank.

"Rochester Home of Many Tutors." *Illinois State Register* [Springfield] 8 May 1915: 7. Published by GenealogyBank.com, a division of NewsBank.

Sangamon County Schools Annual Report. Journal Co. Printers [Springfield, IL]: 1913-1914.

Sangamon County Schools Annual Report. Edward F. Hartmann Co. Printers [Springfield, IL]: 1916.

1920s References

"Rochester: Robert . . ." *Daily Illinois State Journal* [Springfield] 13 Jan. 1925: 3. Published by GenealogyBank.com, a division of NewsBank.

Vaughn, John E. "A Handful O' Sorts: What do you know . . ." *Illinois State Journal* [Springfield] 20 Jan. 1926: 6. Published by GenealogyBank.com, a division of NewsBank.

"Warn Autoists to Avoid Oiled And Dirt Roads." *Illinois State Journal* [Springfield] 10 Feb. 1924: 17. Published by GenealogyBank.com, a division of NewsBank.

"Flooded Roads Bad for Travel." *Illinois State Journal* [Springfield] 19 Mar. 1922: 24. Published by GenealogyBank.com, a division of NewsBank.

"Will File Road Route Writ in Court Monday." *Illinois State Journal* [Springfield] 4 July 1925: 1. Published by GenealogyBank.com, a division of NewsBank.

"Settle Rochester Road Dispute." *Illinois State Journal* [Springfield] 29 Apr. 1926: 1. Published by GenealogyBank.com, a division of NewsBank.

"Rochester and Edinburg Road Work to Start." *Illinois State Journal* [Springfield] 22 Aug. 1926: 43. Published by GenealogyBank.com, a division of NewsBank.

"The East Gate to Our City." *Illinois State Journal* [Springfield] 19 Aug. 1928: 31. Published by GenealogyBank.com, a division of NewsBank.

"Final Service Held in Church at Rochester." *Illinois State Journal* [Springfield] 5 May 1924: 12. Published by GenealogyBank.com, a division of NewsBank.

Montgomery, W.G. "Names and Amount of Those Who Contributed to New M.E. Church Site." *Rochester Item* [Rochester, IL). 23 June 1922: 1.

"Interesting Service to Mark Dedication of New M.E. Church at Rochester." *Illinois State Journal* [Springfield] 30 Nov. 1924: 9. Published by GenealogyBank.com, a division of NewsBank.

"Report Shows Churches Busy: Lists Many Improvements." *Illinois State Journal* [Springfield] 16 Sep. 1926: 5. Published by GenealogyBank.com, a division of NewsBank.

"Rochester to Build School." *Illinois State Journal* [Springfield] 13 Jan. 1920: 12. Published by GenealogyBank.com, a division of NewsBank.

"New Rochester School Visited." *Illinois State Register* [Springfield] 17 Aug. 1921: 9. Published by GenealogyBank.com, a division of NewsBank.

"School Site is Sold to Masons." *Illinois State Journal* [Springfield] 4 June 1922: 24. Published by GenealogyBank.com, a division of NewsBank.

"Rochester: The Masonic Hall . . ." *Illinois State Journal* [Springfield] 2 Feb. 1923: 11. Published by GenealogyBank.com, a division of NewsBank.

Vaughn, John E. "A Handful O' Sorts: *The Rochester Item*. . . " *Illinois State Journal* [Springfield] 5 Aug. 1922: 6. Published by GenealogyBank.com, a division of NewsBank.

Prices on a Few of the Many Items We Carry in Stock. Advertisement. *Rochester Item*. [Rochester, IL] 23 June 1922: 1.

The Last Will and Testament of William B. Cantrill, Deceased. Sangamon – Probate records, Book 19-20, 1917-1919; Book 21, 1919-1923, 15 June 2016 <http://interactive.ancestry.com/9048/007656271_00205/804174?backurl= http%3a%2f%2fsearch.ancestry.com%2fcgi-bin%2fsse.dll%3fgst%3d-6&ssrc=&backlabel=ReturnSearch Results>.

Vaugh, John E. "A Handful O' Sorts: Historic Rochester cemetery. . ." *Illinois State Journal* [Springfield] 18 Feb. 1924: 6. Published by GenealogyBank.com, a division of NewsBank.

The Trustees of the Rochester Cemetery . . . Advertisement. *Illinois State Journal* [Springfield] 2 Feb. 1924: 15. Published by GenealogyBank.com, a division of NewsBank.

"Centennial Edition." *Rochester Herald*, Rochester, Illinois, 2 July 1969.

Vaughn, John E. "A Handful O' Sorts." *Illinois State Journal* [Springfield] 6 July 1922: 6. Published by GenealogyBank.com, a division of NewsBank.

"Rochester Blaze Perils Village." *Illinois State Journal* [Springfield] 3 Jan. 1927: 1. Published by GenealogyBank.com, a division of NewsBank.

"Louis Persinger, Teacher of Menuhin, Boy Violinist, was Born in Rochester, Ill." *Illinois State Journal* [Springfield] 8 Jan. 1928: 10. Published by GenealogyBank.com, a division of NewsBank.

"Form Woman's Club at Rochester Meet." *Illinois State Journal* [Springfield] 13 Nov. 1924: 4. Published by GenealogyBank.com, a division of NewsBank.

"History of the Rochester Woman's Club: 1924-1984." Provided by the Club to the author 2014.

Bruzan, Ray. Talk to Rochester Women's Club. Rochester, IL. 11 Feb. 2014.

"Boy Prisoner Breaks Holes in Calaboose." *Illinois State Journal* [Springfield] 13 Oct. 1924: 1. Published by GenealogyBank.com, a division of NewsBank.

"Calaboose Wrecker Will Get Hearing." *Illinois State Journal* [Springfield] 14 Oct. 1924: 7. Published by GenealogyBank.com, a division of NewsBank.

"Rochester Boy, 10, Saves Sister, 3, Who Falls into Thirty Foot Farm Well." *Illinois State Journal* [Springfield] 25 Sept. 1927: 1. Published by GenealogyBank.com, a division of NewsBank.

Lodge Members and Friends Husk Corn." *Illinois State Journal* [Springfield] 5 Dec. 1925: 2. Published by GenealogyBank.com, a division of NewsBank.

Springfield Dry Goods Co. Advertisement. *Illinois State Journal* [Springfield] 25 Mar. 1922: 3. Published by GenealogyBank.com, a division of NewsBank.

Dance at Rochester. Advertisement. *Illinois State Register* [Springfield] 19 May 1922: 3. Published by GenealogyBank.com, a division of NewsBank.

Public Dance. Advertisement. *Illinois State Register* [Springfield] 22 Sep. 1921: 6. Published by GenealogyBank.com, a division of NewsBank.

Dance. Advertisement. *Illinois State Journal* [Springfield] 10 June 1922: 3. Published by GenealogyBank.com, a division of NewsBank.

"Mary Neer, 85, Edinburg, Dies." *Illinois State Journal* [Springfield] 16 Mar. 1924: 5. Published by GenealogyBank. com, a division of NewsBank.

"Stroke Fatal To John W. Sturdy." *Illinois State Journal* [Springfield] 12 Sep. 1923: 11. Published by GenealogyBank.com, a division of NewsBank.

"Mrs. C.L. Jones, of Rochester, Dies." *Illinois State Journal* [Springfield] 4 Dec. 1929: 3. Published by GenealogyBank.com, a division of NewsBank.

"Central Illinois Deaths: Miss Florence Twist." *Illinois State Journal* Springfield, 9 Oct. 1929: 8. Published by GenealogyBank.com, a division of NewsBank.

"Winn Fairchilds (sic) of Rochester is Killed out West." *Illinois State Register* [Springfield] 6 Oct. 1921: 3. Published by GenealogyBank.com, a division of NewsBank.

"Miss Ella Barnwell Dies at Rochester." *Illinois State Register* [Springfield] 19 Dec. 1922: 17. Published by GenealogyBank.com, a division of NewsBank.

"Rochester Pastor Reaches Church in Hectic Motor Trip." *Illinois State Journal* [Springfield] 24 Nov. 1923: 2. Published by GenealogyBank.com, a division of NewsBank.

"Rev. T.B. Wright is Dead at 68." *Illinois State Journal* [Springfield] 8 Sep. 1924: 3. Published by GenealogyBank.com, a division of NewsBank.

Bruzan, Ray and Pam. "Houses Have Roots, Too." *Illinois Times*, [Springfield] 2-8 Dec. 1977:22-23.

"Two Persons near Rochester Injured." *Illinois State Register* [Springfield] 13 June 1922: 5. Published by GenealogyBank.com, a division of NewsBank.

"Several Injured As Storm Ravages City and Central Illinois; Damage $300,000." *Illinois State Journal* [Springfield] 14 June 1922: 1 & 5. Published by GenealogyBank.com, a division of NewsBank.

"Bolt Hits Barn; Three Horses Die." *Illinois State Journal* [Springfield] 21 Aug. 1924: 2. Published by GenealogyBank.com, a division of NewsBank.

"Arrest Mayor of Rochester." *Illinois State Journal*." [Springfield] 21 July 1926: 4. Published by GenealogyBank.com, a division of NewsBank.

"Drops Suit against Mayor." *Illinois State Journal* [Springfield] 10 May 1928: 2. Published by GenealogyBank.com, a division of NewsBank.

"Rochester Youth Walks to City, Wins Place in *State Journal* Vaudeville Show." *Illinois State Journal* [Springfield] 16 Feb. 1928: 1. Published by GenealogyBank.com, a division of NewsBank.

"Tiny Dancer Makes Big Hit at Vaudeville Contest Sponsored by *Journal*." *Illinois State Journal* [Springfield] 19 Feb. 1928: 1. Published by GenealogyBank.com, a division of NewsBank.

Bell, Paul. Telephone interview. 5 Nov. 2015.

"Change Made in Elevator Names near Rochester." *Illinois State Register* [Springfield] 4 Dec. 1920: 3. Published by GenealogyBank.com, a division of NewsBank.

Vaughn, John E. "A Handful O' Sorts.: The convention of . . ." *Illinois State Journal* [Springfield] 20 Oct. 1921: 6. Published by GenealogyBank.com, a division of NewsBank.

"Rochester Man is Bound Over to the Grand Jury." *Illinois State Register* [Springfield] 25 Mar. 1922: 3. Published by GenealogyBank.com, a division of NewsBank.

"Attempt to Blow Safe at Rochester." *Illinois State Journal* [Springfield] 25 Mar. 1923: 9. Published by GenealogyBank.com, a division of NewsBank.

"Ford Sedan Stolen." *Illinois State Register* [Springfield] 17 Nov. 1922: 6. Published by GenealogyBank.com, a division of NewsBank.

"Rochester Man Held for Action of Jury." *Illinois State Journal* [Springfield] 6 Jan. 1923: 3. Published by GenealogyBank.com, a division of NewsBank.

"Placed under Bond to Preserve Peace." *Illinois State Journal* [Springfield] 3 Apr. 1920: 7. Published by GenealogyBank.com, a division of NewsBank.

"Small Pox Breaks Out in Rochester; Doctor Sent There." *Illinois State Register,* [Springfield] 19 Aug. 1920: 5. Published by GenealogyBank.com, a division of NewsBank.

"Rochester Rural Mail Carrier for 25 Years is Retired on Pension." *Illinois State Journal* [Springfield] 12 Jan. 1927: 17. Published by GenealogyBank.com, a division of NewsBank.

"Rochester Pioneer, Former Sangamon Official, 88 Today." *Illinois State Journal* [Springfield] 28 Feb. 1925: 5. Published by GenealogyBank.com, a division of NewsBank.

"Awarded Medal by D.A.R. As Best History Student in County." *Illinois State Journal* [Springfield] 17 June 1928: 20. Published by GenealogyBank.com, a division of NewsBank.

"Miss Jeanette Coe Becomes Bride in Pretty Church Rite." *Illinois State Journal* [Springfield] 25 Dec. 1927: 10. Published by GenealogyBank.com, a division of NewsBank.

"Miss Campbell of Rochester Married in City." *Illinois State Journal* [Springfield] 23 Nov. 1922: 7. Published by GenealogyBank.com, a division of NewsBank.

"Will Mark Golden Wedding at Home near Rochester." *Illinois State Journal* [Springfield] 2 July 1922: 23. Published by GenealogyBank.com, a division of NewsBank.

"M'Coys Wed 50 Years Ago Today." *Illinois State Journal* [Springfield] 8 Jan. 1923: 9. Published by GenealogyBank.com, a division of NewsBank.

"Four Klansmen in Robes Enter Church Meeting." *Illinois State Journal* [Springfield] 10 Dec. 1923: 4. Published by GenealogyBank.com, a division of NewsBank.

Hallwas, John E. *Bootlegger: A Story of Small-Town America.* 1998. Urbana and Champaign. Board of Trustees of the University of Illinois, 1999.

"K.K.K. Visits Church at Winchester and Leaves Donation." *Illinois State Register* [Springfield] 4 Dec. 1922: 11. Published by GenealogyBank.com, a division of NewsBank.

"Klansmen Cause Stir When Seen at Jacksonville." *Illinois State Register* [Springfield] 18 Dec. 1922: 11. Published by GenealogyBank.com, a division of NewsBank.

"Rochester: Rochester boasts . . ." *Illinois State Journal* [Springfield] 4 Oct. 1923: 12. Published by GenealogyBank.com, a division of NewsBank.

"Plot to Break Jail is Foiled." *Illinois State Journal* [Springfield] 12 Jan. 1922: 1. Published by GenealogyBank.com, a division of NewsBank.

Vote for J. Bruce Highmore for Sheriff. Advertisement. *Illinois State Journal* [Springfield] 10 Apr. 1922: 4. Published by GenealogyBank.com, a division of NewsBank.

"Official Vote Cast in County for Democrats: Sheriff." *Illinois State Journal* [Springfield] 14 Apr. 1922: 12. Published by GenealogyBank.com, a division of NewsBank.

"Activities among Central Illinois Farmers: Rochester." *Illinois State Journal* [Springfield] 9 July 1927: 8.

"Activities among Central Illinois Farmers: Rochester—C.E. Fairchild . . . " *Illinois State Journal* [Springfield] 27 Aug. 1927: 9. Published by GenealogyBank.com, a division of NewsBank.

"Activities among Farmers of Central Illinois: Rochester." *Illinois State Journal* [Springfield] 17 Sept. 1927: 9. Published by GenealogyBank.com, a division of NewsBank.

"Rochester." *Illinois State Journal* [Springfield] 26 Nov. 1922: 12. Published by GenealogyBank.com, a division of NewsBank.

"To Build Track at Rochester." *Illinois State Journal* [Springfield] 3 June 1920: 3. Published by GenealogyBank.com, a division of NewsBank.

"Seek Right to Build Switch." *Illinois State Journal* [Springfield] 9 May 1920: 5. Published by GenealogyBank.com, a division of NewsBank.

"B&O Would Save Trackage." *Illinois State Journal* [Springfield] 24 July 1927: 11. Published by GenealogyBank.com, a division of NewsBank.

"Emergency Train Speeds Firefighters to C.I.&W. Trestle to Check Blaze." *Illinois State Journal* [Springfield] 8 June 1923: 1. Published by GenealogyBank.com, a division of NewsBank.

"Engineer Hurt in Fall from Cab." *Illinois State Journal* [Springfield] 22 June 1927: 2. Published by GenealogyBank.com, a division of NewsBank.

"Man Dies from Injuries in Car Crash Labor Day." *Illinois State Journal* [Springfield] 23 Sep. 1923: 1. Published by GenealogyBank.com, a division of NewsBank.

Isbell, Chris. "Re: External Bridge." E-mail to the author. 25 Jan. 2017.

"Lady from 'Ole Kaintuck' Takes Reins to Save Day When Mules Run Away." *Illinois State Journal* [Springfield] 3 Feb. 1923: 2. Published by GenealogyBank.com, a division of NewsBank.

"Leaps from Runaway Rig at Rochester; May Succumb." *Illinois State Journal* [Springfield] 15 Apr. 1924: 1. Published by GenealogyBank.com, a division of NewsBank.

"Obituaries: Mrs. Nettie Woodruff." *Illinois State Journal* [Springfield] 6 Oct. 1962: 5. Published by GenealogyBank.com, a division of NewsBank.

"Rochester, Decked in Gala Attire, to Greet Farmers at County Institute Today." *Illinois State Journal* [Springfield] 6 Oct. 1925: 1. Published by GenealogyBank.com, a division of NewsBank.

"Ladies Open Institute Meet at Rochester." *Illinois State Journal* [Springfield] 8 Oct. 1924: 12. Published by GenealogyBank.com, a division of NewsBank.

Vaughn, John E. "A Handful O' Sorts: Walnut trees . . ." *Illinois State Journal* [Springfield] 12 Jan. 1926: 6. Published by GenealogyBank.com, a division of NewsBank.

"Campbell New Head of Rochester Legion." *Illinois State Journal* [Springfield] 16 Dec. 1925: 5. Published by GenealogyBank.com, a division of NewsBank.

"Application for Post of The American Legion: Harry Fogle Post 274." 4 May 1925.

"Post Application For Permanent Charter: Harry Fogle Post No. 274." 3 Sep. 1928.

"Rochester Man Recalls Early Events at 80." *Illinois State Register* [Springfield] 24 Apr. 1921: 2. Published by GenealogyBank.com, a division of NewsBank.

"Sergeant Boyd Views Life from Summit of 90 Years; Recalls Civil War Period." *Illinois State Journal* [Springfield] 22 Dec. 1929: 20. Published by GenealogyBank.com, a division of NewsBank.

1930s References

"427 Persons Reside in Rochester, 1930 Census Shows; 28 Gain in 10 Years." *Illinois State Journal* [Springfield] 11 Apr. 1930: 1. Published by GenealogyBank.com, a division of NewsBank.

"Rochester Has Building Boom." *Illinois State Journal* [Springfield] 5 Nov. 1939: 17. Published by GenealogyBank.com, a division of NewsBank.

"Make Raids Here for Robbery Clues." *Illinois State Journal* [Springfield] 27 Nov. 1930: 1. Published by GenealogyBank.com, a division of NewsBank.

Drillinger, Ruth. Personal interview. 29 Oct. 2015.

"Brown and Patterson Found Guilty." *Illinois State Journal* [Springfield] 2 Apr. 1931: 1 Published by GenealogyBank.com, a division of NewsBank.

"Files Appeal in the Case of Ted Patterson." *Illinois State Journal* [Springfield] 2 June 1932: 1. Published by GenealogyBank.com, a division of NewsBank.

"Confesses Error in Brown Case." *Illinois State Journal* [Springfield] 25 Jan. 1933: 11. Published by GenealogyBank.com, a division of NewsBank.

"Expect Trial of Patterson and Brown to Go to Jury Today." *Illinois State Journal* 17 May 1933: 1. Published by GenealogyBank.com, a division of NewsBank.

"Fire Destroys Big Elevator at Rochester." *Illinois State Journal* [Springfield] 16 Feb. 1930: 1. Published by GenealogyBank.com, a division of NewsBank.

"Funds Assured for Rochester Improvements." *Illinois State Journal* [Springfield] 14 Apr. 1935: 3. Published by GenealogyBank.com, a division of NewsBank.

"Rochester Gets Grant from P.W.A." *Illinois State Journal* [Springfield] 17 Jan. 1935: 4. Published by GenealogyBank.com, a division of NewsBank.

"City Moves to Supply Water to Rochester." *Illinois State Journal* [Springfield] 5 Mar. 1935: 8. Published by GenealogyBank.com, a division of NewsBank.

"To Start Work on Water Line at Rochester." *Illinois State Journal* [Springfield] 20 Oct. 1935: 9. Published by GenealogyBank.com, a division of NewsBank.

Notice of Proposal for Bids; Notice to Contractors. Advertisement. *Illinois State Journal* [Springfield] 18 May 1935: 15. Published by GenealogyBank.com, a division of NewsBank.

"Grant Approved for Project at Rochester." *Illinois State Journal* [Springfield] 28 Apr. 1938: 9. Published by GenealogyBank.com, a division of NewsBank.

Warnke, Art. Personal interview. 2015.

"Rochester Swept by Disastrous Fire." *Illinois State Journal* [Springfield] 29 Feb. 1932: 1. Published by GenealogyBank.com, a division of NewsBank.

"Begin Work on Ruin Caused by Rochester Fire." *Illinois State Journal* [Springfield] 1 Mar.1932: 1. Published by GenealogyBank.com, a division of NewsBank.

"The Old And the New." *Illinois State Register* [Springfield]16 Mar. 1930 p. 8.

"May Start Work on Monday." *Illinois State Journal* [Springfield] 26 Sep. 1931: 1. Published by GenealogyBank.com, a division of NewsBank.

"Most Dirt Roads in County are in Good Condition." *Illinois State Journal* [Springfield] 16 June 1932: 15. Published by GenealogyBank.com, a division of NewsBank.

"State Approves Street Contracts." *Illinois State Journal* [Springfield] 13 July 1939: 7. Published by GenealogyBank.com, a division of NewsBank.

"Allot Funds for Street Projects." *Illinois State Journal* [Springfield] 2 Sep. 1939: 3. Published by GenealogyBank.com, a division of NewsBank.

"Wire Fences Built along Highways." *Illinois State Journal* [Springfield] 3 May 1931: 8. Published by GenealogyBank.com, a division of NewsBank.

"Winter Proves Hard on County and City Roads; Spring Work is Begun." *Illinois State Journal* [Springfield] 16 Mar. 1930: 8. Published by GenealogyBank.com, a division of NewsBank.

"Rochester Votes down Bond Issue." *Illinois State Journal* [Springfield] 7 Sep. 1935: 10. Published by GenealogyBank.com, a division of NewsBank.

"Rochester Women Seek Retention of Covered Bridge." *Illinois State Journal* [Springfield] 12 Nov. 1937: 24. Published by GenealogyBank.com, a division of NewsBank.

"Modern Structure Replaces Covered Bridge on New Highway East of City." *Illinois State Journal* [Springfield] 3 Nov. 1937: 19. Published by GenealogyBank.com, a division of NewsBank.

"Voters Favor High School at Rochester." *Illinois State Journal* [Springfield] 21 June 1936: 5. Published by GenealogyBank.com, a division of NewsBank.

"Court Fixes Price on Rochester School Site." *Illinois State Journal* [Springfield] 120 Oct. 1936: 4. Published by GenealogyBank.com, a division of NewsBank.

"Work to Begin Tomorrow on Rochester High." *Illinois State Journal* [Springfield] 10 Jan. 1937: 11. Published by GenealogyBank.com, a division of NewsBank.

"To Lay Stone for Rochester School." *Illinois State Journal* [Springfield] 9 Apr. 1937: 15. Published by GenealogyBank.com, a division of NewsBank.

"Rochester's New Township High Community Asset." *Illinois State Journal* [Springfield] 3 Dec. 1937: 28. Published by GenealogyBank.com, a division of NewsBank.

"Rochester Class Dedicates Stage with First Play." *Illinois State Journal* [Springfield] 9 Jan. 1938: 24. Published by GenealogyBank.com, a division of NewsBank.

"Blast Safe in Rochester School." *Illinois State Journal* [Springfield] 14 Apr. 1939: 7. Published by GenealogyBank.com, a division of NewsBank.

"Two Filling Stations in Rochester Robbed." *Illinois State Journal* [Springfield] 22 Sep. 1936: 7. Published by GenealogyBank.com, a division of NewsBank.

"Cigarets (sic), Cash and Gas Taken at Filling Station." *Illinois State Journal* [Springfield] 13 Aug. 1938: 9. Published by GenealogyBank.com, a division of NewsBank.

"Thieves Steal Two Calves, Hog." *Illinois State Journal* [Springfield] 7 Nov. 1933: 3. Published by GenealogyBank.com, a division of NewsBank.

"Women See Body near County Line." *Illinois State Journal* [Springfield] 15 July 1930: 1. Published by GenealogyBank.com, a division of NewsBank.

"Widen Probe in the Brown Murder Case." *Illinois State Journal* [Springfield] 14 July 1930: 1. Published by GenealogyBank.com, a division of NewsBank.

"Rochester Marshal Nabs 13 Speeders in Two Days." *Illinois State Journal* [Springfield] 18 May 1930: 1. Published by GenealogyBank.com, a division of NewsBank.

"No Driver Hanged as Yet at Rochester and No 'Speed Traps,' Justices Declare." *Illinois State Journal* [Springfield] 23 May 1930: 1. Published by GenealogyBank.com, a division of NewsBank.

"Girl Speeder, Pretty and Fast on Feet, Walks Out on Justice at Rochester." *Illinois State Journal* [Springfield] 21 May 1930: 1. Published by GenealogyBank.com, a division of NewsBank.

Coontz Bros. Dairy. Advertisement. *Illinois State Journal* [Springfield] 29 Aug. 1939: 5. Published by GenealogyBank.com, a division of NewsBank.

Richardson's Service Station. Advertisement. *Illinois State Journal* [Springfield] 30 May 1939: 13. Published by GenealogyBank.com, a division of NewsBank.

Dr. Frederick Bornstein. Advertisement. *Illinois State Journal* [Springfield] 14 Apr. 1937: 8. Published by GenealogyBank.com, a division of NewsBank.

Hilltop Inn. Advertisement. *Illinois State Journal* [Springfield] 31 Dec. 1937: 28. Published by GenealogyBank.com, a division of NewsBank.

"Rescue Four from River." *Illinois State Journal* [Springfield] 11 Apr. 1938: 4. Published by GenealogyBank.com, a division of NewsBank.

"Official Sangamon County Vote in April 12 Primary." *Illinois State Journal* [Springfield] 19 Apr. 1938: 3. Published by GenealogyBank.com, a division of NewsBank.

"Improvement is Noted in A.M. Dunnavan's Condition." *Illinois State Journal* [Springfield] 22 Sep. 1933: 13. Published by GenealogyBank.com, a division of NewsBank.

Public Sale. Advertisement. *Illinois State Journal* [Springfield] 24 Oct. 1933: 13. Published by GenealogyBank.com, a division of NewsBank.

"Rochester Child Injured in Crash." *Illinois State Journal* [Springfield] 5 Apr. 1931: 1. Published by GenealogyBank.com, a division of NewsBank.

"Circuit Court Jury Debates Damage Case." *Illinois State Journal* [Springfield] 28 Sep. 1933: 2. Published by GenealogyBank.com, a division of NewsBank.

"Taft Given Damages in Auto Crash Suit." *Illinois State Journal* [Springfield] 29 Sep. 1933: 2. Published by GenealogyBank.com, a division of NewsBank.

"Three Injured, 1 Seriously, in Boiler Blast." *Illinois State Journal* [Springfield] 23 July 1937: 2. Published by GenealogyBank.com, a division of NewsBank.

"Rochester Man Hurt in Runaway." *Illinois State Journal* [Springfield] 17 Dec. 1938: 2. Published by GenealogyBank.com, a division of NewsBank.

"Injuries are Fatal to Rochester Man." *Illinois State Journal* [Springfield] 15 May 1938: 18. Published by GenealogyBank.com, a division of NewsBank.

"Rochester Girl Dies as Result of Injuries." *Illinois State Journal* [Springfield] 30 Apr. 1935: 10. Published by GenealogyBank.com, a division of NewsBank.

"Mother, Daughter are Fatally Burned." *Illinois State Journal* [Springfield] 22 July 1935: 1. Published by GenealogyBank.com, a division of NewsBank.

"To Hold Air Circus Today, Tomorrow." *Illinois State Journal* [Springfield] 3 Sep. 1933: 4. Published by GenealogyBank.com, a division of NewsBank.

"Obituaries: Stanley W. Kluzek." *Illinois State Journal-Register* [Springfield, IL] 3 Nov. 1987: 4. Published by GenealogyBank.com, a division of NewsBank.

"Rochester woman Drives School Bus." *Illinois State Journal* [Springfield] 27 Jan. 1939: 9. Published by GenealogyBank.com, a division of NewsBank.

Wanless, Carolyn. Personal interview. Dec. 2015.

"Governor's Scouts Roam Cornfields for Giant Stalks." *Illinois State Journal* [Springfield] 30 July 1937: 4. Published by GenealogyBank.com, a division of NewsBank.

"Rochester Man Grows Big Berries." *Illinois State Journal* [Springfield] 26 June 1938: 10. Published by GenealogyBank.com, a division of NewsBank.

Smith, J. Emil. "Making Conversation: Two rare flags. . . " *Illinois State Journal* [Springfield] 20 Nov. 1935: 8. Published by GenealogyBank.com, a division of NewsBank.

Steufert, Duane. "The 37-Star Flag." *The Flag of the United States of America.* 27 June 2016 <http://www.usflag.org/history/the37starflag.html>.

Iasso, Anthony. "American National Flag 42 Stars, Washington Statehood an Unofficial Star Count, c1890." *Rare Flags* <http://rareflags.com/RareFlags_Showcase_IAS_00276.htm>

"Rochester Gold Star Mother Sails for France Today." *Illinois State Journal* [Springfield] 8 July 1931: 9. Published by GenealogyBank.com, a division of NewsBank.

"The March Lion Roared 9 Years Ago." *Illinois State Journal* [Springfield] 28 Mar. 1939: 10. Published by GenealogyBank.com, a division of NewsBank.

"Lake Springfield and Parks of City Will Attract Many Families for Reunions Today: Twist." *Illinois State Journal* [Springfield] 1 Aug. 1937: 38. Published by GenealogyBank.com, a division of NewsBank.

"Scarlet Fever." *Wikipedia. 1 Dec. 2015.* 4 Dec. 2015 <https://en.wikipedia.org/wiki/Scarlet_fever>.

"Taft Dairy Company Suspends Deliveries." *Illinois State Journal* [Springfield] 7 July 1935: 2. Published by GenealogyBank.com, a division of NewsBank.

"Rochester Group Activities Halted by Scarlet Fever." *Illinois State Journal* [Springfield] 23 Feb. 1936: 5. Published by GenealogyBank.com, a division of NewsBank.

"Stirring Days of Civil War Times Recalled by Coming Anniversary of Emancipation." *Illinois State Journal* [Springfield] 20 Sep. 1937: 4. Published by GenealogyBank.com, a division of NewsBank.

"First Baby Born This Year Dies at Hospital." *Illinois State Journal* [Springfield] 16 Jan. 1938: 5. Published by GenealogyBank.com, a division of NewsBank.

"Shirley Fairchild, Head of Rochester Freshmen, is Dead." *Illinois State Journal* [Springfield] 18 Jan. 1938: 4. Published by GenealogyBank.com, a division of NewsBank.

"Ira F. Twist, 80, Native of County, Dies in Arkansas." *Illinois State Journal* [Springfield] 6 Oct. 1937: 2. Published by GenealogyBank.com, a division of NewsBank.

"Death Claims John A. Twist in Arizona." *Illinois State Journal* [Springfield] 15 Feb. 1935: 12. Published by GenealogyBank.com, a division of NewsBank.

"Ralph Twist Rites to be Held Today." *Illinois State Journal* [Springfield] 1 July 1931: 4. Published by GenealogyBank.com, a division of NewsBank.

"Clarence Twist of Prominent Pioneer Family is Dead." *Illinois State Journal* [Springfield] 2 Apr. 1938: 7. Published by GenealogyBank.com, a division of NewsBank.

"A.H. Burt of Rochester Dies; Heat is Blamed." *Illinois State Journal* [Springfield] 14 July 1936: 3. Published by GenealogyBank.com, a division of NewsBank.

"P.P. Breckenridge, Rochester Farmer Many Years, Dies." *Illinois State Journal* [Springfield] 28 Sep. 1936: 3. Published by GenealogyBank.com, a division of NewsBank.

"Grocer Dies." *Illinois State Journal* [Springfield] 23 Feb. 1936: 5. Published by GenealogyBank.com, a division of NewsBank.

"Henry Taft Dies near Rochester." *Illinois State Journal* [Springfield] 3 Oct. 1930: 11. Published by GenealogyBank.com, a division of NewsBank.

"T. Thornton Dies at Home in Rochester." *Illinois State Journal* [Springfield] 16 Sep. 1931: 17. Published by GenealogyBank.com, a division of NewsBank.

"T.D. Shreve Rites to be Held Today." *Illinois State Journal* [Springfield] 4 Oct. 1931: 7. Published by GenealogyBank.com, a division of NewsBank.

"Margaret Bennett, 90 Years Old, Dies near Rochester." *Illinois State Journal* [Springfield] 5 Mar. 1932: 10. Published by GenealogyBank.com, a division of NewsBank.

"Rochester Vet Who was with U.S. Grant Dies." *Illinois State Journal* [Springfield] 31 Dec.1932: 11. Published by GenealogyBank.com, a division of NewsBank.

"Samuel B. Coe of Rochester Dies at Home." *Illinois State Journal* [Springfield] 21 Dec. 1934: 8. Published by GenealogyBank.com, a division of NewsBank.

"William Dawley of Rochester Dies." *Illinois State Journal* [Springfield] 9 Feb. 1934: 2. Published by GenealogyBank.com, a division of NewsBank.

"H.D. Parker, 81, of Rochester, Dies in Chicago." *Illinois State Journal* [Springfield] 3 Dec. 1934: 3. Published by GenealogyBank.com, a division of NewsBank.

"Former Rochester Woman, Mother of Violinist, is Dead." *Illinois State Journal* [Springfield] 5 Dec. 1930: 15. Published by GenealogyBank.com, a division of NewsBank.

Bank at Rochester Established 1900. Advertisement. *Illinois State Journal* [Springfield] 1 July 1938: 10. Published by GenealogyBank.com, a division of NewsBank.

Notice to our Depositors. Advertisement. *Illinois State Journal* [Springfield] 31 Dec. 1932: 3. Published by GenealogyBank.com, a division of NewsBank.

"Rochester Bank Pays Balance of Waived Deposits." *Illinois State Journal* [Springfield] 14 Mar. 1938: 2. Published by GenealogyBank.com, a division of NewsBank.

"Swiney-Churchhill Wedding Vows are Spoken at Church." *Illinois State Journal* [Springfield] 24 Aug. 1939: 7. Published by GenealogyBank.com, a division of NewsBank.

"Fifty Years of Married Bliss." *Illinois State Journal* [Springfield] 7 Dec. 1937: 2. Published by GenealogyBank.com, a division of NewsBank.

"Wed Fifty Years Today." *Illinois State Journal* [Springfield] 19 Oct. 1930: 23. Published by GenealogyBank.com, a division of NewsBank.

"Approach Golden Wedding Day." *Illinois State Journal* [Springfield] 28 Feb. 1933: 4. Published by GenealogyBank.com, a division of NewsBank.

"To Mark Day." *Illinois State Journal* [Springfield] 8 Feb. 1931: 17. Published by GenealogyBank.com, a division of NewsBank.

"William J. Nutt, Rochester Civil War Veteran, will be Ninety Years Old Tomorrow." *Illinois State Journal* [Springfield] 9 July 1931. Published by GenealogyBank.com, a division of NewsBank.

"S.J. M'Coy, Rochester, 85 Years Old Today." *Illinois State Journal* [Springfield] 3 May 1934: 2. Published by GenealogyBank.com, a division of NewsBank.

1940s References

"Casualty List for County Reveals 529 are Wounded." *Illinois State Journal* [Springfield] 28 Aug. 1945: 7. Published by GenealogyBank.com, a division of NewsBank.

"Rochester Man Awarded Bronze Star." *Illinois State Journal* [Springfield] 9 Mar. 1946: 12. Published by GenealogyBank.com, a division of NewsBank.

"Pvt. Donald E. Ray Dies in Battle." *Illinois State Journal* [Springfield] 14 Sep. 1944: 4. Published by GenealogyBank.com, a division of NewsBank.

"Pfc. Delbert Taft has Typhoid Fever." *Illinois State Journal* [Springfield] 20 July 1945: 12. Published by GenealogyBank.com, a division of NewsBank.

"Pfc. Jack Campbell Home on Furlough." *Illinois State Journal* [Springfield] 30 June 1945: 3. Published by GenealogyBank.com, a division of NewsBank.

"Rochester Man Wins Medal for Bravery." *Illinois State Journal* [Springfield] 25 Feb. 1945: 18. Published by GenealogyBank.com, a division of NewsBank.

"Flying in Italy." *Illinois State Journal* [Springfield] 13 Nov. 1944: 16. Published by GenealogyBank.com, a division of NewsBank.

"Rochester Navy Man in Pacific." *Illinois State Journal* [Springfield] 15 Oct. 1945: 14. Published by GenealogyBank.com, a division of NewsBank.

"Completes 23 Missions against Japs." *Illinois State Journal* [Springfield] 18 Sep. 1944: 18. Published by GenealogyBank.com, a division of NewsBank.

"Rochester Navy Man to Aid in Bomb Test." *Illinois State Journal* [Springfield] 30 June 1946: 13. Published by GenealogyBank.com, a division of NewsBank.

"Newly Modernized Taft & Sons' Dairy." *Illinois State Journal* [Springfield] 15 Mar. 1941: 9. Published by GenealogyBank.com, a division of NewsBank.

Taft, Donald. Personal interview. 13 June 2015.

"New Food Market Opens in Rochester." *Illinois State Journal* [Springfield] 4 Oct. 1940: 15. Published by GenealogyBank.com, a division of NewsBank.

"Store Building, Lots at Rochester Sold." *Illinois State Journal* [Springfield] 3 July 1941: 3. Published by GenealogyBank.com, a division of NewsBank.

"Lightest of All Metals Used at Rochester, Ill." *Illinois State Journal* [Springfield] 28 Nov. 1949: 12. Published by GenealogyBank.com, a division of NewsBank.

"Fire Razes Rochester Church." *Illinois State Journal* [Springfield] 10 Feb. 1947: 1. Published by GenealogyBank.com, a division of NewsBank.

"Four Midstate Fires Leave One Dead and Damage of $150,000." *Illinois State Journal* [Springfield] 10 Feb. 1947: 1. Published by GenealogyBank.com, a division of NewsBank.

"Gymnasium to be Used By Church." *Illinois State Journal* [Springfield] 13 Feb. 1947: 9. Published by GenealogyBank.com, a division of NewsBank.

"To Give Farewell Sermon at Rochester." *Illinois State Journal* [Springfield] 27 Nov. 1955: 12. Published by GenealogyBank.com, a division of NewsBank.

"Aids in Drive." *Illinois State Journal* [Springfield] 24 Nov. 1947: 7. Published by GenealogyBank.com, a division of NewsBank.

"To Break Ground for Rochester Church." *Illinois State Journal* [Springfield] 18 Oct. 1947: 2. Published by GenealogyBank.com, a division of NewsBank.

"I.C.C. Authorizes Line Construction: State House News—The office also. . ." *Illinois State Journal* [Springfield] 22 June 1946: 2. Published by GenealogyBank.com, a division of NewsBank.

"The Beginning: Rochester Fire Protection District." *Herald* [Rochester] 2 July 1969: n.p.

"Rochester Groups Plan 3 Day Event." *Illinois State Journal* [Springfield] 1 Sep. 1948: 11. Published by GenealogyBank.com, a division of NewsBank.

"Buy Resuscitator for Rochester." *Illinois State Journal* [Springfield] 22 May 1949: 6. Published by GenealogyBank.com, a division of NewsBank.

"School Consolidations." *Illinois State Journal* [Springfield] 1 June 1946: 6. Published by GenealogyBank.com, a division of NewsBank.

"Sixteen Schools Will Consolidate." *Illinois State Journal* [Springfield] 2 June 1946: 4. Published by GenealogyBank.com, a division of NewsBank.

"Sell School Supplies." *Illinois State Journal* [Springfield] 29 Aug. 1946: 4. Published by GenealogyBank.com, a division of NewsBank.

B-I-G auction. Advertisement. *Illinois State Journal* [Springfield] 27 Aug. 1946: 15. Published by GenealogyBank.com, a division of NewsBank.

Public Sale. Advertisement. *Illinois State Journal* [Springfield] 15 Jan. 1947: 19. Published by GenealogyBank.com, a division of NewsBank.

"Unused School Makes Comfortable Home." *Illinois State Journal* [Springfield] 20 Sep. 1946: 19. Published by GenealogyBank.com, a division of NewsBank.

"School Building Issues Carry." *Illinois State Journal* [Springfield] 13 Apr. 1947: 35. Published by GenealogyBank.com, a division of NewsBank.

"Rochester to Discuss School Consolidation." *Illinois State Journal* [Springfield] 12 Sep. 1948: 38. Published by GenealogyBank.com, a division of NewsBank.

"Rochester Area Unit District Approved." *Illinois State Journal* [Springfield] 21 Sep. 1947: 11. Published by GenealogyBank.com, a division of NewsBank.

Parents!Taxpayers! Advertisement. *Illinois State Journal* [Springfield] 4 Oct. 1948: 18. Published by GenealogyBank.com, a division of NewsBank.

"School Merger Plan Defeated." *Illinois State Journal* [Springfield] 6 Oct. 1948: 1. Published by GenealogyBank.com, a division of NewsBank.

"Election on School Merger in City Area will be Held Soon." *Illinois State Journal* [Springfield] 18 May 1948: 1. Published by GenealogyBank.com, a division of NewsBank.

"Rochester P.T.A. to Hold Rummage Sale." *Illinois State Journal* [Springfield] 3 Oct. 1948: 23. Published by GenealogyBank.com, a division of NewsBank.

"Rochester Pupils to be Immunized." *Illinois State Journal* [Springfield] 9 Feb. 1947: 24. Published by GenealogyBank.com, a division of NewsBank.

Dave Bakke. "Book Club is a Real Bargain." *Illinois State Journal-Register* [Springfield, IL] 29 Nov. 2010: 11. Published by GenealogyBank.com, a division of NewsBank. Published by GenealogyBank.com, a division of NewsBank.

"6 Hurt as Truck Hits Parked Car." *Illinois State Journal* [Springfield] 7 Sep. 1948: 1. Published by GenealogyBank.com, a division of NewsBank.

"Cropp Charged with Reckless Driving." *Illinois State Journal* [Springfield] 10 Sep. 1948: 21. Published by GenealogyBank.com, a division of NewsBank.

"The Thundering Herd." *Illinois State Journal* [Springfield] 14 Sep. 1948: 6. Published by GenealogyBank.com, a division of NewsBank.

"Big Entertainment Arranged at Air Maneuvers Today." *Illinois State Journal* [Springfield] 13 May 1945: 10. Published by GenealogyBank.com, a division of NewsBank.

"Make Final Plans for Air Show." *Illinois State Journal* [Springfield] 15 Sep. 1946: 4. Published by GenealogyBank.com, a division of NewsBank.

"Say Record Set for Vertical Spins." *Illinois State Journal* [Springfield] 16 Sep. 1946: 3. Published by GenealogyBank.com, a division of NewsBank.

Next Aviation Class. Advertisement. *Illinois State Journal* [Springfield] 25 May 1945: 26. Published by GenealogyBank.com, a division of NewsBank.

"Funeral Tribute to Jerome Patrick Daley." 15 July, 2016.

You Can Rent a Plane: Fleck's Airport. Advertisement *Illinois State Journal* [Springfield] 28 June 1945: 14. Published by GenealogyBank.com, a division of NewsBank.

O'Brien, Adelaide. "Aeronautically Speaking—Fourteen members . . ." *Illinois State Journal* [Springfield] 15 Dec. 1946: 38. Published by GenealogyBank.com, a division of NewsBank.

"Two City Pilots Die as Planes Crash in Midair near Here." *Illinois State Journal* [Springfield] 9 June 1948: 1. Published by GenealogyBank.com, a division of NewsBank.

"Obituaries: Frank J. Fleck." *Illinois State Journal* [Springfield] 28 Oct. 1970: 25. Published by GenealogyBank.com, a division of NewsBank.

"Girl Scout Troop 'Goes to Jail.'" *Illinois State Journal* [Springfield] 19 Nov. 1943: 2. Published by GenealogyBank.com, a division of NewsBank.

"Girl Scout Work Shows Increase." *Illinois State Journal* [Springfield] 20 Nov. 1949: 33. Published by GenealogyBank.com, a division of NewsBank.

"Plan New Boy Scout Troop at Rochester." *Illinois State Journal* [Springfield] 10 Sep. 1941: 3. Published by GenealogyBank.com, a division of NewsBank.

"Scouts Depart for Canoe Trip." *Illinois State Journal* [Springfield] 28 July 1946: 9. Published by GenealogyBank.com, a division of NewsBank.

Beck, Wayne. Personal interview. 10 Dec. 2015.

"Walks 7 Miles On 75th Birthday." *Illinois State Journal* [Springfield] 13 Apr. 1945: 29. Published by GenealogyBank.com, a division of NewsBank.

"Wedded Forty Years." *Illinois State Journal* [Springfield] 5 July 1940: 2. Published by GenealogyBank.com, a division of NewsBank.

"Approve Plans for Rochester Sewage Plant." *Illinois State Journal* [Springfield] 2 Oct. 1946: 4. Published by GenealogyBank.com, a division of NewsBank.

Dallman, V.Y. "Lighter Vein: Fiction and cinema. . ." *Illinois State Journal and Register* [Springfield] 23 Mar. 1947: 6. Published by GenealogyBank.com, a division of NewsBank.

Secretary of State Jason Kander: Missouri Digital Heritage. "The State Board of Health of Missouri: Standard Certificate of Death." July 4, 2016 <http://www.sos.mo.gov/images/archives/deathcerts/1947/1947_00014003. PDF>.

"See Light Vote in Township Elections on Tuesday; Local Option up in Some Districts." *Illinois State Journal* [Springfield] 30 Mar. 1941: 1. Published by GenealogyBank.com, a division of NewsBank.

"Drys Lose Two County Contests." *Illinois State Journal* [Springfield] 2 Apr. 1941: 1. Published by GenealogyBank.com, a division of NewsBank.

"Republicans Elect Mayors in Hot City Fights, Drys Gail Ground in Villages." *Illinois State Journal* [Springfield] 16 Apr. 1941: 1. Published by GenealogyBank.com, a division of NewsBank.

"Gold Rush!" *Illinois State Journal* [Springfield] 1 Aug. 1943: 27. Published by GenealogyBank.com, a division of NewsBank.

"South Fork Church will Hold Reunion." *Illinois State Journal* [Springfield] 3 Oct. 1940. Published by GenealogyBank.com, a division of NewsBank.

"Talk Need of New Highway to Decatur." *Illinois State Journal* [Springfield] 12 Apr. 1942: 1. Published by GenealogyBank.com, a division of NewsBank.

"68 Chickens Stolen, and Fencing Too." *Illinois State Journal* [Springfield] 4 June 1945: 7. Published by GenealogyBank.com, a division of NewsBank.

"Cold Ride." *Illinois State Journal* [Springfield] 18 Dec. 1946: 26. Published by GenealogyBank.com, a division of NewsBank.

"Report Boys Use Stolen Rifles on School Windows." *Illinois State Journal* [Springfield] 8 Apr. 1949: 2. Published by GenealogyBank.com, a division of NewsBank.

"Rochester Man is Kidnaped, Robbed." *Illinois State Journal* [Springfield] 19 June 1941: 2. Published by GenealogyBank.com, a division of NewsBank.

"Blaze Damages Rochester Home." *Illinois State Journal* [Springfield] 13 Dec. 1947: 7. Published by GenealogyBank.com, a division of NewsBank.

"Rochester Blaze Causes Damage." *Illinois State Journal* [Springfield] 4 July 1949: 3. Published by GenealogyBank.com, a division of NewsBank.

"Sprains Ankle in 40 Foot Plunge." *Illinois State Journal* [Springfield] 16 Aug. 1949: 2. Published by GenealogyBank.com, a division of NewsBank.

"Six More Cases of Polio Reported." *Illinois State Journal* [Springfield] 4 Oct. 1946: 13. Published by GenealogyBank.com, a division of NewsBank.

"Poliomyelitis." *Wikipedia*, 13 Dec. 2015. <https://en.wikipedia.org/wiki/Poliomyelitis>.

"To Train Surgical Dressings Instructors." *Illinois State Journal* [Springfield] 13 Jan. 1944: 4. Published by GenealogyBank.com, a division of NewsBank.

"Arrange Red Cross Drive at Rochester." *Illinois State Journal* [Springfield] 12 Jan. 1942: 11. Published by GenealogyBank.com, a division of NewsBank.

"Red Cross Drives toward Goal." *Illinois State Journal* [Springfield] 7 Mar. 1945: 13. Published by GenealogyBank.com, a division of NewsBank.

"Twist Estate Given Approval of Court." *Illinois State Journal* [Springfield] 16 Feb. 1940: 3. Published by GenealogyBank.com, a division of NewsBank.

"Famous Twist Plantation Sought for U.S. Project." *Illinois State Journal* [Springfield] 23 Feb. 1940: 5. Published by GenealogyBank.com, a division of NewsBank.

"To Launch Tin Can Drive in County." *Illinois State Journal* [Springfield] 14 Oct. 1942: 9. Published by GenealogyBank.com, a division of NewsBank.

"Open Grease Drive in Cotton Hill Township." *Illinois State Journal* [Springfield] 27 Oct. 1942: 5. Published by GenealogyBank.com, a division of NewsBank.

"Many Basketball Contests Will Assist March of Dimes." *Illinois State Journal* [Springfield] 31 Jan. 1947: 24. Published by GenealogyBank.com, a division of NewsBank.

"Fox Hunt to Aid March of Dimes." *Illinois State Journal* [Springfield] 29 Jan. 1947: 10. Published by GenealogyBank.com, a division of NewsBank.

"Springfield C. of C. Opposes Flood Control Project." *Illinois State* Journal [Springfield] 17 Apr. 1946: 17. · Published by GenealogyBank.com, a division of NewsBank.

"Farm Bureau Asks State Probe on Flood Control." *Illinois State Journal* [Springfield] 13 Mar. 1946: 11. Published by GenealogyBank.com, a division of NewsBank.

"5 Meetings Held to Protest Flood Control Project." *Illinois State Journal* [Springfield] 20 Apr. 1946: 2. Published by GenealogyBank.com, a division of NewsBank.

"Mrs. Josephine Derry Dies at Residence of Long Illness." *Illinois State Journal* [Springfield] 30 Dec. 1940: 2. Published by GenealogyBank.com, a division of NewsBank.

"Mollie C. Wolford Dies at Rochester." *Illinois State Journal* [Springfield] 11 Jan. 1941: 2. Published by GenealogyBank.com, a division of NewsBank.

"John E. Fogle, 83, Dies at Residence." *Illinois State Journal* [Springfield] 16 Oct. 1948: 3. Published by GenealogyBank.com, a division of NewsBank.

"James Bell, 94, of Rochester, Dies." *Illinois State Journal* [Springfield] 22 Oct. 1948: 2. Published by GenealogyBank.com, a division of NewsBank.

"Obituaries: Charles Jones." *Illinois State Journal* [Springfield] 2 Nov. 1949: 24. Published by GenealogyBank.com, a division of NewsBank.

"4-H Beef Winner." *Illinois State Journal* [Springfield] 28 Feb. 1945: 22. Published by GenealogyBank.com, a division of NewsBank.

Smith, J. Emil. "Making Conversation: During the winter months . . ." *Illinois State Journal* [Springfield] 22 Jan. 1946: 6. Published by GenealogyBank.com, a division of NewsBank.

"Note Dropped from B-29 is Given to Kin." *Illinois State Journal* [Springfield] 10 Sep. 1944: 1. Published by GenealogyBank.com, a division of NewsBank.

"Winner." *Illinois State Journal* [Springfield] 19 Aug. 1941: 8. Published by GenealogyBank.com, a division of NewsBank.

"Bags Fox." *Illinois State Journal* [Springfield] 17 Dec. 1940: 4. Published by GenealogyBank.com, a division of NewsBank.

"Scholarship Winners." *Illinois State Journal* [Springfield] 17 Aug. 1941: 2. Published by GenealogyBank.com, a division of NewsBank.

"Rochester in the News—The ther Rochester . . ." *Illinois State Journal* [Springfield] 17 Dec. 1941: 9. Published by GenealogyBank.com, a division of NewsBank.

"City and County Marbles Championships are Decided." *Illinois State Journal* [Springfield] 11 May 1941: 40. Published by GenealogyBank.com, a division of NewsBank.

"St. Louisan Wins in Marbles Finals." *Illinois State Journal* [Springfield] 4 July 1941: 11. Published by GenealogyBank.com, a division of NewsBank.

Smith, J. Emil. "Making Conversation . . . J.E. Campbell . . ." *Illinois State Journal* [Springfield] 5 July 1943: 6. Published by GenealogyBank.com, a division of NewsBank.

"Never Far from the Farm." *Illinois State Journal* [Springfield] 30 Jan. 1997. Published by GenealogyBank.com, a division of NewsBank.

1950s References

"Former City Woman Author of Novel." *Illinois State Journal* [Springfield] 4 June 1952: 24. Published by GenealogyBank.com, a division of NewsBank.

Stafford, Marjorie. "'The Lemon Jelly Cake' is Story of Small Town Life." *Illinois State Journal* [Springfield] 15 Aug. 1952: 29. Published by GenealogyBank.com, a division of NewsBank.

"Plan Funeral for Novelist." *Illinois State Journal* [Springfield] 17 Dec. 1952: 5. Published by GenealogyBank.com, a division of NewsBank.

Smith, Madeline Babcock. *The Lemon Jelly Cake. 1952.* Urbana: University of Illinois Press, 1998.

Watson, Kenneth. "Strike Oil near Rochester." *Illinois State Journal* [Springfield] 15 Dec. 1959:1. Published by GenealogyBank.com, a division of NewsBank.

"Geologist's Prediction Proves Correct." *Illinois State Journal* [Springfield] 15 Dec. 1959: 2. Published by GenealogyBank.com, a division of NewsBank.

"Find Oil Again at Rochester." *Illinois State Journal* [Springfield] 17 June 1960: 25. Published by GenealogyBank.com, a division of NewsBank.

"Second Rochester Oil Well 'Shows Sign.'" *Illinois State Journal* [Springfield] 21 Jan.1960: 4. Published by GenealogyBank.com, a division of NewsBank.

Rochester Christian Church Dedication Service Program. "A Brief History of the Rochester Christian Church." 18 June 1955.

"South Fork Church Plans Rededication." *Illinois State Journal* [Springfield] 16 Aug.1959: 21. Published by GenealogyBank.com, a division of NewsBank.

"Sewer Plan is Discussed at Rochester." *Illinois State Journal* [Springfield] 17 May 1955: 1. Published by GenealogyBank.com, a division of NewsBank.

"Water Tank Contracts Let." *Illinois State Journal* [Springfield] 11 Feb. 1956: 5. Published by GenealogyBank.com, a division of NewsBank.

"Rochester Water Plan Approved." *Illinois State Journal* [Springfield] 17 Jan. 1956: 3. Published by GenealogyBank.com, a division of NewsBank.

"Sewer System Permit Granted." *Illinois State Journal* [Springfield] 4 Feb. 1956: 4. Published by GenealogyBank.com, a division of NewsBank.

"Rochester Gets U.S. Sewer Grant." *Illinois State Journal* [Springfield] 19 June 1959: 15. Published by GenealogyBank.com, a division of NewsBank.

"Rochester Given New Sewer Grant." *Illinois State Journal* [Springfield] 31 July 1959: 1. Published by GenealogyBank.com, a division of NewsBank.

"Rochester Schools to Open Next Week." *Illinois State Journal* [Springfield] 26 Aug. 1952: 10. Published by GenealogyBank.com, a division of NewsBank.

"Report Rochester Schools Crowded." *Illinois State Journal* [Springfield] 8 Sep. 1957: 12. Published by GenealogyBank.com, a division of NewsBank.

"Rochester Approves $125,000 for School." *Illinois State Journal* [Springfield] 2 July 1950: 31. Published by GenealogyBank.com, a division of NewsBank.

"Let Contract for Rochester School." *Illinois State Journal* [Springfield] 3 Sep. 1950: 2. Published by GenealogyBank.com, a division of NewsBank.

"Architect's Drawing Shows Proposed High School at Rochester." *Illinois State Journal* 2 Apr. 1958: 6. Published by GenealogyBank.com, a division of NewsBank.

"Rochester Board to Award Contract." *Illinois State Journal* [Springfield] 28 Aug. 1958: 9. Published by GenealogyBank.com, a division of NewsBank.

"Rochester Has More Students." *Illinois State Journal* [Springfield] 4 Sep. 1959: 27. Published by GenealogyBank.com, a division of NewsBank.

"Rochester Board, Teachers Sign Non-Communist Oath." *Illinois State Journal* [Springfield] 31 Mar. 1953: 9. Published by GenealogyBank.com, a division of NewsBank.

"Rochester School's Example." Editorial. *Illinois State Journal* [Springfield] 2 Apr. 1953: 12. Published by GenealogyBank.com, a division of NewsBank.

"Joseph McCarthy." *Wikipedia* 31 Dec. 2015 <https://en.wikipedia.org/wiki/Joseph_McCarthy>.

"Rochester Coach Resigns Position." *Illinois State Journal* [Springfield] 27 Mar. 1950: 15. Published by GenealogyBank.com, a division of NewsBank.

"Return to Class, Rochester Coach Urges Students." *Illinois State Journal* [Springfield] 29 Mar. 1950: 3. Published by GenealogyBank.com, a division of NewsBank.

"Students Lodge Protest." *Illinois State Journal* [Springfield] 28 Mar. 1950: 1. Published by GenealogyBank.com, a division of NewsBank.

"Coach's Plea Fails to End Students' Strike." *Register-Republic* [Rockford] 29 Mar. 1950: 1. Published by GenealogyBank.com, a division of NewsBank.

"Striking Students Will Go to School, Fight at Polls." *Illinois State Journal* [Springfield] 31 Mar. 1950: 1. Published by GenealogyBank.com, a division of NewsBank.

"Rochester Students to Rally Support for 3 Candidates." *Illinois State Journal* [Springfield] 6 Apr. 1950: 5. Published by GenealogyBank.com, a division of NewsBank.

"Anti-Starks Faction at Rochester School Wins." *Illinois State Journal* [Springfield] 9 Apr. 1950: 1. Published by GenealogyBank.com, a division of NewsBank.

"To Vote on Fire District May 27." *Illinois State Journal* [Springfield] 2 May 1950: 4. Published by GenealogyBank.com, a division of NewsBank.

"Rochester to Show Its New Fire Equipment." *Illinois State Journal* [Springfield] 28 Mar. 1951: 4. Published by GenealogyBank.com, a division of NewsBank.

"More Fire Apparatus." *Illinois State Journal* [Springfield] 7 Oct. 1953: 5. Published by GenealogyBank.com, a division of NewsBank.

"Estimated Loss at $75,000 in Rochester Elevator Fire." *Illinois State Journal* [Springfield] 14 June 1959: 4. Published by GenealogyBank.com, a division of NewsBank.

"Fiery Elevator at Rochester Falls in Ruins." *Illinois State Journal-Register [Springfield, IL]* 14 June 1959: 3. Published by GenealogyBank.com, a division of NewsBank.

Reck, Don. "Owner Places Firm's Loss At $160,000." *Illinois State Journal* [Springfield] 4 Nov. 1959: 1. Published by GenealogyBank.com, a division of NewsBank.

"Plan New Dial Telephone System for Rochester Area." *Illinois State Journal* [Springfield] 7 May 1953: 19. Published by GenealogyBank.com, a division of NewsBank.

"Rochester to go on Dial Telephone System Today." *Illinois State Journal* [Springfield] 18 Nov. 1953. Published by GenealogyBank.com, a division of NewsBank.

"Rochester Gets New Markers." *Illinois State Journal* [Springfield] 26 Apr. 1959: 16. Published by GenealogyBank.com, a division of NewsBank.

"Open Bids on Materials for Road Job." *Illinois State Journal* [Springfield] 19 Apr. 1956: 31. Published by GenealogyBank.com, a division of NewsBank.

"Reroute Buses to Avoid Unsafe Bridges." *Illinois State Journal* [Springfield] 4 Jan. 1950: 3. Published by GenealogyBank.com, a division of NewsBank.

"Relocating Stretch of Route 29." *Illinois State Journal* [Springfield] 23 July 1954: 20. Published by GenealogyBank.com, a division of NewsBank.

"Proposed Route 66 Bypass for Springfield." *Illinois State Journal* [Springfield] 8 Jan. 1956: 2. Published by GenealogyBank.com, a division of NewsBank.

"State and City Planning Groups Debate Proposed Locations of Route 66 Bypass." *Illinois State Journal* [Springfield] 11 Jan. 1956. Published by GenealogyBank.com, a division of NewsBank.

"Cilco (sic) Seeks to Operate Gas System at Rochester." *Illinois State Journal* [Springfield] 7 June 1956: 9. Published by GenealogyBank.com, a division of NewsBank.

Journal Capital Bureau. "I.C.C. Approves Expansion of Gas Facilities." *Illinois State Journal* [Springfield] 6 July 1956: 15. Published by GenealogyBank.com, a division of NewsBank.

"Thieves Get over $4000 at Rochester." *Illinois State Journal* [Springfield] 28 July 1956: 20. Published by GenealogyBank.com, a division of NewsBank.

"Couple in Cadillac Steal Man's Wallet." *Illinois State Journal* [Springfield] 4 Feb. 1957: 9. Published by GenealogyBank.com, a division of NewsBank.

"Rochester Station Robbed of $78.50." *Illinois State Journal* [Springfield] 5 June 1957: 14. Published by GenealogyBank.com, a division of NewsBank.

"Boys Admit Vandalism in Cemetery." *Illinois State Journal* [Springfield] 15 Apr. 1958: 4. Published by GenealogyBank.com, a division of NewsBank.

Candidate. Advertisement. *Illinois State Journal-Register* [Springfield, IL] 19 Jan. 1958: 4. Published by GenealogyBank.com, a division of NewsBank.

"Obituaries: Hugh A. Campbell." *Illinois State Journal-Register* [Springfield, IL] 19 Nov. 1983: 22. Published by GenealogyBank.com, a division of NewsBank.

"Lucille McCormick and Carl J. Rule Wed in Rushville." *Illinois State Journal* [Springfield] 13 Mar. 1950: 18. Published by GenealogyBank.com, a division of NewsBank.

"To Celebrate Date: Mr. and Mrs. Alonzo N. Wilson." *Illinois State Journal-Register* [Springfield, IL] 5 Dec. 1954: 52. Published by GenealogyBank.com, a division of NewsBank.

"Golden Wedding Day Nears." *Illinois State Journal* [Springfield] 21 Aug. 1955: 8. Published by GenealogyBank.com, a division of NewsBank.

"Mrs. Mary Miller, Rochester, is 96." *Illinois State Journal-Register* [Springfield, IL] 22 Feb. 1953: 5. Published by GenealogyBank.com, a division of NewsBank.

"To Mark Day: Jasper Easley." *Illinois State Journal* [Springfield] 31 Mar. 1950: 2. Published by GenealogyBank.com, a division of NewsBank.

"Does It Hurt?" *Illinois State Journal* [Springfield] 26 Apr. 1955: 18. Published by GenealogyBank.com, a division of NewsBank.

"History of Salk." 2016. Salk Institute for Biological Studies, La Jolla, CA. 9 July 2016 <http://www.salk.edu/about/history-of-salk/jonas-salk/>.

"Polio Vaccine." *Wikipedia* 16 Jan. 2016 <https://en.wikipedia.org/wiki/Polio_vaccine>.

Oak Hills. Advertisement. *Illinois State Journal-Register* [Springfield, IL] 31 Mar. 1957: 66. Published by GenealogyBank.com, a division of NewsBank.

Oak Hills Estates Offers Open House. Advertisement. *Illinois State Journal-Register* [Springfield, IL] 23 Aug. 1959: 26. Published by GenealogyBank.com, a division of NewsBank.

"Oak Hills Project under City Plan." *Illinois State Journal* [Springfield] 12 Aug. 1959: 1. Published by GenealogyBank.com, a division of NewsBank.

"City Passes Ordinance for Control of Subdivisions." *Illinois State Journal* [Springfield] 14 Aug. 1957: 4. Published by GenealogyBank.com, a division of NewsBank.

"Council Approves Park Ticket Plan: The Commission . . ." *Illinois State Journal* [Springfield] 26 Aug. 1959: 1. Published by GenealogyBank.com, a division of NewsBank.

"Obituaries: Roy T. Shreve." *Illinois State Journal* [Springfield] 4 Aug. 1950: 18. Published by GenealogyBank.com, a division of NewsBank.

"Woodruff Funeral Set." *Illinois State Journal* [Springfield] 5 Jan. 1952: 3. Published by GenealogyBank.com, a division of NewsBank.

"Driver Killed in Arizona." *Illinois State Journal* [Springfield] 30 Oct. 1951: 7. Published by GenealogyBank.com, a division of NewsBank.

"Obituaries: Albert E. Mavis." *Illinois State Journal* [Springfield] 6 June 1955: 9. Published by GenealogyBank.com, a division of NewsBank.

"G.A. Wolford of Rochester Dies at Age 88." *Illinois State Journal* [Springfield] 6 Jan. 1959: 2. Published by GenealogyBank.com, a division of NewsBank.

"Wolford to Manage Farm Bureau Nine." *Illinois State Journal* [Springfield] 21 Apr. 1932: 10. Published by GenealogyBank.com, a division of NewsBank.

Grand opening. Advertisement. *Illinois State Journal* [Springfield] 24 July 1953: 2. Published by GenealogyBank.com, a division of NewsBank.

$3,500.00 Inventory! Public Auction Restaurant Close-Out. Advertisement. *Illinois State Journal-Register* [Springfield, IL] 29 Sep. 1957: 43. Published by GenealogyBank.com, a division of NewsBank.

The Rumen Story. Advertisement. *Illinois State Journal* [Springfield] 13 Dec. 1954: 3. Published by GenealogyBank.com, a division of NewsBank.

"Dog Lives After Marble is Cut from Lung." *Illinois State Journal* [Springfield] 13 May 1954: 38. Published by GenealogyBank.com, a division of NewsBank.

Auction Sale of Business Property. Advertisement. *Illinois State Journal-Register* [Springfield, IL] 10 Dec. 1950: 58. Published by GenealogyBank.com, a division of NewsBank.

Big Community Sale. Advertisement. *Illinois State Journal-Register* [Springfield, IL] 3 Dec. 1950: 27. Published by GenealogyBank.com, a division of NewsBank.

Raney Close Out Auction Continues. Advertisement. *Illinois State Journal* [Springfield] 2 Aug. 1951: 25. Published by GenealogyBank.com, a division of NewsBank.

Executor's Auction Sale: Residential and Personal Property of Woodruff Estate. Advertisement. *Illinois State Journal-Register* [Springfield, IL] 3 Feb. 1952: 48.

Estate Auction Sale: Estate of Mabelle Raney Mayes, Deceased. Advertisement. *Illinois State Journal-Register* [Springfield, IL] 7 July 1957: 39. Published by GenealogyBank.com, a division of NewsBank.

Estate Auction Sale: Real Estate and Personal Property—Easley. Advertisement. *Illinois State Journal-Register* [Springfield, IL] 18 May 1958: 47. Published by GenealogyBank.com, a division of NewsBank.

"Neighbors Harvest 30 Acres of Wheat for Injured Rochester Farmer." *Illinois State Journal-Register* [Springfield] 6 July 1952: 2. Published by GenealogyBank.com, a division of NewsBank.

"Neighbors Aid Sick Farmer at Rochester." *Illinois State Journal-Register* [Springfield, IL] 10 Oct. 1954: 41. Published by GenealogyBank.com, a division of NewsBank.

"Combine Oats for Ailing Rochester Man." *Illinois State Journal* [Springfield] 14 July 1955: 32. Published by GenealogyBank.com, a division of NewsBank.

"Rochester Band Club Plans Benefit Sale." *Illinois State Journal* [Springfield] 6 Dec. 1950: 10. Published by GenealogyBank.com, a division of NewsBank.

"Rochester Community Will Aid Hospital Fund Drive." *Illinois State Journal* [Springfield] 31 May 1955: 10. Published by GenealogyBank.com, a division of NewsBank.

"Hospital Drive Tops Quota." *Illinois State Journal* [Springfield] 24 June 1955: 1. Published by GenealogyBank.com, a division of NewsBank.

"Porchlight Parade Set." *Illinois State Journal* [Springfield] 24 Jan. 1956: 8. Published by GenealogyBank.com, a division of NewsBank.

"Play Program at Rochester Will Begin Next Week." *Illinois State Journal* [Springfield] 3 June 1955: 20. Published by GenealogyBank.com, a division of NewsBank.

"Civil Defense to Offer Home Protection Class." *Illinois State Journal* [Springfield] 26 Nov. 1957: 10. Published by GenealogyBank.com, a division of NewsBank.

"Rochester Artist Paints Scenes of Middle West." *Illinois State Journal* [Springfield] 28 Aug. 1950: 2. Published by GenealogyBank.com, a division of NewsBank.

"Neal's Grove Settled by Pioneers." *Illinois State Journal* [Springfield] 28 Feb. 1951: 25. Published by GenealogyBank.com, a division of NewsBank.

"Other Area Memorials." *State Journal-Register* [Springfield, IL] 26 May 2008: 17. Published by GenealogyBank.com, a division of NewsBank.

Taft, Justin. *As I Saw It*. Bloomington, IN: 1st Books Library, 2004.

1960s References

Kious, Roberta. "Rochester Gets Cable-Tv Proposal." *Illinois State Journal* [Springfield] 20 Nov. 1966: 16. Published by GenealogyBank.com, a division of NewsBank.

"Rochester Approves Cable Tv Franchise." *Illinois State Journal* [Springfield] 5 Oct. 1966: 6. Published by GenealogyBank.com, a division of NewsBank.

"Village Board Agrees on Annexation Issue." *Illinois State Journal* [Springfield] 27 Oct. 1967: 15. Published by GenealogyBank.com, a division of NewsBank.

Lexington Heights Has Advantages. Advertisement. *State Journal-Register* [Springfield, IL] 26 Aug. 1962: 46. Published by GenealogyBank.com, a division of NewsBank.

"Rochester Trustees Okay South Walnut Subdivision." *Illinois State Journal* [Springfield] 3 Nov. 1965: 22. Published by GenealogyBank.com, a division of NewsBank.

"Board Approves Plans for New Sub-Division." *Illinois State Journal* [Springfield] 10 June 1965: 43. Published by GenealogyBank.com, a division of NewsBank.

"Rochester Board Okays Final Plat." *Illinois State Journal* [Springfield] 8 May 1968: 5. Published by GenealogyBank.com, a division of NewsBank.

"Rochester Board OKs Use of Water, Sewers." *Illinois State Journal* [Springfield] 4 Dec. 1968: 6. Published by GenealogyBank.com, a division of NewsBank.

"Rochester Plans Stable Ordinance." *Illinois State Journal* [Springfield] 8 July 1965: 17. Published by GenealogyBank.com, a division of NewsBank.

"Rochester Board Sets Meeting." *Illinois State Journal* [Springfield] 10 Sep. 1965: 23. Published by GenealogyBank.com, a division of NewsBank.

"Rochester Board Hears Cost of Plan." *Illinois State Journal* [Springfield] 8 Dec. 1965: 5. Published by GenealogyBank.com, a division of NewsBank.

"New Marshal, Improvements Top Discussion." *Illinois State Journal* [Springfield] 7 Dec. 1966: 27. Published by GenealogyBank.com, a division of NewsBank.

"Rochester Board to Take Action on Tax Petitions." *Illinois State Journal* [Springfield] 9 Apr. 1969: 26. Published by GenealogyBank.com, a division of NewsBank.

"Rochester Gets Urban Plan Grant." *Illinois State Journal* [Springfield] 3 June 1968: 26. Published by GenealogyBank.com, a division of NewsBank.

"Village Sets May 15-21 to 'Clean Up.'" *Illinois State Journal* [Springfield] 4 May 1966: 13. Published by GenealogyBank.com, a division of NewsBank.

"Rochester, City Sign Water Pact." *Illinois State Journal* [Springfield] 13 Apr. 1960: 10. Published by GenealogyBank.com, a division of NewsBank.

"Rochester Families Protest Water Rates." *Illinois State Journal* [Springfield] 3 Oct. 1960: 9. Published by GenealogyBank.com, a division of NewsBank.

"Plant Equipment Bids Open." *Illinois State Journal* [Springfield] 16 Feb. 1966: 19. Published by GenealogyBank.com, a division of NewsBank.

"City Firm Makes Low Bid on Project." *Illinois State Journal* [Springfield] 20 Apr. 1966: 16. Published by GenealogyBank.com, a division of NewsBank.

"Water Projects Okayed By Board." *Illinois State Journal* [Springfield] 27 July 1966: 7. Published by GenealogyBank.com, a division of NewsBank.

"Rochester Gets Loan for Water Facilities." *Illinois State Journal* [Springfield] 17 May 1969: 3. Published by GenealogyBank.com, a division of NewsBank.

"Rochester Looks to Future." *Illinois State Journal* [Springfield] 10 Nov. 1960: 2. Published by GenealogyBank.com, a division of NewsBank.

"Rochester Planning for Sewers." *Illinois State Journal* [Springfield] 25 July 1965: 6. Published by GenealogyBank.com, a division of NewsBank.

"Rochester Board Approves Phase 1 of Sewer Plans." *Illinois State Journal* [Springfield] 23 Sep. 1969: 4. Published by GenealogyBank.com, a division of NewsBank.

"County Enrollment up by 4.4 Per Cent." *Illinois State Journal* [Springfield] 12 Sep. 1963: 1. Published by GenealogyBank.com, a division of NewsBank.

"Rochester Bond Issue, Taxes Win." *Illinois State Journal* [Springfield] 20 Dec. 1964: 8.

"Tomorrow's Leaders Walk From Old to New." *Illinois State Journal* [Springfield] 31 Jan. 1967: 3. Published by GenealogyBank.com, a division of NewsBank.

"School Tennis Courts Planned for Rochester." *Illinois State Journal* [Springfield] 1 Apr. 1967: 25. Published by GenealogyBank.com, a division of NewsBank.

"Board to Participate in Vocational School." *Illinois State Journal* [Springfield] 7 May 1969: 2. Published by GenealogyBank.com, a division of NewsBank.

"Students Revive Art of Madrigal Singing." *Illinois State Journal* [Springfield] 11 Dec. 1969: 45. Published by GenealogyBank.com, a division of NewsBank.

"Lack of Classroom Space Reviewed." *Illinois State Journal* [Springfield] 11 Sep. 1969: 20. Published by GenealogyBank.com, a division of NewsBank.

"Dedicate New Church at Rochester." *Illinois State Journal* [Springfield] 6 Nov. 1966: 27. Published by GenealogyBank.com, a division of NewsBank.

"Rochester Methodist Church Fund Drive Passes Goal." *Illinois State Journal* [Springfield] 12 May 1960: 10. Published by GenealogyBank.com, a division of NewsBank.

"Site For Rochester Church Purchased." *The State Journal-Register* [Springfield, IL] 3 Dec. 1967: 17. Published by GenealogyBank.com, a division of NewsBank.

"Rochester to Dedicate Post Office." *Illinois State Journal* [Springfield] 23 May 1962: 7. Published by GenealogyBank.com, a division of NewsBank.

"Dedicate Rochester Post Office." *Illinois State Journal* [Springfield] 28 May 1962: 19. Published by GenealogyBank.com, a division of NewsBank.

"Sun Brightens Road Prospects." *Illinois State Journal* [Springfield] 25 Sep. 1965: 6. Published by GenealogyBank.com, a division of NewsBank.

"Bridge Contract Given to Decatur Firm." *Illinois State Journal* [Springfield] 8 Sep. 1966: 17. Published by GenealogyBank.com, a division of NewsBank.

"Rochester Witnesses UFO Debut." *Illinois State Journal* [Springfield] 31 Mar. 1966: 1. Published by GenealogyBank.com, a division of NewsBank.

"Malfunctioning Oil Burner Causes Blaze." *Illinois State Journal* [Springfield] 3 Apr. 1968: 24. Published by GenealogyBank.com, a division of NewsBank.

Hugh Fire Sale. Advertisement. *Illinois State Journal* [Springfield] 12 Apr. 1968: 33. Published by GenealogyBank.com, a division of NewsBank.

Lumber Yard Big Salvage Sale." *Illinois State Journal* [Springfield] 17 Apr. 1968: 27. Published by GenealogyBank.com, a division of NewsBank.

"Radiology Test Station Slated for Rochester." *Illinois State Journal* [Springfield] 13 Nov. 1969: 46. Published by GenealogyBank.com, a division of NewsBank.

"'Project Alert' Held in Rochester." *Illinois State Journal* [Springfield] 10 Nov. 1961: 10. Published by GenealogyBank.com, a division of NewsBank.

"Rochester Lanes Nears Completion." *Illinois State Journal* [Springfield] 15 June 1960: 10. Published by GenealogyBank.com, a division of NewsBank.

Strub, Dick. "Afterthoughts." *Illinois State Journal* [Springfield] 10 Sep. 1961: 21. Published by GenealogyBank.com, a division of NewsBank.

Grand Opening. Advertisement. *Illinois State Journal* [Springfield] 5 Oct. 1961: 2. Published by GenealogyBank.com, a division of NewsBank.

"City Man Buys Herald Papers." *Illinois State Journal* [Springfield] 13 May 1967: 5. Published by GenealogyBank.com, a division of NewsBank.

Wood, Bill. "Outdoor with Wood." *The State Journal-Register [Springfield, IL]* 7 July 1963: 44. Published by GenealogyBank.com, a division of NewsBank.

Order B&O Train Halt at Crossing." *Illinois State Journal* [Springfield] 15 Oct. 1960: 7. Published by GenealogyBank.com, a division of NewsBank.

Fugate, Dennis. "Fire Destroys B&O Sugar Creek Bridge." *Illinois State Journal* [Springfield] 1 May 1968: 1. Published by GenealogyBank.com, a division of NewsBank.

"New Oil Pool Discovered near Rochester." *Illinois State Journal* [Springfield] 20 Oct. 1967: 5. Published by GenealogyBank.com, a division of NewsBank.

"New Area Oil Field Tapped." *Illinois State Journal* [Springfield] 11 Sep. 1969: 2. Published by GenealogyBank.com, a division of NewsBank.

"Back Rochester Reassessment." *Illinois State Journal* [Springfield] 2 Mar. 1960: 4. Published by GenealogyBank.com, a division of NewsBank.

"Rochester Project Decision Due Soon." *Illinois State Journal* [Springfield] 19 Dec. 1960: 1. Published by GenealogyBank.com, a division of NewsBank.

"Thoman Reveals New Plan for Checking Assessments." *Illinois State Journal* [Springfield] 30 Mar. 1961: 1. Published by GenealogyBank.com, a division of NewsBank.

"Rochester Man Named County Tax Supervisor." *Illinois State Journal* [Springfield] 3 Mar. 1962: 4. Published by GenealogyBank.com, a division of NewsBank.

"Farm Family Plans for Foreign Guest." *Illinois State Journal* [Springfield] 7 May 1965: 14. Published by GenealogyBank.com, a division of NewsBank.

"Rochester Junior to Attend Conference." *Illinois State Journal* [Springfield] 21 Nov. 1968: 18. Published by GenealogyBank.com, a division of NewsBank.

"Just a Touch Here and There." *Illinois State Journal* [Springfield] 22 July 1967: 3. Published by GenealogyBank.com, a division of NewsBank.

"Democratic Candidates in Election Nov. 8: Sheriff Hugh A. Campbell." *The State Journal Register* [Springfield, IL] 6 Nov. 1966: 35. Published by GenealogyBank.com, a division of NewsBank.

Muraro, Joan. "Bit of Ireland near Rochester." *The State Journal-Register* [Springfield, IL] 31 July 1966: 31. Published by GenealogyBank.com, a division of NewsBank.

Kelly, Judith. "Spinners Revive Bygone Era." *The State Journal-Register* [Springfield, IL] 2 Apr. 1967: 41. Published by GenealogyBank.com, a division of NewsBank.

Kious, Roberta. "Small Muscle Disease Victim Fights to Gain Use of Her Body." *Illinois State Journal* [Springfield] 6 Feb. 1969: 14. Published by GenealogyBank.com, a division of NewsBank.

"Rochester Charters Newest Lions Club." *Illinois State Journal* [Springfield] 23 July 1965: 7. Published by GenealogyBank.com, a division of NewsBank.

"Music, Literary Clubs: Chicken Bristle Chapter of Questers," *Illinois State Journal* [Springfield] 27 May 1969: 38. Published by GenealogyBank.com, a division of NewsBank.

"Rochester Lodge to Mark 100th Anniversary." *Illinois State Journal* [Springfield] 17 Oct.1969: 15. Published by GenealogyBank.com, a division of NewsBank.

"Area Man Killed in Viet Combat." *Illinois State Journal* [Springfield] 9 Jan. 1969: 1. Published by GenealogyBank.com, a division of NewsBank.

Vietnam Veterans Memorial Fund. "The Wall of Faces." 30 July 2016 <http://www.vvmf.org/Wall-of-Faces/52014/RICHARD-G-THUNMAN>.

"Obituaries: Thomas Bennett." *Illinois State Journal* [Springfield] 15 Mar. 1962: 48. Published by GenealogyBank.com, a division of NewsBank.

"Obituaries: Dr. Lyman D. Wright." *Illinois State Journal* [Springfield] 4 Jan. 1962: 40. Published by GenealogyBank.com, a division of NewsBank.

"Obituaries: Richard O. Coe." *Illinois State Journal* [Springfield] 1 June 1966: 6. Published by GenealogyBank.com, a division of NewsBank.

"New Phone Exchange Now in Use." *Illinois State Journal* [Springfield] 18 Sep. 1960: 4. Published by GenealogyBank.com, a division of NewsBank.

"Start Work on Strip at Dragway." *Illinois State Journal* [Springfield] 4 May 1961: 24. Published by GenealogyBank.com, a division of NewsBank.

Opening of the Pleasant Grove Drag Strip." Advertisement. *Illinois State Journal* [Springfield] 17 Apr. 1960: 16. Published by GenealogyBank.com, a division of NewsBank.

Davis, Norman. "Best Season at Drag City." *Illinois State Journal* [Springfield] 4 July 1964: 7. Published by GenealogyBank.com, a division of NewsBank.

Bonefeste, Joseph. Personal interview. n.d. 2015.

Jostes, David. Personal interview. n.d. 2015.

"DDD System Begins in Area Sunday." *Illinois State Journal* [Springfield] 20 Jan. 1962: 3. Published by GenealogyBank.com, a division of NewsBank.

"Rochester Names New Supervisor." *Illinois State Journal* [Springfield] 15 Nov. 1962: 56. Published by GenealogyBank.com, a division of NewsBank.

"Taft Takes Absence Leave to Campaign." *Illinois State Journal* [Springfield] 1 May 1968: 4. Published by GenealogyBank.com, a division of NewsBank.

Taft, Justin. *As I Saw It*. Bloomington, IN: 1st Books Library, 2004.

"These Men are Candidates for Con-Con: Maurice Scott." *Illinois State Journal* [Springfield] 11 Sep. 1969: 10. Published by GenealogyBank.com, a division of NewsBank.

"Scott, Maurice: Interview and Memoir." *Illinois Digital Archives* Illinois State Library and Office of the Illinois Secretary of State. Springfield, IL. 1981. 21 Jan. 2016 <http://www.idaillinois.org/cdm/ref/collection/uis/id/3983>.

"Some Sangamon County Elections . . . The Citizens Ticket." *Daily Illinois State Journal* [Springfield] 18 Apr. 1888: 1. Published by GenealogyBank.com, a division of NewsBank.

"Louis Persinger, Great Violinist." *Illinois State Register* [Springfield] 16 June 1912: 13. Published by GenealogyBank.com, a division of NewsBank.

Persinger, Brandon L. Telephone interview with the author. Dec. 2015.

"Wins Laurels with His Violin." *Illinois State Journal* [Springfield] 2 Dec. 1912: 5. Published by GenealogyBank.com, a division of NewsBank.

"Plays Violin for Woman near Death." *Illinois State Journal* [Springfield] 14 Feb. 1914: 7. Published by GenealogyBank.com, a division of NewsBank.

"Boy Violinist Taught by Former Rochester Man Thrills Gotham." *Illinois State Journal* [Springfield] 29 Dec. 1928: 3. Published by GenealogyBank.com, a division of NewsBank.

"Louis Persinger." *Wikipedia*. 26 Sep. 2015 <https://en.wikipedia.org/wiki/Louis_Persinger>.

Violinhunter. "Prone to Violins: Louis Persinger." Feb. 2011. 26 Sep. 2015 <http://pronetoviolins.blogspot.com/2011/02/persinger.html>.

"Rochester Centennial Preview: 1869-1969." *Rochester & Lake Springfield Herald* [Rochester, IL] 27 June 1969: np.

"Findley to Dedicate Military Memorial." *Illinois State Journal* [Springfield] 28 June 1969: 18. Published by GenealogyBank.com, a division of NewsBank.

"Rochester Centennial: 1869-1969." Rochester, Illinois: 1969.

"Rochester Selects July Days for Centennial Celebration." *Illinois State Journal* [Springfield] 8 Mar. 1969: 5. Published by GenealogyBank.com, a division of NewsBank.

"Rochester to Sell Centennial Wares." *Illinois State Journal* [Springfield] 26 Mar. 1969: 30. Published by GenealogyBank.com, a division of NewsBank.

Opening of the Pleasant Grove Drag Strip." Advertisement. *Illinois State Journal* [Springfield] 17 Apr. 1960: 16. Published by GenealogyBank.com, a division of NewsBank.

1970s References

Duffey, Helen. "Narrative for the Slide Segement of Bi-Centennial Program – Entitled 'Rochester – Yesterday and Today.'" Chicken Bristle Chapter of Questers. 1 Apr. 1976.

Ramblewood Rochester. Advertisement. *Illinois State Journal* [Springfield] 10 Nov. 1974: 51. Published by GenealogyBank.com, a division of NewsBank.

Bruzan, Pam. "Rochester Board Talks about Street Lights." *Illinois State Journal* [Springfield] 4 Oct.1972: 4. Published by GenealogyBank.com, a division of NewsBank.

Bruzan, Pam. "Village Growth Planned." *Illinois State Journal* [Springfield] 26 July, 1973: 13. Published by GenealogyBank.com, a division of NewsBank.

Bruzan, Pam, and Ray Bruzan. "Houses Have Roots, Too." *Illinois Times* [Springfield] 2-8 Dec. 1977: 22.

Bruzan, Pam. "Rochester Leash Law Sets Stiff Fines for Violators." *Illinois State Journal* [Springfield] 6 Sep. 1973: 13. Published by GenealogyBank.com, a division of NewsBank.

Bruzan, Pam. "Actions by Rochester Village Board Reflect Growth, Point toward Expansion." *Illinois State Journal* [Springfield] 6 Jan. 1976: 14. Published by GenealogyBank.com, a division of NewsBank.

Bruzan, Pam. "Rochester to Inspect Commercial Buildings During Construction." *State Journal-Register* [Springfield, IL] 4 May 1978: 17. Published by GenealogyBank.com, a division of NewsBank.

Bruzan, Pam. "Permits Come before Building: Rochester Acts on Zoning Policy." *State Journal Register* [Springfield, IL] 6 Dec. 1978: 15. Published by GenealogyBank.com, a division of NewsBank.

"Name 2 to Rochester Planning Panel." *State Journal-Register* [Springfield, IL] 7 Mar. 1978: 15. Published by GenealogyBank.com, a division of NewsBank.

Notice to Contractors: Camelot Sub-Division. Advertisement. *State Journal-Register* [Springfield, IL] 25 June 1971: 36. Published by GenealogyBank.com, a division of NewsBank.

Notice to Contractors: Camelot Sub-Division. Advertisement. *State Journal-Register* [Springfield, IL] 25 Nov. 1973: 50. Published by GenealogyBank.com, a division of NewsBank.

"Rochester Water Pressure Low." *Illinois State Journal* [Springfield] 3 Aug. 1972: 11. Published by GenealogyBank.com, a division of NewsBank.

"Second Leak is Repaired in Rochester Water Main." *Illinois State Journal* [Springfield] 14 Sep. 1972: 31. Published by GenealogyBank.com, a division of NewsBank.

"Rochester, East Lake Areas Must Continue to Boil Water." *Illinois State Journal* [Springfield] 16 Nov. 1972: 21. Published by GenealogyBank.com, a division of NewsBank.

"Rochester 'Water War' Settled." *State Journal-Register* [Springfield, IL] 15 Sep. 1976: 60. Published by GenealogyBank.com, a division of NewsBank.

"Rochester Water Again Low." *State Journal-Register* [Springfield, IL] 24 Aug. 1976: 16. Published by GenealogyBank.com, a division of NewsBank.

Bruzan, Pam & Jim Lukas. "Rochester Asked to Conserve Water after CWLP Cuts off Auxiliary Main." *State Journal-Register* [Springfield, IL] 28 May 1976. Published by GenealogyBank.com, a division of NewsBank.

"New Police Chief Named: Water Usage Restrictions Approved at Rochester." *State Journal-Register* [Springfield, IL] 9 Feb 1977: 31. Published by GenealogyBank.com, a division of NewsBank.

Bruzan, Pam. "Rochester Water Customers Face 50% or More Rate Boost." *State Journal-Register* [Springfield, IL] 13 July 1977: 2. Published by GenealogyBank.com, a division of NewsBank.

Bruzan, Pam. "Rochester Rates Go up 80 Per Cent." *State Journal-Register* [Springfield, IL] 19 July 1977: 17. Published by GenealogyBank.com, a division of NewsBank.

Bruzan, Pam. "Rochester Approves Water Pact." *State Journal-Register* [Springfield, IL] 28 June 1977: 18. Published by GenealogyBank.com, a division of NewsBank.

"Rochester Talks Pact, Own Water Source." *State Journal-Register* [Springfield, IL] 19 Jan. 1977: 32. Published by GenealogyBank.com, a division of NewsBank.

"Rochester Board Oks Sale of Sewage Bonds." *Illinois State Journal* [Springfield] 5 May 1971: 2. Published by GenealogyBank.com, a division of NewsBank.

Bruzan, Pam. "Rochester Board Covers Multiple Topics at Meeting." *Illinois State Journal* [Springfield] 8 Nov. 1972: 42. Published by GenealogyBank.com, a division of NewsBank.

Bruzan, Pam. "Area Sewer Problem Inching to Solution." *State Journal-Register* [Springfield, IL] 17 Sep. 1975: 30. Published by GenealogyBank.com, a division of NewsBank.

Bruzan, Pam. "Sewer System Changes Recommended by Study." *State Journal-Register* [Springfield, IL] 25 May 1978: 35. Published by GenealogyBank.com, a division of NewsBank.

"Meeting to Upgrade Sewage Facilities Set." *State Journal-Register* [Springfield, IL] 13 June 1978: 30. Published by GenealogyBank.com, a division of NewsBank.

"Road Project Gets Attention." *Illinois State Journal* [Springfield] 6 July 1973: 10. Published by GenealogyBank.com, a division of NewsBank.

"County to Request Rural Road Construction Funds." *Illinois State Journal* [Springfield] 11 Aug. 1973: 5. Published by GenealogyBank.com, a division of NewsBank.

Carstens, Caryl. "Taylor-Stevenson Extension Target of County Road Work." *State Journal-Register* [Springfield, IL] 14 Dec. 1974: 36. Published by GenealogyBank.com, a division of NewsBank.

Bruzan, Pam. "Rochester Board Votes to Award Contract for Street Improvements." *State Journal-Register* [Springfield, IL] 8 July 1975: 10. Published by GenealogyBank.com, a division of NewsBank.

"Discuss Main Street Relocation at Rochester." *State Journal-Register* [Springfield, IL] 21 Jan. 1975: 9. Published by GenealogyBank.com, a division of NewsBank.

"West Main Improvement Set to Start July 28." *Rochester Times* [Rochester, IL] 28 July 1975: 1.

"Woman's Club Ecology Pickup Saturday 'Good as Ever.'" *Rochester Times* [Rochester, IL] 14 Mar 1975: 4.

"Your Energy Fair." Rochester Woman's Club. 26 Oct. 1979.

"Village Board Will Let Rochester Vote on Liquor Licenses Issue." *State Journal-Register* [Springfield, IL] 15 Sep. 1976: 60. Published by GenealogyBank.com, a division of NewsBank.

Bruzan, Pam. "But Referendum Required to go 'Wet:' Rochester Repeals Liquor Law." *State Journal-Register* [Springfield, IL] 3 Oct. 1976: 12. Published by GenealogyBank.com, a division of NewsBank.

"Rochester Liquor License." *State Journal-Register* [Springfield, IL] 12 Nov. 1976. Published by GenealogyBank.com, a division of NewsBank.

"Rochester Still Unsure of its Wet or Dry Status." *State Journal-Register* [Springfield, IL] 24 Nov. 1976: 12. Published by GenealogyBank.com, a division of NewsBank.

Bruzan, Pam. "Rochester Seeks to Retain 'Dry' Status in Liquor Sales." *State Journal-Register* [Springfield, IL] 7 Dec. 1976: 16. Published by GenealogyBank.com, a division of NewsBank.

"Sale of Liquor May be on Rochester Ballot." *State Journal-Register* [Springfield, IL] 9 Jan. 1979: 5. Published by GenealogyBank.com, a division of NewsBank.

"Village Dry since 1941: Legal Snags Wash out Rochester 'Wet' Move." *State Journal-Register* [Springfield, IL] 1 Feb. 1979: 8. Published by GenealogyBank.com, a division of NewsBank.

"Rochester May Add Classrooms." *Illinois State Journal* [Springfield] 20 Jan. 1970: 13. Published by GenealogyBank.com, a division of NewsBank.

"Rochester Board Okays Spending." *Illinois State Journal* [Springfield] 8 Apr. 1970: 11. Published by GenealogyBank.com, a division of NewsBank.

"Rochester Buys Land by School." *Illinois State Journal* [Springfield] 15 Apr. 1970: 23. Published by GenealogyBank.com, a division of NewsBank.

Bruzan, Pam. "Rochester School Board Adopts Limited Busing Plan." *Illinois State Journal* [Springfield] 18 Oct. 1972: 37. Published by GenealogyBank.com, a division of NewsBank.

Bruzan, Pam. "Rochester Board Sees 12 Month Schooling—Someday." Illinois State Journal [Springfield] 6 Oct. 1972: 11. Published by GenealogyBank.com, a division of NewsBank.

Bruzan, Pam. "Board Eyes Building Cost." *Illinois State Journal* [Springfield] 2 May 1973: 43. Published by GenealogyBank.com, a division of NewsBank.

Bruzan, Pam. "Rochester Voters Must Make Double Decision on Schools." *Illinois State Journal* [Springfield] 17 Oct. 1973: 45. Published by GenealogyBank.com, a division of NewsBank.

Bruzan, Pam. "Despite Bond Success, Growing Pains are Felt." *Illinois State Journal* [Springfield] 4 Feb.1974: 25. Published by GenealogyBank.com, a division of NewsBank.

Bruzan, Pam. "Rochester School Construction Program Moves to Second Stage." *State Journal-Register* [Springfield, IL] 24 Sep. 1974: 14. Published by GenealogyBank.com, a division of NewsBank.

Bruzan, Pam. "Tri-City School Head to Rochester Post." *State Journal-Register* [Springfield, IL] 1 Feb. 1975: 32. Published by GenealogyBank.com, a division of NewsBank.

Taylor, Jack K. Personal interview. 23 Apr. 2017.

Bruzan, Pam. "Citizens' Committee Will Study Finances of Rochester Schools." *State Journal-Register* [Springfield, IL] 14 Sep. 1976: 16. Published by GenealogyBank.com, a division of NewsBank.

"Rochester Board Eyes Location of New Track." *State Journal-Register* [Springfield, IL] 27 Apr. 1976: 18. Published by GenealogyBank.com, a division of NewsBank.

Bruzan, Pam. "Rochester School Board Votes to Cut Four Teaching Positions." *State Journal-Register* [Springfield, IL] 16 Mar. 1976: 23. Published by GenealogyBank.com, a division of NewsBank.

Bruzan, Pam. "Possible Teacher Cutbacks Draws Crowd at Rochester." *State Journal-Register* [Springfield, IL] 30 Mar. 1976: 11. Published by GenealogyBank.com, a division of NewsBank.

"Rochester Unit Cutting Its Budget." *State Journal-Register* [Springfield, IL] 24 Nov. 1976: 9. Published by GenealogyBank.com, a division of NewsBank.

Bruzan, Pam. "School Board to Start Paring." *Times* [Rochester, IL] 26 Nov. 1976: 1.

"Budget Cut Reaction Worries Rochester Board of Education." *State Journal-Register* [Springfield, IL] 18 Jan. 1977: 3. Published by GenealogyBank.com, a division of NewsBank.

"Rochester School Budget Cuts Meeting Draws Crowd Estimated at 500 Persons." *State Journal-Register* [Springfield, IL] 9 Feb. 1977: 25. Published by GenealogyBank.com, a division of NewsBank.

Bruzan, Pam. "Rochester Board Considers School Tax Boost Referendum." *State Journal-Register* [Springfield, IL] 7 Sep. 1977: 22. Published by GenealogyBank.com, a division of NewsBank.

Bruzan, Pam. "Rochester to Vote Nov. 19 on Proposed School Tax Boost." *State Journal-Register* [Springfield, IL] 10 Nov. 1977: 52. Published by GenealogyBank.com, a division of NewsBank.

Bruzan, Pam. "If Nov. 19 Referendum Fails: School Board Votes $90,000 in Budget Cuts Including Sports." *Times* [Rochester] 28 Oct 1977: 1.

"School Tax Referendum Passes 1012-721." *Times* [Rochester] 25 Nov. 1977: 1.

Bruzan, Pam. "Rochester School Board Votes to Restore Several Programs." *State Journal-Register* [Springfield, IL] 22 Feb. 1978: 23. Published by GenealogyBank.com, a division of NewsBank.

Bruzan, Pam. "Rochester School Budget Looks Healthier." *State Journal-Register* [Springfield, IL] 15 Sep. 1978: 23. Published by GenealogyBank.com, a division of NewsBank.

Bruzan, Pam. "Rochester Gets Bid On Bonds." *Illinois State Journal* [Springfield] 8 Feb. 1972: 17. Published by GenealogyBank.com, a division of NewsBank.

Bruzan, Pam. "Rochester Discusses Space Offer." *Illinois State Journal* [Springfield] 4 Apr. 1972: 13. Published by GenealogyBank.com, a division of NewsBank.

"Legion Hall To Be Leased: Rochester Board Okays Offices." *Illinois State Journal* [Springfield] 11 Apr. 1972: 13. Published by GenealogyBank.com, a division of NewsBank.

Bruzan, Pam. "How to Get a Traffic Light Installed: The Story of How One Village Did It." *Illinois Issues* Jan. 1975: 19. Published by GenealogyBank.com, a division of NewsBank.

"Rochester Talks Highway Crossing." *Illinois State Journal* [Springfield] 20 June 1973: 16. Published by GenealogyBank.com, a division of NewsBank.

Bruzan, Pam. "Rochester to Install Signal Lights." *Illinois State Journal* [Springfield] 19 Sep. 1972: 13. Published by GenealogyBank.com, a division of NewsBank.

"Rochester Trustee Resigns." *State Journal-Register* [Springfield, IL] 6 Feb. 1974: 10. Published by GenealogyBank.com, a division of NewsBank.

"Policeman Considered." *Illinois State Journal* [Springfield] 7 Mar. 1972: 4. Published by GenealogyBank.com, a division of NewsBank.

Bruzan, Pam. "Rochester Hires Full, Part-Time Policemen." *Illinois State Journal* [Springfield] 3 May 1972: 31. Published by GenealogyBank.com, a division of NewsBank..

Bruzan, Pam. "Rochester Innovates Reserve Police Plan." *Illinois State Journal* [Springfield] 19 Feb. 1974: 13. Published by GenealogyBank.com, a division of NewsBank.

Bruzan, Pam. "Rochester's Police Department is Being Restructured." *State Journal-Register* [Springfield, IL] 7 Apr. 1976: 24. Published by GenealogyBank.com, a division of NewsBank.

Bruzan, Pam. "Rochester Police Dept. will be Adding Two Men." *State Journal-Register* [Springfield, IL] 22 Apr. 1978: 6. Published by GenealogyBank.com, a division of NewsBank.

Liken, Ruth. "Construction Depends on Grant: Rochester Eyes Community Center." *State Journal-Register* [Springfield, IL] 7 Dec. 1979: 28. Published by GenealogyBank.com, a division of NewsBank.

Bruzan, Pam. "Rochester Gets 30 Acres For New City Park." *Illinois State Journal* [Springfield] 3 Apr. 1974: 41. Published by GenealogyBank.com, a division of NewsBank.

"Rochester Recreation Board Established." *State Journal-Register* [Springfield, IL] 6 Nov. 1974: 35. Published by GenealogyBank.com, a division of NewsBank.

"Rochester Will Have a New Park." *State Journal-Register* [Springfield, IL] 7 Apr. 1976: 30. Published by GenealogyBank.com, a division of NewsBank.

"Okay Plan for Park West of Rochester." *State Journal-Register* [Springfield, IL] 5 Oct. 1976: 23. Published by GenealogyBank.com, a division of NewsBank.

Bruzan, Pam. "Rochester Getting 'Do-It-Yourself' Park." *State Journal-Register* [Springfield, IL] 5 Nov. 1978: 21. Published by GenealogyBank.com, a division of NewsBank.

Liken, Ruth. "Rochester Park Dedication Scheduled on Fourth of July." *State Journal-Register* [Springfield, IL] 8 Mar. 1979: 15. Published by GenealogyBank.com, a division of NewsBank.

"Rochester Bike Path Proposed, But Some Questions Still Remain." *State Journal-Register* [Springfield, IL] 26 Oct. 1977: 26. Published by GenealogyBank.com, a division of NewsBank.

Bruzan, Pam. "Rochester Board Defers Action on Bicycle Path." *State Journal-Register* [Springfield, IL] 9 Nov. 1977: 13. Published by GenealogyBank.com, a division of NewsBank.

"Rochester Village Board Endorses Bicycle Path." *State Journal-Register* [Springfield, IL] 8 Feb. 1978: 27. Published by GenealogyBank.com, a division of NewsBank.

Bruzan, Pam. "Rochester Gets $29,000 Matching Grant for Bike Path." *State Journal-Register* [Springfield, IL] 8 Feb. 1979: 11. Published by GenealogyBank.com, a division of NewsBank.

To Build Bike Path: Woman's Club Sets Oct. 29 Bike-a-Thon." *Rochester Times* [Rochester, IL] 21 Oct 1977: 1.

Bruzan, Pam. "Meyer, Higgins Win Bicycles." *Rochester Times* [Rochester, IL] 4 Nov. 1977: 1.

Liken, Ruth. "Rochester Invites Bikers to Help Mark Dedication of Path." *State Journal-Register* [Springfield, IL] 4 Oct. 1979: 10. Published by GenealogyBank.com, a division of NewsBank.

Bruzan, Pam. "Rochester Village Board Views Pedestrian Safety Problems." *State Journal-Register* [Springfield, IL] 5 Apr. 1978: 35. Published by GenealogyBank.com, a division of NewsBank.

Bruzan, Pam. "Pedestrian Safety Again before Rochester Board." *State Journal-Register* [Springfield, IL] 5 Oct. 1978: 51. Published by GenealogyBank.com, a division of NewsBank.

Bruzan, Pam. "Rochester Board Fills Vacancies, OKs Money for Guard." State Journal-Register [Springfield, IL] 8 Nov. 1978: 33. Published by GenealogyBank.com, a division of NewsBank.

"Rochester Board To Install Radar for Traffic Control." *Illinois State Journal* [Springfield] 15 Sep. 1971: 12. Published by GenealogyBank.com, a division of NewsBank.

McDaniel, Toby. "School Daze." *State Journal-Register* [Springfield, IL] 24 Jan. 1979: 17. Published by GenealogyBank.com, a division of NewsBank.

"Three Arrests Made in Library Vandalism." *State Journal-Register* [Springfield, IL] 28 Apr. 1976: 31. Published by GenealogyBank.com, a division of NewsBank.

"Rochester Hikes Water Deposit Fee." *Illinois State Journal* [Springfield] 9 May 1974: 12. Published by GenealogyBank.com, a division of NewsBank.

Bruzan, Pam. "An Exciting Saturday in Rochester." *State Journal-Register* [Springfield, IL] 7 Dec. 1977: 69. Published by GenealogyBank.com, a division of NewsBank.

Bruzan, Pam. "Rochester Rescue Unit May be One of Area's Best-Kept Secrets." *State Journal-Register* [Springfield, IL] 27 Nov. 1978: 6. Published by GenealogyBank.com, a division of NewsBank.

Liken, Ruth. "Rochester OKs Fencing Large Swimming Pools." *State Journal-Register* [Springfield, IL] 14 Sep. 1979: 20. Published by GenealogyBank.com, a division of NewsBank.

Michael L. Hawk, D.M.D. Advertisement. *State Journal-Register* [Springfield, IL] 25 Feb 1979: 27. Published by GenealogyBank.com, a division of NewsBank.

Vittal Chapa, M.D. Advertisement. *State Journal-Register* [Springfield, IL] 20 Jun 1979: 6. Published by GenealogyBank.com, a division of NewsBank.

Cronin, Dan. "Business Outlook: Quilting Bee Purchased." *State Journal-Register* [Springfield, IL] 22 Apr 1979: 81. Published by GenealogyBank.com, a division of NewsBank.

Cronin, Dan. "Business Outlook: Another Law Office." *State Journal-Register* [Springfield, IL] 13 May 1979: 82. Published by GenealogyBank.com, a division of NewsBank.

Cronin, Dan. "Business Outlook: Land Surveyors." *State Journal-Register* [Springfield, IL] 7 Feb. 1979: 53. Published by GenealogyBank.com, a division of NewsBank.

Custom Frames and Fine Art Gallery. Advertisement. *State Journal-Register* [Springfield, IL] 31 Aug. 1979: 6. Published by GenealogyBank.com, a division of NewsBank.

Country Peddler. Advertisement. *State Journal-Register* [Springfield, IL] 23 Nov. 1979: 24. Published by GenealogyBank.com, a division of NewsBank.

Notice Under Assumed Business Name Act State of Illinois. Advertisement. *State Journal-Register* [Springfield, IL] 21 July 1979: 39. Published by GenealogyBank.com, a division of NewsBank.

"Grand Opening Celebration." *State Journal-Register* [Springfield, IL] 25 Apr. 1976: 16. Published by GenealogyBank.com, a division of NewsBank.

"Groundbreaking Ceremonies." *State Journal-Register* [Springfield, IL] 30 Mar. 1975: 28. Published by GenealogyBank.com, a division of NewsBank.

Joe's Italian Village. Advertisement. *State Journal-Register* [Springfield, IL] 14 Sep. 1977: 54. Published by GenealogyBank.com, a division of NewsBank.

"New Home of Rochester State Bank." *Rochester Times* [Rochester, IL] 31 Oct. 1975: 1.

"Rochester Property Rezoned." *State Journal-Register* [Springfield, IL] 6 Apr. 1977: 52. Published by GenealogyBank.com, a division of NewsBank.

"Rochester Policeman is Midwife." *State Journal-Register* [Springfield, IL] 24 Mar. 1979: 4. Published by GenealogyBank.com, a division of NewsBank.

"Rochester Man Killed." *Illinois State Journal* [Springfield] 1 Sep. 1971: 2. Published by GenealogyBank.com, a division of NewsBank.

"Police Beat: A Rochester Man was Injured. . . " *State Journal-Register* [Springfield, IL] 28 Jan. 1979: 31. Published by GenealogyBank.com, a division of NewsBank.

Buell, Barbara. "Rochester Boy Drowns in Fall from Train Trestle." *State Journal-Register* [Springfield, IL] 31 Mar. 1979: 36. Published by GenealogyBank.com, a division of NewsBank.

"Rochester Looks at Summer Plan for Youngsters." *Illinois State Journal* [Springfield] 7 Nov. 1973: 27. Published by GenealogyBank.com, a division of NewsBank.

"Officials Attend Flag Dedication in Rochester." *Illinois State Journal* [Springfield] 3 July 1971: 16. Published by GenealogyBank.com, a division of NewsBank.

Bruzan, Pam. "Tuesday is Election Day for Graders." *Rochester Times* [Rochester, IL] 26 Sep. 1975: 1.

"President to Receive Hand Made Quilt from 5th Grade." *Rochester Times* [Rochester, IL] 7 May 1976: 1.

"Whatever Happened To." *Rochester & Lake Springfield Herald* [Rochester, IL] 19 Sep. 1984: 1.

"Fifth graders Receive Letter from President." *Rochester Times* [Rochester, IL] 15 Oct. 1976: 1
"Flag Pole Plaque in Place." *Illinois State Journal* [Springfield] 14 Dec. 1972: 15. Published by GenealogyBank.com, a division of NewsBank.

"Tornado Damage at Rochester." *State Journal-Register* [Springfield, IL] 15 Aug. 1975: 21. Published by GenealogyBank.com, a division of NewsBank.

"Weather Disasters." *Sangamon Link*. 2014. Sangamon County Historical Society. 1 Mar 1016. <http://sangamoncountyhistory.org/wp/?p=4345>.

Bruzan, Pam. "Rochester Board Discusses Trampoline Use at Schools." *State Journal-Register* [Springfield, IL] 24 Aug. 1978: 28. Published by GenealogyBank.com, a division of NewsBank.

Taft, Robin. Re: "Rochester History." E-mail to the author. 6 Mar. 2016.

Bruzan, Pam. "Rochester School Board OKs Budget, Tax Levy." *Illinois State Journal* [Springfield] 19 Sep. 1973: 42. Published by GenealogyBank.com, a division of NewsBank.

"'Old Fashioned' July 4th Event Set at Rochester." *State Journal-Register* [Springfield, IL] 22 Jun. 1978: 9. Published by GenealogyBank.com, a division of NewsBank.

"Residents Get Wrong Signal on Tower." *Illinois State Journal* [Springfield] 12 Feb. 1971. Published by GenealogyBank.com, a division of NewsBank.

"Dedication Set Sunday for Church Building." *Illinois State Journal* [Springfield] 20 Nov. 1970: 4. Published by GenealogyBank.com, a division of NewsBank.

"Groundbreaking Sunday in Rochester: New Building Will House Auditorium." *State Journal-Register* [Springfield, IL] 7 July 1979: 6. Published by GenealogyBank.com, a division of NewsBank.

"Rochester Church Opens This Year." *Illinois State Journal* [Springfield] 29 Aug. 1973: 17. Published by GenealogyBank.com, a division of NewsBank.

"New St. Jude's Construction to Start as Weather Permits." *Rochester Times* [Rochester, IL] 26 Nov. 1976: 6.

"Cemetery Society Asks Township OK." *Illinois State Journal* [Springfield] 10 Apr. 1973: 13. Published by GenealogyBank.com, a division of NewsBank.

Billingsley, Gordon. "Rochester Farmer Grows up to be One of Best in Country." *State Journal-Register* [Springfield, IL] 17 Nov. 1978: 88. Published by GenealogyBank.com, a division of NewsBank.

"Conservation Family of Year is Honored." *Illinois State Journal* [Springfield] 2 July 1972: 22. Published by GenealogyBank.com, a division of NewsBank.

"Tour of Two Farms Starts at 1 p.m. Sunday." *State Journal-Register* [Springfield, IL] 13 Sep. 1974: 42. Published by GenealogyBank.com, a division of NewsBank.

Bernard, Fran. "Maurice W. Scott: Profile of the Taxpayers' Friend." *State Journal-Register* [Springfield, IL] 31 May 1976: 13. Published by GenealogyBank.com, a division of NewsBank.

"Area Man Honored by Engineers." *Illinois State Journal* [Springfield] 13 June 1972: 7. Published by GenealogyBank.com, a division of NewsBank.

"People in the News: Rochester." *Illinois State Journal* [Springfield] 23 June 1972: 7. Published by GenealogyBank.com, a division of NewsBank.

Bruzan, Pam. "Rochester Native Works Metal Magic." *Illinois State Journal* [Springfield] 22 Apr. 1973: 9. Published by GenealogyBank.com, a division of NewsBank.

"Rochester Man Appointed to FHA Committee." *Illinois State Journal* [Springfield] 29 Oct. 1970: 19. Published by GenealogyBank.com, a division of NewsBank.

"Dana Ross Elected State CAR President." *Rochester Times* [Rochester, IL] 4 Apr. 1975:1.

"Dana Ross Elected to National Office of NSCAR." *Rochester Times* [Rochester, IL] 7 May 1976: 1.

"People in the News: Dana Ross. . ." *State Journal Register* [Springfield, IL] 20 May 1977: 27.

"Rochester Man Heads Truck Firm." *Illinois State Journal* [Springfield] 27 Aug. 1971: 35. Published by GenealogyBank.com, a division of NewsBank.

Liken, Ruth. "Rochester Pair Cited for Civic Work." *State Journal-Register* [Springfield, IL] 10 July 1979: 9. Published by GenealogyBank.com, a division of NewsBank.

"Mr and Mrs. L. K. Kyes. . ." *Rochester Times* [Rochester, IL] 30 Dec. 1977: 1.

"Monday, April 4: Fred Braners Mark 60th Wedding Date." *Rochester Times* [Rochester, IL] 18 Apr. 1977: 1.

"Obituaries: Edith Fairchild." *State Journal-Register* [Springfield, IL] 17 Feb. 1978: 97. Published by GenealogyBank.com, a division of NewsBank.

"Mrs. Edith Fairchild 100 Years of Age." *Rochester Times* [Rochester, IL] 14 Nov. 1975: 1.

"Obituaries: J. Earl Bell." *Illinois State Journal* [Springfield] 9 June 1971: 10. Published by GenealogyBank.com, a division of NewsBank.

"Reunions: Bailey." *Illinois State Journal* [Springfield] 23 July 1972:11. Published by GenealogyBank.com, a division of NewsBank.

King, Dollie B. "A Short History of the Bailey Family in Whose Honor We are Having iur Thirty-ninth Annual Reunion Here in the Park at Beautiful Lake Springfield." 29 July 1951.

Bruzan, Pam and Ray Bruzan. "House Have Roots, Too." *Illinois Times* [Springfield] 2-8 Dec. 1977: 22.

"Rochester Reception Honors Walker." *Rochester and Lake Springfield Herald* [Rochester, IL] 19 Aug. 1971: np.

Manning, Al. "Project Poll Faces Early Demise: Gov. Walker's Campaign . . . " *State Journal-Register* [Springfield, IL] 6 Oct. 1976: 8. Published by GenealogyBank.com, a division of NewsBank.

1980s References

"Rochester's Growth Puts Pressure on Village Government, Residents." *State Journal-Register* [Springfield, IL] 8 Aug. 1988: 2. Published by GenealogyBank.com, a division of NewsBank.

"Rochester Library Panel Meets Tonight." *State Journal-Register* [Springfield, IL] 25 Oct. 1984: 18. Published by GenealogyBank.com, a division of NewsBank.

"Rochester Library Informational Meeting Monday." *State Journal-Register* [Springfield, IL] 16 Feb. 1985: 19. Published by GenealogyBank.com, a division of NewsBank.

Bakke, Dave. "Rochester Library 'Checks in' May 25." *State Journal-Register* [Springfield, IL] 16 May 1985: 11. Published by GenealogyBank.com, a division of NewsBank.

"Who-What-When-Where: Events — Rochester Public Library. . . ." *State Journal-Register* [Springfield, IL] 24 May 1985:28. Published by GenealogyBank.com, a division of NewsBank.

"Library Taxing District Passes in Rochester." *State Journal-Register* [Springfield, IL] 19 Mar. 1986: 15. Published by GenealogyBank.com, a division of NewsBank.

"Acting Assessments Supervisor Named: Seven people . . . ." *State Journal-Register* [Springfield, IL] 10 Apr. 1986: 11. Published by GenealogyBank.com, a division of NewsBank.

"Historical Society Begins Log Cabin 'Digs.'" *Rochester and Lake Springfield Herald* [Rochester, IL]. 26 Oct 1988: n.p.

Sears, Polly. "Researchers Try to Solve Puzzle about Life in Rochester in 1840s." *State Journal-Register* [Springfield, IL] 31 Oct. 1988: 2. Published by GenealogyBank.com, a division of NewsBank.

Krasnowski, Matt. "Historic Cabin Uncovered During Demolition of House." *State Journal-Register* [Springfield, IL] 15 Dec. 1987: 7. Published by GenealogyBank.com, a division of NewsBank.

Log House Photos. *Rochester & Lake Springfield Herald* [Rochester, IL] 28 Dec. 1988: 1.

Jenkins, Carol S. "Notes on the History of the Log House: Who Built the Original Log Structure?" Rev. 1 June 1988.

Jenkins, Carol S. Archeology in Rochester." *Rochester & Lake Springfield Herald.* [Rochester, IL] 2 Nov. 1988: 1.

"Historic Group Plans Meeting in Rochester." *State Journal-Register* [Springfield, IL] 14 Feb. 1988: 30. Published by GenealogyBank.com, a division of NewsBank.

Moore, Carolyn, and David Grubb. "RHPS history." c1990. Rochester Historical Preservation Society. 19 Oct. 2015. < http://rochesterhistoricalsociety.org/images/PublicationHomePage.htm>.

"Hello, Rochester." *Rochester Hello* [Rochester, IL] 2 Apr. 1981: 1.

"Hello: One Last Time." *Rochester Hello* [Rochester, IL] 30 Sep. 1982: 1.

"Rochester School Board Approves Use of Educational TV for Next Year." *State Journal-Register* [Springfield, IL] 21 May 1980: 18. Published by GenealogyBank.com, a division of NewsBank.

"Rochester Curriculum Changes Made." *State Journal-Register* [Springfield, IL] 24 Jan. 1980: 34. Published by GenealogyBank.com, a division of NewsBank.

School Personnel Needed. Advertisement. *State Journal-Register* [Springfield, IL] 4 July 1985: 12. Published by GenealogyBank.com, a division of NewsBank.

"School Board Disposes of Football Issue." *Rochester Hello* [Rochester, IL] 21 Jan. 1982: 1.

"School Board Approves Girls Basketball Program." *Rochester Hello* [Rochester, IL] 4 Feb. 1982: 2.

"School Merger Forum Slated at Rochester." *State Journal-Register* [Springfield, IL] 8 Feb. 1986: 24. Published by GenealogyBank.com, a division of NewsBank.

Pokosrski, Doug. "Area Consolidation Plans Put on Hold." *State Journal-Register* [Springfield, IL] 6 Mar. 1986: 13. Published by GenealogyBank.com, a division of NewsBank.

Pokorski, Doug. "Mediation Session Set on Rochester Teacher Pay." *State Journal-Register* [Springfield, IL] 3 Oct. 1986: 9. Published by GenealogyBank.com, a division of NewsBank.

"Rochester Teachers OK 3-Year Pact." *State Journal-Register* [Springfield, IL] 15 Oct. 1986: 11. Published by GenealogyBank.com, a division of NewsBank.

"Talks Set Today at Rochester in Bid to Avert Teachers Strike." *State Journal-Register* [Springfield, IL] 2 Dec. 1989: 9. Published by GenealogyBank.com, a division of NewsBank.

Price, Jacqueline. "Rochester Teachers Approve Contract." *State Journal-Register* [Springfield, IL] 5 Dec.1989: 2. Published by GenealogyBank.com, a division of NewsBank.

Pokorski, Doug. "Study Calls for New School in Growing Rochester." *State Journal-Register* [Springfield, IL] 12 Dec. 1988: 1. Published by GenealogyBank.com, a division of NewsBank.

Finke, Doug, and Doug Pokorski. "Rochester School Bond Issue Passes." *State Journal-Register* [Springfield, IL] 5 Apr. 1989: 13. Published by GenealogyBank.com, a division of NewsBank.

"Sangamon County Election Results: School Referendums, 233 of 233 Precincts Reporting." *State Journal-Register* [Springfield, IL] 6 Apr. 1989: 20. Published by GenealogyBank.com, a division of NewsBank.

Sangamon County Election Results: Christian 51 pf 51 Precincts Reporting." *State Journal-Register* [Springfield, IL] 6 Apr. 1989: 8. Published by GenealogyBank.com, a division of NewsBank.

"Math Club Plans to Buy Computer." *Rochester Hello* [Rochester, IL] 13 July 1981: 1.

"First RSA Meeting Sees Apple Computer." *Rochester Hello* [Rochester, IL] 1 Oct. 1981: 6.

Brody, Jeff. "Taylorville Leaders Call for Four-Lane Illinois 29." *State Journal-Register* [Springfield, IL] 8 Jan. 1988: 10. Published by GenealogyBank.com, a division of NewsBank.

"Thumbs up to Finished Illinois 29 Project." *State Journal-Register* [Springfield, IL] 20 Jan. 2017: 6. Published by GenealogyBank.com, a division of NewsBank.

Hebron, Anthony. "Benefits of Improved 911 System to be Shown." *State Journal-Register* [Springfield, IL] 4 Oct. 1989: 10. Published by GenealogyBank.com, a division of NewsBank.

Hebron, Anthony. "46 Bridges in County Need Repairs." *State Journal-Register* [Springfield, IL] 5 July 1989: 1. Published by GenealogyBank.com, a division of NewsBank.

Liken, Ruth. "Rochester Pay Increased." *State Journal-Register* [Springfield, IL] 10 Apr. 1980: 13. Published by GenealogyBank.com, a division of NewsBank.

"Rochester Village Hall to be Remodeled." *State Journal-Register* [Springfield, IL] 7 Jan. 1981: 30. Published by GenealogyBank.com, a division of NewsBank.

Rominger, Jim. "Spotlight on Home: Village Hall Holds Unusual History." *Hello* [Rochester, IL] 15 Apr. 1982: 11.

·Carsten, Caryl. "Rochester Board OKs Joining Sanitary District." *State Journal-Register* [Springfield, IL] 23 Mar. 1983: 10. Published by GenealogyBank.com, a division of NewsBank.

"County Ballots: What the Voters will Face: Rochester." *State Journal-Register* [Springfield, IL] 3 Apr. 1983: 12, 13. Published by GenealogyBank.com, a division of NewsBank.

"Rochester Turns down Sewer Annex." *State Journal-Register* [Springfield, IL] 13 Apr. 1983: 84. Published by GenealogyBank.com, a division of NewsBank.

Bakke, Dave. "EPA Gives Rochester New 'Set of Directions.'" *State Journal-Register* [Springfield, IL] 23 Apr. 1983: 19. Published by GenealogyBank.com, a division of NewsBank.

"Rochester Sewers, Streets, Water to be Studied." *State Journal-Register* [Springfield, IL] 13 Sep. 1989: 3. Published by GenealogyBank.com, a division of NewsBank.

Hebron, Anthony. "Rochester Starting Tough Rules on Dogs and Cats." *State Journal-Register* [Springfield, IL] 3 Dec. 1988: 13. Published by GenealogyBank.com, a division of NewsBank.

Hebron, Anthony. "Rochester Pet Owners Want New Village Law Changed." *State Journal-Register* [Springfield, IL] 15 Mar. 1989: 11. Published by GenealogyBank.com, a division of NewsBank.

"Home Building in Area is Thriving Once AgainThis Year." *State Journal-Register* [Springfield, IL] 17 Apr. 1988: 47. Published by GenealogyBank.com, a division of NewsBank.

"Pork Producers Expanding Facility." *State Journal-Register* [Springfield, IL] 30 Aug. 1989: 23. Published by GenealogyBank.com, a division of NewsBank.

"Municipal Elections in Sangamon County: Village of Rochester." *State Journal-Register* [Springfield, IL] 8 Apr. 1981: 20. Published by GenealogyBank.com, a division of NewsBank.

"Toby McDaniel: Last Word . . ." *State Journal-Register* [Springfield, IL] 21 Dec. 1988: 11. Published by GenealogyBank.com, a division of NewsBank.

Johnson, Zion. "Rochester Residents Voice Opposition to Nuclear Site." *State Journal-Register* [Springfield, IL] 8 Jan. 1988: 2. Published by GenealogyBank.com, a division of NewsBank.

Johnson, Zion. "Students Studying Nuclear Waste Disposal." *State Journal-Register* [Springfield, IL] 19 Jan. 1988: 13. Published by GenealogyBank.com, a division of NewsBank.

"Area Briefs: Rochester." *State Journal-Register* [Springfield, IL] 12 June 1980: 21. Published by GenealogyBank.com, a division of NewsBank.

"Who-What-When-Where: Statesmen." *State Journal-Register* [Springfield, IL] 13 June 1980: 22. Published by GenealogyBank.com, a division of NewsBank.

"Who-What-When-Where: Fun Run." *State Journal-Register* [Springfield, IL] 13 June 1980: 22. Published by GenealogyBank.com, a division of NewsBank.

"Troop 40 Scouts Build Bridge in Village Park." *Rochester Hello* [Rochester, IL] 4 June 1981: 11.

"Anniversaries: Watkins." *State Journal-Register* [Springfield, IL] 20 Dec. 1987: 42. Published by GenealogyBank.com, a division of NewsBank.

"Anniversaries: Coe." *State Journal-Register* [Springfield, IL] 4 Oct. 1987: 28. Published by GenealogyBank.com, a division of NewsBank.

"Anniversaries: Scott." *State Journal-Register* [Springfield, IL] 12 June 1988: 28. Published by GenealogyBank.com, a division of NewsBank.

"Mr. & Mrs. Ralph Cox Celebrate 50th Anniversary." *Rochester Hello* [Rochester, IL] 22 Apr. 1982: 3.

"Anniversaries: Foster." *State Journal-Register* [Springfield, IL] 23 Oct. 1988: 23. Published by GenealogyBank.com, a division of NewsBank.

"Anniversaries: Simpson." *State Journal-Register* [Springfield, IL] 24 Apr. 1988: 51. Published by GenealogyBank.com, a division of NewsBank.

"Birthdays: Story." *State Journal-Register* [Springfield, IL] 27 Nov. 1988: 25. Published by GenealogyBank.com, a division of NewsBank.

"Anniversaries: Story—70th." *State Journal-Register* [Springfield, IL] 29 Jan. 1984: 36. Published by GenealogyBank.com, a division of NewsBank.

Spencer, Clark. "The Heat is on—and It'll Continue." *State Journal-Register* [Springfield, IL] 21 July 1983: 1. Published by GenealogyBank.com, a division of NewsBank.

Hebron, Anthony. "Rochester, Leland Grove, OK Water Restrictions." *State Journal-Register* [Springfield, IL] 24 Aug. 1988: 9. Published by GenealogyBank.com, a division of NewsBank.

Murphy, Michael. "The Big Dry of 1988 Could Become the Worst on Record." *State Journal-Register* [Springfield, IL] 17 July 1988: 1. Published by GenealogyBank.com, a division of NewsBank.

Murphy, Michael. "Drought Fears Ease as Lake is Replenished." *State Journal-Register* [Springfield, IL] 24 Nov. 1988: 31. Published by GenealogyBank.com, a division of NewsBank.

McDaniel, Toby. "Show Biz." *State Journal-Register* [Springfield, IL] 11 Jan. 1984: 8. Published by GenealogyBank.com, a division of NewsBank.

Schwarz, K. Robert. "Music Industry: Isaac Stern." *The Guardian* 23 Sep. 2001. 27 Jan. 2016. <https://www.theguardian.com/news/2001/sep/24/guardianobituaries>.

"Circus to Perform at Rochester Church." *State Journal-Register* [Springfield, IL] 23 May 1987: 10. Published by GenealogyBank.com, a division of NewsBank.

Liken, Ruth. "Cable TV Marching into Rochester." *State Journal-Register* [Springfield, IL] 10 Nov. 1979: 6.

Liken, Ruth. "Some TV Cable Work Delayed at Rochester." *State Journal-Register* [Springfield, IL] 10 Jan. 1980: 4. Published by GenealogyBank.com, a division of NewsBank.

"City to Get New Arby's Restaurant." *State Journal-Register* [Springfield, IL] 8 June 1988. Published by GenealogyBank.com, a division of NewsBank.

Fargo, Charlyn. "Hog processing Plant Proposed for Rochester." *State Journal-Register* [Springfield, IL] 6 Mar. 1980: 29.

Miller, Judy. "Bank President Killed in Crash of Light Plane." *State Journal-Register* [Springfield, IL] 22 Mar. 1983: 13. Published by GenealogyBank.com, a division of NewsBank.

"Man Killed in Freak Accident." *State Journal-Register* [Springfield, IL] 1 June 1980: 15. Published by GenealogyBank.com, a division of NewsBank.

"Police Beat: An Off-Duty. . ." *State Journal-Register* [Springfield, IL] 18 Nov. 1987: 9. Published by GenealogyBank.com, a division of NewsBank.

"Police Beat: Two Rochester Youths . . ." *State Journal-Register* [Springfield, IL] 30 Jan. 1988: 7. Published by GenealogyBank.com, a division of NewsBank.

"Underpass Mishap." *Rochester Hello* [Rochester, IL] 16 July 1981:2.

"Police Beat: A Construction Worker. . ." *State Journal-Register* [Springfield, IL] 11 May 1984: 15. Published by GenealogyBank.com, a division of NewsBank.

"Towering Rescue." *State Journal-Register* [Springfield, IL] 12 May 1984: 1. Published by GenealogyBank.com, a division of NewsBank.

"Rochester Plans Parade, Concert, Auction, Fireworks." *State Journal-Register* [Springfield, IL] 29 June 1989: 13. Published by GenealogyBank.com, a division of NewsBank.

Green, Chris. "Bicycle Trail Project Awaits Governor's Action." *State Journal-Register* [Springfield, IL] 7 July 1989: 8. Published by GenealogyBank.com, a division of NewsBank.

Murphy, Michael. "Questions Remain on C&IM Buyers." *State Journal-Register* [Springfield, IL] 13 Feb. 1987: 23. Published by GenealogyBank.com, a division of NewsBank.

Pokorski, Doug. "Hey Kids! Here's How to Make the Principal Kiss a Pig." *State Journal-Register* [Springfield, IL] 9 Mar. 1989: 1. Published by GenealogyBank.com, a division of NewsBank.

"Rash of Grass Fires Breaks out in Area." *State Journal-Register* [Springfield, IL] 8 Oct. 1983: 5. Published by GenealogyBank.com, a division of NewsBank.

"Rochester Home Destroyed; Fire Believed Cause by Short." *State Journal-Register* [Springfield, IL] 19 Aug. 1980: 19. Published by GenealogyBank.com, a division of NewsBank.

"Police Beat: Fire Engulfed the Old Chapel . . ." *State Journal-Register* [Springfield, IL] 19 Oct. 1989: 13. Published by GenealogyBank.com, a division of NewsBank.

"Fire-Damage Cemetery Chapel to be Restored." *State Journal-Register* [Springfield, IL] 15 Nov. 1989: 11. Published by GenealogyBank.com, a division of NewsBank.

Hahn, Steve. "Little Damage Seen from Oil Slick on River." *State Journal-Register* [Springfield, IL] 24 July 1981: 11. Published by GenealogyBank.com, a division of NewsBank.

"Suit vs. Oil Firm Seeks Clean-up Costs." *State Journal-Register* [Springfield, IL] 16 June 1984: 5. Published by GenealogyBank.com, a division of NewsBank.

Cronin, Dan. "Apartment Project." *State Journal-Register* [Springfield, IL] 30 Jan. 1980: 39. Published by GenealogyBank.com, a division of NewsBank.

"McDaniel, Toby: Graffiti Department." *State Journal-Register* [Springfield, IL] 13 June 1980: 13. Published by GenealogyBank.com, a division of NewsBank.

Miller, Judy. "Two Attempt Suicide at County Jail." *State Journal-Register* [Springfield, IL] 6 Mar. 1987: 17. Published by GenealogyBank.com, a division of NewsBank.

"Public Safety Day Sunday in Rochester." *State Journal-Register* [Springfield, IL] 28 Apr. 1983: 23. Published by GenealogyBank.com, a division of NewsBank.

Banks, Carmelita. "2 Area Communities Offer Safe Houses to Protect Their Kids." *State Journal-Register* [Springfield, IL] 15 Dec. 1985: 38. Published by GenealogyBank.com, a division of NewsBank.

"McDaniel, Toby: Note Pad." *State Journal-Register* [Springfield, IL] 4 July 1980: 9. Published by GenealogyBank.com, a division of NewsBank.

"Obituaries: Helen C. Prather." *State Journal-Register* [Springfield, IL] 6 Apr. 1981: 21. Published by GenealogyBank.com, a division of NewsBank.

"Obituaries: Ernest J. Rentschler." *State Journal-Register* [Springfield, IL] 1 Apr. 1982: 21. Published by GenealogyBank.com, a division of NewsBank.

"Obituaries: Anthony T. Mazzara." *State Journal-Register* [Springfield, IL] 14 June 1984: 15. Published by GenealogyBank.com, a division of NewsBank.

"Obituaries: D. Gilson Taft." *State Journal-Register* [Springfield, IL] 31 May 1987: 50. Published by GenealogyBank.com, a division of NewsBank.

"Obituaries: Marshall F. Beck." *State Journal-Register* [Springfield, IL] 11 May 1988: 11. Published by GenealogyBank.com, a division of NewsBank.

"Fay Beck Receives First Citizen Award." *Rochester Hello* [Rochester, IL] 8 July 1982: 1.

"Obituaries: Meryl Fairchild." *State Journal-Register* [Springfield, IL] 13 Jan. 1989: 33. Published by GenealogyBank.com, a division of NewsBank.

"Obituaries: R. Earl Sidener." *State Journal-Register* [Springfield, IL] 30 Jan. 1989: 16. Published by GenealogyBank.com, a division of NewsBank.

"Obituaries: Carl E. Moore." *State Journal-Register* [Springfield, IL] 30 Nov. 1981: 3. Published by GenealogyBank.com, a division of NewsBank.

Fargo, Charlyn. "Well Witcher Finds Water to Help People." *State Journal-Register* [Springfield, IL] 21 July 1985: 30. Published by GenealogyBank.com, a division of NewsBank.

"Ross Named to DAR Conservation Post." *State Journal-Register* [Springfield, IL] 23 June 1989: 21. Published by GenealogyBank.com, a division of NewsBank.

"Celebrates 97th Birthday." *Rochester Hello* [Rochester, IL] 14 May 1981: 2.

"Toby McDaniel: School Days." *State Journal-Register* [Springfield, IL] 15 July 1988: 11. Published by GenealogyBank.com, a division of NewsBank.

"Best of Springfield." *State Journal-Register* [Springfield, IL] 6 Feb. 1987. Published by GenealogyBank.com, a division of NewsBank.

Fitzgerald, Jay. "Langfelder Names Top Mayoral Aides for Administration." *State Journal-Register* [Springfield, IL 17 Nov. 1987: 7. Published by GenealogyBank.com, a division of NewsBank.

"Rochester Attorney Leads Cancer Campaign." *State Journal-Register* [Springfield, IL] 30 Jan. 1981: 16. Published by GenealogyBank.com, a division of NewsBank.

"Newhouse is Lions Governor." *Rochester Hello* [Rochester, IL] 2 Apr. 1981: 1.

"Rubik's Cube Team Competes." *Rochester Hello* [Rochester, IL] 3 Dec. 1981: 1.

"Stephanie Brogdon: Championship Baker." *Rochester Hello* [Rochester, IL] 15 Oct. 1981: 1.

Taft, Robin and Steve Taft. Notes to the author. Abt. 2013.

1990s References

"Rochester High Band To Play At Disney World." *State Journal-Register* [Springfield, IL] 16 Feb. 1990: 9. Published by GenealogyBank.com, a division of NewsBank.

"Enrollment Record Seen as Rochester School Term Starts." *State Journal-Register* [Springfield, IL] 22 Aug. 1991: 26. Published by GenealogyBank.com, a division of NewsBank.

"Leininger to Dedicate Rochester School." *State Journal-Register* [Springfield, IL] 27 Oct. 1991: 42. Published by GenealogyBank.com, a division of NewsBank.

"Rochester Makes up For Days Lost to Strike." *State Journal-Register* [Springfield, IL] 16 Sep. 1992: 14. Published by GenealogyBank.com, a division of NewsBank.

Noble, Sean. "Rochester Teachers OK Strike if Agreement Not Reached." *State Journal-Register* [Springfield, IL] 11 Aug. 1992:10. Published by GenealogyBank.com, a division of NewsBank.

"Illinois Report: Rochester." *State Journal-Register* [Springfield, IL] 8 Apr. 1993: 10. Published by GenealogyBank.com, a division of NewsBank.

Cappasso, Tony. "Head Lice Pose Problem." *State Journal-Register* [Springfield, IL] 19 Apr. 1997: 6. Published by GenealogyBank.com, a division of NewsBank.

Kernek, Lisa. "Partial Recount Yields Same Result/Referendum Supporters Ponder Future." *State Journal-Register* [Springfield, IL] 1 Apr. 1998: 9. Published by GenealogyBank.com, a division of NewsBank.

Landis, Debra. "Rochester School Board Candidate Tells Forum He Opposed Bond Issue." *State Journal-Register*, [Springfield, IL] 24 Mar. 1999: 10. Published by GenealogyBank.com, a division of NewsBank.

"Illinois Report: Rochester." *State Journal-Register* [Springfield, IL] 21 Sep. 1999:12. Published by GenealogyBank.com, a division of NewsBank.

"Rochester Board OKs Plan for Complex." *State Journal-Register* [Springfield, IL] 2 Feb. 1994: 14. Published by GenealogyBank.com, a division of NewsBank.

Building dedication and Open House Set." *Rochester Times* [Rochester, IL] 14 Sep. 1995: 1.

McDaniel, Toby. "Dumb-De-Dumb-Dumb!" *State Journal-Register* [Springfield, IL] 23 Sep. 1995: 9. Published by GenealogyBank.com, a division of NewsBank.

England, Pat. "Judge Won't Dismiss 'Impact Fees' Suit." *State Journal-Register* [Springfield, IL] 16 Apr. 1994: 16. Published by GenealogyBank.com, a division of NewsBank.

"Rochester Group Wants Fee Ordinance Reviewed." *State Journal-Register* [Springfield, IL] 12 Jan. 1994: 26. Published by GenealogyBank.com, a division of NewsBank.

Landis, Tim. "State Appeals Court Upholds Rochester Impact Fee." *State Journal-Register* [Springfield, IL] 2 Nov. 1995: 18. Published by GenealogyBank.com, a division of NewsBank.

"Rochester Trustees OK New Street Names." *State Journal-Register* [Springfield, IL] 10 Mar. 1995: 12. Published by GenealogyBank.com, a division of NewsBank.

"Rochester Buys 26.6 Acres from School District." *State Journal-Register* [Springfield, IL] 16 Aug. 1995: 10. Published by GenealogyBank.com, a division of NewsBank.

England, Pat. "Rochester's Water Rates Lawsuit against City Dismissed." *State Journal-Register* [Springfield, IL] 7 Apr. 1994: 7. Published by GenealogyBank.com, a division of NewsBank.

"Water Advisory Team: Evaluate and Recommend." Untitled news release. 16 Jan. 1998. [Rochester, IL] 23 Sep. 2016.

Lawrence, Jerry. "New Law Will Allow Rochester, Chatham to Form Water District." *State Journal-Register* [Springfield, IL] 25 June 1998: 12. Published by GenealogyBank.com, a division of NewsBank.

Rogers, Lesley. "Rochester Water Deal nears Approval / Council Expected to Vote Next Week." *State Journal-Register* [Springfield, IL] 28 Jan. 1999: 10. Published by GenealogyBank.com, a division of NewsBank.

Matulis, Mike. "Rochester Faces Expensive Sewer Solution." *State Journal-Register* [Springfield, IL] 1 Aug. 1990: 7. Published by GenealogyBank.com, a division of NewsBank.

"Threat of EPA Action Puts Rochester on Spot." *State Journal-Register* [Springfield, IL] 22 Oct. 1990: 13. Published by GenealogyBank.com, a division of NewsBank.

"Is It Time to SOS?" Village of Rochester IL. 30 Oct. 1990.

Bruzan, Pam. "Rochester Sewer Referendum." Report to Rochester Village Board. 6 Nov. 1990.

"Rochester to Get Loan from State EPA to Hook Up, Improve Sewers." *State Journal-Register* [Springfield, IL] 12 Sep. 1992: 11. Published by GenealogyBank.com, a division of NewsBank.

Humphrey, Gregg. Personal interview. 2 May 2017.

Illinois Department of Transportation. "Lost Bridge Trail: Springfield to Rochester Illinois." Springfield: 1997. [Springfield] Aug. 1997.

Landis, Debra. "Recreational Trail a Possibility: Project Line: Rochester to Springfield." *State Journal-Register* [Springfield, IL] 15 June 1991: 8. Published by GenealogyBank.com, a division of NewsBank.

"Plans for Recreational Trail Take Another Step Forward." *State Journal-Register* [Springfield, IL] 12 Aug. 1992. Published by GenealogyBank.com, a division of NewsBank.

"Plans on Track for Bike Trail from Rochester to Springfield." *State Journal-Register* [Springfield, IL] 6 Aug. 1994: 9. Published by GenealogyBank.com, a division of NewsBank.

McDaniel, Toby. "Bridge Mystery Solved." *State Journal-Register* [Springfield, IL] 23 May 1997: 11. Published by GenealogyBank.com, a division of NewsBank.

"Springfield, Rochester to Share One Million Dollars for More Bike Paths." *State Journal-Register* [Springfield, IL] 1 Nov. 1999. Published by GenealogyBank.com, a division of NewsBank.

"Coalition to Celebrate Trail's Completion Today." *State Journal-Register* [Springfield, IL] 23 Aug. 1997. Published by GenealogyBank.com, a division of NewsBank.

McDaniel, Toby. "Trail Blazing Bicycle Trails are for Young and Old Alike." *State Journal-Register* [Springfield, IL] 11 Aug. 1997: 15. Published by GenealogyBank.com, a division of NewsBank.

Beaven, Stephen. "Study Paves Way for Rochester-Riverton Highway." *State Journal-Register* [Springfield, IL] 3 May 1995: 9. Published by GenealogyBank.com, a division of NewsBank.

Robbins, Jefferson. "Riverton-Rochester Road Proposal Inches Forward." *State Journal-Register* [Springfield, IL] 2 May 1996: 9. Published by GenealogyBank.com, a division of NewsBank.

"County to Present Latest Riverton-Rochester Road Plans." *State Journal-Register* [Springfield, IL] 21 Mar. 1999: 1. Published by GenealogyBank.com, a division of NewsBank.

Robbins, Jefferson. "Riverton-Rochester Road Rage Continues: Landowners along Corridor Still Miffed at Plans." *State Journal-Register* [Springfield, IL] 2 Apr. 1999: 23. Published by GenealogyBank.com, a division of NewsBank.

"Votes to bypass Oak Street: Village Endorses Its Option for Rochester-Riverton Road." *Rochester Times* [Rochester, IL] 14 Sep. 1995: 1.

"Several County, Township Bridges to be Closed." *State Journal-Register* [Springfield, IL] 23 Mar. 1991: 28. Published by GenealogyBank.com, a division of NewsBank.

"2 Area Bridges to Close Sunday for Replacement." *State Journal-Register* [Springfield, IL] 20 Apr. 1991: 9. Published by GenealogyBank.com, a division of NewsBank.

Hebron, Anthony. "Democrats Urge Probe of Loss of Court Files." *State Journal-Register* [Springfield, IL] 11 July 1990: 11. Published by GenealogyBank.com, a division of NewsBank.

"Rochester Road Work to Restrict Traffic Flow." *State Journal-Register* [Springfield, IL] 17 May 1991: 40. Published by GenealogyBank.com, a division of NewsBank.

Bush, Bill. "County Will Spend $2.7 Million on '92 Highway Projects." *State Journal-Register* [Springfield, IL] 23 Dec. 1991: 1. Published by GenealogyBank.com, a division of NewsBank.

Finke, Doug. "Funds Pledged to Widen Illinois 29: Edgar OKs Money for Rochester to Taylorville Stretch." *State Journal-Register* [Springfield, IL] 17 Sep. 1994: 1. Published by GenealogyBank.com, a division of NewsBank.

Finke, Doug. "Christian County Group Pushes for Wider Illinois 29 / IDOT: Other Roads More Dangerous, Carry More Traffic." *State Journal-Register* [Springfield, IL] 16 Sep. 1994: 11. Published by GenealogyBank.com, a division of NewsBank.

"Heat Pops Pavement on Illinois 29." *State Journal-Register* [Springfield, IL] 15 June 1994: 9. Published by GenealogyBank.com, a division of NewsBank.

Robbins, Jefferson. "Bridge Replacement Postponed Until August." *State Journal-Register* [Springfield, IL] 24 June 1998: 9. Published by GenealogyBank.com, a division of NewsBank.

"Rochester Road to Close for Repairs Monday." *State Journal-Register* [Springfield, IL] 22 Aug. 1998. Published by GenealogyBank.com, a division of NewsBank.

"Illinois 29 Construction between Springfield, Rochester Begins Monday." *State Journal-Register* [Springfield, IL] 17 Oct. 1999: 16. Published by GenealogyBank.com, a division of NewsBank.

"Major Rehabilitation Work on Illinois 29 Starts Monday." *State Journal-Register* [Springfield, IL] 15 Aug. 1999: 12. Published by GenealogyBank.com, a division of NewsBank.

Finke, Doug. "Way Paved for Road Projects to Begin: IDOT Maps Out Details of 5-Year, $1.13 Billion Plan." *State Journal-Register* [Springfield, IL] 12 May 1995:1. Published by GenealogyBank.com, a division of NewsBank.

Crouse, Brenda. "Re: Route 29 and Walnut Street in Rochester." E-mail to Ray Bruzan. 25 Mar. 2016.

"Internet Now Available at Rochester Library." *State Journal-Register* [Springfield, IL] 31 Dec. 1997: 15. Published by GenealogyBank.com, a division of NewsBank.

Fargo, Charlyn. "Rochester Residents Continue Search for Perfect Lemon-Jelly Cake." *State Journal-Register* [Springfield, IL] 15 July 1998: 13. Published by GenealogyBank.com, a division of NewsBank.

"Toby McDaniel: Last Month's Daring Rescue. . . " *State Journal-Register* [Springfield, IL] 1 Aug. 1990: 7. Published by GenealogyBank.com, a division of NewsBank.

"4 Local Rescuers among 13 Honored for Heroic Acts." *State Journal-Register* [Springfield, IL] 18 Sep. 1990: 6. Published by GenealogyBank.com, a division of NewsBank.

"Rochester Rescue Open House Saturday." *State Journal-Register* [Springfield, IL] 3 June 1999: 38. Published by GenealogyBank.com, a division of NewsBank.

" Rescue Workers to Search River for Missing Rochester Man." *State Journal-Register* [Springfield, IL] 23 June 1999: 12. Published by GenealogyBank.com, a division of NewsBank.

"Weather Dampens Search of Sangamon for Missing Man." *State Journal-Register* [Springfield, IL] 27 June 1999: 8. Published by GenealogyBank.com, a division of NewsBank.

"Search for Missing Man Continues Saturday." *State Journal-Register* [Springfield, IL] 4 July 1999: 11. Published by GenealogyBank.com, a division of NewsBank.

"Historical Society of Rochester Sets June 24 Meeting." *State Journal-Register* [Springfield, IL] 17 June 1996: 21. Published by GenealogyBank.com, a division of NewsBank.

Pokorski, Doug. "Rochester Society Seeks Help Preserving History." *State Journal-Register* [Springfield, IL] 24 Jan. 1997: 9. Published by GenealogyBank.com, a division of NewsBank.

Fuhrig, Frank. "A Stiff Wind Blows at the Old Stone House." *State Journal-Register* [Springfield, IL] 9 Apr.1997: 11. Published by GenealogyBank.com, a division of NewsBank.

"Album Provides Pictorial Look at Early 20th Century Rochester." *State Journal-Register* [Springfield, IL] 15 June 1997: 50. Published by GenealogyBank.com, a division of NewsBank.

Beitl, Gail. "A Muddy, Dry Town." *State Journal-Register* [Springfield, IL] 9 June 1991: 9.

Landis, Debra. "Rochester's Alcohol-Free Fourth a 'Selling Point:' Village and Town Always Been Dry." *State Journal-Register* [Springfield, IL] 3 July 1994: 9. Published by GenealogyBank.com, a division of NewsBank.

"Battling Fire and Wind: Rochester and Berry Firefighters Battling." *State Journal-Register* [Springfield, IL] 19 Mar. 1994: 1. Published by GenealogyBank.com, a division of NewsBank.

"Police Beat: Fire Gutted. . ." *State Journal-Register* [Springfield, IL] 30 Jan.1996: 7. Published by GenealogyBank.com, a division of NewsBank.

Kane Dave. "Rochester Boosters Launch Renewed Effort for Football." *State Journal-Register* [Springfield, IL] 10 Jan. 1994: 24. Published by GenealogyBank.com, a division of NewsBank.

"School Board Gives Okay to High School Football." *Rochester Times* [Rochester, IL] 21 Apr. 1994: np.

Wildrick, Jim. "Jacobs Excited about Rochester Football Job." *State Journal-Register* [Springfield, IL] 20 Jan. 1995: 25. Published by GenealogyBank.com, a division of NewsBank.

"Rochester Police to Start Wearing New Blue Uniforms." *State Journal-Register* [Springfield, IL] 18 July 1991: 24. Published by GenealogyBank.com, a division of NewsBank.

"Illinois Report: Rochester Police Get New Computer Equipment." *State Journal-Register* [Springfield, IL] 8 Feb. 1992: 9. Published by GenealogyBank.com, a division of NewsBank.

Antonacci, Sarah. "Local Police Glad to See Their Speed Traps Listed on the Net." *State Journal-Register* [Springfield, IL] 5 Nov. 1999: 1. Published by GenealogyBank.com, a division of NewsBank.

"Religion News: Dedications." *State Journal-Register* [Springfield, IL] 7 Apr. 1990: 24. Published by GenealogyBank.com, a division of NewsBank.

"Religion News: A dedication service. . ." *State Journal-Register* [Springfield, IL] 28 Apr. 1990: 20. Published by GenealogyBank.com, a division of NewsBank.

"Toby McDaniel: Hardly anyone. . ." *State Journal-Register* [Springfield, IL] 27 Sep. 1995: 11. Published by GenealogyBank.com, a division of NewsBank.

"Merle Haggard Bio." *Rolling Stone* 9 May 2017 <http://www.rollingstone.com/music/artists/merle-haggard/biography>.

Hebron, Anthony. "Gasoline Prices Explode: Increases Range from 10 to 27 Cents a Gallon." *State Journal-Register* [Springfield, IL] 8 Aug. 1990: 10. Published by GenealogyBank.com, a division of NewsBank.

Hebron, Anthony. "Gas Prices are Going up Again." *State Journal-Register* [Springfield, IL] 25 Sep. 1990: 1. Published by GenealogyBank.com, a division of NewsBank.

"A Real Welcome: Rochester Police Officer Lonnie Stivers Shows off a Sign . . ." *State Journal-Register* [Springfield, IL] 25 Oct. 1994: 7. Published by GenealogyBank.com, a division of NewsBank.

Pokorski, Doug. "Subdivision Lies on Indian Mound / Rochester Property Will Be Studied to Determine Contents." *State Journal-Register* [Springfield, IL] 20 Nov. 1994: 19. Published by GenealogyBank.com, a division of NewsBank.

Pokorski, Doug. "Indians: Don't Disturb Rochester Mounds." *State Journal-Register* [Springfield, IL] 3 Dec. 1994: 11. Published by GenealogyBank.com, a division of NewsBank.

Pokorski, Doug. "Prehistoric Indian Burial Ground Safe—for Now: Rochester Development's Ultimate Fate Uncertain." *State Journal-Register* [Springfield, IL] 27 Dec. 1994: 1. Published by GenealogyBank.com, a division of NewsBank.

Beaven, Stephen. "Vigil Promotes Awareness of Indian Remains." *State Journal-Register* [Springfield, IL] 23 Jan. 1995: 7. Published by GenealogyBank.com, a division of NewsBank.

Davis, Jenni. "Understanding Indians: Pow Wow Held to Highlight Traditions." *State Journal-Register* [Springfield, IL] 29 Jan. 1995: 19. Published by GenealogyBank.com, a division of NewsBank.

"Vigils by American Indian Movement Set." *State Journal-Register* [Springfield, IL] 13 Dec. 1995: 12. Published by GenealogyBank.com, a division of NewsBank.

Craig, Joseph. "The Olcott Mounds Site: Mortuary Site Investigations in the Sangamon River Drainage." Environmental Compliance Consultants, Inc., 1997.

Hebron, Anthony. "Discouraging Words for Homes on the Range: Developing More Rural Subdivisions Could Be Difficult." *State Journal-Register* [Springfield, IL] 11 Mar. 1990: 1. Published by GenealogyBank.com, a division of NewsBank.

"Capers Restaurant Will Move into Space at Quality Inn: Around Town." *State Journal-Register* [Springfield, IL] 4 Mar. 1990: 33. Published by GenealogyBank.com, a division of NewsBank.

"Rochester Approves New Subdivision Plan." *State Journal-Register* [Springfield, IL] 9 May 1991: 16. Published by GenealogyBank.com, a division of NewsBank.

Dettro, Chris. "Infrastructure Work Set for Subdivision." *State Journal-Register* [Springfield, IL] 28 Aug. 1994: 55. Published by GenealogyBank.com, a division of NewsBank.

Fargo, Charlyn. "Staking a Name: Subdivisions Should Be Named Creatively—and Carefully." *State Journal-Register* [Springfield, IL] 21 Oct. 1995: 9. Published by GenealogyBank.com, a division of NewsBank.

Dettro, Chris. "Christmas Shop Will Mark Anniversary." *State Journal-Register* [Springfield, IL] 27 June 1993: 41. Published by GenealogyBank.com, a division of NewsBank.

"Local Real Estate Market is Very Healthy." *State Journal-Register* [Springfield, IL] 23 Oct. 1994: 51. Published by GenealogyBank.com, a division of NewsBank.

Fargo, Charlyn. "Problems Get Deeper and Deeper for Those With Dry Wells." *State Journal-Register* [Springfield, IL] 21 Jan. 1990: 1. Published by GenealogyBank.com, a division of NewsBank.

"License Needed for Water Hauling." *State Journal-Register* [Springfield, IL] 21 Jan. 1990: 4. Published by GenealogyBank.com, a division of NewsBank.

"Business Owners Form Association in Rochester." *State Journal-Register* [Springfield, IL] 1 Apr. 1990: 43. Published by GenealogyBank.com, a division of NewsBank.

Penner, Diana. "Recycling Just Do It." *State Journal-Register* [Springfield, IL] 10 Mar. 1991: 9. Published by GenealogyBank.com, a division of NewsBank.

Shenfeld, Hilary. "Sangamon County Ready to Start Recycling: Six Cities Slated to Begin Program within the Month." *State Journal-Register* [Springfield, IL] 4 Feb. 1993: 7. Published by GenealogyBank.com, a division of NewsBank.

Village of Rochester, IL. "Rochester Recycles Responsibly: And So Do We!" Feb. 1993.

Village of Rochester, IL. Rochester Recycles Responsibly: Newsletter. Feb. 1993.

"Rochester's Crackdown on Teen Smoking Laudable." *State Journal-Register* [Springfield, IL] 20 Feb. 1997: 6. Published by GenealogyBank.com, a division of NewsBank.

Beaven, Stephen and Chris Green. "Burglar Shot to Death in Area Home." *State Journal-Register* [Springfield, IL] 23 Nov. 1991: 1.

Green, Chris. "Third Suspect Arrested in Rochester Burglary, Killing." *State Journal-Register* [Springfield, IL] 6 Dec. 1991: 11. Published by GenealogyBank.com, a division of NewsBank.

"Information on Tire Slashing Needed." *State Journal-Register* [Springfield, IL] 24 July 1999: 7. Published by GenealogyBank.com, a division of NewsBank.

"Illinois Report: Rochester Police ID Vandals Who Painted Sign." *State Journal-Register* [Springfield, IL] 14 Dec. 1994: 7. Published by GenealogyBank.com, a division of NewsBank.

Shenfeld, Hilary. "Woman Wiggles Out of Arrest, Takes Squad Car." *State Journal-Register* [Springfield, IL] 8 June 1993: 7. Published by GenealogyBank.com, a division of NewsBank.

"Saying Goodbye: Five Area Educators' Last Days in the Schools are Filled with Fond Memories—and a Little Sadness." *State Journal-Register* [Springfield, IL] 8 June 1990: 6A. Published by GenealogyBank.com, a division of NewsBank.

Bush, Bill. "Policing the Mind: James Chandler Hopes His New Book Can Become the Bible Of Police Psychology." *State Journal-Register* [Springfield, IL] 18 Sep. 1990: 15. Published by GenealogyBank.com, a division of NewsBank.

Wood, Kathy. "Letters from Readers: Let's Hear from Local Expert on Alcohol Fuel." *State Journal-Register* [Springfield, IL] 24 June 1991: 4. Published by GenealogyBank.com, a division of NewsBank.

Kernek, Lisa. "A Little Book Work: Germ of an Idea Growing with Children." *State Journal-Register* [Springfield, IL] 30 Oct. 1994: 51. Published by GenealogyBank.com, a division of NewsBank.

"Former Area Man Runs Arizona Visitors Center." *State Journal-Register* [Springfield, IL] 21 Feb. 1995: 10. Published by GenealogyBank.com, a division of NewsBank.

"Sangamon County Fair Crowns Queen." *State Journal-Register* [Springfield, IL] 16 June 1994: 20. Published by GenealogyBank.com, a division of NewsBank.

Harty, Rosalynne. "Task Force Expected to Focus on Horse Racing: Declining Revenues at Tracks Eyed By County Fair Officials." *State Journal-Register* [Springfield, IL] 24 Jan. 1995. Published by GenealogyBank.com, a division of NewsBank.

"On October 21, the Rochester VFW Post 11463. . ." *Rochester Times* [Rochester, IL] 2 Dec. 1999: np.

"Police Beat: A worker at the. . ." *State Journal-Register* [Springfield, IL] 12 Feb. 1991: 14. Published by GenealogyBank.com, a division of NewsBank.

"And Yet Another 'Chutist Hits the Taylorville Trees." *State Journal-Register* [Springfield, IL] 6 Aug. 1990: 12. Published by GenealogyBank.com, a division of NewsBank.

Fargo, Charlyn. "Education the Key to Preventing Farm Accidents." *State Journal-Register* [Springfield, IL] 7 Apr. 1991: 45. Published by GenealogyBank.com, a division of NewsBank.

Landis, Deb. "Up and At 'Em Again." *State Journal-Register* [Springfield, IL] 20 July 1991: 6.

Green, Chris. "Charges Sought in Triple Fatal Accident: Suspect in Hit-Run Faces Three Counts of Reckless Homicide." *State Journal-Register* [Springfield, IL] 30 Apr. 1991: 1. Published by GenealogyBank.com, a division of NewsBank.

England, Pat. "Coroner's Jury: Rochester Youth's Death Accidental." *State Journal-Register* [Springfield, IL] 13 June 1991: 18. Published by GenealogyBank.com, a division of NewsBank.

Noble, Sean and Hilary Saperstein. "Springfield Clinic Blast Kills Boiler Serviceman: Gas Explodes in Nearly Done Addition." *State Journal-Register* [Springfield, IL] 23 Jan. 1992: 1. Published by GenealogyBank.com, a division of NewsBank.

"Obituaries: Robert L. Ritterbusch." *State Journal-Register* [Springfield, IL] 15 Jan. 1996: 5. Published by GenealogyBank.com, a division of NewsBank.

"Obituaries: Nelson V. Campbell." *State Journal-Register* [Springfield, IL] 12 Mar. 1990: 8. Published by GenealogyBank.com, a division of NewsBank.

"Obituaries: William B. Pfeiffer." *State Journal-Register* [Springfield, IL] 11 Sep. 1996: 20. Published by GenealogyBank.com, a division of NewsBank.

"Obituaries: William R. Mayer." *State Journal-Register* [Springfield, IL] 4 Sep. 1996: 4. Published by GenealogyBank.com, a division of NewsBank.

Obituaries: Delores A. Mayer." *State Journal-Register* [Springfield, IL] 5 Sep. 1997: 12. Published by GenealogyBank.com, a division of NewsBank.

"Village President of Rochester Found Dead at His Home." *State Journal-Register* [Springfield, IL] 26 Apr. 1991: 36. Published by GenealogyBank.com, a division of NewsBank.

"Obituaries: Ruby T. Bell." *State Journal-Register* [Springfield, IL] 29 Mar. 1992: 40. Published by GenealogyBank.com, a division of NewsBank.

"Obituaries: Harrison Earl Wilcoxson." *State Journal-Register* [Springfield, IL] 22 Apr. 1992: 10. Published by GenealogyBank.com, a division of NewsBank.

"Obituaries: Charles M. Newhouse." *State Journal-Register* [Springfield, IL] 29 Sep. 1993: 16. Published by GenealogyBank.com, a division of NewsBank.

"Obituaries: Edwin S. Waldmire." *State Journal-Register* [Springfield, IL] 7 Aug. 1993: 15. Published by GenealogyBank.com, a division of NewsBank.

"Obituaries: Ross E. Fairchild." *State Journal-Register* [Springfield, IL] 3 July 1993: 12. Published by GenealogyBank.com, a division of NewsBank.

"Obituaries: H. Wayne Taft." *State Journal-Register* [Springfield, IL] 27 Sep. 1993: 16. Published by GenealogyBank.com, a division of NewsBank.

"Obituaries: Doris H. Campbell." *State Journal-Register* [Springfield, IL] 17 Jan. 1994: 16. Published by GenealogyBank.com, a division of NewsBank.

"Obituaries: James M. Bell." *State Journal-Register* [Springfield, IL] 15 Dec. 1994: 11. Published by GenealogyBank.com, a division of NewsBank.

"Obituaries: Thomas E. Scott." *State Journal-Register* [Springfield, IL] 5 Nov. 1996: 17. Published by GenealogyBank.com, a division of NewsBank.

"Obituaries: Raymond W. Woodruff, Sr." *State Journal-Register* [Springfield, IL] 4 Jan. 1996: 7. Published by GenealogyBank.com, a division of NewsBank.

"Obituaries: Dora S. Lovejoy." *State Journal-Register* [Springfield, IL] 22 Nov. 1998: 42. Published by GenealogyBank.com, a division of NewsBank.

Bettendorf, Elizabeth. "Dora's Legacy: Dora Lovejoy Parting with Home Where Generations of Her Family Were Raised." *State Journal-Register* [Springfield, IL] 7 Apr. 1996: 9.

"Obituaries: Delbert D. Taft." *State Journal-Register* [Springfield, IL] 23 Mar. 1998: 10. Published by GenealogyBank.com, a division of NewsBank.

"Obituaries: Hazel J. Park." *State Journal-Register* [Springfield, IL] 28 Jan. 1998: 31. Published by GenealogyBank.com, a division of NewsBank.

"Obituaries: Wilbern W. Dugger." *State Journal-Register* [Springfield, IL] 10 Aug. 1999: 26. Published by GenealogyBank.com, a division of NewsBank.

"Birthdays: Dora Lovejoy." *State Journal-Register* [Springfield, IL] 18 Aug. 1998: 24. Published by GenealogyBank.com, a division of NewsBank.

"Birthdays: Hazel J. Park." *State Journal-Register* [Springfield, IL] 18 Apr. 1995: 14. Published by GenealogyBank.com, a division of NewsBank.

"Birthdays: Lucile Fairchild." *State Journal-Register* [Springfield, IL] 26 Oct. 1999: 18. Published by GenealogyBank.com, a division of NewsBank.

"Anniversary: Al and Joan Mavis." *State Journal-Register* [Springfield, IL] 5 June 1990: 18. Published by GenealogyBank.com, a division of NewsBank.

"Anniversary: Ross and Elizabeth Fairchild." *State Journal-Register* [Springfield, IL] 5 Mar. 1991: 16. Published by GenealogyBank.com, a division of NewsBank.

"Anniversary: Ralph and Alice Leach." *State Journal-Register* [Springfield, IL] 20 Aug. 1991: 16. Published by GenealogyBank.com, a division of NewsBank.

"Anniversary: Fred and Ruth Drillinger." *State Journal-Register* [Springfield, IL] 25 June 1996: 18. Published by GenealogyBank.com, a division of NewsBank.

"Anniversary: Justin and Mardell Taft." *State Journal-Register* [Springfield, IL] 16 Dec. 1997: 24. Published by GenealogyBank.com, a division of NewsBank.

"Anniversary: Dean and Sarah Wisleder." *State Journal-Register* [Springfield, IL] 21 Sept. 1999: 20. Published by GenealogyBank.com, a division of NewsBank.

"Anniversary: Robert and Jane Fairchild." *State Journal-Register* [Springfield, IL] 26 Oct. 1999: 18. Published by GenealogyBank.com, a division of NewsBank.

"Anniversary: Marshall and Pauline Watkins." *State Journal-Register* [Springfield, IL] 9 Feb. 1993: 7. Published by GenealogyBank.com, a division of NewsBank.

"Anniversary, Thomas and Ann Scott." *State Journal-Register* [Springfield, IL] 8 June 1993: 7. Published by GenealogyBank.com, a division of NewsBank.

"Anniversary: Charles and Ruby Beam." *State Journal-Register* [Springfield, IL] 19 Nov.1991: 10. Published by GenealogyBank.com, a division of NewsBank.

"Toby McDaniel: Calendar Event. . ." *State Journal-Register* [Springfield, IL] 28 July 1990: 4. Published by GenealogyBank.com, a division of NewsBank.

"Rochester Winners Give Awards to Injured Friend." *State Journal-Register* [Springfield, IL] 24 Apr. 1991: 8. Published by GenealogyBank.com, a division of NewsBank.

Rodriguez, J Michael. "Community Pitches in for Fire Victims." *State Journal-Register* [Springfield, IL] 6 July 1999: 7. Published by GenealogyBank.com, a division of NewsBank.

"Rochester plans benefit for Rachel Sperry." *State Journal-Register* [Springfield, IL] 4 Oct. 1997. Published by GenealogyBank.com, a division of NewsBank.

"Benefit Slated to Help Rochester Cancer Patient." *State Journal-Register* [Springfield, IL] 12 July 1997. Published by GenealogyBank.com, a division of NewsBank.

"Donations Sought for Area CF Victim." *State Journal-Register* [Springfield, IL] 1 Feb. 1997: 17. Published by GenealogyBank.com, a division of NewsBank.

Noble, Sean. "Many Tying One on in Response To War." *State Journal-Register* [Springfield, IL] 19 Jan. 1991: 1. Published by GenealogyBank.com, a division of NewsBank.

Orange Judd Farmer. *Pictorial Community Album of Rochester Township and Village*. Chicago: Orange Judd Company, 1918. Maps, index, township section numbers. Compass Point Productions, Rochester IL, 1995.

2000s References

"Population Fluctuation: Most Sangamon County Towns Lost Population." *State Journal-Register* [Springfield, IL] 16 July 2008: 1. Published by GenealogyBank.com, a division of NewsBank.

"Building Permits: Commercial Construction." *State Journal-Register* [Springfield, IL] 26 Jan. 2007: 26. Published by GenealogyBank.com, a division of NewsBank.

Kernek, Lisa. "Portion of Route 29 Nearly Done: Officials Gather for Opening Ceremony." *State Journal-Register* [Springfield, IL] 27 Aug. 2004: 13. Published by GenealogyBank.com, a division of NewsBank.

Reynolds, John. "Getting Connected: First Part of New Road Opens in Rochester." *State Journal-Register* [Springfield, IL] 15 Nov. 2007: 11. Published by GenealogyBank.com, a division of NewsBank.

"Road Work Set in Rochester." *State Journal-Register* [Springfield, IL] 25 Sep. 2006: 15. Published by GenealogyBank.com, a division of NewsBank.

"Road Work Completed on East Main Street." *State Journal-Register* [Springfield, IL] 31 Oct. 2008: np. Published by GenealogyBank.com, a division of NewsBank.

Landis, Debra. "Rochester Has Grown Despite Controversial Fee." *State Journal-Register* [Springfield, IL] 28 Dec. 2004: 15. Published by GenealogyBank.com, a division of NewsBank.

"Impending ICC Decision Could Lead to Higher Phone Rates." *State Journal-Register* [Springfield, IL] 6 June 2004: 19. Published by GenealogyBank.com, a division of NewsBank.

Landis, Debra. "County Voters Will be Asked to Raise Property Tax Rates." *State Journal-Register* [Springfield, IL] 6 Mar. 2006: 19. Published by GenealogyBank.com, a division of NewsBank.

"Rochester Voters Give Early 'No' to Tax for IMRF." *State Journal-Register* [Springfield, IL] 22 Mar. 2006: 27. Published by GenealogyBank.com, a division of NewsBank

"Rochester Village Board Approves Sidewalk Project." *State Journal-Register* [Springfield, IL] 10 Nov. 2009: np. Published by GenealogyBank.com, a division of NewsBank.

Landis, Debra. "Zoning OK'd for Duplexes in Rochester: Planned Subdivision Allowed to Have 16." *State Journal-Register* [Springfield, IL] 11 Apr. 2000: 9. Published by GenealogyBank.com, a division of NewsBank.

Landis, Debra. "Oak Mills Subdivision Planned for Rochester." *State Journal-Register* [Springfield, IL] 25 Jan. 2005: 31. Published by GenealogyBank.com, a division of NewsBank.

"Rochester Planning Commission to Reveal Survey Results." *State Journal Register* [Springfield, IL] 1 May 2009: np. Published by GenealogyBank.com, a division of NewsBank.

Reavy, Amanda. "Rochester Board Outlaws Video Game Terminals in Village." *State Journal-Register* [Springfield, IL] 11 Aug. 2009: np. Published by GenealogyBank.com, a division of NewsBank.

Landis, Debra. "New Chapter about to Begin: Rochester Middle School Wired for the Information Age." *State Journal-Register* [Springfield, IL] 26 Nov. 2000: 11. Published by GenealogyBank.com, a division of NewsBank.

Landis, Debra. "Rochester Voters Approve Bond Issue." *State Journal-Register* [Springfield, IL] 20 Mar. 2002: 12. Published by GenealogyBank.com, a division of NewsBank.

"Illinois report: Rochester - New Track Status." *State Journal-Register* [Springfield, IL] 27 June 2003: 13. Published by GenealogyBank.com, a division of NewsBank.

Landis, Debra. "Teachers, Parents Raise $125,000 to Enlarge Rochester Auditorium." *State Journal-Register* [Springfield, IL] 3 Aug. 2004: 11. Published by GenealogyBank.com, a division of NewsBank.

Landis, Debra. "Rochester Voters Back School Plan." *State Journal-Register* [Springfield, IL] 6 Apr. 2005: 10. Published by GenealogyBank.com, a division of NewsBank.

Landis, Debra. "Rochester Census Will Raise Tax Revenues: Town Has Grown by 550 People Since 2000." *State Journal-Register* [Springfield, IL] 5 Nov. 2006: 9. Published by GenealogyBank.com, a division of NewsBank.

Landis, Debra. "New Subdivisions Strain Village as Population Booms." *State Journal-Register* [Springfield, IL] 14 Nov. 2007: 43A. Published by GenealogyBank.com, a division of NewsBank.

Landis, Debra. "Water, Sewer Service Issues Stunt Rochester's Expansion." *State Journal-Register* [Springfield, IL] 11 Feb. 2008: 5. Published by GenealogyBank.com, a division of NewsBank.

Landis, Debra. "Rochester School Board OKs Bond Referendum." *State Journal-Register* [Springfield, IL] 30 Nov. 2007: 9. Published by GenealogyBank.com, a division of NewsBank.

"Rochester School District Plans at a Glance." *State Journal-Register* [Springfield, IL] 26 Jan. 2009. Published by GenealogyBank.com, a division of NewsBank.

Landis, Debra. "Broken Main Floods Rochester School." *State Journal-Register* [Springfield, IL] 18 Aug. 2005: 19. Published by GenealogyBank.com, a division of NewsBank.

Landis, Debra. "Rochester School, Field House Construction Could Begin This Month." *State Journal-Register* [Springfield, IL] 2 Mar. 2009: np. Published by GenealogyBank.com, a division of NewsBank.

Landis, Debra. "Rochester's Cool School / Junior High Students Move into Their New Building." *State Journal-Register* [Springfield, IL] 8 Jan. 2008: 1. Published by GenealogyBank.com, a division of NewsBank.

Colindres, Adriana. "Rochester Schools One Step Closer to $10M in State Funds." *State Journal-Register* [Springfield, IL] 5 Mar. 2009: np. Published by GenealogyBank.com, a division of NewsBank.

Landis, Debra. "Rochester OKs Alcohol Sales." *State Journal-Register* [Springfield, IL] 18 Apr. 2007: 21. Published by GenealogyBank.com, a division of NewsBank.

"Election and Referendum Results 2007." *State Journal-Register* [Springfield, IL] 18 Apr. 2007: 23. Published by GenealogyBank.com, a division of NewsBank.

Reavy, Amanda. "Rochester Businesses Can Now Sell Alcohol They Make." *State Journal-Register* [Springfield, IL] 18 Aug. 2009: np. Published by GenealogyBank.com, a division of NewsBank.

Landis, Debra. "Rochester Water Use Curbed: Broken Main Finally Found." *State Journal-Register* [Springfield, IL] 28 Jan. 2003: 1. Published by GenealogyBank.com, a division of NewsBank.

Landis, Debra. "Rochester Repairs Water Main Break." *State Journal-Register* [Springfield, IL] 29 Jan. 2003: 36. Published by GenealogyBank.com, a division of NewsBank.

Reavy, Amanda. "Rochester Plans Sewer Line Update." *State Journal-Register* [Springfield, IL] 18 Jan. 09: np. Published by GenealogyBank.com, a division of NewsBank.

Landis, Debra. "Chatham, Rochester Examine Report on Proposed Water Plant." *State Journal-Register* [Springfield, IL] 23 Apr. 2003: 10. Published by GenealogyBank.com, a division of NewsBank.

Landis, Debra. "Aquifer for Proposed Water Plant Sufficient." *State Journal-Register* [Springfield, IL] 7 Sep. 2003: 17. Published by GenealogyBank.com, a division of NewsBank.

"Village Likely to Join Rochester for Water Plant." *State Journal-Register* [Springfield, IL] 29 Apr. 2004: 13A. Published by GenealogyBank.com, a division of NewsBank.

Landis, Debra. "Chatham, Rochester End Water Board." *State Journal-Register* [Springfield, IL] 20 May, 2005: 11. Published by GenealogyBank.com, a division of NewsBank.

Reavy, Amanda. "Rochester OKs Water Deal with Springfield." *State Journal-Register* [Springfield, IL] 10 Feb. 2009: np. Published by GenealogyBank.com, a division of NewsBank.

"Hoax in Rochester Ties Police Up for Two Hours: Dozens of Officers from at Least Three Agencies Involved." *State Journal-Register* [Springfield, IL] 21 Dec. 2006: 1. Published by GenealogyBank.com, a division of NewsBank.

Reavy, Amanda. "Detective Gives Rochester Police an Advantage: Lack of Resources Often Makes it Hard for Small Towns to Fill Position." *State Journal-Register* [Springfield, IL] 7 July 2008: 1. Published by GenealogyBank.com, a division of NewsBank.

"Rochester Plans to Hold First Citizens Police Academy." *State Journal-Register* [Springfield, IL] 15 Jan. 2009: np. Published by GenealogyBank.com, a division of NewsBank.

Reavy, Amanda. "Other Villages Experience Road Troubles, Too." *State Journal-Register* [Springfield, IL] 21 Dec. 2009. Published by GenealogyBank.com, a division of NewsBank.

"Report of the Rochester Rescue Squad Study Committee: Presented to Rochester Village President Grant Blasdell, Rochester Village Board, Rochester Fire Protection District Board." [Rochester] 22 May 2000.

Landis, Debra. "Rochester Considers Merger of Fire, Rescue Units." *State Journal-Register* [Springfield, IL] 13 Sep. 2000: 13. Published by GenealogyBank.com, a division of NewsBank.

Landis, Debra. "Rochester to Vote on Doubling Fire Tax." *State Journal-Register* [Springfield, IL] 21 Mar. 2001: 11. Published by GenealogyBank.com, a division of NewsBank.

Landis, Debra. "Rochester Fire Station to be Auctioned: Richard Rentschler Named New Chief." *State Journal-Register* [Springfield, IL] 24 Feb. 2003: 17. Published by GenealogyBank.com, a division of NewsBank.

Landis, Debra. "Rochester Opens New Firehouse." *State Journal-Register* [Springfield, IL] 8 June 2003: 18. Published by GenealogyBank.com, a division of NewsBank.

"Rochester Adds New Rescue Truck." *State Journal-Register* [Springfield, IL] 1 Dec. 2004: 12. Published by GenealogyBank.com, a division of NewsBank.

Landis, Debra. "Fire District Tax Will be on Rochester Ballots Again." *State Journal-Register* [Springfield, IL] 12 June 2006: 8. Published by GenealogyBank.com, a division of NewsBank.

Landis, Debra. "Rochester Fire Tax Defeated." *State Journal-Register* [Springfield, IL] 9 Nov. 2006: 9. Published by GenealogyBank.com, a division of NewsBank.

Landis, Debra. "Reinstated Rochester Firefighter to Apologize to Full Department." *State Journal-Register* [Springfield, IL] 9 Oct. 2007: 18. Published by GenealogyBank.com, a division of NewsBank.

Landis, Debra. "Two More Rochester Firefighters Resign." *State Journal-Register* [Springfield, IL] 16 Oct. 2007: 17. Published by GenealogyBank.com, a division of NewsBank.

Landis, Debra. "Former Rochester Firefighters File Rights Complaints / Two Women Allege Sexual Discrimination by District, Co-worker." *State Journal-Register* [Springfield, IL] 12 Feb. 2008. Published by GenealogyBank.com, a division of NewsBank.

Reavy, Amanda. "Rochester Fire Board OKs Harassment Policies, Formal Job Descriptions." *State Journal-Register* [Springfield, IL] 22 April 2008: 15. Published by GenealogyBank.com, a division of NewsBank.

Landis, Debra. "Proponents of an Elected Rochester Fire Board Respond to Questions." *State Journal-Register* [Springfield, IL] 12 Jan. 2009: np. Published by GenealogyBank.com, a division of NewsBank.

Landis, Debra. "Background Checks Urged for Volunteer Firefighters." *State Journal-Register* [Springfield, IL] 24 May 2009: np. Published by GenealogyBank.com, a division of NewsBank.

Landis, Debra. "Lost Bridge Trail to Extend through Rochester." *State Journal-Register* [Springfield, IL] 10 Feb. 2003: 18. Published by GenealogyBank.com, a division of NewsBank.

"Wind Causes Snow 'Rollers.'" *State Journal-Register* [Springfield, IL] 12 Feb. 2003: 9. Published by GenealogyBank.com, a division of NewsBank.

"Snow Roller." *Wikipedia* 25 Oct. 2015. 8 Feb. 2016 <https://en.wikipedia.org/wiki/Snow_roller>.

Sanner, Ann. "Rain Leads to Road Closers: Many Area Rivers above Flood Stage." *State Journal-Register* [Springfield, IL] 7 Jan. 2005: 11. Published by GenealogyBank.com, a division of NewsBank.

Bolinski, Jayette. "Fallen Tree Limbs Main Cause of Power Loss during Storms: Center Park and Macoupin County Hit Hardest." *State Journal-Register* [Springfield, IL] 15 June 2005: 1. Published by GenealogyBank.com, a division of NewsBank.

"Religion News: Events—A new church. . ." *State Journal-Register* [Springfield, IL] 20 Dec. 2003: 14. Published by GenealogyBank.com, a division of NewsBank.

"Rochester Church Celebrates 125th Year." *State Journal-Register* [Springfield, IL] 14 Nov. 2001: 20. Published by GenealogyBank.com, a division of NewsBank.

Browning, Tamara. "A Time to Celebrate: South Fork Church of Christ Marks 175 Years." *State Journal-Register* [Springfield, IL] 1 Apr. 2007: 17. Published by GenealogyBank.com, a division of NewsBank.

"Rochester Christian Church Earns Charter for Boy Scott Troop 58." *State Journal-Register* [Springfield, IL] 2 June 2003: 14. Published by GenealogyBank.com, a division of NewsBank.

Reynolds, John. "Blessed be Thy Travels: Pastor Shares Words of God to Protect Motorsyclists." *State Journal-Register* [Springfield, IL] 30 Mar. 2008: 1. Published by GenealogyBank.com, a division of NewsBank.

"Illinois Report: Rochester—Forum for Library Proposal Set March 4." *State Journal-Register* [Springfield, IL] 25 Feb. 2004: 9. Published by GenealogyBank.com, a division of NewsBank.

"Election and Referendum Results." *State Journal-Register* [Springfield, IL] 17 Mar. 2004: 8. Published by GenealogyBank.com, a division of NewsBank.

"Rochester Author Plans Book Signing." *State Journal-Register* [Springfield, IL] 21 Mar. 2004: 45. Published by GenealogyBank.com, a division of NewsBank.

"Moon Rock Will be Displayed July 20." State Journal-Register [Springfield, IL] 12 July 2004: 19. Published by GenealogyBank.com, a division of NewsBank.

McDaniel, Toby "Bookworms! Forward . . . March!" *State Journal-Register* [Springfield, IL] 2 July 2003: 9. Published by GenealogyBank.com, a division of NewsBank.

"Rochester Police Report Jump in Property Crimes, Ask Public's Help." *State Journal-Register* [Springfield, IL] 30 Sep. 2009: np. Published by GenealogyBank.com, a division of NewsBank.

Reynolds, John. "Friendly Rivals: Teacher Loses Election to Former Student." *State Journal-Register* [Springfield, IL] 10 Nov. 2002: 19. Published by GenealogyBank.com, a division of NewsBank.

"Worker Still in Intensive Care after Falling from Cellular Phone Tower." *State Journal-Register* [Springfield, IL] 15 June 2006: 8. Published by GenealogyBank.com, a division of NewsBank.

"Police Beat—A man who fell . . ." *State Journal-Register* [Springfield, IL] 28 June 2006: 10. Published by GenealogyBank.com, a division of NewsBank.

Poole, Deana. "City Getting Impatient for Hunter Lake Answer." *State Journal-Register* [Springfield, IL] 13 Nov. 2009: np. Published by GenealogyBank.com, a division of NewsBank.

"Hunter Lake." *Wikipedia. 2016.* 5 April 2016 <https://en.wikipedia.org/wiki/Hunter_Lake>.

Landis, Debra. "Historical Society Seeks Support for Rochester Building Project." *State Journal-Register* [Springfield, IL] 27 Nov. 2000: 9. Published by GenealogyBank.com, a division of NewsBank.

"History Rebuilt Stone by Stone: House Originally Erected in 1834 East of Rochester." *State Journal-Register* [Springfield, IL] 22 Sep. 2003: 8. Published by GenealogyBank.com, a division of NewsBank.

Landis, Debra. "A Salute to Spuds: Festival Organizers Pick Potatoes to Highlight History." *State Journal-Register* [Springfield, IL] 20 Sep. 2004: 1. Published by GenealogyBank.com, a division of NewsBank.

"Rochester Historical Society Seeks Items for Old Stone House." *State Journal-Register* [Springfield, IL] 1 May 2005: 27. Published by GenealogyBank.com, a division of NewsBank.

Landis, Debra. "Dedication Set for Stone House." *State Journal-Register* [Springfield, IL] 17 Oct. 2005: 17. Published by GenealogyBank.com, a division of NewsBank.

Landis, Debra. "Rochester Honoree Takes Opportunity to Promote Stone House." *State Journal-Register* [Springfield, IL] 4 July 2006: 12. Published by GenealogyBank.com, a division of NewsBank.

Sauders, Rhys. "Lincoln Tied to Rochester's Old Stone House." *State Journal-Register* [Springfield, IL] 13 July 2009: np. Published by GenealogyBank.com, a division of NewsBank.

Landis, Debra. "Gift of History: Rochester's Past, Depicted on Wooden Blocks, on Display at Town's Library." *State Journal-Register* [Springfield, IL] 6 Feb. 2008: 19. Published by GenealogyBank.com, a division of NewsBank.

Reynolds, John. "Path's Historical Status under Consideration: Van Buren Train Runs East of City into Rochester." *State Journal-Register* [Springfield, IL] 9 May 2007: 11. Published by GenealogyBank.com, a division of NewsBank.

Landis, Debra. "Meeting Place: Signs, Mural Mark Lincoln, Van Buren's Introduction in 1842." *State Journal-Register* [Springfield, IL] 17 June 2007: 23. Published by GenealogyBank.com, a division of NewsBank.

Pokorski, Doug. "Springfield Gets Wrapped up in 'Net.'" *State Journal-Register* [Springfield, IL] 8 Jan. 1996:1. Published by GenealogyBank.com, a division of NewsBank..

Landis, Tim. "Verizon Shows off Wireless Internet." *State Journal-Register* [Springfield, IL] 5 Oct. 2006: 13. Published by GenealogyBank.com, a division of NewsBank.

Landis, Debra. "Battle over a Hog Farm at a Standstill." *State Journal-Register* [Springfield, IL] 17 Aug. 2007: 10. Published by GenealogyBank.com, a division of NewsBank.

Landis, Debra. "High Court Allows Hog Farm near Rochester." *State Journal-Register* [Springfield, IL] 26 Sep. 2008: np. Published by GenealogyBank.com, a division of NewsBank.

Landis, Debra. "Rochester Hog Farmer Entitled to Damages Because of Lawsuit, Court Rules." *State Journal-Register* [Springfield, IL] 12 Sep. 2009: np. Published by GenealogyBank.com, a division of NewsBank.

Landis, Debra. "Rochester Youth Gets a New Heart: Electronic Device Has Been Helping to Pump His Blood." *State Journal-Register* [Springfield, IL] 9 Dec. 2006: 1. Published by GenealogyBank.com, a division of NewsBank.

Landis, Debra. "Six Months after Heart Transplant, Teen Feels 'Great.'" *State Journal-Register* [Springfield, IL] 11 June 2007: 1. Published by GenealogyBank.com, a division of NewsBank.

Landis, Debra. "Full of Heart: Matt Felts Lives Vigorously a Year after Transplant." *State Journal-Register* [Springfield, IL] 5 Dec. 2007: 1. Published by GenealogyBank.com, a division of NewsBank.

"Obituary: Matt Kenneth Felts." *State Journal-Register* [Springfield, IL] 9 Dec. 2012: 55.

"Quilt Show Slated for Rochester." *State Journal-Register* [Springfield, IL] 10 July 2003: 14. Published by GenealogyBank.com, a division of NewsBank.

Landis, Debra. "Coin Shop in Old Rochester State Bank Opens Today." *State Journal-Register* [Springfield, IL] 24 Jan. 2004: 17. Published by GenealogyBank.com, a division of NewsBank.

"Local scene: Dollars & Cents Coin Shop Reopening." *State Journal-Register* [Springfield, IL] 30 July 2008: 8. Published by GenealogyBank.com, a division of NewsBank.

"Longtime Rochester Gasoline Outlet Changes Hands." *State Journal-Register* [Springfield, IL] 4 July 2004: 17. Published by GenealogyBank.com, a division of NewsBank.

"Local Scene: Store Ends Gas Service." *State Journal-Register* [Springfield, IL] 22 Jan. 2008: 8. Published by GenealogyBank.com, a division of NewsBank.

Landis, Debra. "Bank and Trust Opens. . . with Cappuccino." *State Journal-Register* [Springfield, IL] 10 May 2005: 31. Published by GenealogyBank.com, a division of NewsBank.

Landis, Debra. "Get It And Go to the Bank: Bank & Trust Co. May Retain Service of Coffee, Soft Drinks." *State Journal-Register* [Springfield, IL] 25 Sep. 2004: 19. Published by GenealogyBank.com, a division of NewsBank.

Landis, Debra. "Helping Hand: Assisted-Living Facility Opening in Rochester." *State Journal-Register* [Springfield, IL] 8 Nov. 2005: 31. Published by GenealogyBank.com, a division of NewsBank.

"Architect Buys, Plans to Renovate Rochester Station." *State Journal-Register* [Springfield, IL] 9 Sep. 2007: 47. Published by GenealogyBank.com, a division of NewsBank.

Shanle, Loren. "History of the Walnut Street Winery." 2012. Walnut Street Winery, Rochester, IL. 2 July 2015. <http://www.walnutstreetwinery.com/the-history-of-the-walnut-street-winery/>.

Reavy, Amanda. "Florists' Decorations to be Backdrop for Obama." *State Journal-Register* [Springfield, IL] 9 Feb. 2009: np. Published by GenealogyBank.com, a division of NewsBank.

Landis, Tim. "Marketing Network Helps Farmers: Illinois Stewardship Alliance Promotes Farms, Healthy Foods." *State Journal-Register* [Springfield, IL] 23 May 2008: 21. Published by GenealogyBank.com, a division of NewsBank.

"News Briefcase: Rochester Business is Finalist in Competition." *State Journal-Register* [Springfield, IL] 7 Jan. 2009: np. Published by GenealogyBank.com, a division of NewsBank.

Kane, Dave. "Easy Does It: Laid-Back Derek Leonard Takes Charge of Young Rochester Team." *State Journal-Register* [Springfield, IL] 19 Aug. 2005: 33. Published by GenealogyBank.com, a division of NewsBank.

Kane, Dave. "Rockets Hire Football Coach: Derek Leonard is the Son of SHG Coach Ken Leonard." *State Journal-Register* [Springfield, IL] 29 Mar. 2005: 27. Published by GenealogyBank.com, a division of NewsBank.

"Obituaries: John R. Foster." *State Journal-Register* [Springfield, IL] 1 July 2000: 44. Published by GenealogyBank.com, a division of NewsBank.

"Obituaries: Virginia Waldmire." *State Journal-Register* [Springfield, IL] 3 Feb. 2002: 35. Published by GenealogyBank.com, a division of NewsBank.

"Obituaries: Lucile C. Fairchild." *State Journal-Register* [Springfield, IL] 25 May 2003: 14. Published by GenealogyBank.com, a division of NewsBank.

"Obituaries: Charles L. Drillinger." *State Journal-Register* [Springfield, IL] 10 Jan. 2003: 34. Published by GenealogyBank.com, a division of NewsBank.

Landis, Debra. "Rochester Library Director Shaw Dies: Also Served as Village Manager." *State Journal-Register* [Springfield, IL] 4 July 2003: 14. Published by GenealogyBank.com, a division of NewsBank.

"Obituaries: Raymond L. Ramsey." *State Journal-Register* [Springfield, IL] 21 Feb. 2003: 37. Published by GenealogyBank.com, a division of NewsBank.

"Obituaries: Marshall H. Watkins." *State Journal-Register* [Springfield, IL] 5 Oct. 2003: 54. Published by GenealogyBank.com, a division of NewsBank.

"Obituaries: Esther M. Taft." *State Journal-Register* [Springfield, IL] 5 Aug. 2004: 30. Published by GenealogyBank.com, a division of NewsBank.

"Obituaries: Alvin M. Mavis." *State Journal-Register* [Springfield, IL] 29 Mar. 2004: 32. Published by GenealogyBank.com, a division of NewsBank.

"Obituaries: Helen L. Campbell." *State Journal-Register* [Springfield, IL] 27 Nov. 2004: 17. Published by GenealogyBank.com, a division of NewsBank.

"Obituaries: Helen K. Newhouse." *State Journal-Register* [Springfield, IL] 3/30/2004: 26. Published by GenealogyBank.com, a division of NewsBank.

"Obituaries: Lacey C. Brooks." *State Journal-Register* [Springfield, IL] 27 Oct. 2005: 32. Published by GenealogyBank.com, a division of NewsBank.

Wetterich, Chris. "Palmatier Laid to Rest / City Man Remembered as a 'Powerful Life Force.'" *State Journal-Register* [Springfield, IL] 8 Mar. 2005: 1. Published by GenealogyBank.com, a division of NewsBank.

"F. North Ross." *State Journal-Register* [Springfield, IL] 20 Jan. 2008: 18. Published by GenealogyBank.com, a division of NewsBank.

Landis, Tim. "Watts Funeral Set for Friday at Calvary." *State Journal-Register* [Springfield, IL] 5 Mar. 2009: np. Published by GenealogyBank.com, a division of NewsBank.

"Route 66 Legend Bob Waldmire Reaches End of Road." *State Journal-Register* [Springfield, IL] 17 Dec. 2009: np. Published by GenealogyBank.com, a division of NewsBank.

"Anniversaries: Mavis-60th." *State Journal-Register* [Springfield, IL] 6 June 2000: 20. Published by GenealogyBank.com, a division of NewsBank.

"Anniversaries: Watkins-65th." *State Journal-Register* [Springfield, IL] 18 Feb. 2003: 15. Published by GenealogyBank.com, a division of NewsBank.

"Building Permits: Commercial Construction." *State Journal-Register* [Springfield, IL] 26 Jan. 2007: 26. Published by GenealogyBank.com, a division of NewsBank.

Gorman, Ann. "New Lincoln Statue Unveiled: Sculpture Depicts Former President as a Surveyor." *State Journal-Register* [Springfield, IL] 5 Oct. 2003: 33. Published by GenealogyBank.com, a division of NewsBank.

Baber, Adin. *A Lincoln With Compass and Chain*. [Kansas, IL]. 1968. Annotated by Robert E. Church. Illinois Professional Land Surveyors Association. [Springfield, IL] 2002.

Landis, Debra. "Rochester Honors Two Residents / Neighbors Win Awards for Contributions to Town." *State Journal-Register* [Springfield, IL] 11 July 2004: 11. Published by GenealogyBank.com, a division of NewsBank.

Kernek, Lisa. "Hanging up His Hat: Columnist Toby McDaniel Closes Book on Journalism Career of 40-Plus Years." *State Journal-Register* [Springfield, IL] 17 Oct. 2004: 19. Published by GenealogyBank.com, a division of NewsBank.

"Birthdays: Dill 102nd." *State Journal-Register* [Springfield, IL] 17 Oct. 2006: 18. Published by GenealogyBank.com, a division of NewsBank.

McDaniel, Toby. "Chili Circuit." *State Journal-Register* [Springfield, IL] 23 July 2004: 13. Published by GenealogyBank.com, a division of NewsBank.

Colindres, Adriana. "Photo Finish: State Retiree Recalls His Career Behind the Camera." *State Journal-Register* [Springfield, IL] 30 Jan. 2005: 17. Published by GenealogyBank.com, a division of NewsBank.

Martinez, Marcia. "Old Yeller: Jostes is a Picture-Perfect Rochester Supporter." *State Journal-Register* [Springfield, IL] 29 June 2005: 37. Published by GenealogyBank.com, a division of NewsBank.

"Personnel File: The Illinois Society of Professional Engineers. . ." *State Journal-Register* [Springfield, IL] 17 Aug. 2005: 32. Published by GenealogyBank.com, a division of NewsBank.

Illinois Society of Professional Engineers. "Illinois Award." Accessed 6 Oct 2016. <https://www.illinoisengineer.com/IllinoisEngineer/ISPEAwards/Illinois_Award.aspx>.

Crown, Dianne. "In to the Woods." *State Journal-Register* [Springfield, IL] 25 Feb. 2006: 16. Published by GenealogyBank.com, a division of NewsBank.

Landis, Debra. "Area Funeral Director Helping / Park Heading for Louisiana." *State Journal-Register* [Springfield, IL] 10 Sep. 2005: 4. Published by GenealogyBank.com, a division of NewsBank.

Reavy, Amanda. "Longtime Urban Planner Dies: Harry Hopkins' Projects Included ALPLM, Rezoning of White Oaks Mall." *State Journal-Register* [Springfield, IL] 3 Feb. 2008. Published by GenealogyBank.com, a division of NewsBank.

"Beekeeper to Speak Monday." *State Journal-Register* [Springfield, IL] 27 Jan. 2008: 60. Published by GenealogyBank.com, a division of NewsBank.

Reavy, Amanda. "Bench to Commemorate Rochester's Bill Roy." *State Journal-Register* [Springfield, IL] 1 Aug. 2009: np. Published by GenealogyBank.com, a division of NewsBank.

2010s References

"IDOT, Rochester Collaborate on Sidewalk Project." *State Journal-Register* [Springfield, IL] 16 May 2010: np. Published by GenealogyBank.com, a division of NewsBank.

Reavy, Amanda. "Sidewalks, Recreation Part of Rochester Plan." *State Journal-Register* [Springfield, IL] 9 June 2011: np. Published by GenealogyBank.com, a division of NewsBank.

Petrella, Dan. "Village Center: Incentives Help Rochester Secure Development." *State Journal-Register* [Springfield, IL] 19 Aug. 2013: 6. Published by GenealogyBank.com, a division of NewsBank.

Leone-Cross, Lauren. "Home-Rule Question to be Put to Voters." *State Journal-Register* [Springfield, IL] 11 Dec. 2013: 8. Published by GenealogyBank.com, a division of NewsBank.

Petrella, Dan. "Area Referendums: Mergers of School Districts,Tax Hikes Rejected . . ." *State Journal-Register* [Springfield, IL] 19 Mar. 2014: 3. Published by GenealogyBank.com, a division of NewsBank.

Menderski, Maggie. "Unlike Booming Neighbors, Rochester Planning for Steady Population Increase." *State Journal-Register* [Springfield, IL] 7 June 2015: 1. Published by GenealogyBank.com, a division of NewsBank.

Landis, Tim. "Kerasotes Filled with Attorneys, Energy Firm: The Catholic Diocese . . ." *State Journal-Register* [Springfield, IL] 20 Sep. 2015: 26. Published by GenealogyBank.com, a division of NewsBank.

Landis, Tim. "Springfield-Area Population Growth Expected to Slow." *State Journal-Register* [Springfield, IL] 7 June 2015: 1. Published by GenealogyBank.com, a division of NewsBank.

Landis, Tim. "Video Gambling: Rochester to Get Gaming Terminals." *State Journal-Register* [Springfield, IL] 25 Feb. 2016: 1.

Landis, Tim. "Video Gaming: $1.1M Wagered in Town's First Year." *State Journal-Register* [Springfield, IL] 26 Mar. 2017: 1.

"Village Board Approves Rezoning in Oak Mills Estates Subdivision on 4-3 Vote." *Rochester Times* [Rochester, IL] 17 Mar. 2016: 1.

"The 2015 Christmas holiday . . . " *Rochester Times* [Rochester, IL] 31 Dec. 2015:1.

Reynolds, John. "Taylorville Teens Missing; Petersburg, Riverton in Peril." *State Journal-Register* [Springfield, IL] 31 Dec. 2015: 19.

"The end of the rain . . ." *Rochester Times* [Rochester, IL] 7 Jan. 2016: 1.

"Flooding Report Highlights Village Board Agenda Monday." *Rochester Times* [Rochester, IL] 14 Jan. 2016: 1.

Landis, Debra. "Rochester School Board Studying How to Use Delayed Construction Funds." *State Journal-Register* [Springfield, IL] 22 June 2010: np. Published by GenealogyBank.com, a division of NewsBank.

Landis, Debra. "New Intermediate School in Rochester Nearly Complete." *State Journal-Register* [Springfield, IL] 3 Dec. 2010: 5. Published by GenealogyBank.com, a division of NewsBank.

Landis, Debra. "Rochester Intermediate School Dedicated." *State Journal-Register* [Springfield, IL] 10 Jan. 2011: 13. Published by GenealogyBank.com, a division of NewsBank.

Petrella, Dan. "Rochester Sues Over Defective Bleachers." *State Journal-Register* [Springfield, IL] 23 May 2012: 19. Published by GenealogyBank.com, a division of NewsBank.

Petrella, Dan. "Rochester Schools - New Bleacher System Expected to be Complete by late February." *State Journal-Register* [Springfield, IL] 15 Jan. 2014: 17. Published by GenealogyBank.com, a division of NewsBank.

Bertrand, Tom. "Rochester Embraces Digital Learning." *State Journal-Register* [Springfield, IL] 26 Aug. 2012:11. Published by GenealogyBank.com, a division of NewsBank.

"Editorial Horseshoe." *State Journal-Register* [Springfield, IL] 6 May 2013: 6. Published by GenealogyBank.com, a division of NewsBank.

Petrella, Dan. "Classroom Technology: Rochester Schools to Expand Laptop Use - Pilot Program Gets High Marks." *State Journal-Register* [Springfield, IL] 5 May 2013: np. Published by GenealogyBank.com, a division of NewsBank.

Reynolds, John. "Follow-up File: Last Piece of Illinois 29 Project Moves Forward." *State Journal-Register* [Springfield, IL] 4 Nov. 2013: 15. Published by GenealogyBank.com, a division of NewsBank.

Menderski, Maggie. "Illinois 29 Widening: Projected for Completion." *State Journal-Register* [Springfield, IL] 3 July 2014: 1. Published by GenealogyBank.com, a division of NewsBank.

Robbins, Brian. "Project 29 - Long Road to Success: Completion of Highway Widening Project 'Big Team Effort'" *State Journal-Register* [Springfield, IL] 18 Jan. 2017: 1.

Landis, Tim. "Illinois 29 Speed Limit Raised to 65 mph." *State Journal-Register* [Springfield, IL] 4 Nov. 2016: 15.

"News in Brief: Electronic Alert System to be Available in 2011." *State Journal-Register* [Springfield, IL] 30 Nov. 2010: 15. Published by GenealogyBank.com, a division of NewsBank.

"News in Brief: Police Plan Youth Academy." *State Journal-Register* [Springfield, IL] 13 Mar. 2011: 17. Published by GenealogyBank.com, a division of NewsBank.

"Former Rochester Firefighter Pleads Guilty to Child Porn Charges." *State Journal-Register* [Springfield, IL] 28 Jan. 2011: np. Published by GenealogyBank.com, a division of NewsBank.

Saunders, Rhys. "Former Rochester Firefighter Gets 30 Years for Child Porn." *State Journal-Register* [Springfield, IL] 13 Aug. 2011: np. Published by GenealogyBank.com, a division of NewsBank.

Petrella, Dan. "Homicide Investigation: No Suspect in Rochester Woman's Death." *State Journal-Register* [Springfield, IL] 1 Aug. 2013: 1. Published by GenealogyBank.com, a division of NewsBank.

Nevel, Jason. "Follow-up File: Police Pursuing Leads in Rochester Homicide." *State Journal-Register* [Springfield, IL] 4 Aug. 2014: 17. Published by GenealogyBank.com, a division of NewsBank.

"Skeletal Remains are Those of 30- to 40-Year-Old Woman." *State Journal-Register* [Springfield, IL] 24 July 2014: 18. Published by GenealogyBank.com, a division of NewsBank.

Nevel, Jason. "2010 Death: Man Pleads Guilty to Concealing Homicide." *State Journal-Register* [Springfield, IL] 10 Jan. 2015: 9.

Spearie, Steven. "Same-Sex Marriage: First Licensees Formalize Civil Unions in County." *State Journal-Register* [Springfield, IL] 31 May 2014: 1. Published by GenealogyBank.com, a division of NewsBank.

Browning, Tamara. "Rochester: Celebrating 150 Years." *State Journal-Register* [Springfield, IL] 26 Feb. 2017: 17.

Browning, Tamara. "Holiday Helpers Women's Club Assistance Lights up Village." *State Journal-Register* [Springfield, IL] 22 Dec. 2013: 29. Published by GenealogyBank.com, a division of NewsBank.

Menderski, Maggie. "Lions Club Fundraiser: New Haunt—Boo Crew Relocated to Larger, Permanent Home." *State Journal-Register* [Springfield, IL] 3 Oct. 2014: 1. Published by GenealogyBank.com, a division of NewsBank.

Landis, Debra. "Seven Seek Five Seats on Rochester Fire Board." *State Journal-Register* [Springfield, IL] 14 Dec. 2010: 20. Published by GenealogyBank.com, a division of NewsBank.

"Newcomer Leads 5 Winners." *State Journal-Register* [Springfield, IL] 6 Apr. 2011: 16. Published by GenealogyBank.com, a division of NewsBank.

Petrella, Dan. "Dry Conditions Complicate Efforts for Firefighters." *State Journal-Register* [Springfield, IL] 28 July 2012: 1. Published by GenealogyBank.com, a division of NewsBank.

Petrella, Dan. "Hunter Lake—CWLP Asks City for Water Study: Would Project Usage 50 Years into Future." *State Journal-Register* [Springfield, IL] 16 Feb. 2014: 1. Published by GenealogyBank.com, a division of NewsBank.

Hansen, Mary. "Springfield Buying More Land for Hunter Lake." *State Journal-Register* [Springfield, IL] 27 Sep. 2016. 14 Oct 2016 <http://www.sj-r.com/news/20160927/springfield-buying-more-land-for-hunter-lake>.

"Village Board Approves Increase in Sewer Rate, Purchases Backhoe." *Rochester Times* [Rochester, IL]12 May 2016: 1.

Petrella, Dan. "SangChris Co-op: Water Group Lowers Fee to Sign Up." *State Journal-Register* [Springfield, IL] 10 Oct 2013: 18. Published by GenealogyBank.com, a division of NewsBank.

Reavy, Amanda. "Rochester Utility Fees Set to Jump." *State Journal-Register* [Springfield, IL] 25 Apr. 2011: 1. Published by GenealogyBank.com, a division of NewsBank.

Nevel, Jason. "Rochester OKs Increases in Water, Sewer Rates." *State Journal-Register* [Springfield, IL] 26 Apr. 2011. Published by GenealogyBank.com, a division of NewsBank.

Reavy, Amanda. "No Rocket on Rochester Water Tower without Donation." *State Journal-Register* [Springfield, IL] 10 May 2011: 18. Published by GenealogyBank.com, a division of NewsBank.

Reavy, Amanda. "Leaky Pipes to Cost Rochester More Than Expected." *State Journal-Register* [Springfield, IL] 12 July 2011: 12. Published by GenealogyBank.com, a division of NewsBank.

Petrella, Dan. "New Plant's Water to Start Flowing Thursday: Delays, Other Issues Pushed Back Date of Operation Several Times." *State Journal-Register* [Springfield, IL] 9 May 2012: 25. Published by GenealogyBank.com, a division of NewsBank.

Petrella, Dan. "Water Plant Taps into Rural Market: Rural Residents Crowd into Meeting to Learn How to Hook up to the South Sangamon Water Commission." *State Journal-Register* [Springfield, IL] 26 May 2012: 1. Published by GenealogyBank.com, a division of NewsBank.

Hendrickson, Harry. Letter. *State Journal-Register* [Springfield, IL] 23 Sep. 2012: 13. Published by GenealogyBank.com, a division of NewsBank.

Petrella, Dan. "Water service: Proposed Agreement Ties Rochester to CWLP until 2029." *State Journal-Register* [Springfield, IL] 5 Aug. 2013: 1. Published by GenealogyBank.com, a division of NewsBank.

Reynolds, John. "Rochester: Board Approves Increases in Water Rates." *State Journal-Register* [Springfield, IL] 13 Aug. 2013: 8. Published by GenealogyBank.com, a division of NewsBank.

Landis, Tim. "Area Home Prices Hold up during Downturn." *State Journal-Register* [Springfield, IL] 11 Feb. 2011: 11. Published by GenealogyBank.com, a division of NewsBank.

Landis, Tim. "Springfield-Area Population Growth Expected to Slow." *State Journal-Register* [Springfield, IL] 7 June 2015: 1. Published by GenealogyBank.com, a division of NewsBank.

Capital Area Association of Realtors. Interview with Ray Bruzan. 13 Apr. 2016.

"Misfortune of a Mule Turns into Quite a Story." *State Journal-Register* [Springfield, IL] 9 June 2013: 17. Published by GenealogyBank.com, a division of NewsBank.

Duffey, Helen. "The Legend of Chicken Bristle." 24 Sep. 1969.

"Photo Genealogy to be Subject of Talk." *State Journal-Register* [Springfield, IL] 21 Sep. 2012: 23. Published by GenealogyBank.com, a division of NewsBank.

Menderski, Maggie. "Home Renovation Project Reveals Remnants of Log Cabin." *State Journal-Register* [Springfield, IL] 16 July 2014: 1. Published by GenealogyBank.com, a division of NewsBank.

Reavy, Amanda. "Planting Ready in Rochester Arboretum." *State Journal-Register* [Springfield, IL] 22 Aug. 2011: np. Published by GenealogyBank.com, a division of NewsBank.

Reavy, Amanda. "Fishing Derby to Take Advantage of Rochester Pond Renaissance." *State Journal-Register* [Springfield, IL] 1 July 2011: 11. Published by GenealogyBank.com, a division of NewsBank.

"Arboretum Classroom Dedication April 26." *Rochester Times* [Rochester, IL] 21 Apr. 2016:1.

"Residents Get Answers on Proposed TIF District Tuesday." *Rochester Times* [Rochester, IL] 28 July 2016: 1.

Landis, Tim. "Would be for Infrastructure, Business Growth." *State Journal-Register* [Springfield, IL] 7 Aug. 2016: 21. Published by GenealogyBank.com, a division of NewsBank.

Reavy, Amanda. "Comfort Station Planned for Lost Bridge Trail." *State Journal-Register* [Springfield, IL] 14 July 2009: np. Published by GenealogyBank.com, a division of NewsBank.

Reavy, Amanda. "Lost Bridge Trail Restroom to Open Saturday." *State Journal-Register* [Springfield, IL] 1 July 2010: np. Published by GenealogyBank.com, a division of NewsBank.

Reavy, Amanda. "Comfort Station Planned for Lost Bridge Trail." *State Journal-Register* [Springfield, IL] 25 Mar 2016: np. <http://www.sj-r.com/article/20090714/News/307149870>.

Landis, Tim. "Dunkin' Donuts Coming to Habitat Property / A bicycle repair . . ." *State Journal-Register* [Springfield, IL] 7 May 2017: 28.

Olsen, Dean. "Open House Planned at New Rochester Health Center." *State Journal-Register* [Springfield, IL] 4 Apr. 2010: np. Published by GenealogyBank.com, a division of NewsBank.

Petrella, Dan. "Fitness Center, Restaurant Project Awaits OK / Owners Hope to be Open by Year's End." *State Journal-Register* [Springfield, IL] 9 July 2013: 1. Published by GenealogyBank.com, a division of NewsBank.

Morris, Natalie. "Planning for Commercial Growth: Zoning Updates on Agenda in Rochester." *State Journal-Register* [Springfield, IL] 28 July 2013: 23. Published by GenealogyBank.com, a division of NewsBank.

Young, Chris. "Rochester Scouts Have Winter Wilderness Adventure." *State Journal-Register* [Springfield, IL] 20 Mar. 2010: np. Published by GenealogyBank.com, a division of NewsBank.

Nevel, Jason. "Heat Doesn't Stop Boy Scouts Camping Trip." *State Journal-Register* [Springfield, IL] 8 July 2012: 17. Published by GenealogyBank.com, a division of NewsBank.

"Illinois High School Association: Records & History." 27 Sep. 2016. 18 Oct. 2016 <http://www.ihsa.org/SportsActivities/BoysBaseball/RecordsHistory.aspx>.

"'Something Special' - Back-to-Back State Titles." *Rochester Times* [Rochester, IL] 9 June 2016: 1.

"Reload and repeat." *Rochester Times* [Rochester, IL] 4 Dec. 2014: 1.

Lunt, Jane and Andy. Personal interview. April 2016.

"Vikings Agree to Terms with 13 Rookie Free Agents." *Minnesota Vikings.* 3 May 2017 <http://www.vikings.com/news/article-1/Vikings-Agree-To-Terms-With-13-Rookie-Free-Agents/acab5bd9-7eb6-4ded-a361-a8ca130c5f4e>.

"Obituaries: Theodore L. (Ted) McCoy." *State Journal-Register* [Springfield, IL] 15 July 2011: 13. Published by GenealogyBank.com, a division of NewsBank.

"Obituaries: Sarah "Sally" Grace Wisleder." *State Journal-Register* [Springfield, IL] 12 May 2012: 22. Published by GenealogyBank.com, a division of NewsBank.

"Margaret Beck." Ellinger-Kunz & Park Funeral Home & Cremation Service. 29 August 2016. <http://www.wilsonparkfuneralhome.com/notices/Margaret-Beck>.

"Obituaries: Sharon Kay McDaniel." *State Journal-Register* [Springfield, IL] 3 Mar. 2013: 57A. Published by GenealogyBank.com, a division of NewsBank.

Spearie, Steven. "Gregory Fultz: 1963-2013 - Rochester Native Made His Mark in Cancer Research." *State Journal-Register* [Springfield, IL] 6 July 2013: 17. Published by GenealogyBank.com, a division of NewsBank.

"James F. Waters: 1922-2015." *State Journal-Register* [Springfield, IL] 15 Aug. 2015: 21.

"Larry Louise Churchill: 1916-2016." *State Journal-Register [Springfield, IL]* 25 Jan. 2016: 7.

"Melvin L. "Crevy" Creviston: 1946-2016." *State Journal-Register* [Springfield, IL] 7 Dec. 2016: 28.

Bakke, Dave. "Darneille Family Copes with Second Death in Two Months." *State Journal-Register* [Springfield, IL] 30 Aug. 2-15: 1. Published by GenealogyBank.com, a division of NewsBank.

Sanders, Rhys. "Klickna Elected President of Illinois Education Association." *State Journal-Register* [Springfield, IL] 13 Mar. 2011: 26. Published by GenealogyBank.com, a division of NewsBank.

"Illinoisan of the Day Award Winners for 2012." *State Journal-Register* [Springfield, IL] 12 Aug. 2012: 25. Published by GenealogyBank.com, a division of NewsBank.

Petrella, Dan. "Rochester Native Wins First USO Award for Guardsman." *State Journal-Register* [Springfield, IL] 2 Nov. 2012: 15. Published by GenealogyBank.com, a division of NewsBank.

Browning, Tamara. "Top Guard Members Include Area Residents: Braun, Clemens among Airmen Honored." *State Journal-Register* [Springfield, IL] 13 Jan. 2013: 11. Published by GenealogyBank.com, a division of NewsBank.

Olsen, Dean. "SIU School of Medicine: City Doctor Lauded for Teaching Future Practitioners." *State Journal-Register* [Springfield, IL] 25 Nov. 2013: 1. Published by GenealogyBank.com, a division of NewsBank.

Wall, Tobias. "Bertrand Superintendent of Year." *State Journal-Register* [Springfield, IL] 23 Nov. 2014: 9. Published by GenealogyBank.com, a division of NewsBank.

Browning, Tamara. "Illinois' Top Mom." *State Journal-Register* [Springfield, IL] 10 Apr. 2016: 17.

Bakke, Dave. "Illinois News." *State Journal-Register* [Springfield, IL] 30 July 2014: 14. Published by GenealogyBank.com, a division of NewsBank.

Bakke, Dave. "Bob Waldmire Takes One Last Ride." *State Journal-Register* [Springfield, IL] 21 Apr. 2010: np. Published by GenealogyBank.com, a division of NewsBank.

Bakke, Dave. "Rochester Car on its Way to Harley Museum." *State Journal-Register* [Springfield, IL] 7 Mar. 2014: 15. Published by GenealogyBank.com, a division of NewsBank.

"Follow-up File: Haitian Twins Settle into New Life in Rochester." *State Journal-Register* [Springfield, IL] 16 June 2010: np. Published by GenealogyBank.com, a division of NewsBank.

"Just Desserts: Rochester Chef Part of Super Bowl Team." *State Journal-Register [Springfield, IL]* 2 Feb. 2011: np. Published by GenealogyBank.com, a division of NewsBank.

Reavy, Amanda. "Families of Area Residents Thought Safe after Quake and Tsunami." *State Journal-Register* [Springfield, IL] 12 Mar. 2011: np. Published by GenealogyBank.com, a division of NewsBank.

(Untitled Photo) "Brad Sturdy . . ." *Rochester Times* [Rochester, IL] 27 April, 2017: 1.

Landis, Tim. "Bee Industry Buzzing." *State Journal-Register* [Springfield, IL] 16 June 2014: 1. Published by GenealogyBank.com, a division of NewsBank.

Howard, Clare. "Christmas Trees without the Toxins: Rochester Farm Uses Natural Way to Keep Pests at Bay." *State Journal-Register* [Springfield, IL] 9 Dec. 2012: 37. Published by GenealogyBank.com, a division of NewsBank.

Bakke, Dave. "Catching up with Former Columnist / We Still Say It: 'That's a Toby!'" *State Journal-Register* [Springfield, IL] 5 May 2014: 17. Published by GenealogyBank.com, a division of NewsBank.

"Reynolds, John. "Award Recipient: Local Guard Member Helps Save Trucker." *State Journal-Register* [Springfield, IL] 6 May 2013: np. Published by GenealogyBank.com, a division of NewsBank.

Leone-Cross, Lauren. "Most Interesting: Rochester Science Teacher Got His Start in War-Torn Laos." *State Journal-Register* [Springfield, IL] 10 July 2013: 17. Published by GenealogyBank.com, a division of NewsBank.

"Birthdays: David L. Jostes." *State Journal-Register* [Springfield, IL] 13 Mar. 2016: 11.

Wallin, Richard. E-mail interview. 24 June 2016.

Browning, Tamara. "Knitting Project No Sweat for Rochester Woman." *State Journal-Register* [Springfield, IL] 4 Dec. 2010: 9. Published by GenealogyBank.com, a division of NewsBank.

Reavy, Amanda. "Gift of reading: Local Teachers Organize Book Drive for Friend-In-Deed." *State Journal-Register* [Springfield, IL] 9 Dec. 2010: 1. Published by GenealogyBank.com, a division of NewsBank.

Saunders, Rhys. "Six Year Old Rochester Girl Donates Her Birthday Presents to Toys for Tots." *State Journal-Register* [Springfield, IL] 25 Dec. 2011: 29. Published by GenealogyBank.com, a division of NewsBank.

"Pana Photographer Never Met His Heroes." *State Journal-Register* [Springfield, IL] 21 Oct. 2012: 21A. Published by GenealogyBank.com, a division of NewsBank.

Ball, A. Marie. "Beating MD." *State Journal-Register* [Springfield, IL] 13 Mar. 2012: 11. Published by GenealogyBank.com, a division of NewsBank.

Hardy, Emma. "Top Teen 2014: A Voice and Face for a Disease Rochester's Runions Helps Others Like Her Battling Muscular Dystrophy." *State Journal-Register* [Springfield, IL] 15 Apr. 2014: 11. Published by GenealogyBank.com, a division of NewsBank.

INDEX

Index entries with an "f" denote a figure.